# FINANCIAL ECONOMICS

# FINANCIAL ECONOMICS

Frank J. Fabozzi
Edwin H. Neave
Guofu Zhou

WILEY

John Wiley & Sons, Inc.

| | |
|---|---|
| Vice President/Publisher: | George Hoffman |
| Acquisitions Editor: | Lacey Vitetta |
| Project Editor: | Jennifer Manias |
| Editorial Assistant: | Erica Horowitz |
| Associate Director of Marketing: | Amy Scholz |
| Marketing Assistant: | Courtney Luzzi |
| Production Manager: | Janis Soo |
| Assistant Production Editor: | Pauline Tan |
| Designer: | Seng Ping Ngieng |

This book was set in 10/12 Times Roman by MPS Limited, a Macmillan Company and printed and bound by Courier Westford.

This book is printed on acid free paper.

Founded in 1807, John Wiley & Sons, Inc. has been a valued source of knowledge and understanding for more than 200 years, helping people around the world meet their needs and fulfill their aspirations. Our company is built on a foundation of principles that include responsibility to the communities we serve and where we live and work. In 2008, we launched a Corporate Citizenship Initiative, a global effort to address the environmental, social, economic, and ethical challenges we face in our business. Among the issues we are addressing are carbon impact, paper specifications and procurement, ethical conduct within our business and among our vendors, and community and charitable support. For more information, please visit our website: www.wiley.com/go/citizenship.

***Library of Congress Cataloging-in-Publication Data***

Fabozzi, Frank J.
    Financial economics/Frank J. Fabozzi, Edwin H. Neave and Guofu Zhou.
      p. cm.
    Includes index.
    ISBN 978-0-470-59620-3 (hardback)
      1. Finance. 2. Economics. I. Neave, Edwin H. II. Zhou, Guofu. III. Title.
    HG173.F28 2012
    332—dc23                 2011022695

Printed in the United States of America
10 9 8 7 6 5 4 3 2 1

# TABLE OF CONTENTS

MATHEMATICAL AND STATISTICAL APPENDICES

\* Web-Appendix A to P are online only—please go to www.wiley.com/college/fabozzi

# PREFACE

$\mathcal{T}$here are many excellent finance textbooks for undergraduate and MBA courses. However, to us those textbooks could benefit from offering more economic reasoning and from showing how that reasoning derives from theoretical models. On the other hand, books at the doctoral level can be too detailed and unnecessarily complex. Hence, this textbook attempts to fill a gap by providing rigorous coverage aimed at assisting undergraduate and master's level students to understand better the principles and practical application of financial economic theory. In addition, the book can serve as a supplemental reference for doctoral students in economics and finance, as well as for practitioners who are interested in knowing more about the theory and intuition behind many common practices in finance. The book selectively covers recent research findings and presents them within a structured framework. In short, the book focuses on economic principles and on putting these principles to work in the various fields of finance—financial management, investment management, risk management, and asset and derivatives pricing.

After our introductory chapter sketches the book's approach, we organize our survey in eight parts. The traditional findings of neoclassical financial economics, the subject of Part I, examine finance in a certainty world with a perfect capital market. In Part II we sketch the real-world institutional setting of financial economics, describing the essential elements of a modern financial system and providing a unified theory of how those elements function in relation to each other and to the rest of the economy. Modern financial economics is largely a study of risk management, and Part III examines tools for measuring and coping with risk. Part IV, concerned with portfolio theory and its recent developments, examines the selection and pricing of risky assets, particularly corporate securities. Continuing to examine risk management, Part V is concerned with the nature and pricing of derivative instruments. Research in modern financial economics is progressing well beyond the findings of its original neoclassical perspectives, and in recognition of this progress, Part VI examines the effects of capital market imperfections and limits to arbitrage. Part VII considers capital structure decisions in the presence of capital market imperfections, while the final part of this book, Part VIII, examines the tasks of making capital budgeting decisions under conditions of risk. Background information regarding both institutional aspects of finance and a variety of technical issues is presented in a series of 16 web appendices. Web-Appendix A to P are online only at www.wiley.com/college/fabozzi and referred to as web-Appendix throughout this book.

In order to provide additional detail, we now consider the contents of each of the eight parts. In our presentation of neoclassical financial economics in Part I, we examine the theory of consumer financial decisions, how wealth is created by investing in productive opportunities, how investors value firms, the nature and importance of firms' financing decisions in a perfect capital market, as well as the nature and importance of firms' investment decisions in the same neoclassical environment. This part intends particularly to emphasize the great contributions of neoclassical financial analysis, both as intellectual contributions in their own right and as a set of guidelines to financial decision making in the more complex world of market imperfections. Although financial economics is sometimes discussed as if there were on the one hand a theoretical world divorced from reality, and on the other a real world in which actual finance is studied, we contend that the two form a complementary whole. In our view, the road maps provided by neoclassical analysis provide the structure that has and will continue to guide both further research and practical applications.

In our discussion of a modern financial system's institutional nature, Part II, we introduce the notion of financial governance. We present a theory of financial system organization arguing that the three main types of financial governance—financial markets, financial intermediaries, and the internal financial decisions administered by firms—are complementary ways of overseeing financial arrangements. In the complex world beyond the domain of neoclassical economics, all three administrative mechanisms are needed to carry out financial system activity and to monitor that activity effectively. Indeed, recognizing how these mechanisms complement each other is necessary to progress beyond the findings of neoclassical economics to a broader understanding of how applied financial decisions are made in practice, as well as of their implications for the firms and investors who make them.

In our coverage of the tools for coping with risk in Part III, we discuss topics that include the microeconomic foundations of financial economics, the roles of both contingent claims analysis and contingency strategies, the nature of risk and risk management, and the recently burgeoning field of choosing risk measures.

The selection and pricing of risky assets in Part IV begins with the topics of mean-variance portfolio choice and the capital asset pricing model, then turns to the arbitrage pricing theory and factor models. Next, the guiding principles of asset pricing theory are examined, closing with a review of how these theories contribute to our current understanding of pricing corporate securities.

Part V examines the nature and valuation of derivative instruments—both derivatives with linear payoff functions (such as forward and futures contracts) and more complex types of derivatives with nonlinear payoff functions (such as options). We show how both types of contracts can be valued by assuming the absence of arbitrage opportunities. These valuation tasks can either be carried out directly or with the aid of the risk-neutral probabilities that the absence of arbitrage opportunities implies.

Although the first five parts of the book acknowledge and sketch out the roles of market imperfections, they recognize imperfections largely as requiring extensions and modifications of the neoclassical theory. Part VI turns explicitly to a more detailed recognition of capital market imperfections, the limits to arbitrage, and the detailed consequences of recognizing these complications.

The themes of recognizing and understanding complications presented by market imperfections are continued in Part VII. Here we consider why market imperfections mean that capital structure decisions matter, and the kinds of decisions that are needed to cope with these complications. In addition, we consider the implications of making financing decisions in practice, as contrasted with their implications in a neoclassical environmment. Finally, we examine the importance of financial contracting and contract terms for coping with different kinds of market imperfections. In its early days, neoclassical analysis assumed away these complications in order to develop an initial understanding of the complex financial world with which practice contends. In those earlier days, financial economics was necessarily concerned with getting the large-scale maps of the territory correct. Once those tasks had been accomplished, it became possible to grapple systematically with the effects of imperfections and hence to fill in the details of smaller-scale maps that fitted within the large-scale context.

Part VIII is a parallel to Part VII, focused this time on capital budgeting decisions rather than on capital structure issues. We consider capital expenditure plans in a risky world and the implications for capital budgeting decisions of recognizing project risk.

The web appendices provide both institutional and technical information. The first 10 appendices, Web-Appendices A through J, are concerned with institutional complications that arise in the practice of finance, and the remaining six appendices (Web-Appendices K through P) are concerned with topics of a mathematical background nature. All of the appendices are intended to provide supplementary information where we think it would be helpful, and to provide it in a form that does not distract the reader from the main presentation.

Most of the chapters in this book were written to be readily accessible to undergraduate students, and we believe that the remaining chapters are also accessible to those readers if they are willing to take on modest challenges. To us, the more challenging chapters are 12, 16, 24, and 25. We have included this material not only for the sake of completeness but also to give students a perspective on where we see the field of financial economics currently moving forward.

The material in the book lends itself to a number of different presentations. We provide the suitability of chapters for undergraduates and graduate students on the next page. Also provided is a list of selected chapters that can be used for various courses.

LEVEL COVERAGE AND SUGGESTED USAGE BY TYPE OF COURSE

Suitability

| | |
|---|---|
| UT | Theory suitable for undergraduates |
| UA | Applications suitable for undergraduates |
| GT | Theory suitable for graduates |
| GA | Applications suitable for graduates |

Course

| | |
|---|---|
| 1 | One semester undergraduate or introductory graduate course in financial economics |
| 2 | Two semester undergraduate course in financial economics |
| 3 | One semester undergraduate or introductory graduate course focusing on financial management |
| 4* | One semester advanced undergraduate or advanced graduate course focusing on financial management |
| 5 | One semester undergraduate or introductory graduate course focusing on asset pricing and derivatives pricing |
| 6* | One semester advanced undergraduate or advanced graduate course focusing on asset pricing and derivatives pricing fundamentals |
| 7* | One semester quantitative finance course |
| 8* | Introductory doctoral finance course |

*  Assumes students are familiar with the fundamentals

| Chapter | Course No. | Suitability | 1 | 2 | 3 | 4 | 5 | 6 | 7 | 8 |
|---|---|---|---|---|---|---|---|---|---|---|
| 1 | Introduction | All | X | X | X | X | X | X | X | X |
|  | **PART I: FINANCE IN A CERTAINTY WORLD WITH A PERFECT CAPITAL MARKET** |  |  |  |  |  |  |  |  |  |
| 2 | Consumer Financial Decisions | UT | X | X | X |  | X |  |  |  |
| 3 | Creating Wealth by Investing in Productive Opportunities | UT | X | X | X |  | X |  |  |  |
| 4 | How Investors Value Firms | UT | X | X | X |  | X |  |  |  |
| 5 | Firm Financing Decisions in a Perfect Capital Market | UT | X | X | X |  | X |  | X |  |
| 6 | Firm Investment Decisions | UT | X | X | X |  | X |  | X |  |
|  | **PART II: FINANCIAL SYSTEM** |  |  |  |  |  |  |  |  |  |
| 7 | Financial Systems, Governance, and Organization | UA | X | X | X | X | X | X |  | X |
| 8 | Market, Intermediary, and Internal Governance | UA | X | X | X | X | X | X |  | X |
|  | **PART III: TOOLS FOR COPING WITH RISK** |  |  |  |  |  |  |  |  |  |
| 9 | The Microeconomic Foundations of Financial Economics | UT | X | X | X | X | X | X | X | X |
| 10 | Contingent Claims and Contingent Strategies | UT | X | X | X | X | X | X | X | X |
| 11 | Risk and Risk Management | UA |  | X |  | X | X | X | X | X |
| 12 | On Choosing Risk Measures | GT |  |  |  | X | X | X | X | X |
|  | **PART IV: SELECTION AND PRICING OF RISKY ASSETS** |  |  |  |  |  |  |  |  |  |
| 13 | Mean-Variance Portfolio Choice | UT | X | X | X | X | X | X | X | X |
| 14 | Capital Asset Pricing Model | UT | X | X | X | X | X | X | X | X |
| 15 | The APT and Factor Models | UT | X | X |  |  | X | X | X | X |
| 16 | General Principles of Asset Pricing | GT |  |  |  |  | X | X | X | X |
| 17 | Pricing Corporate Securities | GT |  | X |  |  | X | X | X | X |
|  | **PART V: DERIVATIVE INSTRUMENTS** |  |  |  |  |  |  |  |  |  |
| 18 | Pricing Derivatives by Arbitrage: Linear Payoff Derivatives | UT | X | X |  |  | X | X | X | X |
| 19 | Pricing Derivatives by Arbitrage: Nonlinear Payoff Derivatives | UT | X | X |  |  | X | X | X | X |

# ACKNOWLEDGMENTS

*T*he idea for this book was proposed to us by George Lobell, former acquisitions editor of Blackwell. George argued the need for a book that focused on the principles of financial economics, fully using the mathematical and statistical training that economics students now acquire, and at the same time assisting those students with the practicalities of applying their economics training. George was especially keen on providing the students both with unusual intellectual challenges and with exciting new research results. We have attempted to achieve those goals.

George handed the reins to Lacey Vitetta, the acquisitions editor at Wiley who guided us to the completion of this project. Along the way she obtained helpful comments from the following reviewers:

Turan G. Bali, Baruch College
Gerard Caprio, Williams College
Martin Cherkes, Columbia University
Ahmet Duran, University of Michigan-Ann Arbor
Brian Henderson, George Washington University
Thomas Jeitschko, Michigan State University
Alexander Koch, Royal Holloway, University of London
Lenny Kostovetsky, University of Rochester
Alex Michaelides, London School of Economics
Andrew Samwick, Dartmouth College
Emanuela Sciubba, Birkbeck University of London
Koray D. Simsek, Sabanci University, Turkey
Anne Villamil, University of Illinois at Urbana-Champaign
Brian Wright, The University of Nottingham, China

There are end-of-chapter questions for each chapter. For a good number of chapters, these questions were prepared by graduate students who also provided the solutions, which appear in the book's *Solutions Manual*. In addition, the students provided us with helpful feedback and suggestions for improving the exposition in the chapters. These students and the chapters that they worked on are listed below:

Faye (Fei) Wu (New York University): Chapters 1–5
Peter Kelly (Yale): Chapters 7 and 8
Li Cai (University of Massachusetts): Chapters 9 and 12
Chen Chang (New York University): Chapters 10 and 11
Dashan Huang (Washington University at St. Louis): Chapters 13–16
Chao Guo (New York University): Chapters 17 and 18
Taym Moustapha (New York University): Chapters 20 and 21
Jian Du (University of Massachusetts): Chapters 22–24
Li (Luke) Tian (New York University): Chapters 25 and 26

We are grateful to Pamela P. Drake, Gray Ferguson Professor of Finance and Department Head at James Madison University, for allowing us to use the illustrations in Chapter 26 from her joint work with one of the authors and for coauthoring several of the web-appendices. We also thank Sergio M. Focardi, Professor of Finance at EDHEC Business School, for coauthoring Web-Appendix O.

Some of the earlier results presented in this book represent extracts from Edwin H. Neave and John C. Wiginton, *Financial Management: Theory and Strategies* published in 1982 by Prentice Hall. We are grateful to Prentice Hall and to John C. Wiginton for transferring their copyrights of the book to one of the present book's coauthors.

Frank J. Fabozzi, New Hope, Pennsylvania
Edwin H. Neave, Kingston, Ontario
Guofu Zhou, St. Louis, Missouri
June 2011

# ABOUT THE AUTHORS

**Frank J. Fabozzi** is Professor of Finance at EDHEC Business School and a member of the EDHEC-Risk Institute. He held various professorial positions in finance at Yale University's School of Management from 1994 to 2011 and from 1986 to 1992 was a visiting professor of finance and accounting at MIT's Sloan School of Management. He earned a doctorate in economics from the City University of New York in 1972. In 2002, he was inducted into the Fixed Income Analysts Society's Hall of Fame and is the 2007 recipient of the CFA Institute's C. Stewart Sheppard Award. He has authored and edited numerous books in finance. His research papers have been published in *Journal of Finance*, *Journal of Financial and Quantitative Analysis*, *Econometric Theory*, *Econometric Journal*, *Operations Research*, *Journal of Banking and Finance*, *Journal of Economic Dynamics and Control*, and *European Financial Management*.

**Edwin H. Neave**, B. Comm., Ph. D., is a Professor Emeritus in the Queen's University School of Business. He has held the positions of Assistant Professor, Northwestern University; Bank of Montreal Professor of Business and Finance, School of Business, Queen's University; Director, Queen's Financial Economics, Queen's University; and Professor of Economics, Queen's University. A former Finance Departmental Editor for *Management Science*, he is the author of almost 60 articles and 17 books focusing on asset pricing, derivatives pricing, financial system theory, and financial system practice. His book *Financial Systems: Principles and Organisation* (Routledge) has been translated into Chinese and published by Renmin University Press, Beijing. In recognition of his banking education programs being used in more than 40 countries, he has been appointed an Honorary Fellow of the Institute of Canadian Bankers, being the only academic ever to receive this honor.

**Guofu Zhou** is Frederick Bierman and James E. Spears Professor of Finance at Olin Business School of Washington University in St. Louis. He has a BS degree from Chengdu College of Geology, China, and a PhD in economics from Duke University. Prior to his PhD studies, he was interested in mathematics with publications in number theory, function theory, and numerical solutions to partial differential equations. His current research interests are primarily in asset pricing and investments. He has published numerous papers in *Journal of Financial Economics*, *Review of Financial Studies*, *Journal of Financial and Quantitative Analysis*, and *Journal of Finance*, as well as in industry journals such as *Journal of Portfolio Management* and *Financial Analyst Journal*. He has won awards for teaching MBA and MSF students and for his research.

# INTRODUCTION

$T$his book presents the foundations of financial economics, a specialized area within economics that utilizes many of the analytical tools developed in the field of microeconomics. Common to both financial economics and microeconomics is a theoretical framework for analyzing the decisions by individuals and managers of firms, and also the interplay of these decisions on the prices of financial assets. In studying these decisions, both fields look at the allocation of limited resources to optimize some measure, with the optimization subject to some constraints. In fact, because of the commonality of topics and tools in the chapters of this book, some consider financial economics a specialized area within microeconomics rather than as a separate branch of economics.

In this chapter, we provide a broad overview of the major types of decisions with which the field of financial economics is concerned. We begin this chapter with the decisions made by individuals and managers, along with the role of markets in which these agents transact. These decisions fall into the area of microeconomics. Then we look at the same kinds of decisions and markets that fall under the purview of financial economics.

## 1.1  MICROECONOMIC THEORY: INDIVIDUALS, MANAGERS, AND MARKETS

Microeconomic theory provides a theoretical framework for analyzing the economic behavior of individuals who are regarded either as consumers of products or as managers of firms. Let's look at the types of decisions these agents make.

*Consumer choice* describes the economic behavior of consumers who, based on their preferences, allocate an expenditure budget amongst alternative products. Those preferences are described mathematically by the individual's *utility function*. Consumer choice theory states that individuals seek to maximize their utility function subject to a budget constraint. It is from this theory that the individual's demand curve for products is derived and, through aggregation, the market's demand curve is obtained. Individuals are assumed to take prices as given when they address these maximization problems.

1

Product prices are determined by the interaction of market demand and market supply. Consumer choice theory provides the framework for obtaining the demand for products, both for individual consumers and, by aggregation, for the markets in which consumers purchase the products. The supply of products is determined by the decisions made by managers of firms, and market supply is the aggregate of firms' individual supply functions.

The branch of microeconomics that looks at how managers should make their operating decisions is called *production theory*. Again, the decision-making agent, the manager in this case, is assumed to maximize an objective function subject to constraints. In production theory, the objective function is profits and the constraints are the production inputs and production technology. In classical production theory it is often assumed that managers cannot influence the prices of inputs and outputs.

Microeconomic theory then puts demand and supply together to analyze equilibrium in both the markets for production inputs (such as labor) and the product markets. Microeconomics is sometimes referred to as *price theory* because it explains how product prices and production costs are determined in equilibrium.

### 1.1.1 Risk and Uncertainty and Economic Decisions

The scope of microeconomic theory has been extended to real-world situations in which individuals and managers face either risk or uncertainty. In the first half of the eighteenth century, Daniel Bernoulli, a mathematician known for his work in probability and statistics, introduced risk in the context of the theory of choice.[1] Almost 200 years later, in his book *Risk, Uncertainty and Profit*, Frank Knight suggested that both risk and uncertainty are important in economics.[2] Moreover, he differentiated between "risk" and "uncertainty," the former being defined as circumstances where the decision maker is able to assign probabilities to the potential outcome of the decision whereas the latter is one in which probabilities cannot usefully be assigned (often referred to as "Knightian uncertainty").

Between 1921 and 1944, several economists began to recognize the importance of risk in economic decisions involving profit maximization, production planning, inventory management, firm financing decisions, and investment decisions. For example, Sir John Hicks, the 1972 corecipient of the Nobel Prize in Economic Sciences,[3] was one of several economists who saw the need to separate the attitudes of individuals towards risk from their preferences for different outcomes.[4] However, the

---

[1] See Bernoulli (1738).

[2] Knight (1921).

[3] The official title for this most prestigious award in economics has changed over the years. Presently, it is the "Sveriges Riksbank Prize in Economic Sciences in Memory of Alfred Nobel." Previously, it was the "Bank of Sweden Prize in Economic Sciences in Memory of Alfred Nobel." Other translations of the official title, which in Swedish is *Sveriges riksbanks pris i ekonomisk vetenskap till Alfred Nobels minne*, are "Prize in Economic Science dedicated to the memory of Alfred Nobel," "Prize in Economic Science," "Prize in Economic Science in Memory of Alfred Nobel," and "Prize in Economic Sciences in Memory of Alfred Nobel." We shall simply refer to it as the Nobel Prize in Economic Sciences and to the winner of this prestigious award as a Nobel Laureate.

[4] See Hicks (1931).

incorporation of risk into economic theory was not formally introduced until the early 1940s when John von Neumann and Oskar Morgenstern provided expected utility rules for decision making in their book *Theory of Games and Economic Behavior*.[5] The probabilities in their framework were *objective probabilities*, that is, probabilities determined by the long-run relative frequency of an event occurring. In 1954, Leonard Savage's book *Foundations of Statistics* brought in the notion of *subjective probabilities*,[6] wherein expected utility theory uses probabilities based on an individual's judgment of a particular event occurring. Another framework, known as the *state-preference framework*, did not rely on decision makers' assigning probabilities—objective or subjective—to events. Rather, state-preference theory assigns values directly to outcomes that can be realized in different states of the world. The state-preference framework was introduced by two Nobel Laureates: Kenneth Arrow,[7] corecipient of the prize with Hicks in 1972, and Gerard Debreu, recipient of the 1983 prize.[8]

## 1.1.2  Market Failure and Economic Decisions

The classical perfect market is one in which (1) buyers and sellers of products are assumed to be price takers and cannot influence the price of a product by their decisions, and (2) buyers and sellers are assumed to make rational decisions based on complete and accurate information that is costless to obtain.[9] When either of these assumptions is violated, a *market failure* is said to have occurred. Studying the economic behavior of market participants in the context of market failure is another important way (in addition to considering risk or uncertainty) that microeconomics has advanced our understanding of real-world decision making.

In the first type of market failure at least one of the parties to the exchange exhibits some form of market power. *Market power* means that individual parties transacting in the market can influence the market price. Examples of market power are monopolies (a single seller), monopsonies (a single buyer), oligopolies (a few sellers), and oligopsonies (a few buyers).

The second type of market failure deals with what is popularly referred to as *information economics*. Information economics recognizes that different parties to a transaction may have different information about the environment in which they are transacting. The treatment of risk described earlier falls under the purview of information economics, but traditionally it has evolved as a separate field within microeconomic theory. As we will see in this book, many of the findings in information economics are applied to the study of financial markets.

The 1978 recipient of the Nobel Prize, Herbert Simon, linked the notion of rationality in decision making under uncertainty to both information availability and the limits of decision makers' capability to process information.[10] James Mirrlees

---

[5] Von Neumann and Morgenstern (1944).

[6] Savage (1954).

[7] See Arrow (1953).

[8] See Debreu (1959).

[9] Market agents making decisions that will maximize some criterion function are often described as market agents who act "rationally."

[10] See Simon (1947).

and William Vickrey, the corecipients of the 1996 prize, and George Akerlof, Michael Spence, and Joseph Stiglitz, who shared the 2001 prize, contributed to our understanding of economic behavior in markets where there is *asymmetric information*. Mirrlees, for example, developed the notion of private information, adverse selection, and moral hazard that we will describe in later chapters in this book.

## 1.2 FINANCIAL ECONOMIC THEORY: INDIVIDUALS, MANAGERS, AND MARKETS

As in microeconomics, financial economics examines the behavior of individuals and managers along with the roles of the markets in which these agents transact. However, in financial economics, the decisions made by individuals and managers are decisions involving monetary outcomes, and the prices established in financial markets are the prices of financial assets. As we did in our discussion of microeconomics in the previous section, let's look at the types of decisions made by individuals and managers in the area of financial economics.

### 1.2.1 Financial Decisions by Individuals

Financial decisions made by individuals in their roles as capital market participants can be grouped into three types. The first type is how, given an initial amount of wealth and a set of investment opportunities, the individual decides to allocate consumption over time. Financial economics assumes the allocation decisions are chosen to maximize individual satisfaction.

As in consumer choice theory, the measure of satisfaction is once again represented by the individual's utility function. Unlike in consumer choice theory, the consumer here trades off between the satisfaction derived from current consumption and that deriving from investing to finance future consumption. Specifically, the individual must select how much of current income to consume, and how much to invest today so as to maximize utility over some time horizon, given the available investment opportunities. The factors that influence an individual's behavior regarding intertemporal choice at different times are the individual's preferences for current and future consumption, and the effects of interest rates on these trade-offs. The role of interest rates is to measure the costs and benefits of shifting consumption intertemporally.[11]

Individuals who elect to consume more than they have available from current income and savings must decide how to finance that consumption. Thus, the second type of financial decision is the *household finance decision*. Obvious examples of financing instruments used by individuals to attain their objectives are residential mortgage loans, credit card borrowings, automobile loans, and student loans. These are claims individuals issue against themselves. The field of financial economics that investigates this behavior by individuals is called *household finance*, and is relatively new. As John Campbell stated in his 2006 Presidential Address to the American

---

[11] Traditionally, this intertemporal consumption decision by individuals is covered in a microeconomics course.

Finance Association, household finance "has attracted much recent interest but still lacks definition and status within our profession."[12] Although this book provides the tools and a description of financial instruments for aiding individuals in making the household financing decision, it does not cover more general issues that are now being tackled in this field. Such issues include, for example, explaining how individuals' incomes and educational characteristics influence participation in the stock market and the degree of diversification in their investment portfolios.

Given an amount to be invested, the third type of individual financial decision is how to allocate that amount amongst the investment oppportunities available in the capital markets. The investment opportunities can involve the direct purchase of physical assets that are expected to generate income (such as a commercial property) or financial claims such as securities (i.e., stocks and bonds). The branch of financial economics that deals with this allocation decision, *portfolio selection theory*, is one of the principal topics covered in this book.

## 1.2.2 Financial Decisions by Firm Managers

An appropriate goal for a firm's management is to place the firm's owners in as satisfactory a financial position as possible. This book will show that in many circumstances the goal can be interpreted as one of maximizing the value of the owners' investment in the firm. The principal task of the firm's management, then, can frequently be expressed as one of raising capital to invest in productive enterprise, with a view to maximizing the value of the owners' investment. Essentially, managers of firms create wealth by generating returns more favorable than those demanded by investors. The details of how and why the wealth creation process can and should be managed form one of the principal subjects of this book.

Thus, we see the two major types of financial decisions that managers make are:

- How to finance the firm.
- How to select productive assets the firm needs to operate in a value maximizing fashion.

The first type of managerial finance decision involves deciding on the firm's capital structure. The *capital structure of a firm* is the mix of debt (i.e., borrowed funds) and equity that management decides to employ to finance the operations of the firm. For example, Apple Inc. as of September 2010 had no long-term debt and therefore was financed primarily by equity. However, most firms do use long-term debt in financing. For example, as of 2010, Duke Energy Corporation (an energy company operating in North America) was financed with about 45% debt and 55% equity. In 2010, the capital structure of Parker Hannifin Corporation, a firm that manufactures fluid power systems, electromechanical controls, and related components, was about 70% debt and 30% equity.

As explained in this book, there are advantages and disadvantages to both sources of financing. The branch of economic theory that deals with this financing decision is

---

[12] Campbell (2006, p. 1553).

referred to as *capital structure theory*. One of the principal questions in this field is whether there is an optimal capital structure for a firm that managers should seek to target. That is, can managers select a mix of debt and equity such that the value of the firm is maximized?

One of the first major theories in financial economics addressed precisely this issue. The theory, referred to the *Modigliani-Miller theory*—named after the two Nobel Laureates who proposed it, Franco Modigliani (winner of the 1985 prize) and Merton Miller (cowinner of the 1990 prize)—showed that in a perfect capital market the capital structure of a firm is irrelevant.[13] That is, under the idealized conditions first examined by Modigliani and Miller there is no optimal capital structure. However, once Modigliani and Miller considered the impact of taxes on the cost of borrowing (i.e., the fact that in the United States interest payments on debt are tax deductible, and those deductions have economic value, where dividend payment to owners are not tax deductible), they showed that there is an optimal capital's payments structure, and the firm should be financed entirely by debt! Obviously, firms are not 100% debt financed, so that economists must look carefully at the conditions assumed by Modigliani and Miller to explain why managers do not behave according to those initially established findings. One of the major reasons is that the cost of bankruptcy is not zero.

Related to the capital structure decision is the question of management's *dividend policy*. The dividends of a firm are the amount of earnings or profits distributed to the owners. Any earnings or profits not distributed to the owners are retained within the firm and thereby represent additional equity in the firm. As such, retention decisions affect the firm's capital structure. Miller and Modigliani (1961) found that in a perfect capital market where there is no uncertainty, the dividend policy does not affect the value of the firm—it is irrelevant. In less restricted circumstances than those examined by Miller and Modigliani, finance theory offers some explanations for why dividend policy is indeed likely to affect firm value.

The second type of managerial financial decision concerns a firm's investments. Management continually invests funds in assets and these assets are expected to produce income and cash flows that the firm may then either employ to reinvest in more assets or distribute to the owners in the form of dividends. The assets include physical assets (such as land, buildings, equipment, and machinery), as well as assets that represent property rights (such as accounts receivable, securities, patents, and copyrights).

*Capital* in this context refers to the company's total assets, both tangible and intangible, and *capital investment* refers to the firm's investment in those assets. There are two principal types of capital investment decisions that management must make: capital budgeting decisions and working capital decisions. *Capital budgeting decisions* involve the selection of investments in long-lived assets, or assets expected to produce benefits over more than one year. The investment projects themselves are referred to as *capital projects*. There are analytical techniques based on maximization of owners' wealth that can be used to determine whether or not to invest in a capital project, and these techniques comprise an area of financial economics referred to as *capital budgeting theory*.

---

[13] Modigliani and Miller (1958, 1963).

Managers also invest in short-term assets, referred to as *working capital* or *current assets*, for the same reason they invest in capital projects: to maximize owners' wealth. However, because managers evaluate current assets over a shorter time frame (less than a year), they focus more on the cash flows from these types of assets rather than on the impact of receiving cash flows over time.

## 1.2.3  Capital Market, Risk, and Asset Pricing

The financial decisions made by individuals (or funds managed on their behalf) in their role as investors result both in the funds supplied to the capital market and the demand for funds stemming from those individuals requiring financing. Further, the supply and demand for funds stem from the financial decisions made by the management of firms in their investment and financing decisions. The resulting aggregates—the demand for and the supply of funds—jointly determine the market rate of return required for investing (or equivalently, the prices of financial assets). In theory, the decisions of individuals in their roles as investors and borrowers, of managers in their roles of making financial decisions, and of the market in signalling the allocation of capital leads to the efficient allocation of capital in the economy. Moreover, the signals provided by the capital market provide guidance to firm managers in making financial decisions that will maximize the weath of the owners of the firm.

As with microeconomic theory, the baseline behavior of individuals and managers is studied under the assumptions of idealized market conditions, in what is referred to as a *perfect capital market*. When these assumptions are violated, alternative theories are needed to explain the financial decision-making behavior of individuals and managers. This study parallels the development of microeconomic theory.

The first extension of perfect capital market theory has been to the consideration of risk in financial decision making. The major contributions here were by Nobel Laureates Harry Markowitz and William Sharpe, two of the three corecipients of the 1990 prize. In 1952, Markowitz showed how investors should determine their optimal investment portfolio in the face of risk.[14] In 1960, building on Markowitz's portfolio selection framework, Sharpe showed how portfolio allocations should be made when investors can choose among both risky and risk-free assets.[15] Sharpe's model shows both how capital asset prices should be determined in a perfect capital market, and the types of risk that investors should and should not be compensated for taking on. Another asset pricing model, based on the arbitrage pricing theory formulated by Stephen Ross (1976), predicts the relationship between return and risk factors that affect portfolio return and its risk. More recent work has examined the issues involved in developing appropriate measures of risk to extend the circumstances considered by Sharpe and by Ross.

The second extension considers the impacts of market failure on financial decision making by individuals and, in particular, managers. For example, if markets fail and it is consequently not possible to maximize the firm's market value, what criterion should managers adopt to make financial decisions? These and similar extensions

---

[14] Markowitz (1952).
[15] Sharpe (1964).

draw from the areas of decision making and information economics that we described earlier in this chapter.

---

### ❖ ❖ ❖    1.3   ROAD MAP FOR THE BOOK

This section explains how the book will pursue the investigations covered in the foregoing broad overview of financial economics.

#### 1.3.1 Development Strategy

The two basic financial decisions, made by both individuals and managers, involve choosing investment and financing strategies. One time-honored method for cutting difficult topics down to size starts by examining an imagined situation from which complicating details have been removed. Then, once the simplified problem has been investigated, a statement of principles can be developed. Next, complicating details can be reintroduced without losing sight of the basics. This is the program we shall follow. As the circumstances we consider are allowed gradually to become more complex, so do the financial decisions made by individuals and managers. But it remains true that our understanding of simple situations carries over to help enlighten us about the same tasks in the more complex real-world situations we eventually consider.

A considerable amount can be learned by following this program. First, our approach will both emphasize key questions for individuals and managers to ask, and will also explain why these are key questions. Second, it will indicate the kinds of information about financial decisions that financial economic theory currently offers, thus providing a sense of the circumstances within which the key questions are asked. Finally, the points at which knowledge must be supplemented by judgment are discussed, in order to impart information as to what aspects of a financial decision are well understood, in contrast to those that cannot be resolved by theory. In essence, by learning what financial economic theory can do, one gains an appreciation for how in practice individuals and managers face the problem of combining understanding with informed judgment.

The first stage of our program is therefore considering a simple certainty world with a perfect capital market. In Part I we consider the tasks faced by individuals and managers in this certainty world within a perfect capital market. We learn how the price of investment funds is determined by the interaction of lender (or investor) preferences and borrower needs. We explain how the managers of firms can combine knowledge of security pricing processes with information about opportunities for investing in a firm. We learn that in those circumstances wealth maximization can be an appropriate goal for a firm's management to pursue. We develop principles that guarantee attainment of the wealth maximization goal, and we learn why the principles work.

In Part II we look at financial systems. Here we explain how financial systems are organized and how individual financial transactions are governed or administered. Although at first financial systems may appear to be complicated, financial economics provides a straightforward analytical and descriptive picture of how all such systems work by performing a set of functions. These functions differ, however, in the relative importance of how they are organized, that is, the different financing mechanisms (which we refer to as governance choices), employed by financial market agents, by financial intermediaries, and by managers using internal allocations of funds. The study of financial systems involves an examination of the differing arrangements reached between financiers and their clients. This process of alignment is studied principally in the context of financial deals that involve either commitments of financial resources (i.e., fund-raising), reallocation of risks (risk transfer), or both.

Building on the principles set forth in a certainty world with a perfect capital market, Part III moves on to the second stage of the program—incorporating risk into the financial decision making process. We provide analytical tools and techniques, along with various traditional and recently proposed risk measures.

In Part IV we cover portfolio selection using the Markowitz mean-variance framework and present different asset pricing theories. The pricing of derivative assets (forwards, futures, and options) is the subject of Part V.

In the financial decisions we analyze in Part I and in the pricing models we present in Parts IV and Vs, we assume a perfect capital market in which we assume that any differences between theoretical asset prices and actual asset prices can be arbitraged away. In Part VI we look at how the criteria for financial decision making may change when there are capital market imperfections. We also examine the impediments to arbitrage activity in real-world capital markets. In Part VII we then apply the principles in Part VI to the capital structure decisions when there are capital market imperfections. In the final part of the book, Part VIII, we look at capital budgeting decision making when risk is taken into consideration.

## 1.3.2  Practical Application

Throughout this book, we discuss how the theory we present is used in practical applications. Indeed, the foregoing discussion has already suggested many ways in which theoretical reasoning and application questions are related in both personal and corporate finance. But questions of personal and corporate financing planning are by no means the only questions with which students of finance are concerned. For example, what were the causes of the 2007–2009 financial crisis, and how did those causes interact to affect the financial system? How is the crisis related to the 2010–2011 concerns of the G20 with governmental deficits and the reactions of financial markets to policies affecting those deficits? Since this book is an introduction to financial economics, a full discussion of these matters is beyond its scope. Nevertheless the material in the book will help the reader to get started answering such larger questions, as we indicate next.

The 2007–2009 financial crisis began with the U.S. subprime market, but the problems in that market were actually indicators of much deeper financial difficulties. The subprime problems began with an upsurge of residential and commercial mortgage loans whose repayment terms exceeded the ability of borrowers to repay their loans, particularly as economic times became more stringent after the loans had been granted. (The book's discussion of financial governance in Chapter 7 expands this point more fully.) Many of these quality problems were disguised because the mortgage originators sold the original loans off to entities that in turn sold instruments to finance the mortgage portfolios to investors using a process known as securitization. (Securitization is explained in Chapter 23.) Although securitization should not have disguised either the underlying loans' poor quality or their inadequate governance, it had the effect of doing so because it provided incentives for weaker governance than had previously been employed in securitization transactions. Moreover the securities used were complex, the default insurance that often accompanied an issue of the securities further weakened governance incentives, and rating agencies sometimes overrated the securities' quality.[16] (The book sketches the kinds of instruments used in the securitization process.)

After the crisis in the U.S. subprime market began to take hold, it spread rapidly throughout the world as additional financial system weaknesses were uncovered in many different places. Financial institutions and their clients were overborrowing (their leverage, a concept discussed in this book under capital structure, reached unprecedented levels) and the forms of default insurance used by many institutions suffered from the fallacy that no matter how much risk was taken on, the defaults could effectively be insured. The fallacy in this belief was that the issuers of the insurance would remain solvent. However, the issuers of the insurance actually assumed liability for large proportions of the world's financial risks, meaning that during a crisis their liability far exceeded their ability to repay.

The world's governments were brought into the crisis because ultimately they had to underwrite the world's financial institutions in order to prevent financial system collapse. To underwrite financial institutions, governments borrowed to finance their activities, even though they were already coming under financial pressure for a multitude of other reasons.

While the crisis may be subsiding in 2010–2011, recovery from the resulting economic downturn continues to be slow and uneven. At the same time and throughout much of the world, government indebtedness is of growing concern, and many governments are trying to balance the use of stimulus to aid the recovery against the increasing indebtedness they are incurring to do so.

---

## QUESTIONS

1. In microeconomic theory, what types of decisions are made by agents?

2. How are the preferences of consumers expressed in economics?

3. The following two excerpts are from an article by M. Basili published in 2001 in *Economic Notes* entitled "Knightian Uncertainty in Finance Markets: An Assessment."

---

[16] In the United States, a U.S. Treasury Department report released on June 27, 2009 ("Financial Regulatory Reform—A New Foundation: Rebuilding Financial Supervision and Regulation") identified poor underwriting standards as a chief reason for the collapse of the securitization market. The report went on to make the following five recommendations to strength the securitization market: (1) modifying the incentive structure, (2) bringing compensation in line with the long-term performance of assets, (3) enhancing the transparency of the securitization market, (4) strengthening performance of credit rating agencies, and (5) reducing overreliance on credit ratings.

If information is too vague and imprecise to be summarized by a unique additive probability measure, an agent faces Knightian uncertainty or ambiguity rather than risk.

It is proved that an agent's attitude towards ambiguity has a crucial role in asset price determination and portfolio choice. Knightian uncertainty attitude provides an alternative explanation of financial market failures and enables puzzles to be solved, such as market breakdowns, price indeterminacy and volatility, bid and ask spreads, portfolio inertia, violation of call and put parity.

  a. What is meant by Knightian uncertainty?

  b. Why do you think that Knightian uncertainty plays a "crucial role in asset price determination and portfolio choice"?

  c. What is meant by financial market failure?

4. In a May 2009 research paper, Matthew Pritsker, a senior economist in the Risk Analysis Section at the Board of Governors of the Federal Reserve, in a paper titled "Knightian Uncertainty and Interbank Lending" wrote the following about the recent financial crisis:

> The collapse of the housing price bubble during 2007 and 2008 was accompanied by high interbank lending spreads, and a partial collapse of interbank lending. This paper models how Knightian uncertainty over risk exposures affects interbank lending spreads, and may have contributed to the collapse of interbank lending.

How does the above statement tie into your answer to part c of the previous question?

5. What is meant by a classical perfect market?

6. What is meant by a subjective probability and how is it used in economics in conjunction with expected utility theory?

7. In finance, what does the consumer choice theory deal with?

8. What is meant by the household finance decision?

9. What does the area of portfolio selection theory deal with?

10. What is an appropriate financial goal for a firm's management to pursue?

11. A firm's capital structure is the sum of its debt plus equity. Below is the debt to equity ratio for three corporations. For each corporation, determine the percentage of the capital structure that is debt and the percentage that is equity.

  a. IBM     1.23

  b. Xerox   0.83

  c. 3M Co. 0.37

12. What does financial theory tell us about the optimal capital structure of a firm?

13. Why is the dividend policy established by management related to the firm's capital structure?

---

### ❖ ❖ ❖ REFERENCES

Arrow, Kenneth J. (1953). "The Role of Securities in the Optimal Allocation of Risk-Bearing," *Review of Economic Studies* **31**: 91–96.

Bernoulli, Daniel. (1738). "Specimen Theoriae Novae de Mensara Sortis," *Commentarii Academiae Scientiarum Imperialis Petropolitanae*. (Translated in 1964: "Exposition of a New Theory on the Measurement of Risk," *Econometrica* **22**(1): 23–36.

Campbell, John Y. (2006). "Household Finance," *Journal of Finance* **61**: 1533–1604.

Debreu, Gerard. (1959). *The Theory of Value: An Axiomatic Analysis of Economic Equilibrium*. New York: Wiley.

Hicks, John. (1931). "Theory of Uncertainty and Profit," *Economica* **11**: 170–189.

Knight, Frank H. (1921). *Risk, Uncertainty, and Profit*, Hart, Schaffner, and Marx Prize Essays, No. **31**. Boston: Houghton Mifflin.

Markowitz, Harry M. (1952). "Portfolio Selection," *Journal of Finance* **7**(1): 77–91.

Miller, Merton H., and Franco Modigliani. (1961). "Dividend Policy, Growth, and the Valuation of Shares," *Journal of Business* **34**(4): 411–433.

Modigliani, Franco, and Merton H. Miller. (1958). "The Cost of Capital, Corporation Finance and The Theory of Investment," *American Economic Review* **48**(3): 261–297.

Modigliani, Franco, and Merton H. Miller. (1963). "Corporate Income, Taxes and The Cost of Capital: A Correction," *American Economic Review* **53**(3): 433–443.

Ross, Stephen A. (1976). "The Arbitrage Theory of Capital Asset Pricing," *Journal of Economic Theory* **13**(3): 343–362.

Savage, Leonard J. (1954). *The Foundations of Statistics*. New York: Dover.

Sharpe, William F. (1964). "Capital Asset Prices," *Journal of Finance* **19**(3): 425–442.

Simon, Herbert A. (1947). *Administrative Behavior: A Study of Decision-Making Processes in Administrative Organizations*. New York: Macmillan.

Von Neumann, John, and Oskar Morgenstern. (1947). *Theory of Games and Economic Behavior*. Princeton: Princeton University Press.

# PART I

# FINANCE IN A CERTAINTY WORLD WITH A PERFECT CAPITAL MARKET

# 2

# Consumer Financial Decisions

$C$onsumer behavior plays a key role in determining what and how much is produced in a developed economy. For this reason, a convenient starting point in microeconomic theory is to understand the basic principles of how consumers make consumption and investment decisions. In arranging their expenditure and finance planning, consumers both spend and invest in the financial obligations of firms and governments. Firms and governments are thus borrowing from consumers who decide both how much to consume at a given time and how much to lend or invest (through the purchase of financial assets) for financing future consumption. Ultimately, the price of investment funds is determined by the interaction of lender preferences and borrower needs. Thus, consumer behavior with respect to financial decisions is critical to understanding financial economic theory.

In this chapter, we describe the basic features of consumers' financial decisions. As we do throughout this book and as explained in Chapter 1, we begin by considering the decisions made by consumers in a certainty world with a perfect capital market.[1]

## 2.1 The Consumption-Investment Problem

In a typical developed economy, consumers' purchases determine the outcome of more than two-thirds of the output produced. Indeed, since consumer decisions are the foremost means by which goods and services are distributed in any developed economy, it is important to understand consumer behavior. To do so, we employ what is termed the *theory of consumer choice*. The theory of consumer choice examines the trade-offs consumers must make, because their income is limited and choices of consumption goods and services are numerous. That is, consumers must consider what they can afford and what they would like to consume. The former consideration is expressed mathematically by a budget constraint and the latter by a function that expresses their preferences.

---

[1] We will explain what we mean by an imperfect capital market later in this chapter and in more detail in later chapters.

In order to emphasize the essential features of a consumer's financial decisions, the theory of consumer choice employs a number of simplifying assumptions.[2] The setting we first examine has these features:

1. Every consumer lives in a world of certainty; that is, all decision-relevant information is known exactly to the consumer, now and for all future time.
2. Only two points in time are of importance, the present time and a later time that accounts for effects that may persist into many future periods. (We subsequently show how this two-period orientation satisfactorily represents financial decision problems involving many time periods.)
3. There are many transactors in the capital market, and no single transactor is large enough to affect prices or interest rates. (Sometimes, but not always, we make similar assumptions about markets for other inputs and outputs such as capital equipment.)
4. Every market participant has the same (certain) information about market prices and the relevant terms of any transaction.
5. Transactions in the capital market can be made without payment of charges other than the ruling market rate of interest.

The last three conditions together describe what is called a *perfect capital market.* An important consequence of a perfect capital market under circumstances of certainty is that every financial instrument is the same as every other in terms of its credit risk and the rate of interest it yields when that rate is computed on the instrument's market price. In a world of certainty, no money is lent or invested unless it is known that the borrower will repay, so credit risk does not exist at all. No user of funds need pay a higher rate of interest than any other because there are many lenders and the borrower knows the rates they all charge. Hence, there is no reason to borrow at rates in excess of the market interest rate. Also, no lender will provide credit at interest rates lower than the market rate because the market rate can always be obtained on alternative transactions.

A further implication of the foregoing is that any profile of cash receipts (or disbursements) having a given present value leaves its owner in the same wealth position as does any other profile with the same present value. That is, if market interest rates are 10% per time period, $1 available now is exactly equivalent to $1.10 available one period later, because at the same point in time either cash flow profile has the same value in the capital market. This means that in the world just described, financial decisions are easy to make, and the principles on which they are based are easy to discern. Because everyone borrows or lends at the same market interest rate (a rate that may differ from one time period to the next), financial transactions can be reduced to a single measure, that of their present value.

---

[2] Simplifying assumptions is unrealistic in that such assumptions create a simpler world than actually exists. But financial decision making in the complicated real world is difficult to understand unless one has a good grasp of first principles. We try first to gain an approximate understanding by examining simple settings. Complications can then be introduced in easy stages.

## 2.1.1  Describing Individuals' Preferences

To explain why consumers decide to borrow or lend at different points in time, we describe both their preferences and their opportunities to reach preferred positions. Individuals' preferences can be described in terms of their attitudes toward bundles of consumption goods available at different points in time. In our context, the satisfaction provided by consuming various goods is summarized by their market value, which we refer to as a consumption standard.[3] Hence, we wish to represent, in a convenient way, a consumer's preferences for money expenditures at different points in time.

Preferences can be represented conveniently, using what is called a *utility function*, if a consumer is able to make consistent statements about what is preferred. The technical meaning of making such statements is as follows:

1. The consumer can compare one pair of consumption standards $(C_1, C_2)$ with another, say $(C_1^0, C_2^0)$, and state which, if either, is preferred.
2. The consumer can make the comparisons transitively; that is, if one consumption standard is preferred to a second, and if the second is in turn preferred to a third, then the first is also preferred to the third.

As long as the consumer's preferences satisfy the two foregoing assumptions, attitudes toward different consumption standards can be represented by a numerical utility function that assigns a larger number to the preferred alternative, if either, of a given pair. Such a utility function also assigns equal numbers to equally preferred alternatives. Thus, a consumer who tries to attain the most preferred position available to him can be represented as trying to maximize utility.

The form of the utility function can be illustrated as in Figure 2.1, using contour lines called *indifference curves*. The indifference curves represent loci of points at equal height on a utility surface defined above a plane on which time 1 and time 2 consumption standards are measured. Any point on any indifference curve represents a combination of time 1 and time 2 consumption expenditures that is as satisfactory as any other point on the same curve, as reflected by the fact that each indifference curve is a set of points for all of which the utility function attains the same value. To be sure the indifference curves will have the shape shown in Figure 2.1, we must also assume that:

3. The higher the consumption expenditure, the greater the consumer satisfaction.

This means that increasing satisfaction is represented in the diagram by movements in north, east, or northeast directions. Finally, we assume that:

4. Any average over two equally satisfactory different consumption combinations yields a higher level of satisfaction than either of the combinations comprising the average.

---

[3] The consumption standards reflect the satisfaction inherent in optimally choosing bundles of commodities at prices fixed in the commodities markets. This fact need not be examined here closely, given our present purposes of explaining only the consumer's financial decisions.

**FIGURE 2.1**
INDIFFERENCE CURVES FOR PERIOD 1 AND PERIOD 2 CONSUMPTION STANDARDS

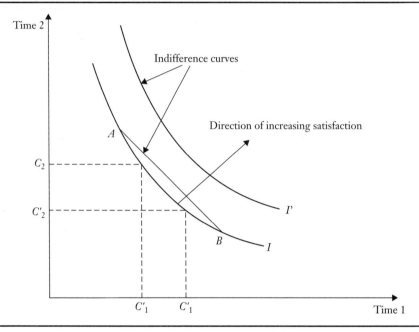

The purpose of this assumption is to render the indifference curves strictly convex. Strict convexity means that the straight line between points like $A$ and $B$ in Figure 2.1, indicating averages over consumption standards represented by points $A$ and $B$, lies inside indifference curve $I$ and hence actually touches curves higher than $I$. This assumption is used to remove any ambiguity about which set of consumption standards a consumer actually will select when the possible choices are limited.

The slope of an indifference curve at any point is called the *marginal rate of substitution between present and future consumption*. This rate indicates the consumer's preference for trading off consumption at the present time against consumption in the future. It will be noted by virtue of our last two assumptions that the marginal rate of substitution for consumption in a given period diminishes as that period's consumption increases. Hence, the larger is present consumption, the lower becomes the consumer's preference for additional present, rather than future, consumption. For example, as time 1 consumption increases, the indifference curves in Figure 2.1 become more nearly horizontal. This means that the higher the level of consumption in time 1, the more consumption must increase in time 1 to compensate (in the sense of leaving the consumer on the same indifference curve) for a given decrease in time 2 consumption.

## 2.1.2 Opportunities for Financing Consumption Expenditures

Consumers' choices are subject to the limitations of what they can afford. The resources individual consumers can expend on consumption are assets already available and incomes that will be received. The value of available assets at a given time $t$ is referred to as *wealth at time t, $w_t$,* and consists of the market value of stocks of real durable goods and financial assets carried over from previous periods. Income consists of wages, salaries, or other payments received at time $t$ and will be denoted as $y_t$. Individuals may purchase either durable or nondurable goods, where by a durable good we mean one that lasts longer than a single time period. Nondurables have a one-period life because they are merely purchased and consumed. For the time being we assume that any durable good a consumer might wish to buy can be rented on a period-by-period basis.[4] This means that any assets consumers hold from one period to the next will take the form of financial instruments.

Since we are presently considering a certainty world, future income is known exactly at any time. But the problem with future income (even if it is known with certainty) is that it cannot be used to finance current consumption unless the individual can somehow borrow against it. Hence, we suppose there are arrangements to permit this. These arrangements are, of course, dependent upon the ability to transact in the capital market.

As already noted, in the present analysis the capital market is assumed to be perfect. In such a market only a single equilibrium price for credit can prevail. Denote this price by $p$, where $p$ is the time 1 price for delivery of \$1 at time 2 (i.e., one time period later). While $p$ indicates that there is a price for money borrowed or lent, it is usually more convenient to express this price as an interest rate. Note first that if $p$ is the time 1 price of \$1 to be delivered at time 2, we can say alternatively that \$1 is the time 1 price of a sum $1/p$ to be delivered at time 2. The sum initially borrowed or lent increases if individuals prefer to spend money now rather than later, as will usually be the case. Assuming this to be so, $p$ will be less than 1 and $1/p$ greater than 1. Then we can rewrite:

$$\frac{1}{p} = 1 + \frac{1-p}{p} \equiv 1 + r \qquad (2.1)$$

That is, we define $(1 - p)/p$ as $r$, where $r$ is the *rate of interest* between times 1 and 2. Just as there is only one equilibrium value of $p$ in a perfect market, there will be only one interest rate $r$. We may also rewrite equation (2.1) to obtain:

$$p = \frac{1}{1 + r} \qquad (2.2)$$

showing that the price $p$ represents the value of \$1 discounted at interest rate $r$.

Considering now the question of the opportunities facing an individual consumer in such a world, suppose an individual has an income stream, fixed and unalterable, of $y_1$ and $y_2$ to be received at times 1 and 2, respectively, as shown in Figure 2.2. (If the individual has any financial assets, their market value can be assumed to be included in the magnitude $y_1$.) We next wish to determine the present value of this income combination. It is the sum of time 1 income $y_1$ plus the present value

---

[4] In a perfect market for durable goods, there is no difference between renting and owning, because rents will always equal the change in an asset's market values over the period it is used by a consumer.

**FIGURE 2.2**
INDIVIDUAL'S WEALTH CONSTRAINT

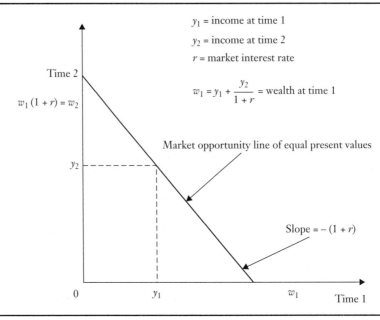

$y_1$ = income at time 1

$y_2$ = income at time 2

$r$ = market interest rate

$w_1 = y_1 + \dfrac{y_2}{1+r}$ = wealth at time 1

of income $y_2$; that is, $y_1 + y_2/(1 + r)$. This sum represents wealth at time 1, and is denoted by $w_1$.

The relation between incomes and wealth is shown in Figure 2.2, with the value of $w_1$ being given as the intercept on the period 1 axis of the straight line passing through the point $(y_1, y_2)$. If wealth $w_1$ were all invested at time 1, it would amount to $w_2 = w_1(1 + r)$ at time 2, so the line joining the points $w_1$ and $w_2$ must have a slope of $-(1 + r)$. Moreover, any point plotting along the line $w_1w_2$ in Figure 2.2 has the same period 1 intercept $w_1$ and thus the same present value. The line $w_1w_2$ is thus a line of income combinations all having equal present values. Since $w_1w_2$ goes through the point $(y_1, y_2)$, it follows that the income profile $(y_1, y_2)$ also has present value $w_1$.

The line $w_1w_2$ is called the *individual's wealth constraint* because it defines the maximum present value of different consumption expenditures that can be purchased by spending all available resources. It is also called the *market opportunity line* because it represents different combinations of funds, available at times 1 and 2, that can be obtained by arranging financial transactions whose net present value is $w_1$. The entire triangle $0w_1w_2$ is called the consumer's opportunity set, because any combination of consumption expenditures lying in or on the triangle is attainable given the consumer's initial wealth. Accordingly, any consumption expenditure pattern the consumer can choose lies within, or on the boundaries of, $0w_1w_2$.

## 2.1.3 Reconciling Preferences with Opportunities

The individual's problem is to choose a pattern of consumption expenditures that maximizes utility given the wealth constraint. The problem can be represented by combining Figures 2.1 and 2.2 as shown in Figure 2.3. If the consumer could not borrow or lend, expenditures would be restricted to the point $(y_1, y_2)$ lying on indifference curve $I'$ in Figure 2.3. With the ability to make financial transactions, the consumer can move to the higher indifference curve $I$. In the particular example of Figure 2.3, the consumer will borrow $c_1^* - y_1$ at time 1 and repay $y_2 - c_2^* = (c_1^* - y_1)(1 + r)$ at time 2. (The amount repaid is the amount borrowed plus interest.) The amounts expended satisfy the consumer's wealth constraint, as they are required to do. To see this, note that:

$$y_2 - c_2^* = (c_1^* - y_1)(1 + r) \tag{2.3}$$

may be rewritten as:

$$\frac{y_2 - c_2^*}{1 + r} = c_1^* - y_1$$

or

$$c_1^* + \frac{c_2^*}{(1 + r)} = y_1 + \frac{y_2}{(1 + r)} = w_1 \tag{2.4}$$

In other words, the present value of optimal consumption choices is just equal to initial wealth.

## FIGURE 2.3
### INDIVIDUAL'S CONSTRAINED UTILITY-MAXIMIZING CHOICE OF CONSUMPTION STANDARDS

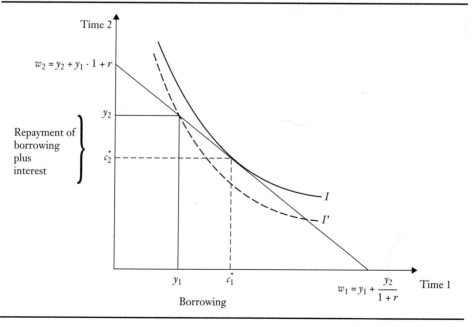

The optimal consumption choices $(c_1^*, c_2^*)$ are found[5] at the point of tangency between the highest attainable indifference curve and the wealth constraint, where optimal choices mean those the consumer most prefers (among the affordable ones). The spending pattern $(c_1^*, c_2^*)$ will not usually correspond to the consumer's income stream $(y_1, y_2)$. For this reason, the consumer will either borrow (sell a claim against future income) or lend (purchase a claim against future income) through the capital markets thus transferring funds between times 1 and 2 (the slope of the wealth constraint equal to 1 plus the market interest rate).

When the consumer chooses consumption standards optimally, an indifference curve just tangent to the wealth constraint is reached. This is the highest indifference curve the person can reach. This means that at the optimum rate at which the consumer is willing to trade off consumption between times 1 and 2 (the slope of the indifference curve) is just equal to the rate at which the market tells us the market value, at time 1, of $1 to be delivered in period 2. The amount $1/(1 + r)$ is called the *present value of $1* payable at time 2.

The theory of consumers' financial decisions thus explains that consumers enter into financial transactions to obtain a more satisfactory time profile of consumption expenditures than they could if they merely spent income when received. However, in using the financial markets, they cannot spend more than the present value of their wealth plus future incomes. In a world of certainty, this arrangement means that all consumer lending can and will be repaid; defaults are not permitted. The theory also indicates a consumer is better off if an increment to initial wealth is obtained, because this shifts the wealth constraint to the right. Thus, to leave the consumer as well off as possible, initial wealth should be made as large as possible. This is an important result that we use frequently in the rest of this book.

## 2.1.4 Numerical Example

In this section we present a numerical example illustrating further aspects of the theory. Consider the following two income streams and a market rate of interest of 10%:

$$(y_1, y_2) = (\$1,000, \$660) \quad \text{and} \quad (y_1^0, y_2^0) = (\$300, \$1,430)$$

Then

$$w_1 = \$1,000 + \frac{660}{1.1} = \$1,600$$

and

$$w_1^0 = \$300 + \frac{1430}{1.1} = \$1,600$$

---

[5] It can now be seen that strict convexity of the indifference curves, as assumed in Section 2.1, is useful for eliminating the possibility of multiple solutions to the utility maximization problem. For if the indifference curve had a linear portion, more than a single set of consumption choices might be optimal.

In a perfect capital market the consumer will be indifferent between these two income streams because their present values are equal, so that $w_1$ and $w_1^0$ are perfect substitutes. This means the consumer can obtain the optimal consumption pattern $(c_1^*, c_2^*)$, also required to have a present value of $1,600, with either income stream. For example, suppose the optimal consumption pattern is ($800, $880), which does have a present value of $1,600 at the assumed 10% rate of interest. If the consumer has the first income stream, $200 is lent at time 1. When repaid with interest at time 2, the loan yields $220. Then expenditure at time 2 can be $880, equal to $660 + $220. If the consumer has the second income stream, $500 is borrowed to finance time 1 consumption, and $550 is repaid at time 2. This leaves $1,430 − $550 = $880 to spend on consumption at time 2.

## 2.1.5 Mathematical Example

The theory can be presented a little more formally by solving a problem like the following one:

$$\max_{c_1, c_2} c_1 c_2^{0.6}$$

subject to $y_1 = \$1,000$, $y_2 = \$648$, and $r = 0.08$, so that:

$$w_1 = y_1 + \frac{y_2}{1+r} + r = \$1,000 + \frac{648}{1.08} = \$1,600$$

Here we have assumed a specific form of the utility function and specific values for incomes and the interest rate, so that we can obtain a numerical answer to the consumption-investment problem. The function $c_1 c_2^{0.6}$ is the utility function; $c_1 c_2^{0.6} = $ constant represents the equation of an indifference curve.

The consumer's problem is to maximize utility by finding the optimal consumption pattern $(c_1^*, c_2^*)$ with a present value of $1,600. That is, the solution to the problem must satisfy:[6]

$$c_1 + \frac{c_2}{1.08} = \$1,600$$

We can rewrite the last condition as:

$$c_2 = (\$1,600 - c_1)(1.08)$$

Then, substitution into the original maximization problem gives:

$$\max_{c_1} c_1 [(\$1,600 - c_1)(1.08)]^{0.6}$$

---

[6] Actually, it cannot exceed $1,600. But since spending more money on consumption is assumed to give greater satisfaction, the consumer will always spend all available funds. Incidentally, some of this spending can be interpreted as a bequest, so the consumer, although a materialist, need not be lacking in altruism.

A solution to the last problem can be found by setting the derivative taken with respect to $c_1$ equal to zero. Taking the derivative gives:

$$(\$1{,}600 - c_1)^{0.6} - c_1(0.6)(\$1{,}600 - c_1)^{-0.4} = 0$$

We then have:

$$(\$1{,}600 - c_1)^{0.6} = 0.6c_1(\$1{,}600 - c_1)^{-0.4}$$

or

$$(\$1{,}600 - c_1) = 0.6c_1$$

so that

$$1.6c_1 = \$1{,}600$$

and hence, the solution for time 1 consumption is:

$$c_1^* = \$1{,}000$$

**FIGURE 2.4**
INCOME AND CONSUMPTION PATTERNS FOR MATHEMATICAL EXAMPLE

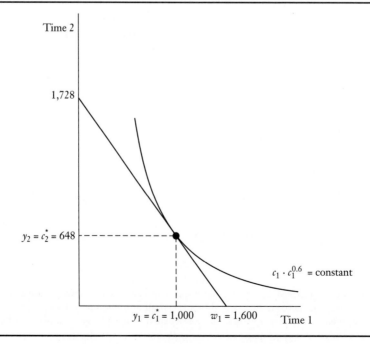

Moreover, since

$$c_1^* + \frac{c_2^*}{1.08} = \$1,600, \quad \frac{c_2^*}{1.08} = \$600$$

so that

$$c_2^* = \$600(1.08) = \$648$$

This consumer is atypical in neither borrowing nor lending; that is, the optimal consumption pattern is exactly the same as the income stream. Formally,

$$c_1^* = y_1 \quad \text{and} \quad c_2^* = y_2$$

A geometrical representation of the problem and its solution is given in Figure 2.4.

## 2.2 INITIAL WEALTH IS THE ONLY CONSTRAINT ON CONSUMER DECISIONS

It is clear from the foregoing analysis that the wealth constraint keeps the consumer from reaching higher indifference curves. But since this constraint is a line describing combinations of time 1 and time 2 cash flows having equal present values, the analysis also says that the limitation on consumption is entirely reflected by the magnitude of $w_1$. This is because all cash flow profiles having the same present value leave the consumer with the same opportunities, as we have already argued. We now ask whether these conclusions are altered if either the individual holds durable goods or the capital market is not perfect.

### 2.2.1 Income and Initial Wealth Combined

We previously mentioned that the consumer might have an initial wealth endowment as well as an income stream. If the initial wealth endowment is in the form of financial assets that can be freely bought and sold in the capital market without payment of transaction costs, their value can be interpreted as included in $y_1$.[7]

If wealth is in the form of durable goods or other real commodities, we assume they are sold in their respective markets, the proceeds added to current income, and the goods, if needed, rented on a period-by-period basis.[8] Thus, initially held assets serve only to shift the wealth constraint by the market value of the assets, a movement to the right in Figures 2.2 and 2.3. Hence, the individual's wealth expressed as the

---

[7] In some analyses this is written as $y_1 + a_1$, where $a_1$ represents an initial endowment of real assets.

[8] A problem arises if real goods markets are not assumed to be perfect, because the per period rents of the durable goods might then differ from their changes in market value. In this case, renting on a period-by-period basis might have financial consequences different from those of ownership. For the present, we assume perfect markets for durable goods, leaving the difficulty for later consideration.

present value of the period income stream plus the market value of other initial assets becomes the effective constraint on the choice of consumption patterns over time. Otherwise the analysis is unchanged.

## 2.2.2　Effects of Capital Market Imperfections

The foregoing analysis showed that individuals in economies with a perfect capital market are never made worse off, and are usually made better off, by their ability to borrow or lend freely in choosing consumption patterns. By implication we can infer that the general level of well-being in such economies is higher than it would be if borrowing and lending were not possible. For these reasons, the presence of *capital market imperfections* is generally regarded unfavorably. For example, transactions charges such as brokerage fees restrict the amount of initial wealth available and consequently reduce the level of a consumer's well-being. Similarly, other kinds of imperfections such as unequally distributed information can inhibit or even prevent certain financial transactions from taking place.

Although we explore the consequences of market imperfections at length in later chapters, even the simple theory developed so far allows us to develop some conclusions. For example, consider the effects of regulatory constraints that restrict lending. Such an intervention has a potential for leaving at least some individuals worse off, as illustrated in Figure 2.5. Here the individual is affected by a lending restriction that permits borrowing only up to a fixed maximum amount $c_1' - y_1$, an amount less than the $c_1^* - y_1$ that would be borrowed if there were no constraint. Thus,

**FIGURE 2.5**
A LENDING RESTRICTION REDUCING INDIVIDUAL SATISFACTION

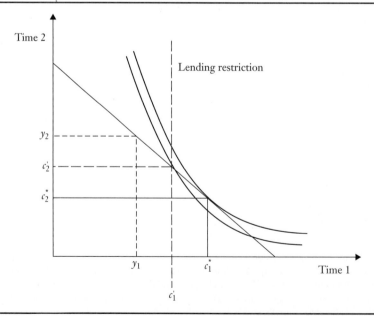

the consumer can only attain the consumption standard $(c_1', c_2')$, which is tangent to an indifference curve at a lower level of satisfaction than that reached by $(c_1^*, c_2^*)$.

The kinds of lending constraints illustrated in Figure 2.5 are observed in actuality. For example, in times of national emergency, credit restrictions may be justified on grounds of the social benefits they bring through restricting purchases of consumer goods and hence freeing the economy's resources for use in dealing with the emergency. In ordinary times, legislation such as a small loans act sometimes stipulates maximum amounts that individual clients can borrow, a position usually justified on the grounds that some individuals may, if unrestricted, borrow more than is desirable, either for them or society.

## 2.3 THE MEANING OF THE MARKET RATE OF INTEREST

If we suppose that on balance consumers are net lenders (as is typically the case in developed economies), and if we assume the economy's total borrowing is a given fixed amount, the aggregate supply of credit provided by consumers will determine the market rate of interest. In determining how much to lend, each individual chooses her total consumption expenditures such that the ratio of marginal utilities for consumption at times 1 and 2 is equal to $1 + r$, the slope of the market opportunity line. The aggregate of decisions like this will determine the total amount of lending and thus, in turn, the market interest rate. Thus, in a certain sense the market interest rate reflects society's preferences for trading off between consumption at times 1 and 2, respectively.

Moreover, the market interest rate is the reward consumers receive for deferring consumption and is thus the price those demanding funds (e.g., businesses and governments) must pay in order to bid funds away from consumer spending. By paying this price, firms induce saving, which then provides funds necessary for purchasing investment goods. Such investments are worthwhile if they yield a return greater than the market rate of interest, because that means the future consumption made possible by the initial investment will have a higher present value than the consumption originally deferred.

## 2.4 PRACTICAL IMPORTANCE OF CONSUMPTION-INVESTMENT THEORY

We have seen that most households will be better off in economies with smoothly working financial markets. A practical circumstance reflecting the theory's predictions is that many householders make contributions to pension funds; that is, by saving (and hence lending to others) they are able to arrange a more satisfactory profile of anticipated consumption expenditures than would be available if there were no such arrangements.

Household investment decisions are important to firms in real-world economies because households are the primary source of finance capital; that is, in most developed economies households are on balance net lenders. Most of these household funds are in financial institutions like life insurance companies and pension and mutual funds. The funds raised by these institutions are reinvested in corporate and government securities. Households also make some direct purchases of corporate and government securities, thus acting directly as lenders to business and government. Households' desires to finance future consumption thus provide the main source of funds that firms can use to finance their investment activities.[9] The price firms must pay for these funds is the price that households require to defer present consumption until some future time.

The theory developed so far provides a criterion for managers of firms. In a certainty world with a perfect capital market the only constraint on consumer decisions is wealth, and the greater the wealth, the greater the consumer satisfaction. Accordingly, the best that management of corporations can do for their owners is to maximize the present value of their ownership interests in these corporations. That is, management's task is to create as much wealth as possible, which is what all the owners of firms require their management to do. Management performs its wealth creation task by reinvesting funds raised at rates higher than the market rate of interest. In the next chapter we turn to the details of how management performs this task.

---

### KEY POINTS

- The behavior of consumers as both demanders of goods and services and as suppliers of funds to the capital market is important in developed economies.
- The theory of consumer choice examines the trade-offs and decisions consumers make in their purchase decisions. The preference of consumers is expressed in their utility functions.
- It is assumed that consumers operate in a perfect capital market in which: (1) there are many transactors, and no single transactor is large enough to affect prices or interest rates; (2) the same (certain) information about market prices and the relevant terms of any transaction are available to all parties; and (3) there are no costs of transacting other than the ruling market rate of interest.
- In a perfect capital market there is no need for borrowers to borrow at a rate in excess of the market interest rate or for lenders to provide credit at a rate below the market interest rate.
- Preferences of consumers can be expressed mathematically by means of a utility function where equally satisfactory consumption patterns are depicted as points on an indifference curve.
- The marginal rate of substitution between present and future consumption is the slope of an indifference curve at any point and indicates the consumer's preference for trading off consumption at the present time against consumption in the future.

---

[9] The technical specialist will notice that monetary expansion and the attendant credit expansion are ignored in this simplified exposition.

- The value of available assets at a given time consists of the market value of stocks of real durable goods and financial assets carried over from previous periods.
- The theory of consumers' financial decisions explains that consumers enter into financial transactions to obtain a better time profile of consumption expenditures than they could by spending their entire income at each time point when it is received.
- A perfect capital market means consumers can never be worse off by having the freedom to borrow or to lend. This result implies that capital market imperfections are regarded as unfavorable.
- Capital market imperfections include transactions charges, unequally distributed information, and regulatory constraints.
- As each consumer decides how much to lend or borrow, the aggregate of consumer decisions will determine the total amount of lending or borrowing and thus in turn the market interest rate. The market interest rate is the reward consumers receive for deferring consumption and is thus the price those needing funds must pay in order to bid funds away from consumers spending funds in a given period.

## QUESTIONS

1.  a.  What are the implications for credit risk in a perfect capital market under circumstances of certainty?
    b.  In a perfect capital market, would an entity in need of funds pay an interest rate in excess of the market interest rate? Why or why not?

2.  Why is financial decision making made easier in a perfect capital market?

3.  a.  What is meant by a utility function?
    b.  What is an indifference curve?
    c.  What is meant by the marginal rate of substitution between present and future consumption?

4.  Draw a line of equal present values for the cash flow profile of $100 now and $210 next period, interest rates at 5%. What is the maximum amount that can be realized in the first period if, in addition to interest charges, 1% commission is collected from the proceeds of any borrowings? Show the effect of the commission on your graph, and explain the importance of this exercise for the consumer's well-being.

5.  Suppose interest rates are zero and the consumer's utility is $u(c_1, c_2) = (c_1, c_2)$, while the two incomes are $(y_1, y_2) = (75, 125)$. Find the optimal consumption in each period, and also indicate what financial transactions the consumer makes. Show the answers on a diagram.

6.  Suppose an investment of $40 now will return $110 one period later, interest rate 10%. Then:

$$w_1 = \frac{110}{1.10} - 40 = 60$$

In a perfect market the owner of such an income stream can create any cash flow profile that satisfies:

$$c_1 + \frac{c_2}{1.10} = 60$$

Hence, if this person is offered another investment opportunity that costs $10 now but pays $77 one period later, it is as satisfactory as the first. Why might this reasoning not work if there were a 1% brokerage charge on amounts borrowed?

7. **a.** Use a diagrammatic analysis to show why a consumer facing a two-period planning problem under certainty may benefit from the existence of a capital market. Explain the different features of your diagram, and list important assumptions of your analysis (other than those already mentioned).

   **b.** Use a similar diagram to show why some individuals would be worse off if (in the world described in part a) lenders restricted the amount an individual could borrow to a fixed percentage of his current (first-period) income.

   **c.** Might such a restriction be a good policy in the real world? Why or why not?

8. Is it possible to say anything, on the basis of the certainty theory of consumption-investment decisions, about whether consumers will borrow more (less) as interest rates rise? Why? Use a diagram.

9. Try to explain why an investor might be indifferent between dividends (cash payments at time 1) and capital gains (cash payments at time 2) in a certainty world with a perfect capital market and no taxes. The proposition means that a change in dividends is offset by a change in capital gains having the same present value. Use a diagram, clearly labeled, and keep your explanations as short as possible.

10. A consumer's consumption-utility function for a two-period horizon is $u(c_1, c_2) = c_1 c_2^{0.6}$; the income stream is $y_1 = 2,000$; $y_2 = 1,296$; and the market rate of interest is $0.08$. Determine values for $c_1$ and $c_2$ that maximize utility. Is the consumer a borrower or a lender?

11. In a two-period problem, a consumer whose preferences satisfy the assumptions of this chapter will consume more of at least one good as income rises. True or false? Show diagrammatically why your answer is correct.

12. Show diagrammatically how an individual earning income at time 1 could provide for consumption at time 2, where time 2 represents retirement and no income is earned.

13. Explain whether you agree or disagree with the following statement: In a perfect capital market, individuals are made worse off by their ability to borrow or lend freely in choosing consumption patterns.

14. What is meant by a capital market imperfection? Give two examples.

# 3

# CREATING WEALTH BY INVESTING IN PRODUCTIVE OPPORTUNITIES

*I*n this chapter we study how management can invest in firms so as to create wealth and thus enhance individuals' satisfaction. We first study *proprietary firms* in which the owner and manager are the same person. Then we consider productive firms with many owners. In both cases the firms make investment and financing decisions that can augment the wealth positions of their owners.

We shall see that in a perfect capital market management can maximize the wealth of a firm's owners by using a rule called the *market value rule*. This rule requires management to make decisions that maximize the market value of the firms they operate. After studying the details of how market value is maximized, we conclude the chapter by stating important generalizations, called *separation principles*, that both define the task of financial management and provide insight into how that task can best be performed.

## 3.1 THE ENTREPRENEURIAL FIRM—PRODUCTION AND INVESTMENT DECISIONS

A firm with a single owner-manager can be regarded as a wealth-creating device capable of increasing its owner's well-being so long as the firm is properly operated. Proper operation means setting production and financing decisions in such a way as to maximize the owner's wealth. We begin by assuming the entrepreneur has knowledge of a production technology. An initial supply of resources is also available that can either be sold for cash or used in a productive process whose outputs are sold for cash. At first we do not worry about where the entrepreneur's original resources stem from, but later we consider what might be done if the entrepreneur has a marketable product and no initial resources whatever.

### 3.1.1 The Entrepreneur's Opportunities

As in the previous chapter we continue to consider two points in time. The problem we now face is how to represent the entrepreneur's opportunity set, given that some resources are owned and can be used in productive activity. There are a large number of different sorts of productive opportunities that appear to be different but are actually the same when regarded in terms of opportunity sets. Such diverse activities as storing a commodity at time 1 for sale at time 2 and the operation of a farm or manufacturing firm both have similar characteristics when depicted in terms of the productive opportunities they represent.

Regardless of which kind of productive opportunity we are considering, it can be represented by a *transformation curve* having the general form $T(K_1, K_2) = 0$, where $K_1$ represents the dollar value of funds invested in the firm at time 1 and $K_2$ the dollar value of funds generated at time 2. The funds generated derive from using the resources and technology available at time 1 to produce goods that are then sold at time 2. The transformation curve is assumed to reflect efficient use of funds in the sense that the capital investment is put to its best possible use; no resources are wasted by the rational entrepreneur.

We shall assume that the transformation curve has the form shown in Figure 3.1, where $0K_1$ represents the current market value of initial resources, which may either be used in productive opportunities or sold for cash. The meaning of the transformation curve may be understood by considering point $A$, which represents the strategy of selling $0X$ of initial resources immediately and investing $XK_1$ in the productive opportunity at time 1. The amount of funds generated at time 2 from the investment $XK_1$ is denoted by $0K_2'$; $0K_2$ indicates the time 2 yield if all resources were to be invested.

The slope of a transformation curve may be interpreted as indicating the firm's marginal rate of return, because it shows the amount realized at time 2 from an increment of funds invested at time 1. Note that the shape of the transformation curve in Figure 3.1 implicitly assumes that the marginal rate of return falls steadily as the level of investment increases. (Increasing investment is shown by moving from $K_1$ to the left in the figure.) The declining slope of the transformation curve of Figure 3.1 can result from either or both of two phenomena. On the one hand, the demand curve for the firm's output may be downward sloping, so that output price must decline if more output is to be sold.[1] In this case the transformation curve will have a decreasing slope as long as average production costs do not fall as fast as output price. On the other hand, the marginal cost of production may rise due to diminishing marginal physical product of invested capital. This is sufficient to cause the transformation curve to have a decreasing slope even if average sales revenue is constant, and will of course be sufficient if average sales revenue is declining. In either case, the rate of return on invested capital will decline as increasing amounts of capital investment are undertaken.

The firm's productive opportunity set is the region enclosed by the line $0K_1K_2$. However, since the firm's owner is concerned with making the most of available

---

[1] The downward-sloping demand curve reflects finite elasticity of demand for the output and perhaps also diminishing marginal returns to advertising.

**FIGURE 3.1**
PRODUCTIVE OPPORTUNITIES

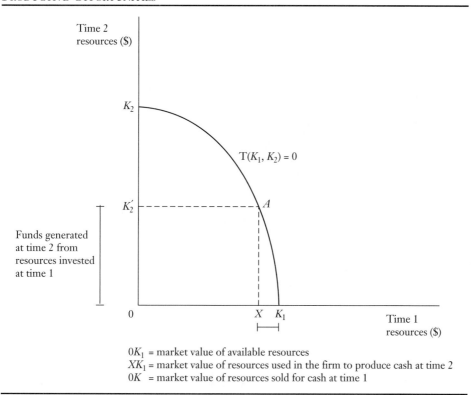

$OK_1$ = market value of available resources
$XK_1$ = market value of resources used in the firm to produce cash at time 2
$OK$ = market value of resources sold for cash at time 1

resources, the relevant portion of the productive opportunity set is the transformation curve $K_1K_2$. We next show how the owner chooses a combination of financial and productive opportunities to maximize initial wealth. For by maximizing initial wealth, the entrepreneur also maximizes the present value of available consumption opportunities, thus becoming as well off as possible given the circumstances faced. These matters may perhaps best be illustrated by some examples.

Suppose at time 1 a farmer can sell 1,000 units of a commodity (e.g., wheat), which is now in storage. The current price of wheat is $1.00 per unit. Alternatively, the farmer can wait until time 2 and sell the 1,000 units at $1.30 per unit. Assuming no spoilage and no storage charges, the situation implies a linear transformation curve as shown in Figure 3.2. Note that in such a case the farmer will either sell all the commodity at time 1 or keep it all until time 2 (unless the market opportunity line has a slope exactly equal to the transformation curve, in which case differing amounts may be sold at either time 1 or time 2 without affecting wealth). As shown in the diagram, if market rates of interest are less than 30%, the market opportunity lines are less steeply sloped than the transformation curve, and the commodity should be stored for sale at time 2. In this case the farmer can borrow at the market rate to finance current consumption, repaying the loan at time 2 from the proceeds of the commodity then

**FIGURE 3.2**

COMMODITY STORAGE EXAMPLE

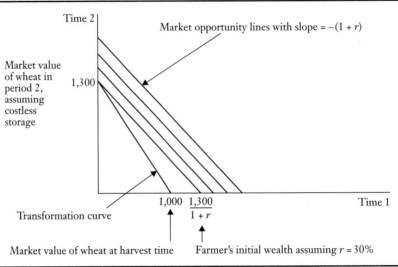

sold. In this way the farmer is better off than if the commodity is completely sold at time 1, as the figure also shows.[2] If interest rates exceed 30%, the commodity should be sold at time 1, and any funds not expended on consumption should be reinvested.

Let us now consider a second example, where productive opportunities are represented by a transformation curve of the nonlinear type first introduced. Referring to Figure 3.3, if an individual immediately liquidates the initial endowment of resources $0K_1$, an initial cash position (available for either consumption or investment at time 1) with a value of $K_1$ is obtained. This wealth can be converted into time 1 and time 2 cash flows as indicated by the straight line of slope $-(1 + r)$ passing through $K_1$. If, however, the individual liquidates only a portion of initial resources $(0K_1)$ and uses the rest $(K_1'K_1)$ for investment in some productive activity, we can represent the new set of attainable combinations by a straight line of slope $-(1 + r)$ passing through the points $w_0$ and $A$. Note that, since $w_0$ is an intercept on the time 1 axis, it represents wealth exceeding the value of the initial resources. Wealth has increased because the individual can earn a higher than market rate of return by investing some of the initially available resources in the firm.

By repeated application of the foregoing reasoning, we discover the investment policy that dominates all others is represented by point $B$, where the straight line with slope $-(1 + r)$ is exactly tangent to the productive opportunity set. This policy calls for liquidating $0K_1^*$ and investing $K_1^*K_1$ to obtain an initial wealth of $w_1$. The important implication of the tangency condition is that the marginal rate of return is

---

[2] Incidentally, the diagram is not consistent with commodity market equilibrium. For in the present circumstances, commodity speculators will have an incentive to buy and hold the commodity, thus bidding up the price at time 1 until the transformation curve and market opportunity lines have equal slopes.

**Figure 3.3**
PRODUCTIVE AND CAPITAL MARKET OPPORTUNITIES

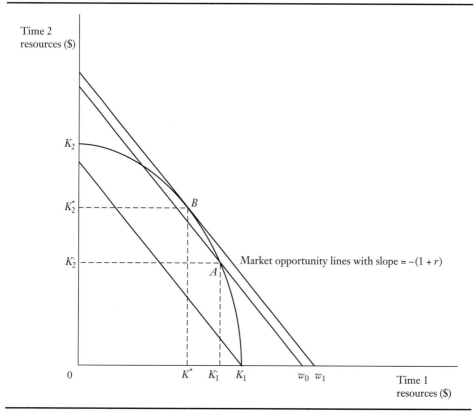

exactly equal to the market rate of interest, as may be seen by noting that at point $B$ the slope of the transformation curve (one plus the marginal rate of return) is equal to the slope of the highest attainable market opportunity line (one plus the market interest rate). The purpose of reaching this highest market opportunity line is, of course, to enable the individual to attain the highest possible initial wealth, a value indicated by $w_1$. Thus, a policy of investing funds in the firm until their rate of return falls to equality with the market rate of interest is a policy that maximizes the entrepreneur's initial wealth.

We can now consider simultaneous choice of both production-investment and consumption decisions by adding indifference curves to diagrams like Figure 3.3. The preferred consumption choices are indicated by point $A^*$ in Figure 3.4, which indicates that to maximize satisfaction the entrepreneur should first maximize initial wealth. This involves (1) liquidating and withdrawing $0K_1^*$ of the initial resources and (2) investing the remaining $K_1^* K_1$ in the productive opportunity at time 1 to yield proceeds of $K_2^*$ at time 2. Then the wealth $w_1$ so generated is allocated to consumption in the two periods. This is done by (3) consuming $0c_1^*$ at time 1, borrowing $0c_1^* - 0K_1^*$ dollars to finance the gap between desired consumption and the proceeds of resources

**FIGURE 3.4**
JOINT CHOICE OF PRODUCTION AND CONSUMPTION DECISIONS

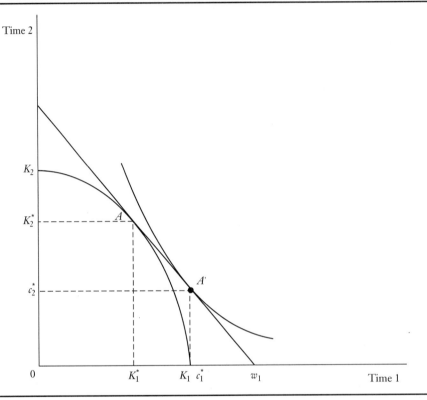

sold for cash, and (4) consuming $0c_2^*$ at time 2, repaying the loan, plus interest, $(0c_1^* - 0K_1^*)(1 + r) = 0K_2^* - 0c_2^*$, from the proceeds of the productive opportunity established by the initial investment.

By virtue of combining borrowing in the capital market with the productive opportunity this entrepreneur is clearly better off than if either the productive or the market opportunity were faced alone. Note also that once the individual has determined the value of investment, $0K_1 - 0K_1^*$, no more can be done to increase total wealth. From that point on, all the entrepreneur can do is determine the most satisfactory consumption pattern having a present value that is also equal to the $w_1$ generated from following an optimal investment policy.

The decision process can be viewed as encompassing two distinct steps:

*Step 1*: Choose the optimum production by equating the marginal rate of return on investment with the market required rate of return.

*Step 2*: Choose the optimum consumption pattern by borrowing or lending in the capital market until the consumer's subjective rate of time preference equals the market rate of return.

**FIGURE 3.5**
ENTREPRENEUR BORROWS INITIAL CAPITAL

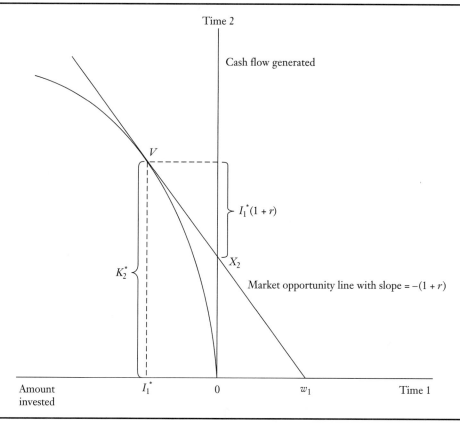

This separation of investment and consumption decisions is sometimes referred to as the *Fisher separation theorem.*[3] We discuss this principle's importance at greater length in Section 3.4.

## 3.1.2  The Entrepreneur with No Initial Resources

Suppose we now consider an aspiring entrepreneur who has a marketable product and understands the necessary productive technology but has no resources to finance the undertaking. Would the entrepreneur be prevented from realizing the value of the technical possibilities? Under the assumptions of a perfect capital market, the answer is no. For, as Figure 3.5 shows, the entrepreneur with no initial resources will be able to go to the capital market at time 1 and borrow all the funds needed to finance production ($0I_1^*$, to be paid back from the cash flow generated by production and received at time 2). Because the individual starts with no financial resources, the

---

[3] Because it first appears in Fisher (1930), Irving Fisher's insights have had a substantial impact on the contemporary economic theory of finance.

**FIGURE 3.6**
ENTREPRENEUR BORROWS SOME OF THE REQUIRED CAPITAL

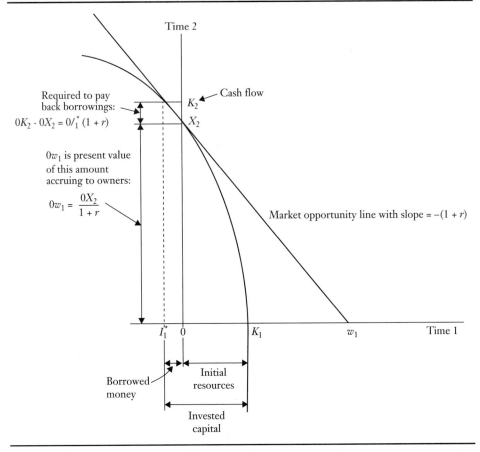

transformation curve is shown as emanating from the diagram's origin. As the amount $0I_1^*$ is borrowed, it is shown as a negative amount. At time 2, the firm repays $I_1^*(1 + r)$, leaving $0X_2$ accruing to the owner. The time 1 value of $0X_2$ is, of course, $w_1$ as shown. Thus, we see that in a perfect capital market entrepreneurs with economically viable ideas can create wealth for themselves even though they do not initially have the funds to finance their ventures—ideas can have a marketable value that can be realized by borrowing from others.

We can also imagine circumstances in which the entrepreneur has some of the funds needed for investment but must borrow the balance. We represent this by appropriately positioning the transformation curve as shown in Figure 3.6. Note that in this case the increment to the entrepreneur's wealth $K_1w_1$ is the same irrespective of whether $0I^*$ is borrowed and $0K_1$ invested or whether $0K_1$ is sold and the entire amount of $I^*K_1$ is borrowed. We conclude that in these circumstances the method of financing a productive investment is irrelevant to determining the value of the opportunity, a principle whose importance we shall consider later in some detail.

## 3.2  INVESTMENT DECISIONS MADE BY MANAGERS ON BEHALF OF OWNERS

Although the previous section provided worthwhile statements of optimal decision principles for proprietary firms (or entrepreneurial firms as we referred to them), business entities that are responsible for investing most of the funds put to work in an economy are corporations. (Some investing businesses are unincorporated entities with more than a single owner, but for simplicity in what follows, we shall refer only to corporations.) This fact leads us to consider two additional issues:

*Issue 1:*  Corporations have many owners, and there is no reason to assume that the owners' preferences are all the same.

*Issue 2:*  The owners of a corporation do not make the operating decisions of the firm but rather hire professional managers and delegate decision-making power to these managers.

No problems arise if the corporation can be managed to yield present values of owners' wealth that are exactly the same as if the owners were making the decisions themselves. For we know that $w_1$ constitutes the only restriction on individuals' consumption decisions. That is, in a perfect capital market the corporation is regarded only as a means of generating wealth, because the present value of the dollar returns it generates is the only feature relevant to its owners. Even if the owners have different marginal rates of substitution between time 1 and time 2 consumption, in a perfect capital market the present value of initial wealth is the only thing constraining their consumption choices. Since this initial wealth is maximized when the market value of individuals' investments is maximized, in a perfect capital market managers (acting on behalf of the firms' stockholders) should maximize the market values of the firms they operate. For if the market value of a firm is maximized, so is the market value of any owner's proportional share of the firm's earnings.

### 3.2.1  Corporations and the Market Value Criterion

To see in greater detail that managers should employ the market value criterion in operating a productive firm, we reconsider the results of the previous section. An entrepreneur's optimal consumption, production, and financing decisions were characterized by the simultaneous satisfaction of two tangency conditions between:

1.  The transformation curve and the capital market opportunity line and
2.  The capital market opportunity line and an indifference curve.

The first condition can be satisfied without needing to know anything about the individual preferences characterizing the second condition. On the presumption that a professional manager is hired on the basis of technical competence (that is, knowledge of the firm's technology), such a person can determine a production plan that will maximize the market value of the firm by relating knowledge of the firm's rate of return on investment to the universally available information regarding the market rate of interest.

The next step in our argument is key to understanding much of the power of financial economic theory. Recall that market opportunity lines are lines of equal present value. Thus, when we instruct the manager to find a tangency between a transformation curve and a market opportunity line, this is equivalent (if returns always diminish with more investment) to maximizing the time 1 market value of cash withdrawals that current owners can realize from the firm. Hence, management following this prescription will maximize the combined wealth of the firm's current owners and also any individual owner's proportional interest in that sum.

The management of a corporation can leave consumption decisions to individuals because an individual's current wealth is the only constraint on consumption opportunities over time. The individual meets the second condition for the optimum through personal transactions in the capital market. In a perfect capital market any set of consumption choices with a given present value can be exchanged for any other set with the same present value. In particular, this implies that any set of consumption possibilities a stockholder can derive from a firm can be converted to a wealth that is equal to this present value. Thus, if any given management decision increases the stockholders' current wealth, the stockholders are unequivocally better off. Hence, a market-value-maximizing decision leaves every stockholder as well off as possible.

### 3.2.2 Maximizing Market Value Is Equivalent to Maximizing Profits

The market value criterion is actually more general than has been apparent so far. For when properly interpreted, the market value rule is also a rule that requires managers to maximize profits at each point in time. To see the equivalence between value maximization and properly interpreted profit maximization, consider the following example, which for the sake of greater generality also contemplates three points in time.

Let $I_1^*$ be the total amount invested in a firm at time 1, $K_2$ be cash flow net of operating expenses at time 2, and $K_3$ be cash flow net of operating expenses at time 3. Assume $r$ is the market rate of interest in both periods. Then the firm's market value at time 1 is:

$$\text{MV}_1 = \frac{K_3}{(1+r)^2} + \frac{K_2}{1+r} - I_1^* \tag{3.1}$$

Now suppose the outlays for investment $I_1^*$ are all borrowed and that a loan repayment schedule is established requiring payment of principal and interest in amounts $I_2$ and $I_3$ at times 2 and 3 respectively such that:

$$\frac{I_2}{1+r} + \frac{I_3}{(1+r)^2} = I_1^* \tag{3.2}$$

Such a schedule ensures, of course, that the lender receives the market rate of interest on the loan. Then we can write:

$$MV_1 = \frac{K_2}{1+r} - \frac{I_2}{1+r} + \frac{K_3}{(1+r)^2} - \frac{I_3}{(1+r)^2} \qquad (3.3)$$

by substituting equation (3.2) into equation (3.1). Furthermore, if the loan repayments are just equal to economic depreciation, then $K_2 - I_2 = \pi_2$ and $K_3 - I_3 = \pi_3$ so that $\pi_2$ and $\pi_3$ are economic profits in the two periods. Hence, we can rewrite equation (3.3) as:

$$MV_1 \frac{\pi_2}{1+r} + \frac{\pi_3}{(1+r)^2}$$

Therefore, maximizing the present value of all (properly interpreted) profits is the same as maximizing the market value of the firm.

The criteria of maximizing market value and of individually maximizing profits in each period are not equivalent when decisions can increase profits in some periods but reduce them in others. In such circumstances, correct decisions will certainly be made if they are made using the market value criterion. Moreover, even in this case a proper interpretation of profits in each period will still yield the result that their present value will be maximized. This issue is discussed at greater length in Chapter 6.

## 3.3  EXAMPLE: AGING WINE

In this section we present a mathematical example as supporting detail for the graphical reasoning presented above. Consider the problem of a businessperson trying to decide whether to sell a product now or refine it further and sell it later at a higher price. For example, assume a vintner who is trying to maximize the market of initially available resources in the form of new wine either by selling the current vintage of wine at time 1 or aging it for sale at time 2. Let the market rate of interest be 6%.

The objective function of the vintner will be:

$$\max K_1 + \frac{K_2}{1.06} \qquad (3.4)$$

where $K_1$ = value of new wine sold at time 1
$\quad K_2$ = value of aged wine sold at time 2

Assume the maximization is subject to $K_1^2 + K_2^2 = 212.36$, a transformation curve chosen for its mathematical tractability rather than for its interpretive realism. The transformation curve implies that the time 1 cash value of all the raw wine is $(\$212.36)^{1/2}$, or approximately \$14.60.

Proceeding by substitution, we can rewrite equation (3.4) as:

$$\max_{K_2} \left(212.36 - K_2^2\right)^{1/2} + \frac{K_2}{1.06} \tag{3.5}$$

Taking the derivative of equation (3.5) with respect to $K_2$ and setting the result equal to zero, we obtain:

$$\frac{\frac{1}{2}(-2K_2)}{\left(212.36 - K_2^2\right)^{1/2}} + \frac{1}{1.06} = 0 \tag{3.6}$$

This step is equivalent to saying "choose a production plan such that the marginal rate of return equals the market rate of interest." Rewriting equation (3.6), we obtain the following sequence of calculations:

$$\frac{1}{1.06} = \frac{K_2}{\left(212.36 - K_2^2\right)^{1/2}}$$

$$K_2(1.06) = \left(212.36 - K_2^2\right)^{1/2}$$

$$K_2^2(1.06)^2 = \$212.36 - K_2^2$$

$$K_2^2\left[1 + (1.06)^2\right] = \$212.36$$

$$K_2^2(\$2.1236) = \$212.36$$

$$K_2^* = \$10.00$$

therefore

$$K_1^* = (\$212.36 - \$100.00)^{1/2} = \$10.60$$

and

$$MV_1 = \$10.60 + \frac{10.00}{1.06} = \$20.03$$

This situation is shown graphically in Figure 3.7. Note the following: (1) The vintner has increased initial wealth ($MV_1$) to $20.03 from the original $14.60 available by selling all the raw wine at time 1; (2) the vintner will employ wine in the aging process up to the point where the marginal rate of return on aging wine just equals the market rate of interest.

**FIGURE 3.7**
WINE AGING EXAMPLE

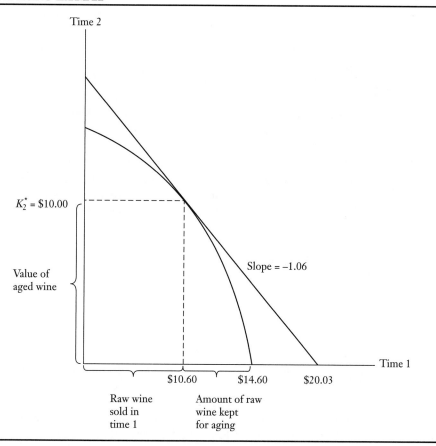

## 3.4 CONSEQUENCES FOR INVESTMENT AND FINANCING DECISIONS

The consequences of this chapter's theoretical investigation are of considerable importance to understanding financial decision making. Thus, we next summarize our four major findings along with two general principles that flow from them:

1.  The market-value-maximizing firm will invest up to the point where the marginal rate of return equals the market rate of interest. This is also consistent with long-run profit maximization when profits are correctly calculated. Note that the decisions involve determining how much to invest, that is, a matter of scale (or total capital budget[4]), rather than a simple accept–reject assessment for a given project of fixed size.

---

[4] We discuss capital budgeting in Chapter 6.

2. Determination of the total investment in a firm depends on two things: (1) the technology and the cash flow it yields and (2) the market rate of interest. Value is created when, on the average, the firm's rate of return exceeds the market rate of interest. Value is maximized when these last two rates are brought into equality by the final marginal amount of investment. Since the market rate of interest is the firm's cost of capital in a certainty world with a perfect capital market, value is maximized when funds are invested up to the point where the marginal rate of return falls to equal the firm's cost of capital.

3. It does not matter whether the firm is owned by many stockholders or a single owner, since if the market value of the firm is maximized so is any stockholder's proportional interest in that market value.

4. Whether the firm uses its own money (retained earnings) or external financing makes no difference. Under assumptions of certainty and a perfect capital market, all sources of financing have the same cost, the market rate of interest. This is true even for retained earnings, since the market rate of interest is the opportunity cost for those retained earnings.

Our last conclusion may be difficult for the practical-minded to accept because it is generally believed that in more complex situations than the one now being examined, the source of financing does make a difference and that optimal capital structures do exist. We emphasize that our present conclusion applies to a certainty world with a perfect capital market. But our finding is valuable nonetheless, because it gives us a hint as to what conditions (market imperfections) might render valid the belief that capital structure does indeed matter in certain kinds of practical circumstances. Indeed, when we later introduce market imperfections, our conclusions will not only approach those acceptable to conventional wisdom, but we shall know why there is truth in the old beliefs.

Finally, we note that while the market value criterion requires management to concern itself only with the technical aspects of production, managers are not computers. They may have their own preferences that may conflict with those of the stockholders. How can we ensure that the market value rule will be followed by such managers? While it is beyond the scope of our discussion at this point, the *economic theory of agency* is one way in which this problem can be approached (Chapter 20).

### 3.4.1  Separation of Operating and Financing Decisions

Given its production plans, in a perfect capital market a firm's financing of the investments needed to carry out these plans is a matter of indifference to its owners. That is, the market value of the firm is determined only by the cash flows it can generate and not by the source of funds used to finance those operations. This also means that the firm's cost of capital is independent of its financing sources. This separation principle follows from the fact that once the operating plans of the firm have been fixed (that is, once the point of tangency between the transformation curve and the market opportunity line has been found), it is irrelevant whether financing is from one source or another because the cost of any type of financing arrangement is the same and is equal to the market rate of interest.

The operational importance of the foregoing separation principle is that the firm's operating plans and the attendant investment decisions need not be considered

**FIGURE 3.8**
SEPARATION OF OPERATING AND FINANCING DECISIONS

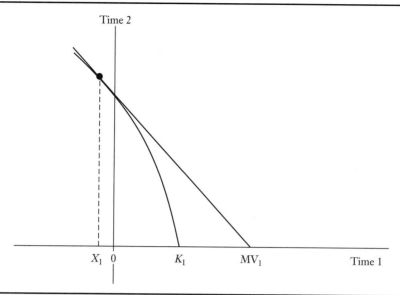

simultaneously with decisions as to how to finance the investment. This is the same thing as saying that all investment decisions can be evaluated using the market rate of interest because this interest rate is the firm's cost of capital.[5]

We show the separation of operating and financing decisions graphically in Figure 3.8. By an operating decision, we mean the decision to invest $X_1K_1$, which determines the amount of the firm's output it will produce and sell. By saying that financial decisions are separate from this operating decision we mean that if the existing owners of the firm originally had resources $0K_1$, the amount of those resources that they personally invest in the firm is irrelevant to the determination of its value. Properly operated, the firm is worth $MV_1$. The existing owners can arrange any profile of cash withdrawals from the firm at times 1 and 2 as long as the profile has a present value equal to $MV_1$. If the existing owners do not wish to provide the required investment funds $X_1K_1$, the funds can be raised in the capital market.

In a perfect capital market every economically viable proposition is always financed by some investor, and an outside investor always receives the market rate of interest on his investment. If the investors are the original owners, they receive a higher rate of return from investing in the firm. However, they value the cash flows so generated using the market rate of interest, because that is their opportunity cost. In other words, the firm's management creates value for the original owners by investing funds at rates that exceed, on average, the market rate of interest. But to determine

---

[5] Most capital expenditure decision criteria implicitly assume this separation principle holds in that they talk first about choosing a criterion, such as the present value of cash flows, and then using the cost of capital in order to determine the present value.

how much wealth was created, the original owners discount the firm's cash flows at the market rate of interest.

## 3.4.2 Separation of Managers' and Owners' Decisions

The second major principle resulting from our findings is that there are no disparities between the goals of managers and owners as long as the firm's managers maximize the market value of the owners' investment in the firm. If the firm has only a single owner, an entrepreneur, we argued that the appropriate criterion for determining satisfaction is the time 1 value of the owner's consumption expenditures. But we also saw that the only constraint on the entrepreneur's consumption decisions is the market opportunity line, which is fixed by the value of initial wealth. Hence, the process of creating wealth can be delegated to a manager who need not know what the owner's consumption preferences are.

A similar result holds for multi-owner firms operating in a perfect capital market. The market value rule requires managers to maximize the current market value of the firm, subject to the technological constraints imposed by the transformation curve. Value maximization is all that managers can do for stockholders, irrespective of their preferences, because the market value of all investments is the owners' wealth, and wealth is the only constraint on owners' consumption decisions.

The importance of this result is that in order to act in the owners' best interests, the firm's managers need not have information about the owners' utility functions. The task of corporate management is thus to create wealth by finding productive opportunities with average rates of return exceeding the market rate of interest. Managers maximize this wealth using the market value rule, which says that market value is maximized by investing in the productive opportunity up to the point where

**FIGURE 3.9**
SEPARATION OF MANAGERS' AND OWNERS' DECISIONS

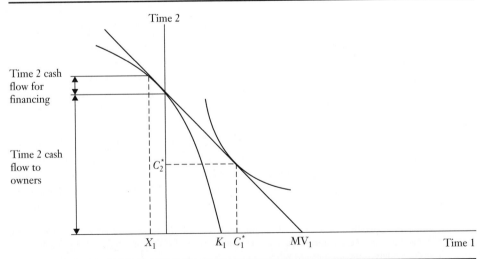

the marginal rate of return declines to equality with the market rate of interest. The separation principle states that the market value rule impounds all the information with which managers need to be concerned.

To see the essence of this separation principle graphically, consider Figure 3.9. The separation principle says the firm's managers determine the optimal investment $X_1K_1$ and hence its market value $MV_1$. In other words, the firm's managers determine the intercept $MV_1$ of the owners' market opportunity line. If the firm has a single owner, the latter then decides what consumption standards, with a present value of $MV_1$, are preferred; that is, the owner chooses a position on the market opportunity line. If the firm has many owners, a given owner is entitled to only some proportion of market value, say $\alpha MV_1$ ($0 \leq \alpha \leq 1$). This then defines the market opportunity line along which that particular owner can move.

# KEY POINTS

- In a perfect capital market, management can maximize the wealth of a firm's owners by using the market value rule. This rule requires management to make decisions aimed at maximizing the market value of the firms they operate.

- A firm with a single owner-manager (referred to as a proprietary firm) can be regarded as a wealth-creating device capable of increasing its owner's well-being if the owner sets production and financing decisions in such a way as to maximize the owner's wealth.

- The productive opportunity set of a proprietary firm is graphically depicted by a transformation curve that shows efficient use of funds. Efficiency means that the capital investment is put to its best possible use and there are no resources wasted by the rational entrepreneur. The slope of the transformation curve may be interpreted as indicating the firm's marginal rate of return.

- A management policy of investing funds until their rate of return falls to equality with the market rate of interest is a policy that maximizes the entrepreneur's initial wealth.

- Combining borrowing in the capital market with a productive opportunity results in an entrepreneur being better off than if either the productive or the market opportunity were faced alone.

- The owner's decision process can be viewed as encompassing two distinct steps: (1) selecting the optimum production by equating the marginal rate of return on investment with the market required rate of return and (2) selecting the optimum consumption pattern by borrowing or lending in the capital market until the consumer's subjective rate of time preference equals the market rate of return.

- The separation of investment and consumption decisions is sometimes referred to as the Fisher separation theorem.

- Unlike proprietary firms, managers of corporations are responsible for most of the funds invested in an economy. Corporations have many owners, and there is no reason to assume that the owners' preferences are all the same. The owners of a corporation do not make the operating decisions of the firm but rather hire professional managers and delegate decision-making power to these managers.

- In a perfect capital market, the market value of individuals' investment is maximized by managers acting on behalf of firms' stockholders. The managers will serve the stockholders' best interests if they maximize the market values of the firms they operate. If the market value of a firm is maximized, so is the market value of any owner's proportional share of the firm's earnings.

- In a perfect capital market, the separation of operating and financing decisions for a corporation still holds; that is, given its production plans, a firm's financing of the investments needed to carry out these plans is a matter of indifference to its owners.

- In a perfect capital market, the market value of the firm is determined only by the cash flows it can generate and not by the source of funds used to finance those operations. The task of management is to create wealth by finding productive opportunities with average rates of return exceeding the market rate of interest.

## QUESTIONS

1. What is meant by the market value rule?

2. a. What is the transformation curve?
   b. What is the interpretation of the slope of the transformation curve?

3. What is meant by the Fisher separation theorem and its implications for financial decision making?

4. Explain why the total investment that management should make for a firm depends on the cash flow that can be generated by the existing technology and the market rate of interest.

5. Explain whether you agree or disagree with the following statement: Value is maximized when the market rate of interest exceeds the rate of return that can be earned by a firm on its invested funds.

6. Under assumptions of certainty and a perfect capital market, explain why it makes no difference whether the firm uses its own money (retained earnings) or external financing.

7. With respect to the separation principle, explain whether you agree or disagree with the following statement: The firm's operating plans and attendant investing and financing decision need not be considered simultaneously.

8. What is the major finding regarding disparities between the goals of owners and managers that results from the separation principle?

9. Consider the example in Section 3.3 but now assume that the market rate of interest is 10%. Graphically show the operating plan for the following two transformation curves:

a. $3K_1 + 2K_2 = 30$

b. $(K_1 + 1)^2 + K_2^2 = 21$

Using the transformation curve in part b, find the firm's optimal financing decision if the firm's initial resources at time 1 is:

c. 5

d. 0

e. Find the optimal consumption decision assuming the transformation curve in part b and further assuming that the only owner of the firm has the following utility function:

$$u(K_1, K_2) = K_1 K_2^{1/2}$$

## REFERENCES

Fisher, Irving. (1930). *The Theory of Interest.* New York: Macmillan.

# 4

# How Investors Value Firms

*I*n this chapter we consider how investors value firms under certainty in a perfect capital market. We show that the value of a firm whose managers follow the market value rule is given by the sum of (1) the present value of cash flows to be generated by the firm's existing assets plus (2) the present value of cash flows to be generated from future growth opportunities. This result holds true even when the growth opportunities have not yet been initiated. The equivalence of earnings and dividend approaches to valuing the firm is also established as a part of the general valuation result. In addition, the question of who benefits from investments yielding returns in excess of market rates is explored. We consider the meaning of a growth stock and the restricted circumstances under which it is possible for stockholders to earn returns in excess of market rates of interest. We discuss returns on investments when an investor's planning horizon might differ from the term to maturity of the investment in which the funds are invested, a matter of concern both in valuing assets and in relating interest rates over time periods of different length.

All the foregoing results are of considerable importance to understanding financial decisions in more complex circumstances, because they show who benefits from wealth-creating new investments that a firm undertakes and when the benefits are realized. Although the results are established under certainty, they also help us to clarify how expectations affect the price of risky securities, as we will show in later chapters.

In our discussion in this chapter, we assume a very simple capital structure—that the firm only obtains capital from the sale of common stock. (In the next chapter, we will cover the important question of how a firm should design its capital structure that is, the relative amount of common stock and debt.) The present capital structure assumption implies that terms such as earnings, cash flow, and profit can be used interchangeably throughout the chapter, since cash flow and the earnings are the same from the perspective of the owners of the firm. In addition, the terms *profit* and *earnings* are used interchangeably. For example, cash flow is equal to the amount of cash available to distribute to the suppliers of capital to the firm.[1] The earnings of a firm are the amount available for the owners (stockholders) of the firm after all expenses.

---

[1] While there are more technical differences in the meaning of cash flow, the definition here is sufficient for our purpose.

# 4.1 Value Based in a Firm's Capacity to Generate Investor Returns

At any point in time, the value of a firm to its stockholders is based on the firm's capacity to generate investor returns. This value may be determined by capitalizing either the dividends or the future earnings to which the original stockholders are entitled. *Dividends* are cash payments[2] made by a corporation to its owners and the determination of their amount, if any, is solely at the discretion of the corporation's board of directors.

The management decisions that will generate the dividend and earnings patterns are assumed to be specified in advance, a condition usually expressed by saying that the firm's value is determined on the basis of operating decisions that are assumed to be fixed. In so valuing the firm, the present value of earnings to be generated by assets already acquired is added to the present value of earnings to be generated from future growth opportunities. To see this, we begin by showing that in a perfect capital market, whether a firm decides to pay a dividend or not has no impact on its market value. Next we show how a firm is valued on the basis of its total earnings, adjusted for the costs of any new investment expenditures. This is another way of saying that the firm is valued in terms of its current earnings generation capacity plus its (already specified) future growth opportunities. Finally, we demonstrate that this adjusted earnings value equals the present value of all future dividends to which the original stockholders of record will be entitled.

## 4.1.1 Why the Size of a Dividend Does Not Affect the Firm's Value

When funds can be raised at the same interest rate as is used to discount the firm's cash flow (without paying transactions charges other than the market rate of interest), the size of a dividend paid is irrelevant to determining the firm's market value. In this circumstance, the firm's value depends only on its future earnings stream and not on the source of funds needed to finance creation of the earnings stream, even if the source is retention financing obtained by not paying a dividend. In the present analysis we interpret dividends as payments made out of resources available at time 1 and capital gains as money received from winding up[3] the firm at time 2. (In general, a *capital gain* is the amount realized before taxes from the sale of an asset at a price higher than the cost of purchasing that asset.) Our purpose is to show that because any money paid out as dividends can be raised again at the market rate of interest, and also because the market rate of interest is the opportunity cost for discounting dividends, the size of a dividend does not affect the market value of the firm.

---

[2] Dividends can also be in the form of products of the firm and although that has occurred historically, today dividends are typically only cash payments. The record date is the date specified by the board such that any shareholders who are on record as owning shares on this date are eligible to receive the dividend.

[3] Alternatively, we can think of selling the ongoing enterprise to another owner at time 2.

**FIGURE 4.1**
FIRST STEP IN ESTABLISHING THAT EARNINGS AND DIVIDEND APPROACHES TO VALUING THE FIRM ARE EQUIVALENT IN A PERFECT CAPITAL MARKET

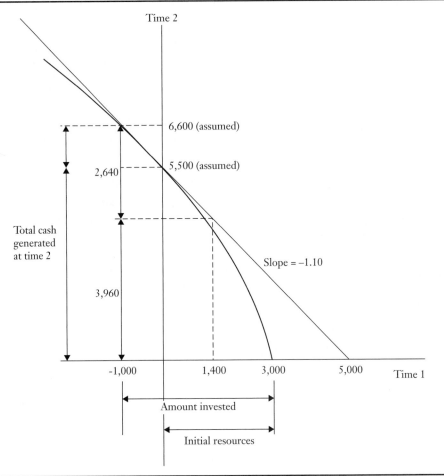

Consider the situation, shown in Figure 4.1, of a firm with initial resources equal to $3,000. That amount is assumed to be generated from previous operations. Optimal operation of the firm, according to management's estimates, requires an investment of $4,000, so the firm needs $1,000 in additional capital. The firm investment creates $6,600 in time 2 cash flow that can be distributed to the various parties financing the operation (which we assume are only new stockholders). We assume the market rate of return required by investors is 10%. If the original stockholders receive none of the initially available resources as a dividend, the firm must raise the entire $1,000 to carry out the optimal investment program. We will demonstrate with the following calculations that, in this case, the value of the firm is equal to $5,000.

If, on the other hand, we assume the board of directors agree to distribute to the stockholders at time 1 a dividend of, say, $1,400, leaving the firm with $1,600 in resources, then the firm's initial capital needs will be $2,400 (i.e., the difference between the $4,000 needed and the $1,600 of available resources after the dividend is paid). What we will demonstrate is that, in this case, the value of the firm remains $5,000, the same as in the case where no dividends are distributed at time 1. In other words, the example shows that the value of the stockholders' investment depends on the cash flow the firm can generate and not on the amount raised in the capital markets to generate this cash flow. This is because amounts not raised in the capital market are effectively raised from retained earnings (i.e., by foregoing dividends), and in the presently assumed circumstances the opportunity cost of the latter equals the market rate of return required by investors that is paid on new financing. The same result obtains if the stockholders invest their own cash in the firm. For, in this case, they regard the required market rate of return of 10% as an opportunity cost (since 10% could be earned by distributing earnings and investing in market investments), and the calculations proceed as before.

The data used in deriving the conclusions of the previous example are shown in Figure 4.1 and worked out in detail here. We suppose the following data characterize the problem irrespective of the size of dividend that may be paid:

| | |
|---|---|
| Initial resources | $3,000 |
| Optimal time 1 investment required | $4,000 |
| Cash generated at time 2 by investment | $6,600 |
| Market rate of return required | 10% |

The value of the firm at time 1 equals the $3,000 current value of the assets (the current resources) plus the $6,600 present value of the cash flow at time 2 minus by the $4,000 investment cost. The cash flow at time 2 must be discounted at the market rate of return required by investors of 10%. Thus, the value of the firm at time 1 is:

$$\$3,000 + \frac{\$6,600}{1.10} - \$4,000 = \$5,000$$

If we assume no dividend is paid at time 1, additional data are as follows:

| | |
|---|---|
| All initial resources invested | $3,000 |
| Funds raised in the market at a cost of 10% | $1,000 |
| Cost of funds obtained in the market (0.10 × $1,000) | $ 100 |
| Available to original stockholders at time 2 ($6,600 − $1,000 − $100) | $5,500 |

The cash flow for the original stockholders in this case is then 0 at time 1 and $5,500 at time 2. Discounting the time 1 cash flow by 10%, the present value is $5,000. Therefore, for the original stockholders, the value of the firm is $5,000.

If, on the other hand, we assume a $1,400 dividend is paid at time 1, the additional data are as follows:

| | |
|---|---|
| Initial resources invested by original stockholders ($3,000 − $1,400) | $1,600 |
| Funds raised in the market at a cost of 10% | $2,400 |

Cost of funds obtained in the market (0.10 × $2,400)                    $   240
Available to original stockholders from time 2 flows ($6,600 − $2,640) $3,960

For the original stockholders, the case flow in this case is $1,400 at time 1, which is the assumed dividend payment, and $3,960 at time 2. Discounting the time 1 cash flow of $3,960 at 10% and adding that to the $1,400 time 1 cash flow gives a present value of $5,000. Thus, the value of the firm is $5,000 the same as in the case where no dividends are paid.

The foregoing results are useful because they force us to focus attention on the primary determinant of a firm's market value—its ability to generate cash flow. The result regarding dividend irrelevance also suggests our next finding: The firm may be valued using either the discounted stream of future earnings available to the initial stockholders or the discounted stream of future dividends.

The irrelevance of a firm's dividend policy was first demonstrated by Franco Modigliani and Merton Miller in 1961. Their results form one of the cornerstones of modern corporate finance and are derived from analyzing the capital structure decision of the firm in a perfect capital market and the absence of uncertainty.[4] However, keep in mind that under more complex circumstances firms pay dividends because management believes that such corporate action will enhance the value of the firm. When we discuss imperfect capital markets in later chapters of this book, we attempt to find a plausible explanation as to why dividends might be relevant in more complex circumstances than we have considered to this point.

## 4.1.2   A Valuation Model Based on Earnings

In a perfect capital market, the equilibrium price of a share at time 1 obeys the condition:

$$s(1) = \frac{d(2) + s(2)}{1 + r} \tag{4.1}$$

where $s(t)$ = ex-dividend price of a share,

   $d(t)$ = dividend accruing to stockholders of record at time $t - 1$ ($t = 2, 3$), and

   $r$ = market interest rate from investing between times 1 and 2.

Note that above we adopted the lowercase notation to denote magnitudes on a per share basis. We will use uppercase notation to denote their aggregates.

Let $N(1)$ be the number of shares outstanding at $t = 1$ (i.e., the number of shares held by the original stockholders of record). Then the market value of the firm at time 1, denoted by $V(1)$, assuming all funds are financed by the sale of common stock,[5] is:

---

[4] Their results appear in three papers, Modigliani-Miller (1958, 1963) and Miller and Modigliani (1961). As already indicated, the latter paper deals with the irrelevance of dividend policy.

[5] In a perfect capital market under certainty, every financial arrangement involves repaying with certainty the principal plus interest at the market rate. Hence, all instruments are effectively the same. Thus, at this point we use the term *equity* merely for its suggestive implications. Later, when risk is considered, debt and equity will be different kinds of financial instruments.

$$V(1) = N(1)s(1) = \frac{N(1)d(2) + N(1)s(2)}{1+r} \tag{4.2}$$

At time 2 the value of the firm, denoted by $V(2)$, is:

$$V(2) = N(2)s(2) = [N(1) + M(2)]s(2)$$

where $M(2)$ refers to the number of new shares (if any) issued at time 2. Therefore, by substitution we can write:

$$V(1) = \frac{N(1)d(2) + V(2) - M(2)s(2)}{1+r} \tag{4.3}$$

But $N(1)d(2) = D(2)$ is the entire time 2 dividend, because at time 2 dividends are paid only to stockholders of record at time 1. Moreover, the firm either invests funds or pays them out as dividends,[6] so that total funds available equal dividends plus investment expenditures; that is,

$$M(2)s(2) + X(2) = D(2) + I(2) \tag{4.4}$$

In other words, the sum of the proceeds from the new issues $M(2)s(2)$ plus net cash earnings $X(2)$ equals dividends $D(2)$ plus investment expenditures $I(2)$. Then equation (4.4) may be rewritten as:

$$M(2)s(2) = -X(2) + D(2) + I(2) \tag{4.5}$$

Substituting equation (4.5) into equation (4.3), we obtain:

$$V(1) = \frac{D(2) + V(2) + X(2) - D(2) - I(2)}{1+r}$$

$$= \frac{X(2) - I(2) + V(2)}{1+r} \tag{4.6}$$

Then using equation (4.6) for all[7] $t$, assuming each period's market interest rate $r$ is the same, and proceeding to eliminate $V(2)$, $V(3)$, . . . by successive substitution, we obtain:

$$V(1) = \sum_{t=1}^{\infty} \frac{X(t+1) - I(t+1)}{(1+r)^t} \tag{4.7}$$

---

[6] This holds because under certainty any excess cash could be invested at the market rate of interest with a net effect of zero on the present value of the firm. Similarly, a cash deficiency can be borrowed at the market rate.

[7] This is because the relationship just established holds between each two successive points in time.

where $X(t)$ = net cash earnings at time $t$ and

$\quad\quad I(t)$ = cost of new investments at time $t$.

Equation (4.7) says the value of the firm (to the stockholders of record at time 1) is the value of all future earnings, from which is subtracted the cost of any additional investment expenditures used to generate those earnings. The latter is equal to the present value of the new shares or borrowings used to finance purchases of additional investment goods.

We can also conclude that equation (4.7) may be read as saying that the time 1 value of the firm equals the present value of existing earnings plus the present value (net of investment cost) of the future growth opportunities that the firm plans to adopt. That is, cash earnings $X(t)$ account for all earnings, both existing and those resulting from new investments, while the $I(t)$ reflect the costs of adopting the new investments.

### 4.1.3 Why the Dividend and Earnings Valuation Models are Equivalent

The preceding argument can now be used to establish an equivalence between dividend and earnings valuation approaches to the firm. To see this, recall that the value of a share of stock at time 1 is equal to the present value (discounted at the market rate) of what will be received at time 2—the dividend per share distributed at time 2 plus the value per share of the stock at time 2. That is,

$$s(1) = \frac{d(2) + s(2)}{1 + r}$$

But similarly, if the market rate continues to be $r$,

$$s(2) = \frac{d(2) + s(3)}{1 + r}$$

and so on for all future periods so that:

$$s(1) = \frac{d(2)}{1 + r} + \frac{d(3) + s(3)}{(1 + r)^2}$$

becomes, by successive substitution,

$$s(1) = \frac{d(2)}{1 + r} + \frac{d(3)}{(1 + r)^2} + \cdots + \frac{d(n) + s(n)}{(1 + r)^{n-1}}$$

But for $r > 0$, as $n \to \infty$ the term $s(n)/(1 + r)^{n-1} \to 0$ so long as $s(n)$ is never greater than some fixed magnitude. Thus, we may write:

$$s(1) = \sum_{t=1}^{\infty} \frac{d(t + 1)}{(1 + r)^t} \tag{4.8}$$

Equation (4.8) means the following: The value of a share is the present value of the dividends to which its owners are entitled. But the value of the firm to the stockholders of record at time 1 is the market value of all such shares; that is,

$$V(1) = N(1)s(1) = N(1) \sum_{t=1}^{\infty} \frac{d(t+1)}{(1+r)^t}$$

Hence, the value of the firm at time 1 is just the present value of dividends accruing to the stockholders of record at that time. But we also know from equation (4.7) that $V(1)$ equals the present value of earnings adjusted for new investment expenditures, so the two approaches to determining the value of the firm must be equivalent.

To put the matter another way, in a certainty world, the stockholders of record at time 1 know the firm's present value because they can perfectly forecast the firm's total future earnings and the market rate at which those earnings will be discounted. If the original stockholders do not have enough money to carry out investment expenditures needed to generate those potential earnings, they can borrow the funds in the marketplace. But in so doing there is no reason for the existing stockholders to pay interest rates higher than the prevailing market rate at the time. That is, the firm's existing stockholders sell shares to any new stockholders at prices high enough to ensure that the shares will yield the new investors just the market rate of return and no more. Moreover, new investors will buy shares at these prices because the market rate of return is the highest (and only) rate that can be earned on financial assets. Hence, any new shares that a firm issues will have a present value just equal to the cost of the investment expenditures financed thereby, and the value of the firm to the original stockholders of record can therefore be expressed as the present value of all earnings less the cost of any new investment expenditures needed to finance them. However, at the same time the market value of the firm to the original stockholders of record is the value of their shares, given by the present value of the dividends to which they are entitled. Hence, the two approaches to valuation are equivalent.

As an example, consider a new firm in which earnings will be $110 at time 2 and the value of any assets then remaining will be zero.[8] The market rate of interest is 10%. Suppose also that the time 1 investment required is $73. If the stockholders invest their own funds in the firm, the net addition to their wealth from making the investment is ($110/1.10) − $73 = $27. Suppose, however, the owners decide to sell shares to others to finance the operation. Since the original stockholders must raise $73 in the marketplace at the market rate of interest, they have to promise new stockholders a payment of $80.30 at time 2 (i.e., $73 × 1.1). One way of doing this is to issue 100 shares at time 1, selling 73 in the financial markets for $1 each. The original owners retain the other 27 shares for themselves. Every share will sell for $1 because each is worth $1.10 at time 2. Moreover, the new purchasers will, by virtue of holding the shares they have bought, be entitled to ($73/100)(110) = $80.30. The present value of the remaining shares represents the increment to the original

---

[8] Alternatively, we could assume the firm will be sold to new owners at time 2 for a market price of $110 (assuming any earnings realized at time 2 would also pass to the new purchasers).

stockholders' wealth, which equals ($110 − $80.30)/1.10 = $29.70/1.10 = $27 as before. The point is that in the valuation equation (4.7), specialized so that only time $t = 1$ is used, investment expenditures are subtracted from earnings. But the expenditures are just equal to the present value of the earnings that have to be promised to raise that amount of money, so subtracting the cost of the new investment is the same thing as subtracting the present value of dividends to which the new stockholders are entitled.

## 4.2 WHAT GROWTH STOCKS ARE AND WHAT RETURNS THEY YIELD

In this section we consider the meaning of a growth firm and whether it is possible to earn returns in excess of market rates by buying growth stocks (i.e., the stocks of growth firms). Since we have already seen that existing investors will not give up something of value unless they receive equal value in exchange, we should be skeptical about the possibility of earning excess returns on stocks whose growth has been anticipated. But the results are counterintuitive enough to merit detailed attention.

### 4.2.1 The Meaning of a Growth Firm

A *growth firm* is one in which the expanding assets generate returns in excess of the market rate of interest.[9] To see this, consider the time 1 value of the original stockholders' investment in a firm which will exist for just one more period,[10] so that it is valued as follows:

$$V^0(1) = \frac{X^0(2)}{1 + r} \tag{4.9}$$

where $V^0(1)$ = market value of existing operations at time 1

$X^0(2)$ = earnings from existing operations, including disposal value, if any, of assets at time 2

$r$ = market interest rate between time 1 and time 2

Now suppose earnings can be augmented through additional investment according to $X(2) = X^0(2) + I(1)(1 + r^*)$, where $r^*$ is the internal rate of return on the new investments that increase these earnings. That is, any new investment has an internal rate of return equal to $r^*$. (As explained in Chapter 6, the internal rate of return is the

---

[9] It should be noted that in the investment community, a growth firm has a different meaning. Investors classify stocks according to what is popularly referred to as "investment style" with two of those styles being growth and value. A growth firm in the style context means a firm that is expected to grow at a rate that is greater than other firms in the industry or the market overall.

[10] Alternatively, we can reinterpret $X^0(2)$ as containing terms that value continued operations of the firm into several future periods.

interest rate that makes the present value of the cash flow from an investment equal the initial investment outlay.) Then we may rewrite equation (4.9) as:

$$V(1) = \frac{X(2)}{1+r} - I(1) = \frac{X^0(2) + I(1)(1+r^*)}{1+r} - I(1)$$

or

$$V(1) = \frac{X^0(2) + I(1)(r^* - r)}{1+r} \tag{4.10}$$

The last result shows that if $r^* = r$, then the firm's market value will not change even if the firm's assets increase because new investment expenditures are undertaken.[11] If, however, $r^* > r$ and $I(1) > 0$, then the firm's assets are both growing and earning more than the market rate of interest, so that the value of the firm to the original stockholders increases accordingly. This is a true growth firm from which the original stockholders receive more than the market rate of return on their investment. We hasten to observe, however, that the beneficiaries of growth in this firm would be only the original stockholders. Because the rewards to growth can be perfectly anticipated and incorporated in share price, other persons investing in the firm by way of purchasing a new share issue would receive only market rates of return on their investment, for the same reasons as developed earlier.

## 4.2.2 Constant Dividend Growth and Some Implications

We now examine the case of a firm whose assets grow continuously, earning rates of return in excess of the market, with the result that management increases dividends at the same rate. For analytic simplicity, we consider a firm with earnings and dividends that grow at a constant rate for all future time periods.[12] While the assumptions probably seem quite unrealistic, even in a certainty world, they will nonetheless permit us to gain some further insights into the effects of growth and who benefits from it.

The value of a share is given in this case by the following specialized form of equation (4.8):

$$s(1) = \sum_{t=1}^{\infty} \frac{d(2)(1+g)^{t-2}}{(1+r)^{t-1}} \tag{4.11}$$

where $s(1)$ = ex-dividend share price at time 1
$d(2)$ = dividend paid at time 2 to a stockholder of record at time 1
$g$ = rate of growth of dividend
$r$ = market rate of interest

---

[11] When $r^* = r$, $I(1)(r^* - r) = 0$ so that equation (4.10) collapses to equation (4.9). This is the case of simple asset growth. The balance sheet shows a larger asset base, but the value of the firm does not change. No wealth is created when funds are reinvested at a rate of return equal to their cost.

[12] The notion of "growing forever" is an approximation to the idea of a going concern. We use it mainly because, from a mathematical point of view, it is easy to work with.

Equation (4.11) can be rewritten as:

$$s(1) = \frac{d(2)}{1+g} \sum_{t=2}^{\infty} \left(\frac{1+g}{1+r}\right)^{t-1}$$

Summing the infinite series, we obtain:

$$s(1) = \frac{d(2)}{1+g} \left\{ \frac{1}{1 - [(1+g)/(1+r)]} - 1 \right\}$$

and, through more algebraic manipulation,

$$s(1) = \frac{d(2)}{r-g} \tag{4.12}$$

where $g < r$. The condition $g < r$ (dividends increase at a slower rate than the discount factor) is necessary for the value of the shares to remain finite. The model given by equation (4.12) is called the *Gordon growth model*.[13]

We now apply equation (4.12) to the study of price-earnings ratios and how they are reflected in a stock's income and capital gains.

### 4.2.3 Price-Earnings Ratios

The *price-earnings ratio*, denoted by *P/E*, is the ratio of the current market price of the stock to the firm's earnings per share of common stock.[14] Price-earnings ratios for firms with constantly growing dividends may conveniently be expressed for our present purposes using a specialized form of equation (4.12). We rewrite $d(2)$ as $ke(2)$ so that:

$$s(1) = \frac{ke(2)}{r-g} \tag{4.13}$$

where $k$ refers to the proportion of earnings paid as dividends (payout ratio) and $e(2)$ to time 2 earnings per share.[15] In these circumstances, the price-earnings ratio may be written as:

---

[13] See Gordon (1959).

[14] The price-earnings ratio is sometimes referred to as the earnings multiple or the price multiple.

[15] Thus, $e(2) = X(2)/N(2)$ in our earlier notation. Note that if $k = 0$, this implies no dividends *forever* in the present model, which in turn means that the firm never plans to distribute funds. So, while (mechanically speaking) the formula seems to break down in this case, it actually correctly describes the logical outcome of an implausible situation. Moreover, in a rationally managed firm dividends not paid at time 2 would at the minimum be reinvested at rate $r$, so that in order to describe what happens to a firm not paying dividends over a *finite* time horizon one should amend the derivation of such formulae as equation (4.8), from which the present equation is derived.

$$\frac{P}{E} = \frac{s(1)}{e(2)} = \frac{ke(2)}{e(2)(r - g)} = \frac{k}{r - g} \qquad (4.14)$$

To see how equation (4.14) helps us to understand the meaning of a price-earnings ratio, we consider some numerical examples. First, let us suppose that:

$$r = 20\%, \ k = 30\%, \ e(2) = \$10, \ \text{and} \ s(1) = \$100$$

and ask at what rate must the earnings be growing for the price-earnings ratio of 10 to be obtained? Employing equation (4.14), we have:

$$\frac{P}{E} = \frac{\$100}{\$10} = 10 = \frac{0.3}{0.2 - g} \quad \text{so that} \ g = 0.17 = 17\%$$

Note that if one buys this share at a $P/E$ of 10, or a price of $100, the return on the investment is 20% per annum, the assumed market rate of interest. To verify the last observation, observe that with an earnings growth rate of 17%, $e(3)$ will be $11.70, and hence, $s(2)$ will be $117. The dividend $d(2)$ will be 30% of $10 or $3. Hence, for $100 invested at time 1, one obtains $117 + $3 = $120 at time 2, for a return of 20%.

In the perfect capital market now being considered, the equilibrium return on investment will be the same for all firms, even though price-earnings ratios for two stocks differ substantially. To see this, we consider a second example with:

$$r = 20\%, \ k = 30\%, \ e(2) = \$10, \ s(1) = \$200$$

and again ask at what rate must the earnings be growing for a price-earnings ratio of 20 to be obtained?

$$\frac{P}{E} = \frac{\$200}{\$10} = 20 = \frac{0.3}{0.2 - g} \quad \text{so that} \ g = 18.5\%$$

Note that $P/E$ ratio has doubled, although the growth rate increased only by about 10% over that of the previous example. Moreover, since in both cases dividends are discounted at 20%, the purchaser of this stock, if the stock is bought after its growth rate has been reflected in the stock price, receives the same 20% return as does the purchaser of the lower $P/E$ stock in the preceding example.

The results of both examples show that the new purchaser of a stock will earn only a 20% return because in a perfect capital market the price of a stock reflects all publicly available information. There is no reason for the original stockholders to sell stocks at prices that will yield more than the market rate of interest; hence, new stockholders can only receive that market rate of interest. Simply put, the original stockholders ensure that they do not surrender any returns in excess of market rates to other investors.

### 4.2.4 Are Low P/E Stocks Underpriced?

An investment strategy touted by some investment advisors is to purchase stocks with low *P/E* ratios. By "low" it meant a price-earnings ratio less than the industry or market average. The argument is that a *P/E* ratio is a gauge of how cheap (or underpriced) a stock is and that in the long-run low *P/E* stocks will outperform high *P/E* stocks. This a strategy that is favored by investors who are called "value investors."

Let's demonstrate why low *P/E* stocks are not necessarily underpriced. Indeed, in a perfect capital market they cannot be cheap. Let:

$$r = 20\%, \ k = 30\%, \ e(2) = \$10, \ s(1) = \$20$$

and once again ask at what rate must earnings be growing? Since:

$$\frac{P}{E} = \frac{\$20}{\$10} = 2 = \frac{0.3}{0.2 - g}$$

we have $g = 0.05 = 5\%$.

This low *P/E* stock is not a bargain because it returns the same 20% market rate of interest as the others. The stock's low price-earnings ratio merely reflects the fact that earnings are growing slowly while the investor is still receiving the 20% market rate of return.

The foregoing examples in this and the previous section suggest that getting a bargain (returns in excess of the market rate) depends in the real world on receiving extraordinary returns resulting from future events not yet reflected in market prices. Even in an imperfect capital market where investors face risk, the holders of shares are not likely to sell those shares for less than the owners' estimate of fair market value. Hence, to make extraordinary returns, new investors must correctly outguess existing stockholders when forecasting the earnings potential of the firm. This would not be possible in a world of perfect certainty but might sometimes be possible in imperfect capital markets, either under risk or under uncertainty. The conclusion might well be that there are few genuine bargains in the financial markets and that these few are hard for most investors (perhaps even professionals) to find.

### 4.2.5 Capital Gains and Dividends

Let's now consider relations between capital gains and income earned on the shares of the kinds of firms we have been examining. In the first instance, we show that even a firm that does not grow can issue shares yielding capital gains. Consider a firm that will pay just one dividend and that dividend is paid at time 3. The value of a share at time 1, assuming that the market rate of interest is constant, is then:

$$s(1) = \frac{d(3)}{(1 + r)^2}$$

and at time 2:

$$s(2) = \frac{d(3)}{1+r}$$

so that $s(2) = s(1)(1 + r)$. Hence, in this case the owner of a share receives a capital gain of $rs(1)$ if the share is held from time 1 to time 2. The rate of capital gain is, of course, just the market rate of return, as it necessarily must be in the presently assumed circumstances.

We next consider a sustained dividend growth model. In the infinite stream model with a constant payout ratio [equation (4.13)], we have:

$$k = \frac{d(2)}{e(2)} = \frac{d(3)}{e(3)} = \frac{d(2)(1+g)}{e(2)(1+x)}$$

where $g$ = dividend growth rate and
$\quad x$ = earnings growth rate

Note that we must have $x = g$ in order for the payout ratio to remain constant. Assuming this to be the case, we then obtain, using equation (4.13),

$$s(1) = \frac{ke(2)}{r-g}$$

and similarly:

$$s(2) = \frac{ke(3)}{r-g} = \frac{ke(2)(1+g)}{r-g}$$

Therefore, $s(2) = s(1)(1 + g)$, and capital gains are $gs(1)$.
Given that:

$$s(1) = \frac{d(2) + s(2)}{1+r} \quad \text{and} \quad s(2) = s(1)(1+g)$$

it is also easy to show that the ratio of dividends to capital gains is a constant:

$$\frac{d(2)}{gs(1)} = \frac{r-g}{g}, \quad g \neq 0$$

The results of this section, as indeed of this entire chapter, depend on the assumptions either of no taxes or of taxation at the same rates on both capital gains and dividends. For if this assumption were not made, dividends and capital gains would not be the perfect substitutes we have assumed they are in the above formulations. In other words, if dividends and capital gains are taxed at differential rates, the price-earnings ratios and equations for stock values of this chapter must be amended to take into account the different forms in which stockholders' returns are received.

### 4.3  MARKET VALUES AND DIFFERENT PLANNING HORIZONS

As we have seen, the value of a firm is determined from the present value of its earnings over all future periods. Accordingly, one of the central considerations relevant to a firm's management involves explicit recognition of the effects of all future periods. Yet in the discussion of previous chapters, as well as in many examples in the present chapter, we have considered only two points in time. Thus, the question arises as to whether our condensed examples really reflect the principles appropriate for recognizing all future periods' effects. We now show that market prices at different points in time adjust in order to eliminate differences in value due only to the maturity dates of financial instruments. Then, applying this result to value the firm in the marketplace, we show that we can assess the effects of an investment decision in terms of present payoff and effects on the next period's market value, even if the investment actually yields payoffs over many future periods.

#### 4.3.1  Returns on Financial Instruments Outstanding for Several Periods

In this section we show that financial instruments outstanding over several periods must, in a perfect capital market, sell at such prices such that the instruments yield the market rates of interest prevailing in each time period. However, in practice the rates to be earned are frequently reported as averages over all periods up to the instrument's maturity—a potentially misleading figure unless it is carefully interpreted.

Consider a simple numerical example with interest rates as shown in the following diagram:

$$
\begin{array}{ccc}
| \underline{\hspace{2cm} 7\% \hspace{2cm}} | \underline{\hspace{2cm} 8\% \hspace{2cm}} | \\
1 \qquad\qquad {}_1r_2 \qquad\qquad 2 \qquad\qquad {}_2r_3 \qquad\qquad 3
\end{array}
$$

Note that the interest rate now has two time subscripts to indicate the particular time interval over which it obtains: The left subscript indicates the start of the time period and the right subscript the end of the period to which the interest rate applies.

Suppose $100 is invested on the terms indicated by the diagram for two periods (i.e., from time 1 to time 3). The value of the investment at the end of two periods will be:

$$\$100(1 + {}_1r_2)(1 + {}_2r_3)$$

The returns on this type of investment are frequently reported using an average rate as follows:

$$\$100(1 + {}_1r_3)^2$$

where

$$1 + {}_1r_3 = [(1 + {}_1r_2)(1 + {}_2r_3)]^{1/2}$$

Thus, $_1r_3$ is defined as the *geometric mean rate of interest* (or *geometric average rate of interest*) earned in each of the two periods. Substituting in the values of the example, we obtain:

$$1 + {}_1r_3 = [1.07(1.08)]^{1/2}$$
$$= 1.07499$$

so that the average interest rate earned over each of the two periods is 7.499%. This rate is frequently termed the instrument's *average yield to maturity*.

To see that the two-period investment actually yields 7% in the first period and 8% in the second period, consider the investment's value at time 3:

$$V(3) = \$100(1.07)(1.08)$$

But its value at time 2 is $V(3)$ discounted at 8%, so that:

$$V(2) = \frac{V(3)}{1.08} = \frac{100(1.07)(1.08)}{1.08} = \$100(1.07) = V_1(1 + {}_1r_2)$$

The yields of 7% and 8% are called the investment's *holding period yields* (for the first and second periods, respectively). The results indicated by the example demonstrate that the maturity structure of an investment does not affect the holding period yields it offers (i.e., if the above investment were bought at time 1 and sold at time 2, it would yield 7% and not 7.499%). Similarly, if held from time 2 to time 3, the instrument yields 8%. Thus, the rates of return earned on holding the investment over any given period of time are the market rates of return over that time period. If the investor's planning horizon is two periods, either the geometric average yield to maturity or the two one-period rates (i.e., holding period yields) may be used to reflect the market rate of return, but if the holding period is only for one of the two periods, the use of the average would be misleading.

## 4.3.2 Market Values and Time Horizons

The foregoing notions can also be used to determine the market value of a firm at different points in time, and this allows us to consider decisions (whose effects might be registered over many periods) just in terms of their present effects plus those on market values one period hence.

To see this, observe that a firm's market value can be determined in two ways. The first is by the stream of earnings accruing to the original stockholders,[16]

$$MV(1) = \frac{\pi(1)}{1 + {}_1r_2} + \frac{\pi(2)}{(1 + {}_1r_2)(1 + {}_2r_3)} + \frac{\pi(3)}{(1 + {}_1r_2)(1 + {}_2r_3)(1 + {}_3r_4)} + \cdots$$

where $MV(1)$ is the market value at the beginning of period 1 and $\pi(t)$ is the net earnings for period. The second is by the discounted current earnings plus the period 1 equivalent of the firm's market value one period later,

---

[16] Here it is assumed that the funds are actually distributed to the stockholders at the indicated times.

$$MV(1) = \frac{\pi(1)}{1 + \,_1r_2} + \frac{MV(2)}{1 + \,_1r_2}$$

where MV(2) is the market value at the end of time period 2. This second way of looking at market value says that it can be considered in terms of the current period results plus a term incorporating the effect of all future periods' results. Clearly, the market value at time 2 is the time 2 value of all earnings accruing to the original stockholders from time 2 onwards. Thus, we can look at market value either in terms of an entire earnings stream or in terms of current earnings plus a future market value. Some additional examples will illustrate this reasoning further.

### 4.3.3   Application to Share Price Determination

In our first example we explore the relations between a many-period analysis and a present versus future period orientation, as applied to the determination of share prices. We consider a firm that has issued 50 common shares and has the following dividend stream that represents all earnings and includes the disposal value, if any, of assets at time 4:

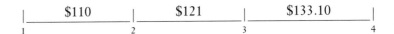

Let $r = 10\%$ over all three time periods (in our notation it would be $_1r_4$) and suppose that the firm has zero value after time 4. Then the stock's value at the beginning of period 1 is the firm market value at the beginning of period 1 divided by the number of shares outstanding (50). That is,

$$s(1) = \frac{1}{50} MV(1)$$

which using the stream of all future earnings is:

$$s(1) = \frac{1}{50} \left[ \frac{\$110}{1.1} + \frac{121}{(1.1)^2} + \frac{133.10}{(1.1)^3} \right] = \frac{1}{50} (\$300) = \$6 \text{ per share}$$

The value of a share can also be computed as follows:

$$s(1) = \frac{1}{50} \left[ \frac{D(2)}{1.10} + \frac{MV(2)}{1.10} \right]$$

where $D(2)$ is the dividend payment at time 2, distributed to stockholders of record at time 1. But,

$$MV(2) = \frac{\$121}{1.1} + \frac{\$133.10}{(1.1)^2} = \$220$$

Therefore,

$$s(1) = \frac{1}{50}\left[\$100 + \frac{1}{1.10}(\$220)\right]$$

$$= \frac{d(2)}{1.10} + \frac{s(2)}{1.10}$$

where $d(2)$ is the time 2 dividend to a single share and

$\quad\quad s(2)$ is the price of the share

Of course, the market price of a share at time 2 reflects the present value of dividends accruing to it after time 2, so that in effect the two calculations incorporate exactly the same information and in exactly the same way. However, for analytic purposes it is frequently useful to represent the situation in the second, more compact way.

## 4.3.4 Applications to Valuing the Growing Firm

In this section we show that the present versus future orientation also applies to the analysis of growth stocks. Moreover, it helps to show, by developing a timing convention for the realization of returns in excess of market rates, how a firm's existing owners capture these excess returns for themselves. In the examples we show that the owners of a growth stock know the firm's earnings will grow at a high rate but discount this stream at the market rate of interest in determining the value of firm. The original owners then sell new shares at this market value, so that the new investor can realize only the market rate of return.

Let us first consider a proposition in which the founders of a firm put up $140 at time 1, to be withdrawn completely at time 2 by selling the firm to new stockholders. Suppose, moreover, that the firm will, using the $140, generate cash earnings of $55.00, $72.60, and $93.17 at times 2, 3, and 4, respectively, and that the market rate of interest is 10%. This proposition is illustrated in Figure 4.2.

What are the market values of the firm at each point in time, the rate of return earned by the original stockholders from time 1 to time 2, and the rates of return

FIGURE 4.2
VALUING THE GROWING FIRM

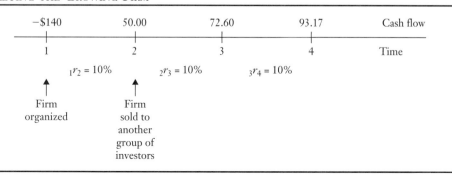

**TABLE 4.1**
VALUES OF THE FIRM AT TIMES 1 THROUGH 4

| Time | Market value of incomes not yet received[a] |
|---|---:|
| 1 | \$50.00 + \$60.00 + \$70.00 = \$180.00 |
| 2 | \$55.00 + \$66.00 + \$77.00 = \$198.00 |
| 3 | \$72.60 + \$84.70 = \$157.30 |
| 4 | \$93.17 = \$ 93.17 |

[a]Note that the data are obtained by appropriate discounting of the cash flows. For example, \$93.17/1.10 = \$84.70, and so on.

earned by the new purchasers? Table 4.1 exhibits the data. The entries in the table's "middle" column include the current period's earnings as their first term and the discounted values of future earnings, if any, at that point in time as their remaining terms. Thus, the market values reported to the right of the equality signs reflect the prices at which the firm can be sold at each of these points in time. We see that the firm's founders could sell the firm immediately at time 1 for \$180, representing *a* for a profit to them of \$40 over the original investment. If the founders sold the firm at time 2 for \$198, their return over that period would be (\$198 − \$140)/\$140 = 41.4%. If, however, new stockholders bought the firm at time 2 for resale at time 3, they would pay \$198 and receive \$55 immediately and \$147.30 at time 3. The rate of return of the new stockholders would be [\$157.30 − (\$198 − \$55)]/(\$198 − \$55) = \$14.30/\$143.00 = 10%. Similarly, investors buying the firm at time 2 for \$198 and collecting the earnings generated by the firm would receive only a 10% return on their investment. Again, this illustrates the principle that the original stockholders can earn returns in excess of the market, but new investors cannot, unless the firm's future earnings have been improperly anticipated by the original stockholders.

To show that the foregoing results apply equally to an existing firm making a new investment, we present the following example. Since we have already, and will again, show that several time points can be incorporated in our analyses, the present example uses only two time points so as to focus more sharply on other matters. Suppose that a firm announces an investment of \$2,200 at time 1, that the cash flow realized at time 2 on this investment will be \$3,520, and that the investment will be financed by a new share issue. How many shares must be issued, and what will the market price of *all* shares be after the new issue?

Let us denote with a superscript 0 the values for the variables before the announcement of the new investment. Let's assume the following in our example:

$$V^0(2) = \$11,000 \quad r = 0.10 \quad N^0(1) = 1,000 \text{ shares} \quad s^0(1) = \$10 \text{ per share}$$

After the announcement, we will then have:

$$V(2) = \$11,000 + \$3,520 = \$14,520$$
$$I(1) = \$2,200$$

where $I(1)$ is the amount of the new investment.

We now have to determine simultaneously the number of new shares to issue and the issue price. Denoting the number of new shares as $M(1)$, we write the time 1 value of each share (new and old) outstanding after the new issue as:

$$\frac{V(2)}{1.10}\left[\frac{1}{N^0(1)+M(1)}\right]$$

Then this value multiplied by the number of new shares must equal the required investment. Thus,

$$I(1) = \frac{V(2)}{1.10}\left[\frac{M(1)}{N^0(1)+M(1)}\right]$$

or

$$\$2,200 = \frac{\$14,520}{1.10}\left[\frac{M(1)}{100+M(1)}\right]$$

so that

$$M(1) = 200$$

What is the issue price? All shares must earn the market rate of interest from period 1 to period 2; therefore,

$$V(1) = V(2)/1.10 = \$13,200$$
and
$$s(1) = \$13,200/\$1,200 = \$11.00$$

The original stockholders realize a capital gain of $1.00 per share (on each of the originally outstanding 1,000 shares) and thus capture all the present value of the investment.

Note that:

$$s(2) = \$14,520/\$1,200 = \$12.10 = \$11.00(1.10)$$

implies that all shares earn the market rate after the price has been adjusted to take into account the returns from the new investment and the additional share issue. This suggests that the original stockholders (i.e., the founders) can be regarded as partners who shared in the capital gains created by the new investment, while the new stockholders can be regarded as investors who merely receive the market rate of return on their shares. The original partners do not share their excess gains with the new investors because they can raise money in a perfect capital market without paying premium rates for the funds.

### 4.3.5 Mathematical Example

In this example we show how the earnings a firm generates are related to its investment policies. Suppose, as in the previous example, new investors can buy the stock only at time 2, 3, and 4; time 1 is an organizing time before the founders sell any shares in the financial markets:

Also, let:

$$K_1 = \text{capital stock at time } 1$$
$$\pi_t = \text{earnings at time } t + 1, \ t = 1, 2, 3$$

The firm's objective is to maximize the present value of the original owners' investment, a value determined by earnings it can generate through setting up the firm and producing and selling a single product. Production is given by:

$$q_t = K_1^{1/2} \ \text{ in each of the three time periods,}$$

where $K_1$ is the capital stock purchased at time 1, a level that cannot subsequently be altered, and $q_t$, $t = 2, 3, 4$, the outputs produced from the capital stock at those times.

Only capital equipment is assumed to be used in producing the product; no other resources are needed. Investment expenditures are incurred at the beginning of time 1, and revenues from selling the product are received at times 2, 3, and 4. Formally, the problem may be written as:

$$\max_{K_1} \frac{p_2 K_2^{1/2}}{1 + \ _1 r_2} + \frac{1}{1 + \ _1 r_2}\left(\frac{p_3 K_1^{1/2}}{1 + \ _2 r_3}\right) + \frac{1}{1 + \ _1 r_2}\left(\frac{1}{1 + \ _2 r_3}\right)\left(\frac{p_4 K_1^{1/2}}{1 + \ _3 r_4}\right) - c_1 K_1 \quad (4.15)$$

where $p_t$ = price of output at time $t$, $t = 2, 3, 4$
  $c_1$ = unit cost of capital stock acquired at time 1

The owners achieve their objectives by selecting an optimal value for $K_1$ (i.e., by determining the firm's initial capital investment). Since equation (4.15) includes the present value of all the firm's future cash flows as well as the cost of the initial investment, it indicates the market value of the firm at time 1.

Now if we assume that:

$$p_2 = p_3 = p_4 = 3$$
$$c_1 = 1$$

and

$$_1r_2 = {}_2r_3 = {}_3r_4 = \frac{1}{2} \quad \text{(i.e., 50\%)}$$

we can rewrite the objective function as:

$$\max_{K_1} \frac{3K_1^{1/2}}{\frac{3}{2}} + \frac{3K_1^{1/2}}{\left(\frac{3}{2}\right)^2} + \frac{3K_1^{1/2}}{\left(\frac{3}{2}\right)^3} - K_1 = \max_{K_1} \frac{38}{9} K_1^{1/2} - K_1 \qquad (4.16)$$

The assumed prices and interest rates are chosen for computational convenience and are not intended to represent realistic values. Taking the derivative of equation (4.16) and setting it equal to zero will yield the optimal amount of capital $K_1^*$:

$$\frac{1}{2} \left(\frac{38}{9}\right) K_1^{-1/2} - 1 = 0$$

$$\frac{19}{9} K_1^{-1/2} = 1$$

$$\frac{19}{9} = K_1^{1/2}$$

$$K_1^* = \left(\frac{19}{9}\right)^2$$

To obtain the market value of the firm at time 1, we substitute $K_1^*$ into equation (4.16):

$$MV(1) = \frac{38}{9} \left(\frac{19}{9}\right) - \left(\frac{19}{9}\right)^2 = \left(\frac{19}{9}\right)^2$$

Assuming that the firm distributes earnings to stockholders as quickly as the earnings are generated, the market value of the firm at time 2 is the present value, at that time, of all future earnings the firm can generate:

$$\left[\frac{3}{\frac{3}{2}} + \frac{3}{\left(\frac{3}{2}\right)^2}\right] \left(\frac{19}{9}\right) = \frac{30}{9} \left(\frac{19}{9}\right)$$

Similarly, MV(3) would be:

$$\frac{3}{\frac{3}{2}} \left(\frac{19}{9}\right) = \frac{18}{9} \left(\frac{19}{9}\right) = 2 \left(\frac{19}{9}\right)$$

Now suppose the firm was sold by the founders at time 2. What would be the returns made by the firm's founders? First, let us calculate the one-period return on the original owner's investment:

$$\text{Return} = \frac{\text{revenues in period 1} + \text{sales price of firm} - \text{original investment}}{\text{original investment}}$$

$$= \frac{p_1 K_1^{*(1/2)} + \text{MV}(2) - K_1^*}{K_1^*}$$

$$= \frac{3\left(\frac{19}{9}\right) + \left(\frac{30}{9}\right)\left(\frac{19}{9}\right) - \left(\frac{19}{9}\right)^2}{\left(\frac{19}{9}\right)^2}$$

$$= 100\%$$

We can interpret this result as saying that once the original owners have determined the firm's prospects, they make an immediate excess return on their investment. If they continue to hold shares in the firm after period 1, their subsequent returns, when calculated on the basis of the firm's market values, just equal market rates of interest. For example, the rate of return between times 3 and 4 is:

$$\text{return} = \frac{p_1 K_1^{*(1/2)} - \text{MV}(3)}{\text{MV}(3)}$$

$$= \frac{3\left(\frac{19}{9}\right) - \frac{18}{9}\left(\frac{19}{9}\right)}{\frac{18}{9}\left(\frac{19}{9}\right)} = 50\%$$

exactly the market rate of interest.

The foregoing example shows the following:

1. The value of the firm at any point in time can be viewed as the sum of two terms: the value of current period earnings on the one hand and the discounted future value of the firm on the other.
2. The discounted future value used for planning over more than a single period is the market value of the firm at the end of that single planning period. For comparison purposes, it and the current earnings are usually discounted to time 1.
3. The original owners of the firm get any excess returns because, as and when they sell the firm, they demand and can obtain a market price such that the new owners receive only the market rate of interest on their investment.

We showed that, because we used the market value at time 2 to calculate the return on the original investment, the excess returns could be regarded[17] as earned between times 1 and 2. This interpretation, coupled with the assumption that the original owners can only sell the firm at time 2 or later, highlights the fact that

---

[17] Alternatively, we could regard them as spread out over the first two or more periods. We made the arbitrary choice indicated simply to emphasize that the original stockholders get the excess returns.

the excess returns are captured by the original owners rather than by the new investors subsequently purchasing the firm.

If we know or can compute the firm's market value at the end of the current period, then planning over many periods can be done correctly in a "one-period-at-a-time fashion" by determining the effects on the future market values and current periods' earnings in doing the planning.

## 4.3.6 Relations to Profit Maximization

The example of the last section can be used to indicate how period-by-period profit (or earnings in the terminology we have used throughout this chapter) maximization can, if correctly carried out, lead to the same result as maximization of present value. The key to obtaining the same results lies in the interpretation of period earnings.

It is evident from the previous example that buying capital equipment at time 1 affects the firm's earning power at times 2, 3, and 4. Hence, a correct computation of earnings over the first period must take all these future effects into account. This can be done by considering as a part of period 1 earnings the value of assets held by the firm at time 2. Hence, a time 1 decision yields time 2 earnings composed of both current earnings and future capital gains. In the example, period 1 earnings are thus, when evaluated in time 1 magnitudes, equal to the time 1 values of earnings received at time 2, plus asset value at time 1, less asset acquisition costs on the market value of the firm at time 1:

$$\frac{3\left(\frac{19}{9}\right)}{\frac{3}{2}} + \frac{\frac{10}{3}\left(\frac{19}{9}\right)}{\frac{3}{2}} - \left(\frac{19}{9}\right)^2 = \left(\frac{19}{9}\right)^2$$

That is, this view of earnings takes into account the fact that the time 1 decision creates earnings at times 2, 3, and 4. The time 2 earnings are considered directly; the time 3 and 4 earnings are considered in terms of their time 2 value.

If this treatment of earnings is carried forward consistently into future periods, we discount end-of-period earnings and asset values to the beginning of the period and subtract from this magnitude the beginning-of-period asset acquisition costs. When correctly done, this gives zero earnings at times 2, 3, and 4. This seems counterintuitive at first, but the zero-earnings calculation says:

1. The rate of return on invested assets valued at market prices is the market rate of return, and
2. No new value is created subsequent to the initial asset acquisition decision. Moreover, the initial value creation stemmed from acquiring assets at a cost less than the present value of the earnings those assets could generate.

Although the numbers do not reflect the way financial statements are kept in practice,[18] they do indicate economic earnings, and they also give interpretations

---

[18] In particular, the income or profit and loss statement.

consistent with our earlier views of who receives excess returns. Original owners, receiving excess returns, may be said to earn economic rents (positive economic profits); other investors, getting merely the market rate of return on their investments, receive no economic rent (zero economic earnings).

## KEY POINTS

- When management follows the market value rule, the value of the firm is equal to the present value of cash flows to be generated by the firm's existing assets plus the present value of cash flows to be generated from future growth opportunities.
- In a perfect capital market, when funds can be raised at the same market rate of interest as is used to discount the firm's earnings, the size of a dividend is irrelevant to determining the firm's market value. This is because the firm's value depends only on its future earnings stream and not on the source of funds needed to finance creation of the earnings stream, even if the source is retention financing obtained by foregoing a dividend.
- The irrelevance of the dividend decision in a perfect capital market means the firm may be valued using either the discounted stream of future earnings available to the initial stockholders or the discounted stream of future dividends.
- A growth firm is one in which the expanding assets generate returns in excess of the market rate of interest.
- The price-earnings ratio is the ratio of the current market price of the stock to the firm's earnings per share. In a perfect capital market, the equilibrium return on investment will be the same for all firms, even though price-earnings ratios for stocks differ substantially.
- In practice, purchasing a stock at a bargain depends on receiving extraordinary returns resulting from future events not yet impounded into the market price.
- In a perfect capital market, the original stockholders can earn returns in excess of the market, but new investors cannot unless the firm's future incomes have been improperly anticipated by the original stockholders. This principle applies even to stock of growth firms.
- In a perfect capital market, financial instruments outstanding over several periods must have market prices such that they yield the market rates of interest prevailing in each time period.

## QUESTIONS

1. Who determines the amount and timing of earnings that are distributed to shareholders?

2. On the website of a financial consultant the following appears:

   "Since dividend stocks make regular cash payments to shareholders, you can score a worthwhile return even if the overall market peters out. If the market stays strong, you'll probably enjoy share price appreciation plus the steady dividend income." (www.winninginvesting.com/picking_ dividend_stocks.htm)

    **a.** Based on the theory described in this chapter, explain why you agree or disagree with this statement.

    **b.** What might be a reason why this consultant is correct in his assessment?

**3.** The following appears in an investor relations website for Amazon.com:

> "We have never declared or paid cash dividends on our common stock. We intend to retain all future earnings to finance future growth and, therefore, do not anticipate paying any cash dividends in the foreseeable future."

Do you think this statement will adversely impact the value of the stock of Amazon.com?

**4.** Atech Industries Inc. has initial resources equal to $150 million. Because management estimates that optimal operation requires an investment of $200 million, the firm must raise an additional $50 million in capital and that amount will be financed through retention of some or all of the existing resources rather than distribution to stockholders as dividend. Management projects that the investment of $200 million in time 2 will create $330 million in cash flow at time 2. Assume the market rate of interest is 8% for funds raised.

    **a.** If the original stockholders receive none of the initially available resources as a dividend and must raise the entire $50 million to carry out the optimal investment program, what is the present value of the Atech Industries Inc.?

    **b.** Suppose that the board of directors decides to pay out to existing stockholders $80 million at time 1 so that only $70 million of the $150 million of the firm's initial resources are available to meet the future operational needs. What is the present value of the Atech Industries Inc. for the original stockholders if the amount needed is raised in the capital markets?

**5.** Two investors are discussing the procedure that they employ to value the share of a firm's common stock. Investor A believes that a firm should be valued based on the dividends that are expected to be distributed in the future. Investor B believes that the proper valuation approach is to look at expected earnings per share and not dividends. Comment on the two approaches for valuation.

**6.** The history of the stock market shows that there are a large number of start-up corporations whose stock price traded at high market values despite large losses and never any positive earnings. Why would investors be willing to pay a high price for the stock of a corporation that has never reported positive earnings?

**7.**   **a.** What is meant by a growth firm?

    **b.** A common belief by investors is that investors who can identify growth firms can realize superior market returns by investing in them if their expectations about growth prospects are correct. Comment on this view.

8. What are the assumptions of the Gordon growth model?

9. Assume the following data for the KW firm:

    Earnings per share at time 2: $4

    Share price at time 1: $71

    Portion of earnings paid out as dividends: 40%

    What is the growth rate necessary to support a price-earnings ratio of 7 assuming the following market rate of interest:

    a. 8%
    b. 10%
    c. 15%

10. a. Why do investors believe that low price-earnings stocks are trading cheap in the market?

    b. An investment strategy that seeks to create a portfolio of stocks with low price-earnings ratios is believed to be able to earn excess market returns. Explain why this is not the case in a perfect capital market under certainty.

    c. Explain how in an imperfect capital market where there is risk, that a low price-earnings ratio strategy may be able to generate excess market returns.

11. Why are the tax rates that are applied to capital gains and dividends important in stock valuation?

12. Consider the following market conditions for a two-period investment:

    Market rate of interest for period 1 (i.e., beginning of period 1 to the end of period 1) = 5%

    Market rate of interest for period 2 (i.e., beginning of period 2 to the end of period 2) = 7%

    a. What is the value of the investment at the end of the two periods?
    b. What are the holding period yields?
    c. What is the average yield to maturity for this investment?

13. The founder of RX Widgets started the firm five years ago. The business has been profitable. Today he is looking to sell additional shares in the firm in order to expand the business and take advantage of new investment opportunities. Explain why the founder shares in the capital gains created by the new investments made by the firm, while the new stockholders can be regarded as investors who merely receive the market rate of return on their shares.

14. The value of a firm at a given point in time can be viewed as consisting of two terms. Explain each of the terms.

# REFERENCES

Gordon, Myron J. (1959). "Dividends, Earnings and Stock Prices," *Review of Economics and Statistics* **41**: 99–105.

Miller, Merton H., and Franco Modigliani. (1961). "Dividend Policy, Growth and The Valuation of Shares," *Journal of Busines* **34**: 411–433.

Modigliani, Franco, and Merton H. Miller. (1958). "The Cost of Capital, Corporate Finance and The Theory of Investment," *American Economic Review* **48**: 261–297.

Modigliani, Franco, and Merton H. Miller. (1963). "Corporate Income Taxes and The Cost of Capital: A Correction," *American Economic Review* **53**: 433–443.

# 5

# FIRM FINANCING DECISIONS
# IN A PERFECT CAPITAL MARKET

*A* firm's managers invest in new plant and equipment to generate additional revenues and income. Earnings generated by the firm belong to the owners and can either be paid to them or retained within the firm. The portion of earnings paid to the firm's owners is referred to as *dividends*; the portion retained within the firm is referred to as *retained earnings*. The owners' investment in the company is referred to as *owners' equity* or, simply, *equity*.

If earnings are plowed back into the company, the owners expect it to be invested in projects that will enhance the firm's value, and hence, the value of the owners' equity. Consequently, one way to pay for new investments is to use some of the previously retained earnings. But earnings may not be sufficient to support all profitable investment opportunities, and if so, management must either forego the investment opportunities or raise additional capital. New capital can be raised by borrowing, by selling additional ownership interests, or both. Borrowing can be in the form of bank loans or the issuance of debt obligations such as bonds. When we discuss additional ownership interests, we will usually assume that additional ordinary shares of common stock are issued.[1]

Decisions about how the firm should be financed, whether with debt or equity, are referred to as *capital structure decisions*. In this chapter, we explain both the basic issues associated with capital structure decisions and how corporate management should choose a capital structure in a perfect capital market. The principal issue faced by management is whether there is a capital structure that maximizes the firm's value, referred to as an *optimal capital structure*. This chapter examines a theory, known as the Modigliani-Miller theory, explaining the influence of capital structure on firm value in the context of a perfect capital market. In a perfect capital market and the absence of corporate taxation, the value of the firm will not change as capital structure is altered: The Modigliani-Miller theory argues that capital structure is irrelevant.

---

[1] More complex kinds of equity issues are discussed in Chapter 23.

The demonstration in this chapter should be regarded as a first step in disentangling the effects of capital structure choice.[2] In Part VII, we find that capital market imperfections can provide reasons for capital structure to matter, and provide analyses of the effects of capital structure decisions in a world of imperfect capital markets.

## 5.1 DEBT VS. EQUITY

A firm's capital structure is some mix of three sources: debt, equity already accumulated (from previous equity issues or from accumulated earnings), and new equity. If management elects to finance the firm's operations with debt, the creditors (lenders) expect the interest and principal—fixed, legal commitments—to be paid back as promised. Failure to pay may result in legal actions by the creditors. If the firm finances its operations with equity, the owners expect a return in the form of dividends, an appreciation of the value of their equity interest (i.e., capital gain), or, as is most likely, some combination of both.[3]

Returning to the effects of a debt issue, suppose a firm's management elects to borrow $100 million for one year at an interest rate of 10%. By doing so, the firm is promising to repay the $100 million plus $10 million in interest in one year. That is, satisfying the debt obligation means that $110 million must be paid. Consider the following three possible outcomes for the firm's *operating earnings* (i.e., earnings from operations before interest expense) generated by the $100 million invested and any returns on it, and the associated consequences for lenders and owners.

| Operating earnings | Implication for lenders | Implication for owners |
| --- | --- | --- |
| More than $10 million | Debt obligation satisfied | Profit generated equal to the operating earnings reduced by $10 million |
| $10 million | Debt obligation satisfied | No profit or loss |
| Less than $10 million | Shortfall in required repayment, equals $110 million less the amount of operating earnings generated | Loss equal to the difference between $10 million and the operating earnings generated |

As indicated, if management can invest the amount borrowed so as to realize both a return of the invested capital—$100 million—plus operating earnings in excess of the $10 million the firm must pay in interest (the cost of the funds), the company keeps all the profits. But if the investment generates operating earnings of $10 million or less for the firm, the lender still gets either $10 million or whatever the operating earnings happen to be.

---

[2] In Chapter 10 we provide another interpretation of why the firm's capital structure is irrelevant in a perfect capital market without corporate taxation. The framework we use is contingent claims analysis, an especially convenient way of disentangling the meaning of capital structure change.

[3] A value maximizing capital structure will depend on several factors that we discuss later in this chapter.

The foregoing example illustrates the basic idea behind *financial leverage*—the use of financing that has fixed, but limited, payments. If the company has abundant earnings relative to the debt payments that must be made, the owners reap all that remains of the earnings after the creditors have been paid. If earnings are low relative to the debt payments that must be made, the creditors still must be paid what they are due, possibly leaving the owners nothing. Failure to pay interest or principal as promised may lead to financial distress. *Financial distress* is the condition where management makes decisions under pressure to satisfy its legal obligations to its creditors—decisions that may not be in the best interests of the company's owners. Although management may and often does choose to make dividend payments to shareholders, with equity financing there is no legal obligation to do so. Furthermore, under U.S. tax law, interest paid on debt is deductible for tax purposes, whereas dividend payments are not tax deductible.

One measure of the extent to which debt figures in the capital structure is the *debt ratio*:

$$\text{Debt ratio} = \text{Par value of debt/Market value of equity}$$

The greater the debt ratio, the greater the use of debt relative to equity financing. Another measure is the *debt-to-assets ratio*, which is the extent to which the firm's assets are financed with debt:

$$\text{Debt-to-assets ratio} = \text{Par value of debt/Market value of total assets}$$

This is the proportion of debt in a company's capital structure.

---

## 5.2  CAPITAL STRUCTURE AND FINANCIAL LEVERAGE

Capital structure decisions can affect the risks stemming originally from the company's business decisions. As explained in Section 5.1, debt and equity financing create different types of obligations for the company. The concept of *leverage* plays a role in affecting the company's financial risk because leverage amplifies the effects of outcomes, good or bad. The fixed and limited nature of a debt obligation affects the risk of the earnings available for distribution to the owners. Consider a firm that has $20 million of assets, all financed with equity. We refer to such a firm as "100% equity financed" or "unlevered." Suppose that there are 1 million shares of stock of this firm outstanding, valued at $20 per share. In this case, the equity is $20 million, equal to the value of the assets, and the debt is zero.

Suppose further that the firm's management (1) has identified investment opportunities requiring $10 million of new funds and (2) can raise the funds in one of the following three ways:

*Financing package 1*:  Issue $10 million equity (500,000 shares of stock at $20 per share)

*Financing package 2:* Issue $5 million of equity (250,000 shares of stock at $20 per share) and borrow $5 million with an annual interest of 10%

*Financing package 3:* Borrow $10 million with an annual interest of 10%

For each financing package, the resulting post-financing capital structure is summarized in Table 5.1.

Note that it may be unrealistic to assume that the interest rate on the debt in financing package 3 will be the same as the interest rate for financing package 2 because there is more credit risk in financing package 3. However, for purposes of illustrating the effects of leverage, let's keep the interest rate unchanged for now. We shall revisit this assumption later in the chapter.

Suppose the firm has $4.5 million of operating earnings. We refer to the return that the firm earns on its operating assets as the *return on assets* (ROA). For our hypothetical firm, the ROA is 15% (=$4.5/$30). And suppose there are no taxes. To illustrate the concept of financial leverage, consider the effect of this financial leverage on the company's earnings per share. The *earnings per share* (EPS) is the ratio of the earnings available to the owners divided by the number of shares outstanding. The EPS for the three financial packages are shown in Table 5.2 assuming a 15% ROA.

Similarly, different EPS can be computed for different assumptions about the ROA. Table 5.3 shows the EPS for each of the three financing packages based on three assumptions about the ROA—15%, 10%, and 5%:

Notice that if the ROA is the same as the cost of debt, 10% in our illustration, the EPS is not affected by the choice of financing, because in that case the EPS is $2.00 regardless of the financing package. If the ROA is 15%, greater than the cost of debt,

## TABLE 5.1
### SUMMARY OF THE CAPITAL STRUCTURE FOR THREE FINANCING PACKAGES

| Financing package | Assets (millions) | Debt | Equity | No. of shares (millions) | Debt-to-equity ratio | Debt-to-assets ratio |
|---|---|---|---|---|---|---|
| 1 | $30 | $ 0 | $30 | 1.50 | 0.0% | 0.0% |
| 2 | $30 | $ 5 | $25 | 1.25 | 20.0% | 16.7% |
| 3 | $30 | $10 | $20 | 1.00 | 50.0% | 33.3% |

## TABLE 5.2
### EARNINGS PER SHARE RESULTING FROM THREE FINANCING PACKAGES

| | Financing package | | |
|---|---|---|---|
| | 1 | 2 | 3 |
| Operating earnings in millions | $ 4.5 | $ 4.5 | $ 4.5 |
| − Interest expense in millions | 0.0 | 0.5 | 1.0 |
| = Earnings available to owners in millions | $ 4.5 | $ 4.0 | $ 3.5 |
| No. of shares in millions | 1.5 | 1.25 | 1.0 |
| Earnings per share | $3.00 | $3.20 | $3.50 |

**TABLE 5.3**
EARNINGS PER SHARE FOR DIFFERENT RETURN ON ASSETS
FOR THREE FINANCING PACKAGES

| | Financing package | | |
|---|---|---|---|
| Assumed ROA | 1 (least leverage) | 2 | 3 (most leverage) |
| 15% | $3.00 | $3.20 | $3.50 |
| 10% | $2.00 | $2.00 | $2.00 |
| 5% | $1.00 | $0.80 | $0.50 |

financing package 3 (with the greatest financial leverage) has the highest EPS. In stark contrast, if the ROA is 5%, less than the cost of debt, financing package 3 has the lowest EPS while financing package 1 with the least amount of financial leverage has the highest EPS.

This example illustrates the effect of debt financing on operating risk (as measured by the variability of operating earnings): The greater the use of debt vis-à-vis equity, the greater the operating risk. Additionally, by comparing the outcomes for the different operating earnings scenarios—$4.5, $3.0, and $1.5 million—the effect of adding financial risk to the operating risk magnifies the risk to the owners. Comparing the results, each of the alternative financing packages shows that as more debt is used in the capital structure, the greater the variability[4] of the EPS.

When debt is used instead of equity (financing package 3), the owners do not share earnings over and above the contractual interest on the debt. But when equity financing is used instead (financing package 1), the original owners must share the increased earnings with the holders of newly issued shares, diluting their return on equity and EPS.

Another way to view financing effects is to calculate the *degree of financial leverage*, DFL:

$$DFL = \frac{\text{Earnings before interest and taxes}}{\text{Earnings before interest and taxes} - \text{Interest}}$$

The DFL for the three financing packages at a 10% ROA, or $3 million in operating earnings, is:

| Financing package | 1 | 2 | 3 |
|---|---|---|---|
| DFL at 10% ROA | 1.0 | 1.2 | 1.5 |

From the above, we can see that financing package 3 has the highest degree of financial leverage. Recall that increased leverage means more debt is used in the capital structure relative to equity, and consequently the greater the volatility of the EPS.

---

[4] Variability is commonly called volatility, and sometimes the swing. It is usually measured by either the variance or the standard deviation of the measure in question, in this case the EPS.

## 5.2.1   Financial Leverage and Financial Flexibility

The use of debt also reduces a company's financial flexibility. A company with unused debt capacity, sometimes referred to as *financial slack*,[5] is more prepared to take advantage of investment opportunities in the future. The ability to exploit future strategic options is valuable and, hence, taking on debt decreases slack, with the result that the company may not be sufficiently nimble to act on valuable opportunities.

Empirical evidence provided by Booth and Cleary (2006) suggests that companies with more cash flow volatility tend to build up more financial slack and, hence, their investments are not as sensitive to the companies' ability to generate cash flows internally. Rather, financial slack allows them to exploit investment opportunities quickly without the need to generate additional cash. Consequently, companies with highly volatile operating earnings may want to maintain some level of financial flexibility by keeping their debt financing relatively low.

## 5.2.2   Governance Value of Debt Financing

The *free cash flow* of a company is, basically, its gross cash flow less any capital expenditures and dividends. One management problem is how effectively a company uses its free cash flows. Jensen (1986) argues that by using debt financing, a firm reduces its free cash flows and, hence, the firm must reenter the debt market to raise new capital. Jensen theory, known as *Jensen's free cash flow theory*, contends that the need to issue debt benefits the firm in two ways.

First, there are fewer resources under control of management and less chance of wasting these resources in unprofitable investments. Second, being continually dependent on the debt market to raise new capital imposes a governance discipline on management that would not have been there otherwise. That is, a company's use of debt financing may help to reduce agency costs. Agency costs, discussed further in the next chapter, are the costs that arise from the separation of the management and the ownership of a company. They include all costs of resolving agency problems between management and shareholders, and also include the cost of monitoring company management. Agency costs further include costs associated with operating and informing a board of directors, as well as with providing financial information to shareholders and other investors.

## 5.3   CAPITAL STRUCTURE AND TAXES

We've seen how the use of debt financing increases the risk to the firm's shareholders: The greater the use of debt financing (relative to equity financing), the greater the financial risk. Another factor to consider is the role of taxes. In the United States, income taxes play an important role in a company's capital structure decision because, as mentioned above, a firm's payments to its creditors and its owners are taxed

---

[5] It is not always easy to define financial slack: Its size is really determined by creditors and their attitudes towards the firm.

differently. In general, interest payments on debt obligations are deductible for tax purposes, whereas dividends paid to shareholders are not deductible. Because taxes affect the cost of financing, tax law naturally affects capital structure decisions.

## 5.3.1   Interest Deductibility and Capital Structure

The deductibility of interest represents a government subsidy of debt financing: By allowing interest to be deducted from taxable income, the government is sharing the cost of a debt issue with the borrowing company. To see how this subsidy works, let's compare three capital structures for a firm that is assumed to have operating earnings of $5 million and the total assets of $35 million. The debt requires an annual payment of 10% and the tax rate is 30%. The three capital structures and the earnings available to the owners are shown in Table 5.4.

By financing its activities with debt, paying interest of $1 million, capital structure B reduces the company's tax bill by $0.3 million. The firm's creditors receive $1 million of the earnings, the government receives $1.2 million of the earnings, and the owners receive the balance of $2.8 million. The $0.3 million represents money the firm would not have to pay because it is allowed to deduct the $1 million of interest expense. This reduction in the tax bill is a type of subsidy. With capital structure C, the interest expense is $2 million and earnings available to owners are $2.1 million. Comparing capital structure C to A, we see that the interest expense is more, taxes are less, and earnings available to owners are less.

Consider the distribution of income between creditors and owners. The total income to the suppliers of capital increases from the use of debt. For example, the difference in the total income paid to creditors and equity owners under capital structure B compared to capital structure A is $0.3 million. This difference is due to a tax subsidy by the government: By deducting $2 million in interest expense, the firm benefits by reducing taxable income by $1 million and reducing taxes by $2 million $\times$ 30% = $0.3 million.

If we assume that there are no direct or indirect costs to financial distress, the firm's cost of capital should be the same, no matter the method of financing. It usually makes no difference to the firm's credit standing, and consequently to its creditors, whether the government does or does not subsidize the firm's owners. It is those

TABLE 5.4
THREE CAPITAL STRUCTURES AND THEIR IMPACT ON EARNINGS

| $ in millions | *A* | *B* | *C* |
|---|---|---|---|
| | | *Capital Structure* | |
| Debt | $0.0 | $10.0 | $20.0 |
| Operating earnings | 5.0 | 5.0 | 5.0 |
| − Interest expense | 0.0 | 1.0 | 2.0 |
| = Taxable income | 5.0 | 4.0 | 3.0 |
| − Taxes | 1.5 | 1.2 | 0.9 |
| = Earnings available to owners | 3.5 | 2.8 | 2.1 |

owners who benefit from the tax deductibility of interest. We can see this by computing the return on equity (ROE)—the ratio of earnings available to owners divided by equity. Under capital structure A, the owners would have an ROE of 10% (= $3.5 million/$35 million). Compare this to the ROE under capital structure B, which is 11.2% ($2.8 million/$25 million) and 14% (= $2.1 million/$15 million) under capital structure C. For the two levered capital structures, the owners benefit from the tax deductibility of interest in that ROE increases.

## 5.3.2 Interest Tax Shield

The benefit from tax deductibility of interest expenses is referred to as the *interest tax shield*, so named because it shields operating earnings from taxation. The tax shield from interest deductibility is:

$$\text{Tax shield} = \text{Tax rate} \times \text{Interest expense}$$

Recognizing that the interest expense is the interest rate on the debt, which we will denote by $r_d$, multiplied by the par value of debt, denoted by $D$, the tax shield for a company with a tax rate of $\tau$ is:

$$\text{Tax shield} = \tau \times r_d \times D$$

This tax shield affects the value of the company by reducing the firm's operating earnings that would otherwise go to pay taxes. The tax rate $\tau$ here refers to the *marginal tax rate*—the tax rate on the next dollar of income.

Of course, the value of the tax shield depends on whether the company can use an interest expense deduction. In general, if a company has deductions that exceed operating earnings, the result is a *net operating loss.* The company does not have to pay taxes in the year of the loss and may "carry" this loss to previous tax years, where (with some limits) it may be applied against those years' taxable incomes.[6] If the previous years' taxable incomes are insufficient to absorb the entire loss, any remaining portion can (again with some limits) be carried over into future years, reducing future years' taxable incomes. In such cases, the tax shield must be discounted at a rate that reflects both the uncertainty of realizing its benefit and the time value of money. Thus, the benefit from interest deductibility of debt depends on whether or not the company can utilize the interest deduction, and if so when.

## 5.4 THE COST OF CAPITAL

The capital structure of a company both affects and is affected by the company's cost of capital. The *cost of capital* is the return that must be provided for the use of investors' funds. In raising new funds, the relevant cost of capital is a *marginal* concept. That is, the cost of capital is the cost associated with raising one more dollar of capital. If the

---

[6] The previous years' taxes are recalculated and a refund of taxes previously paid is requested.

funds are borrowed, the cost is the interest that must be paid to the holder of the debt instrument (a loan or bond). If the funds are equity, the cost is the return that investors expect to obtain, whether from stock price appreciation, dividends, or both.

In addition to affecting capital structure decisions, there are two other important roles played by a corporation's cost of capital. First, the cost of capital is often used as a starting point (a benchmark) for determining the cost of capital for a specific capital project in which management contemplates investing. Since many of a firm's projects present risks similar to the business risk of the firm as a whole, the firm's cost of capital may be a reasonable approximation for the cost of capital of a project with roughly similar business risk. However, if a project's risk differs from the firm's business risk, the project's cost of capital should be adjusted upward or downward, depending on whether the project's risk is more than or less than the firm's typical project.

A firm's cost of capital is the cost of its long-term sources of funds: debt, common stock, and such other forms of financing as preferred stock. The cost reflects the risk of the assets in which the firm invests. A firm that invests in assets having little risk will usually have lower costs of capital than a firm that invests in assets having a higher risk. Moreover, the cost of each source of funds reflects the hierarchy of the financial risk associated with its seniority over the other sources. For a given firm, the cost of funds raised through debt is normally less than the cost of funds from preferred stock,[7] which, in turn, is less than the cost of funds from common stock. This is because creditors have seniority over preferred shareholders, who have seniority over common shareholders. If there are difficulties in meeting obligations, the creditors receive their promised interest and principal before the preferred shareholders, who, in turn, receive their promised dividends before the common shareholders.

Estimating the cost of capital requires management to estimate the cost of each source of capital along with the amounts raised from each source. Putting together all these pieces, the firm can then estimate the marginal cost of raising additional capital in the following three steps. In the first step, the proportion of each source of capital to be used in the calculations is determined. This should be based on the capital structure selected by the firm.

The cost of each financing source is calculated in the second step. The cost of debt and preferred stock is fairly simple to obtain, but the cost of equity is by far much more difficult to estimate. Several models are available for estimating the cost of equity, as described in later chapters. What is critical to understand is that these different models can generate significantly different estimates for the cost of common stock and, as a result, the estimated cost of capital can be highly sensitive to the model selected. The proportions of each source must also be determined before calculating the cost of each source since the proportions may further affect the costs of the sources of capital.

The last step is to weight the cost of each source of funding by the proportion of that source in the target capital structure.

For example, suppose the firm's capital structure as selected by management is as follows: 40% debt, 10% preferred stock, and 50% common stock. Assume further that management estimates the costs for raising an additional dollar of debt, preferred stock, and common equity are 5%, 6%, and 12%, respectively. If the company's

---

[7] Preferred stock is not available in all countries.

marginal tax rate is 40%, the after-tax cost of debt is $5\% \times (1 - 0.4) = 3\%$. Returning to the illustration, the average cost of raising funds, referred to in this context as the *weighted average cost of capital*, is:

$$(40\% \times 3\%) + (10\% \times 6\%) + (50\% \times 12\%) = 7.8\%$$

This means that for every $1 the firm plans to obtain from financing, the cost is 7.8%. As management adjusts the firm's capital structure, the cost of capital for the firm would be expected to change. How the conditions under which the cost of capital changes when financial leverage is increased will be discussed in the next section as well as in Part VII of this book.

## 5.5 CAPITAL STRUCTURE IN A PERFECT CAPITAL MARKET: THE IRRELEVANCE THEORY

In this section we demonstrate that in an idealized financial environment, capital structure does not affect the firm's market value, a result that has come to be known as the *Modigliani-Miller theorem*.[8] Since the theorem logically depends on the assumptions it employs, properly interpreting and using its findings in more complex circumstances requires further investigation, as we show in this section.

The Modigliani-Miller theorem assumes a perfect capital market under conditions of risk. In such a market, the following is assumed to hold:

- Buyers and sellers are all assumed to use the same probability distributions to characterize future uncertain returns (i.e., investor expectations are homogeneous). Financing decisions are further assumed to have no effect on the business risk of the firm.
- Buyers and sellers of securities cannot individually affect ruling market interest rates.
- There is no tax advantage associated with debt financing relative to equity financing.
- There are no costs associated with voluntary liquidation or bankruptcy, where bankruptcy is defined as a state when the value of the firm's debt exceeds the value of the firm's total assets.
- Although financial instruments must yield market returns commensurate with their risks, no transactions charges are paid on their purchase or sale.
- Any financial arrangements available to firms are assumed to be available to individuals on the same terms.
- Financial transactions capable of adversely affecting the positions of creditors relative to owners are not permitted, thus preventing involuntary expropriation of particular investors' wealth positions.

---

[8] Modigliani and Miller (1958).

## 5.5.1 Me-First Rules

The last assumption above means that debt holders protect themselves by including protective covenants, conditions that Fama and Miller (1972, p. 169ff) term *me-first rules*. In the context now being studied it is assumed that me-first rules can be enforced without costs. We illustrate the rules' importance using several examples.

Consider first the case where a firm has some risky debt outstanding and also elects to raise additional debt at time 1. Both the outstanding debt and the new issue take the form of a bond. The existing bondholders are referred to as original bondholders, purchasers of the new issue as new bondholders. We assume the original bond has a par value of $1,000 requiring a 10% annual interest payment, and further that the new bond is issued on the same terms. Both bonds are assumed to mature at time 2, when each requires a payment of $1,100 (par value of $1,000 plus interest of $100). Moreover, it is assumed that the two bond issues have equal claims on the firm's assets in the event of bankruptcy: The two classes of creditors (i.e., bondholders) are said to be paid *pari passu*.

Suppose that the operating earnings of the firm are realized at time 2, that only two possible states of the world can occur, and that distribution of the two outcomes is:

| State | Probability[9] | Operating earnings |
|---|---|---|
| 1 | $p$ | $2,500 |
| 2 | $1-p$ | $ 800 |

Consider first the claim of the original bondholders if there was no additional bond financing. In state 1, the firm will have sufficient operating earnings to satisfy the claim of the original bondholders (i.e., $1,100). However, in state 2, the firm can only distribute $800 and by the terms of their contract, the original bondholders have a claim on that entire amount. Thus, the distribution of the claim of the original bondholders and the stockholders given the operating earnings is:

| State | Probability | Operating earnings | Original bondholders | Stockholders |
|---|---|---|---|---|
| 1 | $p$ | $2,500 | $1,100 | $300 |
| 2 | $1-p$ | $ 800 | $ 800 | $ 0 |

When a scheduled bond payment cannot be fully met from the operating earnings, the firm is technically insolvent. For purposes of the examples in this chapter, we suppose that under insolvency the bondholders receive whatever the firm is worth (i.e., all of the operating earnings), and no additional costs are incurred in liquidating the firm.

Now consider the claim of all the bondholders if new bonds are issued. In state 1 the firm has sufficient operating earnings to satisfy the claim of both bondholders

---

[9] The probabilities referred to in this chapter are the underlying or objective probabilities of the states.

($2,200). However, in state 2 the operating earnings are only $800—not a sufficient amount to pay either class of bondholder. But the original and new bondholders are usually both paid based on the percentage of the par value of their claims. Since we are assuming that the obligation to either class of bondholders is $1,100, the $800 is distributed equally, $400 to each class. Thus, the distribution of the claims to the original and new bondholders is:

| State | Probability | Operating earnings | Old bondholders | New bondholders | Stockholders |
|---|---|---|---|---|---|
| 1 | $p$ | $2,500 | $1,100 | $1,100 | $300 |
| 2 | $1 - p$ | $ 800 | $ 400 | $ 400 | $ 0 |

Comparing the distribution of claims of the original bondholders with and without the issuance of the new bonds, we see that this financing arrangement effectively expropriates a part of the wealth position of the original bondholders. At the same time, the financing arrangement does not change the distribution of funds available to the stockholders.

To prevent such an adverse occurrence for the original bondholders, the appropriate me-first rule in this case requires subsequent debt issues to be subordinated to the first (original) bondholder so as to leave the claim distribution of the original bondholders unchanged. Subordination of the new bondholders' claim means that in state 2, the original bondholders have the first claim against the $800 operating earnings and, as a result, the new bondholders receive nothing. With these terms affecting the new bondholders, the claim distribution for all the suppliers of capital is:

| State | Probability | Operating earnings | Old bondholders | New bondholders | Stockholders |
|---|---|---|---|---|---|
| 1 | $p$ | $2,500 | $1,100 | $1,100 | $300 |
| 2 | $1 - p$ | $ 800 | $ 800 | $ 0 | $ 0 |

Stockholders also have rules that prohibit the firm changing its capital structure in ways that would affect them adversely. To see the me-first rule in this case, suppose that the operating earnings in time 2 remain the same as in our previous illustration for state 1 ($2,500) but that in state 2 they are $1,100 instead of the previous $800. Now we will assume that there are two bond issues outstanding, which we will refer to as bond issue 1 and bond issue 2. We will assume that the face value and interest on both bond issues is $1,000 and $100, respectively, and that the bonds are repaid *pari passu* at time 2. The distribution of claims for the bondholders and the stockholders is then:

| State | Probability | Operating earnings | Bondholder 1 | Bondholder 2 | Stockholders |
|---|---|---|---|---|---|
| 1 | $p$ | $2,500 | $1,100 | $1,100 | $300 |
| 2 | $1 - p$ | $1,100 | $ 550 | $ 550 | $ 0 |

However, suppose that bond issue 1 is retired by management at time 1. Then, unless other conditions were imposed, the claims for the holders of bond issue 2 and the stockholders would become:

| State | Probability | Operating earnings | Bondholder 2 | Stockholders |
|---|---|---|---|---|
| 1 | $p$ | $2,500 | $1,100 | $1,400 |
| 2 | $1-p$ | $1,100 | $1,100 | $ 0 |

In this event, the remaining bondholders would certainly be better off, and would become so at the expense of the stockholders. The remedy is to arrange that the stockholders receive compensation for leaving the bondholder in this better position. This effect can be brought about either by retiring all the bonds at the outset or by regarding the claims represented by the retired bonds as the property of the stockholders.

When me-first rules ensure that uncompensated shifts in wealth positions are ruled out, and when the capital market is also perfect in all other respects, the Modigliani-Miller theorem establishes that changes in capital structure do not affect the market value of the firm, and are consequently a matter of indifference to the individual classes of investors in the firm. Put another way, in a perfect capital market with no corporate taxation, the cost of capital to the firm (the market's required rate of return) remains constant as the debt-equity ratio changes.

## 5.5.2 Consequences of the Modigliani-Miller Theorem

The Modigliani-Miller theorem says stockholders' wealth cannot be affected by changes in the firm's capital structure because the capital structure changes envisioned are prevented from affecting redistributions of the wealth positions to which individual investor classes lay claim. Rather, changes in capital structure merely repackage the earnings stream that determines the firm's market value. As long as the repackaging does not itself create additional costs or benefits, it cannot affect the firm's market value.[10]

One way of explaining that the market value of the firm is unaffected by capital structure changes in a perfect capital market is to show that under the foregoing assumptions any claims represented by financial instruments can be undone by investors. Recall that one of the assumptions of the previous section is that any financial arrangement available to firms is also available to individuals on the same terms. To understand the importance of this assumption, let's use another example. Suppose a firm, with a value of $1,500 at time 1, has a capital structure consisting of $1,000 in par value of bonds and $500 in equity. We'll refer to this capital structure of the firm as the "levered structure." Suppose the bonds bear interest at a 12% interest rate[11] and at time 2 the distribution of operating earnings is as follows:

---

[10] The theorem also implicitly assumes that markets are so constituted that decisions made by a firm's management cannot restrict investor opportunities. When these conditions are relaxed, the Modigliani-Miller predictions require modification. But since these matters are of greater concern to the welfare theory of financial markets than they are to corporate finance, we do not consider them further here.

[11] Note that (1) the bonds are not riskless as interest and principal cannot be fully paid and (2), if technical insolvency caused by default on the bonds should occur, it does not lead to any extra costs.

| State | Probability | Operating earnings |
|---|---|---|
| 1 | $p$ | $1,700 |
| 2 | $1 - p$ | $ 800 |

Then the time 2 distributions of values to which bondholders and stockholders are entitled are as follows:

| State | Probability | Operating earnings | Bondholders | Stockholders |
|---|---|---|---|---|
| 1 | $p$ | $1,700 | $1,120 | $580 |
| 2 | $1 - p$ | $ 800 | $ 800 | $ 0 |

Now let's consider an alternative capital structure, to be called the "equity structure" because the firm issues only equity. To simplify the illustration, assume that one individual purchases all the equity, and hence is entitled to receive the entire operating earnings at time 2, earnings that have the distribution shown above. The time 1 market value of the equity remains at $1,500, since under present assumptions different capital structures do not affect firm value.

For the stockholder to create the same distribution as in the levered structure, the individual can issue bonds as a claim upon himself. Moreover, it is assumed that this can be done on the same terms as the firm so that $1,000 of par value bonds can be issued with a 12% interest rate. This possibility is referred to as "homemade leverage." After the stockholder issues the bonds (which we also assume are bought by the same investors as those who purchase the firm's bonds), the positions of both the bondholders and the stockholder are the same as in the levered structure. Because it is assumed that investors can, on their own, costlessly reverse or otherwise alter the effects of capital structure decisions made by management, the market value of the firm is determined only by operating earnings and not by how management elects to divide up that distribution using varying combinations of debt and equity.[12]

## 5.5.3  Business and Financial Risk

Recall that the current discussion assumes operating decisions are given, implying that the business risk of the firm is not permitted to change. Nevertheless, as different financial claims are used by management to obtain funding, the financial risks associated with each class of claims can and usually do change, as illustrated next.

Suppose first that a firm that is financed only by equity and has the following distribution of time 2 operating earnings:

---

[12] That is to say, the focus is on the pie and not on how it is sliced. This is because no crumbs are lost if and when the pie is sliced. Indeed, the pie can also be unsliced without any loss of crumbs.

| State | Probability | Operating earnings |
|---|---|---|
| 1 | 0.5 | $2,500 |
| 2 | 0.5 | $1,100 |

The expected value for the time 2 operating earnings, denoted by $E[V(2)]$, is $1,800, and the standard deviation, denoted by $\sigma[V(2)]$, is $700. Since the firm is 100% equity financed, the stockholders' claims at time 2 have the same distribution, expected value, and standard deviation. The ratio of expected value to standard deviation can be interpreted as a measure of a claim holders' financial risk. The lower this ratio, the greater the financial risk. For this 100% equity-financed firm, the measure is 2.6 (= $1,800/$700).

Now let's change the example. Suppose that at time 1 bonds promising to pay $1,000 (par value plus interest) at time 2 are issued, while the remaining financing of the firm takes the form of equity. Then the distribution of bondholder and stockholder claims is:

| State | Probability | Operating earnings | Bondholders | Stockholders |
|---|---|---|---|---|
| 1 | 0.5 | $2,500 | $1,000 | $1,500 |
| 2 | 0.5 | $1,100 | $1,000 | $ 100 |

Based on the distribution for operating earnings above, the bonds can be seen to be riskless, since the claim of bondholders at time 2 is less than the lowest realizable value of the operating earnings available for distribution. That is, regardless of which of the two states occur, the bondholders will be paid in full. Since the expected value for the stockholders with the issuance of the riskless debt is then $800 and the standard deviation is $700, the ratio of expected value to standard deviation is 1.1 (= $800/$700), suggesting that the risk of the stockholders' earnings stream has been increased by the issuance of riskless debt.

Now suppose that management is considering bond financing alternatives of either $1,100 or $1,500. We will refer to these alternatives as bond issue 1 and bond issue 2, respectively. Based on these assumptions, the distribution of payments to original bondholders, the new bondholders for the two alternative financing arrangements, and for the corresponding claims for the stockholders is as follows:

| State | Probability | Operating earnings | Financing using bond issue 1 Bondholders | Financing using bond issue 1 Stockholders | Financing using bond issue 2 Bondholders | Financing using bond issue 2 Stockholders |
|---|---|---|---|---|---|---|
| 1 | 0.5 | $2,500 | $1,100 | $1,400 | $1,500 | $1,000 |
| 2 | 0.5 | $1,100 | $1,100 | $ 0 | $1,100 | $ 0 |

By comparing these two bond financing alternatives with our first example, we see that there is an upper limit of $1,100 to the promises that can be made using a

**FIGURE 5.1**

COST OF CAPITAL UNAFFECTED BY LEVERAGE

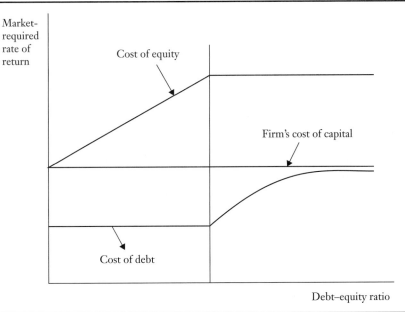

riskless bond. If bonds promising greater repayments are issued, their payoffs become risky. At the same time, as the amount promised to bondholders increases beyond $1,100, the nature of the risk faced by the equity holders is no longer altered.[13]

The situation we have described is illustrated in Figure 5.1, which shows that, if enough bonds are issued, they eventually become risky. Nevertheless, whether the bonds become risky or not, our previous analysis shows that the market required rate of return on the firm as a whole (i.e., its cost of capital) remains unchanged as long as the conditions of the Modigliani-Miller theorem are satisfied. To see this in still another way, consider how the firm's cost of capital behaves as shown next.

## 5.5.4   Cost of Capital in a Perfect Capital Market

Since in a perfect capital market the firm's weighted average cost of capital depends only on the firm's business risk, the cost of capital does not change as the capital structure is altered. But the individual costs of the firm's debt and of its equity capital will depend on capital structure choices because they are affected by financial risks.

---

[13] The precise quantitative results depend on our assumption of a probability distribution with only two possible outcomes (i.e., two possible states). In more complex cases, the effect on the equity as bonds become risky is one of increasing equity risk. However, the increase occurs at a decreasing rate as the debt-equity ratio increases.

To see how this all works, let $E(r_j)$ be the cost of capital for firm $j$ defined as follows:

$$E(r_j) = \frac{E[V_j(2)] - V_j(1)}{V_j(1)} \tag{5.1}$$

where $V_j(2)$ is the distribution of firm $j$ values at time 2 and $V_j(1)$ its market value at time 1. Similarly, the market rate of discount applied to the firm's bonds is:

$$E(r_{j,B}) = \frac{B_j(2) - B_j(1)}{B_j(1)} \tag{5.2}$$

where $B_j(2)$ is the bond principal and interest at time 2 and $B_j(1)$ the market value of the bonds at time 1. Primarily for simplicity of exposition, in this discussion we shall assume that bonds are riskless.

The rate of return on the firm's equity is defined as:

$$E(r_{j,S}) = \frac{E[V_j(2)] - B_j(2) - S_j(1)}{S_j(1)} \tag{5.3}$$

where $V_j(2) - B_j(2)$ represents earnings available to stockholders at time 2 and $S_j(1)$ the time 1 market value of this distribution. We now rewrite equations (5.1) and (5.2), respectively, as:

$$V_j(1)\left[1 + E(r_j)\right] = E\left(V_j(2)\right)$$

and

$$B_j(1)\left(1 + r_{j,B}\right) = B_j(2).$$

We then substitute into equation (5.3) to obtain:

$$E(r_{j,S}) = \frac{V_j(1)[1 + E(r_j)] - B_j(1)(1 + r_{j,B}) - S_j(1)}{S_j(1)} \tag{5.4}$$

Then, since $V_j(1) = B_j(1) + S_j(1)$, we can simplify equation (5.4) to:

$$E(r_{j,S}) = \frac{V_j(1)E(r_j) - B_j(1)r_{j,B}}{S_j(1)}$$

Eliminating $V_j(1)$ then gives:

$$E(r_{j,S}) = \frac{[S_j(1) + B_j(1)]E(r_j) - B_j(1)r_{j,B}}{S_j(1)}$$

which finally simplifies to:

$$E(r_{j,S}) = E(r_j) + [E(r_j) - r_{j,B}] \frac{B_j(1)}{S_j(1)} \tag{5.5}$$

Note that the ratio $B_j(1)/S_j(1)$ is the firm $j$'s financial leverage ratio, and that it increases as additional bonds are issued.

The upshot of the discussion is that in equation (5.5) $E(r_j)$ remains constant, but $E(r_{j,S})$ increases with leverage. In other words, equation (5.5) reiterates that, while the expected return on the firm is constant, the equity risk—and hence, the rate of return required on the equity—can change as more debt is issued. In fact, it's easy to see why: More riskless debt means that equity claims cannot become less risky—either equity risk increases or remains unchanged.[14]

We now consider an example indicating how equation (5.5) reflects the manner in which financial risks change as the firm becomes more highly levered. The example will also exhibit the effects associated with issuing risky bonds. Suppose a firm has $V(1) = \$1,000$ and the following distribution for $V(2)$:

| State | Probability | $V(2)$ |
|---|---|---|
| 1 | 0.5 | $1,675 |
| 2 | 0.5 | $ 525 |

Then $E[V(2)]$ is equal to $1,100, and the cost of capital for firm $j$ is:

$$E(r_j) = \{E[V(2)] - V(1)\}/V(1) = \{\$1,100 - \$1,000\}/\$1,000 = 0.10$$

Now suppose that the firm issues bonds promising to pay $525 at time 2. Since the bonds will be risk free, they can be sold at the risk-free rate of interest, which we will assume is $r_f = 0.05$. Under these circumstances, the market value of the bonds at time 0 is $B(1) = \$500$ (= \$525/1.05). Then, since $V(1) = B(1) + S(1)$, it follows that $S(1) = \$500$ also. Finally,

$$E(r_{j,S}) = \frac{E[V(2)] - B(2) - S(1)}{S(1)} = \frac{(\$1,100 - \$525) - \$500}{\$500} = \frac{\$575 - \$500}{\$500} = 0.15$$

so that the required rate of return on equity is 15%.

If, instead of using both bonds and stocks, the firm had been financed only with equity, the discount rate applying to it would be 10%, since in this capital structure the owners of the equity would be entitled to the entire distribution $V(2)$.

Let us now consider another capital structure where the amount of debt outstanding is large enough for the debt to be risky. Suppose debt with a face amount of

---

[14] As previous examples have shown, in some cases the equity risk can reach a maximum and then cannot increase further beyond that point, even as leverage is further incremented.

$700 and an interest rate of 5% is issued; the distribution for $V(2)$ remains the same as before. For this capital structure, the distributions to which the two investor classes are entitled are:

| State | Probability | B(2) | B(2) | S(2) |
|-------|-------------|------|------|------|
| 1 | 0.5 | $1,675 | $735 | $940 |
| 2 | 0.5 | $ 525 | $525 | 0 |

$S(2)$ is related to the distribution of returns to stockholders in the first example (the present $S(2)$ is $940/$1,150 of the value available in State 1 according to the first distribution). In Chapter 14, we will introduce an asset pricing model called the Capital Asset Pricing Model (CAPM) and we will see that it establishes rates of return independently of a distribution's absolute size. Based on the CAPM we reason that the rate of return on equity in the present example must be 15% as in the first capital structure. This means that:

$$0.15 = \frac{E[S(2)] - S(1)}{S(1)} = \frac{\$470 - S(1)}{S(1)}$$

so that $S(1)$ is approximately $409. Hence, $B(1) = \$1,000 - \$409 = \$591$.

To obtain the discount rate that should be applied to the debt, recall that according to the Modigliani-Miller theorem, the firm's weighted average cost of capital must remain a constant 10%. This allows us to write:

$$0.10 = 0.15 \left( \frac{\$409}{\$1,000} \right) + E(r_{j,B}) \left( \frac{\$591}{\$1,000} \right)$$

so that the discount rate applied to the bonds is now calculated to be 6.6%. We can check this by noting that:

$$E(r_{j,B}) = \frac{E[B(2)] - B(1)}{B(1)} = \frac{\$630 - \$591}{\$591} = 0.066$$

Thus, we see that for the particular firm in question, debt is riskless until the debt-equity ratio reaches unity, after which point the debt becomes risky. The relations between discount rates applied to the firm and to the two classes of securities are shown in Figure 5.2.

Note that even though the cost of equity rises as the firm becomes more highly levered, we do not have (in the absence of the effects of tax differentials or costs for defaulting on the promised debt repayment) any statement to the effect that debt affects the firm's cost of capital. In fact, more debt does not lower the average cost of funds in the present example even though debt always has a lower required return than equity. On the other hand, large issues of debt do not raise the cost of capital either because (as we have assumed) defaulting on the debt involves no bankruptcy costs. In this case, risky debt is, apart from its priority of claim, treated just like equity; that is, it

**FIGURE 5.2**

EFFECT OF LEVERAGE ON REQUIRED RETURNS ON STOCKS AND BONDS

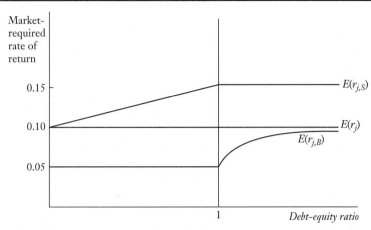

is treated as a risky proposition discounted at a rate reflecting its risk. The constant cost of capital result follows because the rate at which the firm's total income stream is capitalized (discounted) remains constant even though the capital structure is altered.

The managerial implication of these findings is that we have not yet found any reason for management to be concerned with leverage (i.e., the capital structure appears to be irrelevant). However, Part VII will identify features of a firm's capital structure that do affect the firm's value.

## KEY POINTS

- The capital structure decision is usually analyzed by managing the risks associated with financing decisions while taking a company's business risk as given.
- The cost of capital is the return that must be provided for the use of an investor's funds.
- An optimal capital structure is the mix of financing that maximizes the firm's value. If an optimal structure exists it will both maximize firm value and minimize the firm's cost of capital.
- The concept of financial leverage plays a role in affecting investor risk because leverage exaggerates the impacts of either favorable or unfavorable outcomes.
- Financial leverage makes use of additional debt; that is, increased leverage increases the firm's debt-equity ratio.
- Taxes provide an incentive to increase debt financing because interest paid on debt is a deductible expense for tax purposes, and thus, works to shield income from taxation.

- Since the capital structure of a company is intertwined with the company's cost of capital, estimating the latter is important for both capital structure decisions and capital budgeting decisions.
- The weighted average cost of capital is the estimate of a firm's cost of capital found by first computing the after-tax cost of each type of funding source and weighting each cost by the targeted percentage of the funding source sought by management.
- Although the cost of debt and preferred stock is relatively easy to determine for small amounts of new issues, the cost of equity must be estimated using some economic model.
- The Modigliani-Miller theorem asserts that in a perfect capital market, the capital structure decision does not affect the firm's market value; that is, the capital structure decision is irrelevant and therefore, there is no optimal capital structure.
- Under the assumptions of the Modigliani-Miller theorem, changes in capital structure merely repackage the earnings stream that determines the firm's market value. As long as the repackaging can occur without itself creating additional costs or benefits, it cannot affect the firm's market value.
- The main reason the market value of the firm is unaffected by capital structure changes in a perfect capital market is that the capital structures change the way an income pie is divided, but without affecting the size of the pie.
- An assumption in the Modigliani-Miller theorem is that financial transactions capable of affecting adversely the position of creditors vis-à-vis owners are not permitted; that is, involuntary expropriation of particular investors' wealth positions is not allowed.
- Creditors can protect themselves against management taking action that would adversely impact their wealth position by including protective covenants, conditions referred to as me-first rules. It is assumed that creditors can enforce the me-first rules without cost.
- In a perfect capital market the firm's weighted average cost of capital depends only on the firm's business risk. Since altering the capital structure does not change business risk (even though it does change financial risk), the cost of capital does not change as the capital structure is altered.
- For the weighted average cost of capital to stay constant in a perfect capital market when more leverage is added, the cost of equity will rise to offset the effects of lower cost debt being added to the capital structure.

## QUESTIONS

1. What do the investors in a firm expect if a firm retains earnings rather than distributing earnings in the form of dividends?

2. Suppose that the Matrix Corporation has $120 million of assets, all financed with equity, and that the firm has 6 million shares of stock outstanding valued at

$40 per share. Suppose further that management has identified investment opportunities requiring $60 million of new funds and can raise the funds in one of the following three ways:

Financing package 1: Issue $60 million equity (3,000,000 shares of stock at $40 per share)

Financing package 2: Issue $30 million of equity (1,500,000 shares of stock at $40 per share) and borrow $30 million with an annual interest of 8%

Financing package 3: Borrow $60 million with an annual interest of 8%

a. Complete the following table for each financing package after the financing capital structure is completed:

| Financing package | Assets (millions) | Debt | Equity | No. of shares (millions) | Debt-to-equity ratio | Debt-to-assets ratio |
|---|---|---|---|---|---|---|
| 1 | | | | | | |
| 2 | | | | | | |
| 3 | | | | | | |

b. Suppose the Matrix Corporation has $27 million of operating earnings. Show that the firm's return on assets is 15%.

c. Assuming there are no taxes, compute the earnings per share for the three financing packages by completing the table below:

| | Financing package | | |
|---|---|---|---|
| | 1 | 2 | 3 |
| Operating earnings in millions | $27.0 | $27.0 | $27.0 |
| − Interest expense in millions | | | |
| = Earnings available to owners in millions | | | |
| No. of shares in millions | | | |
| Earnings per share | | | |

d. Complete the table below for each of the three financing packages based on three assumptions for the return on assets shown below:

| | Financing package | | |
|---|---|---|---|
| Assumed ROA | 1 | 2 | 3 |
| 15% | | | |
| 12% | | | |
| 8% | | | |

e. Based on the calculation in part d, when is the choice of financing irrelevant?

    f. If operating risk is measured by the variability of operating earnings, what is the relationship between the use of debt relative to equity and the risk associated with operating earnings?

    g. Assuming that the return on assets is 8%, what is the degree of financial leverage for the three financing packages?

    h. In this problem, the interest rate on the debt in financing package 3 is assumed to be the same as the interest rate for financing package 2. Why might this assumption be unrealistic?

3. Why does the use of debt reduce a firm's financial flexibility?

4. The following excerpt is from an article entitled "Valuing Financial Slack in the Steel Sector" by David Merkel in October 15, 2003 (RealMoney.com: http://www.thestreet.com/p/rmoney/davidmerkel/10119562.html)

"As far as investors go, I'm a singles hitter. It can be tough to find investments that more than double your money, but I aim for a pretty high batting average overall. One key to such success is insisting that the companies in which I invest possess financial slack."

What does the author mean by *financial slack*?

5. a. What is meant by free cash flow?

    b. What are the two implications of Jensen's free cash flow theory for debt financing?

6. What is meant by an interest tax shield?

7. XYZ has operating earnings of $40 million and total assets of $280 million. The company's management is considering three alternative capital structures. The debt requires an annual payment of 12% and the tax rate is 40%.

    a. The three capital structures are given the table below. Compute the values in the table:

| | Capital Structure | | |
| --- | --- | --- | --- |
| $ in millions | A | B | C |
| Debt | $ 0.0 | $ 10.0 | $20.0 |
| Operating earnings | | | |
|   − Interest expense | | | |
|   = Taxable income | | | |
|   − Taxes | | | |
|   = Earnings available to owners | | | |

    b. Explain how financing its activities using capital structure B reduces the company's tax liability.

c. Explain how financing its activities using capital structure C reduces the company's tax liability.

d. Based on the calculations above, explain how the total income to the suppliers of capital increases from the use of debt.

8. a. What is meant by a company's cost of capital?

b. Why is the company's cost of capital critical in the financial decisions that management must make?

9. Assume that a firm's capital structure consists of 30% debt and 70% equity. Further assume that the cost of debt and the cost of equity are 6% and 10%, respectively.

a. What is the weighted average cost of capital if the firm pays no taxes?

b. What is the weighted average cost of capital if the firm is in the 30% marginal tax rate?

c. What is the weighted average cost of capital if the firm is in the 40% marginal tax rate?

10. One of the assumptions of the Modigliani-Miller theory regarding capital structure is that debt holders protect themselves by including "me-first rules."

a. What is meant by me-first rules?

b. Give an example of a me-first rule.

11. According to the Modigliani-Miller theorem, what are the implications of changes in the firm's capital structure for stockholders' wealth?

12. a. What is meant by a firm's business risk?

b. According to the Modigliani-Miller theorem, the firm's weighted average cost of capital depends only on the firm's business risk and not its capital structure. Explain why.

## REFERENCES

Booth, Laurence, and Sean Cleary. (2006). "Cash Flow Volatility, Financial Slack, and Investment Decisions," Working Paper, University of Toronto (January).

Fama, Eugene F., and Merton H. Miller. (1972). *The Theory of Finance*. New York: Holt, Rinehart and Winston.

Jensen, Michael C. (1986). "Agency Cost of Free Cash Flow, Corporate Finance, and Takeovers," *American Economic Review* **76**, 2: 323–329.

Modigliani, Franco, and Merton H. Miller. (1958). "The Cost of Capital, Corporation Finance, and the Theory of Investment," *American Economic Review* **48**: 261–267.

# 6

# FIRM INVESTMENT DECISIONS

$F$ irms continually invest funds in assets, and these assets produce cash flows that the company may then either reinvest in more assets or pay to the owners. *Capital* is the company's total assets, including both tangible and intangible assets. Capital includes both physical assets (such as land, buildings, equipment, and machinery) and assets that represent property rights, such as accounts receivable, securities, patents, and copyrights. *Capital investment* refers to a company's investment in new assets, that is, additions to the existing capital stock.[1]

*Capital budgeting decisions* refer to financial decisions regarding the use of a company's scarce resources in making capital investments, and thus represent decisions regarding long-term use of capital. Whereas some capital budgeting decisions are routine and do not change the course or risk of a company, there are also strategic capital budgeting decisions that will either have an impact on the company's future market position in its current product lines or permit it to expand into a new product line. Moreover, capital budgeting decisions may involve large commitments to particular capital projects with widely differing degrees of irreversibility. Thus, capital budgeting decisions can play a prominent role in determining whether a company will be successful over the longer term.

The company's capital budget may involve making a number of distinct decisions, each referred to as a *project*. A capital project is a set of assets that are contingent on one another and are considered together. For example, suppose a company is considering the production of a new product. This capital project requires the company to acquire land, build facilities, and purchase production equipment. And this project may also require the company to increase its investment in its working capital—inventory, cash, or accounts receivable. *Working capital* is the collection of assets needed for day-to-day operations that support a company's long-term investments.

As demonstrated in Chapter 5, in a perfect capital market and under conditions of either certainty or risk, the stream of earnings is still valued by the marketplace so that the manager is able to determine operating and financing decisions separately.

---

[1] The term *capital* also has come to mean the funds used to finance the company's assets. Finally, in some contexts, the term *capital* refers to the sum of equity and interest-bearing debt.

Therefore, in this chapter we will assume a perfect capital market and look at how managers should perform an economic analysis of proposed investments.[2]

## 6.1 INVESTMENT DECISIONS AND OWNERS' WEALTH MAXIMIZATION

Recall that according to the market value rule, management's goals should be to maximize the market value of the firm in order to maximize the owners' current wealth. Managers must evaluate a number of factors in seeking to satisfy the market value rule. Not only does the manager need to estimate how much the firm's future cash flows will change if it invests in a project, but the manager must also evaluate the risk associated with these future cash flows. The firm's value today is the present value of all its future cash flows, discounted in a way that takes account of project risk.[3] Hence, we need to understand where these future cash flows come from. Their sources are both assets that have been accumulated as a result of all past investment decisions and future investment opportunities. The firm's value is the present value of all the firm's future cash flows, where the expected values of the future cash flows are discounted at a rate that represents investors' assessments of the risk involved. As you can see, we need to evaluate the risk of these future cash flows, referred to as *cash flow risk*, in order to understand the risk of any investment opportunity on the value of the company.

Later chapters will show how the distributions of cash flows can be evaluated to take account of their risk. Qualitatively, we can also observe that cash flow risk comes from two basic sources:

- *Sales risk*: The risk related to the firm's output that will be sold and the price of the goods or services; and
- *Operating risk*: The risk concerning operating cash flows that arises from the particular mix of fixed and variable operating costs.

Sales risk is related to the economy and the market in which the company's goods and services are sold. Operating risk, for the most part, is determined by the product or service that the company provides and is related to the sensitivity of operating cash flows to changes in sales. We refer to the combination of these two risks as *business risk*.

As already mentioned, a project's business risk is reflected in the discount rate— the rate of return required to compensate the suppliers of capital (bondholders and owners) for the amount of risk they bear. From the perspective of investors, the discount rate is the *required rate of return* (RRR). From the company's perspective, the discount rate is the *cost of capital* discussed in Chapter 5.

---

[2] For a survey describing how corporate chief financial officers make firm investment decisions, see Graham and Campbell (2002).

[3] In this chapter, we determine the present values of risky cash flows by discounting their expected value at a risk-adjusted discount rate. Later chapters will discuss the valuation of risky cash flows in greater detail.

For example, suppose a firm invests in a new project, Project $X$. How does the investment affect the firm's value?

- If Project $X$ generates cash flows that just compensate the suppliers of capital for the risk they bear on this project (that is, if it just earns the cost of capital), the firm's value does not change.
- If Project $X$ generates cash flows greater than the amounts needed to compensate investors for the risk they take on, it earns more than the cost of capital, increasing the firm's value.
- If Project $X$ generates cash flows less than needed, it earns less than the cost of capital, decreasing the value of the company.

How do we know whether the cash flows are more than or less than are needed to compensate investors for the risk involved? If we suppose that any new cash flows have risks similar to those already on the books, and if we then discount all those cash flows at the cost of capital, we can assess how this project affects the present value of the company. If the expected change in the value of the company from an investment is:

- Positive, the project returns more than the cost of capital.
- Negative, the project returns less than the cost of capital.
- Zero, the project returns the cost of capital.

*Capital budgeting* is the process of identifying and selecting investments in long-lived assets, that is, assets expected to produce benefits over more than one year.

## 6.2 CLASSIFICATION OF INVESTMENT PROJECTS

Managers classify capital investment projects in different ways. One way is by project life, whether short term or long term, largely because the time value of money plays a more important role in long-term than in short-term projects. Another way of classifying projects is by their risk. The riskier the project's future cash flows, the greater the discount rate that must be used and consequently the greater the role of the cost of capital in decision making. We will address how to incorporate risk into project analysis in Chapters 25 and 26. Still another way of classifying projects is by their dependence on other projects. The relationship between a project's cash flows and the cash flows of other company projects must be incorporated explicitly into the analysis since we want to analyze how new projects affect the business risk of the entire company.

### 6.2.1 Classification According to Economic Life

An investment project generally provides benefits over a period of time referred to as its *economic life*. The economic (or useful) life of a project is determined by physical deterioration, obsolescence, and/or the degree of competition in the market for a product. Toward and after the end of its useful life, project revenues tend to decline rapidly while expenses tend to increase.

Typically, an investment project requires an immediate expenditure and provides benefits in the form of cash flows to be received in the future. If benefits are received only within the current period—within one year of making the investment—the investment project is referred to as a *short-term investment*. If these benefits are received beyond the current period, the investment project is referred to as a *long-term investment* and that associated fund outlay is said to be a *capital expenditure*. An investment project may comprise one or more capital expenditures. For example, a new product may require investment in production equipment, a building, and transportation equipment.

Short-term investment decisions involve, primarily, investments in current assets: cash, marketable securities, accounts receivable, and inventory. Decisions regarding short-term investments, or current assets, are concerned with day-to-day operations. A company needs some level of current assets to act as a cushion in case of unusually poor operating periods, when cash flows from operations are less than expected.

The objective of investing in either short-term or long-term assets is the same: maximizing owners' wealth. Nevertheless, we consider them separately for two practical reasons. First, decisions about long-term projects are based on projections of cash flows far into the future and require us to consider the time value of money. Second, long-term projects do not usually figure into the daily operating needs of the company.

## 6.2.2 Classification According to Risk

An investment project's risk of return can be classified qualitatively according to the nature of the project: new products and markets, replacement projects, expansion projects, and mandated projects.

*New products and markets* are projects that involve introducing a new product or entering into a new market.

*Replacement projects* are investments in the replacement of existing equipment or facilities and include the maintenance of existing assets to continue the current level of operating activity. Projects that reduce costs, such as replacing old equipment or improving operating efficiency, are also considered replacement projects. Evaluating replacement projects requires management to compare the firm's value with the replacement project to the firm's value without that same replacement project. There is little risk in the cash flows from replacement projects. Management is simply replacing equipment or buildings already operating and producing cash flows. And the company typically has experience in managing similar new equipment.

*Expansion projects* are investments in projects that broaden existing product lines and existing markets. Often they involve little risk. In contrast, new products and markets projects are investment projects that involve introducing new products or entering into new markets are riskier because management has little or no experience in the new product or market.

Management may be forced or coerced to invest in projects by government laws or agency rules. Such projects, referred to as *mandated projects*, are typically found in "heavy" industries, such as utilities, transportation, and chemicals, all industries requiring a large portion of their assets in production activities. Government agencies, such as the Occupational Safety and Health Agency (OSHA) or the Environmental Protection Agency (EPA), may impose requirements that companies install specific equipment or alter their activities (such as how they dispose of waste).

### 6.2.3  Classification According to Dependence on Other Projects

In addition to considering the future cash flows generated by a project, management must consider how it affects projects already in place—the results of previous project decisions—as well as other projects that may be undertaken. Projects can be classified according to the degree of dependence with other projects: independent projects, mutually exclusive projects, contingent projects, and complementary projects.

An *independent project* is one whose cash flows are not related to the cash flows of any other project. Therefore, accepting or rejecting an independent project does not affect the acceptance or rejection of other projects.

Projects are *mutually exclusive* if the acceptance of one precludes the acceptance of other projects. For example, suppose a manufacturer is considering whether to replace its production facilities with more modern equipment. The company may solicit bids among the different manufacturers of this equipment. The decision consists of comparing two choices, either keeping its existing production facilities or replacing the facilities with the modern equipment of one manufacturer. Because the company cannot use more than one production facility, it must evaluate each bid and choose the most attractive one.

*Contingent projects* are dependent on the acceptance of another project. Suppose a greeting card company develops a new character, Pippy, and is considering starting a line of Pippy cards. If Pippy catches on, the company will consider producing a line of Pippy T-shirts—but *only* if the Pippy character becomes popular. The T-shirt project is a contingent project.

Another form of dependence is found in *complementary projects*, where the investment in one enhances the cash flows of one or more other projects. Consider a manufacturer of personal computer equipment and software. If it develops new software that enhances the abilities of a computer mouse, the introduction of this new software may enhance its mouse sales as well.

## 6.3  A Project's Incremental Cash Flows

The firm's managers should invest only to increase the value of the owners' interests. When a firm invests in new assets, it expects the future cash flows to be greater than without this new investment. The difference between the cash flows of the company with the investment project, compared over the same period of time to the cash flows of the company without the investment project, is referred to as the *project's incremental cash flows*.

How much does the value of the company change as a result of the investment? The change in a company's value is the difference between project benefits and costs:

Project's change in the firm's value = Project's benefits − Project's costs

A second way of evaluating the change in the value of the company is to break down the project's cash flows into two components:

1. The cash flows from the project's operating activities (revenues and operating expenses), referred to as the *project's operating cash flows* (OCF)
2. The *investment cash flows*, that is, the expenditures needed to acquire the project's assets and any cash flows from disposing the project's assets

Web-Appendix G explains how a project's incremental cash flows is calculated. The effect on the value of the company can then be expressed as:

Change in the value of the firm

   = Present value of the change in operating cash flows provided by the project

   + Present value of investment cash flows

The present value of a project's operating cash flows is typically positive (predominantly indicating cash inflows) and the present value of the investment cash flows is typically negative (predominantly indicating cash outflows).

## 6.4 APPLYING THE MARKET VALUE RULE TO INDEPENDENT PROJECTS

The market value criterion deals with the totality of the firm's investments, not with particular projects comprising it. But it is often convenient to assess increments to the firm's assets, and for this purpose we need to understand how incremental investments can contribute to market value.

The problem of assessing an incremental investment is easy to resolve if it is economically independent of the firm's other assets. By "economic independence" we mean that the net cash flows of an opportunity are not affected by the level of operation of any other opportunities. Then management can consider such a project's acceptability and scale without reference to other projects.

Management can either evaluate all projects within the capital budget simultaneously, or, if it is more convenient, each independent project can be evaluated separately. Since the evaluations are to use the market value rule, the appropriate question to ask regarding each such project is what scale of the project provides the greatest increment to market value? If the contribution of a project is negative for all levels at which it can be adopted, then, of course, the firm should not undertake it at all. With these stipulations in mind, we can proceed to consider projects independently and yet ensure that the totality of accepted projects will have the value-maximizing property. The fact that economically independent projects' values add to the market value of the firm is sometimes referred to as the *value additivity principle*; for the rest of this chapter we assume the principle can be used.

## 6.5 COMMONLY USED ASSESSMENT CRITERIA IN A CERTAIN WORLD WITH A PERFECT CAPITAL MARKET

This section describes net present value and internal rate of return as criteria suitable for accept–reject decisions—as long as they are properly interpreted.[4] Accept–reject decisions are correctly contemplated only if a single fixed level of a project can be adopted. If a project's scale can be changed, it is necessary to determine the scale providing the largest increment to the firm's market value. Moreover, scale can be varied more often than first appears to be the case. For example, acquiring a fleet of 100 trucks seems to be an accept–reject decision until the possibility of leasing additional trucks is considered. Further, the trucks might be acquired either all at once or in a series of staged acquisitions.

### 6.5.1 Net Present Value

Using the terminology for the incremental cash flows in Section 6.3, *net present value* (NPV) is defined as follows:

$$\text{NPV} = \text{PV of net cash flows from operations over the project's life}$$
$$- \text{PV of investment cash outflows over the project's life}$$

where PV denotes the present value.

Alternatively, if one computes the net cash flows for each period, the NPV is defined as:

$$\text{NPV} = \text{PV of net cash flows over the project's life}$$

In most books, it is common to break out the initial cash investment outlay and subtract that amount from the present value of the subsequent net cash flows. This can be expressed as:

$$\text{NPV} = \text{PV of net cash flows over the project's life after the initial investment outlay}$$
$$- \text{Initial investment outlay}$$

It is this last formulation of NPV that we will use in this book.

The economic interpretation of the NPV is straightforward. The present value of the net cash flows over the project's life after the initial investment outlay can be viewed as the value added to the firm if the estimated future cash flows are realized and that value is adjusted to take into consideration the time value of money. The difference between this value and the project's initial cost is the present value of the project's profit.

---

[4] There are other criteria that are not covered here. They include the profitability index, modified IRR, payback period, and discounted payback period. For a discussion of these criteria, see Peterson and Fabozzi (2002).

Mathematically, the NPV is calculated as follows:

$$\text{NPV} = \sum_{t=1}^{N} CF_t(1+r)^{-t} - I \tag{6.1}$$

where $CF_t$ = net cash flow for period $t$
$\quad I$ = initial investment outlay
$\quad N$ = number of periods (expected life of the project)
$\quad r$ = one-period required rate of return for the project.

Typically, each period is taken to be one year.

If the NPV is positive, the firm's market value will be increased by acceptance of such a project. Since we are assuming here that the firm is operating in a perfect capital market and there is no shortage of financing in a perfect capital market, projects with a positive NPV should be undertaken.

To illustrate the NPV calculations, assume the following information for a project, which we will refer to as Project $X$, with a four-year life, an initial investment outlay of $10 million, and the required rate of return is 10%.

| Year | Net cash flow ($CF_t$) | Present value of net cash flow at 10% [$CF_t(1+r)^{-t}$] |
|------|------------------------|---------------------------------------------------------|
| 1    | $ 0                    | $ 0                                                     |
| 2    | 2,000,000              | 1,652,893                                               |
| 3    | 3,000,000              | 2,253,944                                               |
| 4    | 9,000,000              | 6,147,121                                               |

Based on the above $I$ = $10,000,000, $N$ = 4, and:

$$\sum_{t=1}^{4} CF_t(1+r)^{-t} = \$10,053,958$$

Using equation (6.1), we have for Project $X$:

$$\text{NPV} = \$10,053,958 - \$10,000,000 = \$53,958$$

This NPV indicates that, by investing in Project $X$, there would be an expected increase in the firm's value by $53,958.

As another example, consider another project, Project $Y$, which also has a four-year life, requires an initial investment outlay of $10 million, a required rate of return of return of 10%, and the following net cash flows for each of the next four years of $3,250,000. For this project, the NPV is $302,063. This NPV indicates that by investing in Project $Y$, there would be an expected increase in the firm's value by $302,063.

A positive NPV means that the project increases the firm's value—the project's return is more than sufficient to compensate for the project's required rate of return. A negative NPV means that the project decreases the firm's value—the project's return does not compensate for the project's required rate of return. A zero NPV means that the project's return just equals the project's return required by owners. This leads to the following rule regarding the accept–reject for *independent* projects based on the NPV criterion:

| If ... | then shareholder wealth is expected to ... | and management should ... |
|---|---|---|
| NPV > $0 | project expected to increase shareholder wealth | accept project |
| NPV < $0 | project expected to decrease shareholder wealth | reject project |
| NPV = $0 | keep shareholder wealth unchanged | be indifferent to project |

Project $X$ is expected to increase the firm's value by $53,958, whereas Project $Y$ is expected to add $302,063 to the firm's value. If these are independent investment projects, both should be taken on because both increase the value of the company.

However, suppose that, instead of being independent projects, Project $X$ and Project $Y$ are mutually exclusive projects. Recall that projects are said to be mutually exclusive if accepting one precludes the acceptance of the other. Then, in this case, Project $Y$ is preferred since it has the greater NPV. So, although both projects would be accepted if they are independent projects and there is a perfect capital market, only Project $Y$ would be accepted if the two projects are mutually exclusive.[5]

### 6.5.1.1 The Investment Profile

Management may want to see how sensitive the decision to accept a project is to changes in the estimate of the project's required rate of return. The *investment profile* (also known as the *net present value profile*) is a depiction of the NPVs for different required rates of return, which allows an examination of the sensitivity in how a project's NPV changes as the rate changes. The investment profile is a graphical depiction of the relation between the NPV of a project and the discount rate: The profile shows the NPV of a project for each rate, within some range.

The NPV profiles for Projects $X$ and $Y$ are shown in Figure 6.1 for rates from 0% to 20%. As shown in the figure, the NPV of Project $X$ is positive for rates from 0% to 10.172%, and negative for rates greater than 10.172%. (As explained later, the 10.172% is the internal rate of return.) Therefore, Project $X$ increases owners' wealth if the project's required rate of return is less than 10.172% and decreases owners' wealth if the project's required rate of return exceeds 10.172%. Comparing the investment profile for Projects $X$ and $Y$, we can see that, if they are mutually exclusive projects, the graph clearly shows the project selected depends on the required rate of return. For higher required rate of return, Project $X$'s NPV is less than that of Project $Y$. This is because most of Project $X$'s present value is attributed to the large cash flows in the last two years. The present value of the more distant net cash flows is

---

[5] We later discuss situations in which the two projects are independent but the capital market is not perfect.

**FIGURE 6.1**
INVESTMENT PROFILES OF INVESTMENTS $X$ AND $Y$

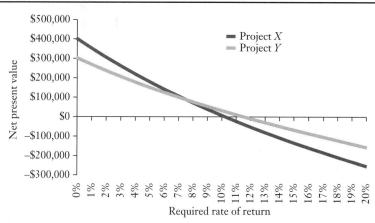

more sensitive to changes in the rate than is the present value of the net cash flows nearer the present. If the rate is less than 7.495%, Project $X$ adds more values than Project $Y$. If the rate is more than 7.495% but less than 11.338%, Project $Y$ increases owners' wealth more than Project $X$. If the rate is greater than 11.338%, management should invest in neither project because both would decrease owners' wealth.

## 6.5.2 Internal Rate of Return

Another criterion used for selecting investment projects is the *internal rate of return* (IRR). The IRR is the discount rate that makes the sum of the present value of the net cash flows equal to zero. Or equivalently, it is the discount rate that makes the NPV equal to zero. We can represent the IRR as the discount rate that solves:

$$0 = \sum_{t=1}^{4} CF_t(1+r)^{-t} - I \tag{6.2}$$

The IRR is a yield—what is earned, on average, per year.

Let's use Project $X$ to illustrate the calculation of the IRR. The IRR for this project is the discount rate that solves:

$$0 = \frac{\$0}{(1+\text{IRR})^1} + \frac{\$2,000,000}{(1+\text{IRR})^2} + \frac{\$3,000,000}{(1+\text{IRR})^3} + \frac{\$9,000,000}{(1+\text{IRR})^4} - \$10,000,000$$

Using a calculator or a computer, we get the answer of 10.172% per year for Project $X$. For Project $Y$, the IRR is equal to 11.388%.

Looking back at the investment profiles of Projects $X$ and $Y$ in Figure 6.1, each profile crosses the horizontal axis (where NPV = 0) at a discount rate corresponding to the project's IRR. This is no coincidence: By definition, the IRR is the discount rate that causes the project's NPV to equal zero.

The decision rule for the IRR is to invest in a project if it provides a return greater than the required rate of return. The required rate of return, in the context of the IRR, is a *hurdle rate*—the minimum acceptable rate of return. For independent projects and situations in where a perfect capital market is assumed, then the accept–reject decision is as follows:

| If ... | then shareholder wealth is expected to ... | and management should ... |
|---|---|---|
| IRR > RRR | project expected to increase shareholder wealth | accept project |
| IRR < RRR | project expected to decrease shareholder wealth | reject project |
| IRR = RRR | keep shareholder wealth unchanged | be indifferent to project |

### 6.5.2.1  The IRR Criterion and Mutually Exclusive Projects

What if management is forced to choose between Projects $X$ and $Y$ because the projects are mutually exclusive? Project $Y$ has a higher IRR than Project $X$—so at first glance management might want to accept Project $Y$. What about the NPV of Projects $X$ and $Y$? What does the NPV tell management to do? If management uses the higher IRR, it tells management to go with Project $Y$. If management uses the higher NPV and the required rate of return is 10%, management should once again select Project $Y$. However, if instead of 10% the required rate is 7%, then the answer is not straightforward. With a 7% discount rate the NPV of Projects $X$ and $Y$ are \$61,828 and \$8,047, respectively, making Project $X$ more attractive than Project $Y$ based on the NPV criterion. Which is correct? Choosing the project with the higher NPV is consistent with maximizing owners' wealth. Why? Because if the required rate of return is 7%, we would calculate different NPVs and come to a different conclusion, as shown using the investment profiles in Figure 6.1.

It is possible to make a value-maximizing decision by using the IRR method, but the method can also be misleading. When evaluating mutually exclusive projects, the project with the highest IRR may not be the one with the largest NPV as we have just shown. The IRR method assumes cash flows may be reinvested at the IRR, while the NPV method assumes cash flows may be reinvested at the required rate of return. The reinvestment assumption may cause different decisions in choosing among mutually exclusive projects when:

- The timing of the cash flows is different among the projects.
- There are scale differences (that is, very different cash flow amounts).
- The projects have different useful lives.

With respect to the role of the timing of cash flows in choosing between two projects: Project $Y$'s cash flows are received sooner than Project $X$'s. Part of the return on either is from the reinvestment of its cash inflows. And in the case of Project $Y$, there is more return from the reinvestment of positive cash flows. The question is what is done by the management with the positive cash flows from a project when they are received? It is generally assumed that when there are positive cash flows, management reinvests in other assets. Then for projects with an IRR above the required rate of return, management's analysis would be overstating the return on the investment using the IRR criterion. However, if the reinvestment rate is assumed to be the required rate of return, then evaluating projects on the basis of the NPV means selecting projects that maximize owners' wealth.

### 6.5.2.2  The IRR Criterion and Capital Rationing

Capital rationing means that there is a limit on the capital budget. This is a typical restriction imposed on management when there are capital market imperfections. Suppose Projects $X$ and $Y$ are independent projects. And suppose the capital budget is limited to $10 million. In our example, management would therefore be forced to choose between Projects $X$ or $Y$. Choosing the project with the higher IRR, Project $Y$ should be chosen. But Project $Y$ is expected to increase owners' wealth less than Project $X$ if the required rate of return is 7%. Therefore, ranking investments on the basis of their IRRs may not maximize wealth.

This dilemma is similar to that in the case of mutually exclusive projects using the projects' investment profiles. The discount rate at which Project $X$'s NPV is zero is where that project's IRR is 10.172%, where the project's investment profile crosses the horizontal axis. Likewise, the discount rate at which Project $Y$'s NPV is zero is where that project's IRR is 11.388%. The discount rate at which Project $X$'s and Project $Y$'s investment profiles cross is at 7.495% (see Figure 6.1). For discount rates less than 7.495%, Project $X$ has the higher NPV. For discount rates greater than 7.495%, Project $Y$ has the higher NPV. If Project $Y$ is chosen because it has a higher IRR and if Project $Y$'s required rate of return is less than 7.495%, management would not have chosen the project that produces the greatest increase to owners' wealth. In the case of capital rationing the source of the problem is that the IRR is a percentage, not a dollar amount. Because of this, management cannot determine how to distribute the capital budget to maximize owners' wealth using NPV or IRR. However, there are techniques that can be employed to aid management in such situations but they are not covered here.

### 6.5.2.3  Multiple Internal Rates of Return

The typical project usually involves only one large negative cash flow initially, followed by a series of future positive cash flows. But that's not always the case. Suppose management is considering a project that uses environmentally sensitive chemicals. The project may involve costly disposal of residual assets, meaning a negative cash flow at the end of the project.

Suppose we are considering a three-year project requiring an initial investment outlay of $100 million that has net cash flows:

| Year | Net Cash Flow ($) |
| --- | --- |
| 1 | +100 million |
| 2 | + 50 million |
| 3 | −210 million |

What is this project's IRR? One possible solution is IRR = 7.77%, yet another possible solution is IRR = 33.24%. That is, both IRRs will make the NPV equal to zero.

The NPV of these cash flows are shown in Figure 6.2 for discount rates from 0% to 40%. Remember that the IRR is the discount rate that causes the NPV to be zero. In terms of Figure 6.2, this means that the IRR is the discount rate where the NPV is zero, the point at which the present value changes sign—from positive to negative or from negative to positive. In the case of this project, the present value changes from negative to positive at 7.77% and from positive to negative at 33.24%.

**FIGURE 6.2**
THE CASE OF MULTIPLE IRRS

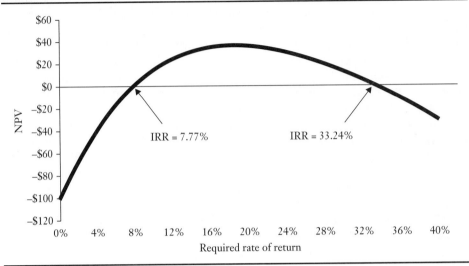

The IRR given in equation (6.2) is a polynomial of degree $N-1$ in the terms $1 + \text{IRR}$ with coefficients $CF_t$, as may be seen by multiplying equation (6.2) by $(1 + \text{IRR})^{N-1}$. Since the coefficients $CF_t$ are unrestricted as to sign, equation (6.2) can have more than a single root, and hence, a project's IRR is not uniquely defined.[6] In the general case involving $N$ periods, the polynomial in $1 + \text{IRR}$ will have terms up to the power $N-1$; hence, there could be as many as $N-1$ distinct roots. Notice that when considering the initial investment cash outlay (a negative sign), for our project there is a positive sign for the next two net cash flows, and a negative sign for the last net cash flow. That gives three changes for the signs. Hence, the number of possible solutions is two possible IRRs $(3-1)$. In fact, there are two in this example.

Is it reasonable to expect in real-world projects that a project's cash flows will experience only one sign change during its useful life? It depends on the type of project. For example, projects requiring environmental mitigation or significant retooling may have negative cash flows during or at the end of the project's useful life.

### 6.6 INVESTMENT CRITERIA IN PRACTICE

Just as with the theory of capital structure, the theory of investment under certainty provides a point of departure for analyzing investment decisions in the more complex circumstances presented in practice. In practice, of course, investments are contemplated under conditions of risk or uncertainty, and one of the most important advances in investment theory recognizes the value of being able to postpone investments.[7] Postponement value is of particular importance under both risk and uncertainty. It

---

[6] Indeed, by Descartes's rule of signs, the number of possible distinct roots (candidates for IRR) is given by the number of sign changes between the coefficients $CF_t$.

[7] See Dixit and Pindyck (1994).

affects the timing of new investment, a matter that depends both on investment opportunities and the possibility of waiting to obtain new information. These issues are discussed at several later points in the book, particularly in Chapters 25 and 26.

## KEY POINTS

- One of the most important strategic functions in managing a firm is the evaluation of capital projects. Decisions relating to a firm's capital projects are known as capital budgeting decisions.
- Capital budgeting decisions commit funds for a time period longer than one year and may have an impact on a firm's strategic position within its industry.
- In making firms' investment decisions, management should seek to maximize the market value of the firm in order to maximize the owners' current wealth.
- Classifying capital projects along different dimensions (that is, economic life, risk, and dependence on other projects) is helpful because these characteristics affect the analysis of the projects.
- Investment projects can be classified according to their degree of dependence as independent projects, mutually exclusive projects, contingent projects, and complementary projects.
- Two commonly used criteria for evaluating investment projects are net present value and internal rate of return.
- The net present value method is the preferred method because it considers all the project's cash flows, involves discounting, and assumes reinvestment of cash flows at the project's required rate of return.
- The net present value method calculates the present value of the project's expected cash flows.
- The internal rate of return is the yield on the investment. It is the discount rate that causes the net present value to be equal to zero.
- The internal rate of return is hazardous to use when selecting among mutually exclusive projects or when there is a limit on capital spending (a form of capital market imperfection or self-imposed by management).
- It is possible for the internal rate of return to have multiple values depending on how many times the sign of the cash flows change.

## QUESTIONS

1. Suppose a toy manufacturer is faced with the following collection of investment projects:
   a. Opening a retail outlet
   b. Introducing a new line of dolls
   c. Introducing a new action figure in an existing line of action figures
   d. Adding another packaging line to the production process
   e. Adding pollution control equipment to avoid environmental fines

    **f.** Computerizing the doll molding equipment

    **g.** Introducing a child's version of an existing adult board game

      Classify each project into one of the four categories: expansion, replacement, new product or market, or mandated.

2. A shoe manufacturer is considering introducing a new line of boots. When evaluating the incremental revenues from this new line, what should be considered?

3. Suppose that management estimates that a project's net present value to be $6.5 million. What does this mean?

4. Consider two projects, AA and BB, that have identical, positive net present values, but Project BB is riskier than AA. If these projects are mutually exclusive, what is your investment decision?

5. Can the net present value method of evaluating projects always identify the ones that will maximize wealth? Why?

6. The net present value method and the internal rate of return method may produce different decisions when selecting among mutually exclusive projects. What is the source of this conflict?

7. Management is evaluating an investment project, Project ZZ, with the following cash flows:

| Period | Cash Flow |
|---|---|
| 1 | −$100,000 |
| 2 | 35,027 |
| 3 | 35,027 |
| 4 | 35,027 |
| 5 | 35,027 |

Calculate the following:

    **a.** Net present value assuming a 10% required rate of return

    **b.** Net present value assuming a 16% required rate of return

    **c.** Internal rate of return

8. Management is evaluating two mutually exclusive projects, Thing 1 and Thing 2, with the following cash flows:

| Year | End of Year Cash Flows | |
|---|---|---|
| | Thing 1 | Thing 2 |
| 1 | −$10,000 | −$10,000 |
| 2 | 3,293 | 0 |
| 3 | 3,293 | 0 |
| 4 | 3,293 | 0 |
| 5 | 3,293 | 14,641 |

a. If the required rate of return on both projects is 5%, which project, if either, should management choose? Why?

b. If the required rate of return on both projects is 8%, which project, if either, should management choose? Why?

c. If the required rate of return on both projects is 11%, which project, if either, should management choose? Why?

d. If the required rate of return on both projects is 14%, which project, if either, should management choose? Why?

e. On a graph, draw the investment profiles of Thing 1 and Thing 2. Indicate the following items:
   - crossover discount rate
   - NPV of Thing 1 if the required rate of return is 5%
   - NPV of Thing 2 if the required rate of return is 5%
   - IRR of Thing 1
   - IRR of Thing 2

9. Consider these three independent projects:

| Period | FF | GG | HH |
|---|---|---|---|
| 1 | −$100,000 | −$200,000 | −$300,000 |
| 2 | 30,000 | 40,000 | 40,000 |
| 3 | 30,000 | 40,000 | 40,000 |
| 4 | 30,000 | 40,000 | 40,000 |
| 5 | 40,000 | 120,000 | 240,000 |
| Required rate of return | 5% | 6% | 7% |

a. If there is no limit on the capital budget, which projects would you choose? Why?

b. If there is a limit on the capital budget of $300,000, which projects would you choose? Why?

10. Mr. Anderson is a trainee on the capital acquisition staff of a major manufacturer. In the process of evaluating several capital acquisitions, he determines that one of the projects has two IRRs. He checked his calculations several times but did not find any error. He is puzzled by this finding. Explain to Mr. Anderson why more than one IRR is possible for a capital project.

# REFERENCES

Dixit, Avinash K., and Robert S. Pindyck. (1994). *Investment under Uncertainty*. Princeton, NJ: Princeton University Press.

Graham, John, and Campbell R. Harvey. (2002). "How Do CFOs Make Capital Budgeting and Capital Structure Decisions?" *Journal of Applied Corporate Finance* **15**: 8–23.

Peterson, Pamela, and Frank J. Fabozzi. (2002). *Capital Budgeting: Theory and Practice*. New York: John Wiley & Sons.

# PART II

# FINANCIAL SYSTEM

# 7

# FINANCIAL SYSTEMS, GOVERNANCE, AND ORGANIZATION

*I*n this chapter and the one to follow, we explain how financial systems are organized and why they assume those forms. This material is intended to provide a practical context for the financial transactions examined in the rest of the book. Even though financial systems may initially appear to be complicated entities, financial economics offers a straightforward analytical and descriptive picture of how such systems work. A financial system performs a set of tasks, called *functions*. One way to study financial systems[1] involves examining the arrangements reached between financiers and their clients in a process called *alignment*. These alignments are studied principally in the context of *financial deals* that involve either commitments of financial resources (i.e., fund-raising), reallocation of risks[2] (risk transfer), or both.

All financial systems perform similar functions, but differ in the relative importance of the three major forms of governance they use: (1) financial markets, (2) financial intermediaries, and (3) internal allocations. *Governance* is the process of suitably contracting a financial arrangement at the beginning and of tailoring the arrangement to ensure, as far as possible, its profitable conclusion. Some deals depend on continuing supervision to strengthen the possibility of their profitable conclusion. At any point in time, the attributes of financial deals, the organizations funding them, and the capabilities of the organizations' governance methods jointly determine the financial system's organization.

Analyzing the workings of a financial system thus involves identifying (1) the major attributes of proposed financial deals; (2) the capabilities of the organizations (financial entities) that provide financing, risk transfer, or both; and (3) how the attributes of clients' deals can be aligned with financial entities' governance capabilities. Since the entities and their clients both strive to achieve cost-effective

---

[1] This "bottom up" approach to analyzing markets and organization was first suggested by Williamson (1975). A "top-down" approach is advocated by Crane et al. (1995).

[2] A risky financial deal is one whose earnings cannot be determined exactly in advance. Rather, they are known only in terms of a probability distribution.

forms of funding, a financial system's static organization is determined principally by economic considerations. Although in practice not every type of financial deal is governed cost-effectively from the outset, governance choices typically evolve toward greater efficiency as economic agents learn. That is, both a system's static organization and its evolution are largely determined by a combination of learning and the changing economics of performing different financial functions.

In comparing financial systems, it becomes evident that each of the three major financing mechanisms complements the other two. Hence, explaining the allocation of financial resources necessarily involves examining these complementary roles. For example, in some economies financial markets are not very important, and most financial resources are allocated through financial intermediaries. In these economies, an analysis of financial markets would give a very incomplete picture of how the financial system works. As a second example, studying the financial intermediaries in a financial system does not show how intermediaries complement both market and internally provided forms of finance. Even for developed economies such as those of the United States and the United Kingdom, a comprehensive understanding of the financial system requires examining the complementary roles played by the principal types of external finance—market and intermediated transactions—as well as the complementarities between external and internal finance.

The study of financial systems is worthwhile both for its own sake and because financial activity contributes importantly to economic well-being. Yet these beneficial effects are rarely apparent to casual observers. Indeed, some readers of the financial press may have the misleading impression that a financial system is principally a set of markets in which shares of stocks and exotic instruments such as financial derivatives are traded. But in fact, financial activity generates a significant share of national income in many economies, and most of this income is generated by performing everyday functions, such as transferring funds between economic agents, investing accumulated wealth, funding viable new projects, and managing risks.

At the same time, a financial system's economic importance extends well beyond performing everyday functions. Macroeconomic theory explains that while consumption, investment, and government spending are the major determinants of economic activity over the near term, changes in the rate of investment (capital formation) importantly affect the rate of economic growth. Moreover, different amounts and types of capital formation can also affect an economy's productivity and its international competitiveness. A financial system plays an important role in determining these effects, since capital formation is affected by conditions for obtaining financing.

In this chapter, we begin with a functional approach of the permanent features of financial systems and then examine financial activity at the level of individual deals. After outlining the concepts of deal attributes and financing capabilities, the chapter contends that agents strive to negotiate cost-effective alignments and that financial structure represents groupings of these alignment activities. We then turn to financial system governance, the types of governance, and the mechanisms for governance of financial systems. In Web-Appendix A, we provide a description of how the terms of a financial deal can perfect the capabilities utilized in its governance.

## 7.1 FINANCIAL SYSTEM FUNCTIONS

The unchanging functions[3] performed by every financial system include:

- Clearing and settling payments
- Pooling resources
- Transferring resources
- Managing risks
- Producing information
- Managing incentives

Although every financial system performs these functions, the organizations carrying them out are determined endogenously in response to the characteristics of the local economic environment and currently available transactions technology. Thus, the observed structures of financial systems can differ, both at any point in time and also over time.

In this section, we examine these six functions that comprise relatively permanent features of financial systems. Identifying the unchanging features of financial activity is a useful exercise for two reasons. First, when the present discussion of relatively permanent functions is combined with the analysis of financial deals and their governance later in this chapter, we will be able to describe financial activity comprehensively, using differing combinations of a few basic financial deal attributes and a few basic governance capabilities. Second, identifying these basic dimensions helps understand how financial system organization emerges endogenously from the economics of governing deals, as well as indicating how it is likely to evolve in the future.

### 7.1.1 Clearing and Settling Payments

One principal financial function involves *clearing and settling payments*, both domestically and internationally. In essence, clearing and settling payments mean that a payment order requiring one agent to pay another is executed by a third party who effects a transfer of funds from the payer's to the payee's institution. Although settlement has been a traditional financial system function throughout history, today funds are mainly transferred electronically, and payments are made much more quickly than they were even as recently as in the 1980s. The financial system now makes it easy and cheap to transfer funds quickly between almost any two points in the world, and usually in whatever currency the payer desires to use. The increasing use of credit cards, debit cards, and cards that function as electronic purses all contribute to an important form of change in the retail payments system.

### 7.1.2 Pooling Resources

*Resource pooling* is a second financial system function. Some of the ways in which savings are pooled at the retail level are through bank deposits, mutual funds, other

---

[3] These functions were first identified in Crane et al. (1995), and our presentation follows that work.

stock investments, and insurance policies. While savers are concerned with the expected return on their funds, most also want to ensure their wealth is invested relatively safely. A well-developed financial system acts to store wealth, not without any risk, but at a risk commensurate with the expected rate of return on the investment. Since investors are usually risk-averse, they normally demand that asset returns increase as the perceived risk of an investment increases. As is well confirmed by empirical research, informed savers profit from one of the most important conclusions of modern financial theory: The expected return on an asset normally increases with the systematic risk the asset bears.

Funds are also pooled at the wholesale and commercial level. The most well-known instruments of this type are securities issued to raise funds for pooled forms of debt that were originally granted by banks and other lenders through a wide range of what are called asset-backed securities. Institutions like insurance companies, pension funds, and hedge funds are willing to invest in asset-backed securities because they are in effect lending against portfolios of loans rather than against individual loans. The securities are likely to be safer than the individual loans in the pool, because the securities have the entire diversified loan pool as collateral.[4]

### 7.1.3  Transferring Resources

A third basic function is to *transfer resources*, not only from one geographical region to another, but more importantly from one time period to another. Resource transfers through time in effect channel funds from savers to borrowers, thereby facilitating lending or investing. The funds used to finance new investment by businesses are typically raised from both domestic and foreign sources. Through financing new productive activity, the financial system stimulates economic growth.

### 7.1.4  Managing Risks

*Managing risks*, a fourth basic financial system function, includes everything from retail transactions such as selling car insurance to wholesale transactions and trading derivative instruments in international markets. Indeed, almost every aspect of economic life is subject to various forms of either risk or uncertainty. Kenneth Arrow (1974), the corecipient of the 1972 Nobel Memorial Prize in Economic Science, notes that pooling, sharing, and shifting risks are pervasive forms of economic activity. The ability of an individual or business enterprise to shift risks of losses from fire or theft to specialized insurance companies provides an obvious example of a retail transaction. The stock and derivatives markets can all be seen as providing certain forms of wholesale risk management.

Historically, a series of institutions and arrangements have evolved to carry out risk management activities, and the arrangements continue to evolve. The concept of risk management has been familiar to providers of funds for a long time. For example,

---

[4] The effects of diversification are only obtained when the loans in the pool retain a degree of statistical independence. If, as in the case of some pools of certain subprime mortgage securities, many were likely to default simultaneously, say because of a change in the macroeconomic climate, risk reduction through diversification would be sharply reduced.

insuring some of the risks of trade was practiced by caravans following the silk routes. From such historical beginnings, insurance companies were formed principally to assume risks that others were unwilling to bear. Other risk instruments such as commodities futures have also been traded actively for a long time.

As the discussion suggests, risk trading is a kind of insurance activity. It is not particularly fruitful to regard it as a form of gambling in which financiers make money at the expense of uninformed players. Indeed, the growth of risk trading represents a valuable economic function aimed at spreading rather than at increasing risk.[5] Probably most people would agree that buying fire insurance can be a good idea, but fewer observers realize that such forms of financial engineering as using derivative instruments to hedge portfolio risk are conceptually similar. Buying fire insurance is a familiar transaction, but hedging portfolio risk seems exotic and strange until one gets to know it better.

## 7.1.5 Information Production

The fifth basic function of a financial system is *information production*. As pointed out earlier, well-functioning markets foster information production. The *efficient markets hypothesis* holds that, when markets are perfectly competitive and trading is not impeded by transactions costs or institutional practices, securities will have equilibrium prices that fully reflect all publicly available information. The differences between instruments traded in efficient markets are captured in their risk-return characteristics.

Exchange trading in derivatives offers a second example of information production, and many derivatives markets are also efficient information producers. Derivatives trading was not originally thought of as an information-producing activity, but option pricing theory[6] has made it evident that the prices of traded options can be used to obtain estimates of underlying asset volatilities. Volatility information can be used to interpret the degree of earnings uncertainty a given asset presents, and this information can prove valuable for making investment decisions.

Financial intermediaries also perform information production roles, but the information produced by these entities is not usually disseminated publicly. For example, financial intermediaries develop information when they evaluate loan applications, but this information is normally used privately by the intermediaries to decide whether or not credit will be extended to given clients. Nevertheless, skillful production of this information is also essential to economic well-being—without it institutions would be less discriminating in their lending and investment activities, and fewer good projects would be able to obtain funding.

## 7.1.6 Managing Incentives

Still another form of financial system function involves *managing incentives*, especially incentives arising from informational differences. Informational differences can create

---

[5] Risks may be reduced for the agent selling them off, but the same risks are then borne by another party. Financial activity that divides up and trades risks does not alter the underlying physical or economic realities that present the risks in the first place.

[6] We cover option pricing theory in Chapter 19.

situations in which, say, a client has private information that can put the financier at a disadvantage. Managing the potential difficulties presented by informational differences is the essence of everyday financial activity. For example, credit departments of banks investigate borrowers before loans are made, and subsequently monitor the activities of the borrowers to ensure that the terms of the contract are observed. Insurance companies investigate risks before they underwrite them. They also limit the kinds of activities or assets they will underwrite, thus affecting the incentives of the insured.

Incentive considerations affect both lender and borrower. A borrower providing information to a potential lender risks giving away a knowledge advantage. Both the borrower and the lender need protection against exploitation by the other, and in recognition of this possibility, some financiers try to develop reputations for helping rather than exploiting borrowers.

## 7.2 FINANCIAL SYSTEM GOVERNANCE

All financial transactions require governance. By *financial governance* we mean the process of looking after financial transactions with a view to suitably contracting the arrangement at the beginning and with a further view to ensuring, as far as possible, its profitable conclusion. Although all financial transactions require governance, in this chapter and the next we focus on two main types: (1) transactions aimed primarily at raising funds and (2) those aimed primarily at managing risks. Both types are what we refer to generically as financial deals.[7]

Governance capabilities are particularly important for securing the expected profits from financial deals. If funds are being raised, financiers commit resources over time and must subsequently recover the funds invested, with compensation for the expected risk involved, if the financiers are to prosper. Similarly, financiers entering risk management deals must price and govern the risks appropriately. Financial deals that are well governed can be expected on average to reward financiers for assuming risks, while ineffectively governed financial deals have substantially greater probabilities of making losses.

The mechanisms for governing financial deals are variations of financial market, financial intermediary, and internal funding arrangements. Cost-effective alignments of financial deals with the most suitable types of mechanisms depend on both deals' attributes and financiers' governance capabilities. While each alignment of a financial deal and a mechanism is likely to have some distinctive features, financial system analysis is simplified by recognizing that deals can be grouped according to their combinations of attributes, and the economics of governance usually leads financiers to select a particular mix of capabilities for the deals' governance.

### 7.2.1 Types of Financial Governance

In the previous section, we discussed the main functions carried out by the financial system. This section offers a complementary analysis that begins at the level of the

---

[7] In practice, financial deals often combine fund-raising and risk management, but for discussion purposes it helps to distinguish the two.

individual transaction, referred to as the financial deal. Once the processes of agreeing and governing individual transactions have been examined, we then consider how financiers aggregate financial deals, and how the aggregations of deal types endogenously determine the kinds of institutions and markets present in a financial system.

*Financial governance* can be regarded as utilizing a few capabilities drawn from a fixed taxonomy, and financial deals can be described in terms of a few critical attributes, drawn from a second fixed taxonomy. Financiers with given capabilities usually accept financial deals with particular attribute combinations. In addition, financial firms choose a form of business organization that is intended to facilitate cost-effective governance. At the aggregate level, financiers' organizational choices are determined endogenously by the attributes of available details and the economies of governing those attributes. Alignment of attributes and governance capabilities results in the structure of a financial system. That is, the combination of financial markets, financial intermediaries, and internal governance that a financial system represents is also determined endogenously by the economics of governance and the operating economics of the organizations implementing the governance methods.

*External finance* is provided by both financial markets and financial intermediaries, and clients' choices among alternative financing forms depend on both the cost and the perceived stringency of the financing conditions. Differences in financing terms stem from differences in market structure, from differences in borrower and lender information, and from the incentives the informational conditions create. In particular, informational differences between financiers and their clients can create problems that increase the costs of any financial deals that are actually agreed upon. If the problems caused by informational differences are severe enough, external finance may not be obtainable even at a very high cost.[8] Even in an economy with a highly developed financial system, a considerable proportion of business financing is provided internally from business' own resources. Decisions to finance internally rather than externally will usually depend on the perceived risk or uncertainty inherent in the proposal, the cost of the external funding, and the perceived stringency of the funding conditions.

Some financial systems (those of the United States and the United Kingdom, for example) channel a relatively large proportion of external financing through financial markets, while others (those of France, Germany, and Japan, for example) channel a greater proportion through financial intermediaries. These differences in the relative importance of different financing sources are reflected in the terms *market-based systems* and *intermediary-oriented systems*. For example, it is customary to describe the financial systems of the United States and the United Kingdom as "market-oriented"; those of France, Germany, and Japan as "intermediary-based." However, the differences between market-oriented and intermediary-oriented systems are to some extent a function of historical development, and as the global financial system continues to evolve, the search for efficient forms of financing continues to reduce the differences between the two classifications.

Markets and intermediaries utilize different capabilities, and are therefore not equally well suited to governing the same types of financial deals: in a static and

---

[8] The issues of cost and availability are discussed at length in later chapters.

efficiently organized financial system the types of financings arranged in markets will differ from the types arranged with intermediaries.[9] Thus, at the system level, a strongly market-oriented system could exhibit different aggregate performance characteristics than a strongly intermediary-oriented system.

Market-oriented and intermediary-oriented financial systems develop public and private information in different proportions. Through trading, markets aggregate the impact of widely diverse forms of public information. Portfolios composed largely of securities that trade actively in financial markets have readily established values that are frequently described as transparent. On the other hand, intermediaries offer greater potential for in-depth, private development of credit information. Since intermediaries acquire relatively large proportions of nontradable assets, their portfolios have less easily established values that are often referred to as opaque.[10]

## 7.2.2 Governance Mechanisms

The three principal mechanisms for governing the allocation of financial resources are markets, intermediaries, and internal organizations. Internal organizations are also referred to as *hierarchies*. Each type of mechanism utilizes a mix of capabilities drawn from a fixed taxonomy. Here we will explore the differential capabilities of the three main mechanisms.[11] Table 7.1 presents a schematic representation of the differences between governance mechanisms and their capabilities. As the table indicates, the type of allocation mechanism ranges along a continuum indicating that (1) markets typically allocate financial resources using the price mechanism, (2) intermediaries combine allocation by price with some forms of command and control, and (3) hierarchies such as financial conglomerates provide finance primarily using command and control mechanisms. The capabilities of the mechanisms increase in both effectiveness and cost along a continuum having market governance

TABLE 7.1
MECHANISMS AND GOVERNANCE CAPABILITIES

| → Markets | Intermediaries | Hierarchies | → |
|---|---|---|---|

→ Allocation by price . . . . . . . . . . . . . . Allocation by command and control →

Greater screening (*ex ante*) capabilities
Greater monitoring (*ex post*) capabilities
Greater control capabilities
    (auditing, replacement of key personnel)
Greater adjustment capabilities
    (ability to alter contracts on an *ex post* basis)

---

[9] In any observed situation, the economics of governance may not have been fully worked out, and experimentation can mean that what actually might evolve to be a market form of financing is actually arranged as an intermediated form. We distinguish these situations using the terms *static* and *dynamic complementarity*.

[10] See Ross (1989).

[11] For a more in-depth discussion, see Neave (2009).

at one extreme, and internal governance at the other. The ideas underlying the table are examined in the following sections.

### 7.2.2.1 Market Finance

Markets allocate financial resources by price, which in the context of a financial transaction refers to a financial deal's effective funding cost. Market governance works best when a financial deal's essential attributes can be captured by the funding cost it bears. Such financial deals' essentials can be reflected by terms that are fully specified at the outset, meaning that financial deals consummated by market agents can usually be regarded as complete contracts. Most financial deals that market agents entertain require relatively little monitoring after being struck, often because market deals finance the acquisition of assets with a ready resale value in secondary markets.

Typically, market agents carry out trades between parties who do not necessarily know each other. Moreover, market agents often have well-developed research and information-processing capabilities regarding readily observable short-term changes in each financial deal's likely profitability. For example, market trading of a firm's shares determines the value of the firm's underlying assets. As a second example, trading derivatives prices volatility,[12] and thereby produces economic information about how different risks are valued in the marketplace. As Allen and Gale (2000) observe, markets are especially well suited to assessing the economic impact of a variety of disparate forms of information.[13]

Market agents attempt to realize scale economies by standardizing the terms of the deals they take on, and thereby reducing the transactions costs of a financial deal. Market agents can also realize economies of scale if the same specialized information-processing techniques can be used for numbers of similar financial deals. The most active markets usually deal primarily in standardized contracts, a category that includes the public share issues of widely traded companies. On the other hand, less active markets deal principally in contracts that can be more varied in their terms.

Within the markets category, distinctions can be made on the basis of differences in the capabilities of market agents. For example, private markets, in which securities are sold to one or a small group of investors, typically permit more detailed *ex ante* screening and more detailed negotiation of a financial deal's terms than do public markets in which securities are sold to a relatively large number of investors on standard terms.

### 7.2.2.2 Intermediary Finance

*Financial intermediaries* are enterprises that raise funds from savers, mainly house-holders and to a lesser extent businesses. The major financial intermediaries are depository institutions such as banks whose funds are raised via deposits. These financial intermediaries relend the funds to business and personal borrowing custo-mers, and in most developed economies, they provide the largest proportion of loan funds obtained by those ultimate users. The public normally views intermediary deposits as highly liquid, and expects to be able to withdraw the nominal amounts of

---

[12] The relations between derivatives' prices and asset price volatility are examined in Web-Appendix G.

[13] Markets can perform this task well under relatively stable conditions. Their capabilities to do so are much more sharply limited in times of uncertainty.

their deposits on short notice. On the other hand, most of the loans granted by financial intermediaries are illiquid, typically being repaid in installments over months or years. Hence, financial intermediaries must manage a portfolio of relatively illiquid assets that are funded by relatively short-term liabilities.[14]

Loans granted by financial intermediaries specify an interest rate, and therefore, utilize a form of resource allocation by price, but the arrangements also incorporate a greater use of command and control mechanisms than is typically found in market transactions. As a result, intermediaries exercise certain kinds of governance capabilities that are not customarily utilized by market agents. The additional capabilities that financial intermediaries utilize include more intensive *ex ante* screening capabilities, more extensive capabilities for monitoring, control, and subsequent adjustment of financial deal terms. Intermediaries use these combinations of capabilities because they offer cost-effective ways of governing the financial deals they enter. Intermediaries produce private information by screening loan applications *ex ante*, as well as by *ex post* monitoring of deals they have already entered. Information produced by financial intermediaries remains private because they do not normally trade their financial assets.[15] The contracts drawn up for intermediated financial deals are incomplete in comparison to the contracts drawn up for market financial deals. In particular, they may have implicit terms that are not actively invoked unless the originally agreed financial deal appears to be in some danger of producing less revenue for the financier than was first contemplated.

Not all intermediaries can screen all types of financial deals equally well, and differential capabilities help to explain why intermediaries are likely to specialize, at least to a degree. For example, some intermediaries can offer automated screening of credit card and consumer loan applications, thereby enjoying scale economies not available to those with smaller volumes of the same business. As a second example, expert systems and credit scoring techniques are coming to play an increasingly important role in assessing many types of deals, including business lending. Such systems exhibit declining average costs, chiefly because they require a large initial investment, but have relatively small marginal operating costs. As a result, expert systems will most likely be installed by a relatively small number of large firms. If they can negotiate profitable terms, smaller firms may purchase the services from their larger counterparts.

### 7.2.2.3 Internal Governance

*Internal governance*, also referred to as *hierarchical governance*, represents financial resource allocation using command-and-control capabilities to a still greater extent than that used by financial intermediaries. Internal governance offers the greatest potential for intensive *ex ante* screening, *ex post* monitoring, control over operations, and adjustment of financial deal terms. Hierarchical mechanisms typically focus less on the nature of a financial contract and more on the command-and-control

---

[14] This aspect of intermediary structure can create stability problems.

[15] Securitization involves selling beneficial interests in a portfolio and is different from selling the assets themselves, not least because the original lender usually collects the loan repayments and bears some responsibility for defaults.

mechanisms they can use to effect *ex post* adjustment of financing terms. Internal governance is likely to be more expensive than market or intermediated governance, and as a result will normally be used to govern financial deals whose uncertainties are greater than those acceptable to intermediaries.

For example, internal capital market transactions may be the only feasible way of governing financial deals whose problems of incomplete contracting are relatively severe. Internal governance provides highly developed capabilities for auditing project performance, for changing operating management, and for adjusting financing terms if conditions change. On all these counts, internal financing arrangements employ different governance capabilities from those of either market agents or intermediaries, but also at higher administrative costs than those of the former two. Of course, in order to be viable such financial deals must offer a potential for both covering higher governance costs and for returning greater rewards.

## 7.2.3  Types of Financial Deals

Financiers are faced with proposals for what appear to be many different types of financial deals. Indeed, on the surface deals differ so much that it might seem necessary to describe each one separately. However, at a macro level, differences among financial deals can be described as different combinations of a few basic attributes.

### 7.2.3.1  Deal Attributes

Some deals are so familiar to financiers that their successful conclusion depends primarily on the results of an initial screening followed by using a standard form of governance. These simple forms of financings arise either when clients acquire relatively liquid[16] assets, or when collateral with a readily established market value can be used for security. In either case, such kinds of financings are relatively easy to arrange because in the event of difficulty, the underlying asset values can be used to repay most or all of the funding. The simplest kinds of risk management financial deals are similarly standardized. Such financial deals present risks rather than uncertainties, can be formalized using rule-based, complete contracts, and are relatively easy to price. Accordingly, such financial deals can usually be agreed upon after only relatively cursory investigation.

Other financial deals may be unfamiliar to financiers, have unusual terms, and present greater uncertainty regarding the likelihood of repayment. These more complex kinds of financial deals often involve financing the purchase of illiquid assets when there is no collateral to serve as security in the event of a failure to satisfy the terms of the financial deal. For example, financial deals (i.e., investments) made by specialized entities known as venture capitalists whose success rests on the talent and commitment of given individuals are deals in which financiers' rewards will depend on highly uncertain future earnings. There will usually be little in the way of marketable assets available to provide security.

---

[16] Williamson (1987) stresses the importance of asset specificity as a deal attribute. This book uses the related (but not identical) concept of asset liquidity, mainly because financiers are very often concerned with the likelihood that an asset can quickly be sold at or near its secondary market value.

TABLE 7.2
ATTRIBUTES AND GOVERNANCE IMPLICATIONS

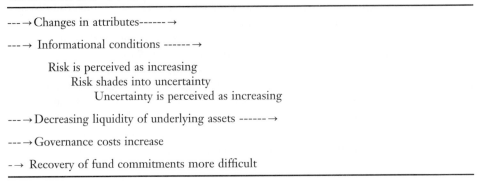

--- → Changes in attributes------ →

--- → Informational conditions ------ →

        Risk is perceived as increasing
           Risk shades into uncertainty
               Uncertainty is perceived as increasing

--- → Decreasing liquidity of underlying assets ------ →

--- → Governance costs increase

- → Recovery of fund commitments more difficult

Table 7.2 indicates that increasing information differences, decreasing asset liquidity, or both make financial deals more costly to govern. Governance costs increase in part because greater informational differences present possibilities of both adverse selection and moral hazard, as explained later in this chapter. The effects of such phenomena can be partially offset by additional governance capabilities, but acquiring such capabilities is costly, as will be discussed further below.

### 7.2.3.2 Asset Liquidity

*Asset liquidity* makes a considerable difference as to whether a financial deal can be classified as simple or complex. If the underlying assets can readily be traded in secondary markets, financiers have two potential sources of repayment. They can recoup their investment with interest if the firm or project being financed turns out well and generates a sufficiently large cash flow. If the firm or project cash flows do not materialize, liquid assets can still be sold to recover at least some of the funds initially put up. In such cases the deal is relatively simple. But if the assets are illiquid, financiers can only expect to recover a return on their investment by working to ensure that the project will operate profitably. Moreover the less liquid the underlying assets, the less the financier can rely on them as a source of repayment.

As will be discussed further below, asset liquidity will not necessarily remain constant over time. Indeed, liquidity depends primarily on the presence of both buyers and sellers. If there are only buyers in a market, there will be an asset demand but no compensating supply, whereas if there are only sellers in a market, there will be an asset supply but no compensating demand. Illiquidity becomes most widespread in markets where asset values can be affected in an uncertain manner by the actions of third parties, as will be discussed further in the next section. A potential buyer and a potential seller will find it difficult to agree on terms if the value of the asset they are attempting to exchange can be affected by the actions of a third party, and if those values are difficult for the potential counterparties to predict.

### 7.2.3.3 Risk versus Uncertainty

A second important attribute of a financial deal is whether its payoffs can usefully be described quantitatively using a probability distribution. If the expected earnings of a financial deal can usefully be described in probabilistic terms, the financial deal can be called risky. Two of the major risks associated with risky financial deals are profitability risk and default risk. *Profitability risk* refers to the probability of earning a relatively low return on the investment. *Default risk* refers to the possibility that a lender or investor faces the risk of the borrower not satisfying the terms of the contract, including both repayment of the amount invested and any accrued interest.[17]

Although profitability risk and default risk can be closely related, it is useful for descriptive purposes to distinguish them henceforth. Profitability risk depends mainly on such features of a financial deal as the possible magnitude of fluctuations in realized earnings, the maturity or termination date of the financial deal, whether the interest rate on it is fixed or floating, and the currency in which the financial deal is expressed. Default risk depends mainly on the probability that cash flows, including any cash that might be raised from selling assets, will be too small to permit making the contracted repayments on the debt. Financial deals that involve financing the purchase of liquid assets are less likely to pose default risk because liquid assets can be seized and sold to repay at least part, and perhaps all, of a loan or investment.

In another type of financial deal, it may not even be possible to quantify the factors critical to profitability. Consider, for example, the press reports of profitability estimates for the Channel Tunnel project connecting England and France that started in 1988 and began operations in 1994. This project's expected profitability changed considerably with the passage of time, even after allowing for some ability to recoup cost overruns through higher toll charges. The range of profitability estimates depends mainly on such variables as the demand for tunnel services, the reactions of competitors, global interest rates, and the like. Even sophisticated profitability models are not very helpful, since they depend critically on assumptions that are extremely difficult to render precise. Moreover, the Channel Tunnel's assets are illiquid, and therefore provide little in the way of collateral against default. That is, the Channel Tunnel's financing essentially represented a financial deal struck under conditions of uncertainty.

Uncertainty means that an economic agent cannot regard himself as understanding a financial deal well. Financial deals most likely to present uncertainty are those involving either a strategic change in business operations, or those financing a technological innovation. A start-up investment in a new, high technology business offers an example of a deal under uncertainty. It is often observed that such projects are particularly difficult to finance, mainly because economic agents find it difficult to assess their likely payoffs. First, neither clients nor financiers may be able to determine a proposed financial deal's key profitability features. Second, the possible reactions of competitors to carrying out the project may be difficult to predict. Despite these difficulties, financial deals presenting uncertainties are the essence of both business and financial innovation, and analyzing how financiers overcome the difficulties is profoundly important to studying financial activity.

Financial deals presenting uncertainties require different governance capabilities than do their merely risky counterparts. First, their successful governance requires greater adaptability to circumstances that are not easy to see when financial deals are first entered. Financial deals entered under uncertainty will require relatively more monitoring, especially if relevant information is likely to be revealed gradually with the passage

---

[17] Default risk is also sometimes categorized as a type of *counterparty risk*.

of time. Moreover, if monitoring indicates that contract adjustments would be in order, the deal terms need to provide for those adjustments, or even for control of underlying operations as and when the needs for change are revealed.[18] As a result, financiers often have to use incomplete contracts when entering deals under uncertainty.

### 7.2.3.4  *Informational Differences*

Financiers and clients do not always have the same information about a financial deal. When there are information differences, economists refer to this situation as *informational asymmetries*, a term used in contract theory where in a financial deal one party has more or better or different information than the other party.[19] Information asymmetries can arise either because the two parties do not have access to the same data, or because they interpret the same data differently. Differences in interpretation can stem from differing levels of competence, or because differing experiences bias the parties' respective views. In addition to views about the financial deal itself, economic agents may form views of how counterparties regard the financial deal, complicating the picture further. Thus, a deal's informational attributes can be classified according to whether agents perceive the risks or uncertainties symmetrically or asymmetrically. Moreover, the information differences between the two may change significantly during the life of a financial deal.

As a result of information asymmetries, there may be two types of problems in financial deals: adverse selection and moral hazard. *Adverse selection* in terms of financial deals means the negotiation of inferior terms relative to what would have been consummated if financiers (the "ignorant party" in the financial deal) had access to the same information as a client.[20] *Moral hazard* in the case of a financial deal means that the ignorant party (the financier in the deal) does not have either (1) sufficient information about the performance of the client to evaluate whether the client is complying with the terms of the deal or (2) the capability to effectively remedy situations where the client has breached the terms of the deal. The classic example is in risk sharing, which as explained is one of the functions of a financial deal. An individual with insurance against the theft of jewelry may not be as careful about safeguarding the insured property because the adverse consequences of its loss are principally borne by the insurer.

Informational differences usually occur in financial deals that do not receive intensive study by a number of economic agents. Even in routine public market transactions, not all parties obtain the same information at the same time. Informational differences can even impede large public market transactions if the firm involved is changing the nature of its business. In both the United States and Canada, stock market trading activity by corporate officers and market specialists based on inside information has been shown to yield abnormal risk-adjusted returns. Whatever the likelihood of informational differences in public market transactions, they are even more likely to occur in private markets or in intermediated transactions. For example, financiers are well aware that some clients will provide biased information in attempts to improve financing terms.

---

[18] The necessary changes may be in the client's operations, the terms of the financing, or both.

[19] George Akerlof, Michael Spence, and Joseph Stiglitz shared the 2001 Nobel Memorial Prize in Economic Sciences for their study of the impact of asymmetric information on markets.

[20] See Akerlof (1970).

Whenever informational asymmetries are perceived to have economically important consequences for a financier, attempts will be made to obtain more information, at least if the information's value is expected to be greater than the cost of gathering it. Cost-benefit analysis of information acquisition can be a challenging task under risk, and is even more so under uncertainty. In the latter case, financiers may not even know how to frame relevant questions regarding any benefits to gathering more information.[21]

### 7.2.3.5  Complete versus Incomplete Contracting

In risky financial deals, the financier's main function is to determine the market price of the assets involved, mainly by using information publicly available to market participants. Such financial deals normally require only a minimal degree of subsequent monitoring, since their terms can be specified relatively completely at the time when funds are first advanced. Financial deals of this type are said to use *complete contracting*.

Only some financial deals can be formalized using complete contracts. Complete contracting is a situation under risk in which all important outcomes can be described fully, and a situation in which actions to be taken can also be described fully, at least on a contingency basis. Some market deals can be described as complete contracts because they have little need of *ex post* monitoring. In some other market deals *ex post* has little value because the monitor has no real capability to effect any necessary changes.

Financial deals under uncertainty are often characterized by incomplete contracting, which refers to situations in which not all important outcomes can usefully be described in terms of a probability distribution. An example of incomplete contracting that arises from a conflict of interest is one between entrepreneurs and outside investors.[22] Consider a situation in which the nature of the conflict cannot satisfactorily be resolved by specifying entrepreneurial effort and reward. To complicate situation further, entrepreneurial effort cannot always be modeled satisfactorily in a quantitative manner. And nor can entrepreneurial effort always be motivated by an incentive scheme: In some cases, it can only be motivated by financiers' threat to liquidate/terminate the financial deal. When earnings prospects are good, the entrepreneur decides whether or not the profits from expansion are worth the effort she must supply. At the same time, if outside investors perceive the earnings prospects as bad, they may sometimes want to liquidate the company when the entrepreneur perceives expansion possibilities to be attractive. Such situations reflect some of the complexities of incomplete contracting.

## 7.2.4  Alignment

Financiers have specialized capabilities and accept deals whose attributes they can govern effectively. Relatively simple[23] deals are usually agreed upon with market

---

[21] If financiers decide that they cannot learn enough about a given deal to assess its profitability even roughly, they may decline to enter the deal.

[22] This illustration is from Aghion and Bolton (1992).

[23] In the specific sense of this chapter, these are financial deals under risk, involving liquid assets, and not being subject to severe informational asymmetries.

agents, while more complex deals are usually agreed upon either with intermediaries or, in extreme cases, internally to the funding organization. Thus, financier capabilities and deal attributes are aligned on the basis of cost-effectiveness. In the aggregate, the specialized capabilities of financiers and the financial deals they agree upon determine the mix of a given financier's business. The numbers and kinds of business organizations formed to carry out financial deals ultimately determine the nature of financial system organization.

### 7.2.4.1 *Principles*

Alignment decisions depend importantly on the kinds of specialized capabilities needed to govern a financial deal cost-effectively. Information about some kinds of deals may be fully available when a financial deal is first prepared, but in other cases pertinent information about the financial deal may also be gained during the time it remains in force. Moreover, in unfamiliar financial deals, financiers may learn how better to govern a financial deal over the time when it remains in force. Financial deals for which learning is important are usually agreed upon either with financial intermediaries or internally to the business firm, because in these cases it can be easier to adapt the terms of the financial deal as learning takes place. The incomplete contracts created are evidence that such financial deals are not usually traded, but are retained by the original lender until the funds advanced have been repaid.

Jensen and Meckling (1976) help illuminate choices among different forms of financial governance. They refer to knowledge that is costly to transfer among economic agents as *specific knowledge*, and knowledge that is cheap to transfer as *general knowledge*. Financial deals whose governance requires specific knowledge are more difficult to arrange than are financial deals whose governance requires only general knowledge. For example, a financial deal whose governance requires specific knowledge is more likely to be held by the originating financial institution rather than being traded in the marketplace, partially because the skills of the personnel originating the financial deal are more likely to be used in its continuing administration.

The packaging of loans (i.e., groups of financial deals) by a financial institution and the sale of securities backed by those loans is one financial technology that helps deal with the difficulties of transmitting specific knowledge. The process of packaging financial deals is referred to as *securitization* and the securities created are referred to as *asset-backed securities*. The original loans have idiosyncratic characteristics that represent specific knowledge, but the asset-backed securities issued against the portfolio of original loans are tradable instruments because investors in these instruments need only general knowledge about portfolio characteristics when they decide whether or not to invest in them. Making sure the portfolio retains its value is usually a job for the original lender, who has specific knowledge of the transaction details involved.[24]

Decision makers are constantly assembling new knowledge, and Jensen and Meckling argue that the more specific the assembled knowledge becomes, the more costly its transfer and the greater the likelihood it will be retained within the

---

[24] If the incentives for the original lender to preserve value are weak, difficulties are likely to result. The subprime mortgage market difficulties and the difficulties of the asset-backed commercial paper market are both partially attributable to attenuated incentives, as discussed at later points in the book.

producing organization. Jensen and Meckling also point out that the initial costs of acquiring idiosyncratic knowledge (learning) can be modest, but the costs of transferring it can be high relative to the benefits. Uncertainty about what pieces of idiosyncratic knowledge might prove valuable *ex post* can actually present high *ex ante* transfer costs, in part because uncertainty implies a need to transfer knowledge that might never turn out to be useful. Thus, idiosyncratic knowledge is also likely to be retained within the producing organization.

To enhance the safety and profitability of a financial deal, financiers typically want to exercise more intensive governance capabilities if a project has uncertain rather than risky returns. When facing uncertainty, financiers (if they agree to put up any funds at all or to insure a financial deal) will try to discover and manage a financial deal's key profitability features. But since they cannot specify exactly what might be required in advance, financiers can only formalize their loan agreements to the extent of citing principles that allow them to respond flexibly to changing conditions. That is, financiers use incomplete contracts to govern the uncertainties with which they grapple. If relatively precise specifications were possible, financiers could write complete contracts when financial deals were agreed upon.

Contrast a public issue of stock with a financing arrangement that a conglomerate headquarters might strike with one of its subsidiaries. In the first case, information is widely shared by many parties; in the second case (internal governance), it is not. Moreover, in the second case, there are much greater opportunities for continuing supervision after financing has initially been provided. Finally, in contrast to a public securities issue whose features are explained in a publicly distributed prospectus,[25] internal governance may be used to keep information about development plans from being revealed to competitors.

### 7.2.4.2 Process

Financiers attempt to make alignment choices as cost-effectively as they are able, and Table 7.3 shows how alignments can be regarded as the results of an interplay between clients presenting deal attributes and financiers' possessing governance capabilities. The financing costs that clients face, and governance costs that financiers incur, are determined as a result of the interplay. The first section of Table 7.3 arranges the three basic governance mechanisms—financial markets, financial intermediaries, and hierarchical arrangements such as internal financing, in increasing order of command-control intensity. For example, public markets are recorded to the left of private markets, because private market agents can muster certain governance capabilities not possessed by public market agents. Private market agents usually have greater investigative capability, and in some cases greater freedom to negotiate terms, than do public market agents. Similarly, even though commercial banks and venture capital firms are both intermediaries, commercial banks usually have less highly developed screening

---

[25] In the United States, a publicly offered security must be registered with the Securities and Exchange Commission (SEC). The type of information contained in the registration statement is the nature of the business of the issuer of the security, key term of the securities, identification and summary of the investment risks about the security, and information about management. The registration is divided into two parts. The prospectus is the first part and is typically distributed to the public as a part of the offering. The second part is supplemental information that can be obtained from the SEC.

TABLE 7.3
GOVERNANCE CAPABILITIES, DEAL ATTRIBUTES, AND ALIGNMENT

**Governance**

| Markets (Market Agents) | Hybrids (Intermediaries) | Hierarchies (Internal Financing) |
|---|---|---|

Public Markets
    Private Markets
           Securities Firms
                Commercial Banks
                    Venture Capital Companies
                        Universal Banks
                          Keiretsu
                              Financial Conglomerates

**Governance Capabilities**

----→ Direction of change ----→

Greater monitoring capabilities
    (particularly on a continuing basis)
Greater control capabilities
    (auditing, replacement of key personnel)
Greater adjustment capabilities
    (ability to alter contracts as circumstances change)

**Governance Costs**

---→ Increasing ------------------------------→

**Deals' Attributes**

----→ Direction of change ----→

Increasing information differences
Perceived greater risk; uncertainty rather than risk
Decreased asset liquidity
Greater need for continued monitoring
Greater need for subsequent adjustment
Increasing cost of default

and monitoring capabilities than do venture capital firms. In particular, venture capital firms make greater use of discretionary arrangements, which usually include obtaining a seat on the board of any company to which they extend funds. Finally, hierarchical governance means governance within a given organization or group. Western financial conglomerates sometimes offer examples of hierarchical organizations, as do the Japanese keiretsu.[26] Similarly, the universal banks[27] found in Germany use something

---

[26] Keiretsu are groups of firms with interrelated shareholdings. The firms within the keiretsu typically give business preference to other keiretsu members, and the keiretsu's main bank often takes a seat on the board of client companies experiencing financial difficulties.

[27] A universal bank is a bank that also performs such other functions as underwriting or selling securities. In Germany universal banks own share positions in some of their larger client companies.

closer to hierarchical governance when they both purchase the shares of, and make long-term loans to, the same clients.

The second section of Table 7.3 indicates that different governance mechanisms can exercise differing degrees of capabilities. For example, internal financing arrangements have greater monitoring and control capabilities than market arrangements. The governance cost section of Table 7.3 is a reminder that greater capabilities cannot be acquired without incurring additional costs.

Reading from left to right in the attributes section of the table shows that deals characterized by greater informational differences between the two parties (the financiers typically having less information) are viewed by financiers as involving higher degrees of risk, or as presenting uncertainty instead of risk. Higher-risk financial deals, and financial deals whose prospects are uncertain, pose greater needs for continuing governance than do lower-risk financial deals. Similarly greater uncertainty, a lower degree of asset liquidity or both make it more difficult to establish market values for the underlying assets. Difficulty in establishing market value leads to difficulty in determining the breakup value of a firm when in financial difficulty. If financiers cannot readily establish a breakup value for the firm, they do not know what they might be able to recover from a sale of assets if the firm should fail. Therefore, financial deals with such firms appear riskier than, say, financial deals that involve financing the purchases of liquid assets with readily established market values.

Financings under uncertainty present the most difficult governance problems, and are therefore likely to be subjected to the most intensive forms of governance. Of course, greater capabilities come at greater costs, and these governance costs must be recovered from gross returns on the investment. For example, administering a portfolio of short-term liquid securities principally requires market governance, while administering the financing of conglomerate subsidiaries that are entering new ventures can require a much more intensive, higher capability form of governance. As a result, the second kind of financial deal must offer higher gross returns if it is to be regarded as capable of generating expected net profits.

## 7.2.4.3   Cost-Effectiveness

Financiers accept a financial deal on the basis of whether they regard themselves as having the capabilities to govern the financial deal profitably. They reject financial deals that do not meet such criteria. Expected profits depend both on the revenue from the financial deal and the cost of its governance. Financiers strive to control costs by only taking on those financial deals they can govern cost-effectively, as illustrated by the arrangements in the different parts of Table 7.3. For example, in comparison to intermediary or hierarchically governed deals, market financial deals tend to be more standardized, and to exhibit less important informational differences between client and financier. As a result, market governance uses relatively few monitoring and control capabilities, and market-governed deals typically present lower administration costs than do hierarchically governed deals. A market agent will not usually take on financial deals that require the specialized governance capabilities of a financial intermediary.

Market governance is generally cheaper than hierarchical governance.[28] In governing standard deals arranged under competitive conditions there is little room to cover the extra resource costs of hierarchical governance, and risk reduction has little importance for assessing profitability. It follows that the profitability[29] of doing a standard deal using market governance usually exceeds the profitability of doing a standard deal using, say, intermediary governance. If intermediaries were to take on such deals, they would do so primarily because they could exercise additional governance capabilities. In such cases, their loan administration costs would be higher than the administration costs of market agents, and the intermediaries would have to charge a higher interest rate to cover the costs.

A form of non-arm's length governance can be a cost-effective alternative to market governance if the benefits of additional monitoring, control, and adjustment capabilities exceed the extra information and monitoring costs involved. Hierarchical governance is especially likely to be cost-effective when the financing environment is uncertain. The reduced risk or increased return from hierarchical governance more than compensates for the greater cost of acquiring the extra governance capabilities.

On the demand side, clients attempt to seek out a financier who offers the most attractive terms available. Clients strive to minimize their costs of obtaining funds, but they will not always find the best available deal terms. For example, a client will not willingly pay a higher fee to an intermediary than the client would have to pay to a market agent. Yet if search costs are high, a client will quite often accept one of the first few feasible arrangements the client can find, maybe even the very first. That is, high search costs bias clients toward exploring familiar sources of funding.

Nevertheless, a client may be able to secure several offers of financing. For example, a client seeking external financing will choose, frequently in consultation with one or more financiers, whether to offer securities in a public marketplace or through private negotiations. The client's eventual choice will depend on the terms offered, including interest costs, the amount of information required to be provided, the parties who will become privy to the information, and the effects of information release on the client's competitive position.

### 7.2.4.4 Asset Specificity

Williamson (2002) models the complementarities of governance structures as a function of asset specificity. Although the two concepts are not identical, for most purposes asset specificity can be thought of as similar to asset illiquidity. Figure 7.1 shows the transactions' cost consequences of organizing financings through markets, through financial intermediaries such as banks, and through financial conglomerates when the transactions vary by asset specificity. Increasing asset specificity is plotted toward the right of the horizontal axis, and costs are plotted on the vertical axis.

---

[28] See, for example, Riordan and Williamson (1985), Williamson (1987), and Jensen and Meckling (1998).

[29] Profitability is defined as expected future net earnings, discounted at a rate adjusted to reflect the risk or uncertainties involved.

FIGURE 7.1
COMPARATIVE COSTS OF GOVERNANCE

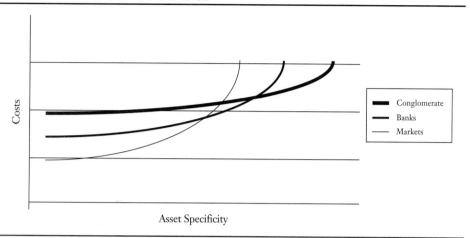

Source: Adapted from Williamson (2002).

When assets have a low degree of specificity, the bureaucratic costs of financial conglomerates place them at a serious disadvantage relative to markets. Similarly the bureaucratic costs of banks place them at a disadvantage relative to markets, albeit a lesser one than conglomerates. However, the cost differences narrow and are eventually reversed as asset specificity increases. Intermediaries are therefore viewed as a hybrid form of governance structure that possesses capabilities somewhere between those of markets and those of conglomerates. With an increase in asset specificity, intermediaries come to offer a cost advantage relative to markets, and as asset specificity increases further still, conglomerates come to offer a cost advantage relative to intermediaries. Because added governance costs accrue on taking a transaction out of the market and supervising it with an intermediary or conglomerate organization, the three are usefully viewed as complements, the more expensive to be substituted for the less expensive as the degree of asset specificity increases. Cost-effective governance choices mean the effective form of cost curve in the circumstances displayed is the envelope reflecting the minimum of the three cost curves displayed.

### 7.2.4.5 Deal Terms

Financiers propose varied deal terms, both in attempts to ensure profitability and to fine-tune governance arrangements. The terms of a financial deal include repayment arrangements, the collateral taken, the currency used, and its maturity (fixed or variable). Along with the amount advanced, these terms also determine the effective interest rate. The effective interest rate on a financial deal increases with its risk, and will be higher for uncertainty than for risk, because financiers require larger returns to compensate for greater risks or for assuming uncertainty rather than risk.[30]

---

[30] The tax status of a deal can also affect both the financier's return and the client's cost of funds.

Terms can alter the nature of a financial deal's original attributes. For example, a deal offering uncertain payoffs can be much easier to finance if the client can offer marketable securities as collateral. In this case, a loan can be made against the value of the securities, and the financier, who can rely on the securities' market value as collateral for the loan, will likely view the deal as merely risky rather than uncertain.

How the terms of a financial deal can perfect the capabilities utilized in its governance is explained in Web-Appendix A. In particular, the informational conditions under which a deal is originated, and the likely evolution of that information, have important implications for selecting deal terms.

## 7.3 FINANCIAL SYSTEM ORGANIZATION

There will usually be a least-cost form of governance for each type of financial deal. Over time, competitive pressures will create a tendency for a least-cost form of governance to emerge for financial deals of a given type. Nevertheless, financiers can sometimes earn above-normal profits[31] on complex financial deals (even after adjusting for differences in risk) because the markets in which some deals are agreed can be less competitive than the markets for more straightforward deals.

A financial firm's size and organization are determined mainly by the economics of the financial deals they take on, and by their operating economics. Scale and scope economies are important features of the latter. *Scale economies* refer to the ability to produce additional units of output at a decreasing average cost per unit, and frequently arise from spreading fixed production costs over a larger number of units of output. *Scope economies* refer to the ability to obtain combinations of goods or services at a lower average cost per unit than can be achieved if the goods or services are produced individually. Scope economies, sometimes called *cost complementarities* or *synergies*, frequently stem from the ability to share common inputs.

### 7.3.1 Markets, Intermediaries, and Internal Finance

The alignment of financial deal attributes and governance capabilities, and the consequent assembly of portfolios to take advantage of the associated firms' operating economies, explain the static organization of the financial services industry. If there were no financial intermediaries, potential borrowers would individually have to seek out willing lenders. Similarly, lenders would individually have to screen borrowers, design financial contracts, and monitor borrower behavior. When financial intermediaries perform the same functions, they may be able to do so more economically by realizing scale and scope economies in their operations. Carey, Post, and Sharpe (1998) argue (1) that markets and intermediaries make different types of corporate loans, and (2) that within the class of intermediaries differently specialized firms make different types of corporate loans. Their evidence further implies that it is

---

[31] The supernormal profits can persist until the deal becomes standard and is governed by competitive market transactions.

not enough to understand the mixture of debt obtained by from public markets and private markets; what also matters is the mixture of the varieties of private debt.

Boot and Thakor (1993) model private banking markets as less competitive than public securities markets. In their model, greater interbank competition reduces banking rents and makes banks more like each other and less likely to specialize. Increased capital market competition tends to reduce both banking rents and entry to the banking industry. Boot and Thakor believe the distinctions between banks and financial markets are likely to become increasingly blurred, but the perspective of this chapter suggests that there will continue to be differences between different types of financial deals, and therefore, different kinds of governance mechanisms will continue to be needed for their administration.[32]

In the aggregate, the organization of a financial system reflects a mix of alignments among the types of deals agreed upon and the capabilities of the economy's financiers. The size of an individual firm is determined by its operating economics. In addition, there is a natural evolution of any particular deal type from the right to the left in Table 7.1 that is due to financier learning, increasing volume of deals, standardization of deals over time, and more nearly precise and cheaper information production. At the same time, a continual infusion of new financial deals means that high capability governance continues to be needed, even in advanced economies. The proportions of deals governed as market arrangements may change relative to the proportions governed by intermediaries or internally, but all three types of governance will continue to be needed.

## 7.3.2 Financial Firms

*Financial firms* assemble agreed financial deals into portfolios whose size and composition are determined by the firms' operating economics. Financiers specialize in particular types of deals as a means of realizing scale economies in both screening and information production. They realize additional scale economies by increasing the numbers of financial deals in their portfolios, and scope economies by taking on related types of financial deals. In other words, these actions reduce unit costs and, if unit revenue remains the same, profitability is improved.

Limits to the size of a financial firm depend mainly on the costs of coordinating the governance of different types of financial deals. When coordination costs begin to rise on a unit basis, taking on more business generating the same unit revenue means that the profitability of additional business begins to fall. When incremental profitability falls to zero, it is uneconomic for a financial firm to take on still further business: Firms can be expected to grow only until coordination costs become large enough to impair the profitability of taking on more financial deals.

There are several economic reasons for specializing. First, specialized skills and experience may be required in order to be able to do financial deals profitably, and only a few intermediaries can justify incurring these expenses. For example, some banks specialize in foreign exchange transactions involving their home currencies, while other banks trade in most major foreign currencies. Second, certain types of

---

[32] See Neave (2009).

financial deals can only be done in relatively small volumes, so that only a few firms can profitably service that market. Venture capital investments offer a case in point. Third, regulation may restrict intermediaries to only certain types of transactions.

On the other hand, there can also be advantages to diversification. When a firm assumes a greater number of financial deals, as well as when it assumes additional types of financial deals, it can usually diversify portfolio risks.[33] Since diversifying portfolio risk reduces earnings risk relative to the expected level of earnings, the firm's performance is thereby improved.

### 7.3.3 Combinations of Mechanisms

There are many instances of governance mechanisms being combined. For example, an intermediary can partially diversify its asset portfolio by issuing securities backed by some of its loans (securitization) and using the proceeds to purchase other unrelated securities. Usually, intermediaries use the funds raised from securitization to fund more of the same type of lending. Nevertheless, some potential for unbundling remains: A bank may have a competitive advantage in screening and monitoring, but an insurance company or mutual fund may have a competitive advantage in raising funds for investment purposes.

Banks can complement the workings of the securities markets in other ways as well. For example, certifying the creditworthiness of borrowing customers makes it easier for those borrowing customers to avail themselves of additional capital market financing.[34] Banks also assist their customers to obtain less costly capital market financing by providing guarantees, particularly in circumstances where a bank might have a competitive advantage in determining a client's creditworthiness.

Intermediaries also provide services that are not reflected on their balance sheets. Traditionally off-balance sheet activities included providing letters of credit, and now include such other activities as arranging risk management services using derivative instruments. In some risk management transactions, corporations can use exchange-traded instruments, but in others they deal with intermediaries that trade the instruments on an over-the-counter basis. The difference in the types of transactions depends on whether it is securities markets or intermediaries that offer a competitive advantage; this in turn depends on the type of instrument, its complexities, and the creditworthiness of the parties involved.

---

### ● ● ● KEY POINTS

- The functions performed by every financial system include clearing and settling payments, pooling resources, transferring resources, managing risks, producing information, and managing incentives.

---

[33] Diversification is only effective if the different deals are not perfectly positively correlated. This topic is examined in Chapter 13.

[34] See Fama (1985).

- Some financial system functions—pooling resources, transferring resources, and managing risks—require special attention because they involve either the commitment of financial resources over relatively long periods of time, significant transfers of risks, or both.

- If financial deals are to work out profitably, they need to be governed appropriately, and the most effective financial system governance mechanisms depend on both the capabilities of the accommodating financier and the attributes of the financial deals themselves.

- The mechanisms for governing financial deals are variations of financial market, financial intermediary, and internal arrangements.

- Financial market governance works best when a financial deal's essential attributes can be captured by the funding cost it bears and within this category of governance distinctions can be made on the basis of differences in the capabilities of market agents.

- Financial intermediaries are enterprises that raise funds from savers and relend the funds to business and personal borrowing customers.

- Financial intermediaries exercise certain kinds of governance capabilities that are not customarily utilized by market agents (more intensive *ex ante* screening capabilities of borrower and more extensive capabilities for monitoring, control and subsequent adjustment of financial deal terms) producing cost-effective ways for governing the financial deals they enter.

- Internal governance (also referred to as hierarchical governance) involves financial resource allocation using command and control capabilities to a still greater extent than that used by financial intermediaries, offering the greatest potential for intensive *ex ante* screening, *ex post* monitoring, control over operations, and adjustment of financial deal terms.

- The focus of internal governance is more on the command and control mechanisms that can be employed to effect *ex post* adjustment of financing terms than on the nature of a financial contract itself.

- Internal governance is likely to be more expensive than governance by financial market or financial intermediaries, and as a consequence will normally be used to govern financial deals whose uncertainties are greater than those acceptable to financial intermediaries.

- Financial deals can be described as different combinations of the basic attributes: asset liquidity, risks, information asymmetries, and complete contracting.

- Once an alignment of financial deal attributes and governance capabilities has been reached, the actual tasks of governance typically involve developing transaction information and managing incentives. However, these tasks receive different emphases according to the financial deal's attributes.

- Financial system organization is influenced by the economics of performing basic functions, by the economics of governing deals, and by the operating economics of the institutions that group financial deals together.

- Both the functional and the governance approaches contend that financial deals of particular types are governed as cost-effectively as possible, subject to the limitations imposed by current financial technology.

- Financial firms with particular governance capabilities usually specialize in financial deals with particular attributes, because that is how the firms can utilize their resources most effectively. The sizes of financial firms are determined by their cost and profitability characteristics.
- Financiers have sharply varying capabilities for funding projects that are backed by uncertain earnings, illiquid assets, or both.

## QUESTIONS

1. What are the components of a financial system?

2. Explain each of the major financing mechanisms found in financial systems.

3. What is meant by risky financial deals?

4. What is meant by financial governance within the financial system?

5. Explain why market governance works best when the essential attributes of a financial deal are incorporated into the funding cost associated with the risk borne by investors.

6. The following excerpts are taken from Reinhard H. Schmidt and Aneta Hryckiewicz, "Financial Systems—Importance, Differences and Convergence," Working Paper Series No. 4 (2006), Institute for Monetary and Financial Stability:

   In most economies, many financial decisions and relationships of the households and the firms involve banks, capital markets, insurance companies and similar institutions in some way. In their totality, those institutions that specialize in providing financial services constitute the financial sector of the economy. Of course, the financial sector is a very important part of almost any financial system. But it should not be taken for the entire financial system. Only some 15 years ago, there were some parts of the so-called developing world and some formerly socialist countries in which almost no financial institutions existed or operated, and still people saved, invested, borrowed and dealt with risks in these countries and regions. Thus there can in principle even be financial systems almost without a financial sector. But also in advanced economies, many financial decisions and activities completely bypass the financial sector. Examples are real saving, self-financing and self-insurance and informal and direct lending and borrowing relationships.

   a. Explain how "real saving, self-financing and self-insurance and informal and direct lending and borrowing relationships" are examples of bypassing the financial sector.

      Most theoretical models presented in the literature focus either on banks or financial markets, and they emphasize either the function of fostering capital accumulation or that of promoting innovation and increasing the productivity of the use of capital.

**b.** Explain the two functions in the preceding quote.

> Some contributions point out that banks can have some positive effects or perform certain functions very well, while markets are good at performing other functions well. As an example, banks seem to be particularly good at creating and using private information. On the other hand markets seem particularly well suited to aggregating diverse pieces of public information.

**c.** Explain why banks and markets perform their respective functions well.

> The statistical data and the descriptions of national financial systems . . . show two trends that seem rather contradictory. One is that in almost all financial systems the values taken on by those financial sector indicators that represent the role of capital markets increase over time. This suggests a tendency of a general convergence towards the Anglo-Saxon model of a capital market–based financial system, although this is no conclusive evidence since systems are more than collections of individual elements. The other trend is that in many countries the characteristics remain largely intact. As the descriptions show, the German financial system still seems to be bank-dominated, and the Anglo-Saxon countries USA and UK still have capital market–dominated financial systems.

**d.** What is meant by a "capital market–based financial system" and "bank-dominated" financial system?

7. The following excerpts are from Section 802 of the U.S. *Payment, Clearing, and Settlement Supervision Act of 2009*:

   **(1)** The proper functioning of the financial markets is dependent upon safe and efficient arrangements for the clearing and settlement of payment, securities and other financial transactions.

   **(2)** Financial market utilities that conduct or support multilateral payment, clearing, or settlement activities may reduce risks for their participants and the broader financial system, but such utilities may also concentrate and create new risks and thus must be well designed and operated in a safe and sound manner.

   **(3)** Payment, clearing and settlement activities conducted by financial institutions also present important risks to the participating financial institutions and to the financial system.

   **(4)** Enhancements to the regulation and supervision of systemically important financial market utilities and the conduct of systemically important payment, clearing, and settlement activities by financial institutions are necessary to provide consistency, to promote robust risk management and safety and soundness, to reduce systemic risks, and to support the stability of the broader financial system.

a. What is meant by "payment, clearing, and settlement"?

b. Explain what is meant by Point 2 above.

c. Explain what is meant by Point 3 above.

d. Explain what is meant by Point 4 above.

8. At a conference ("Perspectives on Managing Risk for Growth and Development") held at the University of the West Indies on March 4, 2010, the following comments were made by Brian Wynter, a governor of the Bank of Jamaica:

> Let me begin by emphasizing the critical importance of good risk management for the each firm, its industry and the economy as a whole and say that an efficient risk management system is one of the key ingredients for increasing the productivity of investment in Jamaica. Financial markets promote economic growth by channeling capital to the entrepreneurs with high-return projects. A robust and stable financial system capable of directing capital to its most efficient use is therefore a necessary condition for economic growth. The efficient allocation of capital underlies economic efficiency, international competitiveness, and economic stability. The level of efficiency of capital allocation derives in part from sound risk management.
>
> As a financial system supervisor, the Bank of Jamaica is committed to facilitating sound risk management in the financial system. Our responsibilities are discharged by focusing on both firm-specific and system-wide elements, both of which support overall macroeconomic stability and growth.
>
> From the perspective of the central bank, therefore, the early identification and measurement of risk, the development and enforcement of sound liquidity risk management practices, good corporate governance and risk control are the critical components of sound risk management.
>
> . . .
>
> Generally, financial intermediaries play a vital role in facilitating growth and economic development by pooling household savings and channeling them to the real sector. They also economize on information costs associated with the monitoring of investment risk and minimize uncertainty about rates of return. Indeed, countries with financial intermediaries which are better at acquiring information and more adept at implementing and enforcing corporate governance principles in order to increase investor participation as well as manage risk typically grow faster than countries with less developed financial systems. Jamaica's financial intermediaries can therefore increase the efficiency of investments and improve the potential for growth by improving their risk management capabilities.

a. What does Governor Wynter mean by "Financial markets promote economic growth by channeling capital to the entrepreneurs with high-return projects"?

b. How do "financial intermediaries play a vital role in facilitating growth and economic development by pooling household savings and channeling them to the real sector"?

  **c.** How do financial intermediaries "economize on information costs associated with the monitoring of investment risk and minimize uncertainty about rates of return"?

  **d.** Why are "countries with financial intermediaries which are better at acquiring information and more adept at implementing and enforcing corporate governance principles in order to increase investor participation as well as manage risk typically grow faster than countries with less developed financial systems"?

**9. a.** What is meant by informational asymmetries?

  **b.** What adverse consequences to a financial system are created by informational asymmetries?

**10. a.** What is meant by complete contracting in a financial deal?

  **b.** What is meant by incomplete contracting in a financial deal?

  **c.** Why are financial deals under uncertainty usually characterized by incomplete contracting?

**11. a.** What is meant by alignment of parties to a financial deal?

  **b.** What are the special capabilities needed to cost-effectively govern financial deals?

**12.** What is volatility information used for by participants in financial markets?

**13.** What type of information is produced by financial intermediaries but is not made available to the public?

**14.** The financing costs that clients face, and the governance costs that financiers incur, are determined as a result of the interplay between clients and financiers. Explain why.

**15.** Why is market governance generally less expensive than hierarchical governance?

**16.** How does decreasing asset liquidity make financial deals more costly to govern?

**17.** Explain why scale economies and scope economies are key determinants of the financial deals that a financial firm takes on.

---

# REFERENCES

Aghion, Philippe, and Patrick Bolton. (1992). "An Incomplete Contracts Approach To Financial Contracting," *Review of Economic Studies* **59**: 473–494.

Akerlof, George A. (1970). "The Market For 'Lemons': Quality Uncertainty and The Market Mechanism," *Quarterly Journal of Economics* **84**: 488–500.

Allen, Franklin D., and Douglas Gale. (2000). *Comparing Financial Systems*. Cambridge: MIT Press.

Arrow, Kenneth J. (1974). *Essays in the Theory of Risk-Bearing*. Amsterdam: North-Holland.

Boot, Arnoud, and Anjan Thakor. (1993). "Security Design," *Journal of Finance* **48**: 1349–1378.

Carey, Mark, Mitch Post, and Steven A. Sharpe. (1998). "Does Corporate Lending By Banks and Finance Companies Differ? Evidence on Specialization in Private Debt Contracting," *Journal of Finance* **53**: 845–878.

Crane, Dwight B., Kenneth A. Froot, Scott P. Mason, Andre E. Perold, Robert C. Merton, Zvi Bodie, Erik R. Sirri, and Peter Tufano. (1995). *The Global Financial System: A Functional Perspective*. Boston: Harvard Business School Press.

Fama, Eugene F. (1985). "What's Different about Banks?" *Journal of Monetary Economics* **15**: 29–39.

Jensen, Michael C., and William H. Meckling. (1976). "Theory of the Firm: Managerial Behavior, Agency Costs, and Ownership Structure," *Journal of Financial Economics* **3**: 305–360.

Neave, Edwin H. (2009). *Modern Financial Systems: Theory and Applications*. Hoboken, NJ: John Wiley & Sons.

Riordan, Michael, and Oliver E. Williamson. (1985). "Asset Specificity and Economic Organization," *International Journal of Industrial Organization* **3**: 365–378.

Ross, Stephen A. (1989). "Institutional Markets, Financial Marketing, and Financial Innovation," *Journal of Finance* **44**: 541–556.

Williamson, Oliver E. (1985). *The Economic Institutions of Capitalism*. New York: Free Press.

Williamson, Oliver E. (1987). "Transaction Cost Economics: The Comparative Contracting Perspective," *Journal of Economic Behavior and Organization* **8**: 617–627.

Williamson, Oliver E. (2002). "The Theory of the Firm as Governance Structure: From Choice to Contract," *Journal of Economic Perspectives* **16**: 171–197.

# 8

# Market, Intermediary, and Internal Governance

*A*s explained in the previous chapter, financial markets, financial intermediaries, and internal finance play complementary roles within the financial system. With respect to financial markets, performance is usually assessed in terms of market efficiency, market liquidity, and information production, and forms of marketplace organization are chosen in attempts to enhance these performance characteristics. Understanding the advantages and disadvantages of market governance is aided by examining the principal capabilities of different market types. For example, public versus private markets, primary versus secondary markets, dealer versus broker markets, and wholesale versus retail markets all display different combinations of capabilities, and as a result align cost-effectively with different classes of deals presenting particular attribute combinations. Under some circumstances, financial markets are the most cost-effective way of allocating financial resources, and these circumstances are examined in greater detail in this chapter.

Intermediary and internal capital allocations provide cost-effective governance in circumstances where market arrangements cannot fully incorporate the complexities of financial deal governance. Here are several reasons why this is so. First, financial intermediaries aggregate information differently than do market agents. Consequently, the aggregate liquidity demands of a group of clients, for example, can be important for some kinds of investment planning, but market agents are not always able to assemble this kind of information. Second, information about a financial deal can be asymmetrically distributed,[1] and deals exhibiting these attributes need continuing governance of a type not easily arranged in market transactions. Finally, in circumstances such as capital rationing, command, and control allocation through the

---

[1] Many of the discussions of perfect competition also assume no transactions costs, meaning that the market rate of interest will be charged on the deal, but that no other kinds of charges such as application fees or compensating balance requirements will be applied. Some of the results derived for perfect competition need not be heavily qualified in the presence of moderate transactions costs, and in any event asymmetrically distributed information is much more important for our present purposes.

internal capital markets of organizations such as financial conglomerates can prove more cost-effective than either market or intermediary allocations. This chapter discusses the principal circumstances in which financial intermediaries and internal capital allocations can provide more cost-effective governance than market agents.[2]

## 8.1 FINANCIAL MARKET GOVERNANCE

There are often many different specialized kinds of financial markets within financial systems, but financial markets can be distinguished analytically using just a few characteristics. These characteristics include:

- The cost and revenue functions of markets
- The economics of producing information about market-traded assets
- The economics of trading firms

Economics determines the operating and allocative efficiency of any given financial market, the type and number of market agents trading in it, the liquidity of the instruments traded in it, and the extent to which price information is revealed by trading. In this section, we examine the nature of governance in financial markets and consider how it is affected by market economics.

### 8.1.1 Functions of Financial Markets

The principal function of any financial market is to create a central location where buyers and sellers (or their agents) can meet to trade. In the past, markets were usually described by their physical locations, but as Internet access and electronic trading have increased in importance, markets are now frequently described in terms of their Internet addresses. Electronic access to markets continues to become more readily available and both market agents and investors are increasingly trading from their homes or offices. Hence, the physical location of the computers processing market trading information is less important than the kind of Internet access available to prospective traders.

Finding counterparties in a highly active marketplace is less time consuming and less costly than in a relatively inactive market. The more prominent the instruments traded in the market, the greater their liquidity, and the lower the market's trading costs, the greater trading volumes are likely to be. A market in which it is cheap and easy to find counterparties is also likely to be a market in which the assets exchanged are relatively liquid.

Two of the most prominent dimensions of marketplace activity are the volume and frequency of trading.[3] Some of the larger public stock markets transact at least some shares in large volumes (thousands of shares) on an almost minute-by-minute basis, while some other markets handle only relatively small transactions,

---

[2] For a more detailed discussion of the topics covered in this chapter, see Neave (2009).
[3] As will be explained later, these two dimensions are closely related to market liquidity.

and infrequently at that. The types of instruments traded constitute another dimension. Markets trade instruments such as bonds and equities that are initially sold (i.e., floated) to raise capital, as well as other instruments such as derivatives whose principal function is to exchange risks. Some market instruments are highly liquid, others relatively illiquid. Markets also differ in the degree to which agents doing financial deals either have or will be able to acquire the same information about the values of the instruments they are trading.

The organizers of a financial market strive to enhance its profitability by increasing the market's trading volume. To attract greater volumes of business, market organizers work to reduce unit trading costs through standardizing the instruments traded, through processing trades efficiently, through executing trades quickly and as near to ruling market prices as possible. The charges market organizers collect take the forms of trading commissions, bid-ask spreads (i.e., the difference between the price at which they are willing to pay for an instrument and sell that same instrument),[4] or both.

A financial market's total operating costs usually have a fixed component so that unit trading costs fall as trading volume increases. These scale economics to market operations mean that larger and more active markets can typically offer lower trading costs than their smaller, less active counterparts. Although in the past many markets have specialized, say in either securities or derivatives, contemporary mergers of different types of markets as well as mergers of markets in different jurisdictions both suggest the presence of scope economies to trading many different types of instruments on the same facility. Thus, established markets strive both to attract large volumes of trades in individual instruments, and to expand the number of instruments in which they deal.

Historically, financial markets have been organized as associations of traders who share market revenues and costs, usually in proportion to the amounts of business done. The goals of marketplaces organized in this way have not always been easy to specify, and in some case have been subject to considerable debate. During the first decade of the 2000s, many of the larger stock and derivatives markets were reorganized as for-profit businesses that were accountable to their shareholders. A profit-oriented marketplace has clearly defined goals and can use profitability criteria to determine whether it should specialize or combine different forms of trading, the amount and kinds of technology it should acquire, and other operating issues.

Financial markets are much less likely to be organized for instruments that trade in small volumes, or for deals that require individual attention.[5] On a per unit basis, trade in small volumes is more costly, and infrequent trading is most likely to be completed on a negotiated rather than a standardized basis. In addition, some types of transactions cannot be completed at all. This phenomenon, known as *market failure*, can occur when the demand for trading an instrument is not sufficiently large to induce market agents to take a position in it.

---

[4] That is, by purchasing instruments at lower prices than they are currently selling them.

[5] Markets for these kinds of trades may be less costly to organize using the Internet, but in some cases even Internet trading may not prove profitable. The auction services provided by eBay offer one example of how such markets can successfully be set up.

Technological change offers potentials for cost reduction that can both stimulate the creation of new markets and enhance access to existing markets. The rapid growth of electronic trading, including Internet trading, means that electronic marketplaces can and do now provide strong competition for organized exchanges. Parties who assemble bid and ask information from potential buyers and sellers can sometimes complete exchanges quickly at or near market prices, even if the computer network on which they trade has no established dealers[6] in the instrument.

## 8.1.2 Descriptive and Economic Characteristics

The discussion that follows relates descriptive market classifications to the principal underlying economics of marketplace operations.

### 8.1.2.1 Public versus Private Markets

The term *public market* refers to any member of a class of securities markets in which issues are both initially sold to and subsequently traded by the public at large. Information about the nature of public market securities is usually widely and relatively evenly distributed, and regulations are usually in place to ensure that agents potentially have access to new or evolving information. The New York Stock Exchange, the London Stock Exchange, and the NASDAQ are examples of public markets.

The term *private market* refers to any member of a class of markets in which instruments are traded among a small number of parties on a negotiated basis. Information about private market transactions is usually less widely distributed than it is for public market transactions. A negotiated sale of company debt to an insurance company that buys the whole issue is an example of a private market transaction.

Holding aside regulatory requirements that must be satisfied by the issuer,[7] public and private markets differ mainly in the types of screening that market agents use and in information distribution among participants. Assessing the underwriting risks of a public market issue usually involves determining whether a sufficient number of securities purchasers can be attracted to the new issue, and setting a price at which they are likely to be attracted. For example, if a bond issuer is widely known to a large prospective group of purchasers, it is quite likely that a public issue will prove successful in raising the needed funds at or near market rates of interest.

In contrast, the underwriter of a private market issue needs to find particular clients who will be willing to buy and hold the securities. Thus, private issues can require more lengthy negotiations than their public market counterparts, but the small number of purchasers will also permit more intensive screening. For example,

---

[6] Markets like the NASDAQ have market-makers who act as both dealers and brokers. Dealers take positions in instruments, while brokers arrange transactions between counterparties. The economic differences of these functions are discussed in the market agents section in this chapter.

[7] In the United States, the Securities Act of 1933 and the Securities Exchange Act of 1934 require all securities offered to the general public be registered with the SEC unless given a specific exemption. Section 4(2) of the 1933 Act exempts from registration "transactions by an issuer not involving a public offering." In such offerings, referred to as private offerings or private placements, the issuer must still furnish information deemed by the SEC to material in a private placement memorandum as opposed to the more detailed information disclosure in prospectus filing for a public offering.

a less-well-known firm will be more likely to use a private rather than a public issue because the deal can be examined in detail by one or a few prospective buyers. Moreover, if the trade is between sophisticated parties, regulations do not usually require public disclosure of the information necessary to assess the trade.

### 8.1.2.2 *Primary versus Secondary Markets*

*Primary market* transactions involve selling new issues of securities. Primary public market issues of securities are sold to large numbers of purchasers who have potentially equal access to public information regarding an issuing firm. In order both to comply with disclosure regulations and to attract investors, underwriters usually distribute information about new public issues as widely as possible.

Primary private market issues, in contrast, are sold to a smaller number of possible investors. The information produced for analyzing and selling private issues is not usually required to be released to the public at large, because there is usually no need to inform a wide group of potential investors if the issue is to be sold to a relatively small number of sophisticated parties. Primary market agents are concerned mainly with raising new funds, and depend on an effective distribution network to do so successfully. Firms that can successfully capture the business of underwriting primary issues are also usually skilled at reselling the securities to investors.

Primary transactions are particularly important to financing new capital formation and hence for contributing to economic growth. If a domestic financial system does not finance certain kinds of financial deals, capital formation will be inhibited— unless the necessary funds can be raised offshore. If neither domestic nor foreign financing is available, the proposed capital formation will either be postponed until it can be financed from internal operations (i.e., retained earnings) or even abandoned. In either case, economic growth is likely to be affected adversely.[8]

Trades in outstanding instruments are called *secondary transactions*. Most secondary market transactions involve rearrangements of outstanding securities or derivatives. Secondary transactions are used both to invest surplus funds and to raise cash, and are usually finalized in the stock markets, the bond markets, or the money markets. Instruments representing individual bank loans are not often resold in the marketplace, but securities issued against portfolios of individual loans are very often resold.[9]

Secondary transactions help evaluate new information about firms and other entities (such as municipal governments and sovereign governments) that issue publicly traded securities and also improve the liquidity of both secondary and primary securities issues. Secondary transactions evaluate new publicly distributed information by trading firms' securities at prices set to recognize the impact of the informational developments. They enhance primary market liquidity by making it easier to trade outstanding securities. Secondary market agents are concerned mainly with carrying out trades at or near existing market prices. Successful performance of

---

[8] See, for example, King and Levine (1993).

[9] Banks securitize a loan portfolio (or a part of one) by selling new securities that normally use the whole portfolio (or the relevant part), and not individual loans in it, as collateral.

these functions depends largely on the ability of market agents to find counterparties quickly and relatively cheaply, and to keep their trading costs as low as those of their competitors.

### 8.1.2.3 Dealer versus Broker Markets

Traders act as *dealers* by taking instruments into inventory, and as *brokers* when they arrange transactions between counterparties without taking a position themselves. The existence of dealers, and consequently the degree to which the market provides liquidity, depends in part on the inventory risk-trading reward ratio for a typical transaction. In other words, economic analysis explains both why and how brokers differ from dealers.

### 8.1.2.4 Wholesale versus Retail Markets

*Wholesale markets* can either be part of an exchange, as with the upstairs (institutional) market on the NYSE, or a separate market operated by institutions to conduct their own trading. Securities are usually traded in large volumes in these wholesale markets, and large-volume trades may not always take place at the prevailing market price, for at least two reasons. First, the counterparty to a large trade may be concerned about possible adverse selection. The buyer might, for example, ask why the seller is willing to dispose of a large number of securities. If the buyer does not know the reasons, he may only be willing to buy a large number at a discount from the prevailing market price. The second reason large trades can affect the price is that the demand curve for large amounts of a given security is usually thought to be downward-sloping rather than flat—that is, to exhibit a degree of price inelasticity that is in part attributable to difficulty that might be encountered in reselling that security. Analogously, the supply curve of a given security is usually thought to be upward-sloping rather than flat.

In contrast, *retail market* transactions are usually completed at or near the current market price (after allowing for agents' fees such as commissions and bid-ask spreads). Retail trades are not usually thought to be subject to a significant degree of adverse selection, partly because they occur much more frequently than wholesale trades, and the number of agents carrying out retail trades is usually large.

## 8.1.3 Types of Firms

The nature and size of firms acting as market agents are determined by their operating economics. Securities firms exhibit two dominant forms of organization: either large and multipurpose, or small and specialized. Large firms emerge because they can realize scale and scope economies through the activities they conduct. For example, large firms can realize scale economies in their sales activities, in their research functions, and in their data-processing and accounting activities. They can realize scope economies through combining such activities as underwriting on the one hand, arranging mergers and acquisitions on the other. Large firms can also obtain benefits from diversification. For example, by combining retail sales and wholesale activities, large firms may be able to improve the return-risk ratio of their earnings. Small, specialized firms are set up primarily to exploit niche markets, usually by assembling particular combinations of skills that are not possessed by larger firms.

In part, smaller firms may be able to provide more attractive incentives to their employees, and as a result operate a highly productive specialized business.

### 8.1.4 Market Efficiency

A perfectly competitive financial market is both allocatively and operationally efficient. Consider each in turn.

*Allocative efficiency* means that equally risky proposals can be funded at the same rate of return that has to be paid to providers of funds. If an allocatively efficient financial system is not in equilibrium, atypical funding cost differentials signal that profit opportunities are available. If atypical rate of return differentials emerge, they will be exploited by trading that continues until the differentials have been eliminated. Arbitrage opportunities are eliminated in perfectly competitive markets because, by assumption, there are no transactions costs or other impediments to arbitraging.

The *efficient market hypothesis* maintains that, when markets are perfectly competitive and trading is not impeded by transactions costs or institutional practices, the markets will be allocatively efficient in the sense that the equilibrium prices of securities fully reflect all publicly available information. The only real difference between instruments traded in allocatively efficient markets is in their risk-return characteristics: On average, securities with higher systematic risk command relatively higher rates of return than their less risky counterparts.

Market trading is most active, and consequently markets most nearly approach allocative efficiency when the terms of financial deal are standardized and when market agents have ready access to the same information. As explained in Chapter 16, the prices (or rates of return) on securities that are close substitutes are likely to be kept aligned through active trading. In such cases, the markets are said to be *linked by arbitrage*. Any persistent price differences between apparently close substitutes are attributable to a market consensus regarding differences in their risk or in the details of the instruments' terms. For example, if interest earned on some instruments receives different tax treatment than interest earned on other instruments of similar risk and maturity, there will be a price differential reflecting the value of the different tax treatment on interest earned.

Turning now to *operational efficiency*, a financial market is said to be operationally efficient if it performs financial services at the lowest possible cost, given existing technology and best practice. A perfectly competitive market is operationally efficient by definition, because the definition assumes that all financial deals can be completed without payment of transactions costs.[10] However, perfect competition is also operationally efficient in a deeper sense. Traders in perfectly competitive markets must recover their costs either from the trading commissions they charge or from the bid-ask spreads at which they trade. If a given trader's costs are higher than the costs incurred by the most efficient traders, either that trader's commissions will be higher or their bid-ask spreads greater than those of efficient traders. In these circumstances, the less efficient traders will have difficulty competing to attract business and are likely to be driven out of business.

---

[10] In such a market all deals have to pay, or earn, the ruling market interest rate appropriate for the deal's risk.

Under competition, any financial deal whose costs were above the minimum would also have to yield above-market returns in order to cover the higher costs. But, the only way to earn returns over and above their competitive levels is to buy securities at less than their market prices, and this is not possible in the presence of a competitive equilibrium. If a market agent does not have costs as low as other market agents, then a return less than a competitive return will be realized. But then unless a market agent can find ways of reducing costs to below competitive levels, the business will not survive. Similarly, if a firm cannot perform its financial services at the lowest possible cost, any securities it sells would have to be overpriced to cover the higher costs. But then nobody would buy the securities from such a firm. In order to survive, the firm would have to trim its costs back to the same levels as those of other firms.

The larger and more active secondary securities markets are usually regarded as allocatively efficient. They are capable of conducting both small or retail trades and large institutional trades at very nearly the same market prices. Since about 1960, financial institutions have accounted for increasingly larger proportions of securities trading, and from time to time observers have expressed concern as to whether the larger individual trades of institutions are compatible with retail trading in the same market. However, the most active securities markets can handle both institutional and retail trading without loss of allocative efficiency. For example, the trading of large institutions does not appear to influence stock price variability.[11]

Research suggests further that most developed countries have allocatively and operationally efficient markets in government securities, albeit to varying degrees in different economies and in markets for different governments' securities, even within the same economy. The public securities markets in many advanced economies exhibit a high degree of operating efficiency, partly because of scale economies to market operations.[12] Moreover, transactions costs are typically lower in national markets with greater volumes of activity, a finding that indirectly confirms smaller exchanges have higher unit operating costs.

## 8.1.5 Information Production

Securities firms develop research information both for their own trading purposes and for the use of their clients. If the cost of producing research information has a fixed component, information production is subject to scale economies. The more deals of the same type for which information is produced, the lower the unit cost of producing the information. At the same time, it may be possible to sell the information to more than one client, increasing the revenue obtained from its production.

Research information affects the market value of securities, but not all traded securities receive the same degree of research attention. The amount of research conducted, and the revenue that can be derived from selling the research results, both depend on the kinds of securities traded and the clientele who would likely use the information. Information regarding traded instruments is only produced if its value in use at least equals its cost. Value will be greater than cost in markets where securities information has a degree of heterogeneity and a number of market agents will benefit

---

[11] See Gemmill (1996).
[12] See Tinic and West (1974).

from reducing the heterogeneity.[13] On the other hand, the value of producing some information may not equal its cost, either because the cost is relatively high or the information cannot be used to produce much revenue.

The most homogeneous instruments are traded in the money markets, while the most heterogeneous are found in such markets as the primary mortgage markets. In the money markets, high-quality debt instruments with a maturity of one year or less are traded. In this market, there is little uncertainty regarding the value of a particular instrument and additional research is unlikely to produce enough revenue to make its production profitable. In markets where there is little trading, information might have large potential value for a few purchasers, but with just a few sales it is not always possible to recover the cost of producing the information. Most economically worthwhile research in the public securities markets seems to be aimed at developing information about actively traded securities whose value is subject to some controversy.

## 8.1.6 Liquidity

For any given type of instrument, markets can differ substantially in their liquidity. Liquidity differences among markets depend on such factors as differences in market structure, in the nature of the instruments traded, and in the kinds of obligations those instruments represent. Most importantly, the economics of market making creates important differences in liquidity. In essence, *highly liquid markets* are markets in which there are competing dealers willing to take positions in the instruments traded. Dealers are likely to be present if they can generate a trading profit that is commensurate with the risk of taking an inventory position in the traded asset. For example, most economies have dealers in short-term government securities, but few if any economies have secondary market dealers in residential housing.

## 8.1.7 Funding Illiquid Asset Portfolios

Since the 1970s financial intermediaries have been active in funding illiquid asset portfolios using a mechanism known as *asset securitization*.[14] As practiced by intermediaries, asset securitization involves selling new securities representing claims against[15] a portfolio of specialized and usually illiquid loans. The typical buyers of the new securities are financial institutions, such as pension funds, mutual funds, and insurance companies with a need for specialized investments. Asset securitization releases funds that would otherwise be tied up in illiquid assets, permitting intermediaries such as banks to continue lending rapidly even if traditional forms of

---

[13] Allen and Gale (2000) argue that securities markets are good at reconciling diverse forms of information, while intermediaries can be better at producing information that is less diverse.

[14] There are actually two practices referred to as asset securitization. The first refers to the corporate practice of raising funds in financial markets rather than borrowing from banks; the second refers to intermediaries' practice of funding asset portfolios through selling securities to financial institutions.

[15] The practice of selling claims against illiquid assets is much more common than the actual sale of the loans themselves. When claims against the illiquid assets are sold, the default risk on the original loans usually, but not always, continues to be borne by the intermediary originally making the loans.

deposit growth have tailed off. Asset securitization provides not only a funding source for banks, but also a form of risk management as illiquid loans are removed from the balance sheet of the issuing banks. That is, the credit risk and market risk of the loans that are included in a securitization are legally sold by issuing banks such that, with the exception of a small portion, the bulk of the risk is transferred to the buyer of the debt instruments created from the securitization.

During the 2000s, securitization has increasingly been used in new and more complex ways. For example, the large international investment banks have become financial-liquidity factories, turning loans into tradable securities, selling the loans on and profiting from the transactions. Some of the fastest growth has been in funding traditional portfolios such as commercial and residential mortgages and business and consumer using products such as mortgage-backed securities, asset-backed securities, and collateralized debt obligations. More generally, these vehicles are referred to as *credit risk transfer instruments*.

The newer forms of financial innovation reallocate risks between investment banks and their clients. The practices can make the banks more diversified as they search for unrelated portfolios that have little correlation, such as credit instruments and government bonds. However, the new instruments create problems as well as opportunities. Bank portfolios have always been opaque, and with the new instruments it has become even more difficult for investors and analysts to understand the nature of the portfolios. As a result, banks face greater incentives to take excessive risks in their activities, risks such as those leading to the subprime mortgage and credit crisis that began in the summer of 2007.

## 8.2 NON-MARKET GOVERNANCE: FINANCIAL INTERMEDIARIES

In practice financial markets offer competitive advantage for some types of financial deals, while financial intermediaries can do so for others. Nevertheless, it is useful to begin by outlining theoretical circumstances in which the latter offer no advantage, as it is then easier to identify circumstances in which they do. This chapter begins by examining the major types of intermediaries in a financial system, and offers theoretical explanations for the different types. It then considers in greater detail some of the advantages offered by financial intermediaries such as providing liquidity insurance, and reducing transactions costs.

### 8.2.1 When and Why Financial Intermediaries Cannot Create Value

Financial governance is comparatively simple under the assumptions of the *neoclassical paradigm*. Analysis using the neoclassical paradigm usually begins by assuming that markets are perfectly competitive, that all transaction information is homogeneously distributed, and that transacting is costless. The numerous agents in a perfectly competitive market strive to maximize their profits by trading on the basis of their common information. According to the Efficient Markets Hypothesis outlined earlier in this chapter, market agents establish equilibrium securities prices that, through trading, fully reflect all publicly available information.

In an efficient market equilibrium, funds are supplied at the market rate of return commensurate with a given financial deal's risk, and clients can only obtain funds by agreeing to pay that market rate of return. Moreover, only the most cost-effective forms of governance can remain viable at equilibrium, and hence, each type of financial deal must be governed by those comparatively efficient methods. No financier's governance costs can be persistently greater than those of the most efficient competitor, because inefficient financiers will be driven out of the market by competition.

If all financial deals are of the same type, intermediaries cannot create value by doing things differently than market agents. One of the theories implying this no-value-creation result is the Capital Asset Pricing Model (CAPM) that we describe more fully in Chapter 14. The CAPM assumes a perfectly competitive market in which financial deals differ only in terms of their risk. The CAPM assumes further that all investors have the same information about the risks, and that the risks can be measured using the variance of portfolio return. Usually, the CAPM also assumes that a risk-free security can be purchased by any investor. Under these circumstances all investors will choose the same (best available) combination of risky securities, a combination referred to as the *market portfolio*. Investors with different attitudes toward risk combine the market portfolio and the risk-free security in differing proportions to reflect their individual preferences.

Under the assumptions of the CAPM, securities with different risks bear different equilibrium rates of return that reflect each security's contribution to the risk of the market portfolio. If two securities make the same contribution to the risk of the market portfolio, they bear the same equilibrium rate of return. The result means that all traders, individuals, and intermediaries face the same diversification possibilities and at the same costs. Since individuals are assumed to incur no transaction costs while doing so, financial intermediaries cannot create value because they can only perform services that investors could duplicate on their own.

Since the CAPM defines circumstances in which financial intermediaries offer no advantage over market transactions under idealized conditions, it becomes necessary to consider more complex circumstances in order to explain why intermediaries can create value. In the remainder of this chapter we will show there are several such sets of circumstances, including possibilities for providing nonmarket diversification, for reducing transactions costs, for taking positions in illiquid assets, and for performing certain kinds of information-processing activities.

## 8.2.2 When and Why Financial Intermediaries Can Create Value

In practice, different types of financial governance are employed because financial deals differ in several ways not recognized in developing theories such as the CAPM.[16] For example, some financial deals are consummated when different information is available

---

[16] For certain purposes the descriptions of reality conveyed by the CAPM may be perfectly adequate. But those descriptions do not fulfill our present purpose of explaining how a financial system with intermediaries and internal capital markets can arise.

to interested parties. Governing such financial deals in a cost-effective manner requires the use of screening and monitoring techniques different from those used by parties who all have the same information. Moreover, as explained earlier in this chapter when we covered financial market governance, different governance techniques employ different combinations of resources, and the techniques therefore have different costs. In other words when the full complexities of financial arrangements are recognized, financial markets, financial intermediaries and internal financing can be viewed as offering complementary forms of finance governance.[17]

One of the most common ways that financial intermediaries create value is through using forms of non-arm's length transactions.[18] In performing these governance functions, intermediaries produce different kinds of information than financial market agents, largely because of their capabilities for intensively screening individual deal applications *ex ante*, and because of their capabilities for continued monitoring *ex post*. Financial intermediaries can also realize cost savings on some types of financial deals, in particular scale economies in portfolio administration.

In addition, by transacting with groups of clients, intermediaries can coordinate liquidity services differently than can market agents. First, financial intermediaries can usually issue liquid claims in amounts greater than the liquid assets they need to redeem those claims, because not all clients wish to redeem their funds invested with financial intermediaries (such as deposits in banks) at the same time. As a result, financial intermediaries can use some of their funds (usually most of them) to finance illiquid loans. This role played by a financial intermediary is called *maturity intermediation*. The benefit of maturity intermediation is that those providing funds to financial intermediaries have more choices with respect to the maturity for the financial deals in which they invest and fund-seeking entities have more alternatives for the maturity of their financial arrangement. Second, financial intermediaries can create additional value through producing information that is largely a by-product of their governance activities.

### 8.2.3 Successful Financial Intermediaries

While there are a relatively large variety of financial intermediaries, here it suffices to mention the major types and their principal distinguishing characteristics. For this purpose, we shall discuss insurance companies, banks, and venture capital firms.

*Insurance companies* collect premiums from purchasers of insurance policies, and invest the collected funds in asset portfolios whose value is intended to cover their liabilities plus generate a spread (income). Insurance companies provide financial deals that transfer risk when they sell pure insurance products but they also have investment-oriented products. Much of the work done by insurance companies involves the ways they invest assets to fund their long-term liabilities and the analysis of the risks associated with the insurance products they sell (i.e., analysis of underwriting risks).

---

[17] Most of the complementarities examined in this chapter are static in nature and coexist on a continuing basis. The first treatments of functional analysis only recognized dynamic complementarities.

[18] Similarly, conglomerates create value by governing financial allocations even more intensively than intermediaries.

*Banks* principally collect deposits from individual clients, gather these deposits together, and lend them to business and households. The liabilities of banks are relatively liquid, while their loan portfolios are for the most part illiquid. Thus, banks are relatively short-term borrowers and longer-term lenders. Much of the work done by banks consists of screening loan applications and subsequently, governing the loans on their books. Beginning in the 1970s, the asset management tasks of banks shifted as they learned to securitize their loan portfolios and to sell off some of their assets through securitization. In addition, they have learned to sell off some of their default risks through a special type of instrument called a credit derivative.

*Venture capital firms* principally acquire long-term high-risk investments in new or growing ventures, and fund their investments through equity issues. Even less liquid than banks, venture capital firms principally recover their investments by taking their client companies public. Conglomerate operations take the close supervision of investments even further as they conduct them within the framework of a given organization.

The above very brief sketch of financial intermediary types demonstrates that all intermediaries face asset-liability management challenges, and that the nature of the challenges varies considerably from one type of specialized business to another. Even in today's world of financial mergers, firms continue to specialize largely because the challenges of running many different kinds of combined businesses can prove more complex than the firms' managements find it profitable to meet.[19]

Bond (2005) examines financial conglomerates, banks, and trade credit arrangements as three different instances of financial intermediation. In the language we have adopted in this and the previous chapter, Bond analyzes discriminating alignments of project attributes with financier capabilities. To Bond, financial intermediaries differ in the types of projects they fund, the types of claims they issue to investors, and the costs of transmitting information between parties to the arrangement. Furthermore, he emphasizes a link between the fate of a project's financing and the possibility that the financial intermediary itself can run into financial trouble.

Bond describes how different types of intermediaries emerge from the kinds of asset and liability portfolios they hold and the costs of information sharing.[20] One class of intermediaries, financial conglomerates, finances high-risk/low-quality projects and raises funds through offering investors high-risk securities. Investors attempt to guard their interests in a conglomerate through risk sharing: Borrowers from the conglomerate partially absorb each others' losses. In essence, this risk sharing among borrowers will permit the conglomerate to better manage some of the moral hazard and adverse selection problems that might otherwise arise.

Banks and near banks form a second class of financial intermediaries. These operations fund low-risk/high-quality projects. Banks issue low-risk liabilities and

---

[19] As one example, Citigroup was formed to combine the banking business of Citibank with the insurance businesses of Travelers Insurance. The principal arguments favoring the merger focused on the ability to conduct international business and to realize scale economies. Since the merger took place in 1997, the combined company has sold off, in separate transactions, two types of its insurance business.

[20] Bond implements the costs of information sharing by assuming an agent's output is private information unless a verification cost is incurred to disclose it to another agent.

borrowers from banks do not gain from absorbing each others' risks. Rather, it is efficient for bank investors to absorb project financing losses. If low-risk financial intermediaries are funded by many depositors, it will be economic for the intermediaries to specialize in information processing.

## 8.2.4 Information Sharing

Financial intermediaries can also create value by managing the effects of informational asymmetries. An *ex ante* asymmetry exists when management of the entity seeking funds knows more than the lender about the probability distribution of future returns from a project. An *ex post* asymmetry arises when a lender or investor is unable to observe management's choice of investment project or the effort expended in attempting to make the project a success. As explained in the previous chapter, the impacts created by asymmetries include both adverse selection, an aggregate phenomenon, and moral hazard, a difficulty that can affect individual deals. It may be possible to resolve an asymmetry—sometimes partially, sometimes wholly—by screening.[21] Here we examine managing the aggregate effects of adverse selection.

### 8.2.4.1 *Informational Asymmetries and Adverse Selection*

Adverse selection involves relations between a financier and a group of clients whose quality is indistinguishable to the financier. It can affect a financier's profitability by discouraging the best credit risks, while at the same time attracting lower-quality ones. For example, suppose financiers announce a set of terms on which they will deal with potentially indistinguishable clients whose proposals represent a range of different risks. If the terms are unattractive to the lowest risks in the client pool, those clients will turn to other financing sources and the average risk of the pool of clients who continue to be attracted to the terms offered by the financial intermediary will increase.[22]

A financial intermediary can sometimes mitigate the impact of adverse selection by creating incentives for clients truthfully to signal their otherwise undistinguishable qualities. It is convenient to illustrate the issues with a model from Freixas and Rochet[23] (1997). Suppose risk-averse entrepreneurs would prefer to obtain outside financing rather than use their own resources to fund a risky project. However, they will not do so at any cost: Rather, they will only use outside financing if they can obtain it on sufficiently favorable terms. Suppose that different entrepreneurs seek financing for projects that have different means, but that all have the same variance. Suppose also that entrepreneurs value projects using the following preference function:

$$\mu = \theta - \rho\sigma^2/2 \tag{8.1}$$

---

[21] A profit-maximizing lender will incur screening costs only if they produce at least commensurate improvements to the profitability of the deal.

[22] The adverse selection effect could be exacerbated if the announced terms attracted more high-risk clients to the pool.

[23] One of the classic signaling models is due to Leland and Pyle (1977).

where $\theta$ is the project mean, $\sigma^2$ its variance, and $\rho > 0$ is a coefficient reflecting the entrepreneur's attitude toward risk.[24] When considering whether or not to self-finance, the entrepreneur determines whether he would be better off retaining his shares or selling them to financiers. Equation (8.1) implies that a project with mean $\theta$ and risk $\sigma^2$ is the same as a project with mean $\theta - \rho\sigma^2/2$ and zero risk. So, equation (8.1) is the certainty equivalent value[25] of the firm to the entrepreneur.

Suppose that interest rates are zero, and that risk-neutral financiers (such as a venture capital firm) can set the price $S_0^*$ at which they will buy a firm's shares. The assumptions imply that projects are valued at the financiers' estimate of project means—a quantity denoted $E(\theta)$—and the price of securities is set accordingly. That is,

$$S_0^* = E(\theta)$$

Because financiers cannot distinguish good firms from bad ones, they will offer $S_0^*$ to all firms.

If $S_0^*$ were an equilibrium price at which all firms sold their shares, financiers purchasing the shares for $S_0^*$ would earn an expected return of zero (equal to the assumed interest rate). But $S_0^*$ is not an equilibrium price, because the reasoning to this point has not recognized the effects of adverse selection. The entrepreneur will choose the better of two deals—the price $S_0^*$ or the certainty equivalent value of the firm:

$$\theta - \rho\sigma^2/2$$

whichever is greater. That is, the entrepreneur will only sell his shares to the financiers if:

$$S_0^* \geq \theta - \rho\sigma^2/2 \tag{8.2}$$

Inequality equation (8.2) implies that only the entrepreneurs of lower-quality firms will offer their shares for sale. Let $\theta_0^*$ be the value for which equation (8.2) holds with equality. Then entrepreneurs of firms with expected return $\theta \leq \theta_0^*$ will sell their shares to financiers but other entrepreneurs of higher-quality firms will regard $S_0^*$ as too low and will choose not to sell. In other words, the financiers offer a form of insurance against downside risk, but entrepreneurs of high-quality firms regard the insurance as too costly to be worth purchasing.

Understanding these reactions, financiers will set their offer price $S_0^{**}$ at:

$$S_0^{**} = E[\theta | \theta \leq \theta_0^*] \tag{8.3}$$

where $\theta_0^*$ is the value for which equation (8.2) holds with equality when the left-hand side of equation (8.2) is equal to $S_0^{**}$. This is the meaning of adverse selection: Since the price defined by equation (8.3) will discourage some firms (those with values

---

[24] One frequently used set of assumptions leading to this valuation is that the random prospect is normally distributed and that the investor has a negative exponential utility function.

[25] The concept of certainty equivalent value is explained in Chapter 11.

of $\theta \geq \theta_0^*$), $S_0^{**}$ as defined by the conditional expectation in equation (8.3) takes this into account. Nevertheless, $S_0^{**}$ is an equilibrium price since it ensures the financiers will earn their required expected profits (of zero) and since the financiers are assumed to be able to act as price setters.

### 8.2.4.2 Signalling

The effects of adverse selection can be mitigated if potential clients can credibly signal their quality. Suppose there are only two types of firms, high and low quality, indicated by $H$ and $L$, respectively. Let the firms' mean returns be indicated by $\theta_H$ and $\theta_L$. Assume that $H$ firms signal their quality by retaining a proportion $\alpha$ of the shares while selling off the remaining $(1 - \alpha)$. Assume further that $L$ firms signal their low quality by selling all of their shares. In order for both signals to be credible, $L$ firms must not be able to benefit by misrepresenting themselves as $H$ firms. Therefore, the price received by $L$ firms that retain no shares must be a price $S_L = \theta_L$ such that:

$$\theta_L \geq (1 - \alpha)\theta_H + \alpha\theta_L - \rho\sigma^2\alpha^2/2 \qquad (8.4)$$

where the utility of wealth function takes the same form as in equation (8.1). Inequality equation (8.4), called the *no-mimicking condition*, means it is better for a low-quality firm to classify itself truthfully and to sell all its equity for $S_L$ rather than receive the proceeds $S_H(1 - \alpha)$ through misrepresentation. If a low-quality firm were to retain proportion $\alpha$ of its shares, thereby representing itself as a high-quality firm, it would get the high-quality firm price $S_H = \theta_H$, but only for proportion $(1-\alpha)$ of the shares. Inequality equation (8.4) states that this outcome would leave the low-quality firm less well off than if it had represented itself as a low-quality firm and sold all its shares.

Since equation (8.4) provides no incentive for $L$ firms to retain any proportion of their equity, any firms that do retain $\alpha$ will be $H$ firms. High-quality firms get:

$$(1 - \alpha)S_H = (1 - \alpha)\theta_H > (1 - \alpha)\theta_L$$

However, the certainty equivalent value of H firms' wealth is only:

$$\theta_H - \rho\sigma^2\alpha^2/2 \qquad (8.5)$$

because they have to retain proportion $\alpha$ of their shares in order to signal their higher quality. The minimum proportion $\alpha$ that entrepreneurs of high-quality firms must retain is defined as the proportion that reduces the no-mimicking condition equation (8.4) to an equality. We can then rewrite the equality as:

$$\alpha^2/(1 - \alpha) = 2(\theta_H - \theta_L)/\rho\sigma^2 \qquad (8.6)$$

So long as equation (8.6) is satisfied, then at equilibrium, low-quality firms get full outside financing, at price $S_L$. High-quality firms get $(1 - \alpha)S_H$.

### 8.2.4.3  A Cooperative Lending Association

To see how an intermediary could improve the present situation, it is first necessary to determine how $\alpha$ varies with $\sigma^2$. From equation (8.5), the certainty equivalent value of the loss to entrepreneurs of high-quality firms can be measured by:

$$\rho\sigma^2\alpha^2/2 \tag{8.7}$$

Combining equations (8.6) and (8.7) gives:

$$\rho\sigma^2\alpha^2/2 = (\theta_H - \theta_L)(1 - \alpha) \tag{8.8}$$

To see how $\alpha$ varies with $\sigma^2$, note that the right-hand side of equation (8.6) increases as $\sigma^2$ decreases. By evaluating the left-hand side of equation (8.6) for $\alpha$ near zero, finding that it is higher for $\alpha$ near one, then checking to make sure the left-hand side increases everywhere on the interval between zero and one, we see the left-hand side increases in $\alpha$. Thus, we conclude that $\alpha$ increases as $\sigma^2$ decreases. Moreover the right-hand side of equation (8.8) decreases as $\alpha$ increases, at least assuming that $0 < \alpha < 1$, as we do throughout. But since $\alpha$ increases as $\sigma^2$ decreases, this also means that the cost, that is, the left-hand side of equation (8.8), decreases as $\sigma^2$ decreases.

The foregoing results can now be used to examine what would happen if borrowers formed a credit cooperative or coalition; that is, if they combined to form a financial intermediary. Assume the coalition members combine statistically independent projects with the same mean,[26] so that the weighted combination of projects has a lower variance than does any single project with the same value as the weighted combination. Since $\alpha$ increases as $\sigma^2$ decreases, the credit cooperative can credibly signal that it has a lower standard deviation and hence, a lower variance of return than any individual firm. As a result of this signal, the credit cooperative's cost of raising external finance is lower than that of any individual firm. The importance of this conclusion is not just that a portfolio of loans can have a lower variance than any individual loan, but that the credit cooperative can credibly signal that its portfolio risks are lower than those of the individual borrowers in the coalition. Thus, setting up the credit cooperative (i.e., setting up a financial intermediary) can create value so long as the reduction in interest costs covers the cooperative's operating expenses.

## 8.2.5  Delegated Monitoring

Diamond (1984) argues that lenders may be able to realize scale economies by delegating some of their governance functions, thus inferring that delegated monitoring can be a factor explaining the existence of financial intermediaries. In the following model the monitor verifies realized earnings to determine whether or not borrowers can repay their loan, either fully or to the extent permitted by realized earnings. Each lender could monitor earnings individually, but to do so would incur greater cost than

---

[26] A similar result could be obtained if the projects were only imperfectly correlated. It is simpler, but not necessary, to assume they are independent.

delegating the responsibility to a central authority, here thought of as a bank. However, delegating the monitoring function presents a new set of incentive problems, since the lenders must be able to satisfy themselves that the monitor acts properly on their behalf.

Suppose that any lender who monitors a borrowing account incurs a unit cost $K$. Suppose in addition that the number of borrowing accounts ($n$) is large, so that to finance the demands of a given borrower requires $m$ lenders, each of whom advances an equal fraction of the funds. If each lender monitors accounts individually, the total cost of monitoring is $nmK$. Table 8.1 summarizes the situation of direct finance where each lender monitors its own borrower.

If the lenders delegate the monitoring to a bank, the bank will spend $K$ per individual borrower, plus some other costs $C_n$, which depend on the number of borrowers. The total cost would be $nK + C_n$. If the reduction in monitoring costs more than offsets the increase in operating costs, it will be worthwhile to have the bank monitor on behalf of the former individual lenders. In this setting, bank depositors are regarded as the parties who would otherwise have been the individual lenders. This situation where this is intermediated finance is summarized in Table 8.2.

One issue remains. How do the depositors know the bank will monitor as arranged, and will report its earnings truthfully to the depositors? Clearly, the depositors must employ some kind of contract that provides penalties if the bank fails to report accurately. Sometimes the economics literature proposes nonpecuniary penalties to ensure the bank will monitor in a manner consistent with depositor interests. Diamond (1984) shows that each depositor's monitoring costs can grow arbitrarily small as the bank's assets grow sufficiently large. Moreover, using the law of large numbers it is possible to define the likely fraction of loan defaults with increasing accuracy. In such cases, as noted by Lewis (1995), "Default is unlikely because the intermediary lowers its default losses on loans by careful screening and the monitoring of loans and investments, and then reduces its own probability of bankruptcy by exploiting advantages of size and diversification."

**TABLE 8.1**
DIRECT FINANCE: EACH LENDER MONITORS ITS OWN BORROWER. TOTAL COST $nmK$

| | |
|---|---|
| Borrower 1 | Lender 1 |
| | Lender $m$ |
| Borrower $n$ | Lender $(n-1)m + 1$ |
| | Lender $nm$ |

**TABLE 8.2**
INTERMEDIATED FINANCE: LENDERS DELEGATE MONITORING TO BANK. TOTAL COST $nK + C_n$

| | | |
|---|---|---|
| Borrower 1 | Bank | Lender 1 ... Lender $m$ |
| Borrower $n$ | | Lender $(n-1)m + 1$ ... Lender $nm$ |

### 8.2.5.1 Intermediary Information Processing

Intermediary differences in information processing have long been recognized. DeLong (1991) and Ramirez (1995) argue that the U.S. banking firms of the later nineteenth and earlier twentieth century resolved external financing problems by mitigating principal-agent problems, including those arising from asymmetric information. Similarly, Gorton and Kahn (2000) argue that bank loans have features quite distinct from those of bonds sold in the public market, features that arise from the ways banks govern their outstanding loans. They argue that banks perform important functions between the time they extend a loan and collect the repayments on it. In particular, banks have the ability, not possessed by market agents, to renegotiate credit terms with borrowers, and to create a tight link between renegotiation and monitoring.

## 8.3 INTERNAL GOVERNANCE

Finally, we turn to internal governance. Stein (1997) develops a model that shows how an internal capital market can add value to certain kinds of financial deals when the amount of available financing is limited. If it has the authority and the incentive to reallocate scarce funds across projects, a corporate headquarters operation can create value in a credit-constrained setting where not all profitable projects can be financed. (The profitability of a project is determined by its net present value, a metric that is described in Chapter 6 where we discuss the valuation of investment projects by firms. A project is profitable if it has a positive net present value.) The internal capital market created by the headquarters division can create value when credit constraints imposed by uninformed outsiders do not permit the optimal size of a project to be undertaken, as shown below.

Stein's model provides both an economic rationale for setting up an internal capital market and determines the optimal size of a conglomerate corporation's capital budget.[27] Stein also addresses the determinants of the internal capital market's optimal scope. Assume the scale of the projects is defined by their initial investment, which can be either 1 or 2 units of capital. The projects are one-period ventures with two possible payoffs—a high payoff in state G, and a lower payoff in state B. The state G payoff is $\theta y_i$ and the state B payoff is $y_i$; $i = 1, 2$. The states obtain with probabilities $p$ and $(1-p)$, respectively, and $\theta > 1$. Project managers observe the actual state; outside investors know only the probabilities with which the states obtain. Interest rates are assumed to be zero. Investments and investment returns are shown in Table 8.3.

TABLE 8.3
INVESTMENTS AND INVESTMENT RETURNS

| Investment | State G (probability p) | State B (probability 1−p) |
|---|---|---|
| 1 | $\theta y_1$ | $y_1$ |
| 2 | $\theta y_2$ | $y_2$ |

---

[27] Stein also addresses the determinants of the internal capital market's optimal scope.

Assume that $y_1 > 1$, so that even in state B the project yields a positive return to an investment of 1. As a result, there would never be any difficulty in obtaining external funding for an investment of 1. However, Stein also assumes that project returns are diminishing, and that the net present value in state B is no longer positive if the investment is equal to 2:

$$1 < y_1 < y_2 < 2 \qquad (8.9)$$

In an example that is continued for the rest of this section, we set $y_1 = 1.0100$, $y_2 = 1.9400$, and $\theta = 1.1000$.

Returning to the more general setting, we also assume:

$$\theta(y_2 - y_1) > 1 \qquad (8.10)$$

so the optimal investment in state G is 2, as may be seen from the fact that equation (8.10) implies $\theta y_2 > \theta y_1 + 1$. Note that condition equation (8.10) is satisfied for the example data just given: $1.1000(1.9400 - 1.0100) = 1.0230$.

Suppose that in the absence of setting up a corporate headquarters each project has its own project manager. Project managers have an incentive to over invest because projects yield private benefits as well as benefits to the firm. The private benefits whose realizations are displayed in Table 8.4 are assumed not to be verifiable by outsiders. (The $s$ denotes the coefficient of private benefits.) Nevertheless, they present a moral hazard problem because the private benefits mean that project managers have an incentive to misrepresent a project as being in state G when it is not.

TABLE 8.4
PRIVATE BENEFITS

| Investment/Private Benefit | State G (probability p) | State B (probability 1− p) |
|---|---|---|
| 1 | $s\theta y_1$ | $s y_1$ |
| 2 | $s\theta y_2$ | $s y_2$ |

To begin the analysis, suppose project managers' information is not revealed, either to outside investors or to other parties within the corporation. If a project receives one unit of financing, its expected net cash flow is:

$$[p\theta + (1 - p)]y_1 - 1 \qquad (8.11)$$

And, as already mentioned, financing of 1 can always be obtained from outside financiers [see equation (8.1)]. To continue the example given above, let $p = 0.3$ and $1 - p = 0.7$. Using these data along with the previous values, equation (8.11) becomes:

$$1.0100 \times [0.3 \, (1.1000) + 0.7] - 1 = 0.0403$$

However, suppose the project manager desired to invest 2. Then the expected net return is:

$$[p\theta + (1 - p)]y_2 - 2 \qquad (8.12)$$

For a given value of $\theta$, equation (8.12) can be less than equation (8.11) if $p$ is sufficiently small, as is henceforth assumed. Indeed, if:

$$[p\theta + (1 - p)][y_2 - y_1] < 1 \tag{8.13}$$

outside financing for the larger project will not be obtainable since inequality equation (8.13) implies:

$$\{[p\theta + (1 - p)]y_2 - 2\} - \{[p\theta + (1 - p)]y_1 - 1\} = [p\theta + (1 - p)][y_2 - y_1] < 1$$

Again in terms of the example data, equation (8.12) becomes:

$$1.9400 \times [0.3(1.1000) + 0.7] - 2 = -0.0018$$

Suppose the corporate headquarters can screen and therefore obtain (possibly noisy) information about project success. Then the presence of a corporate headquarters' division can improve the situation both with respect to financing individual projects and to obtaining funds from outside financiers. Assume corporate headquarters has no financial resources of its own, but has an incentive to monitor because it can capture a fraction of the private benefits that project managers get. If publicly verifiable cash flows are $y$, and total private benefits are $sy$, assume that corporate headquarters can appropriate $\phi sy$, leaving $(1 - \phi)sy$ to be retained by project managers. The ability of corporate headquarters to expropriate private benefits reduces the incentives affecting project managers, as reflected by a factor $k < 1$ that reduces cash flows in all states of the world and at either level of initial investment. In other words, the existence of a corporate headquarters absorbs $(1 - k)$ of any realized cash flow.

Since a corporate headquarters' operation reduces cash flows as well as private benefits, it is always value reducing in a one-project setting. Moreover, because corporate headquarters realizes private benefits from projects, its operation presents the same moral hazard problems as do the individual project managers. Despite these costs, however, corporate headquarters can create value on a net basis if there are two or more projects.

Corporate headquarters' span of control allows it to derive private benefits from several projects simultaneously, and it therefore has an incentive to channel funds toward the more productive investments. Assume that corporate headquarters is entitled to redistribute investments across projects. If corporate headquarters is controlling $n$ projects and can therefore raise $n$ units of financing, it can reallocate the $n$ units across projects in any way it likes. Some projects may be allocated 2, others 1, and still others zero units of capital. Corporate headquarters therefore differs from a bank that only has the authority to accept or reject individual financing proposals without making any reallocations.

Suppose there are two projects $i$ and $j$ whose states are realized independently, and suppose in addition that corporate headquarters can observe the state perfectly by screening the projects. Since there are two projects, corporate headquarters can raise 2 units of capital from outside financiers. Suppose the marginal returns to investing the second dollar in, say, project $i$, are greater than the marginal returns to investing one dollar in each of projects $i$ and $j$ when $i$ is in the good state and $j$ is in the bad state. That is, $\theta y_2 > (\theta + 1)y_1$, from which it follows that:

$$\theta(y_2 - y_1) > y_1 \tag{8.14}$$

To assess the benefits of operating an internal capital market, note first that expected returns to external market (denoted by EM) investors are:

$$\text{EM} = 2[y_1(p\theta + (1 - p)) - 1] \tag{8.15}$$

Again reverting to the example data, the calculation following equation (8.11) can be used to show that for these data EM $= 2(0.0403) = 0.0806$.

Since corporate headquarters can reallocate funds to the more productive project, internal market returns are:

$$\text{IM} = 2(1 - p)^2 ky_1 + 2p^2 k\theta y_1 + 2p(1 - p)k\theta y_2 - 2 \tag{8.16}$$

The term $2p(1-p)k\theta y_2$ in equation (8.16) means that when the two projects are in different states, whichever project is in state G receives both units of financing. (Recall that establishing a corporate headquarters operation means that proportion $(1-k)$ of any realized cash flow is absorbed by that operation.) Continuing to use the example data previously given, along with $k = 0.9999$, equation (8.16) becomes:

$$2(0.7)^2(0.9999)(1.0100) + 2(0.3)^2(1.1000)(1.0100)$$
$$+ 2(0.7)(0.3)(0.9999)(1.9400) - 2 = 0.0859$$

verifying that for the data in question the internal market solution generates greater value than the external market solution.

It is also possible to determine the optimal size of the capital budget that corporate headquarters should allocate. Suppose that the ability of corporate headquarters to monitor decreases with the number of projects, and for simplicity suppose further that the projects are statistically independent. Let $M(n)$ be the probability that monitoring is successful, and suppose that $M(n)$ is a decreasing function of $n$. To calculate the optimal number of projects, begin by picking an arbitrary value of $n$, from which a value $M(n)$ can be determined. For an arbitrary level of funding $F$ the *ex ante* expected profit is:

$$\pi(n, F) = M(n)\pi^M(n, F) + [1 - M(n)]\pi^N(n, F) \tag{8.17}$$

where $\pi^M(n, F)$ is the per project profits if monitoring is successful and $\pi^N(n, F)$ is the per project profits if monitoring is unsuccessful and corporate headquarters learns nothing. For each fixed value of $n$, optimize equation (8.17) over $F$ to obtain $F^*(n)$. Finally, pick the value of $n$ that maximizes:

$$\pi[n, F^*(n)] \tag{8.18}$$

Improvements to the monitoring technology will not always imply an increase in the optimal size of the internal capital market, mainly because the calculation involves two offsetting effects: the increased profits from using a better monitoring technology, versus the increased profits that come from having more money to invest. When the monitoring technology improves, it may be possible to generate a substantial easing of credit constraints with a smaller number of projects. In such a case it becomes less important to add projects in an effort to boost the level of per project funding.

Stein (2002) discusses how different organizational structures generate different forms of information about investment projects. A decentralized approach—with small, single-manager firms—is most likely to be attractive when project information is difficult to transmit credibly. In contrast, large hierarchies perform better when information can be cheaply and easily transmitted within the firm. Stein argues that the model helps one to think about the consequences of consolidation in the banking industry, particularly the documented tendency for mergers to lead to declines in small business lending. Since small business lending information is difficult to transmit, it can be relatively more expensive for larger hierarchical organizations to process.

## KEY POINTS

- The principal function of any financial market is to create a forum where buyers and sellers (or their agents) can trade financial claims.
- Usually market performance is evaluated in terms of market efficiency, liquidity, and information production, and marketplaces are typically organized so as to enhance these performance characteristics.
- Two of the most prominent dimensions of marketplace activity are the volume and frequency of trading.
- The different kinds of markets within financial systems can be distinguished in terms of three characteristics: (1) their cost and revenue functions, (2) the economics of producing information about market-traded assets, and (3) the economics of trading firms.
- Economic considerations also determine the operating and allocative efficiency of any given financial market, the type and number of market agents trading in it, the liquidity of the instruments traded in it, and the extent to which price information is revealed by trading.
- Public versus private markets, primary versus secondary markets, dealer versus broker markets, and wholesale versus retail markets all display different combinations of capabilities. As a result, they are cost-effectively aligned with different classes of financial deals, each class presenting different attribute combinations.
- The nature and size of firms acting as market agents are determined by their operating economics.
- A perfectly competitive financial market is both allocatively and operationally efficient.

- A financial market is said to be allocatively efficient when equally risky proposals can all be funded at the same rate of return. It is not necessarily at the rate of return that the providers raise funds, because they have to cover their costs and produce a return to capital.
- According to the efficient market hypothesis, when a financial market is perfectly competitive and there are no trading costs or institutional impediments, it will be allocatively efficient in the sense that the equilibrium prices of securities fully reflect all publicly available information.
- Usually larger and more active secondary securities markets are viewed as allocatively efficient.
- If, given prevailing technology and best practice, a financial market performs financial services at the lowest possible cost, it is said to be operationally efficient.
- Liquidity differences among markets depend on such factors as differences in market structure, in the nature of the instruments traded, and in the kinds of obligations those instruments represent (e.g., debt, equity).
- Asset securitization is a mechanism used by securities firms to fund illiquid asset portfolios and involves selling new securities representing claims against a portfolio of specialized and usually illiquid loans.
- Financial intermediaries create value when they (1) govern financial deals using different capabilities than are used by market agents, (2) are involved in non-arms' length financial deals that require them to produce different kinds of information than financial market agents, (3) manage the effects of informational asymmetries, and (4) realize cost savings on some types of financial deals due to scale economies in portfolio administration.
- Internal governance (i.e., internal capital markets) can add value to certain kinds of financial deals that require intensive forms of high-capability governance. For example, they can allocate funds using command and control mechanisms, and thus overcome agency problems in situations where the amount of external financing would otherwise be limited.

---

## ♦ ♦ ♦   QUESTIONS

1. Give three reasons why financial market arrangements cannot fully incorporate the complexities of financial deal governance.

2. What is the principal function of any financial market?

3. What are the two most important measures of marketplace activity?

4. What is meant by scale economies in market operations?

5. What is meant by a market failure?

6. Why are primary market issues important for new capital formation?

7. Why are secondary market transactions useful in evaluating new information about firms?

8. What are the differences between wholesale and retail markets?

9. What are the two dominant forms of organization for firms acting as market agents?

10. a. Give three examples of the types of markets that would be expected to be allocatively efficient.

   b. Give three examples of markets that would be expected to be less than fully efficient in an allocative sense.

   c. Do you think that the time horizons of financial deals are related to whether the markets for the deals are or are not allocatively efficient?

11. Following is an excerpt from a commentary by Professor Lasse H. Pedersen of New York University, "Saving Free Markets from Market Failure," that appeared on Forbes.com (http://www.forbes.com/2009/09/29/free-markets-liquidity-opinions-contributors-lasse-h-pedersen.html):

   The recent economic crisis is changing the way we think about economics and finance, but what is the key lesson to be learned? Some economists argue for the critical importance of a large fiscal stimulus, while others suggest that the government should not intervene at all. It is neither; the real lesson is that we need to save the free markets from market failure. Market efficiency relies on liquidity and well-functioning institutions.

   a. What is meant by market failure?
   b. What is meant by market efficiency?
   c. What is meant by liquidity?

12. What is the difference between an efficient capital market and an operationally efficient capital market?

13. What are the factors that cause differences in liquidity among different financial instruments?

14. What does asset securitization involve?

15. What is assumed about markets in neoclassical economic analysis?

16. Under what circumstances can financial intermediaries create value?

17. Explain how the effects of adverse selection can be mitigated.

18. How can internal governance add value to certain types of financial deals?

# REFERENCES

Allen, Franklin D., and Douglas Gale. (2000). *Comparing Financial Systems*. Cambridge, MA: MIT Press.

Bond, Philip. (2004). "Bank and Nonbank Financial Intermediation," *Journal of Finance* **59**: 2489–2529.

DeLong, Bradford. (1991). "Did J. P. Morgan's Men Add Value? An Economist's Perspective on Financial Capitalism," in Peter Temin, ed., *Inside the Business Enterprise: Historical Perspectives on the Use of Information*. Chicago: University of Chicago Press.

Diamond, Douglas. (1984). "Financial Intermediation and Delegated Monitoring," *Review of Economic Studies* **51**: 393–414.

Freixas, Xavier, and Jean-Charles Rochet. (1997). *Microeconomics of Banking* (1st ed.). Cambridge, MA: MIT Press.

Gemmill, Gordon. (1996). "Transparency and Liquidity: A Study of Block Trades on the London Stock Exchange under Different Publication Rules," *Journal of Finance* **51**, 1765–1790.

Gorton, Gary, and James Kahn. (2000). "The Design of Bank Loan Contracts," *Review of Financial Studies* **13**: 331–364.

King, Robert G., and Ross Levine. (1993). "Financial Intermediation and Economic Development," in Colin Mayer and Xavier Vives (eds.) *Financial Intermediation in the Construction of Europe*. London: Centre for Economic Policy Research, 156–189.

Leland, Hayne, and David H. Pyle. (1977). "Informational Asymmetries, Financial Structure, and Financial Intermediation," *Journal of Finance* **32**: 371–387.

Lewis, Mervyn K., (1995). *Financial Intermediaries*. Aldershot: Elgar.

Neave, Edwin H. (2009). *Modern Financial Systems: Theory and Applications*. Hoboken, NJ: John Wiley & Sons.

Ramirez, Carlos D. (1995). "Did J.P. Morgan's Men Add Liquidity? Corporate Investment, Cash Flow, and Financial Structure at the Turn of the Century," *Journal of Finance* **50**: 661–678.

Stein, Jeremy C. (1997). "Internal Capital Markets and the Competition for Corporate Resources," *Journal of Finance* **52**: 111–133.

Stein, Jeremy C. (2002). "Information Production and Capital Allocation: Decentralized versus Hierarchical Firms," *Journal of Finance* **57**: 1899–2002.

Tinic, Seha M., and Richard R. West. (1974). "Marketability of Common Stocks in Canada and the USA: A Comparison of Agent versus Dealer Dominated Markets," *Journal of Finance* **29**: 729–749.

# PART III
# TOOLS FOR COPING WITH RISK

# 9

# THE MICROECONOMIC FOUNDATION OF FINANCIAL ECONOMICS

$A$s pointed out in Chapter 1, financial economics is concerned with explaining the nature of financial decision making and with determining the economic effects of those decisions. As the discussions of Chapters 2 through 8 have already suggested, financial economics explains decision making both in terms of how agents should decide, referred to as *prescriptive theory*, and in terms of how agents actually decide in practice, referred to as *descriptive theory*. In effect, financial economics attempts to combine the prescriptive and the descriptive to provide useful insights both as to how things can be explained in theory, and as to how things actually work in practice.[1]

Since financial economics is an empirically oriented discipline, the prescriptive and descriptive approaches are often used in combination. However, both approaches employ their own framework, and it is probably most helpful to understand each individually before attempting to consider their combination. *Prescriptive financial economics* has largely been developed using a framework known as the *neoclassical paradigm* in which rational agents interact in competitive markets under conditions of homogeneously distributed information and in the absence of transactions costs. (The neoclassical paradigm has been introduced in Chapter 8; further details are provided later in Section 9.2.1.)

The assumptions of the neoclassical paradigm have led to the development of an impressive, unified set of theoretical results. In particular, financial economics has been very successful at showing how economic agents, acting rationally under conditions of risk, establish equilibrium asset prices. It has been equally successful at identifying some of the factors determining those prices. In addition, it has shown that prices and price relations provide information about asset risk premia (i.e., the amount that investors should be compensated for taking on the risk associated with investing in an asset). Furthermore, the paradigm shows how equilibrium prices are

---

[1] The two are not contradictory. Rather, theory can be thought of as a road map, and concerns about the applicability of theory are concerns regarding how well the road map describes the territory. The adequacy of the description depends, of course, on the purposes of the observer.

related to each other in the absence of arbitrage opportunities. Finally, and also under the assumption of no-arbitrage opportunities, the paradigm establishes the existence of a risk-neutral probability measure that can be used to calculate the prices of financial instruments relative to each other.[2]

With regard to empirical work, researchers conduct rigorous and ongoing tests of financial economics' theoretical implications. Where empirical research uncovers relations that differ from accepted theoretical findings, financial economics responds by expanding its original prescriptive assumptions to include additional descriptively oriented possibilities. The resultant approaches attempt to explain additional observed characteristics of financial market prices and transactions.

Two of the more notable evolutionary thrusts are theories explaining the practical limits of arbitrage,[3] and theories describing the importance of behavioral approaches to trading and pricing securities. The topics covered by these extensions include recognizing that information production is costly, and that agents may incur different costs to obtain particular forms of information. As a result, transacting parties may be differently informed, and their particular perspectives can affect the prices at which they will trade.[4] Recognizing differences in information further leads to characterizing and explaining situations (using what is known as *agency theory*) in which informed persons make decisions on behalf of uninformed persons. Still further, recognizing the costs to decision making and to transacting leads to theories of how those costs might be reduced, as well as to explanations of what such actions imply for the descriptive power of financial economics. Each of these topics is introduced in this chapter.

Finally, this chapter offers examples that help illustrate both the flavor of the original neoclassical prescriptive approach and its evolution toward recognizing additional behavior characteristics.[5] These examples are intended to suggest the range of the book's topics in the chapters ahead, and will be expanded upon and developed further in the rest of the book.

## 9.1  PRESCRIPTIVE AND DESCRIPTIVE APPROACHES

Financial economics begins with a number of fundamental concepts that are used as building blocks both for developing theory and for devising empirical tests. First, financial economics uses *expected utility theory* to prescribe the behavior of economic agents.[6] Second, financial economics uses concepts arising from observation and

---

[2] In this description of the neoclassical paradigm, we have mentioned terms such as arbitrage opportunities, equilibrium prices, and risk-neutral measures without formally defining them. However, as we continue to develop our understanding of financial economics in the chapters, formal definitions will be provided.

[3] To be discussed further in Chapters 15 and 16.

[4] In this book, we refer to *prescriptive behavior* as carried out by decision makers called "economic agents" and *descriptive behavior* as carried out by decision makers called "people," "persons," or "parties."

[5] There can be conditions under which prescriptive theory captures financial phenomena quite adequately, and other circumstances in which it does not. Specifying the circumstances and the applicable forms of theory form much of the current work of financial economics.

[6] Agents who conform to the underpinnings of expected utility theory are frequently described as acting rationally. The meaning of rational behavior is discussed further shortly.

empirical research to describe how people actually behave, and then compares and contrasts this description with predictions derived from the assumptions of prescriptive behavior. To indicate the nature of the two research thrusts, this section first presents the underpinnings of expected utility theory and then outlines some of the questions currently addressed by descriptively oriented research, frequently referred to as *behavioral finance*.

## 9.1.1 Utility Theory: Prescriptive Approach to Preference and Choice

This section considers choice under conditions of risk, conditions that include choice with respect to certainty outcomes as a special case.[7] The view presented here was first developed by von Neumann and Morgenstern in *The Theory of Games and Economic Behavior* (1944). The von Neumann–Morgenstern theory represents individual preferences using a numerical scale called *utility*. That is, a *utility function* maps preferences among choices to the numerical scale. Decision makers are viewed as rational in the sense they are assumed to maximize the expected value of a utility function.[8]

For example, under situations of certainty, where the outcomes of choices are known in advance, the utility function indicates the relative satisfaction the individual gains from selecting a particular alternative. If an individual prefers good A to good B, then the utility assigned to alternative A is higher than the utility assigned to B, symbolically $u(A) > u(B)$. Under conditions of risk, choices have consequences whose possible realizations are weighted by a *probability distribution*. The importance of each possible consequence is reflected by the utility assigned to it. Von Neumann and Morgenstern then show that preferences among risky prospects[9] can be ranked by calculating their expected utilities; that is, by the probability-weighted expectation of the utilities of possible outcomes.[10]

In expected utility theory, the probability distributions employed reflect objective probabilities, an assumption consistent with the view that randomness is inherent in the choices of a neutral nature. In the von Neumann–Morgenstern framework, all individuals are assumed to observe the same objective probability distribution of payoffs to a lottery.

The appeal of expected utility theory stems both from the generality with which it approaches choice under risk and from its convenient representation of preferences. In particular, utility theory permits reflecting agents' preferences through the shapes of their utility functions. For example, it is possible to describe risk-averse, risk-loving, and risk-neutral agents by respectively using concave, convex, and linear utilities, as will be illustrated further. Moreover, it is possible to prescribe choice behavior for entire classes of agents using properties of utility functions that reflect salient aspects of those agents' preferences. Again, for example, if all agents in a given

---

[7] The *theory of decision making under uncertainty*, still in its infancy, is introduced in Parts VI, VII, and VIII.

[8] Firms are often characterized as profit maximizers. As will later become evident, the profit-maximizing firm can be modeled as employing a utility function that is linear in monetary rewards.

[9] Subsequently we shall refer to such prospects as "lotteries."

[10] The work of von Neumann and Morgenstern proved that only expected utility can characterize preferences over lotteries.

class are *risk-neutral*, then they will rank lotteries solely by their expected values. We show further that several rules, called *dominance orderings*, can be established and used to define efficient choice sets for a given class of agents whose preferences are specified in a relatively minimal sense.

### 9.1.1.1  St. Petersburg Paradox

The von Neumann–Morgenstern approach to choice theory was foreshadowed by the work of Daniel Bernoulli, who in 1738 proposed a resolution to the famous *St. Petersburg Paradox*.[11] The paradox is illustrated by a lottery stipulating that a fair coin will be tossed until a head appears. If the head appears on the first toss, the payoff is \$1. If it appears on the second toss, then the payoff is \$2. If the head appears on the third toss, the payoff is \$4; on the fourth toss, it is \$8. If the head appears on the $n$-th toss, the payoff is $2^{n-1}$ dollars.

At the time Bernoulli proposed his resolution, it was commonly accepted that the fair value of a lottery would be the expected value of its payoff. Since a fair coin is tossed, the probability of having a head on the $n$-th toss equals $1/2^n$, and the expected payoff to the lottery is:

$$\$1(1/2) + \$2(1/4) + \$4(1/8) + \cdots + \$2^{n-1}/2^n + \cdots$$

an infinite sum of terms, each of which is equal to 1/2. The expected value of the lottery is therefore infinite, and implies that people should be willing to participate in the game no matter how large the ticket price. However, in practice very few people appeared to be willing to pay substantial sums for such tickets.

To explain the paradox, Bernoulli suggested that rather than the actual payoff, its utility should be considered. With this change of perspective, the fair value would be calculated by:

$$u(1)(1/2) + u(2)(1/4) + u(4)(1/8) + \cdots$$

In order to get the infinite sum to converge, Bernoulli considered utility functions with diminishing marginal utility; that is, for which the utility gained from an extra dollar diminishes with the sum of money one has. For example, if $u(x) = \log x$, the fair value of the lottery equals approximately \$2 rather than the infinite amount originally proposed.[12]

### 9.1.1.2  Von Neumann–Morgenstern Expected Utility

Technically, a *lottery* is a probability distribution[13] defined on the set of payoffs, and the lottery in the St. Petersburg Paradox is given in the following table:

---

[11] The rest of this section closely follows the development in Rachev, Stoyanov, and Fabozzi (2009).

[12] Solutions like Bernoulli's are not completely satisfactory because the lottery can be changed so that the fair value becomes infinite even with choices of utility functions such as the log function. Nevertheless, the resolution of the St. Petersburg Paradox uses concepts later developed into theories of decision making under uncertainty.

[13] Lotteries can be discrete, continuous, or mixed, but for present purposes, we shall only use discrete lotteries.

| Probability | ½ | ¼ | 1/8 | ,,, | $1/2^n$ |
|---|---|---|---|---|---|
| Payoff | 1 | 2 | 4 | . . . | $2^{n-1}$ |

Let $P_X$ denote the probability distribution of a lottery whose payoffs are described by the random variable $X$. Denote the following:

1. Particular outcomes of the lottery by lowercase letters, $x$
2. The probability that the payoff is no greater than $x$ by $P(X \leq x) \equiv F_X(x)$
3. The probability of the outcome $x$ by $p_x$

If we need to refer to a particular outcome $i$, we employ notation such as $x_i$ for the particular outcome and $p_i$ for the corresponding probability.

Von Neumann and Morgenstern define *rational behavior* as behavior conforming to the following four principles, usually referred to as axioms:

*Axiom 1*: Completeness of ranking

*Axiom 2*: Transitivity of ranking

*Axiom 3*: Continuity of ranking

*Axiom 4*: Independence

Assuming a decision maker conforms to the above four axioms, von Neumann and Morgenstern prove that a numerical scale can be used to describe any preference ordering. Denote by **X** the set of all lotteries. Any element $X$ of **X** (i.e., any lottery) is considered a choice available to an economic agent. The numerical scale is a real-valued function $u$ that maps a decision maker's attitude toward $X$ into a numerical value $u(X)$. The scheme is set up to reflect the notion that lottery $Y$ is not preferred to lottery $X$ if and only if:

$$E\left[u(X)\right] \geq E\left[u(Y)\right]$$

where E denotes expected value.

Even though the preference ordering is defined by the economic agent and different agents are likely to have different preference orders, in applications it is usually more convenient to use a numerical scale rather than to deal directly with the preference order. The numerical scale is not unique, but it is rather like a temperature scale in being defined only up to a positive linear transformation. That is, if $u(X)$ orders a set of possible outcomes $X$, then so does $a + bu(X)$, where $a$ can take on any value (positive, negative, or zero) and $b$ can take on any positive value.

The formula for the fair value in the resolution of the St. Petersburg Paradox has the form:

$$E\left[u(X)\right] \equiv E\left[\log(X)\right]$$

meaning that the St. Petersburg Paradox is resolved by defining the lottery's value to a potential purchaser as its expected utility.

### 9.1.1.3 Types of Utility Functions

Some properties of utility functions reflect preferences likely to be displayed by an entire class of agents. For example, all agents who prefer certainty payoffs with higher payoffs are called *nonsatiable*, and their utility functions are nondecreasing over the range of possible outcomes. Thus, if there are two lotteries, one with a certainty payoff of $100 and another with a certainty payoff of $200, a *nonsatiable agent* would never prefer the first opportunity (although in some cases it is possible that the agent would be indifferent to the two opportunities). This preference is reflected by writing $u(200) \geq u(100)$. We can generalize the foregoing as:

$$X \leq_u Y \text{ for any } X,Y \in \mathbf{X} \leftrightarrow E[u(x)] \leq E[u(y)]$$

where the symbol $\leq_u$ means a preference ordering that is reflected by the utility function $u$. If we assume further that agent preferences can be reflected by a differentiable utility function, the function for a nonsatiable agent will have a nonnegative first derivative, $u'(x) \geq 0$, defined at each outcome $x$ of the lottery $\mathbf{X}$.

Other characteristics of agent preferences can also be described by the shape of the utility function. Suppose the agent prefers to receive a certainty outcome that is equal to the expected value of a lottery, rather than the lottery itself. In such a case we say the agent is *risk averse*. Assume that the lottery has two possible outcomes, say $x_1$ with probability $p_1$ and $x_2$ with probability $p_2 = 1 - p_1$, $p_1 \in (0, 1)$.[14] Then the lottery's expected payoff equals:

$$x_1 p_1 + x_2(1 - p_1)$$

In terms of the utility function, the risk-aversion property can be expressed as:

$$u[x_1 p_1 + x_2(1 - p_1)] \geq u(x_1)p_1 + u(x_2)(1 - p_1), \forall x_1, x_2 \,^{15}$$
and                                                                                                           (9.1)
$$p_1 \in (0, 1)$$

where the left-hand side on the inequality corresponds to the utility of the certainty outcome and the right-hand side is the expected utility of the lottery.

A function that satisfies equation (9.1) is called a *concave function*, and the utility functions of all risk-averse agents are concave. If the utility function is twice differentiable, the concavity property is reflected by a nonpositive second derivative, $u''(x) \leq 0$, for all values $x$ in the domain of $u$.

In a local sense, it is possible to describe the curvature of a risk-averter's utility functions as reflected by the function's derivatives. One such description uses the *Arrow-Pratt coefficient of absolute risk aversion*,[16] defined by:

---

[14] The symbol $\in$ is used to denote an element of a set.
[15] The symbol $\forall$ means "for any."
[16] The Arrow-Pratt measure of absolute risk aversion is discussed further in Chapters 11 and 12.

$$r_A(x) = -u''(x)/u'(x) \qquad (9.2)$$

This measure increases with the curvature of the utility function; that is, the greater the coefficient, the more pronounced the inequality in equation (9.1) becomes.[17] The coefficient of absolute risk aversion is also related formally to the sizes of the risk premia and to the kinds of portfolios selected by individuals exhibiting those kinds of preferences (see Chapter 12 for additional details).

Some common examples of utility functions are given next:

1. *Linear utility function.* $u(x) = a + bx.$

   The linear utility function always satisfies equation (9.1) with equality and, therefore, represents a risk-neutral agent. If $b > 0$, the utility represents the preferences of a nonsatiable agent. The coefficient of absolute risk aversion for a linear utility is zero.

2. *Quadratic utility function.* $u(x) = a + bx + cx^2.$

   If $c < 0$, then the quadratic utility function is concave and represents a risk-averse agent, at least up to the point where the quadratic reaches its maximum. The local measure of risk aversion for a quadratic utility increases with the argument of the function.

3. *Logarithmic utility function.* $u(x) = \log x, \qquad x > 0.$

   The logarithmic utility represents a nonsatiable, risk-averse agent. It exhibits decreasing absolute risk aversion since $r_A(x) = 1/x$ and the coefficient of absolute risk aversion decreases with $x$.

4. *Negative exponential utility function.* $u(x) = -e^{-ax}, \qquad a > 0.$

   The exponential utility represents a nonsatiable, risk-averse agent. It exhibits constant absolute risk aversion since $r_A(x) = a$; that is, the coefficient of absolute risk aversion does not depend on $x$.

5. *Power utility function.* $u(x) = -x^{-a}; \qquad x > 0, \ a > 0.$

   The power utility represents a nonsatiable, risk-averse agent. It exhibits decreasing absolute risk aversion since $r_A(x) = a/x$; the coefficient of absolute risk aversion decreases as $x$ increases.

### 9.1.1.4 Types of Stochastic Dominance

There are some circumstances in which an agent can make decisions without knowing a great deal about the clients' utilities. Thus, when a decision maker can make only weak assumptions about individual preferences rather than postulate the exact nature of a utility function, some decisions can still be made correctly. For example, some, but not all, probability distributions can be compared for any utility function that, say, merely exhibits risk aversion.

Consider first a situation applying to nonsatiable decision makers, regardless of whether or not they are risk averse. (After having considered this case, we will then

---

[17] Note that the Arrow-Pratt measure of absolute risk aversion is not affected by the change of scale $u^*(x) = a + bu(x)$. Thus, in a certain sense, it is more fundamental than the numbers produced by a given utility function.

discuss rules for use by risk-averse decision makers.) Some lotteries are clearly better than others for all nonsatiable decision makers. For example, consider two lotteries A and B with the following payoffs and associated probabilities:

| | Lottery A | | Lottery B | |
|---|---|---|---|---|
| Payoff | Probability | | Payoff | Probability |
| $1 | 0.5 | | $0 | 0.6 |
| $3 | 0.5 | | $2 | 0.4 |

Lottery A would be preferred to lottery B, because the former always offers outcomes below a given fixed amount with lower probability than does the latter (i.e., the downside risk of lottery A is lower). To verify that this result is true for any decision maker whose utility increases with wealth, consider:[18]

$$E[u(\text{A})] = u(1)\frac{1}{2} + u(3)\frac{1}{2}$$

$$E[u(\text{B})] = u(0)\frac{6}{10} + u(2)\frac{4}{10}$$

Then, under the assumption that utility increases in wealth,

$$E[u(\text{B})] = u(0)\tfrac{6}{10} + u(2)\tfrac{4}{10} < u(1)\tfrac{6}{10} + u(3)\tfrac{4}{10} < u(1)\tfrac{1}{2} + u(3)\tfrac{1}{2} = E[u(\text{A})]$$

so that $E[u(\text{A})] \geq E[u(\text{B})]$. As this example suggests, a choice between two lotteries can be made on the basis of these ideas whenever their respective probability distributions do not cross.[19] Hence, if this were the only available ranking rule, in many cases it would mean that no comparisons could be made.

Sometimes the inability to compare distributions whose graphs cross can be resolved by imposing additional assumptions about decision makers' preferences. We suppose all decision makers are both risk averse and nonsatiable, and that we wish to compare lottery C and lottery D with the following payoffs and associated probabilities:

| | Lottery C | | Lottery D | |
|---|---|---|---|---|
| Payoff | Probability | | Payoff | Probability |
| $0 | 1/3 | | $1 | 1/2 |
| $2 | 1/3 | | $4 | 1/2 |
| $4 | 1/3 | | | |

---

[18] Note that we have omitted the dollar signs in the utility function. We will follow this practice throughout the book.

[19] The relationship between A and B is, in this case, expressed by saying A dominates B in the first degree.

**FIGURE 9.1**
SECOND-DEGREE STOCHASTIC DOMINANCE (START EVALUATION AT LEFT-HAND SIDE OF
THE DIAGRAM BECAUSE RISK-AVERSE INVESTORS ATTACH A GREATER NEGATIVE WEIGHT
TO DOWNSIDE RISK THAN THEY DO TO UPSIDE POTENTIAL)

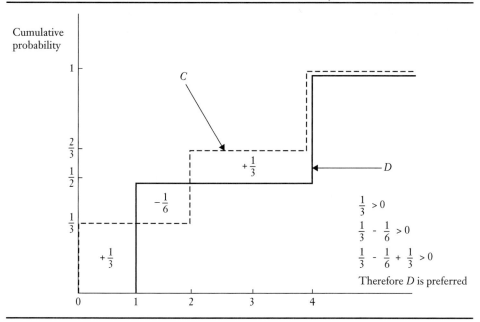

These are lotteries whose cumulative distributions cross as shown in Figure 9.1.
Notice first that the expected payoff of lottery D is $2.5 and the expected payoff of
lottery C is $2, so the risk-neutral agent at least would prefer lottery D. Note also that
the worst outcome of lottery D is at least as good as (in fact, better than) the worst
outcome for lottery C.[20] This means that in terms of the greatest possible downside
risk, lottery D is never quite as bad as lottery C.

To see how it might be shown formally that lottery D is actually preferred by any
risk-averter, let us ask if $E[u(D)] \geq E[u(C)]$. If it were, we would have:

$$u(1)\tfrac{1}{2} + u(4)\tfrac{1}{2} > u(0)\tfrac{1}{3} + u(2)\tfrac{1}{3} + u(4)\tfrac{1}{3}$$

which may also be written as:

$$u(1)(\tfrac{1}{3} + \tfrac{1}{6}) + u(4)(\tfrac{1}{3} + \tfrac{1}{6}) > u(0)\tfrac{1}{3} + u(2)(\tfrac{1}{6} + \tfrac{1}{6}) + u(4)\tfrac{1}{3}$$

---

[20] These are necessary conditions for the ranking we are now establishing, second-degree dominance.
They are necessary to prevent lottery D being rejected by risk-averters who are especially heavily influenced
by worst-case thinking. Note that these necessary conditions do not imply $\sigma^2(D)$ must always be smaller
than $\sigma^2(C)$ where $\sigma^2$ denotes the variance of the outcome for the lottery.

Then, after cancelling common terms and regrouping, we would have:

$$[u(1)-u(0)]\tfrac{1}{3} + [u(4)-u(2)]\tfrac{1}{6} > [u(2)-u(1)]\tfrac{1}{6}$$

But $u(1) - u(0) > u(2) - u(1)$ by the diminishing marginal utility characteristic of risk-averters, so the original inequality will certainly be satisfied if we can show that:

$$[u(1) - u(0)](1/6) + [u(2) - u(1)] (1/6) + [u(4) - u(2)] (1/6) > [u(2) - u(1)](1/6)$$

But this expression reduces to:

$$[u(1) - u(0)] (1/6) + [u(4) - u(2)](1/6) > 0$$

which is obviously true. Accordingly, it is now easy, by working backward from the last line, to verify that $E[u(D)] > E[u(C)]$; that is, lottery D is preferred to lottery C by all risk-averse decision makers. A test for this relationship, known as *second-degree stochastic dominance*,[21] will be given in Chapter 12.

Not everything can be ranked by second-degree stochastic dominance, for there are pairs of distributions such that the area of the difference between the distributions does change sign as these areas are cumulated from the left. For example, consider the following two lotteries, F and G:

| Lottery F | | Lottery G | |
|---|---|---|---|
| *Payoff* | *Probability* | *Payoff* | *Probability* |
| $0 | 1/6 | $1 | 2/3 |
| $2 | 1/2 | $4 | 1/3 |
| $4 | 1/3 | | |

These two lotteries have the same payoffs as lotteries C as D, but with different probability distributions. Note that $E(F) = \$2\tfrac{1}{3} > E(G) = \$2$, so that on the basis of the expected value (but not on the basis of lowest outcomes) lottery F might prove to be a dominant lottery. But we cannot choose between lotteries F and G without knowing more about the decision maker's preferences. A risk-neutral decision maker would prefer lottery F, but lottery G has a better lowest outcome than lottery F, so that a highly risk-averse[22] decision maker would prefer lottery G. Hence, neither lottery F nor lottery G satisfies the two conditions necessary for one lottery to dominate the other.

Rothschild and Stiglitz (1970, 1971) introduce a dominance ordering that sharpens the notion of comparing lotteries' risks. Their ordering requires agents to be risk averse,[23] with preferences that can be represented by the set of all concave utility

---

[21] This is also referred to as second-order stochastic dominance.

[22] That is to say, if the decision maker's index of absolute risk aversion is sufficiently large. See Chapter 3.

[23] However, the agents may be satiable (i.e., need not satisfy nonsatiability).

functions, and further requires that the class of random variables to be ordered will have equal expected values. The conditions are thus similar to the conditions for second-degree stochastic dominance, but with the additional requirement that the expected payoffs from the lotteries be equal. The importance of the Rothschild-Stiglitz ordering is that it provides additional economic insight. As discussed further in Chapter 12, *Rothschild-Stiglitz dominance* means a dominated variable can be written as the dominating variable plus noise terms reflecting pure risk, that is, random variables having a mean of zero.

## 9.1.2 Behavioral Theory: Descriptive Approach to Individual Preference and Choice

Financial economics has been founded largely on prescriptive theory, but since about the 1950s research has shown that in many circumstances agents do not conform to prescriptive theory. Since numerous financial phenomena cannot fully be explained by the prescriptive foundations of financial economics,[24] the field has become increasingly concerned with descriptive approaches that further its capability to explain anomalous observations.

Behavioral finance examines how psychology affects the agents' decisions. The implications of behavioral finance for the theories of asset pricing and for portfolio selection are sketched in this chapter and dealt with more fully in later chapters. Barberis and Thaler (2003) identify two building blocks of behavioral finance:

1. Limits to arbitrage theories
2. Psychological explanations of decision making

The *limits to arbitrage theories* argue that it can be difficult for fully rational traders to undo the pricing anomalies created by less rational traders. (Arbitrage theories are discussed in Chapter 15, and limits to arbitrage in Chapter 21.) The psychological explanations literature identifies departures from neoclassical rationality that might be likely to affect financial market prices, and the findings that have so far proved useful in the study of financial economics are described next.

### 9.1.2.1 Beliefs

In the von Neumann–Morgenstern theory, agent expectations are described using objective probabilities. In contrast, psychology has identified several features of how agents choose probability distributions in practice. The features that appear to be of special relevance to financial economists are:

- Overconfidence
- Optimism and wishful thinking
- Representativeness
- Conservatism

---

[24] Of course, the prescriptive theory remains of great value, both for its explanations and for the benchmarks it provides for comparison with descriptive theory.

- Perseverance of belief
- Anchoring
- Availability bias

We briefly discuss each in turn.

Peoples' *overconfidence* in their own judgment has two principal dimensions. First, the confidence limits they assign to judgments are substantially narrower than the confidence limits revealed by statistical studies. Second, in practice agents overestimate the probabilities of relatively likely events, and underestimate the probabilities with which relatively unlikely events occur.

*Optimism and wishful thinking* are also displayed, again in two ways. Most people display unrealistically optimistic estimates of personal capabilities such as driving skills, as well as unrealistically optimistic estimates of personal qualities such as a sense of humor. They often predict that tasks can be completed much more quickly than usually proves to be the case.

*Representativeness* means that people use *heuristic methods*[25] to conclude that the more closely phenomenon A represents phenomenon B, the more likely people are to believe that the probability of A's occurring approximates the probability of B's occurring. In other words, people put too much weight on apparent similarities and too little weight on the underlying probability of the event. People also tend to neglect sample size effects and put too much faith in small samples. *Conservativeness* is a phenomenon opposite to representativeness, in which, because of past experience, people put too much weight on data that are not representative of models with which they are familiar.

*Belief perseverance* is manifest by peoples' holding on to opinions for too long in the face of disconfirming evidence. The term *anchoring* means that people first estimate the probability of an event by using an initial and possibly arbitrary value. They then adjust their estimates away from that value in the face of evidence. Estimates can thus be heavily weighted by the initial choice of anchor. Consequently, different anchors will generate widely different concluding estimates in the face of the same evidence. *Availability biases* mean that more recent and more salient events will weigh most heavily in, and therefore distort, estimates.

### 9.1.2.2 Subjective Expected Utility

Leonard Savage's *Foundations of Statistics* published in 1954 shows that under certain consistency conditions individual's preferences for risky outcomes can be described by an expected utility calculated as a probability-weighted sum of outcomes' utilities. In Savage's approach the weights are subjective probabilities of the outcomes. These subjective probabilities and outcomes' utilities both arise from individual's preferences, as long as those preferences are expressed consistently. Unfortunately, Savage's theory has not been well supported by empirical evidence.

---

[25] By a heuristic method is meant a rule of thumb strategy or good guide to follow in order to shorten the time it takes to make a decision.

### 9.1.2.3 Preferences: Prospect Theory

In contrast to the prescriptions of normative utility theory, behavioral financial theory attempts to explain observed behavior. One of the most successful theories in describing experimental results relevant to financial economics is *cumulative prospect theory*. This theory[26] employs a value function that measures payoff differences—payoffs relative to a reference point—along with a weighting function that adjusts the cumulative objective probabilities of the prospect.

By focusing on gains or losses, cumulative prospect theory offers an explanation of why different people make different choices that differs from the explanations provided by von Neumann–Morgenstern utility. As one example, cumulative prospect theory explains simultaneous preferences for buying both insurance (risk-averse behavior) and lottery tickets (risk-loving behavior). To do so, the theory postulates a utility function with both concave and convex regions. The convexity of the utility function occurs in the region of losses, and typically leads to risk seeking. At the same time the overweighting of small probabilities leads to risk aversion with respect to lotteries that offer a small chance of a large loss.

### 9.1.2.4 Preferences: Ambiguity Aversion

Another aspect of observed behavior is that people appear to dislike situations in which they are uncertain about the probability distribution of a lottery. *Ambiguity aversion* seems to have much to do with how competent an individual feels about assessing a probability distribution. The less competent an individual feels about their ability to assess a lottery, the more likely that person is to avoid a lottery. On the other hand, the more confident an individual feels about a lottery, the more likely that person is to take it.

### 9.1.2.5 Identifying Preferences: Shefrin's Approach

Traditional asset pricing theory, to be covered in Chapter 15, assumes that asset prices are set as if agents held correct beliefs about the objective probabilities governing returns, and have preferences that conform to expected utility theory. On the other hand, *behavioral asset pricing theory*—asset pricing as set forth by those who support behavioral finance—assumes that agents are subject to systematic psychologically induced errors, and have preferences that violate the assumptions of expected utility theory. In particular, Shefrin (2005) argues that people are heterogeneous.

1. They hold different beliefs.
2. They differ in their tolerance for risk.
3. They differ in their levels of patience.

Individual differences are typically large, and the differences can affect both prices and trading volume. Moreover, differences of opinion widen after extreme market movements.

Shefrin (2005) argues that behavioral phenomena affect asset prices through their impact on a market pricing method using a concept known as the *stochastic discount*

---

[26] See Kahneman and Tversky (1979) and Tversky and Kahneman (1982).

*factor.*[27] Shefrin provides a theoretical structure to recognize the impact of behavioral beliefs and preferences on the stochastic discount factor. Shefrin's central concept is *agent sentiment*, a notion that captures the market pricing impact of different behavioral influences that affect the investing public. The logarithm of the stochastic discount factor decomposes into the sum of (1) a fundamental component and (2) a sentiment component, where the fundamental value is determined by the methods of neoclassical pricing theory and the sentiment component represents a deviation from fundamental value determined by behavioral influences. When sentiment is zero, prices reflect fundamentals, and market pricing accords with the neoclassical paradigm. When sentiment is not zero, the prices of some assets deviate from their fundamental values. Moreover, the market error may not bear a close resemblance to the errors made by any of the individual agents, because market pricing effects can be driven by the aggregate effects of agent errors, agent preferences, and a combination of the two.

## 9.2  ASSUMPTIONS UNDERLYING FINANCIAL ECONOMICS

By examining the assumptions customarily used in financial economics, this section outlines the conditions underlying different forms of analyses. It begins by sketching the tenets of the *neoclassical paradigm*: an approach embodying the most frequently used assumptions of prescriptive economics. It then considers how these assumptions have been relaxed to recognize the impacts of such complexities as costly information, asymmetric information, transactions costs, and principal-agent relations. As new assumptions have been introduced, financial economics has begun to evolve from a purely prescriptive field to a combination of prescriptive and descriptive analyses.

### 9.2.1  Neoclassical Paradigm

The neoclassical paradigm refers to formal economic analysis whose results depend on assumptions of individual rationality, homogeneously (symmetrically) distributed information, the absence of transactions costs, and (usually) the assumption of competitive markets. The paradigm focuses principally on modeling the rational behavior of economic agents and on determining the nature of financial market equilibrium prices that these agents establish through exchange. As earlier chapters have already indicated, the theoretical results cited in this book all begin with the findings obtained under the neoclassical paradigm, but then continue with amended results obtained under assumptions aimed at reflecting additional complexities of observed financial phenomena. In the book's extensions to the neoclassical paradigm, we will consider how the original theoretical results are altered by differing assumptions: how decisions are affected when information is distributed asymmetrically, when transactions costs must be incurred, and how decisions are affected when assumptions of prescriptive rationality are replaced by behavioral characterizations.

---

[27] The stochastic discount factor can here be thought of as a risk-adjusted discount rate. It will be discussed in greater depth in Chapter 16.

## 9.2.2 Costly Information

Although the neoclassical paradigm assumes that the same information is costlessly available to all economic agents, since the writings of Marschak and Radner (1972) economists have recognized that financial information can be both costly to acquire and costly to use. One of the consequences of recognizing costs to information production is that not all economic agents have the same information when they make decisions.[28] Moreover, differently informed agents may not agree on asset prices, precisely because they do not have the same information.

## 9.2.3 Asymmetric Information

*Information asymmetry* arises when, possibly because of information costs as already recognized, one party to a transaction has payoff-relevant information[29] that the counterparty does not have. Information asymmetries lead to problems of both *adverse selection* and *moral hazard*. In transactions subject to adverse selection, the uninformed party does not have the same information as the informed parties with which he deals, and must perforce deal with the informed parties on the basis of their average characteristics. In transactions involving moral hazard, the uninformed party lacks information about whether an agreed-upon transaction is actually carried out.

In financial transactions, the uninformed party is usually regarded as providing resources to the informed party. Spence (1973) originally proposed the idea of *signaling*, arguing that information asymmetries might sometimes be resolved by having informed parties signal uninformed parties, thus credibly transferring information to the counterparty. Stiglitz (2002) pioneered the *theory of screening*, a process by which an under-informed party can induce a counterparty to reveal additional information.

A classic paper by Akerlof (1970), aptly titled "The Market for Lemons," considers solutions to asymmetric information problems that involve signaling and screening. Some forms of screening involve purchasing conditional probability distributions, while others involve defining a menu of choices so that the informed party's private information is credibly transmitted to the uninformed counterparty.

## 9.2.4 Principal-Agent Relations

*Agency theory* studies the relationship between a principal and an agent who acts on the principal's behalf.[30] Agency theory arises from costly information transmission in that informed agents are viewed as making decisions on behalf of others. Thus, agency theory involves both aligning the interests of principal and agent and determining the costs of resolving conflicts between them. As one example, the portfolio manager of a mutual fund (a pooled investment vehicle) trades on behalf of the many shareholders in the fund. The portfolio manager is the agent and the shareholder is the principal in

---

[28] Information differences are usually introduced as different probability distributions defined on the same, given set of states.

[29] Marschak and Radner interpret information in terms of conditional probability distributions defined on states of the world. Payoff-relevant information refers to conditional probability distributions whose nature affects positively the expected value of taking decisions using such information.

[30] One of the classic papers underlying agency theory is Alchian and Demsetz (1972).

this relationship. In order to satisfy shareholder priorities as fully as possible, the portfolio manager may attempt to make a rough estimate of the average shareholder's risk aversion. However, the portfolio manager will be unable to make precise estimates of each shareholder's attitude toward risk, and thus the decisions taken by management will not necessarily be optimal for any single shareholder. As a second example, the management of a firm can be regarded as agents for the firm's shareholders, in which case the shareholders will likely employ incentive schemes that will help motivate management to act in the shareholders' interest.

## 9.2.5 Costly Transactions

*Transactions costs* can explain many different types of organization. Demsetz (1968), one of the first to outline some of the implications of transactions costs, pointed out that in a world of zero transactions costs, many of the economic arrangements we observe in fact would not be necessary. To take just one example, if information production were free, every economic agent could make decisions on the basis of full rather than partial information. Demsetz further pointed out that in practice many economic organizations are set up to minimize the effects of transactions costs. For example, and as already mentioned in the previous chapter, some forms of resource allocation are performed internally to a corporation rather than in a marketplace because the cost of doing so is less. Further, transactions costs impede arbitrage possibilities and therefore, contribute to financial market prices' continuing to deviate from the fundamental values[31] predicted by neoclassical economics.

Suppose, for example, that a stock is trading at $48.25, while its fundamental value is $49. If the cost per share of transacting exceeds $0.75, it would not pay a decision maker to purchase the undervalued stock even though she knows it to be undervalued. As a second example, if a particular piece of information has a one-time monetary value of, say, $100 but if it costs more than $100 to develop the information, the rational agent will make a choice in the absence of the information. Again, in such cases equilibrium prices do not necessarily reflect all publicly available information.

Once transaction costs are recognized, the issues of *scale economies* must also be considered.[32] The unit costs paid by an individual to transact may well be larger than the unit costs paid by a financial institution capable of realizing scale economies to transacting. For example, the cost per share of transacting might be $0.75 for an individual, but very much less than that for a financial institution. As a result, the financial institution could, through large transactions, eliminate price effects that individuals would not find it economic to exploit.

## ◈ ◈ ◈ KEY POINTS

- Financial economics uses prescriptive approaches to provide explanations of what the financial world might look like if all agents behaved rationally, and contrasts

---

[31] The notion of fundamental value will be discussed further in Chapter 16 on asset pricing.

[32] Scale economies refers to a situation in which the average cost of producing an item, or of conducting a transaction, decreases as the volume of the activity increases.

that view with descriptive approaches intended to determine what the financial world is actually like.

- When the prescriptive and descriptive approaches give different predictions, financial research attempts to resolve the findings.
- Expected utility theory is used to prescribe how agents might select among lotteries with different risks and payoffs.
- Different forms of utility functions can be chosen to reflect different agents' underlying preferences. For example, some agents may be represented as risk-neutral, while others may be represented as highly averse to risk.
- Stochastic dominance orderings can rank some risks using only minimal assumptions about agent preferences. For example, if agents are assumed to be risk-neutral, risks can be ranked in terms of just their expected values.
- Behavioral (psychological) approaches to finance attempt to describe how agents actually choose among risky alternatives. For example, they may be overconfident, or they may use wishful thinking.
- Behavioral approaches have identified a number of ways in which agents interpret risks and choose among them. For example, some agents may be highly conservative, either in their interpretations of what is likely to happen or in their willingness to change their views.
- The neoclassical paradigm that underlies prescriptive approaches to financial economics makes a number of specific assumptions regarding how agents make financial decisions. Essentially, it assumes agents are highly logical, excellent at calculation, and know the exact probabilities with which risky events are likely to occur.
- The neoclassical paradigm also assumes information is equally available to all decision makers, but in fact decision makers are not usually equally well informed.
- The neoclassical paradigm further assumes information is freely available, but in practice gathering information is costly. The costs affect both the information that agents actually have, and ways they make their financial decisions.
- In many situations principals make financial decisions on behalf of agents whom they represent.

# QUESTIONS

1.  a. What do von Neumann and Morgenstern show about preferences among risky prospects and their ranking?
    b. How is the expected utility of a risk project defined?
    c. In the von Neumann–Morgenstern framework, what is assumed about objective probability distribution of payoffs to lotteries for all investors?
    d. What is the appeal of using expected utility theory?

2.  a. What is the St. Petersburg Paradox?
    b. How did Daniel Bernoulli propose solving this paradox?
    c. How is the approach for solving the St. Petersburg Paradox suggested by Bernoulli useful in making decisions under uncertainty?

3. How do economists define a lottery?

4. In the von Neumann–Morgenstern framework how is a rational behavior defined?

5. What is meant by a nonsatiable preferences?

6. Charlie Brown's utility function is $50w - w^2$; his current wealth $w$, measured in cents, is zero. Lucy has a penny and wants Charlie to take the following bet: Charlie will owe Lucy 2 if the penny is tossed and comes up heads. Lucy will give Charlie the penny and owe him another if it comes up tails.

   a. Should Charlie Brown take the bet? Why, or why not?

   b. Draw a diagram, and show your calculations.

   c. Lucy, exasperated by her failure to persuade Charlie to take the bet she proposed in above, is wondering if he is more daring than she had thought. This leads her to wonder whether Charlie Brown might gamble if the stakes were doubled. By calculating another expected utility, show that Lucy is not thinking correctly. Verify your calculations using a diagram.

   d. Compute the variances of the old and new bets in above, and using these variances as measures of risk, explain in one sentence why Charlie Brown is even more unwilling to make the new bet.

   e. Suppose Lucy were to propose a third bet as follows. Charlie will owe Lucy 2 cents if the penny is tossed and comes up heads. Lucy will give Charlie $y$ if it comes up tails where $y$ is a number yet to be determined. Show that Charlie Brown will certainly take the new bet if $y$ is at least equal to 3. (In fact, he will take the bet if $y$ is greater than $[50(2084)^{1/2}]/2 \approx 2.2$. You do not have to determine this last number; it is included just in case you were curious about its size.)

7. The following two excerpts are from a paper by Lars Tyge Nielsen, "Differentiable von Neumann–Morgenstern Utility," published in *Economic Theory* (Vol. 14, No. 2, 1999).

   > Differentiability is a convenient property of von Neumann-Morgenstern utility functions which is almost always imposed but has not been translated into behavioral terms. (p. 285)

   a. What is meant by differentiability is a "property of von Neumann–Morgenstern utility functions"?

   > In most applications in economics and finance, the utility function is assumed to be risk averse. (p. 286)

   b. What does that type of behavior mean?

8. The following excerpt is from "Deal or No Deal? Decision Making under Risk in a Large-Payoff Game Show" by Thierry Post, Martijn J. van den Assem, Guido Baltussen and Richard H. Thaler and published in the *American Economic Review* (Vol. 98, No. 1, March 2008):

A wide range of theories of risky choice have been developed, including the normative expected utility theory of John von Neumann and Oskar Morgenstern (1944) and the descriptive prospect theory of Daniel Kahneman and Amos Tversky (1979). Although risky choice is fundamental to virtually every branch of economics, empirical testing of these theories has proven to be difficult. (p. 38)

    **a.** What is meant by the "descriptive prospect theory of Daniel Kahneman and Amos Tversky (1979)"?

    **b.** How does the normative expected utility theory of von Neumann and Morgenstern differ from prospect theory?

    **c.** Why do you think these theories might require different forms of empirical testing?

**9.** What is the shape of the utility function of risk-averse agents? In answering this question you can assume that the agents always prefer more wealth to less.

**10.** What is meant by the coefficient of absolute risk aversion and what does it seek to measure?

**11.** For each of the following utility functions, explain what type of agent its preferences reflect and the economic interpretation of each and derive the coefficient of absolute risk aversion:

    **a.** linear utility function

    **b.** quadratic utility function

    **c.** logarithmic utility function

    **d.** negative exponential utility function

    **e.** power utility function

**12.** **a.** What is meant by stochastic dominance and how it is used in decision making?

    **b.** What is meant by Rothschild-Stigliz dominance?

**13.** **a.** What is behavioral finance?

    **b.** What are the two building blocks of behavioral finance?

**14.** In behavioral finance, what is meant by

    **a.** representativeness?

    **b.** anchoring?

**15.** What are some of the implications for financial decision making once it is recognized that financial information can be both costly to acquire and costly to apply?

**16.** **a.** What is meant by information asymmetry?

    **b.** What problems do information asymmetry lead to?

**17.** What is meant by signaling and its importance in dealing with information asymmetry?

18. **a.** What is meant by agency theory?

    **b.** Give two examples where agency theory is applied?

19. What is the principal impact of transaction costs on arbitrage possibilities and the pricing of financial assets?

---

# REFERENCES

Akerlof, George. (1970). "The Market For Lemons: Quality Uncertainty and The Market Mechanism," *Quarterly Journal of Economics* **84**: 488–500.

Alchian, Armen, and Harold Demsetz. (1972). "Production, Information Costs, and Economic Organization," *American Economic Review* **62**: 777–795.

Arrow, Kenneth J. (1971). *Essays in the Theory of Risk-Bearing*. Chicago: Markham.

Barberis, Nicholas, and Richard Thaler. (2003). "A Survey of Behavioral Finance," in George M. Constantinides, Milton Harris, and Rene Stulz (eds.), *Handbook of the Economics of Finance*. Burlington, MA, Elsevier.

Demsetz, Harold. (1968). "The Cost of Transacting," *Quarterly Journal of Economics* **82**: 33–53.

Freixas, Xavier, and Jean-Charles Rochet. (2008). *Microeconomics of Banking* (2nd ed.). Cambridge: MIT Press.

Kahneman, Daniel, and Amos Tversky. (1979). "Prospect Theory: An Analysis of Decision under Risk," *Econometrica* **47**: 263–299.

Knight, Frank H. (1933). *Risk, Uncertainty, and Profit*. Chicago: University of Chicago Press.

Marschak, Jacob, and Roy Radner. (1972). *The Economic Theory of Teams*. New Haven, CT: Cowles Foundation, Yale University Press.

Pratt, John W. (1964). "Risk Aversion in the Small and in the Large," *Econometrica* **32**: 122–136.

Rachev, Svetlozar T., Stoyan V. Stoyanov, and Frank J. Fabozzi. (2008). *Advanced Stochastic Models, Risk Assessment, and Portfolio Optimization*. Hoboken, NJ: John Wiley & Sons.

Rothschild, Michael, and Joseph E. Stiglitz. (1970). "Increasing Risk I: A Definition," *Journal of Economic Theory* **2**: 225–243.

Rothschild, Michael, and Joseph E. Stiglitz. (1971). "Increasing Risk II: Its Economic Consequences," *Journal of Economic Theory* **3**: 66–84.

Shefrin, Hersh. (2005). *A Behavioral Approach To Asset Pricing*. Burlington, MA: Elsevier.

Spence, A. Michael. (1973). "Job Market Signaling," *Quarterly Journal of Economics* **87**: 355–374.

Stiglitz, Joseph E. (2002). "Information and The Change in The Paradigm in Economics," *American Economic Review* **92**: 460–501.

Tversky, Amos, and Daniel Kahneman. (1986). "Rational Choice and The Framing of Decisions," *Journal of Business* **59**: 251–278.

Tversky, Amos, and Daniel Kahneman. (1992). "Advances in Prospect Theory: Cumulative Representation of Uncertainty," *Journal of Risk and Uncertainty* **5**: 297–323.

# 10

# CONTINGENT CLAIMS
# AND CONTINGENT STRATEGIES

*T*his chapter introduces the concepts of contingent claims and contingent strategies. Both are tools for analyzing and valuing the effects of risky financial decisions, and both are used extensively in the rest of the book. Indeed, we later show how contingent claims can be used to value any financial instrument, including such apparently exotic instruments as put and call options and convertible securities. We also provide further examples of how contingent strategies can be used to improve payoffs from risky decision making, as well as how they can be interpreted as ways of valuing real options.

We begin by explaining the notion of states of the world, a way of classifying risky outcomes whose value can then be represented using contingent claims. After providing examples of valuation using contingent claims, we introduce the concept of incomplete markets, and consider its importance for explaining real-world financial arrangements. We then examine some financial instruments and arrangements that can be used to trade or to manage risks. We also show how contingent claims analysis provides an alternative way to establish the Modigliani-Miller theorem about capital structure explained in Chapter 5. Finally, we discuss using contingent strategies: how decisions can differ in different states of the world, and how payoffs may be improved by making decisions that are contingent on the currently prevailing state of the world.

## 10.1 STATES OF THE WORLD

The idea of *states of the world* is useful for thinking about convenient ways to model risky payoffs. In a two-time-point model, states of the world are defined as those future events that matter to the decision problem being considered. These states of the world are defined by the decision maker to be mutually exclusive and collectively exhaustive. Using an example given by Savage (1951), if one is about to break a ninth egg into a bowl already containing eight other eggs, the relevant states of the world could be whether or not the ninth egg is rotten and would hence spoil the others.

(Here we presume the rottenness of an egg is not discernible until the egg has been broken and fallen into the bowl.)

In a second example more closely related to finance, an investor might be concerned with the future price of a share of stock, and this price might in turn depend on economic conditions. Suppose the investor defines (1) "states" to represent economic conditions and (2) "future prices" to be the following list of possible stock prices that may be realized at the time a given state is actually realized:

| State | Future Prices |
|---|---|
| 1 | $10 |
| 2 | $ 8 |
| 3 | $ 6 |

For example, state 1 might mean that the industry in which the firm operates faces buoyant market conditions; state 2, conditions that are neither good nor bad; and state 3, conditions that are depressed. In each state, the effect is registered on the stock price. We shall usually associate probabilities with the states; for example, $p_i$ might represent the probability that state $i$ will actually occur; that is, $i = 1, 2, 3$. Because the states are mutually exclusive, only one can actually occur; because they are collectively exhaustive, one of the three must occur. Hence, $\Sigma p_i = 1$.[1]

## 10.2  CONTINGENT CLAIMS AND THEIR VALUE

A *unit contingent claim* is a security that will pay an amount of $1 if a certain state of the world is actually realized, but nothing otherwise. A claim that pays $1 if state $i$ is realized is frequently called a *unit claim on state i*. A unit contingent claim is also referred to as a *primary security* or *Arrow-Debreu security*.[2] Accordingly, the future stock price described in Section 10.1 may be regarded as equivalent to a package containing all of the following:

Ten unit claims on state 1
Eight unit claims on state 2
Six unit claims on state 3

The idea of a contingent claim is thus useful for expressing, in terms of fundamental units, exactly what a given security's payoff may be in different possible states of the world.

[1] Although throughout this book we make less use of multiperiod models using contingent claims, we can also define states at different points in time, for example, the states of the world at different times. Since these time-state definitions are used relatively infrequently, we shall develop them further in specific contexts encountered later in the book.
[2] So-named after the economists who introduced them—Arrow (1964) and Debreu (1959).

It may take a little imagination to come up with real-world examples of claims, and those real-world examples are not numerous.[3] But packages of unit claims represent perfect substitutes for the more ordinary types of securities such as stocks or bonds, and we shall frequently find it useful to employ claims to help understand price relations between securities. For example, if we assume a perfectly competitive financial market along with a description of future events in terms of states of the world, certain price relationships between securities and contingent claims must be obtained. This means in turn that certain predictable relationships between securities prices must also be obtained, as introduced next and as examined further in Chapter 16.

To see these relationships, suppose that we can describe the world using two states and that two stocks are available, stock A and stock B. We assume the stocks' future prices have the following distributions:

| State | Future Prices Stock A | Future Prices Stock B |
|---|---|---|
| 1 | $10 | $7 |
| 2 | $ 8 | $9 |

Let $A(1) = \$6$ denote the time 1 price of stock A, $B(1) = \$5$ the time 1 price of stock B, and suppose these prices admit no arbitrage opportunities. Now, if we let $C_1$ and $C_2$ represent the time 1 prices of unit claims on states 1 and 2, we can use the foregoing information about stock prices and payoffs to find the time 1 prices $C_1$ and $C_2$. Purchasing stock A for $6 is equivalent to buying a package of 10 unit claims on state 1 and 8 unit claims on state 2, while buying stock B for $5 is equivalent to buying a package of 7 unit claims on state 1 and 9 unit claims on state 2. Since the unit claims comprising the two stocks are perfect substitutes, they must sell for the same prices in a perfect market. Hence, we can write:

$$10C_1 + 8C_2 = \$6$$
$$7C_1 + 9C_2 = \$5$$

which can be solved to obtain:

$$C_1 = \$\frac{7}{17}, \quad C_2 = \$\frac{4}{17}$$

We can use the same reasoning to find the risk-free rate of return that must be obtained in this market. Since a risk-free instrument is one that offers the same payoff irrespective of which state of the world obtains, we wish to find a combination of the two stocks that gives the same time 2 payoff, here denoted $k$, in either state of the world. That is, the following equation must be solved for $\alpha$:

---

[3] A ticket to win on a horse race is an example of a claim; a fire insurance policy is another. One example of a unit claim is an option that pays off $1 if the value of some underlying asset exceeds a fixed dollar value.

$$\alpha \begin{pmatrix} 10 \\ 8 \end{pmatrix} + (1 - \alpha) \begin{pmatrix} 7 \\ 9 \end{pmatrix} = \begin{pmatrix} k \\ k \end{pmatrix}$$

We can write the payoff $k$ as equal to either of the following payoffs:

$$10\alpha + 7(1 - \alpha) = 8\alpha + 9(1 - \alpha)$$

which implies that:

$$2\alpha = 2(1 - \alpha)$$

so that $\alpha = \frac{1}{2}$. The riskless payoff is then $\frac{1}{2}(10) + \frac{1}{2}(7) = \$8.50$, and this can be obtained for a price equal to $\frac{1}{2}(6) + \frac{1}{2}(5) = \$5.50$, since a portfolio composed of equal proportions of the two stocks creates the riskless investment. Accordingly, the risk-free rate of return is:

$$\frac{\$8.50 - \$5.50}{\$5.50} = \frac{6}{11} = 54.55\%$$

Of course, this is not necessarily a realistic number for a risk-free rate of interest.[4] However, our purpose here is to develop illustrative calculations to display relations between contingent claims, and for this purpose particular sizes of numbers are not really important.

Another way of making a riskless investment is to buy one of each available unit claim, that is, one claim on state 1 and one claim on state 2. Such a portfolio gives a certain payoff of $1 for an investment cost:

$$\$\frac{4}{17} + \$\frac{7}{17} = \$\frac{11}{17}$$

The rate of return on this investment is then:

$$\frac{\$1 - \$\frac{11}{17}}{\$\frac{11}{17}} = \frac{\$17 - \$11}{\$11} = \frac{\$6}{\$11} = 54.55\%$$

just as before.

---

### 10.3  INVESTOR'S UTILITY MAXIMIZATION IN CONTINGENT CLAIMS MARKETS

In this section we describe how an investor can solve the utility maximization problem when facing risk in a market for contingent claims. For our illustration, we shall continue with stocks A and B from the previous section. Further, we shall assume the

---

[4] Whether it is realistic or not depends on the length of the time period under consideration, a matter we have left unspecified.

**TABLE 10.1**
SUMMARY OF TERMINAL WEALTH IN TWO STATES

| | No. of shares Purchased | Terminal wealth | |
| --- | --- | --- | --- |
| | | State 1 | State 2 |
| Purchase A only | 100 | $1,000 | $ 800 |
| Purchase B only | 120 | $ 840 | $1,080 |

**FIGURE 10.1**
MARKET OPPORTUNITY LINE SHOWING IMPLIED PRICES OF UNIT CLAIMS

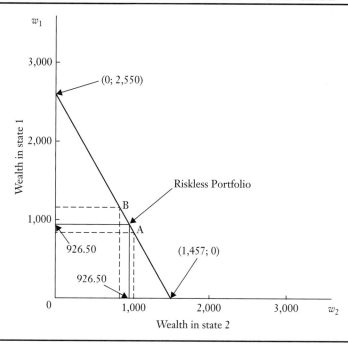

investor's initial wealth to be $600. This scenario is summarized in Table 10.1. We let $w_1$ represent wealth if state 1 occurs and $w_2$ represent wealth if state 2 occurs. We can plot these data in $(w_1, w_2)$ space as shown in Figure 10.1. Note that the previously determined riskless position of dividing the purchases to obtain an equal number of each security (54.5 of each) generates a riskless terminal wealth position of $w_1 = w_2 = \$926.50$.

We can also use another way to calculate the value of the claims' combinations at time 1. We can write the equation of the straight line in Figure 10.1 as:

$$w_2 = a - bw_1$$

so that for the time 1 price of stock A we have:

$$\$800 = a - \$1,000b$$

while for the time 1 price of stock B we have:

$$\$1,080 = a - \$840b$$

Solving these two simultaneous equations, we find $b = 1.75$ and $a = \$2,550$. Thus, when $w_1 = 0, w_2 = \$2,550$, while when $w_2 = 0, w_1 = \$1,457$, which are the two intercepts of the line on their respective axes in Figure 10.1.

Now if $w_2 = 0$, we have the case of a claim (primary security) on state 1. (The security pays $\$1,457$ in state 1 and nothing otherwise.) The price of this claim can be calculated by dividing initial wealth by the maximum wealth obtained if state 1 occurs, or $\$600/\$1,457 = 0.41 (= \frac{7}{17})$. Similarly, the price of primary security 2 is $\$600/\$2,550 = 0.24 (= 4/17)$, the same values as obtained previously.

Note that in Figure 10.1 the investor's time 1 position is some point on the line from $A$ to $B$. How could the investor obtain a terminal wealth position lying beyond these points? The investor could engage in *short sales*, that is, selling shares not currently owned, for delivery when the unknown future state of the world is revealed. In this transaction the investor obtains cash from the time 0 sale of one security and uses it to buy the other. In so doing, the investor promises later to buy the security sold short at whatever price will be prevailing and deliver it. Note that there is a potential for large gains or losses in such transactions. Here the initial wealth will be used as a constraint and we shall require that at worst the investor will have zero terminal wealth if he guesses incorrectly. That is, no net borrowing is permitted at the end of the period so that the investor cannot go beyond the intercepts in Figure 10.1.

To illustrate, consider point $w_1 = \$1,457, w_2 = 0$. Let $n_A$ be the number of shares of stock $A$ and $n_B$ the number of shares of stock $B$ purchased. If state 1 occurs, the terminal wealth will be:

$$10n_A + 7n_B = \$1,457$$

while if state 2 occurs, we must have:

$$8n_A + 9n_B = 0$$

Solving these equations simultaneously, we find $n_B = -343$. If the investor sells short 343 shares of stock B at the current price of $5, he will receive $1,715. Combining this with the initial wealth of $600 gives $2,315, so this investor may buy $2,315/$6 = 386 $n_A$ at $6 per share. If state 1 eventuates, the investor will receive $3,860 ($10 times 386 shares) but now must pay $2,401 ($7 times 343 shares) for stock B shares to cover the short position. The net terminal wealth is $3,860 − $2,401 = $1,459 (difference due to rounding), as required. In state 2, the terminal wealth will be equal to $3,088 (386 shares times $8 per share) reduced by the cost to repurchase stock B to cover the short position, 343 shares at $9 per share or $3,087. Therefore, the net terminal wealth is equal to zero (the calculations show it is $1 but that is due to rounding).

Note that none of the points we have considered will necessarily be a utility-maximizing point. To determine this point, it is necessary to know the investor's utility function in $(w_1, w_2)$ space. Given a utility function, the investor's utility-maximizing position is the familiar one discussed in Chapter 2. The optimal portfolio for the investor satisfies the tangency condition that the slope of the wealth constraint (the ratio of the prices of the unit claims) equals the slope of the indifference curve (marginal rate of substitution of state 1 consumption for state 2 consumption).

The immediate purpose of the foregoing demonstration is to show that every security can be viewed as a bundle of unit claims and thus represents a combination of positions regarding future states of the world. Moreover, in these circumstances an investor can attain any point along the market opportunity line. If, on the other hand, there are fewer securities than the number of distinct states, the individual's optimal consumption choices may not be attainable. The significance of this will be explored in the next section.

The second purpose, although it is not yet clearly revealed, is to demonstrate that contingent claim analysis provides a powerful method for valuing complex financial instruments and financial arrangements, as will be shown in Chapters 17 through 19.

---

## 10.4 INCOMPLETE MARKETS FOR CONTINGENT CLAIMS

A market is said to be a *complete market* when economic agents can structure any set of future state payoffs by investing in a portfolio of unit continent claims (i.e., primary securities). A financial market is said to be *incomplete* if the number of (*linearly*) *independent securities* traded in it is smaller than the number of distinct states of the world. Clearly, market incompleteness depends on how states of the world are defined. However, since the number of states of the world used to describe a typical financial market is likely to be large,[5] the possibility that real-world financial markets will be incomplete is a very real one.

The importance of market incompleteness is best introduced by an example. Let us consider an economy with three possible states of the world and suppose only two securities (taking the form of unit claims for ease of exposition) are traded in it. Table 10.2 describes the securities in terms of their time 1 payoffs for each state of the world. It is apparent from the table that weighted averages of the two unit claims can

TABLE 10.2
MARKET VALUES OF TWO SECURITIES AT TIME 1

|          | States of the World | | |
|----------|------|------|------|
| Security | 1    | 2    | 3    |
| 1        | 1    | 0    | 0    |
| 2        | 0    | 1    | 0    |

---

[5] The appropriate number of states depends on the purpose of the analysis.

be used to create packages with time 1 distributions of values ranging between zero and unity, the actual outcome depending on whether state 1 or state 2 is realized. However, by using just the existing two unit claims, an investor cannot create an income claim of other than zero in state 3. Moreover, no investor can arrange a risk-free investment in this example, because it is not possible to guarantee the same return in every state of the world by using the available securities.

The situation is quite different if a third unit claim worth $1 in state 3 and zero in the other states becomes available. Now the number of claims equals the number of distinct states, and a risk-free investment can be arranged.

We are now ready to discuss some practical implications of market incompleteness. It is obvious from the foregoing example that investor choice is restricted in incomplete markets. Moreover if investor choices are restricted, the investors will never be better off, and are likely to be worse off, than would be the case if markets were complete (i.e., if the restrictions were removed). In such situations, it is to be expected that if ways of completing the market can be found, those possibilities are likely to be utilized. That is, in the context of incomplete financial markets the appearance of new instruments might be regarded as attempts to provide investors with financial opportunities not otherwise available. The appearance of derivatives (options, futures, and swaps) can be regarded as examples of such attempts. Mossin (1977) argues that the preference existing firms show for organizing new activities as separate corporations may be another indication of attempts to deal with market incompleteness.

We shall have more to say about recently created financial instruments, their relations to incomplete markets, and their pricing in later chapters. For the present we wish next to indicate some of the ways in which real-world financial instruments and arrangements can be interpreted as contingent claims.

## 10.5 Modigliani-Miller Revisited

Let's revisit the Modigliani-Miller theorem of Chapter 5 using contingent claim analysis. Our purpose is to provide a different illustration of how the securities a firm issues can be regarded as representing only a division of the firm's operating earnings.

Let $p(s)$ be the price at time 1 of receiving $1 at time 2 if state $s$ is realized. That is, $p(s)$ is the time 1 price of a unit claim that pays $1 at time 2, if state $s$ then occurs. Now suppose management raises funds by issuing a bond that promises to pay $500 (which includes interest and face value) at time 2. Continuing to assume that there are only two possible states that can be realized at time 2, and that the firm can generate operating earnings in each state as shown below, the bondholder and stockholder claims are also as shown:

| State | Operating earnings | Bondholders | Stockholders |
|---|---|---|---|
| 1 | $1,700 | $500 | $1,200 |
| 2 | $ 800 | $500 | $ 300 |

Using the prices of the contingent claims, the value of the bond at time 1, denoted by $B(1)$, is:

$$B(1) = \$500\, p(1) + \$500\, p(2)$$

In other words, to rule out the possibility of arbitrage, the value of the bonds must be just equal to the value of a package of contingent claims constituting a perfect substitute for the bonds. Similarly the time 1 value of equity, denoted by $S(1)$, is:

$$S(1) = \$1{,}200\, p(1) + \$300\, p(2)$$

Finally, the value of both securities (a value that also represents the market value of the firm), denoted by $V(1)$, is:

$$V(1) = \$1{,}700\, p(1) + \$800\, p(2)$$

Notice that the market value of the firm is just the sum of the market values of the two securities, as it must be under the Modigliani-Miller assumptions.

The calculation shows that payoffs on the firm's securities, and payoffs on the firm itself, can be regarded as packages of contingent claims. Any different set of packages will have the same combined value, so long as the payoffs add up to the firm's entire earnings. To see this, consider a second case in which bonds promising to pay $1,000 at time 2 are issued. The distribution of the claims is then:

| State | Operating earnings | Bondholders | Stockholders |
|-------|--------------------|-------------|--------------|
| 1     | $1,700             | $1,000      | $700         |
| 2     | $ 800              | $ 800       | $ 0          |

Since these bonds will be partially defaulted in state 2 because the payoff is less than the required bond payment, the time 1 value of the bonds is:

$$B(1) = \$1{,}000\, p(1) + \$800\, p(2)$$

and the time 2 value of equity is:

$$S(1) = \$700\, p(1) + \$0\, p(2)$$

But this still means the time 1 value of both securities together is as given earlier for $V(1)$:

$$V(1) = \$1{,}700\, p(1) + \$800\, p(2)$$

The importance of this discussion is threefold. First, it uses a different method to confirm the irrelevance of capital structure based on the assumptions made by

Modigliani and Miller as established in Chapter 5. Second, it demonstrates that bonds and equity merely represent different ways of packaging the fundamental units (contingent claims) that can be regarded as representing the firm's earnings. Under the assumptions of the Modigliani-Miller analysis, different ways of packaging fundamental units have no effect on the total numbers of each kind of fundamental unit represented by the firm's earnings. Third, the discussion here shows how easy it is to apply contingent claim analysis to valuing different securities. In essence the demonstration shows that financial theory values different kinds of securities, no matter how complex, in exactly the same way. In each case the basis of a security's value is the package of fundamental units it represents.

## 10.6 FINANCIAL INSTRUMENTS AS CONTINGENT CLAIMS

Most financial instruments can be bought or sold, but not all of them are actively traded in financial markets. For example, a common form of contingent claim (and one that is close in concept to a unit claim) is a lottery ticket. In its simplest form this claim results in its holder winning either a positive prize or zero. Accordingly, this lottery ticket represents a claim that can be valued using two states of the world.[6] But lottery tickets, once issued, are rarely traded again. The same is true of such other contingent claims as the tickets obtained when betting on horse races or similar contests.

An insurance policy is a contingent claim that comes closer to our usual notions of a financial instrument, but traditional forms of insurance policies are rarely traded in the financial markets. On the other hand, put or call options, representing contingent claims for selling or buying securities or financial indices at prespecified prices (options will be discussed extensively in Chapters 18 and 19), trade actively on such organized exchanges. Rights and warrants are other examples of contingent claims in that they permit, but do not require, the holder to buy securities on prespecified terms.

There are also securities that have *embedded derivatives* in them, derivatives that are not traded separately from the instrument itself. For example, a *callable bond* is a bond that grants the issuer the right to redeem the bond at some time in the future and at a specified price. That is, a callable bond can be viewed as a straight bond with an embedded call option granted to the issuer. A *putable bond* is a bond that grants the investor the right to sell (i.e., put) the bond to the issuer in the future at a specified price. Hence, the bond structure can be viewed as a straight bond with an embedded put option. *Convertible securities*, which include convertible bonds or convertible preferred stocks, represent contingent claims in that they typically allow the owner to exchange the original issue for other securities, usually common stock, and they are callable. Some convertible securities even include an embedded put option.

A number of other commonplace financial arrangements, again not usually traded in the marketplace, also can be regarded as contingent claims. As suggested by Brennan (1979), these include such possibilities as a firm's tax liability, which is

---

[6] Obviously, if a lottery has several different prizes, several states of the world may need to be defined in order to describe it completely.

dependent on the size of its taxable income.[7] In this case the relevant states of the world are economic conditions that affect reported income. Tax shields on depreciation or leasing expense will be valuable only if there is sufficient operating income. Costs that will be paid only in the event of a firm facing technical insolvency represent another kind of contingent claim on the firm. Finally, the opportunities a firm may have to make future investments (investments with varying degrees of profitability) or to purchase physical assets when a lease expires also represent contingent claims owned by the firm.

The realization of many of these opportunities is often dependent on the firm's using contingent strategies (taking different decisions in different states of the world), a matter to which we next turn.

## 10.7  CONTINGENT STRATEGIES

Just as investor satisfaction can increase if more kinds of contingent claims become available, a firm can improve its earnings distribution[8] by using a *contingent strategy*. To recognize the possibility of taking contingencies into account in decision making, we say a decision maker uses contingent planning when instead of merely saying "I will do $X$," the person announces "I will do $X_1$ if state 1 is realized, $X_2$ if state 2 is realized," and so on.[9] The details of contingency planning are referred to as *formulating a contingent strategy*.

Just as an insufficient number of securities can restrict investor satisfaction in an incomplete market, an absence of contingent planning can lead to less desirable payoff distributions than might otherwise be available. To establish the connection between contingent claims and contingent strategies in greater detail, we first discuss the context in which contingent strategies arise and then provide an example showing how contingent planning can effect improvements over noncontingent decision making.

Consider a firm planning to select a location and build a factory now in the hopes of later expanding its facilities if its products can successfully be marketed. The initial location decision cannot easily be reversed and will affect future payoffs earned by the firm. For example, the kinds of expansion activities that may later take place will very likely depend on the initial location and what may be learned about it in the future. It might be that at one location a complete product would be produced, while at another location components would be produced for assembly still elsewhere. In any event, once a given location has been selected, the type of expansion plan selected will depend on the initial location choice. Furthermore, the details of that type of expansion plan may change as time passes, because more is likely to become known about local conditions after the initial location decision has been made. Accordingly, management

---

[7] In the mid 1980s, the U.S. government effectively allowed the sale of tax benefits under certain conditions via a leasing arrangement. See Fabozzi and Yaari (1983).

[8] If it costs nothing to use a contingent strategy, then even if it does not improve firm payoffs, it can never leave them worse off.

[9] "One if by land, and two if by sea" is an example of how contingent planning was employed in Paul Revere's time.

TABLE 10.3
DECISION SEQUENCES AND THEIR PAYOFFS

| Decision sequence | Payoff in state g | Payoff in state h |
|---|---|---|
| Aa | $3 | $3 |
| Ab | $0 | -$4 |
| Ba | $3 | -$3 |
| Bb | $7 | -$7 |

has a choice: select now the location that offers the highest criterion function value if the future turns out as anticipated, or alternatively, select the location most suitable for taking a variety of possible decisions if the future turns out to differ from the most likely scenario presently anticipated. The latter is a form of contingent planning.

To develop the details of computations related to contingent planning, we present a numerical example. In doing so, we assume the particular decision problem discussed can be considered separately from others faced by the firm. Also, for simplicity we assume that the firm wishes to maximize the expected value of the payoffs involved.[10] Esoteric Electronics is a manufacturer of components used in both industrial applications and in space exploration. At the present time, the company is planning its production for the next two quarterly periods. It has to decide whether to produce either a or b components in each quarter, since it cannot produce both components simultaneously. Steady production of either one component or the other for both quarters eliminates setup charges. On the other hand, revenues from continued production of b will be affected by the success or failure of a space exploration mission, the results of which will become known before the end of the first quarter but after the time for making the first quarter's production decision has passed. The revenue from a, a non-space-industry-utilized component, is independent of the mission's outcome.

The foregoing considerations are captured in Table 10.3, where production plan payoffs are shown to depend on the state of the world (i.e., the mission outcome). A successful mission outcome is denoted by g and an unsuccessful outcome by h. The sequences of events are also displayed in decision tree form in Figure 10.2.

Now suppose that the best presently available estimate of the probability of a successful mission (state g) is 0.65. Management might then make the calculations shown in Table 10.4 and state that they should elect to produce a in both quarters since that gives the highest expected payoff. However, the kind of thinking used to select the strategy of producing a in both quarters proceeds along lines like the following. Long production runs are better because they eliminate setup costs. At the same time, mission success is more likely than failure, so on an expected value basis it pays to produce a in both quarters. At this point, the reader should consider how noncontingent strategies would be displayed on the tree of Figure 10.2.

The problem with noncontingent strategies in the assumed circumstances is that the actual mission outcome will be known before the second-quarter production must

---

[10] In the present example, expected utility maximization can also be assumed merely by interpreting the payoffs as expressed in utility units.

**FIGURE 10.2**
ILLUSTRATION OF A CONTINGENT STRATEGY

**FIGURE 10.2**
ILLUSTRATION OF A CONTINGENT STRATEGY

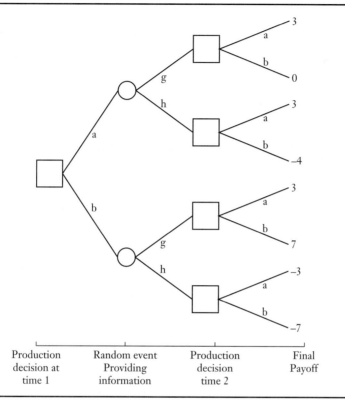

| Production decision at time 1 | Random event Providing information | Production decision time 2 | Final Payoff |

**TABLE 10.4**
NONCONTINGENT STRATEGIES AND EXPECTED PAYOFFS

| Noncontingent Strategy | Expected Payoff |
| --- | --- |
| a(ga, ha) | $3(0.65) + $3(0.35) = $3.00 |
| a(gb, hb) | $0(0.65) + $4(0.35) = $1.40 |
| b(ga, ha) | $3(0.65) + $3(0.35) = $0.90 |
| b(gb, hb) | $7(0.65) + $7(0.35) = $2.10 |

*Note:* The notation *c*(*gd*, *hd*) means that production of *c* is planned for the first quarter, followed by production of *d* in the second quarter regardless of whether the mission succeeds or fails.

be determined. Although it is true that setup costs will have to be incurred a second time if switches in production are made after the first quarter, these increased costs might in some circumstances be offset by the higher payoffs realized from producing whichever product is appropriate once the mission outcome is known. Hence, it can be important to select plans that allow for this possibility of revision, especially if the most likely outcome does not occur.

**TABLE 10.5**
CONTINGENT STRATEGIES AND EXPECTED PAYOFFS

| Contingent Strategy | Expected Payoff |
|---|---|
| a(ga, hb) | $3(0.65) + $4(0.35) = $0.55 |
| a(gb, ha) | $0(0.65) + $3(0.35) = $1.05 |
| b(ga, hb) | $3(0.65) + $7(0.35) = $0.50 |
| b(gb, ha) | $7(0.65) + $3(0.35) = $3.50 |

To see how this type of reasoning may be implemented, we now consider contingent strategies. These kinds of strategies may be denoted by c(gd, he), which means that production of c is planned for the first quarter, followed by production of d in the second quarter if the mission succeeds or by e if the mission fails. Notice that a contingent strategy of the type c(gd, hd) is really degenerate in the sense that it does not differ from a strategy in the noncontingent category already considered. The nondegenerate contingent strategies and their payoffs are given in Table 10.5; the complete contingent solution method considers the strategies in both Tables 10.4 and 10.5. One can use Figure 10.2 to see how a contingent strategy differs from a noncontingent strategy by imposing fewer constraints on the decision maker's choices.

From Table 10.5, we see that the optimal strategy is b(gb, ha). In other words, management begins by producing b and continues with b if the mission is successful but switches to a if the mission is unsuccessful. Note this strategy has a higher expected value than the noncontingent strategy that management initially considered. What we have shown, then, is that incorporating flexibility into the firm's decision making encompasses a wider range of possibilities, and the extra flexibility gained never does any harm (except for the costs of making extra computations). More often than not, the procedure may yield real benefits, as in the example just studied.

In other situations, the increased payoffs to contingent planning may only be available at increased cost. The problem then is to decide whether the expected increased benefits outweigh the increased costs. We shall discuss examples of financial decisions involving these issues at several points in the succeeding development. We shall see that contingent planning provides ways to redistribute both risks and information about risks. In particular, we shall discuss management's use of information about future conditions in relation to making contingent capital expenditure decisions in Chapter 26. We shall also discuss management's provision of information to investors in relation to making contingent financing decisions (e.g., issuing convertible bonds) in Part VII of this book.

## ● ● ● KEY POINTS

- Contingent claims analysis and contingent strategies are tools for dealing with risk in financial decision making.
- Contingent claims analysis uses the notion of states of the world in assessing future risky payoffs.

- A unit contingent claim (also known as a primary security or Arrow-Debreu security) is a security that has a payoff of $1 if a certain state of the world is actually realized, but nothing in all other states.
- A contingent claim that pays off $1 if state $i$ is realized is also referred to as a unit claim on state $i$.
- Although few unit contingent claims exist in reality, claims represent a useful tool to employ in valuing securities and in understanding relations among securities prices.
- An investor facing risk in a market for contingent claims may formulate her decision problem as one of utility maximization.
- Every security can be viewed as representing a bundle of unit claims and thereby further represents a combination of positions (long and short) regarding future states of the world.
- Contingent claims analysis can be used to show how an investor can affect his terminal wealth position by engaging in short sales (i.e., selling shares not currently owned, for delivery when the unknown future state of the world is revealed). The outcomes in this case are riskier than they would be in the absence of short selling.
- If the number of (linearly) independent securities traded is smaller than the number of distinct states of the world, the financial market is said to be incomplete.
- Because the number of states of the world necessary to describe a well-functioning financial market is likely to be large, the possibility that real-world financial markets will be incomplete is a very real one.
- Although many financial instruments representing contingent claims can be bought or sold, not all financial instruments or arrangements are actively traded in financial markets.
- Contingent strategies can be used by a firm's management to recognize the possibility of taking contingencies into account in financial decision making. Contingent strategies can improve the payoffs obtained from financial decision making.

## QUESTIONS

1. What is the purpose of understanding:
   a. contingent claims?
   b. contingent strategies?

2. How is the concept of "states of the world" useful in making decisions under risk? Under uncertainty?

3. What is meant by a unit contingent claim and why is this concept useful in financial economics?

4. Suppose that we can describe the world using two states and that two assets are available, asset $K$ and asset $L$. We assume the assets' future prices have the following distributions:

| State | Future Prices Asset K | Future Prices Asset L |
|-------|----------------------|----------------------|
| 1 | $25 | $21 |
| 2 | $20 | $18 |

Let $K(1) = \$20$ denote the time 1 price of asset $K$ and $L(1) = \$19$ the time 1 price of asset $L$.

    **a.** Assuming no arbitrage opportunities, what are the values of the unit claims at time 1?

    **b.** What is the risk-free rate of return that must obtain in this market?

5. Suppose that we can describe the world using two states. The time 1 prices for contingent unit claims on states 1 and 2 in this market are $0.3 and $0.5, respectively. An investor's utility function in $(w1, w2)$ space is $U(w1, w2) = w1 \times w2$, where U represents the utility level. In addition, the initial wealth of the investor is $420. What is the maximum utility portfolio for this investor?

6. What is meant by a short sale?

7. What is meant by an incomplete financial market?

8. Suppose that the world can be described using two states and two stocks $Y$ and $Z$ are available. We assume the stocks' future prices have the following distributions:

| State | Future Prices Stock Y | Future Prices Stock Z |
|-------|----------------------|----------------------|
| 1 | $10 | $15 |
| 2 | $20 | $11 |

The initial prices for the stocks are: $Y(1) = \$13$, $Z(1) = \$10$. Our utility function in $(w1, w2)$ space is $U(w1, w2) = w1 \times w2$, where U represents the utility level. Now we have an initial endowment of $420. How many shares and what positions of $Y$ and $Z$ should we choose to build our portfolio so that we actually maximize our utility function? (Assume fractional shares are permitted.)

9. What are several types of bonds that have embedded options can be viewed as contingents claims?

10. Why can a firm's tax liability be viewed as a contingent claim?

11. Henry Morton has an initial wealth endowment of $1,200. He considers the future to be risky but completely characterized by only two possible states. Henry has the opportunity to invest in two securities $S$ and $T$ for which the initial prices are $S(1) = \$10$ and $T(1) = \$12$. The payoffs to these securities are:

| State | Future Prices Security S | Future Prices Security T |
|-------|--------------------------|--------------------------|
| 1 | $10 | $21 |
| 2 | $20 | $18 |

a. If Henry buys only security $S$, how many units can he purchase?

b. If Henry buys only security $T$, how many units can he purchase?

c. What will be his final wealth in both cases and in each state?

d. Suppose now Henry can issue as well as purchase securities. However, he must be able to meet all claims under the occurrence of either state (terminal wealth can be zero, but he cannot renege on any promises). Now how many units maximum of $S$ could Henry sell to buy $T$, and conversely, how many units maximum of $T$ could he sell to buy $S$?

e. What now would be Henry's terminal wealth in both cases and in each state?

12. Two securities have the following payoffs:

| State | Future Prices Security S | Future Prices Security T |
|---|---|---|
| 1 | $10 | $30 |
| 2 | $20 | $10 |

The current prices are $G(1) = \$8$ and $H(1) = \$9$. Both future states are equally likely. Your initial endowment (current wealth) is \$720.

a. If you wanted to purchase a completely risk-free portfolio, how many units of $G$ and $H$ would you buy (fractional units are permitted)?

b. What will be the implied risk-free return?

13. Suppose there is a stock S in the market. The terminal price of S can be \$40, \$42, or \$45. Therefore, we can describe the world in three states. There also exists a security has the payoff as follows:

- When the terminal stock price $S_T$ is greater than \$41, it pays $S_T - \$41$.
- When the terminal stock price $S_T$ is equal to or less than \$41, it pays 0.

Show that this security is a contingent claim.

# REFERENCES

Arrow, Kenneth J. (1964). "The Role of Securities in the Optimal Allocation of Risk-Bearing," *Review of Economic Studies* **31**: 91–96.

Brennan, Michael J. (1979). "The Pricing of Contingent Claims in Discrete Time Models," *Journal of Finance* **34**: 55–68.

Debreu, Gerard. (1959). *The Theory of Value*. New York: John Wiley & Sons.

Fabozzi, Frank J., and Uzi Yaari. (1983). "Valuation of Safe Harbor Tax Benefit Transfer Leases," *Journal of Finance* **37**: 595–605.

Mossin, Jan (1977). *The Economic Efficiency of Financial Markets*. Lexington, MA: Heath.

Savage, Leonard J. (1951). *The Foundations of Statistics*. New York: John Wiley & Sons.

# 11

# RISK AND RISK MANAGEMENT

*W*hat do financial economists mean by risk and how is risk to be managed? In this chapter, we explain why risk cannot be described in the abstract, but instead depends on such specifics as the decision maker's preferences, wealth position, and, in many cases, on environmental circumstances as well. For example, a possible monetary loss of $1,000 can mean a great deal to a struggling student, but much less to a wealthy businessperson. Similarly, a possible loss of $1,000 is more serious in a depressed economy than in a buoyant one. Risks can also be characterized according to a number of other features. For example, risks can differ with the decision maker's chosen time horizon. Moreover, those risks can evolve dynamically through time. Decision makers' preferences can also change, both with respect to differing circumstances and over time. As a result of these many factors characterizing risk, management tasks also take on a large variety of forms that may similarly change through time.

In order to present the complexities of risk-management tasks systematically, this chapter approaches them as management problems. We begin the chapter by outlining different kinds of risks and the attitudes of decision makers facing them. We then examine how different combinations of these elements present a variety of optimization problems. In the present discussion, optimization means doing the best you can, given what you already know and what you can find out.[1] While this concept of optimization includes the concept of expected utility maximization, it goes further. Under uncertainty, for example, maximizing choices are ruled out by definition: Uncertainty is taken to refer to situations where it is not possible to attach probability distributions to possible outcomes. But even under uncertain circumstances, attempting to make good rather than poor decisions is still a sensible goal.

The chapter proceeds by defining differences between risk and uncertainty. Then the decision makers' management objectives and the criteria they employ in pursuing those objectives are considered. Once a criterion has been chosen, and assuming the decision maker has some ability to affect the situation being faced, the chapter discusses how the criterion can be used to guide the choice of decisions. For example, a

---

[1] "What you can find out" depends on whether the cost of finding out is reasonable in relation to your goals. It does not mean "getting information at all costs, irrespective of what its benefits might be."

decision maker may be able to formulate a problem under risk as one of maximizing the expected utility of a pre-selected utility function by choosing among risk transfer methods.

In this chapter, different aspects of probability distributions are considered. Moreover, specifically, we (1) describe some of the main features of the probability distributions that decision makers are likely to encounter in practice, (2) discuss how different probability distributions can be incorporated in problem formulations, and (3) examine how the distributions can affect problem solutions. Finally, different forms of utility functions and how choices of utility functions can affect solutions to risk-management problems are explained.

## 11.1 RISK AND UNCERTAINTIES

While the difference between *uncertainty* and *risk* can be stated as a matter of degree, for discussion purposes it is convenient to distinguish the two situations more sharply. Furthermore, uncertainty itself can be divided into two classifications, the first of which refers to situations where qualitative descriptions are so difficult to generate that it is not practical even to define possible future states of the world. The second kind of uncertainty (and the one usually addressed in the financial economics literature) refers to situations in which it is possible to define future states of the world, but not to attach probability distributions to their possible realizations.[2] Risk refers to situations in which it is possible both to define future states of the world and the probabilities[3] with which they might occur. As we have already stated, the categories are matters of degree: It is not easy, or in some circumstances even possible, to distinguish sharply between the two forms of uncertainty, nor is it easy to distinguish between uncertainty and risk. From a problem-solving point of view, distinguishing between types of uncertainty depends on how practically useful it is to define possible future states of the world, and distinguishing risk from uncertainty depends on how practically useful it is to estimate and employ a probability distribution of state outcomes.

Whatever the form of uncertainty or risk faced, the decision maker starts out by considering how the management problem can be modeled, including how decisions can affect the impact of outcomes. That is, decision makers attempt to foresee possible outcomes, structure them, and, if possible, assess their impacts. Depending on the extent of a decision maker's capabilities and knowledge of a situation, the decision maker may adopt different management techniques.

---

[2] Since it is difficult to say much about situations in which not even states of the world can be defined, the first kind of uncertainty cannot be discussed extensively. Nevertheless, it is important to recognize its complications, since decision makers do sometimes face uncertainties of the first kind. After some short remarks on these circumstances, the rest of this chapter's discussion of uncertainty will focus on the second kind.

[3] The probabilities referred to here are the objective probabilities of events' being realized. They are to be distinguished from risk-neutral probabilities, discussed in Chapter 16, that place values on outcomes of events. It is important to be clear about their differences and their different usages.

## 11.1.1 Uncertainty

The first kind of uncertainty is the most difficult to describe and also the most difficult to deal with. It can arise, for example, in such circumstances as new product development. If the success of a product is likely to be affected by the unknown reactions of both consumers and competitive producers, it may well be difficult to define relevant future states of the world with any useful degree of precision. At the same time, attitudes towards the uncertainties cannot be very precisely specified either, not least because the circumstances themselves are not very well defined. As a result, some decision makers might simply decide to avoid such situations.

However, if a decision maker decides to proceed and attempts to manage a situation like that of new product development, the choice of suitable criteria may be relatively crude. For example, the decision maker may attempt either to avoid some of the uncertainties or attempt to control possible losses.[4] To help formulate alternative possible actions, the decision maker might attempt to determine key aspects of the new product's acceptance by consumers, as well as to determine key aspects of competitor reactions. One consideration in deciding to face uncertainty of the first kind might be that losing out to competitors is regarded as an unacceptable outcome. If so, the best the decision maker might be able to do is to go ahead with a (necessarily sketchy) development plan, and simultaneously formulate an exit strategy if things work out badly.

The second type of uncertainty, and the type that is most frequently described in the literature, can be represented by a decision tree that outlines the possible outcomes of a situation (see Chapter 10 for an example). However, by definition uncertainty means it is not practically useful to attempt to attach probabilities to the outcomes.[5] For example, a large financial institution might face bankruptcy if certain asset markets fail to function smoothly. In analyzing these prospects, management of the financial institution might be able to establish possible loss magnitudes in several lines of business, yet still be unable to describe the outcomes probabilistically.[6] In such situations decision makers are likely to place considerable emphasis on loss prevention, possibly attempting to avoid what are seen to be the worst outcomes. For example, in the uncertain world financial environment starting in the summer of 2007, one common response to uncertainty was simply to avoid certain kinds of transactions. This strategy, mainly expressed through purchases of assets viewed as having little credit risk, is often referred to as a "flight to quality."

It is important to bear in mind that uncertain situations can evolve through time, as can decision makers' capabilities for addressing them.[7] Consequently, in practice, managing uncertainty is a dynamic process. It is also important to bear in mind that

---

[4] Attempts to maximize a criterion are unlikely to be helpful because the situation cannot be defined with sufficient precision.

[5] See, for example, Machina and Rothschild (2008).

[6] This is not to deny that probabilities can be defined axiomatically (see, Savage, 1951), but it is to say that any such probability distribution might not prove practically useful. For example, if the probability distribution is uniform over a very large range of possible outcome values it might not be of much help in selecting among possible decisions.

[7] In particular, as some uncertain situations become more familiar, it may be fruitful to model them as risky, at least for purposes of establishing benchmarks.

decision makers can err in their modeling efforts, so that the situations they attempt to address differ from the situations they actually face. This is known as *modeling risk*.

## 11.1.2 Risk

The bulk of the financial economics literature focuses on quantitative approaches that permit structuring and analyzing choices intended to affect the impacts of future state realizations. Situations under risk are usually modeled as maximization problems, and can very often be analyzed to good effect using decision trees. (Again see Chapter 10 for an example.) The decision maker's attitudes toward risk may be represented by one of the utility functions introduced in Chapter 9.[8] Another way of incorporating attitudes toward risks is to value outcomes using risk-neutral probability measures, as will be discussed in Chapter 16. Finally, still other criteria such as chance-constrained approaches may be used, as discussed further below.

## 11.2 DECISION CRITERIA

The possible choices of criteria stem from an interaction between the decision maker and the kind of situation being faced. We have already mentioned how relatively informal criteria may be chosen under conditions of uncertainty. Under risk, decision makers' criteria include expected wealth maximization, minimizing maximum regret, and the customary expected utility maximization. Different choices of criteria will help manage certain aspects of a risk-management problem, but the solutions will not necessarily be consistent with those obtained using other criteria. In fruitfully managing either risks or uncertainties, it may be as important to recognize the implications of criterion choice as it is to formulate other aspects of the problem as clearly and as comprehensively as possible.

### 11.2.1 Wealth-Based and Dispersion-Based Criteria

*Wealth-based criteria* emphasize the distribution of a decision maker's final wealth, usually focusing on such measures of central tendency as expected value. For example, an expected utility-maximizing, risk-neutral decision maker would choose between two portfolios on the basis of their expected outcomes (or expected returns), without regard to any other features of the outcome distribution.

*Dispersion-based criteria* emphasize the spread of a random variable. For example, the variance of final wealth and the variance of the ratio of the return to invested wealth are both measures of dispersion about the mean. They are also both symmetric measures, and as a result consider variation above the mean as serious as variation below the mean. In contrast, many decision makers prefer to use criteria that weight losses more heavily than gains.[9]

---

[8] If utility functions are used, their properties can be further refined in terms of the Arrow-Pratt measures of risk aversion described later in this chapter.

[9] Value maximization using risk-neutral probabilities is one such criteria (see Chapter 16).

Both wealth-based and dispersion-based criteria can give conflicting results. For example, a nonsatiable decision maker would prefer to end up with a wealth distribution that offers outcomes of either of say $2 or $4 with equal probability rather than with a certain outcome of $1. However, a measure of dispersion considered by itself would point to choosing the certain wealth of $1, since that outcome has zero dispersion while the first lottery's dispersion is positive. To resolve these difficulties, measures of final wealth and measures of dispersion may both be incorporated in choosing a criterion function. For example, it is not uncommon to find decision makers using a utility function such as:

$$E(X) - \beta\sigma^2(X)$$

where $\beta > 0$ is used to reflect a degree of risk aversion,[10] while the risk of X is measured by the variance $\sigma^2(X)$.[11]

## 11.2.2 Target-Based Criteria

In some instances, management may exhibit risk aversion through attempts to avoid downside risk (unfavorable outcomes). We shall refer to techniques of this type as *target-based approaches* or *chance-constrained approaches*. The notions are perhaps most easily expressed in terms of an example.

Suppose the management of a firm is trying to allocate liquid assets to two accounts, one of which (e.g., a bank checking account) is riskless but pays no interest, while the other offers a risky return (money market investments, for example, if we assume they will not necessarily be held to maturity). For simplicity we assume the rate of return $r$ on the second account is uniformly distributed over the range $[-0.5, 0.7]$. If $R$ is the amount currently available for allocation to the two accounts, the value of invested resources next period will be:

$$(R - S) + S(1 + r) \tag{11.1}$$

where $S$ is invested in the risky asset and the remainder $R - S$ is kept in the non-interest-bearing riskless account. Note that for simplicity that equation (11.1) can be rewritten as:

$$R + Sr \tag{11.2}$$

Now suppose management would like to make the next period investment value as large as possible but subject to the condition that $R + Sr$ not fall below 95% (an arbitrarily chosen percentage) of the original value of $R$ too often. Of course, this means we also have to define "too often." In this example we mean that if the investment falls below 95% of its original value, it should not do so more than 25% of the time (another arbitrary choice). In other words, management does not wish to find

---

[10] In this context, $\beta$ is used rather informally simply to indicate the degree of importance attached to risky outcomes. A more formal approach, given below, employs the Arrow-Pratt measures of risk aversion.

[11] This criterion is consistent with expected utility maximization using a negative exponential and an assumption of normally distributed outcomes.

the firm in an illiquid position (having lost more than 5% of the original investment value) more than 25% of the time. Formally, this can be expressed by saying that management wishes to:

$$\max_{S} E\left[R\left(1 + \frac{S}{R}r\right)\right] \tag{11.3}$$

subject to:

$$\Pr[R + Sr \geq 0.95R] \geq 0.75 \quad \text{and} \quad 0 \leq S \leq R$$

where Pr means cumulative probability.

Equation (11.3) says that we should maximize expected return subject to a (probabilistic) minimum balance requirement calculated at the end of the period. This problem may be rewritten in a somewhat simpler form as:

$$\max_{\alpha} E(1 + \alpha r)$$

subject to:

$$\Pr[(1 + \alpha r) \geq 0.95] \geq 0.75 \quad \text{and} \quad 0 \leq \alpha \leq 1 \tag{11.4}$$

where $\alpha = S/R$. (The solution to this problem is $\alpha^* = 0.25$.)

The constraint requiring that downside risk be controlled according to equation (11.3) imposes an opportunity cost on the firm, since if more risk were taken, expected return would be higher. One way of assessing this opportunity cost is to allow the probability of losses to increase and recalculate the solution to the original problem. (Another way is to allow for larger losses but with the same probability.) To allow for a larger loss probability, we replace the constraint in (11.4) by

$$\Pr[(1 + \alpha r) \geq 0.95] \geq 0.67 \quad \text{and} \quad 0 \leq \alpha \leq 1$$

The solution to this problem is $\alpha^* = 0.50$. The solution allows the expected return on invested assets to rise to 0.05, but the standard deviation of return also rises. Without further information, it is not possible to say which distribution management ought to choose, but at least the calculations make explicit the trade-offs between risk (in this case, risk of decreased liquidity) and return. Moreover, we have shown that when practical problems arise (for which only a rough risk-return trade-off calculation is required), the chance-constrained approach may provide a useful way of examining the trade-offs involved.

## 11.2.3 Criterion Choice

As mentioned in Chapter 9, expected utility has been offered as a financial decision criterion since the time of Daniel Bernoulli. Moreover, analyses that use other criteria may turn out to be consistent with maximizing expected utility. First, the use of risk-neutral probabilities to calculate the value of a decision can be wholly consistent with expected utility maximization, as will be shown in Chapter 16. As a second example, minimizing the probability of missing a target such as the one described above can also be shown to be consistent with maximizing the expectation of a particular form of utility function.[12]

Some financial research replaces the classic von Neumann–Morgenstern wealth-dependent utility function with more elaborate forms that offer greater flexibility in representing the consequences of choices. For example, *state-dependent utility functions* are utility functions like those introduced in Chapter 9, but are more complex in that they score outcomes according to both wealth and the state in which wealth is received. That is, the utility function is written as $u(w, s)$ where $w$ represents wealth and $s$ represents individual states drawn from a set of possible states $S$. Research using state-dependent utilities is capable of explaining a number of observed asset price features that will be discussed in later chapters in this book.[13]

## 11.3 METHODS OF RISK TRANSFER

*Risk management* often involves transferring risks to the agents best equipped to bear them. *Risk transfer* can make it possible for agents to undertake new risks that they would otherwise avoid, and hence improve an economy's resource allocation. Many attempts to manage risks involve selecting among forms of risk transfer according to a pre-selected criterion. Using the notion of a decision tree to represent the management problem, one can think of risk transfers as actions intended to affect the impacts of certain outcomes.[14] The forms of risk transfer considered next are hedging, insurance, and diversification.[15] In many, but not necessarily all, such analyses we assume the outcomes themselves are not capable of being changed, and we assume further that the probabilities of realizing the outcomes do not react to our choice of risk transfer method. Although most of the agents discussed below are modeled as transferring risks to other parties, their ability to do so depends on the existence of agents who willingly act as counterparties to assume the risks.

### 11.3.1 Hedging

*Hedging* means eliminating the possibility of realizing either a gain or a loss. A hedge can be arranged either by selling the risky prospect to another party, or by buying an offsetting risky prospect. For example, suppose a decision maker has a long position in a random variable $X$ that promises to pay \$4 with probability ½ and −\$2 with

---

[12] See Rachev et al. (2008). However, an appropriate choice of targets is needed to avoid incorrect evaluation of opportunities available to decision makers. For example, in practice little recognition is given to liability targets, and Rachev et al. (2008) suggest this contributed to the underfunding of defined benefit pension plans in the United States.

[13] This includes empirical issues such as a high equity risk premium, high return volatility, volatility clustering, a low risk-free rate, and stock return predictability discussed in Chapter 12.

[14] But in simpler models it does not impact the outcomes themselves. In more sophisticated models, interactions between decisions and outcomes may be recognized.

[15] This classification is proposed in Bodie, Merton, and Cleeton (2009).

probability ½. If the decision maker now sells short the same random variable, that position becomes $X - X$, offering a certainty outcome of zero irrespective of the outcome of $X$. In such a situation the decision maker is said to be fully hedged against the risk. The decision maker has, of course, eliminated the potential for either loss or gain in this example. If the offsetting short position is to be arranged through a market transaction, the hedger must be able to find a suitable counterparty—say, a speculator who might assume a long position in $X$.

Hedging is a form of *risk management* that involves risk sharing. We will discuss financial instruments, called derivatives, that can be used for hedging and other forms of risk management in Chapters 18 and 19.

## 11.3.2  Insuring

*Insuring* means reducing the probability of one or more downside outcomes by buying insurance protection. The price paid for the protection is referred to as an *insurance premium*. Upside outcomes are not usually affected by the purchase of insurance.

To see the difference between hedging and insuring, consider a variant on the above example. Suppose it is now possible to purchase, for price $p$, an insurance contract $P$ that allows the insured to sell to the insurance company the variable $X$ at a price of \$1.5. The decision maker's payoffs, exclusive of the insurance premium $p$, are then:

| Instrument | $X$ | $P$ | $X + P$ |
| --- | --- | --- | --- |
| First outcome | \$4.0 | \$0.0 | \$4.0 |
| Second outcome | −\$2.0 | \$1.5 | −\$0.5 |

The decision maker's loss exposure has now been reduced from \$2 to \$0.5, by paying a price of $p$, so that if things turn out badly, the decision maker's total loss is $\$0.5 + p$. On the other hand, the decision maker's gross gain remains at \$4, and the net gain including the insurance premium (represented by the cost of the insurance contract, in this case a put) is $\$4 - p$. As in the hedging example above, the risk transfer can only be brought about if a counterparty can be found to assume the risk. In this case, the counterparty is the agent who sells the insurance contract $P$ at the assumed price $p$.

In Chapters 18 and 19 we further distinguish insurance-type contracts from risk-sharing type contracts used for risk management. We describe an insurance-type contract in Chapter 19.

## 11.3.3  Diversifying

*Diversifying* means combining different prospects in ways designed to reduce downside risks. To see how diversification can lower risk in relation to return, consider investing in just two finanical instruments, $X$ and $Y$. Denoting realized returns on the two financial instruments by $r_X$ and $r_Y$, Table 11.1 shows the joint probabilities,

TABLE 11.1
JOINT PROBABILITIES OF RETURNS

| $r_X$ | 4% | 7% | 10% |
|---|---|---|---|
| 1% | 1/9 | 1/9 | 1/9 |
| 3% | 1/9 | 1/9 | 1/9 |
| 5% | 1/9 | 1/9 | 1/9 |

*(column group header spanning 4%, 7%, 10%: ——$r_Y$——)*

estimated at time 0, with which the returns might be realized one period later. For example, the joint outcome $r_X = 1\%$, $r_Y = 10\%$ is assumed to occur with probability 1/9, as are all the other combinations shown in the table.

The expected return on either financial instrument in Table 11.1 is given by the sum of the outcomes multiplied by the probability of realizing each possible outcome. The probabilities of the outcomes of $r_X$ are given by the row sums of the joint probabilities, while the probabilities of the outcomes of $r_Y$ are given by the column sums of the joint probabilities. Thus,

$$E(r_X) = (1/3)(0.01) + (1/3)(0.03) + (1/3)(0.05) = 0.03$$

and $E(r_Y) = 0.07$.

The *variance* of returns, and its square root the *standard deviation*, are both measures of how dispersed returns can be—the greater the dispersion, the greater the variance, and hence also the standard deviation. The variance is defined as the expected value of the square of the differences between outcomes and their mean:

$$\text{Var}(r_X) = \sigma^2(r_X) = E[r_X - E(r_X)]^2$$

For example, letting $\sigma^2(r_X)$ denote the variance of return on financial instrument $X$,

$$\sigma^2(r_X) = E[r_X - E(r_X)]^2 = (1/3)[0.01 - 0.03]^2 + (1/3)[0.03 - 0.03]^2 + (1/3)[0.05 - 0.03]^2$$
$$= (2/3)(0.02)^2 = 0.000267$$

For subsequent use, note that the standard deviation of return on financial instrument $X$ is $\sigma(r_X) = (0.000267)^{1/2}$. Similar calculations show that $\sigma(r_Y) = (0.0006)^{1/2}$.

Since the two financial instruments $X$ and $Y$ offer expected returns of 0.03 and 0.07, respectively, any portfolio combining them will have an expected return equal to the weighted average of the two. For example, a portfolio constructed by investing half the available funds in each of the two financial instruments has an expected return equal to:

$$(1/2)[E(r_X) + E(r_Y)] = 0.05$$

The variance of return for a portfolio composed of the two risky financial instruments is given by the formula:

$$\sigma^2(w_X r_X + w_Y r_Y) = (w_X)^2 \sigma^2(r_X) + 2w_X w_Y \, cov(r_X, r_Y) + (w_Y)^2 \sigma^2(r_Y)$$

where
$\sigma^2(r_X)$ = variance of return on financial instrument $X$
$\sigma^2(r_Y)$ = variance of return on financial instrument $Y$
$w_X$ = the proportion of funds invested in financial instrument $X$
$w_Y = 1 - w_X$ = the proportion invested in financial instrument $Y$
$cov(r_X, r_Y)$ = is a measure of the statistical association between the returns on the two financial instrument and is known as the *covariance* between $r_X$ and $r_Y$. Covariance is defined as:

$$cov(r_X, r_Y) = E(r_X \cdot r_Y) - E(r_X)E(r_Y)$$

In the present example this covariance is equal to zero because the two returns for the financial instruments are distributed independently. You can see the returns are statistically independent by noting that regardless of which outcome you consider for $r_X$, the probabilities of the three outcomes for $r_y$ are all equal.[16]

## 11.4 CHARACTERISTICS OF PROBABILITY DISTRIBUTIONS

An important assumption in finance theory is the *probability distribution* assumed for asset returns. Unfortunately, the probability distribution traditionally used in financial theory and the one that dominates statistics textbooks used in business schools—the *normal distribution*—does not correspond closely with the distributions typically found in real-world financial markets.[17] Although in principle any form of probability distribution can be incorporated in a decision-tree analysis, in practice the best choice of probability distribution is not always easy to determine.[18] First, there are many candidate distributions that have to be considered in formulating a risk-management problem. In particular, statistically convenient choices of distributions may simplify modeling the problem, but may also give inaccurate descriptions of the probabilities with which states might be realized. Moreover, estimating the appropriate distribution may be subject to error, and any such errors affect model solutions. Finally, estimating and using a realistic form of probability distribution can involve a considerable amount of computation, an important practical consideration in

---

[16] For statistical independence it would only be necessary that the conditional probabilities have the same ratio to each other.
[17] The normal distribution is also referred to as the *Gaussian distribution*.
[18] Nevertheless, spreadsheet analyses can prove very helpful, even for quite complex problems. See, for example, Benninga (2008).

managing institutional portfolios where large numbers of financial instruments must be valued frequently.[19]

As just explained, financial economics usually assumes that asset returns are normally distributed. Since the normal distribution can be described by two parameters—its mean and its variance—portfolio risk-return relationships (see Chapters 13 and 14) can also be described using the same two parameters.[20] While assuming that portfolio risks and returns can thus be modeled, the appropriateness of using the assumption has been investigated empirically and found wanting. Estimated returns turn out not be normally distributed. Rather, the estimated distributions

1. possess heavier tails (i.e., *fat tails*) than those of the normal distribution
2. are skewed rather than symmetric (i.e., $E\{[X - E(X)]^3\} \neq 0$), and
3. may possibly be *leptokurtic* (i.e., the fourth moment about the mean $E\{[X - E(X)]^4\} > 3$, its value for the normal distribution).

In addition, empirical distributions can have extreme realizable outcomes with higher probability than is reflected even by popular choices of *heavy-tailed distributions*.

The *skewness* parameter has a particularly important impact on portfolios that include such instruments as options (see Chapters 18 and 19), but even recognizing the effects of skewness may not be sufficient to capture all important problem features. A correct analysis can involve working with multivariate distributions whose features are described by the statistical (marginal) properties of all the component random variables in the portfolio. Moreover, the dependence structures among components are likely to be more complex than those capable of being captured by the linear correlation coefficients used in Section 11.3. The distributions needed for full analysis may have to incorporate such features as how different risks combine, how their component dependencies can change through time, and consequently how the entire portfolio's distribution can change through time.

Models can be constructed to display all these realistic features, but they can be both costly to construct and difficult to solve. For example, if one tried to capture all of the foregoing features using decision-tree analyses, the resulting problem representation might be very complex. Indeed, some models are so complex that even today's fastest computers cannot determine solutions to them in short periods of time. For example, the daily marking to market of an institutional portfolio containing thousands of securities can, if carried out fully, actually require more time than is available between trading periods.

## 11.5 EXPECTED UTILITY THEORY AND ARROW-PRATT RISK AVERSION

Just as the choice of probability distribution affects the solution to a risk-management problem, so does the choice of criterion function. This section examines how some

---

[19] These considerations can become particularly important if sensitivity analyses are needed.
[20] These issues are discussed under portfolio theory in Chapter 13.

properties of utility functions affect the solutions they imply. In Chapter 9 we explained that the utility function of a risk averter is concave, and introduced the measure known as the Arrow-Pratt risk aversion coefficient. We continue that investigation here.

An intuitive way to characterize a risk averter's behavior is to say that downside risk is regarded more seriously by a risk averter than an equal upside potential is valued, meaning that the risk-averse investor requires to be compensated if she is to accept risk. To see how upside potential and downside risk are weighted by a risk-averse investor, consider the lottery X: payoff of $10 and −$10 with equal probability. This lottery's mean is zero. One can calculate the *certainty equivalent value* for this lottery, which is defined as an amount of cash, paid or received with certainty, that the decision maker regards as just equal to the value of the lottery. Hence, a risk-averse investor's certainty equivalent value for lottery X will be negative. In the present example (continuing with the practice of not including dollar signs in the utility function),

$$u(c) \equiv E[u(X)] = (1/2)u(10) + (1/2)u(-10) \le u(0)$$

where $c$ is the certainty equivalent value of the lottery and "$\equiv$" means "is defined to be." As already explained, in the case of this example $c$ is a negative number for any risk averter. If the individual were only made as unhappy by downside risk (moving from 0 to −10) as he would be made happier by upside potential (moving from 0 to 10), the certainty equivalent value of the lottery would be zero. But since it is in fact negative, downside risk must be weighted more heavily by an investor who is a risk averter. This situation suggests that the risk-averse investor might be willing to give up some amount of wealth in order to avoid this particular lottery. The maximum amount of wealth that would thus be given up is called a *risk premium*.[21] As a general matter, the amount of the risk premium depends on both the lottery and the precise nature of the utility function.

Recall from Chapter 9 that both risk premia and some aspects of risk-taking behavior can be related to characteristics of utility functions known as the Arrow-Pratt measures of *local risk aversion*. To see this, let us again consider our hypothetical risk-averse investor, now with an initial wealth endowment of $w$ and a more generally specified lottery X. For convenience, we suppose that $E[X]$ is still 0. We then ask what risk premium $\pi(w, X)$ must be deducted from the $E[X]$ to create a certainty equivalent level of wealth that will provide the investor with the same satisfaction as from her original position. That is, we wish to find the risk premium that satisfies

$$E[u(w + X)] \equiv u[w + 0 - \pi(w, X)] \tag{11.5}$$

We can use a Taylor expansion around $w$ to find a local, linear approximation of the function $u(.)$.[22] Starting with the right-hand side of equation (11.5), we shorten the notation for risk premium to $\pi$ and bear in mind that $E(X) = 0$ by assumption. Then the Taylor expansion of $u(w - \pi)$ is:

$$u(w - \pi) = u(w) - \pi u'(w) + O(\pi^2) \tag{11.6}$$

---

[21] As we will see in Chapter 12, this risk premium is referred to as a Markowitz risk premium.

[22] This operation is described in Web-Appendix K. It assumes the outcomes of X are not large relative to $w$.

**Figure 11.1**

Downside Risk is More Important than an Equal Upside Potential to Risk-Averter

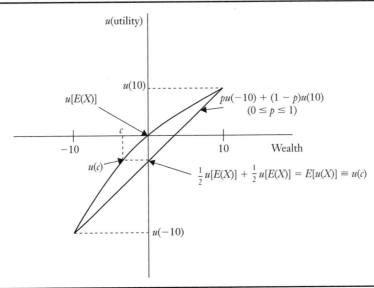

where $u'(w)$ is the first derivative of the utility function and $O(\pi^2)$ refers to a term whose magnitude is at most equal to the order of $\pi^2$, that is, small enough to be ignored. Similarly, the Taylor expansion of the left-hand side, $E[u(W + X)]$, is:

$$E[u(w + X)] = E[u(w)] + E(X)u'(w) + \frac{1}{2}E(X^2)u''(w) + O(X^3)$$
$$= u(w) + \frac{1}{2}\sigma_X^2 u''(w) \tag{11.7}$$

and $O(X^3)$ is also assumed to be small enough to be ignored. Equation (11.7) can then be simplified as shown because $E[u(w)] = u(w)$ (initial wealth is known with certainty) and because $E(X) = 0$, so that $E(X^2) = \sigma_X^2$. Using equations (11.6) and (11.7), and solving for $\pi$, we obtain:

$$\pi = -\frac{1}{2}\sigma_X^2 \frac{u''(w)}{u'(w)} \tag{11.8}$$

The function $-u''(w) / u'(w)$ in equation (11.8) is the Arrow-Pratt *measure of absolute risk aversion*[23] first referred to in Chapter 9.

Since variance is always positive, the sign of the risk premium $\pi$ will depend on the sign of the ratio. We have assumed that utility always increases with wealth so $u'(w) > 0$. For a risk averter, utility of wealth increases at a decreasing rate as wealth increases; that is, $u''(w) < 0$, and therefore $u''(w)/u'(w) < 0$. This type of utility function is shown in Figure 11.1, and for such an individual, the risk premium $\pi > 0$ as would be expected.

---

[23] See Arrow (1971) and Pratt (1964).

In a similar manner, we can show that an individual's attitude toward proportional risks is expressed by the measure of relative risk aversion:

$$\text{relative risk aversion} = -w\frac{u''(w)}{u'(w)} \tag{11.9}$$

An individual's attitude toward risks measured in monetary amounts is reflected by the measure of absolute risk aversion, as we show next. Recall that every consumer's utility may be specified as to origin and scale. If we take a particular lottery, such as a payoff of $10 with a probability of ½ and a payoff of $0 with a probability of ½ and define:

$$u_A(0) = u_B(0) = 0; u_A(10) = u_B(10) = 1$$

where $A$ and $B$ refer to two investors, and if investor $B$'s certainty equivalent $c_B$ for the lottery $X$ is less than $c_A$, $B$ can be said to show greater absolute risk aversion. It can be shown, moreover, that $B$'s measure of absolute risk aversion is, in this case, larger than $A$'s (because $B$'s risk premium is larger).[24] The observation implies that when the utilities are appropriately scaled, the curvature of $B$'s utility is greater than the curvature of $A$'s. That is, when utilities are appropriately scaled for comparability, the measure of absolute risk aversion increases as the utilities' curvature increases.

Another question of interest is how the absolute risk-aversion measure might change with a significant change in the level of initial wealth. It is frequently speculated on the basis of casual empiricism that absolute risk aversion should decrease as the individual's wealth increases, and that relative risk aversion might remain about constant. If absolute risk aversion decreases, it can be shown that a decision maker's investment in a lottery of fixed composition will increase. Similarly, if relative risk aversion decreases, it can be shown that a decision maker's investment in a proportional lottery of fixed composition will increase.

Such properties of utility functions and their implications for risky behavior can be inferred by calculating the Arrow-Pratt measures. For example, a quadratic utility function defined on portfolio returns has been widely used in a portfolio context, as described further in Chapter 13. Let us, following the example of Chapter 9, write a representative quadratic utility function as:

$$u(w) = aw - bw^2 \tag{11.10}$$

having $u'(w) = a - 2bw$, and $u''(w) = 2b$ (for $w \leq a/2b$). The corresponding measures of risk aversion are:

$$\text{absolute risk aversion} = \frac{2b}{a - 2bw}$$

$$\text{relative risk aversion} = \frac{2b}{(a/w) - 2b}$$

---

[24] See Pratt (1971).

Both of these measures are increasing functions of $w$ rather than being decreasing or constant, thus implying that the quadratic decision maker becomes more averse to risk as wealth increases. Some observers reject the use of quadratic utility on the grounds that increasing risk aversion is *a priori* implausible.

The definitions of risk premium and of the risk-aversion measures provide useful ways to examine the properties of various possible utility functions and to make inferences about risky behavior, as we have just seen. Recall, though, that the definitions of absolute and relative risk aversion assume that risks are small, or local. The local property is due to the fact that the measures of risk aversion are derived using a linear Taylor expansion around the current wealth level, and such an approximation is valid for only small changes. In the next chapter, we show how a global measure of riskiness proposed by Aumann and Serrano (2008) can be related to the Arrow-Pratt measures of local risk aversion.

## KEY POINTS

- The environments in which financial decisions are taken can be viewed as either uncertain or as risky.
- Uncertainty refers to an environment that is difficult to specify, even qualitatively. For example, in extreme cases it may not be possible to identify possible outcomes in even a qualitative fashion.
- In less extreme cases of uncertainty it may be possible to identify outcomes qualitatively, but not to attach a meaningful probability distribution to the outcomes (i.e., one that will be helpful in choosing among those outcomes).
- Although some quantitative approaches to modeling choices under uncertainty have been proposed, the results of these approaches are still quite preliminary. Quantitative approaches to modeling have so far not proved very helpful in selecting among actual possible decisions in these contexts.
- In contrast to decision making under uncertainty, decision making under risk allows taking advantage of quantitative problem formulations. For example, it is possible quantitatively to state possible outcomes, say using the form of a decision tree, to attach meaningful estimates of probabilities to the outcomes, and to choose among the possible outcomes according to some form of criterion function.
- Nearly all of the models used in financial economics assume that decisions are taken under risk.
- Modeling financial decisions involves choosing among different criteria, selected according to their usefulness in capturing the essence of particular contexts. For example, one form of criterion function specifies taking actions to maximize expected wealth, while a second form focuses on actions that will minimize the dispersion of final possible outcomes.
- In some contexts, wealth-maximizing criteria may be highly suitable while in other contexts reducing the dispersion of wealth may be more nearly appropriate. In still other contexts it may be necessary to model how expected wealth and wealth dispersion can be traded off, say using a utility function.

- Another approach to modeling financial decisions aims at achieving specified target outcomes. For example, the decision maker may strive achieve a target financial wealth with some prespecified probability.
- Choices among different decision criteria are made by taking account of the context within which a problem arises, and by taking further account of a decision maker's preferences. For example, decision makers facing a high degree of uncertainty may strive to minimize the worst possible outcomes they envision.
- In contrast, a decision maker facing risk may strive to maximize the expected utility of final possible outcomes.
- Many financial decision problems focus on transferring risk.
- There are three main types of risk transfer—hedging, insurance, and diversification.
- Hedging involves eliminating the possibility of making either gains or losses.
- Insurance involves paying premiums to eliminate certain downside outcomes.
- Diversification involves combining different prospects in ways designed to reduce downside risks without selling them off.
- Modeling the impacts of risky choices involves choosing appropriate distributions to reflect outcome probabilities. For example, if there is a possibility of realizing extreme outcomes, using analytically convenient distributions like the normal distribution may understate the probabilities of the extreme outcomes and lead the decision maker to bear greater risks than originally intended.
- Modeling the impacts of risky choices frequently employs expected utility maximization, and in those cases the Arrow-Pratt measures of risk aversion offer guidance regarding the types of preferences being assumed. For example, using a constant absolute risk-averse utility function implies that the decision maker wishes to assume the same proportional levels of risk regardless of the individual's initial level of wealth.

# QUESTIONS

1. How can risk be characterized?

2. What does optimization mean?

3. **a.** What is the difference between uncertainty and risk?
   **b.** What are the two kinds of uncertainty and give an example of each kind?
   **c.** Which kind of uncertainty is usually addressed in the financial economics literature?

4. Why is modeling risk an important task in risk management?

5. With respect to risk management, what is meant by:
   **a.** wealth-based criteria?
   **b.** dispersion-based criteria?

6. What is the disadvantage of symmetric measures of risk?

7. Give an example to illustrate how a wealth-based criteria and dispersion-based criteria can give conflicting results.

8. What are target-based approaches to risk management?

9. Suppose the management of a firm is trying to allocate $1 million of fund between two investment vehicles. One pays a risk-free interest rate of 0.1. The second offers a risky return $r$. Assume that $r$ follows a normal distribution with mean 0.2 and volatility 1, that is, $N(0.2, 1)$. Furthermore, suppose that management would like to make the next period investment value as large as possible but subject to the condition that the total wealth does not decrease with probability more than $N(0.3)$, where $N(\ )$ represents the standard normal cumulative distribution function. How should management allocate the $1 million between the two investment vehicles?

10. What is the difference between the von Neumann–Morgenstern wealth-dependent utility function and state-dependent utility functions?

11. **a.** What is meant by risk management?
    **b.** What is meant by risk transfer?

12. **a.** What is meant by hedging?
    **b.** What are two ways that a hedge can be arranged?

13. **a.** In risk management, what does insuring an asset mean?
    **b.** What is the difference between hedging and insuring an asset?

14. What does the risk-management strategy of diversifying involve?

15. What measures are commonly used to indicate dispersion of return?

16. **a.** What type of probability distribution is typically assumed in financial theory?
    **b.** What is the problem with using a simple probability distribution in risk management when it is not a good descriptor of the real-world probability distribution?

17. **a.** What is meant by fat tails and a heavy-tailed distribution?
    **b.** What are the implications for risk management if the return distribution for an asset is assumed to be normally distributed but in fact has fat tails?
    **c.** What does it mean that a return distribution is skewed?

18. What is meant by the certainty equivalent value of a lottery?

19. What is the term for the maximum amount of wealth that a risk-averse investor might be willing to give up in order to avoid facing risk?

20. How do the definitions of risk premium and risk-aversion measures provide helpful ways to investigate the properties of possible utility functions and to make inferences about risk behavior?

**21.** There are two measures of local risk aversion, absolute risk aversion and relative risk aversion.

    **a.** What are the definitions of the two measures?

    **b.** If an investor has a utility with increasing absolute risk aversion, what can you say about her investments?

    **c.** If an investor has a utility with constant relative risk aversion, what can you say about her investments?

# REFERENCES

Arrow, Kenneth J. (1971). *Essays in the Theory of Risk-Bearing*. Amsterdam: North-Holland.

Aumann, Robert J., and Roberto Serrano. (2008). "An Economic Index of Riskiness," *Journal of Political Economy* **116**: 810–836.

Benninga, Simon. (2008). *Financial Modeling* (3rd ed.). Cambridge, MA: MIT Press.

Bodie, Zvi, Robert C. Merton, and David L. Cleeton. (2009). Financial Economics (2nd ed.). Upper Saddle River, NJ: Pearson Prentice-Hall.

Machina, Mark J., and Michael Rothschild. (2008). "Risk" in Steven N. Durlauf and Lawrence E. Blume (eds.), *The New Palgrave Dictionary of Economics* (2nd ed.). New York: Palgrave Macmillan.

Pratt, John W. (1964). "Risk Aversion in the Small and in the Large," *Econometrica* **32**: 122–136.

Rachev, Svetlozar T., Sergio Ortobelli, Stoyan V. Stoyanov, Frank J. Fabozzi, and Almira Biglova. (2008). "Desirable Properties of an Ideal Risk Measure in Portfolio Theory," *International Journal of Theoretical and Applied Finance* **11**: 19–54.

# 12

# On Choosing Risk Measures

$A$s we explained in the previous chapter, risk-management problems can be viewed as problems aimed at optimizing a variety of criteria.[1] In this chapter, we examine how risk measures are defined and used to help select solutions to the risk-management problems of either individual or institutional investors. There are many different risk measures, but their use is based on the same considerations: Each measure attempts both to describe risks and to provide some information for solving risk-management problems. However, since any risk measure gives a summary description of lottery characteristics, it can only be used correctly in the context of particular optimization problems, as we show in this chapter.

## 12.1 Using Risk Measures

A *risk measure* is a *function*, denoted by $\rho$, that maps lotteries X into the set of real numbers **R**:[2]

$$\rho: X \to \mathbf{R}$$

The function $\rho$ is defined to have a positive range. For example, if a risk management problem is formulated as maximizing an expected utility function $u$, and if $u$ has a positive range,[3] then:

$$\rho(X) \equiv m - E[u(X)]$$

---

[1] If we interpret utility functions broadly enough, we can consider them as describing the preferences of either individual investors or institutional investors, although the particular utility functions chosen in the two cases might well be different. The Foster-Hart riskiness measure discussed later in this chapter eschews the use of conventional utility functions to focus on possibilities of bankruptcy (in effect, that is, on a discontinuous utility).

[2] Real numbers include rational and irrational numbers.

[3] It is always possible to find a utility function with a positive range since utilities are only determined up to a positive linear transformation.

where $m$ is an appropriately large positive constant, could serve as a risk measure. While this observation shows how risk measures are related to risk-management problems, it is not very informative because it simply restates the original problem. Fortunately, there are several other approaches to finding helpful measures, as we demonstrate in the balance of this chapter.

## 12.1.1 Measures Based on the First Two Moments

Financial economics has traditionally focused on using the mean and the variance of probability distributions as descriptive risk measures, in part because these two measures address the essence of expected utility maximization when the utility function is concave. Consider such a utility, and suppose further, for explanatory purposes, that the risk-averse investor faces lottery X with the following two outcomes (referred to as *two-point lotteries*) and probability distribution:

| State | Probability | Outcome |
|-------|-------------|---------|
| 1 | 0.5 | $w - a$ |
| 2 | 0.5 | $w + a$ |

Based on the above, $E(X) = w$ and $\sigma^2(X) = a^2$, where $\sigma^2(X)$ is the variance of the above two-point lottery outcomes. If $a$ increases while the lottery's expected value remains constant, it is easy to show that the certainty-equivalent value of X (see Chapter 11) will decrease for any risk-averse decision maker. That is to say, among symmetric two-point lotteries having equal expected values but differing variances, the risk-averter will prefer the one having the smallest variance.[4]

Thus, we may say, at least for these special kinds of lotteries,[5] that expected utility decreases as variance increases (holding expected value constant), and expected utility increases as $E(X)$ increases (holding variance constant). Expected payoff is a measure of expected future wealth,[6] while variance of payoffs is a measure of wealth dispersion. Moreover, in these cases we can use either the variance $\sigma^2(X)$ or the standard deviation $\sigma(X)$ as risk measures, since either describes the lottery's dispersion. It is equally possible to use other measures of dispersion such as *mean absolute deviation*, defined by:

$$E[|X - E(X)|]$$

Selection among dispersion measures is largely a matter of reflecting significant problem characteristics. For example, the mean absolute deviation measure, defined above, gives less weight to extreme outcomes than does the variance.

---

[4] Some analysts prefer a semi-variance measure that looks only at the downside risks. In the current example, the semi-variance would be measured only by the downward deviation.

[5] It is useful to know this because more complicated lotteries can be thought of as compounds of two-point lotteries.

[6] If W is a random outcome, we can think of it as being determined by V(1 + R) where V is deterministic and R is random. Hence, our discussion can use either W or R interchangeably; the reader can make the appropriate translations as required.

Prior to the development of Markowitzian portfolio theory (see Chapter 13) the effects of risk were recognized by using a discount factor of the form $1/(1 + r + \pi)$, where $r$ represents the risk-free rate of interest and $\pi$ a risk premium that is positive for valuations made by risk-averters. Markowitz proposed determining the risk premium more nearly exactly by using variance of return on the entire portfolio as a measure of risk.[7] Markowitz noted that covariances between pairs of individual investments (i.e., linear correlation coefficients) can be used to examine the effects of diversification on the variance of portfolio return. Markowitz thus explained that diversification is a solution property emerging from calculating the portfolio variance of return.

The Markowitz approach can be used correctly with some distributions and some utility functions. The mean-variance trade-offs described by Markowitz exactly characterize solutions to any expected utility maximization problem whose random returns are jointly normally distributed, and also to quadratic utility maximization problems even if returns are not normally distributed. In both these cases, $\rho(r_X) \equiv \sigma^2(r_X)$ or $\rho(r_X) \equiv \sigma(r_X)$ serve as risk measures that correctly rank portfolios constrained to have the same expected return. Of portfolios with the same expected return, a minimum variance portfolio is preferred. Alternatively, expected return can be used to rank portfolios constrained to have the same variance; in this case a maximal return is sought.[8] Portfolios that offer the best available combinations of mean and variance are said to lie on a mean-variance *efficient frontier*.

Two of the main pricing models in current use, the theoretically oriented Capital Asset Pricing Model (CAPM) and the empirically oriented Arbitrage Pricing Theory (APT), frequently describe return distributions using their first two moments[9]— expected value (mean) and variance. The return variance of the portfolio is then readily related to the return variance of its component securities. For example, if a portfolio is composed of two securities, its risk as assessed by the CAPM is described using:

$$\sigma^2(r_X + r_Y) = \sigma^2(r_X) + \sigma^2(r_Y) + 2\,\sigma(r_X)\,\sigma(r_X)\,corr(r_X, r_Y)$$

where

$$corr(r_X, r_Y) \equiv E\{[r_X - E(r_X)][r_Y - E(r_Y)]\}$$

is the linear correlation coefficient between $r_X$ and $r_y$.

Given either normally distributed random variables or quadratic utilities (or both), desirable risk-return trade-offs can be easily calculated using a solution

---

[7] Variance is only an appropriate measure of risk for symmetric distributions.

[8] Variance alone is not sufficient to render a lottery more or less desirable, as may be shown by comparing a certainty payment of $3 (whose variance is zero) to a lottery of $5 and $7, each with probability $\frac{1}{2}$ (and whose variance is therefore $1). An example presented in Section 12.3 will show that an increase in variance while holding the mean constant can increase the Aumann-Serrano riskiness of a lottery (to be introduced in Section 12.2), but will only rank the lotteries consistently for some utility functions.

[9] The theoretical development of the CAPM explicitly assumes normality, while the theoretical development of the APT assumes returns follow a linear factor structure without further specification of the error term's distribution.

property known as *two-fund separation*. For example, if there is a risk-free asset, the optimal portfolios described by the CAPM are weighted combinations of the risk-free asset and the market portfolio.[10]

Recent research has identified the class of random variables for which it is theoretically correct to use linear correlation as a dependence measure—the class of distributions whose equidensity surfaces are ellipsoids. This class of so-called *elliptical distributions* includes both the normal distributions and the Student *t*-distributions with finite variances.[11]

## 12.1.2 Measures Recognizing Higher Moments

As explained in the previous chapter, empirically estimated return distributions from real-world financial markets are not usually elliptical—rather they are heavy-tailed, skewed, and have kurtosis measures $E[X - E(X)]^4$ different from that of the normal distribution.[12] In addition, some empirically estimated distributions may have extreme outcomes that occur with significantly larger probability than even some choices of heavy-tailed distributions will reflect. A linear correlation coefficient may not correctly describe the dependence between the risks of individual random variables having empirically estimated distributions, and risk-return rankings derived from the CAPM may not correctly characterize solutions to the associated utility maximization problems.[13]

In particular, using a variance-covariance model for non-elliptical distributions can lead to severe underestimates of extreme losses. The difficulties are compounded by the fact that higher moments such as kurtosis can be unstable and must therefore be estimated from relatively large samples. Moreover, it is not known how many parameters are actually necessary to identify a multiparameter efficient frontier.[14] Still further, even if the relevant optimization problems could define optimal choices for a whole class of investors, the problems can be computationally too complex to be solved for large portfolios, and the computational difficulties increase still further if short sales are prohibited.[15] On the other hand, if the optimization problem is simplified to make it computationally more tractable, then only a subset of optimal portfolios will be identified, no matter what risk measure is chosen.

---

[10] The property does not extend easily: Although two-fund separation holds for two-parameter distributions, it is not generally true that *k*-fund separation holds for *k*-parameter distributions. For a discussion of general separation theorems and conditions for separation in the absence of a risk-free rate, see Ingersoll (1987).

[11] Web-Appendix M provides further details of the normal, Student *t*, and other distributions.

[12] The kurtosis of the normal distribution has a value of 3. A distribution with a kurtosis measure greater than 3 is called leptokurtic, and one with a measure less than 3 is called platykurtic.

[13] Tobin (1969, p. 14) wrote that the critics of mean-variance "owe us more than demonstrations that it rests on restrictive assumptions. They need to show us how a more general and less vulnerable approach will yield the kind of comparative-static results that economists are interested in." As do Aumann-Serrano (2008, p. 813)—from whom the foregoing quote is taken—we address Tobin's suggested purpose throughout the rest of this chapter.

[14] Empirically, the APT is usually estimated using three or four risk parameters.

[15] We'll have more to say about short sales in a later chapter.

● ● ●  ## 12.2  MEASURES OF RISKINESS

We turn now to considering risk measures with broader application than mean and variance. This section examines two such measures, the Aumann and Serrano (2008) measure of riskiness and a related measure proposed by Foster and Hart (2008). The Aumann-Serrano measure extends the ranking capabilities of measures based on mean and variance, and of those based on stochastic dominance. Further, the Aumann-Serrano measure provides relations between the riskiness of portfolios and their component securities for arbitrary forms of distributions. It is both a global description of lottery riskiness and related to the Arrow-Pratt measures of local risk aversion explained in Chapter 11.

The Foster-Hart measure is another global description of a lottery's riskiness and is also related to the Arrow-Pratt measures of local risk aversion. However, it is based on a criterion of bankruptcy avoidance, a postulate different from the axioms underpinning the Aumann-Serrano measure.

The next section states the two axioms[16] on which the Aumann-Serrano measure is based and then discusses the measure's main properties. The conceptual underpinnings and purposes of the Aumann-Serrano measure are next compared briefly with the underpinnings and purposes of the related riskiness measure proposed by Foster and Hart (2008).

### 12.2.1  Aumann-Serrano Axioms

A lottery X is said to be riskier than a lottery Y if $\rho^*(X) \geq \rho^*(Y)$, where $\rho^*(\ )$ denotes Aumann-Serrano (2008) riskiness. As will be shown shortly, the function $\rho^*(\ )$ is defined uniquely by a pair of axioms, referred to as the *duality axiom* and the *positive homogeneity axiom*, respectively. To do so, however, it is first necessary to introduce the concept of "uniformly more risk averse," a stronger condition than Arrow-Pratt risk aversion. A utility function $u_i$ is said to be more risk averse than a utility function $u_j$ if $r_{Ai}(w) \geq r_{Aj}(w)$ for some $w$, where $r_{Ai}(.)$ is the Arrow-Pratt measure of absolute risk aversion (see Chapter 11). Aumann-Serrano's stronger condition is as follows. If:

$$\min_w[r_{Ai}(w)] \geq \max_w[r_{Aj}(w)]$$

for all levels of wealth $w$, then $i$ is said to be uniformly more risk averse than $j$, while if:

$$\max_w[r_{Ai}(w)] \leq \min_w[r_{Aj}(w)]$$

for all levels of wealth $w$, then $i$ is uniformly less risk averse than $j$. The concepts of uniformly more (less) risk averse mean that one function's measure of risk aversion is no less (no more) than that of another across the measures' entire domain.

---

[16] The purpose of using axioms is to state clearly the context on which the analysis is based.

"Uniformly risk averse" is therefore a *partial ordering*[17] since it does not characterize relations between measures of risk aversion that can cross each other.

We can now state the axioms on which the Aumann-Serrano measure is based. The first, the duality axiom, refers to two agents, one uniformly more risk averse than the other, and two lotteries, one riskier than the other.

*Duality axiom*: If $u_i(w)$ is uniformly more risk averse than $u_j(w)$, if $\rho^*(X) \geq \rho^*(Y)$, and if $i$ accepts X at wealth level $w$, then $j$ accepts Y at $w$.

The duality axiom stipulates that if the uniformly more risk-averse agent accepts the riskier of the two lotteries, the uniformly less risk-averse agent will accept the less risky lottery.[18]

The second axiom, positive homogeneity, axiom refers to the scale of a lottery.

*Positive homogeneity axiom*: $\rho^*(tX) = t\rho^*(X)$ for all positive numbers $t$.

This axiom says that changing the scale of a lottery will change the risk measure similarly. For example, if a lottery has outcomes measured in thousands of dollars and a risk measure of, say, 7, then measuring the same lottery in hundreds of dollars will produce a risk measure of $10 \times 7 = 70$. In particular, the positive homogeneity axiom means that if one has a riskiness measure for a lottery whose payoffs are measured in dollars, it will be easy to convert both the lottery and the risk measure to reflect payoffs measured in rates of return. The positive homogeneity axiom is also useful in establishing relations between portfolio riskiness and the riskiness of the individual securities composing it.

The next theorem defines the riskiness measure.

*Theorem 12.1.* If the duality and positive homogeneity axioms are satisfied, then for any lottery[19] X, $\rho^*(X)$ is uniquely defined as the solution to:

$$1 - E\left[e^{-X/\rho^*(X)}\right] = 0 \tag{12.1}$$

The proof of Theorem 12.1 is provided in Aumann-Serrano (2008). A practical way of calculating $\rho^*(.)$ is given in the Section 12.2.2, along with several other examples illustrating the measure's properties.

Note that the function in Theorem 12.1 represents the preferences of a decision maker whose utility function is:

$$u(w) = 1 - e^{-\gamma w} \tag{12.2}$$

with risk-aversion parameter $\gamma = 1$. Equation (12.2) displays a constant absolute risk-averse utility function,[20] and if $\gamma = 1$, then $r_A(w) \equiv -u''(w)/u'(w) \equiv 1$ for all $w$.

---

[17] A partial ordering is a method of comparison that only gives meaningful results for some of the items being compared. For example, A is larger than B if A has a certainty outcome of 3 and B has a certainty outcome of 2. But if A offers equally probable outcomes of 3 and 1, then it is neither larger nor smaller than B.

[18] Aumann and Serrano (2008, p. 814).

[19] Schulze (2008) points out that the theorem is true only if the lottery X is bounded below.

[20] Aumann and Serrano also develop a variant of $\rho^*()$ based on a constant relative risk-averse function.

It follows from the next theorem that $\rho^*(.)$ permits comparing the riskiness of lotteries for all decision makers who are uniformly more risk averse than the decision maker in equation (12.2).

*Theorem 12.2.* If $\rho^*(X) \geq \rho^*(Y)$, then Y is weakly preferred to X for all decision makers who are uniformly more risk averse than a decision maker whose utility function is constant absolute risk averse with a risk-aversion parameter $\gamma = 1$.

Again, the proof may be found in Aumann-Serrano (2008).

As an example of Theorem 12.2, a decision maker who is constant absolute risk averse with a risk-aversion parameter of 1.3 is uniformly more risk averse than the decision maker in equation (12.2), and hence, $\rho^*(X) > \rho^*(Y)$ indicates that the decision maker with a risk-aversion parameter of 1.3 (weakly) prefers Y to X, just as does the decision maker with a risk-aversion parameter of 1.

The results can be further extended to other uniformly more risk-averse decision makers. However, although such comparisons are valid for any decision maker who can be described as uniformly more risk averse than the decision maker in equation (12.2), there can still be other decision makers who are not uniformly more risk averse and for whom the comparison will not be valid. That is why the Aumann-Serrano measure is a partial rather than a complete ordering.

## 12.2.2 Properties of $\rho^*(\ )$

Theorem 12.1 shows that $\rho^*(\ )$ relates a lottery's global riskiness measure to the local definition of absolute-risk aversion. Formally, $\rho^*(\ )$ is continuous, subadditive (as defined below), and consistent with dominance orderings. (Consistency is discussed in Section 12.3.) Both the form of $\rho^*(.)$ given in equation (12.1) and the following examples show that riskiness is more sensitive to the loss side of a lottery than to its gain side. Other useful properties of $\rho^*(\ )$ are also illustrated by the examples.

To see that $\rho^*(.)$ recognizes the effects of both mean and dispersion, we consider three lotteries. First, compare a lottery X that offers either a payoff of $5 or a loss of $2 with equal probability to a second lottery Y that offers a payoff of $4 or a loss of $3, also with equal probability. Then:

$$E(X) > E(Y)$$
$$\sigma^2(X) = \sigma^2(Y)$$
$$\rho^*(X) = 3.56 < \rho^*(Y) = 12.10$$

The calculations to find $\rho^*(X)$ and $\rho^*(Y)$ can be performed in an Excel spreadsheet as illustrated in Table 12.1. The table shows how to set up the spreadsheet to incorporate each lottery's outcomes and probabilities, as well as how to calculate the expected utilities. This involves exponentiation of each outcome [divided by a tentatively chosen value for $\rho^*(\ )$], then multiplying the result by the relevant probability. Then, for the specified value of $\rho^*(\ )$, the table shows further how to check whether equation (12.1) is satisfied by the just-calculated expected utility measure. If the

**TABLE 12.1**
CALCULATING RISKINESS MEASURES

|  | First lottery, X |  |  |
|---|---|---|---|
| Outcomes, $\rho^*(X)$ | −2 | 5 | **3.56** |
| Probabilities of outcomes | 0.5 | 0.5 | |
| Exponentiate (-outcome/riskiness measure) | 1.753823 | 0.245491 | |
| Above line times probability | 0.876911 | 0.122746 | |
| Sum of above lines minus 1: Negative of condition (12.1) | | | −0.000 |
|  | Second lottery, Y |  |  |
| Outcomes, $\rho^*(Y)$ | −3 | 4 | **12.10** |
| Probabilities of outcomes | 0.5 | 0.5 | |
| Exponentiate (-outcome/riskiness measure) | 1.281375 | 0.718508 | |
| Above line times probability | 0.640688 | 0.359254 | |
| Sum of above lines minus 1: Negative of condition (12.1) | | | −0.000 |

solution condition is not satisfied for the initially chosen value of $\rho^*(\ )$, then that value is successively increased or decreased until a solution is converged upon.[21] Usually only a few values need to be tried before a solution is found.

Continuing to explore how $\rho^*(.)$ incorporates the effects of both mean and variance, next consider a lottery Z that offers a payoff of $6 or a loss of $3 with equal probability. Then:

$$E(X) = E(Z)$$
$$\sigma^2(X) < \sigma^2(Z)$$
$$\rho^*(X) = \$3.5 < \rho^*(Z) = 6.2^{22}$$

Notice that the foregoing examples weigh both the effects of changing mean in comparing lotteries X and Y, and the effects of changing variance in comparing lotteries X and Z. Clearly, the riskiness measure can quantitatively recognize the effects of changing mean and changing variance simultaneously, thus in effect defining a function whose domain of definition can be taken as mean-variance space. Since each point in mean-variance space can be associated with a value of the riskiness measure for a given family of distributions,[23] the measure constitutes an advance over historical mean-variance methods that cannot assign a quantitative measure to changing both mean and variance simultaneously.[24] Essentially, the simultaneous

---

[21] While the reader familiar with Excel can use "Goal Seek" as an alternative, the trial-and-error method usually does not take very long.

[22] We have used positive mean examples in part because the risk measures for mean-zero two-point lotteries with outcome probabilities of ½ approaches 1 asymptotically.

[23] Say, the family of two-point distributions, or the family of normal distributions.

[24] Of course, the utility functions of the Markowitz approach define indifference curves in mean-variance space, and any point on an indifference curve can be assigned a value of the utility function. In contrast, for a given family of distributions $\rho^*(.)$ assigns a unique numerical score to each point in mean-variance space.

effects are recognized by the expected utility maximization calculation used to define $\rho^*(.)$ [recall equation (12.1)].

Aumann and Serrano (2008) also show that the riskiness measure is defined exactly for normally distributed variables. If X is normally distributed:

$$\rho^*(X) \equiv \sigma^2(X)/2E(X)$$

Consequently, the riskiness of any normally distributed variable X can be compared to an equivalently risky standardized form of normal distribution N. For example, take $E(N) = 1$ and $\sigma^2(N) = 2\rho^*(X)$. Then $N[1; 2\rho^*(X)]$ (where the first argument of N refers to its mean and the second to its variance) has the same riskiness as X. It follows immediately that if X and Y are both normally distributed and $\rho^*(X) < \rho^*(Y)$, then $N[1; 2\rho^*(X)]$ is less dispersed than $N[1; 2\rho^*(Y)]$.

Aumann and Serrano also offer another and more widely applicable benchmark for $\rho^*(.)$. Suppose X is a lottery, no longer restricted to be normally distributed, such that $\rho^*(X) = k$. Then the lottery B having outcome $-k$ with probability $1/e$ where $e^{25}$ is 2.17828 and therefore, its reciprocal is approximately equal to 0.37, and a sufficiently large[26] outcome $m$ with probability $1 - 1/e$, approximately 0.63, has $\rho^*(B) = k$. That is, every lottery with a given riskiness measure can be compared to a standard lottery that offers (1) a loss equal to the riskiness measure $k$ (realized with probability $1/e$) and (2) a gain equal to some large outcome realized with probability $1 - 1/e$. Both the original lottery and the benchmark have the same riskiness measure $k$.

The riskiness measure also helps to relate a portfolio's riskiness to the riskiness of the securities composing it. For any lotteries X and Y:

$$\rho^*(X + Y) \leq \rho^*(X) + \rho^*(Y)$$

That is to say, the riskiness of a sum of lotteries is no greater than the sum of the riskiness measures for the individual lotteries. This property is known as *subadditivity*. Moreover, if the variables X and Y are independent and identically distributed, then not only is $\rho^*(X) = \rho^*(Y)$ but also:

$$\rho^*(X + Y) = \rho^*(X) = \rho^*(Y)$$

That is, $\rho^*(.)$ does not increase when the two independently distributed variables are added together. Still further, if X and Y are totally positively correlated (i.e., if they are the same lottery), then:

$$\rho^*(X + Y) = 2\rho^*(X) = 2\rho^*(Y)$$

---

[25] This is the base of the Naperian logarithm.

[26] The quantity $m$ is required to be large enough to have little influence on an expected utility calculation like that in equation (12.1). For example, $m = 10k$ is a convenient choice, because it leads to considering the value of $e^{-10k/k} = e^{-10}$, a number whose first four decimal places are zero.

Finally, if the two variables are totally negatively correlated (e.g., if $X \equiv -Y$), then $\rho^*(X + Y)$ is minimized, although it need not equal zero.[27]

Applying the positive homogeneity property to the above statements provides immediate portfolio theoretic applications. Let $w$ and $1 - w$ be positive weights. Then for any[28] X and Y:

$$\rho^*(wX + (1 - w)Y) \leq w\rho^*(X) + (1 - w)\rho^*(Y)$$

the riskiness of the portfolio does not exceed the weighted riskiness measures of its components. Still further, the riskiness of an equally weighted sum of independent and identically distributed lotteries decreases:

$$\rho^*(X/2 + Y/2) = \rho^*(X)/2 = \rho^*(Y)/2$$

Thus, $\rho^*(.)$ provides natural generalizations of insights developed by Markowitzian portfolio theory.

The riskiness measure can also be applied to compound lotteries. For example, if X and Y are compounded with probabilities $p$ and $(1 - p)$, respectively, and if $\rho^*(X) \leq \rho^*(Y)$, then Aumann and Serrano (2008, p. 819) show that:

$$\rho^*(X) \leq \rho^*(pX + (1 - p)Y) \leq \rho^*(Y)$$

A compound lottery (a lottery of lotteries) has a riskiness measure that lies between the riskiness measures of the individual lotteries making up the compound lottery.

Finally, to show that $\rho^*(X)$ does not always reflect all aspects of a lottery's desirability, Aumann and Serrano (2008, p. 823) compare a lottery X, with equally probably payoffs \$5 and −\$3, to a lottery Y having payoffs \$15 and −\$1 with probabilities 1/8 and 7/8, respectively. Note that:

$$E(X) = E(Y) = \$1$$
$$\sigma^2(X) = 8 < \sigma^2(Y) = 32$$
$$\rho^*(X) = 7.70 < \rho^*(Y) = 9.20$$

However, even though Y has the greater riskiness, it is possible to find constant absolute risk-averse utility functions $u$ with risk-aversion parameters[29] for which $E[u(Y)] \geq E[u(X)]$. The example shows not only that the riskier lottery is more desirable for some decision makers, but also shows once more that the ranking provided by $\rho^*(.)$ is a partial ordering.[30] In this example, it does not rank the lotteries

---

[27] See Aumann and Serrano (2008, pp. 820−821).

[28] Note further that the foregoing refers to portfolio long positions; relations for portfolio short positions remain to be further investigated. Of course, $\rho^*(.)$ can be calculated from the distribution of a net long position that is itself composed of both long and short positions.

[29] The lottery X is preferred if the agent has a negative exponential utility with a risk-aversion parameter at least equal to 0.2, but Y is preferred for risk-aversion parameters around 0.1.

[30] If the uniformly more risk-averse condition is violated, the rankings will not necessarily hold.

similarly for all decision makers, but only for those who can be ranked as uniformly more risk averse. As with other measures, it is necessary to know the limitations of $\rho^*(.)$ in order to use it correctly.

### 12.2.3 Foster-Hart Operational Measure

Foster and Hart (2008) acknowledge the inspiration of Aumann and Serrano (2008) in developing their own operational measure of riskiness. The *Foster-Hart measure* shares many properties with the Aumann-Serrano measure, and quite often yields very similar rankings. For these reasons we shall not present the Foster-Hart measure's details, but it is still important to note the following. The Aumann-Serrano measure is derived from critical levels of risk aversion and is concerned principally with comparing lotteries' riskiness, while the Foster-Hart measure is derived from critical levels of wealth and is defined separately for each lottery. Foster-Hart develop their measure using only a single assumption: that no bankruptcy is preferred to bankruptcy.[31] They also show how their measure is related to Arrow-Pratt constant relative risk-averse utilities. Foster-Hart further stress their measure's practicality, meaning that it may find use in institutional portfolio choice problems. In particular, the measure can be used to tell when lotteries should be rejected. However, it does not otherwise help with the optimal portfolio selection problem—a limitation similar to many of the other measures discussed in this chapter.

## 12.3 CONSISTENT RISK MEASURES AND STOCHASTIC ORDERINGS

The concept of consistency describes a further link between utility-maximizing portfolios and risk measures. Recall that dominance criteria were introduced in Chapter 9. This chapter will further discuss these dominance criteria and demonstrate how each is consistent with utility maximization for a given class of decision makers.

A risk measure $\rho(.)$ is said to *consistent* with a stochastic-order relation if $E[u(X)] \geq E[u(Y)]$ for all utility functions $u$ belonging to a given category[32] implies that $\rho(X) \leq \rho(Y)$ for all admissible lotteries $X \leq_D Y$, where $\leq_D$ indicates a particular dominance relation. Since consistency can characterize the set of all optimal portfolio choices when either wealth distributions or expected utility satisfy the conditions summarized by a particular order relation, it is useful to examine how consistency can be used with the dominance criteria introduced in Chapter 9 and defined further below. It will be shown that $\rho^*(.)$ extends the orderings provided by each of the dominance criteria.

### 12.3.1 First-Degree Dominance

One form of stochastic dominance that we will describe here is first-degree stochastic dominance, which orders a subset of all possible lotteries for all nonsatiable agents.

---

[31] Or, in a shares context, that infinite growth is preferred to bankruptcy.

[32] Respectively for the dominance relations just mentioned, increasing, increasing and concave, concave but not necessarily increasing.

Denote by $U_1$ the set of all utility functions representing nonsatiable agents; that is, the set containing all nondecreasing utility functions. We say that X dominates Y in the sense of the *first-degree stochastic dominance* (FSD), denoted by $X \geq_{FSD} Y$, if a nonsatiable agent weakly prefers X to Y. In terms of expected utility, $X \geq_{FSD} Y \leftrightarrow E[u(X)] \geq E[u(Y)]$, for any $u \in U_{1.m}$. Formally, the first-order dominance relation is characterized by Theorem 12.3, showing that the test for FSD involves comparing cumulative probability distributions for lotteries.

*Theorem 12.3.* $X \geq_{FSD} Y$ if and only if $F_X(x) \leq F_Y(x)$ for all $x$ in the (assumed common) domain of the distribution functions $F_X$, $F_Y$.

When the conditions of Theorem 12.3 are satisfied, FSD gives a consistent ranking for all nonsatiable decision makers: $X \geq_{FSD} Y$ if and only if $E[u(X)] \geq E[u(Y)]$ for all nondecreasing utility functions $u \in U_1$. Moreover, $\rho^*(.)$ extends the partial ordering provided by FSD. For example:[33]

$$\text{If } X \geq_{FSD} Y, \text{ then } \rho^*(X) \leq \rho^*(Y)$$

To illustrate, suppose X is a lottery that offers either \$3 or $-\$2$ with equal probability; Y a lottery that offers either \$3.2 or $-\$1.8$ with equal probability. Clearly, $X \geq_{FSD} Y$. Moreover, $\rho^*(Y)$ is approximately \$12.20, while $\rho^*(X)$ is approximately \$6.05.

The condition $E(X) \geq E(Y)$ is necessary[34] for $X \geq_{FSD} Y$. On the other hand, ranking by means is not sufficient for FSD. If $E(X) \geq E(Y)$, it does not necessarily follow that every nonsatiable agent would necessarily prefer X. In effect, there can be nonsatiable agents who would choose X and other nonsatiable agents who would choose Y.

First-degree stochastic dominance is a relatively restrictive partial ordering that is only capable of ranking lotteries whose distribution functions do not cross at any point in their respective domains. It is possible to rank more lotteries by imposing additional restrictions on agent preferences.

## 12.3.2 Second-Degree Dominance

We introduced the idea of second-degree stochastic dominance in Chapter 9. Denote by $U_2$ the set of all utility functions that are both nondecreasing and concave. Thus, $U_2$ represents the set of nonsatiable risk-averse agents, and $U_2$ is contained in $U_1$. We say that a lottery X dominates lottery Y in the sense of *second-degree stochastic dominance* (SSD), denoted by $X \geq_{SSD} Y$, if a nonsatiable risk-averse agent weakly prefers X to Y. In terms of expected utility, SSD is also a consistent ordering:

$$X \geq_{SSD} Y \leftrightarrow E[u(X)] \geq E[u(Y)] \text{ for any } u \in U_2$$

---

[33] See, for example, Aumann and Serrano (2008, p. 818).

[34] The result follows by contradiction. Suppose that X is preferred by all nonsatiable agents but that $E(X) < E(Y)$. But by assumption of FSD, X is preferred by the nonsatiable agent with utility function $u(x) = x$, for which $E(X) \geq E(Y)$. The contradiction means the original hypothesis cannot be true.

For example, consider a lottery Y with two possible payoffs—$100 with probability ½ and $200 with probability ½, in comparison to a lottery X yielding $180 with probability one. A nonsatiable risk-averse agent would never prefer Y to X because the expected utility of Y is not larger than the expected utility of X:

$$E[u(X)] = u(180) \geq u(150) \geq u(100)/2 + u(200)/2 = E[u(Y)]$$

where $u(x)$ is assumed to be nondecreasing.

The test for SSD is an integral test.

*Theorem* 12.4. X $\geq_{SSD}$ Y if and only if

$$\int_{-\infty}^{a} F(x)dx \leq \int_{-\infty}^{a} F(y)dy \qquad (12.3)$$

for all $a$ in the (assumed common) domain of $F(x)$, $F(y)$.

Similar to the result of the previous section, $\rho^*(.)$ extends the partial orderings provided by SSD. For example:[35]

If X $\geq_{SSD}$ Y, then $\rho^*(X) \leq \rho^*(Y)$

To illustrate, suppose Y is a lottery that offers either $2 or −$1 with equal probability; X offers either $2.10 with probability 0.27, $1.95 with probability 0.23, and −$1.00 with probability 0.5. Clearly, X $\geq_{SSD}$ Y. Moreover, $\rho^*(X)$ is approximately $2.071, while $\rho^*(Y)$ is approximately 2.075.

As it is with FSD, $E(X) \geq E(Y)$ is a necessary condition for SSD. However, in contrast to FSD, the integral condition for SSD is less restrictive in that, as long as equation (12.3) is satisfied, the distribution functions may cross each other.

### 12.3.3 Rothschild-Stiglitz Dominance

As first mentioned in Chapter 9, Rothschild and Stiglitz (1970, 1971) introduce a dominance ordering that requires agents be risk averse, but not necessarily insatiable. The class of risk-averse agents considered is represented by the set of all concave utility functions, a set that contains $U_2$. The class of random variables ranked by Rothschild-Stiglitz dominance (RSD) is restricted to have the same expected values.

In practical terms RSD and SSD both focus on dispersion, but RSD provides economic insight that is not stressed in the development of SSD. In particular, RSD means that a dominated variable can be written as the sum of a dominating variable plus noise terms with a mean[36] of zero; that is, the dominated variable is more dispersed than the dominating variable. Like FSD and SSD, RSD provides a consistent ordering.

---

[35] See, for example, Aumann and Serrano (2008, p. 818).

[36] A noise term may be conditional on a given outcome of the lottery.

As mentioned in the previous sections, $\rho^*(.)$ extends the partial orderings provided by dominance relations. In the present case:

$$\text{If } X \geq_{\text{RSD}} Y, \text{ then } \rho^*(X) \leq \rho^*(Y)$$

as established in Aumann and Serrano (2008, p. 818); the riskiness measure is also consistent with RSD.

To illustrate, recall an example that has already been investigated. Let X offer either \$5 or −\$2 with equal probability, and Z offer \$6 or −\$3 with equal probability. Then:

$$E(X) = E(Z)$$
$$\sigma^2(X) < \sigma^2(Z)$$
$$\rho^*(X) = \$3.5 < \rho^*(Z) = \$6.2$$

### 12.3.4  Generalizations and Limitations

Dominance orderings are partial rankings, each capable of ranking only a subset of all possible portfolio choices. Nevertheless, successively restricting the set of preferences expands the class of portfolios that can be ranked by a given ordering. For example, SSD ranks more random variables than FSD, but does so for a subset of $U_1$.[37] On the other hand, finding portfolios that satisfy a dominance ordering is not always a trivial computational task, especially if the portfolio can contain many financial instruments with different forms of return distribution. Thus, risk measures based on dominance orderings provide only a partial solution to the problems of selecting optimal portfolios.

Given a class of investors, consistency implies that all the best investments for that class are among the dominating, and therefore the less risky, ones. However, there is no guarantee that the less risky choices are utility maximizing choices when all possible portfolios are considered. For example, the decision maker might find that some portfolio, not capable of being ranked by a given stochastic ordering, could offer a higher expected utility.

---

## 12.4  VALUE AT RISK AND COHERENT RISK MEASURES  ◈ ◈ ◈

In this section we first consider a measure known as Value at Risk, usually referred to as VaR. VaR has been and is still widely used in practice and has also been endorsed by

---

[37] It is possible to develop higher-order stochastic orderings that in effect utilize more parameters [see, for example, Milne and Neave (1994).] The Milne-Neave results are obtained for standardized variables (i.e., variables with outcomes that conform to an originally chosen partition). Counterexamples can be found for distributions whose outcomes do not conform to the originally chosen partition, but they do not remain counterexamples if the original partition is appropriately refined. It is a matter of where the analysis is begun.

bank regulators. However, the use of VaR has also been criticized severely by academics.[38] The section will first discuss the properties of VaR, then the difficulties its use presents. We next consider an axiomatic approach to defining risk measures, developed by Artzner, Delbaen, Eber, and Heath (1999), henceforth ADEH. ADEH developed the concept of coherent measures as a way of resolving some of the difficulties with VaR, and we show below how the choice of coherent measures can be regarded as superior to the choice of VaR measures. In so doing, we also compare and contrast the properties of coherent measures with the concept of Aumann-Serrano riskiness.

## 12.4.1 Value at Risk

VaR, originally developed by JPMorgan in the 1980s, defines the minimum amount of money a portfolio manager can expect to lose with a given probability. As an example, consider a portfolio whose possible value at the end of a 30-day period beginning now can be regarded as a normally distributed random variable with an expected value of $20 million and a standard deviation of $2 million. Then, given the normality assumption, the probability that this portfolio will finish the 30-day period with a realized value of $17 million or less is 0.0668. In VaR terms,[39] this situation would be expressed as a VaR of $3 million with a probability of 0.0668.

In other words, VaR states a loss magnitude that defines the upper limit of a probability distribution's lower tail. However, some important qualifications need to be kept in mind. First, the probability of 0.0668 implies that the portfolio manager could well realize a loss of more than $3 million, because VaR refers only to the tail's upper boundary. Second, the normal distribution used is quite likely to be an approximation of the actual distribution. In practice, portfolio losses of $3 million or more may actually have a probability distribution that is non-normal, with a fatter lower tail (as well as a fatter upper tail) than that of the normal distribution. This means that in practice the probability of losing $3 million or more is likely to be higher than 0.0668. (See Web-Appendix M for a discussion of alternative probability distributions.)

Despite the foregoing qualifications, VaR has been widely used by both portfolio managers and banks as a measure of the risks they face. Although the suitability of VaR is really restricted to business-as-usual periods, VaR measures have also sometimes been relied on in turbulent periods. In practice, VaR calculations are often based on data from the preceding three or four years of business. Hence, if business has operated smoothly for that period, VaR may well understate the dangers of future loss. Indeed, VaR measures based on loss experience during past business-as-usual periods may not even be very useful for predicting future losses in a changed economic environment, and portfolio managers using VaR have sometimes failed to ask what kinds of losses might be incurred if the assumptions underlying their calculations were to change.

---

[38] See, for example, ADEH (1999), Aumann and Serrano (2008), and Foster and Hart (2008).

[39] VaR measures are usually defined for periods from a few days up to a year or so. The probabilities used in assessing VaR are usually round numbers like 1% or 5%. Our choice of a different probability is intended to simplify aspects of the example.

There are still other practical problems with VaR. Attempts to apply VaR to non-elliptical return distributions ignore information contained in the tail of the distribution; that is, VaR ignores extreme events. In addition, attempts to reduce portfolio VaR may actually have the effect of stretching out the tail of losses, increasing the magnitude of losses that might be realized in extreme cases. Still further, portfolio diversification may both increase the risks assumed and prevent adding up component VaRs. Moreover, VaR can be unsuitable for use in many optimization problems, especially if the VaR measure has many local extremes that make rankings unstable. Finally, VaR can provide conflicting results at different confidence levels.

The use of VaR can also create such system problems as the dynamic instability of asset prices. Episodes of volatility increase VaR, which in turn triggers moves to sell, creating still further volatility. Fair-value accounting, which requires assets to be valued at current market prices, also accentuates price movements because marking assets down to lower market prices can stimulate further selling. Despite the foregoing problems, and even though the use of VaR has sometimes led to disastrous results, it still finds favor with regulatory agencies.

VaR has also come under severe criticism for theoretical reasons. First, VaR is not subadditive unless the joint distribution of returns is elliptical. But in the case of elliptical joint distributions, a VaR-minimizing portfolio is also a Markowitz variance-minimizing portfolio, meaning that VaR is no better than the simpler and more traditional variance measure. Finally, VaR is not a coherent measure in the sense discussed in the next section.

But if the decision maker accepts the four coherence axioms presented in the next section, both conditional VaR (CVaR)—a modification of VaR that more carefully takes into consideration tail risk—offers possible choices of measure that does not suffer from the same problems.[40] In particular, a switch from VaR to CVaR essentially requires calculations similar to those used for VaR. In the example at the beginning of this section, CVaR is the conditional expected value of losses described by the tail limit of $3 million, and is clearly a number larger than that $3 million. Since conditional losses are at least $3 million, the appropriate value for CVaR is in fact roughly equal to $3.47 million.[41]

## 12.4.2  Axioms for Coherent Risk Measures

As just mentioned, the concept of coherent measures was developed in an attempt to remedy the deficiencies of using VaR. Artzner, Delbaen, Eber, and Heath (1999, henceforth ADEH) define coherent risk measures as measures that conform to the following four axioms.

---

[40] To date, Foster-Hart have not addressed relations between their measure and either CVaR or expected regret, but they do note that their measure does not satisfy the transition invariance axiom.

[41] The exact value of CVaR is the integral of: the product of outcomes equaling $3 million or less with the conditional probability that those outcomes occur. A discrete approximation to the integral can readily be calculated using a spreadsheet such as Excel, and amounts to roughly $3.47 million. An exercise asking the reader to make such a calculation is given in question 19 at the end of this chapter.

*Positive homogeneity*: $\rho(tX) = t\rho(X)$ for all random variables X and all positive real numbers $t$.

That is, the scale of the risk measure should correspond to the scale according to which the random variables are defined. Recall that positive homogeneity is also one of the two principal axioms used by Aumann-Serrano (2008).

*Subadditivity*: $\rho(X + Y) \leq \rho(X) + \rho(Y)$ for all random variables X and Y. Subadditivity insures that combining random variables cannot increase a risk measure beyond the sum of the measures for individual components.

Subadditivity is assumed by ADEH, whereas this chapter showed earlier that it follows as a consequence of the Aumann-Serrano axioms.

*Monotonicity* : $X \leq Y$ implies $\rho(Y) \leq \rho(X)$ for all random variables X and Y.

The monotonicity axiom rules out any asymmetric form of measure, and for that reason, cannot represent all decision makers. Moreover, monotonicity is not postulated by Aumann and Serrano, and indeed their measure is more sensitive to the downside of a lottery than to its upside. Furthermore, monotonicity rules out measures such as the semi-variance,[42] which deals only with downside risk.

*Translation invariance*: $\rho(X + k) = \rho(X) - \alpha$ for all random variables X, all certainty outcomes $k$, and all real numbers $\alpha$. Translation invariance implies that adding a sure payoff to a random payoff X decreases the risk measure.

Aumann and Serrano do not postulate translation invariance as interpreted by ADEH, but their measure conforms to the same concept: $\rho^*(X) \geq \rho^*(X + a)$, where a is a positive constant.

If all four of the ADEH axioms are satisfied, $\rho$ is said to be a *coherent risk measure*. The four axioms do not define a single measure, but rather allow for a multiplicity of choices. In contrast, the Aumann-Serrano measure is defined uniquely by their choice of axioms.

### 12.4.3  Examples of Coherent Risk Measures

Many different risk measures satisfy the ADEH axioms, and any measure that does so can be termed a coherent measure. One of the most straightforward coherent measures is CVaR, which determines the expected value of losses equal to or exceeding a VaR level. Thus, CVaR attempts to describe expected tail losses rather than their upper limit as indicated by VaR.[43] As already mentioned, for the example at the beginning of this section, a 6.68% VaR is equal to $3 million and a 6.68% CVaR, the conditional expected loss described by the tail of the normal distribution, is roughly $3.47 million. (The calculation is described in footnote 40 and is detailed in question 19 at the end of the chapter.)

Other possible choices of coherent measures include Expected Regret—the expected value of a loss distribution beyond some threshold—and Worst Conditional Expectation.[44] Rachev et al. (2008) note that coherent measures serve mainly to

---

[42] *Semi-variance* is defined by the squares of the negative terms of $X - E(X)$; that is, the squares of the terms that define payoffs to a put. To see this, let $Y \equiv \min [X - E(X), 0]$. Then the non-zero terms of Y define the downside outcomes and the semi-variance is calculated as $E[Y^2]$.

[43] In addition to being a coherent measure, CVaR can be related on a one-to-one basis with deviation measures and with expectation-bounded measures.

[44] There are also spectral risk measures whose discussion is beyond the scope of the present chapter.

identify optimal choices of nonsatiable risk-averse decision makers. On the other hand, the coherence axioms violate Aumann-Serrano duality, and consequently coherence measures need not reflect Aumann-Serrano riskiness.

### 12.4.4 Generalizations and Limitations

As has been shown, only some aspects of any risk-management problem will be recognized by a given risk measure. Moreover, additional problems can arise from model error (e.g., from the ways asset return distributions are modeled), but these problems will not normally be recognized in the risk measure. For example, the potential rewards to diversification can only be measured accurately if asset return distributions are modeled to reflect empirically observed characteristics.

---

## KEY POINTS

- A risk measure provides a numerical characterization of some aspects of a lottery's risk.
- All the measures described in this chapter are partial orderings in that each is unable to rank certain specific forms of lottery.
- Early forms of risk measures were based on lotteries' means and lotteries' dispersion measures.
- Mean-dispersion approaches to measuring risk do not capture all significant aspects of empirically estimated distributions.
- The Aumann-Serrano riskiness measure is the most comprehensive measure found so far. Its capabilities derive from its theoretical foundation in expected utility, extended to describe lotteries globally.
- The Foster-Hart measure of riskiness gives characterizations very similar to those of the Aumann-Serrano measure. However, Foster-Hart use a different theoretical foundation based on the practically oriented criterion of avoiding bankruptcy.
- Consistent risk measures order lotteries in ways that also maximize expected utility, but in restricted circumstances.
- First-degree stochastic dominance, second-degree stochastic dominance, and Rothschild-Stiglitz dominance are all forms of consistent measures capable of ranking certain lotteries. Each measure can compare a differently specified set of lotteries.
- Coherent risk measures are derived from axioms that attempt to provide rankings capable of overcoming certain practical difficulties.
- Coherent risk measures address some of the practical difficulties encountered with using the forms of VaR measures developed by practicing risk managers.
- The proponents of coherent measures suggest a modification of VaR measures to overcome previously encountered practical difficulties.
- There are a large number of possible choices for coherent risk measures, and so coherence gives many descriptions of risks. Nevertheless, none of these descriptions is wholly consistent with the Aumann-Serrano measure.

### ❖ ❖ ❖   QUESTIONS

1. Many risk measures have been proposed in the financial economics literature. What does each measure attempt to do?

2. What is the definition of a risk measure?

3. What are the two risk measures of probability distributions for returns that are traditionally employed in financial economics?

4. In symmetric two-point lotteries having equal expected values, which lottery will a risk-averse decision maker prefer?

5. **a.** What is meant by mean absolute deviation?
   **b.** Why might a decision maker prefer to use mean absolute deviation rather variance as a measure of dispersion?

6. What is meant by the efficient frontier?

7. Assuming that the appropriate asset-pricing model is the capital asset pricing model, what does two-fund separation mean?

8. Explain the link between the class of elliptical distributions and measures of dependence.

9. Explain how using a variance-covariance model for non-elliptical distributions can lead to severe underestimates of extreme losses.

10. **a.** What is the economic meaning of the duality axiom upon which the Aumann-Serrano measure is based?
    **b.** What is the economic meaning of the positive homogeneity axiom upon which the Aumann-Serrano measure is based?

11. Why does the Aumann-Serrano measure of risk provide a partial ordering rather than a complete ordering of risk?

12. A bet is on flipping two independent coins; head gives payoff of $3 and tail gives loss of $2. What is the Aumann-Serrano measure of risk for this bet?

13. How does the Foster-Hart measure of risk differ from the Aumann-Serrano measure?

14. What is meant by a dominance ordering?

15. **a.** What is meant by first-degree stochastic dominance?
    **b.** How does second-degree stochastic dominance differ from first-degree stochastic dominance?

16. **a.** In what sense is Rothschild-Stiglitz dominance similar to second-degree stochastic dominance?

b. In what sense does Rothschild-Stiglitz dominance differ from second-degree stochastic dominance?

17. a. What is meant by a coherent risk measure?
    b. What are the four axioms that must be satisfied for a risk measure to be a coherent risk measure?
    c. Give three examples of coherent risk measures.

18. a. What is meant by value at risk?
    b. Is value at risk a coherent risk measure? Explain.

19. Show how to use a spreadsheet to calculate an approximate value of the 5% CVaR for the example in Section 12.4.1. (See below for an approximate approach.)

| A | B | C | D | E | F |
|---|---|---|---|---|---|
| 0.066807 | 17 | 0.044057 | 0.659466 | 3 | 1.978398 |
| 0.02275 | 16 | 0.01654 | 0.247585 | 4 | 0.99034 |
| 0.00621 | 15 | 0.00486 | 0.072743 | 5 | 0.363716 |
| 0.00135 | 14 | 0.001117 | 0.016724 | 6 | 0.100343 |
| 0.000233 | 13 | 0.000201 | 0.003008 | 7 | 0.021056 |
| 3.17E-05 | 12 | 2.83E-05 | 0.000423 | 8 | 0.003386 |
| 3.4E-06 | 11 | 3.11E-06 | 4.66E-05 | 9 | 0.000419 |
| 2.87E-07 | 10 | 2.87E-07 | 4.29E-06 | 10 | 4.29E-05 |
| Sum of column | | 0.066807 | 1 | | 3.4577 |

Column A: values for NORMDIST(X,20,2,TRUE)
Column B: values of X for Column A function
Column C: incremental values: A1-A2, A2-A3, ...
Column D: incremental values/sum of incremental values
Column E: losses represented by values in Column F: Expected values of individual losses; sum of expected values

# REFERENCES

Artzner, Philippe, Freddy Delbaen, Jean-Marc Eber, and David Heath. (1999). "Coherent Measures of Risk," *Mathematical Finance* **9**: 203–228.

Aumann, Robert J., and Roberto Serrano. (2008). "An Economic Measure of Riskiness," *Journal of Political Economy* **116**: 810–836.

Foster, Dean P., and Sergiu Hart. (2008). "An Operational Measure of Riskiness," Working Paper, Center for the Study of Rationality, The Hebrew University of Jerusalem.

Ingersoll, Jonathan E. (1987). *Theory of Financial Decision Making*. Totowa, NJ: Rowman & Littlefield.

Milne, Frank, and Edwin H. Neave. (1994). "Dominance Relations Among Standardized Variables," *Management Science* **40**: 1343–1352.

Rachev, Svetlozar T., Sergio Ortobelli, Stoyan Stoyanov, Frank J. Fabozzi, and Almira Biglova. (2008). "Desirable Properties of an Ideal Risk Measure in Portfolio Theory," *International Journal of Theoretical and Applied Finance* **11**: 19–512.

Rothschild, Michael, and Joseph E. Stiglitz. (1970). "Increasing Risk I: A Definition," *Journal of Economic Theory* **2**: 225–243.

Rothschild, Michael, and Joseph E. Stiglitz. (1971). "Increasing Risk II: Its Economic Consequences," *Journal of Economic Theory* **3**: 66-84.

Schulze, Klaase. (2008). "How to Compute the Aumann-Serrano Measure of Riskiness," Working Paper, BGSE, University of Bonn, Germany.

Tobin, James. (1969). "Comment on Borch and Feldstein," *Review of Economic Studies* **36**: 13–112.

# PART IV

# SELECTION AND PRICING OF RISKY ASSETS

# 13

# MEAN-VARIANCE PORTFOLIO CHOICE

*I*n this chapter, we provide a detailed and rigorous introduction to the most well-known theory of portfolio selection: mean-variance portfolio theory. We start from the simple case of two risky assets to understand the basic problem, then generalize to an arbitrary number of risky assets. After deriving the mean-variance frontier both graphically and analytically, we apply the theory to a realistic example. We also discuss some practical issues associated with the implementation of mean-variance analysis. Finally, we consider some advanced issues.

## 13.1 TWO RISKY ASSETS

Consider the investment of \$1 in two risky assets, asset 1 and asset 2, whose random returns next period are $r_1$ and $r_2$, respectively. In this section, we assume that the expected returns, variances, and covariances are known, and focus on the portfolio selection problem. In practice, these variables are unknown, and have to be estimated using historical data. An illustration will be given in Section 13.4.3.

### 13.1.1 Portfolio Return

If we let $w_1$ and $w_2$ be the percentage of the portfolio invested in asset 1 and asset 2 respectively, then the total percentage allocated to the two assets must be equal to one, that is,

$$w_1 + w_2 = 1 \tag{13.1}$$

This equation is known as the *budget constraint*. For example, if the investor allocates 40% of the portfolio to asset 1 (i.e., $w_1 = 0.4$), that means the investor allocates 60% of the portfolio to asset 2 (i.e., $w_2 = 0.6$).

Given the allocation of the portfolio between these two assets, let's look at the investor's realized return, referred to as the *portfolio return* and denoted $r_p$. The portfolio return will depend on the return realized on the two assets, which we denote by $r_1$ and $r_2$. The contribution to the portfolio return for asset 1 is $r_1 w_1$. Similarly, the

257

contribution to the portfolio return for asset 2 is $r_2 w_2$. Adding the contributions from both assets gives the portfolio return:

$$r_p = w_1 r_1 + w_2 r_2 \tag{13.2}$$

Equation (13.2) is useful for computing the realized portfolio return if we know $r_1$ and $r_2$. It is equally useful for computing the expected portfolio return, that is, we also have:

$$E[r_p] = w_1 E[r_1] + w_2 E[r_2] \tag{13.3}$$

where $E[r_1]$ and $E[r_2]$ are the expected returns on the two risky assets and $E[r_p]$ is the expected portfolio return.

Notice that we have not said anything about the the sign of the weights. A positive weight for an asset in a portfolio means the investor takes a *long position* in the asset. A negative weight means the investor takes a *short position*, created by *short selling* an asset.

There are some important implications following from restrictions on the weights. First, if weights are restricted to be nonnegative, then the maximum expected portfolio return cannot exceed the expected return of the asset with the largest expected return. If short selling is permitted (i.e., negative weights are allowed), then the expected portfolio return can well exceed the expected return of the asset with the largest expected return.

For example, if $E[r_1] = 5\%$ and $E[r_2] = 10\%$, then the expected return is:

$$E[r_p] = w_1 \ 5\% + w_2 \ 10\%$$

If an investor wants an expected return of 100% (i.e., $E[r_p] = 1$), this means that the investor seeks to satisfy the following equation:

$$1 = \ w_1 \ (0.05) + w_2 \ (0.10)$$

There are two unknowns in this equation. However, the investor needs to satisfy not only the above equation but also the budget constraint given by equation (13.1). Thus, there are two equations and two unknowns. Solving these two equations we obtain the solution $w_1 = -18$ and $w_2 = 19$. How do we interpret these two values for the weights?

Let's assume that the investor has $1 to invest. The weight $w_1 = -18$ means that the investor short sells $18 worth of asset 1. Assuming that the investor receives the $18 from the short sale, then the amount available to invest in asset 2 will be the $18 plus the original investment of $1. That is, $19 will be invested (long position) in asset 2. This is what the solution $w_2 = 19$ means.

In practice, short selling assets is not simple or, for some assets, even possible. For example, there are mechanisms for short selling a common stock by borrowing it from a broker. The lender of the stock, however, can request the return of the stock on demand. This is a risk faced by the investor who shorts sells a stock. Bonds can be sold short either through a mechanism known as a repurchase agreement or through a securities lending transaction just the same as in the case of common stock. However, it is difficult to short sell other types of assets such as real estate and common stock of private companies (i.e., nonpublic companies). Moreover, even if one can short sell, there may be restrictions on how the investor can use the proceeds. For individual investors, the proceeds may not be available from the short sale but, instead, retained by the broker to assure that the funds borrowed from the short sale will be returned. That is, the broker will want to reduce counterparty risk. For institutional investors, the funds may or may not be available depending on the particulars of the deal.

## 13.1.2  Portfolio Risk

Although the expected return of a portfolio is simply a weighted average of the expected return of the two assets in the portfolio, the variance of the portfolio return is more complicated. Based on equation (13.2), the variance of the portfolio return is a weighted sum of the asset variances and covariance, that is:

$$var(r_p) = w_1^2 var(r_1) + 2w_1w_2 cov(r_1, r_2) + w_2^2 var(r_2) \tag{13.4}$$

where $var$ denotes the variance and $cov$ the covariance. Equation (13.4) follows straightforwardly from the variance formula for a linear function of random variables in statistics. In finance, we often use $\sigma^2$ to denote the variance function. Furthermore, if we let $\rho_{12}$ be the correlation between the returns of assets 1 and 2, then:

$$\rho_{12} = \frac{cov(r_1, r_2)}{\sqrt{var(r_1)var(r_2)}} = \frac{cov(r_1, r_2)}{\sigma_1 \sigma_2}$$

Next, we can write equation (13.4) above in a mathematically simpler form:

$$\sigma_p^2 = w_1^2 \sigma_1^2 + 2w_1w_2\rho_{12}\sigma_1\sigma_2 + w_2^2\sigma_2^2 \tag{13.5}$$

Equation (13.5) is the portfolio return variance, which is the risk measure in the mean-variance framework. Very often, the square root of the variance, $\sigma_p$, is also used to denote the risk of a portfolio, but this is the risk in terms of standard deviation. It should be noted that both measures of risk give the same information. This is because one portfolio is riskier than another in terms of $\sigma_p^2$ if and only if it is riskier in terms of $\sigma_p$.

## 13.1.3  Diversification Effect

The *diversification effect* means that the risk of a portfolio can be reduced by combining assets with certain statistical attributes. The simplest way to see this is to assume that the two asset returns are statistically independent, with the same expected return denoted by $\mu$, and the same variance $\sigma_1^2 = \sigma_2^2 = \sigma^2$. In this case, because of the independence of the returns between the two assets, $\rho_{12} = 0$, an equal-weighted portfolio consisting of the two assets with the same expected return, but has a variance of:

$$\sigma_p^2 = \left(\frac{1}{2}\right)^2 \sigma^2 + 2 \times \frac{1}{2} \times \frac{1}{2} \times 0 \times \sigma^2 + \left(\frac{1}{2}\right)^2 \sigma^2 = \frac{1}{2}\sigma^2 \qquad (13.6)$$

An examination of equation (13.6) indicates that by holding the two assets, the portfolio's variance is one half of the variance of a portfolio consisting of just one of the two assets.

When the two assets have different means and variances, the diversification effect is more complex. To see this intuitively, let us analyze the portfolio risk and return obtainable by combining assets 1 and 2 with expected returns of 4% and 8%, and standard deviations of 6% and 10%, respectively. If they are combined in varying proportions $w_1$ and $w_2$, then the expected portfolio return is:

$$E[r_p] = w_1(0.04) + (1 - w_1)(0.08)$$

To see the impact of the correlation ($\rho_{12}$) between the two assets on portfolio variance, let's look at three cases: perfect positive correlation, perfect negative correlation, and imperfect correlation.

*Case 1:* *Perfect Positive Correlation.* In this case, $\rho_{12} = 1$. As $w_1$ varies from 0 to 1, the portfolio risk-return relation, as measured by the standard deviation and expected return, is the straight line AB in Figure 13.1. This is because, when $\rho_{12} = 1$

$$\sigma_p^2 = w_1^2\sigma_1^2 + 2w_1(1 - w_1)\sigma_1\sigma_2 + (1 - w_1)^2\sigma_2^2 = [w_1\sigma_1 + (1 - w_1)\sigma_2]^2$$

which implies:

$$\sigma_p = w_1\sigma_1 + (1 - w_1)\sigma_2 = 0.06w_1 + 0.10(1 - w_1) \qquad (13.7)$$

Now the derivative of $\sigma_p$ with respect to $w_1$ is:

$$\frac{d\sigma_p}{dw_1} = \sigma_1 - \sigma_2$$

so the derivative of the return-risk relation is:

$$\frac{dE[r_p]}{d\sigma_p} = \frac{dE[r_p]/dw_1}{d\sigma_p/dw_1} = \frac{0.04 - 0.08}{0.06 - 0.10} = 1$$

Mathematically, this says that the segment AB must be a straight line with slope 1, because the derivative is independent of $w_1$.

Intuitively, when two assets are perfectly correlated, the risk is the weighted sum of the individual risks. If we restrict the portfolio weights to being nonnegative (i.e., no short selling), the risk cannot be less than the

**FIGURE 13.1**

DIVERSIFICATION WITH TWO RISKY ASSETS

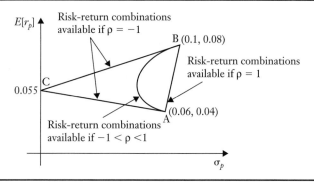

lower of the two, as evident from line AB. This means that diversification is not possible. However, if short selling is allowed, the portfolio risk can be reduced to any desired number. For example, if we want to have $\sigma_p = 2\%$, we solve equation (13.7) to get $w_1 = 2$ and $w_2 = -1$. Then the resulting portfolio will have a standard deviation of 2%. However, the expected portfolio return will be $2 \times 0.04 - 1 \times 0.08 = 0\%$, an undesirable level. In other words, though the portfolio risk can be reduced, we may not want to do so due to the impact on the expected return. Note that Figure 13.1 only shows the case where the weights are nonnegative, that is, the case of no short selling.

As an example showing approximately the meaning of perfect positive correlation in practice, we could think of the shares of two zinc-mining companies of the same size and having the same standard deviation of return (by virtue of being in the same industry) but different expected returns (e.g., one has management that can control its fixed costs better than can the other). Also by virtue of the two firms being in the same industry, we can assume their earnings are perfectly positively correlated.

*Case 2:* *Perfect Negative Correlation.* In this case, $\rho_{12} = -1$, and

$$\sigma_p^2 = w_1^2 \sigma_1^2 - 2w_1(1 - w_1)\sigma_1\sigma_2 + (1 - w_1)^2 \sigma_2^2 = [w_1\sigma_1 - (1 - w_1)\sigma_2]^2$$

It follows that $\sigma_p$ must again be a linear function of $\sigma_1$ and $\sigma_2$. However, it takes on a nonnegative value for the square root above, which is either:

$$w_1\sigma_1 - (1 - w_1)\sigma_2$$

or

$$-[w_1\sigma_1 - (1 - w_1)\sigma_2]$$

When $w_1 = 0.625$ and $w_2 = 0.375$, $\sigma_p$ is exactly equal to zero. When $w_1$ is between 0.055 and 0.10, it can be shown, similar to line AB in Figure 13.1, that the risk-return combination is a line, and is given by CB in Figure 13.1. Likewise, when $w_1$ is between 0.06 and 0.055, the combination is the line segment CA.

*Case 3:* *Imperfect Correlation.* For this case we have $-1 < \rho_{12} < 1$, which is the case most likely to be encountered in practice. In this case, $\sigma_p$ is not a linear function of the return. In fact, the risk-return combinations lie on the curved line shown in Figure 13.1. We can begin to trace this curve by allowing $\rho_{12}$ to move slightly away from $-1$. As $\rho_{12}$ moves closer and closer to 1, the curve gets more and more flat. Eventually, when $\rho_{12} = 1$, it becomes the straight line AB.

Whenever the two assets are imperfectly correlated, portfolio risk can be reduced without short selling. This means that diversification can in general take place even with long positions (i.e., positive weights) for both risky assets. However, the diversification effect is quite limited with two risky assets.

Moreover, it is impossible to reduce the risk if we fix the level of the expected portfolio return. This can be seen in Figure 13.1. At any horizontal line, there is only one unique risk level and nothing else to choose from. Mathematically, this is obvious from the budget constraint. Assume that the two risky assets have different expected returns. Then, for any given $E[r_p]$, there is a unique combination of $w_1$ and $w_2$ such that the portfolio will achieve an expected portfolio return of $E[r_p]$. Because the portfolio is unique, an investor cannot reduce its risk any further. However, as shown in the next section, diversification possibilities are increased when there are $N > 2$ assets. These assets will in general provide infinitely many possible portfolios with the same level of $E[r_p]$. In such circumstances, it makes sense to select the one portfolio that has the minimum risk among all portfolios with the same level of expected return. In practice, risk reduction can be substantial since there are so many assets that provide so many ways to obtain a given level of expected portfolio return.

## 13.2  MANY RISKY ASSETS

Consider now the case for investing in $N > 2$ risky assets, with random returns next period denoted by $r_1, r_2, \ldots, r_N$. Let $w_1, w_2, \ldots, w_N$ be the portfolio weights (i.e., percentage allocations). As an extension of the two-asset case, the budget constraint is:

$$w_1 + w_2 + \cdots + w_N = 1 \tag{13.8}$$

and the return on the portfolio is:

$$r_p = w_1 r_1 + w_2 r_2 + \cdots + w_N r_N \tag{13.9}$$

The expected portfolio return and variance are then given by applying the standard statistics formulas to $r_p$:

$$E[r_p] = w_1 E[r_1] + w_2 E[r_2] + \cdots + w_N E[r_N] \tag{13.10}$$

$$\sigma_p^2 = var(r_p) = \sum_{i=1}^{N} \sum_{j=1}^{N} w_i w_j cov(r_i, r_j) \qquad (13.11)$$

Note that the right-hand side of equation (13.11) simply denotes the sum of the products of all possible covariances with the portfolio weights on the $N$ assets. Including both variances and covariances, there are $N^2$ possible terms. Equation (13.11) is sometimes also written as:

$$\sigma_p^2 = \sum_{i=1}^{N} w_i^2 \sigma_i^2 + \sum_{i=1}^{N} \sum_{i \neq j}^{N} w_i w_j cov(r_i, r_j) \qquad (13.12)$$

where the first term is the sum of the $N$ variances, and the second term is the sum of all $N(N-1)$ covariances between the different assets.

For notational brevity and for reading the vast literature on mean-variance portfolio choice, it is important to be comfortable with vector and matrix expressions. Denote the expected returns on the $N$ risky assets by:

$$\mu = E[r] = \begin{bmatrix} \mu_1 \\ \mu_2 \\ \vdots \\ \mu_N \end{bmatrix} \qquad (13.13)$$

where $r$ is an $N$-vector formed by the risky returns on the $N$ assets, and $\mu_i = E[r_i]$ is the expected return on the $i$-th asset. In vector form, we can write the budget constraint and expected portfolio return as:

$$w' 1_N = 1 \qquad (13.14)$$

and

$$\mu_p = w' \mu \qquad (13.15)$$

where $w = (w_1, w_2, \ldots, w_N)'$ is an $N$-vector formed by the portfolio weights, and $1_N$ is an $N$-vector formed by ones, and the prime ($'$) means the transpose of the vector.

The riskiness of the $N$ risky assets is summarized by the covariance matrix given by:

$$\Sigma = var(r) = \begin{bmatrix} var(r_1) & cov(r_1, r_2) & \cdots & cov(r_1, r_N) \\ cov(r_2, r_1) & var(r_2) & \cdots & cov(r_2, r_N) \\ \vdots & \vdots & \cdots & \vdots \\ cov(r_N, r_1) & cov(r_N, r_2) & \cdots & var(r_N) \end{bmatrix} \qquad (13.16)$$

The covariance matrix is usually assumed to be nonsingular, which is equivalent to the assumption that none of the asset returns is an exact linear combination of the rest. If any asset is a linear combination of the rest, a situation known as existence of a *redundant asset*, it can be eliminated from the asset set since keeping it in the existing asset set will not alter the optimal portfolio choice of any investor.

In terms of matrix notation, the portfolio risk as given by equation (13.12) can be simply written as:

$$\sigma_p^2 = w' \Sigma w \tag{13.17}$$

For mean-variance portfolio selection, $\mu$ and $\Sigma$ summarize all the information we need about the risky assets.

## 13.2.1 Diversification and Its Limits

Risk-averse investors are motivated to reduce portfolio risk without reducing the expected portfolio return. Usually they will attempt to realize this goal by adding additional assets to the portfolio. Consider first the simple and hypothetical case where all the $N$ risky assets have the same expected return, say $\mu_1 = 10\%$, and the same portfolio variance, say $\sigma^2 = 20\%^2$. Assume further that the returns are independent so that the covariances are zero. Then, by equation (13.12), the risk of an equal-weighted portfolio is:

$$\sigma_p^2 = \sum_{i=1}^{N} \left(\frac{1}{N}\right)^2 \sigma^2 = \frac{1}{N}\sigma^2 = \frac{1}{N} 0.20^2 \tag{13.18}$$

Notice that the portfolio risk diminishes to zero as more and more assets are used (i.e., as $N$ increases). On the other hand, the portfolio return remains at 10%. In this example, diversification can potentially eliminate all risks.

The above example is, however, unrealistic. In the real world, asset returns are correlated. For example, economic recessions are likely to affect all stocks and real estate properties. In this case, it will be impossible to eliminate all the risks. To see the intuition, assume all the assets have the same correlation $\rho$ and that $\rho > 0$. Then,

$$\sigma_p^2 = \frac{1}{N}\sigma^2 + \frac{N-1}{N}\rho\sigma^2 \tag{13.19}$$

As $N$ approaches infinity, the portfolio variance approaches $\rho\sigma^2$, a positive number that cannot be lowered any further.

When asset returns have different means and variances,[1] it is natural to ask what is the maximum reduction in risk that can be achieved? In other words, given the level of expected portfolio return at $\mu_p$, what is the minimum risk an investor has to take? While the minimum risk is almost always nonzero in practice, finding portfolio weights that yield this minimum is clearly important. Mathematically, we need to find $w$ to minimize $\sigma_p^2$, that is:

$$\min_{w} \sigma_p^2 = w' \Sigma w \tag{13.20}$$

---

[1] In this chapter we are implicitly assuming that all investors have the same expectations of any asset's return and its variance.

where the portfolio weights have to satisfy two constraints,

$$w'1_N = 1$$
$$w'\mu = \mu_p$$

The first constraint is the budget constraint, and the second is necessary to meet a given level of desired expected portfolio return $\mu_p$.

For example, suppose that an investor can create a $\sigma_p^2 = 0.30^2$ portfolio variance by using 10 risky assets in order to achieve an expected portfolio return of 10%. Suppose further that the investor uses 100 risky assets and wants the same return. The investor will then have to solve the above problem with $\mu_p = 10\%$, and with $\mu$ and $\Sigma$ as the expected portfolio return and covariance matrix of the 100 assets. If the best that the investor can do is to find a set of portfolio weights (the allocation of funds among the 100 assets) that will generate a portfolio variance of $\sigma_p^2 = 0.20^2$ then the diversification effect will be $0.30^2 - 0.20^2 = 0.05$ in terms of the portfolio variance. If the investor uses standard deviation as a measure, the portfolio risk declinces from $\sigma_p = 30\%$ to $\sigma_p = 20\%$.

The optimization problem given by equation (13.20) be solved analytically with the use of calculus, as shown in the next section.

## 13.2.2 Derivation of Optimal Portfolios

Recall from calculus that in order to optimize an objective function, we need only set the first-order derivatives of the function to zero—which are known as *first-order conditions* (FOCs)—and then solve them. The solution to the FOCs is the solution to the optimization problem, which may maximize or minimize the objective function depending on the behavior of the function. In our case here, the variance is a quadratic function, and is clearly unbounded above. Hence, the solution must minimize the function.

Note that minimizing $\sigma_p^2$ is the same as minimizing $\sigma_p^2/2$, which simplifies the FOCs below. In addition, since our optimization problem has two constraints, we need to add them into the objection function with Lagrangian multipliers. Then, we can write the new objective function (or the Lagrangian function) of our problem as:

$$L = \frac{1}{2}w'\Sigma w + \lambda_1(1 - w'1_N) + \lambda_2(\mu_p - w'\mu) \tag{13.21}$$

where $\lambda_1$ and $\lambda_2$ are the Lagrangian multipliers that reflect the two constraints. Taking the first derivatives with respect to $w$, $\lambda_1$, and $\lambda_2$:

$$\frac{\partial L}{\partial w} = \Sigma w - \lambda_1 1_N - \lambda_2 \mu = 0$$

$$\frac{\partial L}{\partial \lambda_2} = 1 - w'1_N = 0 \tag{13.22}$$

$$\frac{\partial L}{\partial \lambda_2} = \mu_p - w'\mu = 0$$

where $\partial L / \partial w$ is the partial derivative of $L$ with respect to the vector $w$, that is, an $N$ vector formed by stacking all the derivatives with respect each individual $w_i$, which is:

$$\frac{\partial L}{\partial w_i} = w_i \sigma_i^2 + \sum_{j \neq i}^{N} w_j \sigma_{ij} - \lambda_1 - \lambda_2 \mu_i = 0$$

with $i = 1, 2, \ldots, N$.

The solution to the FOCs is the solution to our problem. The first of the three equations is:

$$w = \lambda_1 \Sigma^{-1} 1_N + \lambda_2 \Sigma^{-1} \mu \qquad (13.23)$$

but $\lambda_1$ and $\lambda_2$ are unknown. Multiplying both sides of this equation by $1_N'$ and using the second equation of the FOCs, we have:

$$1 = \lambda_1 (1_N' \Sigma^{-1} 1_N) + \lambda_2 (1_N' \Sigma^{-1} \mu) \qquad (13.24)$$

Multiplying both sides of equation (13.23) again by $\mu'$ and using the third equation of the FOCs, we have:

$$\mu_p = \lambda_1 (\mu' \Sigma^{-1} 1_N) + \lambda_2 (\mu' \Sigma^{-1} \mu) \qquad (13.25)$$

Since equations (13.24) and (13.25) are two linear equations with two unknowns, standard algebra yields:

$$\lambda_1 = \frac{B - A\mu_p}{\Delta}, \qquad \lambda_2 = \frac{C\mu_p - A}{\Delta} \qquad (13.26)$$

where $A, B, C$, and $\Delta$ are functions of the expected asset returns and covariance matrix,

$$A = 1_N' \Sigma^{-1} \mu, \quad B = \mu' \Sigma^{-1} \mu, \quad C = 1_N' \Sigma^{-1} 1_N$$

and $\Delta = BC - A^2$.

Plugging the solution to $\lambda_1$ and $\lambda_2$ into equation (13.23), we obtain the optimal portfolio weights:

$$w = g + b\mu_p \qquad (13.27)$$

where

$$g = \frac{1}{\Delta} \left[ B(\Sigma^{-1} 1_N) - A(\Sigma^{-1} \mu) \right], \quad b = \frac{1}{\Delta} \left[ C(\Sigma^{-1} \mu) - A(\Sigma^{-1} 1_N) \right]$$

The minimized portfolio variance is then:

$$\sigma_p^2 = \frac{A\mu_p^2 - 2B\mu_p + C}{\Delta} \qquad (13.28)$$

Both this formula and the formula for the optimal portfolio weights are fundamental in mean-variance portfolio choice.

### 13.2.3 Efficient Frontier

To achieve a desired level of expected portfolio return $\mu_p$, our derivation says that an investor should choose portfolio weights according to equation (13.27). These weights can be computed easily once the expected asset returns and covariance matrix are given. The weights are said to be *optimal* since they produce a portfolio that has the *minimum portfolio risk* among all possible portfolios with the same expected portfolio return $\mu_p$.

The minimized portfolio risk is given by equation (13.28), which is a quadratic function of $\mu_p$. Hence, if we plot $(\mu_p, \sigma_p)$ together for all possible $\mu_p$, we get a hyperbola, which is the curve AGB in Figure 13.2. This curve is known as the *mean-variance frontier*. Those portfolios whose risk and return trade-offs fall on the curve are referred to as *frontier portfolios*. If we plot at the same time the expected return and standard deviation of an individual asset or of any other portfolio, they must lie within the curve. This is because at the same portfolio return level, or on a horizontal line across the expected portfolio return, the optimal portfolio will yield a smaller risk, and be on their left-hand side.

The portfolio that yields the minimum possible portfolio risk, point G on the frontier, is known as the *global mean-variance portfolio*. Mathematically, as $\sigma_p^2$ is a quadratic function, there must be some choice of $\mu_p$ such that $\sigma_p^2$ is the smallest among all possible $\sigma_p^2$'s. Note that GA and GB are symmetric around the horizontal line passing through point G. As a result, the frontier GB will be inefficient. Although the optimal portfolio is on GB for any expected portfolio return below point G, the investor will prefer instead a higher expected portfolio return with the same portfolio risk, a mirror point on GA. Therefore, only frontier portfolios on GA are of interest to investors. The frontier portfolios on curve GA are called *efficient portfolios* and thus curve GA is known as the *efficient frontier* (or the *mean-variance frontier*), representing the risk and return trade-offs available for investors from which to choose.

**FIGURE 13.2**
MEAN-VARIANCE FRONTIER

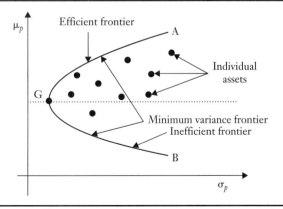

### 13.2.4 Two-Fund Theorem

The derivation for the mean-variance frontier portfolios provides a number of insights into the portfolio choice problem, an important one of which is the so-called *Two-Fund Theorem*. It means that, when there are $N$ risky assets available for investment, then (1) it will be unnecessary to consider all possible portfolios comprised of those risky assets, and (2) two portfolios will be sufficient. All investors will be satisfied by holding a mixture of these two portfolios. In practice, one can imagine that the two portfolios are two mutual funds. In that case, then the mean-variance theory says that only two such mutual funds will be sufficient, and what the investors need to do is to buy some mixture of these two funds.

To understand why the Two-Fund Theorem holds, consider the optimal portfolio weights when $\mu_p = 0$ and $\mu_p = 1$. Equation (13.27) says that the weights are $g$ and $g + h$. In other words, by holding a portfolio with weight $g$, we will obtain a frontier portfolio with expected return 0%, and $g + h$ will produce a frontier portfolio with expected return 100%. Rewrite equation (13.27) as:

$$w = (1 - \mu_p)g + \mu_p(g + h)$$

To produce an arbitrary frontier portfolio with expected portfolio return $\mu_p$, the above equation says that we need hold only $(1 - \mu_p)$ units of $g$ plus $\mu_p$ units of $g + h$, a portfolio of two frontier portfolios. In particular, all frontier portfolios are portfolios of the $g$ and $g + h$, the 0 and 1 expected return portfolios. Since all investors will only hold efficient portfolios, they will be satisfied by holding suitable mixtures of the 0 and 1 expected return portfolios.

Any two distinct frontier portfolios can play the same role of the 0 and 1 expected return portfolios. This is because their portfolio weights can be represented linearly by $g$ and $g + h$. Inverting the relation, $g$ and $g + h$ can be represented by them too. Then, any frontier portfolio, as a portfolio of $g$ and $g + h$, are also a portfolio of these two distinct frontier portfolios.

It should be noted that the mean-variance frontier is the result of choosing an optimal portfolio. But the portfolio risk, when moving along the frontier, is not a linear function of the portfolio return. When we want to double our expected portfolio return, the portfolio risk, as a quadratic function of $\mu_p$, will not necessarily double. In contrast, the portfolio weights, which are how we actually select the assets, do change linearly with $\mu_p$. If we double $\mu_p$, we just double our holdings of $g + h$, but at the same time reduce the holding of $g$ to $(1 - \mu_p)$ units to satisfy the budget constraint.

## 13.3 ADDING A RISK-FREE ASSET

Let's now consider now what happens when a risk-free asset is available and can be included in a portfolio consisting of the $N$ risky ones. This is realistic since investors in practice can invest their money in short-term Treasury bills, which can be regarded as risk-free over the one-period time horizon used to measure the return. It is also important since investors do have available an asset that allows them to earn a return without taking risk. The zero risk return (i.e., the return on the risk-free asset) is the opportunity cost of money and a useful benchmark for assessing the value of any risky investment.

Graphically, we can see the huge improvement brought by having the opportunity to add the risk-free asset to a portfolio. Without it, investors can only choose among the portfolios on the efficient frontier, the AB curve in Figure 13.3. Let $D = (r_f, 0)$ be the risk-return point for the risk-free asset. Intuitively, there is one and only one line that starts from $D$ and is tangent to the efficient frontier. We call the portfolio that is represented by this point the *tangency portfolio* and denote it by P. The risk-return choice along the line DP is achievable by holding a portfolio of the risk-free asset and P. This is because any point on that line must be a linear combination of D and P (in geometry, the usual equation for a line), and this combination associated with D and P provides the portfolio that has the desired risk-return choice. Similarly, the risk-return choice along the line PC is also achievable by borrowing at the risk-free asset (negative holding) and investing in P. Here, we assume for simplicity that investors can borrow and lend at the same interest rate for any amount.

The line DPC is in fact the best new opportunity set for risk-return choices. Any line that begins at D and does not intersect with the frontier is not feasible. With the exception of point D, there will not be any portfolios that can generate such a risk and return relation. On the other hand, for any line that intersects the frontier, and yet is not tangent to it, the choice will be dominated by DPC. This is because for any one of them (except point D), one can find a portfolio on the DPC line with the same expected portfolio return, but lower portfolio risk. Therefore, with the availability of the risk-free asset, investors now will choose a portfolio along the line DPC.

Note that the Two-Fund Theorem is obviously still true with the addition of the risk-free asset. In this case, all investors only hold a mixture of the tangency portfolio and the risk-free asset as they choose along the line DPC. Thus, under the assumption of the mean-variance portfolio theory developed thus far, there need only exist two mutual funds, a money market fund (which is the risk-free asset) and a risky asset fund. Then all investors will be satisfied by holding suitable mixtures of the two mutual funds.

It will be useful to see how the portfolio weights may change with the addition of the risk-free asset. Denote by $r_f$ the rate of return on the risk-free asset. Then, we will

FIGURE 13.3
OPTIMAL PORTFOLIOS WITH A RISK-FREE ASSET

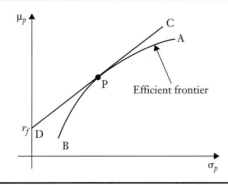

no longer have a budget constraint on the risky assets. This is because the return on our portfolio is:

$$r_p = (w_1 r_1 + w_2 r_2 + \cdots + w_N r_N) + (1 - w_1 - w_2 - \cdots - w_N) r_f \qquad (13.29)$$

where the first term is the total return on the risky assets with $w_1, w_2, \ldots, w_N$ as the portfolio weights, and the second term is the return on the risk-free asset. The total amount invested in the risky assets is $w_1 + w_2 + \cdots + w_N$, which can be any allocation percentage, and $(1 - w_1 - w_2 - \cdots - w_N)$ is the remainder allocated to the risk-free asset. If the remainder is negative, it means we borrow that amount at the risk-free rate. We can then express the desired level of the expected portfolio return as:

$$\mu_p = w'\mu + (1 - w'1_N) r_f \qquad (13.30)$$

This will be the only single constraint in our new optimization problem. The optimal portfolio weights are then obtained the same way as before, and are given by:

$$w = \frac{\mu_p - r_f}{\psi} \Sigma^{-1} (\mu - r_f 1_N) \qquad (13.31)$$

where $\psi^2 = B - 2Ar_f + Cr_f^2$ and the coefficients $A$, $B$, and $C$ were defined after equations (13.26). This formula makes intuitive sense. If $\mu_p = r_f$, we have $w = 0$, or zero positions in all risky assets, and the entire portfolio is invested entirely in the risk-free asset to earn $r_f$. The higher the expected portfolio return, the more we invest proportionally in the risky assets. The proportionality is linear in $\mu_p - r_f$, which is the desired expected portfolio return in excess of the risk-free rate.

The minimized portfolio risk (as measure by the variance) is:

$$\sigma_p^2 = (\mu_p - r_f)^2 / \psi^2$$

In terms of standard deviation, we have:

$$\sigma_p = \frac{\mu_p - r_f}{\psi} \qquad (13.32)$$

where $\mu_p > r_f \geq 0$. This says that the portfolio risk in terms of the standard deviation is exactly a linear function of the desired portfolio excess expected return. The higher the return an investor seeks for the optimal portfolio, the greater the portfoilio risk the investor must take.

Mathematically, equation (13.32) is the equation for the line DPC. At point P, the expected return is:

$$\mu_p^* = \frac{A}{C} - \frac{\Delta/C^2}{r_f - A/C} \qquad (13.33)$$

where $\Delta$ is defined after equations (13.26) and the associated standard deviation is computed from equation (13.32) with this level of expected return.

## 13.4 MARKOWITZ PORTFOLIOS

The portfolios on the mean-variance frontier are also known as *Markowitz efficient portfolios* since the theory is largely due to Markowitz (1952). In this section, we analyze issues associated with applying the Markowitz theory in practice. The Markowitz framework is applied in three ways. First, it used to determine the asset allocation across asset classes (e.g., stocks, bonds, real estate, alternative investments, and so on). Second, within an asset class there are typically different sectors. For example, in the case of common stock, there are various ways sectors can be classified such as defensive and cyclical sectors or within the cyclical sector there are the following nine sectors: capital goods, energy, technology, health care, communications, transportation, basic materials, consumer cyclical, and finance. We'll demonstrate how Markowitz theory is used in this way later in this chapter. Finally, Markowitz theory is used to determine particular investments within an asset class. For example, it is used when constructing a portfolio of stocks; that is, it is used to select the specific stocks that will make up the portfolio from among a universe of $N$ candidate stocks.

### 13.4.1 Preferences

Theoretically, although investors who care about only mean and variance will choose one of the many possible Markowitz efficient portfolios, the precise one is impossible to determine unless we know the preferences or utility function of an investor. For example, if we know that a 20% expected portfolio return corresponds to a 30% portfolio risk (i.e., standard deviation of 30%), and 10% expected portfolio returns correspond to 20% portfolio risk, some investors may prefer the former and some may prefer the latter.

Graphically, Figure 13.4 illustrates the point. The three dotted lines represent the indifference curves of three investors. Investor I, with indifference curve I, is aggressive and will choose a portfolio at a point on line PC at which the indifferent curve is tangent to the line. Investor II may choose exactly the tangency portfolio. Investor III is the most typical, because it involves allocating a portion of the portfolio to the risk-free asset and the remainder in the risky tangency portfolio P.

FIGURE 13.4
DIFFERENT PORTFOLIO CHOICES BY DIFFERENT INVESTORS

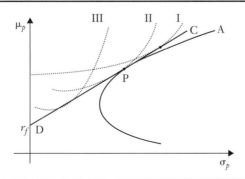

## 13.4.2 Quadratic Utility Function

A common mean-variance preference function is the quadratic utility function given by:

$$u(\mu_p, \sigma_p) = E[r_p] - \frac{\gamma}{2} \, var\,[r_p] = \mu_p - \frac{\gamma}{2}\sigma_p^2 \tag{13.34}$$

where $\gamma$ is often called the risk-aversion parameter, used as a practical means of reflecting risk aversion through affecting the trade-off between risk and return.[2] The utility is an increasing function of the expected portfolio return and a decreasing function of the portfolio risk. It is typical to specify a value of $\gamma = 3$. In this case, a 10% expected portfolio return and a 20% standard deviation will result in a utility level of:

$$u(0.10, 0.20) = 0.10 - 1.5 \times 0.20^2 = 0.04$$

For 30% portfolio risk, the investor requires a return of 17.5%, because:

$$u(0.175, 0.30) = 0.175 - 1.5 \times 0.30^2 = 0.04$$

In other words, the investor is indifferent between choices $(17.5\%, 30\%)$ and $(10\%, 20\%)$.

With a quadratic utility function, the optimal portfolio weights on the risky assets, which make the indifference curve tangent to the DPC line, is:

$$w^* = \frac{1}{\gamma}\Sigma^{-1}(\mu - r_f 1_N) \tag{13.35}$$

which is a particular case of $w$ given by equation (13.31). Note that $w^*$, $w$, and the tangency portfolio all are proportional to $\Sigma^{-1}(\mu - r_f 1_N)$, and they differ only by the proportionality coefficient. So, the formula for $w^*$ reaffirms that the optimal investment in the risky assets is an allocation of a suitable amount into the tangency portfolio with the remainder allocated to the risk-free asset.

Equation (13.35) can also be derived by directly maximizing the utility function (13.34) without using equation (13.31). To see this, we first rewrite the expected portfolio return given by equation (13.30):

$$r_p = r_f + w'(\mu - r_f 1_N)$$

Then, the portfolio variance is:

$$\sigma_p^2 = w'\Sigma w$$

---

[2] Note that $\gamma$ is not the Arrow-Pratt coefficient of risk aversion first introduced in Chapter 9 and discussed further in Chapters 11 and 12. The Arrow-Pratt measure of absolute risk aversion is defined in (11.8), and of relative risk aversion in (11.9).

which is the same as before. Intuitively, adding the risk-free asset will not change the risk for any given $w$. The utility is:

$$U(\mu_p,\sigma_p) = r_f + w'(\mu - r_f 1_N) - \frac{\gamma}{2}w'\Sigma w \tag{13.36}$$

The FOC for the maximization is now much simpler than before, and is given by:

$$\frac{\partial U}{\partial w} = (\mu - r_f 1_N) - \gamma\Sigma w = 0$$

The solution to this is easily obtained as that given by equation (13.35).

With the optimal portfolio weights, the maximized utility of the investor is:

$$U(w^*) = r_f + \frac{1}{2\gamma}(\mu - r_f 1_N)'\Sigma^{-1}(\mu - r_f 1_N) \tag{13.37}$$

which is obtained from equation (13.36) by plugging in the optimal portfolio weights. This is often called the *certainty equivalent return* of the optimal strategy.[3] The reason is that the second term in the utility function plays a risk adjustment role. If $E[r_p]$ is 25%, and the second term is 15%, then the maximized utility is 20%, as a result of accounting for the risk. If the investor were offered a 20% return without any risk, the maximized utility is also 20%. Hence, the 25% risky return is equivalent to a certainty return of 20%.

In practice, $w^*$ is not computable because the expected asset return vector $\mu$ and covariance matrix $\Sigma$ are unknown. To implement the mean-variance theory of Markowitz (1952), the optimal portfolio weights are usually determined by a two-step procedure. Suppose an investor has $T$ periods of observed data on the $N$ returns, $r_1, r_2, \ldots, r_T$, and would like to form a portfolio for period $T+1$. First, the mean and covariance matrix of the asset returns are estimated based on the observed data. Note that only returns in excess of the risk-free rate, $\theta = \mu - r_f 1_N$, matter in the portfolio weights formula, and it is the excess returns (i.e., returns in excess of the risk-free rate) that are commonly used. Let:

$$R_t = r_t - r_{ft} 1_N$$

be an $N$-vector of the asset excess returns in each period, that is, each of its components is the asset return minus that of the risk-free rate at $t$. Then the estimates are:

$$\hat{\theta} = \frac{1}{T}\sum_{t=1}^{T} R_t \tag{13.38}$$

$$\hat{\Sigma} = \frac{1}{T}\sum_{t=1}^{T} (R_t - \hat{\theta})(R_t - \hat{\theta})' \tag{13.39}$$

---

[3] The concept of certainty equivalent value is explained in Chapter 11.

which are the sample excess return and covariance matrix, respectively.

In the second step, the sample estimates are then treated as if they were the true parameters, and are simply plugged into equation (13.35) to compute the optimal portfolio weights,

$$\hat{w}^* = \frac{1}{\gamma} \hat{\Sigma}^{-1} \hat{\theta} \tag{13.40}$$

Although one can update the estimates as time goes by with more data, the optimal portfolio weights are theoretically constant. More data can only make the estimate more accurate. However, if one assumes that true expected asset returns and standard deviations (risk) can vary over time, so will $w^*$. In this case, the estimation will be much more complex and the analysis in such situations is beyond the scope of this book.

### 13.4.3 An Example

As we explained earlier, Markowitz theory can be applied in three ways in determining the allocation of funds. One way is for allocating funds among sectors within an asset class. Let's consider now how to allocate funds among five sectors of the economy. All publicly traded stocks are grouped into five (i.e., $N = 5$) industries:[4]

1. Consumer
2. Manufacturing
3. High Tech
4. Health Care
5. Other

The industry groupings are based on their four-digit Standard Industrial Classification (SIC) code at the end of June of any year. Then, the market value for each indutry group in each month is computed, which can then be used to compute the monthly returns for all five groups. There are now a total of $T = 984$ observations on $N = 5$ assets, that is, the five industy portfolios. Subtracting the observed returns from the risk-free rates, which are approximated by the monthly Treasury bill rates, we obtain the monthly excess returns. The sample mean and covariance matrix of the excess returns are then easily computed using any software, or directly based on equations (13.38) and (13.39).

The monthly excess returns, variances, and covariances for the five industy portfolios are provided in Table 13.1. In terms of matrix notation for the model, the results are:

---

[4] The data, from January 1927 to December 2008, are available from Professor Kenneth French's website, http://mba.tuck.dartmouth.edu.

$$
\hat{\theta} = \frac{1}{100} \begin{bmatrix} 0.654 \\ 0.655 \\ 0.582 \\ 0.758 \\ 0.571 \end{bmatrix}, \quad
\hat{\Sigma} = \frac{1}{100^2} \begin{bmatrix}
29.436 & 26.594 & 25.060 & 24.547 & 31.094 \\
26.594 & 31.381 & 25.841 & 24.357 & 32.673 \\
25.060 & 25.841 & 32.641 & 23.535 & 29.609 \\
24.547 & 24.357 & 23.535 & 33.577 & 28.123 \\
31.094 & 32.673 & 29.609 & 28.123 & 42.635
\end{bmatrix}
$$

We see that the health care industry (industry 4) has the highest monthly mean excess return of 0.758% per month, while the other industry has the lowest of only 0.571% per month. The monthly standard deviation of the health care industry and other industry is 5.791% ($= \sqrt{33.577}/100$) and 6.530%, respectively. Note that the industry group other (industry 5) has a lower return and higher risk than health care. At the sector level, this is possible as is observed from the data. However, at the portfolio level, the optimal portfolio that has a higher expected return must have higher risk.

Plugging the estimates into equation (13.40) and setting $\gamma = 3$, we obtain the estimated optimal portfolio weights:

$$
\hat{w}^* = \begin{bmatrix} 0.571 \\ 0.644 \\ -0.009 \\ 0.575 \\ -0.837 \end{bmatrix}
$$

**TABLE 13.1**
ESTIMATED INPUTS FOR THE EXAMPLE

| | | Expected monthly returns |
|---|---|---|
| 1. | Consumer | 0.00654 |
| 2. | Manufacturing | 0.00655 |
| 3. | High Tech | 0.00582 |
| 4. | Health Care | 0.00758 |
| 5. | Other | 0.00671 |

Variances (diagonal values) and covariances (off-diagonal values) (values must be divided by $100^2$)

| | Consumer | Manufacturing | High Tech | Health Care | Other |
|---|---|---|---|---|---|
| Consumer | 29.436 | 26.594 | 25.060 | 24.547 | 31.094 |
| Manufacturing | 26.594 | 31.381 | 25.841 | 24.357 | 32.673 |
| High Tech | 25.060 | 25.841 | 32.641 | 23.535 | 29.609 |
| Health Care | 24.547 | 24.357 | 23.535 | 33.577 | 28.123 |
| Other | 31.094 | 32.673 | 29.609 | 28.123 | 42.635 |

TABLE 13.2
OPTIMAL PORTFOLIO WEIGHTS (%) FOR THE EXAMPLES
$\hat{w}^* = (0.192, 0.132, -0.106, 0.527, 0.075)'$

| Constraint on Industry | | No Restrictions | No Short Sales | Health Care* |
|---|---|---|---|---|
| 1. | Consumer | 57.1 | 18.6 | 19.6 |
| 2. | Manufacturing | 64.4 | 13.6 | 14.1 |
| 3. | High Tech | −0.9 | 0.0 | 0.0 |
| 4. | Health Care | 57.5 | 51.8 | 50.0 |
| 5. | Other | −83.7 | 0.0 | 0.0 |
| Treasury bills | | 5.6 | 16.0 | 16.3 |
| Total | | 100.0 | 100.0 | 100.0 |

* Constraint $0 \le w_4 \le 0.5$.

The solution is also summarized in the second column of Table 13.2.

The optimal allocation is not surprising given our earlier computation of the mean and standard deviations. Note that the sum of the weights on risky assets here is less than one, implying that we invest the remainder, 5.6% of the funds, in the risk-free asset (U.S. Treasury bills).

## 13.5 PRACTICAL ISSUES

There are many practical issues associated with implementing the mean-variance framework. For simplicity, we analyze these issues in terms of our earlier example and in terms of the quadratic utility function.

### 13.5.1 Restrictions on Portfolio Weights

The first issue is whether the investor is actually able to sell short. The optimal strategy of the example suggests a short sell position in the Other industry by using 83.7% of the portfolio's funds. This position is clearly large relative to the amount invested. In fact, it is typical that the solutions to mean-variance optimal portfolios call for large short positions. In practice, however, it is difficult or impossible for most individuals or institutional investor to short a large value comparable to their wealth. For example, the prospective of most mutual funds limit short selling, as well as SEC regulations. Hedge funds are an exception, however, because they typically have no restrictions on short selling. But it should also be kept in mind that for some asset classes and individual assets it is difficult to short sell in the market even in the absence of any legal or self-imposed restrictions on short selling. Even when short sales are permitted, as noted earlier in this chapter, the investor may not receive the total proceeds from the short sale to invest.

Suppose now that no short sales are allowed. This effectively requires the inclusion another set of constraints:

$$w_i \ge 0, \quad i = 1, 2, \ldots, 5 \tag{13.41}$$

into the utility maximization problem. While there will be no simple analytical solutions as in the earlier case, the problem can be solved numerically and easily with commercially available quadratic programming software.

The solution to our example when no short sales are permitted would then be:

$$\hat{w}^* = (0.186, 0.136, 0.000, 0.518, 0.000)'$$

This solution is summarized in Table 13.2. Note that once no short sales are allowed, we reduce our exposure to the other industries, as well as the amount invested in the Treasury bills. This is intuitive since we do not have the short positions to offset the portfolio risk, and so we have to invest less in other industries to balance out the risk.

A constraint that is often imposed in practice is to specify a range on the weights. In an asset allocation problem where an allocation is to be made from among asset classes, there can be a range imposed for the weight. In the application of the port-folio choice model to a given asset class, sector, or specific issuer, or sector, there may be restrictions on the minimum and maximum that can be allocated. For example, if real estate is one of the asset classes that is a candidate for inclusion in a portfolio, an investor may decide to restrict the amount that can be invested due to the lack of liquidity for that asset class.

The range for the weights is imposed by the following set of constraints:

$$a_i \le w_i \le b_i, \quad i = 1, 2, \ldots, 5 \tag{13.42}$$

that is, for each asset $i$, the position has to be between $a_i$ and $b_i$. For example, our previous solution has a relatively large position in the Health Care industry (industry 4). Suppose that an investor wants to limit no more than 50% invested in Health Care. Then we can solve the problem with the additional constraint that:

$$0 \le w_4 \le 0.5$$

Under this additional constraint, the solution is:

$$\hat{w}^* = (0.196, 0.141, 0.000, 0.500, 0.000)'$$

The optimal allocations, also shown in Table 13.2, are quite intuitive too. Once we limit $w_4$ to be no more than 50%, the solution uses the maximum possible of $w_4 = 0.5$ since it is optimal to use the fourth industry (Health Care) as much as possible up to 51.8%. The 50% constraint limits the total risk exposure of the portfolio. To balance this out, the solution increases the holdings in the first industry from 0.18.6% to 19.6%, and of the third industry from 13.5% to 14.1%. The amount allocated to the risk-free asset increases slightly.

A more general constraint is to impose the following linear relation on the weights:

$$c \le w_1 \beta_1 + w_2 \beta_2 + + \cdots + w_5 \beta_5 \le d \tag{13.43}$$

where $\beta_i$ is the beta risk (see the next chapter) or other characteristic of the $i$-th asset/sector/issuer. The constraint limits the total beta exposure of the portfolio. As before, while analytically the solution is difficult to obtain, in practice the problem is easily solved numerically with commercial software.

## 13.5.2 Portfolio Rebalancing

The mean-variance framework is a one-period model. Consequently, a second practical issue in portfolio choice involves *portfolio rebalancing* each time period. If the optimal portfolio weights are to be held constant, one must trade assets each period to maintain the same constant weights.

For instance, in our previous example with 19.6% as our position in the Consumer industry (the first industry), this industry value can change next period, doubling, say, while other industries remain the same. In this case, our allocation to the consumer industry will then exceed the optimal portfolio weight of 19.6%. This requires that the investor sell enough of the holdings in the Consumer industry so that the portfolio weight remains at 19.6%, and use the proceeds to invest in other assets to maintain their optimal weights too. In practice, because asset values change randomly each period, we have to buy and sell them to maintain the same optimal weights each period too. This action will result in the investor incurring transaction costs every period, and such costs can be substantial.

Considering that in practice investment decisions are usually made starting with a portfolio of specific assets rather than cash, some assets may have to be liquidated to permit investment in others. Chen et al. (1971) were among the first to address this problem by considering the transaction costs to be incurred in the process of portfolio revision. Actually, the costs associated with buying or selling assets should be directly integrated into the portfolio optimization problem. How to optimize a portfolio in the presence of transaction costs is a subject of active research.[5]

## 13.5.3 Estimation Errors

A third practical issue involves *estimation errors* of the parameters of the model for the expected return and variance for every asset, as well as the covariance (correlation) of returns between all pairs of assets. In the real world, the parameters are likely to change over time, and the models for estimation are not perfectly valid. Even assuming that the true parameters are constant and the data are normally distributed, the parameter estimation problem is still complex. This issue will be discussed further in the next section and in future chapters.

## 13.6 Advanced Topics

In this section, we discuss three topics that are of practical importance. They are the more challenging issues in portfolio choice.

---

[5] See Davis and Normal (1990), Adcock and Meade (1994), Yoshimoto (1996), Konno and Wijayanayake (2001), Best and Hlouskova (2005), Lobo et al. (2007), and Chen, Fabozzi, and Huang (2010).

## 13.6.1 Long-Term Investment

In mean-variance portfolio theory, the investment horizon is one period, although the period can be of any length, say a month or a year. Consider now the problem of investing for $H$ periods. Assume today is time 0, and an investor has a wealth of $W_0$. Then, after investing for $H$ periods, the investor's wealth will be:

$$W_H = W_0(1 + R_1)(1 + R_2)\cdots(1 + R_H) \tag{13.44}$$

where $R_t$ is the portfolio return in time period $t$.

Suppose now that the investor cares only about the terminal wealth at the end of period $H$. Let $U(W_H)$ be the investor's utility function. The question of interest here is under what conditions the investor will adopt a one-period constant investment policy; that is, the investor would invest today as if tomorrow were the terminal date, and use the same portfolio weights for all the remaining periods. If so, how is this constant investment policy relate to the mean-variance optimal portfolio weights?

Assume that the returns are independent and identically distributed (IID) over time. If this assumption is not made, the investment policy will clearly vary with time as the investor reacts to the different return distributions at different times. Under the IID assumption, Samuelson (1969) shows that the investor will have a *constant investment policy* if the investor has a power utility of wealth:

$$u(W_H) = \frac{W_H^{1-\gamma}}{1-\gamma} \tag{13.45}$$

where $\gamma > 0$ is the risk-aversion parameter. When $\gamma = 1$, the utility is defined as the limit of $\gamma$ approaching 1, and is the log utility function. With the power utility function, the constant portfolio weights in each period is also approximately given by the mean-variance optimal portfolio weights.

To see why, consider the case of the log utility function. Then the expected utility of wealth is:

$$E[log(W_H)] = log(W_0) + E[log(1+R_1)] + E[log(1+R_2)] + \cdots + E[log(1+R_H)] \tag{13.46}$$

All the terms on the right-hand side of equation (13.46) are uncorrelated, and so maximizing the expected utility, $E[log(W_H)]$, is the same as maximizing each of the terms. Because of the IID assumption, maximizing each term, apart from $log(W_0)$, will yield the same constant investment policy. A quadratic approximation to each of the terms yields the mean-variance portfolio policy.

In general, for an arbitrary utility function and time-varying asset return distributions, it will be difficult to maximize $u(W_H)$ at time 0 (today) since the decision will depend on how the investor will respond in period 1, period 2, and each period until period $H-1$. Dynamic programming, a specialized type of mathematical programming, is usually employed because it solves the problem backwards successively to find the optimal policy at periods $H-1, H-2, \ldots, 2, 1$ and today. Merton (1990) and Campbell and Viceira (2003) provide some of the models and solutions. But the solutions are available only for a few models and a few assets. As a result, despite significant advances in portfolio theory over the years, the mean-variance framework is still the major model used in practice today in asset allocation and active portfolio management.

Grinold and Kahn (1999), Litterman (2003), and Meucci (2005) provide various practical applications of the mean-variance framework. One of the main reasons for the popularity of the mean-variance analysis is that many real-world issues, such as large dimensionality, factor exposures, and trading constraints, can be accommodated easily within a framework that provides analytical insights and fast numerical solutions.

## 13.6.2 Index Tracking

In practice, portfolio managers are often given a task of beating a benchmark index (or simply index), usually a value-weighted portfolio of the underlying assets (typically stocks or bonds). To see how an index works in the case of stocks, consider, for example, the case where there are only two stocks in the economy, $A$ and $B$, whose market values are \$100 and \$200, respectively. Then their value-weighted index will use a weight of $\frac{1}{3}$ in $A$ and $\frac{2}{3}$ in $B$, the proportions of their values in the market. The popular Standard & Poor's 500 (S&P 500) index is such a value-weighted index comprising the stock of 500 large capitalizaton companies that are actively traded.

Let $\overline{w}$ be the portfolio weights of the index, and $w$ be the weights of the managed portfolio. The *active return* is defined as:

$$\begin{aligned} \text{Active return} = &\text{ Total return on the managed portfolio} \\ &- \text{Total return on the index} \end{aligned} \tag{13.47}$$

Clearly, to outperform the index, $w$ must be different from $\overline{w}$. However, investors do not want $w$ to be too different from the benchmark in terms of risk. What they want is to take a comparable risk of the index, and to obtain a higher expected return than the index. To measure the risk of the managed portfolio, the variance of the active returns is often used. This variance, referred to as the *tracking error*, is defined as:

$$\text{Tracking Error} = var[w'r - \overline{w}'r] = (w - \overline{w})'\Sigma(w - \overline{w}) \tag{13.48}$$

While there are many ways by which the mean-variance portfolio theory may be applied in seeking to outperform an index,[6] we focus below on using the tracking error as a criterion. The task of portfolio managers is to outperform the index as much as possible while keeping a limit on the tracking error. The limit is referred to as a *risk budget*, which constrains the risk the portfolio manager can take. It will be of interest to examine the analytical solution to maximizing the expected portfolio return under a target for tracking error. Roll (1992) and Jorion (2003) provide analytical solutions to this and related problems.

Mathematically, the problem is:

$$\begin{aligned} &\max_w w'\mu \\ &\text{s.t. } w'1_N = 1 \\ &(w - \overline{w})'\Sigma(w - \overline{w}) = \tau \end{aligned} \tag{13.49}$$

---

[6] See, for example, Grinold and Kahn (1999).

where $\tau$ is a given amount of tracking error. Recall that the constraint $w'1_N = 1$ is the standard one that implies wealth is fully invested so the weights sum to 1. The solution is then:

$$w_r = \overline{w} + \sqrt{\frac{\tau C}{\Delta}} \Sigma^{-1}(\mu - \mu_{gmv}1_N) \qquad (13.50)$$

where $\mu_{gmv} = B/A$ is the expected portfolio return on the global minimum variance portfolio, A, B, C, and $\Delta$ are as defined earlier in Section 13.2.2. When $\tau = 0$, the managed portfolio must be equal to $\overline{w}$, the benchmark. As $\tau$ increases, the portfolio includes proportionally more of the portfolio $\Sigma^{-1}(\mu - \mu_{gmv}1_N)$.

There are two important observations to note. First, the managed portfolio is obtained by adding the second portfolio to $\overline{w}$. Since $\Sigma^{-1}(\mu - \mu_{gmv}1_N)$ is not proportional to $\Sigma^{-1}(\mu - r_f 1_N)$ unless $\mu_{gmv} = r_f$ (unlikely), the added portfolio is not an efficient portfolio. This says that the tracking error constraint may be questionable as it induces portfolio managers to hold an inefficient portfolio regardless of whether the benchmark is efficient or not. Second, the added portion is independent of $\overline{w}$. This means that in a world of say 5,000 stocks, the portfolio manager uses the same added portfolio to beat an index, whether the index is comprised of 500 stocks or 2,000.

## 13.6.3 Estimation Errors

The expected asset returns and the covariance matrix are needed in order to apply the mean-variance portfolio model, but they are unknown parameters and have to be estimated in practice. Equations (13.38) and (13.39) provide the formulae used for estimation. The estimates have random errors.[7] The two key questions are: (1) how large are the estimation errors and (2) do these errors have a major impact on the portfolio decisions (i.e., the optimal portfolio weights)?

To assess the estimation errors, we have to make an assumption on how the asset returns behave each period. The simplest assumption is that they are well behaved, IID, with the same joint normal distribution. In particular, for each individual asset excess return, we have:

$$R_{it} \sim N(\theta_i, \sigma_i^2) \qquad (13.51)$$

which says that the asset excess return, denoted by $R_{it}$, has a normal distribution with mean $\theta_i$ and variance $\sigma_i^2$. Then, our sample estimate of $\theta_i$, the average of the observations, should also be normally distributed:

$$\hat{\theta}_i \sim N(\theta_i, \sigma_i^2/T) \qquad (13.52)$$

which says that the $\hat{\theta}_i$ has a mean $\theta_i$, and estimation error variance of $\sigma_i^2/T$. In other words, if we play the game of estimating $\theta_i$ infinite times with the same sample size $T$,

---

[7] See Best and Grauer (1991), Black and Litterman (1992), Chopra (1993), and Chopra and Ziemba (1993).

we will get $\hat{\theta}_i$ on average equal to the true $\theta_i$, but the error each time can easily be of magnitude equal to $\sigma_i/\sqrt{T}$. In our earlier example in Section 13.4.3, $T = 984$, and $\sigma_i/\sqrt{T}$ is estimated at the level of 0.185% for the Other industry (the fifth industry).

Now we change the expected monthly asset return for the Other industry to 0.756% by adding the possible error of 0.185% to 0.571%. Using the same values for all other parameters, then the optimal portfolio weights in the case where there are no constraints on the weights become:

$$\hat{w}^* = (0.192, 0.132, -0.106, 0.527, 0.075)'$$

This solution as well as the original solution where the monthly excess return of 0.518% are summarized below:

*Portfolio weights with estimation error*

|  |  | 0.756% | 0. 518% |
|---|---|---|---|
| 1. | Consumer | 19.1% | 57.1% |
| 2. | Manufacturing | 13.2% | 64.4% |
| 3. | High Tech | −10.6% | −0.9% |
| 4. | Health Care | 52.7% | 57.5% |
| 5. | Other | 7.5% | −83.7% |
| Treasury bills |  | 18.1% | 5.6% |
| Total |  | 100.0% | 100.0% |

As can be seen from the above table, instead of shorting Other heavily, the investor now has a long position in that industry. Accounting for the estimation errors completely alters our strategy (i.e., portfolio allocation), a phenomenon arising not only in this example, but in almost all applications of mean-variance portfolio theory. In practice, the expected asset returns are notoriously difficult to estimate. Moreover, the optimal portfolio weights are sensitive to the estimates and can change drastically even with small changes in the estimates.

The estimation errors affect both the portfolio's optimal portfolio weights and its certainty equivalent return (or maximum utility level). To see this, consider the simple case in which an investor knows the true expected asset returns, but just does not know the true covariance matrix. Kan and Zhou (2007) show that the maximum utility with the estimated covariance matrix can only achieve a portion of the maximum utility had the investor known the true covariance matrix. The proportion coefficient is given by:

$$k_1 = \left(\frac{T}{T-N-2}\right)\left[2 - \frac{T(T-2)}{(T-N-1)(T-N-4)}\right] \tag{13.53}$$

For example, if we apply the mean-variance portfolio theory to $N = 200$ assets with $T = 984$, we obtain $k_1 = 52.57\%$. That is, even with the estimation errors in $\Sigma$ alone, we can achieve only about half of what is the possible level of the expected utility.

Because of the substantial impact of the estimation errors on the optimal solution, it is important to develop ways to handle them. The next two chapters will discuss some theoretical structures for the expected asset returns and their covariance matrix. The theories and methods provided there will be useful for reducing the estimation errors.

## KEY POINTS

- In mean-variance theory, the risk and return of a portfolio are determined by the portfolio return variance (or standard deviation) and expected portfolio return, respectively.
- Portfolio risk can be reduced by adding more assets with certain statistical characteristics and is referred to as the diversification effect.
- An efficient portfolio is the one that has the minimum risk among all possible portfolios that have a given level of expected portfolio return.
- There is a trade-off between risk and return: The higher the expected return of an efficient portfolio, the higher the portfolio risk.
- The mean-variance frontier is a plot of the expected portfolio return and the minimum risk a portfolio has to bear to have that level of expected portfolio return.
- In practice, the Markowitz framework is used to determine: (1) the asset allocation across asset classes (e.g., stocks, bonds, real estate, alternative investments, and so on), (2) the allocation of funds across sectors within an asset class the allocation, and (3) the selection of particular investments within an asset class.
- In the absence of a risk-free asset, the efficient frontier is the upper part of the mean-variance frontier, and it contains all the possible portfolios from which an investor may choose.
- In the presence of the risk-free asset, the efficient portfolios are on the straight line that, starting from the point of the risk-free asset return with zero risk, is tangent to the mean-variance frontier of the risky assets.
- The particular efficient portfolio selected by an investor depends on the investor's preference or utility function.
- Given data and a quadratic utility for an investor, the optimal portfolio can be analytically computed based on the historical mean return and the standard deviation of returns for each asset, and the historical covariance of each pair of asset returns.
- Over time, the optimal portfolio must be rebalanced to remain optimal in future periods.
- The estimation errors in estimating the expected asset return, variance, and covariances can have a significant impact on the performance of the estimated optimal portfolio.

## QUESTIONS

1. In mean-variance portfolio theory, what is meant by the budget contraint?

2. If the solution to a mean-variance portfolio problem specifies a negative weight for Asset X, what does that mean?

3. Explain whether you agree or disagree with the following statement: "A portfolio's expected return and variance of return are simply a weighted average of the expected return and variance of all assets in the portfolio."

4. Consider investing money into two stocks. Suppose they have expected returns next year of 10% and 20%, respectively. Assume further that they have standard deviations of 15% and 25%, with a correlation of 50%.

   a. What is the expected return on the equal-weighted portfolio?
   b. How do you get a portfolio with 18% return and what is the risk of this portfolio?
   c. How do you get a portfolio with 100% return and what is the risk of this portfolio?
   d. Suppose the two stocks have realized returns of 30% and −10% next year. What is the realized return of the equal-weighted portfolio, and what will be the value of your wealth if you started with $100?

5. Suppose there are three stocks with the same expected return of 10% per year and the same risk (standard deviation) of 100%. The correlation between any two of them is 50%.

   a. What is the risk of the equal-weighted portfolio of two stocks?
   b. What is the risk of the equal-weighted portfolio of three stocks?
   c. What is the minimum possible risk of a portfolio of the three stocks?
   d. If the third stock has a correlation of −50% instead of 50% with the rest, what is the risk of the equal-weighted portfolio of three stocks, and what is the minimum possible risk?

6. Suppose that you have a risky asset that provides you with an expected return of 12% per year with 20% volatility (standard deviation). Consider a risk-free asset that provides you with a 3% risk-free return.

   a. If you have $100,000 and invest 80% into the risky asset and 20% into the risk-free asset, what is the expected return and risk of your portfolio?
   b. How much will your portfolio be worth if the realized return on the risky asset is 15%?
   c. If you cannot borrow money, what is the maximum possible expected return on your portfolio, and what is the minimum?
   d. If you are allowed to borrow money at the risk-free rate, how can you get a portfolio with an 18% expected return and what is the risk of this portfolio?

7. In the mean-variance framework, what is meant by

   a. global minimum variance portfolio?
   b. an efficient frontier?

8. What is meant by the Two-Fund Theorem and why is it important?

9. Consider the problem of finding the optimal portfolio of three stocks—Johnson and Johnson, Microsoft, and Walmart—whose expected returns and covariance matrix are:

$$\mu_N = \begin{bmatrix} 1.216 \\ 2.408 \\ 1.241 \end{bmatrix}, \qquad \Sigma = \begin{bmatrix} 0.4381 & 0.1751 & 0.1483 \\ 0.1751 & 0.3544 & 0.2361 \\ 0.1144 & 0.2361 & 0.5673 \end{bmatrix}$$

which are monthly values in percentage points, estimated as the sample mean and sample variance/covariance of the data.

a. Are the optimal portfolio weights dependent on the data frequency used to estimate the parameters?

b. If the true parameters are assumed unchanged from this month to the next one, will the optimal portfolio weights change?

c. Once we have bought the stocks today based on the optimal portfolio weights, do we have to do any trading next month?

d. What is the risk and return of the equal-weighted portfolio?

e. Find the optimal portfolio weights with a desired level of expected return 1.7251%.

f. Find the optimal portfolio weights with a desired level of expected return 2.408%.

10. Consider an asset allocation problem faced by an investor who has $1 million to allocate between a stock index and a money market fund. Suppose that the investor believes that the stock index has an annual expected return of 12% with 20% risk. The risk-free interest rate is 3% per year.

a. If the investor has a quadratic utility with risk-aversion parameter $\gamma = 3$, what will be the asset allocation decision?

b. What is the risk and return of the investor's optimal portfolio?

c. If for a portfolio risk of 15%, the investor desires a level of expected return of 9.75%, what is the implied risk-aversion parameter?

11. In the mean-variance framework, what is the practical issue associated with

a. shorting in the mean-variance framework?

b. portfolio rebalancing?

c. estimation of the parameters of the model?

# REFERENCES

Adcock, C. J., and N. Meade. (1994). "A Simple Algorithm to Incorporate Transaction Costs in Quadratic Optimization," *European Journal of Operational Research* **79**: 85–94.

Best, M. J., and R. R. Grauer. (1991). "On the Sensitivity of Mean-Variance Efficient Portfolios to Changes in Asset Means: Some Analytical and Computational Results," *Review of Financial Studies* **4**(2): 315–342.

Best, M. J., and J. Hlouskova. (2005). "An Algorithm for Portfolio Optimization with Transaction Costs," *Management Science* **51**(11): 1676–1688.

Black, F., and R. Litterman. (1992). "Global Portfolio Optimization," *Financial Analysts Journal* **48**: 28–43.

Chen, A. H., F. J. Fabozzi, and D. Huang. (2010). "Models for Portfolio Revision with Transaction Costs in the Mean-Variance Framework." In J.B. Guerard, Jr. (ed.), *The Handbook of Portfolio Construction: Contemporary Applications of Markowitz Techniques.* New York: Springer.

Chen, A. H., F. C. Jen, and S. Zionts. (1971). "The Optimal Portfolio Revision Policy," *Journal of Business* **44**: 51–61.

Chopra, V. K. (1993). "Mean-Variance Revisited: Near-Optimal Portfolios and Sensitivity to Input Variations," *Journal of Investing* **2**(1): 51–59.

Chopra, V. K., and W. T. Ziemba. (1993). "The Effects of Errors in Means, Variances, and Covariances on Optimal Portfolio Choices," *Journal of Portfolio Management* **19**(2): 6–11.

Grinold, R. C., and Kahn, R. N. (1999). *Active Portfolio Management: Quantitative Theory and Applications.* New York: McGraw-Hill.

Jorion, Philippe. (2003). "Portfolio Optimization with Tracking-Error Constraints," *Financial Analyst Journal* **59**: 7–82.

Kan, R., and G. Zhou. (2001). "Optimal Portfolio Choice with Parameter Uncertainty," *Journal of Financial and Quantitative Analysis* **42**: 621–656.

Konno, H., and H. Yamazaki. (1991). "Mean-Absolute Deviation Portfolio Optimization Model and Its Applications to Tokyo Stock Market," *Management Science* **37**: 519–531.

Konno, H., and A. Wijayanayake. (2001). "Portfolio Optimization Problem under Concave Transaction Costs and Minimal Transaction Unit Constraints," *Mathematical Programming* **89**(2): 233–250.

Litterman, B. (2003). *Modern Investment Management: An Equilibrium Approach.* New York: John Wiley & Sons.

Lobo, M. S., M. Fazel, and S. Boyd. (2007). "Portfolio Optimization with Linear and Fixed Transaction Costs," *Annals of Operatons Research* **152**(1): 341–365.

Markowitz, H. M. (1952). "Portfolio Selection," *Journal of Finance* **7**(1): 77–91.

Merton , R. C. (1990). *Continuous Time Finance.* Cambridge, MA: Basil Blackwell.

Meucci, A. (2005). *Risk and Asset Allocation.* New York: Springer-Verlag.

Roll, R. (1992). "A Mean-Variance Analysis of Tracking Error," *Journal of Portfolio Management* **18**: 13–22.

Samuelson, P. A. (1969). "Lifetime Portfolio Selection by Dynamic Stochastic Programming," *Review of Economics and Statistics* **51**(3): 239–246.

Yoshimoto, A. (1996). "The Mean-Variance Approach to Portfolio Optimization Subject to Transaction Costs," *Journal of Operations Research Society of Japan* **39**(1): 99–117.

# 14

# CAPITAL ASSET PRICING MODEL

*T*he theory of portfolio selection developed in the previous chapter together with asset pricing theory described in this and the next two chapters provides the foundations for portfolio management. The goal of portfolio selection is to construct portfolios that maximize expected returns consistent with individually acceptable levels of risk. Portfolio selection theory, popularly referred to as mean-variance portfolio theory, prescribes a standard or norm of behavior that investors should pursue in constructing a portfolio. The theory does not necessarily intend to describe actual investor behavior. In contrast, asset pricing theory goes on to formalize the relationship that should exist between asset returns and risk if investors behave in a hypothesized manner. Thus, asset pricing theory is a positive theory. Based on this hypothesized investor behavior, asset pricing theory derives a model (called the *asset pricing model*) that specifies expected return, a key input in constructing portfolios based on mean-variance portfolio analysis.

In this chapter and the two that follow, major theories about a security's expected return based on asset pricing models are described. It is important to understand that portfolio selection theory is independent of any theories about asset pricing: The validity of prescriptive portfolio selection theory does not rest on the validity of descriptive asset pricing theory.

Together, portfolio selection theory and asset pricing theory provide a framework to specify and measure investment risk and to develop relationships between expected asset return and risk (and hence, between required return and risk on an investment). While we described a variety of risk measures in Chapter 12, the measures described in this chapter and the next two are currently in common use.

This chapter develops the well-known Capital Asset Pricing Model (CAPM), which states that the expected return on any asset is a linear function of its market risk relative to the market and the market risk premium. Credit for the development of the CAPM is generally assigned to a number of individuals, including William Sharpe (1964), John Lintner (1965), Jack Treynor (1962), and Jan Mossin (1966).[1]

---

[1] See Perold (2004) and Rubinstein (2006).

## 14.1 CAPM ASSUMPTIONS

The CAPM is an equilibrium asset pricing model derived from a set of assumptions. The assumptions simplify matters from a mathematical standpoint, even though some of them seem unrealistic. However, what matters are the insights from the theory and how they can be used in practice. For a better understanding of the derivation below, we begin by discussing the six underlying assumptions. These assumptions are:

*Assumption 1:* Investors make investment decisions based on the expected returns and variance of returns and subscribe to the Markowitz method of portfolio diversification.

*Assumption 2:* Investors are rational and risk averse.

*Assumption 3:* Investors all invest for the same period of time.

*Assumption 4:* Investors have the same expectations about the expected returns and return variance of all assets.

*Assumption 5:* There is a risk-free asset and investors can borrow and lend any amount at the risk-free rate.

*Assumption 6:* Capital markets are completely competitive and frictionless.

The first four assumptions deal with the way investors make decisions, and the last two relate to characteristics of the capital market. Assumption 1 tells us how an investor chooses an optimal portfolio. Specifically, the investor is assumed to make decisions based on mean-variance analysis as described in the previous chapter.

Assumption 2 indicates that, in order to accept greater portfolio risk, investors must be compensated by earning a higher rate of expected return. We refer to the behavior of such investors as being risk averse. The assumption means that if an investor faces a choice between two portfolios with the same expected return, the investor will select the portfolio with the lower risk. Certainly, this is a reasonable assumption.

By Assumption 3, all investors are assumed to make investment decisions over some single-period investment horizon. The theory does not specify how long that period is (i.e., one month, one year, two years, and so on). In reality, the investment decision process is more complex, with many investors having more than one investment horizon. Nonetheless, the assumption of a one-period investment horizon is necessary to simplify the mathematics of the theory.

To obtain the efficient frontier (i.e., the set of efficient portfolios as explained in the previous chapter), which we will use in developing the CAPM, it will be necessary to assume that investors have the same expectations with respect to the inputs that are used to derive the efficient portfolios: asset returns, variances, and covariances. This is Assumption 4 and is referred to as the *homogeneous expectations assumption*.

The risk-free rate in Assumption 5 serves as a benchmark return for the opportunity cost of the investor's money when investing in risky assets. Unlimited borrowing and lending at the risk-free rate is a common assumption in many economic models developed in finance despite the fact there is a difference in the rates at which investors can borrow and lend funds in practice. This assumption simplifies the derivation and is the same assumption made in the previous chapter.

Finally, Assumption 6 specifies that the capital market is perfectly competitive. This means that the number of buyers and sellers is large enough, and all investors are small enough relative to the market, that no individual investor can influence an asset's price. Consequently, all investors are price takers, and the market price is determined where there is equality of supply and demand. In addition, according to this assumption, there are no transactions costs or impediments that interfere with the supply of and demand for an asset. Economists refer to these various costs and impediments as *frictions*. The costs associated with frictions generally result in buyers paying more than in the absence of frictions and/or sellers receiving less.

In formulating models that seek to extend the CAPM, one or more of the above assumptions is relaxed. Some of such extensions will be discussed in this chapter. But no matter how the extensions are done, the basic implications of the model are unchanged: Investors are only rewarded for taking on certain types of risks. As we will see, the risks for which investors are compensated are systematic risks. This result applies both to the CAPM and its extensions discussed in this chapter, as well as to the arbitrage pricing theory to be discussed in Chapter 15.

## 14.2  DERIVING THE CAPITAL MARKET

The building blocks of the CAPM are the capital market line and the security market line. In this section, we focus on the derivation of the capital market line.

Under the homogeneous expectations assumption (Assumption 4), and the risk-free asset assumption (Assumption 5), the efficient frontier of investment portfolios is identical for every investor. The frontier is given by the line through $(0, r_f)$ and $[\sigma(r_m), E(r_m)]$ of Figure 14.1, where $m$ is the unique frontier portfolio tangent to the line starting from $(0, r_f)$. This is because each investor views the frontier of available risky portfolios as being in exactly the same place on the graph, and hence, all investors will purchase some combination of the risk-free asset and the portfolio $m$ of risky assets. However, the proportions of the risk-free asset and of portfolio $m$ chosen by a particular investor depend on that investor's attitudes toward risk. Consequently, the particular risk-return combination chosen by a given investor may differ from that

**FIGURE 14.1**
THE CAPITAL MARKET LINE

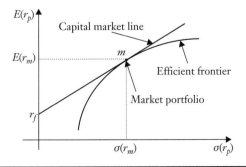

chosen by another. But all investors choose a mixture of the risk-free asset and the market portfolio (*m*). The chosen portfolios are on the straight line and to the right of *m* are borrowing at the riskless rate, investing both their initial capital and borrowed funds in the tangent portfolio.

The tangent portfolio of risky assets is widely known as the *market portfolio*. Suppose again that there are *N* risky assets in the market. The market portfolio weight for the *i*-th asset is defined as:

$$w_{mi} = \frac{\text{Asset } i\text{'s Market Value}}{\text{Total Market Value}} \tag{14.1}$$

that is, the amount invested in the *i*-th asset is value-weighted. For example, if Microsoft has 2% of the total market value, we will allocate 2% of the amount invested in Microsoft if we wish to hold the market portfolio.

Why does the tangent portfolio turn out to be the simple value-weighted market portfolio? Assume that there are only two corporations, Motor and Food, and that both companies have issued stock and no other securities. So, in this highly simplified capital market, the only investable assets are the stocks of the two companies. Assume the total numbers of shares issued by Motor and Food are $100 and $150, respectively, and that the market price per share of Motor is $5 and for Food it is $2. The market value of Motor is then $500 and Food is $300, so that the total market value is $800.

Suppose further that there are only two investors. Let $I_a$ and $I_b$ be their total dollar investments in the two stocks. Since they hold the same proportions of risky assets, we can assume $w$ is the percentage of the total portfolio invested in Motor, and $1 - w$ is the percentage invested in Food. Then, we must have the market clearing conditions:

$$I_a w + I_b w = \$500$$

and

$$I_a(1 - w) + I_b(1 - w) = \$300$$

which says that the total investments of the two investors in the each stock must be equal to total values of the stocks. In addition, their total invested in the stocks must also be equal to the market value, $I_a + I_b = \$800$. Solving the above two equations, we have $w = \$500/\$800$, which is the market portfolio weight on Motor. Similar accounting formulas hold for an arbitrary number of stocks and for an arbitrary number of investors. Thus, as long as investors have the same proportions of risky assets, their common portfolio weights for the risky assets must be the value-weighted market portfolio weights.

Theoretically, the combined actions of all investors imply that both *m* and the risk-free asset will be priced by investors' aggregated demands for risky assets. This implication follows from the theory's prediction that investors' choices always involve purchasing a combination of *m* and the risk-free asset. Hence, the total demand of all investors for the risky portfolio *m* determines the total demand for each asset held in that portfolio. Similarly, the total demand for the risk-free asset is the sum of individuals' demands for it. These choices establish a particular price for every asset, because each investor holds the same proportions of risky assets in the portfolio of risky assets. At this so-called equilibrium price, the market clears in the sense that the optimal holdings by investors are exactly equal to the supply of assets outstanding.

The line representing all the portfolio combinations that can be selected is called the *capital market line* (CML). It describes the equilibrium optimal portfolio choice by investors. The slope of this line is called the *market price per unit of risk*; by reference to Figure 14.1, this price is seen to be:

$$\text{Slope} = \frac{E(r_m) - r_f}{\sigma(r_m)} \qquad (14.2)$$

where $E(r_m)$ = the expected return for the market portfolio

$\qquad r_f$ = the risk-free rate of return

$\qquad \sigma(r_m)$ = standard deviation of the market return

Using the CML, the relationship between risk and return of the portfolio chosen by any investor can be written as:

$$E(r_p) = r_f + \left[ \frac{E(r_m) - r_f}{\sigma(r_m)} \right] \sigma(r_p) \qquad (14.3)$$

where $E(r_p)$ = the expected portfolio return of the individual investor

$\qquad \sigma(r_p)$ = standard deviation of the individual investor's portfolio return

The risk-return relationship given by equation (14.3) can easily be verified since the equation of the line is $E(r_p) = a + b\sigma(r_p)$, where $b$ is the slope and $a$ is the intercept. Because the line passes through $(0, r_f)$ we must have $a = r_f$. Note the following:

- If $p$ is a portfolio consisting of only the risk-free asset, then $E(r_p) = r_f$ with zero risk.
- If $p$ is the market portfolio, then $E(r_p) = E(R_m)$ with risk $\sigma(r_p)$.

The implication of the CML is that, the higher the (optimally chosen) portfolio risk, the higher the expected portfolio return.[2] Moreover, the risk of any individual's (optimally chosen) portfolio per unit of risk, as given by $(Er_p - r_f)/\sigma(r_p)$, must be equal to the market price per unit of risk. The per unit price measure is also known as the portfolio's *Sharpe ratio*, named in recognition of William Sharpe's pioneering work in portfolio theory. The CML states that the Sharpe ratio of any optimal portfolio chosen by an investor is the same as that of the market portfolio. (It cannot be higher than the Sharpe ratio of the market portfolio since the latter is the best available portfolio.) One can obtain the market portfolio's Sharpe ratio by choosing

---

[2] However, the foregoing is not generally true at the asset level.

portfolios along the CML, and an investor will not choose anything worse than it because he is assumed to maximize return for a given level of risk.

Consider now the portfolio weight of an investor when he balances risk and return by choosing the proportions of $m$ and the risk-free asset that he wishes to hold. The expected return and risk of each investor's portfolio are given by:

$$Er_p = (1 - w)r_f + wE(r_m) = r_f + wE(r_m - r_f) \qquad (14.4)$$

and variance:

$$\sigma^2(r_p) = var[(1 - w)r_f + wr_m] = w^2\sigma^2(r_m) \qquad (14.5)$$

where $w$ is the proportion of portfolio wealth the investor allocates to the market portfolio and $1 - w$ is the percentage allocated to the risk-free asset held. To solve $w$, we have to know the investor's objective function. In the previous chapter, we introduced the quadratic utility function which we reproduce below:

$$U(w) = E[r_p] - \frac{\gamma}{2} var[R_p] = r_f + w[E(r_m) - r_f] - \frac{\gamma}{2}\sigma^2(r_m)w^2 \qquad (14.6)$$

where $\gamma$, called the risk aversion coefficient, is used to reflect risk aversion. The larger the $\gamma$ is, the more risk averse the investor.[3]

In our illustration, we will use the quadratic utility function. Taking its derivative with respect to $w$ and setting it to zero, we obtain:

$$w^* = \frac{1}{\gamma} \frac{E(r_m) - r_f}{\sigma^2(r_m)} \qquad (14.7)$$

where $w^*$ is the optimal percentage allocation to the market portfolio.

In words, equation (14.7) says that:

1. The higher the expected market return in excess of the risk-free rate or the lower the market risk, the more the investor will invest in $m$.
2. The higher the risk aversion or the higher the market risk, the less the investor will invest in $m$.

For example, assume the following values for the inputs in equation (14.7):

$$\gamma = 3$$
$$E(r_m) - r_f = 8\%$$
$$\sigma(r_m) = 20\%$$

---

[3] Recall from Chapter 13 that $\gamma$ is not the same as either the Arrow-Pratt measure of absolute risk aversion or the Arrow-Pratt measure of relative risk aversion. Those measures are defined in equations (11.8) and (11.9).

As noted in the previous chapter, we assume that a reasonable value for $\gamma$ is 3. Substituting these values into equation (14.7), we find that this investor will invest $w = 0.08/(3 \times 0.2^2) = 67\%$ of his wealth in the market portfolio.

Let's see what happens for different values of the risk-aversion coefficient. If an investor is more conservative with a risk-aversion coefficient of $\gamma = 6$, he will allocate only 33% of his wealth to the market portfolio, while allocating the balance to the risk-free asset. If, instead, an investor is more aggressive with a risk aversion coefficient of $\gamma = 1$, he will invest 200% of his wealth into the market portfolio, financed with a borrowing of half of the money at the risk-free rate. This is a case where an investor's choice lies on the right-hand side of $m$ along the CML in Figure 14.1.

One of the implications of the CML is that in a perfect market with homogeneous expectations, each investor can, and will, select the market portfolio when choosing the combination of risky assets to enter his portfolio. This is clearly unrealistic because it relies on, among others, Assumption 6 that markets are frictionless so that there are no transactions costs. Then anyone can buy any proportion of an asset in the market, provided the going price for the asset is paid. In addition, there are no costs to supervising investment portfolios since everyone has the same information about asset prices. Thus, the functions of operating a mutual fund, bank, or other financial institution can be performed individually as well as by firms. In such a world, individuals can diversify, as well as lever (borrow using debt), on their own just as efficiently as can financial institutions. For these reasons, one should always keep in mind that the CML only predicts what would happen under idealized conditions.

## 14.3 DERIVING THE CAPM

In this section, we use the ideas underlying the CML to derive an equilibrium risk-return relationship for an individual asset. Assets issued by firms are typically referred to as securities and the equilibrium risk-return relationship for individual securities can tell us how securities are valued. To this end, we wish to examine first how the inclusion of security $j$ affects the risk of the market portfolio.

Consider how the slope of the mean-standard deviation frontier for a portfolio composed of a preselected security $j$ and the market portfolio changes as the proportion invested in $j$ changes. Figure 14.2 shows the equilibrium CML, the efficient frontier of risky securities, as well as the mean and standard combinations for the portfolio including extra proportions of security $j$ with the market portfolio $m$.

Let $w_j$ be the proportion of security $j$ in a portfolio consisting of that security and the market portfolio $m$. When $w = 0$, we have the market portfolio alone (point $m$, which contains the equilibrium amount of security $j$), while when $w = 1$, we have a portfolio containing only security $j$, as shown by point $A$ in the Figure 14.2. When $w$ is positive but less than 1, the portfolio is the same as the market portfolio, except for the fact that a larger amount of security $j$ is included. This is represented by a point like $B$. Point $A'$ indicates a case where $w < 0$ and can be interpreted as a portfolio similar to the market portfolio, except that some of the original proportion of security $j$ has been removed. The frontier $AA'$ is inside the original frontier because any combination of security $j$ with the portfolio $m$ is a special combination of the original assets, and hence, it cannot do better than the earlier case. By the same token, adding

**FIGURE 14.2**
FRONTIER FROM COMBINING THE MARKET WITH ANOTHER ASSET

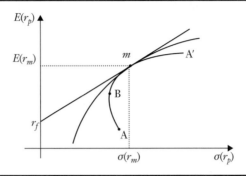

in the risk-free asset cannot do better than the earlier CML. On the other hand, when portfolio $m$ is on the $AA'$ frontier, a combination of this frontier with the risk-free rate can achieve the earlier maximum, so the optimal combination of $AA'$ frontier with the risk-free asset cannot be any worse. Therefore, the $AA'$ frontier must be tangent with the CML at $m$ too.

The expected return and standard deviation of the above hypothetical portfolio are:

$$E(r_p) = wE(r_j) + (1 - w)E(r_m) \qquad (14.8)$$

and

$$\sigma(r_p) = [w^2\sigma(r_j) + 2w(1 - w)cov(r_j, r_m) + (1 - w)^2\sigma(r_m)]^{1/2} \qquad (14.9)$$

where $\sigma(r_j)$ = standard deviation of security $j$
$cov(r_j, r_m)$ = covariance between return on security $j$ and the market portfolio

Now we wish to find:

$$\frac{\partial E(r_p)/\partial w}{\partial \sigma(r_p)/\partial w} = \frac{\partial E}{\partial \sigma} \qquad (14.10)$$

which measures the trade-off between risk and return as we move along line $AA'$ in Figure 14.2. This is one of the fundamental insights of Sharpe (1964). The trade-off links the expected return of individual assets to that of the market.

Taking the derivative with respect to $w$, we obtain

$$\frac{\partial E(r_p)}{\partial w} = Er_j - Er_m$$

and

$$\frac{\partial \sigma(r_p)}{\partial w} = \frac{2w\sigma^2(r_j) + 2(1 - w)\ cov(r_j, r_m) - 2w\ cov(r_j, r_m) - 2(1 - w)\sigma^2(r_m)}{2\sigma(r_p)}$$

In particular, at $w = 0$, we get:

$$\frac{\partial \sigma(r_p)}{\partial w}\Big|_{w=0} = \frac{cov(r_j, \ r_m) - \sigma^2(r_m)}{\sigma(r_m)}$$

This implies that the slope of $AA'$ at $m$ (when $w = 0$) is:

$$\frac{\partial E}{\partial \sigma} = \frac{\sigma(r_m)[E(r_j) - E(r_m)]}{cov(r_j, \ r_m) - \sigma^2(r_m)}$$

Now we equate this slope with the slope of the CML at $m$, and obtain:

$$\frac{E(r_m) - r_f}{\sigma(r_m)} = \frac{\sigma(r_m)[E(r_j) - E(r_m)]}{cov(r_j, \ r_m) - \sigma^2(r_m)}$$

This equation can be rewritten as:

$$E(r_j) = r_f + \beta_j[E(r_m) - r_f] \tag{14.11}$$

where

$$\beta_j = \frac{cov(r_j, \ r_m)}{\sigma^2(r_m)} = \frac{corr(r_j, \ r_m)\sigma(r_j)}{\sigma(r_m)} \tag{14.12}$$

measures the covariation of the $j$-th security with the market.

Let's look at the components of equation (14.11). First, it is common in finance to refer to $\beta_j$ as the security's *beta* and to the measure's value as the security's *beta risk*. It is a relative measure since it measures risk in relation to the risk of the market portfolio. Notice, moreover, that if $\beta_j > 0$, security $j$ moves with the market portfolio, while if $\beta_j < 0$, it moves in the opposite direction. Second, the term $E(r_m) - r_f$ is known as the *market risk premium*. It is the return in excess of the risk-free return, and represents the premium required for taking on market risk.

Equation (14.11) holds for all securities in the market. It says the expected return on security $j$ must be the sum of the risk-free rate and a premium for risk that is the product of the market risk premium and the beta risk of security $j$. A plot of this relation across securities is known as the *security market line* (SML), shown in Figure 14.3. In equilibrium, the expected returns on all securities must lie along the SML together with their beta risks associated with the market. Note that the SML should not be confused with the CML. While the SML is about expected returns on individual securities relative to their beta risks, the CML is about returns on optimal portfolios of investors relative to the portfolio total risks.

One of the fundamental questions in finance is to explain why some firms have higher returns than others. How much return should an investor expect to get out of an individual security? Based on equation (14.11), all investors evaluate the security by how much it contributes to the risk of the market portfolio. This is the key point. Intuitively, if it increases the market risk, the expected return should be higher to

## FIGURE 14.3
### SECURITY MARKET LINE

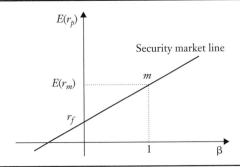

compensate for the extra risk. Equation (14.11) explains that the differences in a cross section of returns for securities such as stocks are due to their differences in beta risk. Equation (14.11) is also known as the Capital Asset Pricing Model (CAPM).

For example, to explain returns on the two stocks we used in our earlier illustration, Motor and Food, assume their respective beta risks are 1.5 and 0.14. Suppose the risk-free rate is 3% and the expected market return is 12%. Then, the market risk premium is 8% (= 11% − 3%). Based on the CAPM, the expected returns on the two stocks will be:

$$\text{For Motor}: \quad 15\% = 3\% + 1.5 \times 8\%$$

and

$$\text{For Food}: \quad 9.4\% = 3\% + 0.8 \times 8\%$$

This says that, in comparison with Food, Motor should have a expected return of 15% due to its higher beta risk.

In the real world, the application of the CAPM is a more challenging task than simply plugging numbers into the equation. All the parameters must be estimated. We'll discuss how the beta risk is estimated, but there could also be considerable difference of opinion as to what the market risk premium is. Moreover, the parameters are not constant over time due to changes in macroeconomic conditions and changes at the firm level that alter a firm's beta risk.

## 14.4  CAPM IN THE ABSENCE OF A RISK-FREE ASSET

In the absence of a risk-free asset, say when the lending rate is lower than the borrowing rate, Black (1972) shows that the CAPM can be modified to:

$$E(r_j) = E(r_z) + \beta_j[E(r_m) - r_z] \tag{14.13}$$

where $r_z$ is the return on a portfolio that is uncorrelated with $r_m$, or has zero beta. For this reason, equation (14.13) is widely known as the *zero-beta CAPM*.

If there is a risk-free asset, $r_z$ can be replaced by it in the above equation, resulting in the standard CAPM given by equation (14.11). Without $r_f$, it can be shown that, adapting our proof earlier for the CAPM, there is a unique $r_z$ on the mean-variance frontier, which has zero beta with respect to $r_m$. Hence, the zero-beta CAPM is an extension of the standard CAPM. However, it is not as widely used as the CAPM partly because of the determination of $r_z$ is not so obvious to practitioners. On the other hand, practitioners often view the returns on U.S. Treasury bills as risk-free and use their yields to approximate $r_f$, and hence, the standard CAPM is much more popular than the zero-beta CAPM.

## 14.5 IMPLICATIONS OF THE CAPM

To understand the CAPM, we can always regress the excess return on security $j$ onto the market excess return:

$$r_j - r_f = \alpha_j + \beta_j(r_m - r_f) + \varepsilon_j \tag{14.14}$$

where $\varepsilon_j$ is the residual that is uncorrelated with the market return. The regression decomposes the random return on $r_j$ into a constant term ($\alpha_j$) plus two components: one that is correlated with the market ($\beta_j$) and one that is not ($\varepsilon_j$).

Taking expectations on both sides of equation (14.14) and rearranging the terms, we have:

$$E(r_j) - r_f = \alpha_j + \beta_j[E(r_m) - r_f] \tag{14.15}$$

which is always true regardless of any financial theory. The constant term $\alpha_j$ is the unexplained expected return by the market, and can potentially be any value. The CAPM says that when investors have homogeneous expectations and when certain additional assumptions (those listed in Section 14.1) hold, in equilibrium the value of $\alpha_j$ must be zero for each security $j$.

### 14.5.1 Decomposition of Total Risk

The total risk of a security or a portfolio is measured by its variance. Based on the regression given by equation (14.14), we can, taking variance on both sides, write:

$$\sigma^2(r_j) = \beta_j^2 \sigma^2(r_m) + \sigma^2(\varepsilon_j) \tag{14.16}$$

where

$\beta_j^2 \sigma^2(r_m)$ measures the total market risk exposure of security $j$, referred to as *systematic risk*, and

$\sigma^2(\varepsilon_j)$ is the remaining risk, referred to as *unsystematic risk*.

FIGURE 14.4
DIMINISHING UNSYSTEMATIC RISK

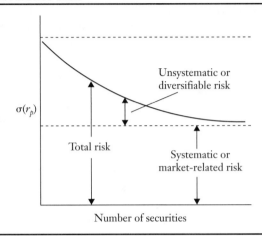

Hence, in words, the risk decomposition can be read:

$$\text{Total Risk} = \text{Systematic Risk} + \text{Unsystematic Risk} \qquad (14.17)$$

Many studies, such as Wagner and Lau (1971), have shown that unsystematic risk can be eliminated via diversification. Theoretically, this is true under the CAPM conditions. However, in the real world, certain unsystematic risks may not be eliminated due to asset mispricing.[4] Nevertheless, typically, for individual stocks in reality, the average ratio of systematic risk to total risk is about 30%. But, on the average, 40% of the single-security risk can be eliminated by forming randomly selected portfolios of about 20 stocks. Additional diversification yields rapidly diminishing reduction in risk. The return on a diversified portfolio usually follows the market closely with the ratio of systematic risk to total risk exceeding 90%. The diversification process works as in Figure 14.4. Unsystematic risk is also referred to as *company-specific risk*, *company-unique risk*, or *idiosyncratic risk*.

In contrast to unsystematic risk, systematic risk cannot be eliminated. The message of the CAPM is that only this part of total risk is rewarded. Investors hold the market portfolio, which finances the economy, for a risk premium reward, and the reward to an individual security only comes from its contribution to the market portfolio. In reality and in theory, one can take all kinds of risks. Not necessarily all will be rewarded.

## 14.5.2 Pricing Portfolios by CAPM

It should be noted that the CAPM relation is trivially valid for the risk-free asset and the market portfolio, which have 0 and 1 beta risks, respectively. Hence, the CAPM

---

[4] A complete elimination of the unsystematic risks implies zero prices for those risks. But they can be mispriced in practice. As argued by Shleifer and Vishny (1997), there are limits to arbitrage because arbitrageurs have limited capital and incur risk. We discuss the limits to arbitrage in Chapter 21.

holds true not only for each individual securiy, but also for the risk-free asset and the market portfolio. In addition, it is also true for an arbitrary portfolio of the securities. To see this, let $w_1, w_2, \ldots, w_n$ be portfolio weights that sum to 1. Multiplying each $w_i$ to each asset excess return and summing over all the products, we get:

$$E[r_q] = \sum_{i=1}^{n} w_i E[r_i] = r_f + \left( \sum_{i=1}^{n} w_i \beta_i \right) [E(r_m) - r_f] \tag{14.18}$$

which is the CAPM relation. In particular, the beta for a portfolio of assets is equal to the portfolio of the asset betas. That is, the portfolio beta risk is *linear* in its component betas. In contrast, the total risk (or variance risk) of a portfolio does not have this property, which is almost always not equal to the portfolio of the total risks.

## 14.6 AN ALTERNATIVE DERIVATION

Consider now another proof of the CAPM based on the quadratic utility assumption as earlier in equation (14.6). It is worthwhile to provide an alternative, since it gives additional insights into the CAPM and on how one can be better off by realizing higher utility if the CAPM is violated.

Recall that when allocating funds between the risk-free asset and the market portfolio, the optimal holding (i.e., weights) in the market portfolio is $w^*$ as given by equation (14.6). Plugging this into the utility function, we obtain the optimized utility (happiness of the investor):

$$u(w^*) = r_f + \frac{1}{2\gamma} \frac{(E(r_m) - r_f)^2}{\sigma^2(r_m)} \tag{14.19}$$

Recall that the Sharpe ratio or market price of risk is the difference between the expected market return and the risk-free rate divided by the variance of the market. Now look at the second term in equation (14.19). That term is the squared Sharpe ratio divided by $2\gamma$. As we discussed in Chapter 13, the utility level— the right-hand side of the above equation— is the certainty-equivalent return.

Now, if $\alpha_j$ in equation (14.12) is not zero for some asset $j$, consider portfolio $q$ consisting of the risk-free asset, the market portfolio, and this asset $j$. The return for portfolio $q$ would be:

$$r_q = (1 - w_1 - w_2)r_f + w_1 r_m + w_2 r_j \tag{14.20}$$

where $w_1$ is the portfolio weight on the market, $w_2$ on $r_j$ and the remaining proportion of the investor's wealth on the risk-free asset. We want to show that for some choice of the portfolio weights, the investor can attain higher utility than $u(w^*)$ due to $\alpha_j \neq 0$. But this is not possible since $u(w^*)$ is already the maximum. The contradiction proves that it must be the case that $\alpha_j = 0$.

To see the proof, we first write:

$$r_q = r_f + w_1(r_m - r_f) + w_2(r_j - r_f)$$
$$= r_f + x_1(r_m - r_f) + x_2(\alpha_j + \varepsilon_j)$$

where $x_2 = w_2$ and $x_1 = w_1 + w_2\beta_j$. Hence, we only need to find $x_1$ and $x_2$ to maximize the utility. The representation in terms of the $x$'s makes the variance of $r_q$ have a simple expression:

$$\sigma^2(r_q) = x_1^2 \sigma^2(r_m) + x_2^2 \sigma_2(\varepsilon_j)$$

where, as we recall, $\sigma^2(\varepsilon_j)$ is the variance of $\varepsilon_j$. Then the utility is:

$$u(x_1, x_2) = r_f + x_1\left[E(r_m) - r_f\right] + x_2\alpha_j - \frac{\gamma}{2}\left[x_1^2\sigma^2(r_m) + x_2^2\sigma^2(\varepsilon_j)\right] \qquad (14.21)$$

Taking derivatives with respect to $x_1$ and $x_2$, the first-order conditions yield:

$$x_1^* = \frac{1}{\gamma}\frac{E(r_m) - r_f}{\sigma^2(r_m)} \qquad (14.22)$$

the same holding of the market portfolio as before, and:

$$x_2^* = \frac{1}{\gamma}\frac{\alpha_j}{\sigma^2(\varepsilon_j)} \qquad (14.23)$$

Hence, if $\alpha_j \neq 0$, the investor will add his position on asset $j$ if $\alpha_j > 0$ and reduce or short it if $\alpha_j < 0$. The maximized utility is:

$$u(x_1^*, x_2^*) = r_f + \frac{1}{2\gamma}\frac{(E(r_m) - r_f)^2}{\sigma^2(r_m)} + \frac{1}{2\gamma}\frac{\alpha_j}{\sigma^2(\varepsilon_j)} \qquad (14.24)$$

where the first two terms are the same as before, and the third term is the additional certainty-equivalent return to the investor. When $\alpha_j \neq 0$, this utility level will be higher than the optimized utility, equation (14.19). This is inconsistent with the earlier assumption that the utility is maximized. Hence, $\alpha_j$ must be zero.

In practice, if an investor can predict the alphas, the investor can make excess returns. For a fund manager to beat a benchmark index, the same alphas can contribute to the so-called value-added portfolio. A general form of the above utility analysis is known as the *Fundamental Law of Active Portfolio Management*, articulated first by Grinold (1989).[5]

While the derivation in this section assumes a quadratic utility, the CAPM can also be derived for an arbitrary utility as long as the returns are identical and

---

[5] Zhou (2008a, 2008b) and references therein provide some of the recent developments.

independently distributed and the distribution is the normal distribution. The proof of the CAPM, due to Rubinstein (1973), is both insightful and elegant. It is provided in Appendix 14.1.

## 14.7 ESTIMATING BETA RISK

The beta of a security can be estimated in practice by computing the covariance and standard deviation in the formula for beta or, numerical equivalently, by running a regression of the stock returns in excess of the risk-free rate on the market returns in excess of the risk-free rate. We explain and illustrate how this is done below.

Consider estimating the beta of the International Business Machines (IBM). An investor can collect 120 monthly returns for IBM stock, and then run the following regression of the IBM excess returns on the market:

$$r_{IBMt} - r_{ft} = \alpha + \beta(r_{mt} - r_{ft}) + \varepsilon_{IBMt} \qquad (14.25)$$

where the subscript $t$ denotes the month ($t = 1, 2, \ldots, 120$). That is, an investor would run a time-series regression of 120 excess IBM returns on the 120 market excess returns (with a constant in the regression). With data from January 1997 to December 2006, standard regression software or Excel can produce the results reported in the first two rows of Table 14.1. The regression coefficients $\alpha$ and $\beta$ are 0.0069 and 1.2828. A beta value greater than 1 indicates that IBM is riskier than the market. The standard error of the beta is 0.1450 (shown in the parentheses in the table), indicating that the true beta is reliably nonzero. The alpha value is 0.69% per month, but estimated with a relatively large standard error of 0.0067. The regression's coefficient of determination, denoted by $R^2$, is 39.87%. For an individual stock, a $R^2$ of this magnitude indicates that the regression provides a reasonably good fit.

In the interest of comparison, we also estimate the betas of Bank of America (BAC) and Merck (MRK). While IBM is in a high technology industry, these two companies are in the banking and pharmaceutical industries, respectively. The results are reported in Table 14.1. Interestingly, BAC has about half the beta of IBM, and yet MRK has in turn about half of the beta of BAC. BAC is more diversified than IBM and so it is less riskier. For MRK, whether the economy is up or down, people will

**TABLE 14.1**
**BETA ESTIMATES**

| Company | $\alpha$ | $\beta$ | $R^2$ |
|---------|----------|---------|-------|
| IBM | 0.0069 | 1.2828 | 0.3987 |
|  | (0.0067) | (0.1450) |  |
| BAC | 0.0078 | 0.7473 | 0.2079 |
|  | (0.0062) | (0.1343) |  |
| MRK | 0.0035 | 0.3375 | 0.0325 |
|  | (0.0078) | (0.1694) |  |

*Note:* The values shown in the parentheses are the standard errors of the coefficient estimates.

consume pharmaceuticals regardless, and hence, MRK has little exposure to the macroecomic risk, which is captured by the market portfolio.[6]

## 14.8 APPLICATION OF CAPM IN INVESTMENT MANAGEMENT

There are two major uses of the CAPM. The first is for investors and/or fund managers for making investment decisions and evaluating fund performance. The second is for a firm's financial managers to make capital budgeting decisions and to conduct project valuation analysis. We will postpone a discussion of this second application until we cover capital budgeting decisions in Part VII of this book.

For the use of the CAPM in investment decisions, we focus on how the CAPM can be used to improve the estimate for the future expected return of a stock. For example, consider the problem of estimating the expected return on IBM, $E[r_{IBM}]$. An investor can do the same as before as estimating the beta by collecting 120 monthly returns for IBM stock, and then run the regression of the IBM excess returns on the market:

$$r_{IBMt} - r_{ft} = \alpha + \beta(r_{mt} - r_{ft}) + \varepsilon_{IBMt}$$

The regression is commonly referred to as the *market model* or the *single-index market model*. The market model is easily estimated by using any linear regression software, which yields the regression coefficients estimates, 0.0069 and 1.2828, as reported earlier in Table 14.1. Since now the investor has more information on both IBM and the market, the investor can in general obtain a more accurate estimate of $E[r_{IBM}]$. In particular, if the CAPM is true, the investor's expected excess return estimate is:

$$E(r_{IBMt} - r_{ft}) = 1.2828 \times E(r_{mt} - r_{ft}) \tag{14.26}$$

which should be more accurate than the sample average in terms of the standard error.

More importantly, if an investor has a view about future expected return on the market or about future variation of IBM's beta, the CAPM can help us to estimate IBM's future expected returns. The same is true for any other asset once we know its beta. Such insights are unavailable by studying IBM in isolation or by using its historical data alone.

The market model, motivated by the CAPM, is useful for estimating not only an asset's expected returns, but also its covariances with all other assets. This is because the residuals are often assumed uncorrelated across assets. Then the covariance between two assets is given by:

$$cov(r_i - r_{ft}, r_j - r_{ft}) = \beta_i \beta_j var(r_{mt} - r_{ft}) \tag{14.27}$$

---

[6] If we include the data up to December 2008 to cover the recent financial crisis, the three beta estimates are little changed: 1.2081, 0.8445, and 0.4497.

and the variance is:

$$var(r_i - r_{ft}) = \beta_i^2 var(r_{mt} - r_{ft}) + var(\varepsilon_{it}) \tag{14.28}$$

In contrast with the sample covariance matrix, which requires the estimation of $N(N+1)/2$ parameters, the market model requires only $2N$ estimates, the $N$ betas and $N$ residual variances. It is a huge reduction in the number of parameters to be estimated, and is feasible for any $N$, making it possible to apply the mean-variance portfolio theory to a large number of assets. Although the market model does not perform well in practice, it can be improved with the inclusion of additional risk factors as discussed in the next section. The next chapter will address the estimation problem in a multifactor asset pricing model.

## 14.9  TESTS OF THE CAPM

As with any other economic theory, it is necessary to test the theory empirically. In this section, we discuss the various tests of the CAPM, first explaining the testing methodology and then providing a simple illustration. Finally, we discuss the major empirical results and their implications.

### 14.9.1  Methodology

There are two main approaches for testing the validity of the CAPM: time-series and cross-sectional approaches, respectively.

#### 14.9.1.1  Time-Series Approach

The time-series approach empirically examines the alphas from a time-series regression of asset excess returns on those of the market excess returns, that is, the regression:

$$r_{it} - r_{ft} = \alpha_i + \beta_i(r_{mt} - r_{ft}) + \varepsilon_{it}, \quad t = 1, \ldots, T \tag{14.29}$$

where $T$ is the sample size for security $i$. If the CAPM is true, all the alphas in the regression model given by equation (14.29) should not be statistically significantly different from zero. That is, the null hypothesis for all assets is:

$$H_0: \quad \alpha_i = 0, \quad i = 1, \ldots, N \tag{14.30}$$

where $N$ is the total number of assets tested. This is a well-defined parametric hypothesis in regression analysis.

There are two ways to test this hypothesis. The first is a univariate method. Given an asset $i$, we compute (1) its excess returns, $r_{it} - r_{ft}$'s, over time, say from time period 1 to $T$ and (2) the excess returns on a market index, which is an approximation of the excess return on the market, the $(r_{mt} - r_{ft})$'s. Then, we apply the standard ordinary least square (OLS) regression approach to equation (14.29), which will provide the estimates of the alphas and betas for each asset. Then, a standard Student $t$ test may be used to assess whether the alpha is statistically significantly different from zero.

The univariate method just described ignores any correlations between the residuals across the assets, which is clearly unrealistic. To account for possible correlations, however, we make use of the information contained in the covariance matrix of the residuals across asset returns. Denote the estimated covariance matrix by $\hat{\Sigma} = (\hat{\sigma}_{ij})$, whose $(i,j)$ element is computed as the average of the cross products of the fitted residuals:

$$\hat{\sigma}_{ij} = \frac{1}{T} \sum_{t=1}^{T} \hat{\varepsilon}_{it} \hat{\varepsilon}_{jt}$$

Then, we can construct a test statistic based on $\hat{\Sigma}$ to test whether all the alphas are simultaneously zero or not. This is known as the multivariate method because all alphas and assets are considered jointly in the test. The resulting test is the known as the *Gibbons, Ross, and Shanken* (GRS) *test.*[7]

To compute the GRS test, let $\hat{\alpha}$ be an $N$-vector of the estimated alphas from the time-series regression, and $\hat{\theta}_m = \bar{r}_m/s_m$ be the sample Sharpe ratio of the market portfolio, where $\bar{r}_m$ and $s_m^2$ are the mean and variance of $r_m - r_f$:

$$\bar{r}_m = \frac{1}{T} \sum_{t=1}^{T} (r_{mt} - r_{ft}), \quad s_m^2 = \frac{1}{T} \sum_{t=1}^{T} (r_{mt} - r_{ft} - \bar{r}_m)^2$$

Then, assuming that the null hypothesis is true, the GRS test statistic follows an $F$ distribution:

$$\text{GRS} = \frac{T - N - 1}{N} \frac{\hat{\alpha}' \hat{\Sigma}^{-1} \hat{\alpha}}{1 + \hat{\theta}_m^2} \sim F_{N, T-N-1} \tag{14.31}$$

Where the tilde indicates the left-hand statistic is distributed as the $F$-distribution given in the right-hand side with degrees of freedom $N$ and $T - N - 1$. Given $\hat{\Sigma}$, the larger the GRS test statistic, the more the estimated alphas deviate from zero. Indeed, GRS show that this test statistic measures how far the market portfolio $m$ deviates from the mean-variance frontier. The $F$ distribution provides a $p$-value of the GRS test statistic that accounts for the sampling errors. When the $p$-value is less than 5%, we usually reject the null hypothesis that the alphas are zero, meaning we reject the CAPM.

### 14.9.1.2 Cross-Sectional Approach

The second approach for testing the CAPM is the more popular cross-sectional approach pioneered by Fama and MacBeth (1973). The *Fama-MacBeth approach* involves a two-step procedure, and is often applied to monthly data too.

In the first step, betas are estimated from individual monthly asset returns regressions on the market portfolio. Then, in the second step, a cross-sectional regression is used to estimate the market risk premiums. Instead of estimating a single

---

[7] See Gibbons, Ross, and Shanken (1989).

cross-section regression of average monthly returns on betas, the Fama-MacBeth approach involves estimating month-by-month cross-sectional regressions of monthly returns on betas. The times-series means of the monthly slopes and intercepts, along with the standard errors of the means, are then used to test whether the average market risk premium $[E(r_{mt}) - r_f]$ is positive and whether the intercepts are zero.

Formally, consider a time-series linear regression of asset excess returns on the market index excess return:

$$r_{it} - r_{ft} = \alpha_i + \beta_i(r_{mt} - r_{ft}) + \varepsilon_{it}, \quad i = 1, \ldots, N, \ t = 1, \ldots, T \qquad (14.32)$$

where $\varepsilon_{it}$ is the disturbances or random errors, $N$ is the number of assets, and $T$ is the number of time-series observations. In the first step of the two-pass procedure, estimates of the betas are obtained by applying OLS to equation (14.32) for each asset. Let $\hat{\beta} = (\hat{\beta}_1, \ldots, \hat{\beta}_N)$ be the resulting $N$-vector of OLS slope estimates for all the assets. In the second step, for each month a cross-sectional regression of $R_t = (r_{1t} - r_{ft}, \ldots, r_{Nt} - r_{ft})'$ on $\hat{X} = [1_N, \hat{\beta}]$:

$$r_{it} - r_{ft} = \gamma_0 + \beta_i\gamma_1 + \varepsilon_{it}, \quad i = 1, \ldots, N \qquad (14.33)$$

is estimated. If the CAPM is true, $\gamma_0 = 0$ and $\gamma_1$ should be the market risk premium $E(r_{mt}) - r_f$.

Using matrix notation, the estimated gammas ($\gamma$) from the regression model given by equation (14.33) in each month are:

$$\begin{pmatrix} \hat{\gamma}_{0t} \\ \hat{\gamma}_{1t} \end{pmatrix} = (\hat{X}'\hat{X})^{-1}\hat{X}'R_t$$

whose times-series averages given by:

$$\begin{pmatrix} \hat{\gamma}_0 \\ \hat{\gamma}_1 \end{pmatrix} = \frac{1}{T}\sum_{t=1}^{T}\begin{pmatrix} \hat{\gamma}_{0t} \\ \hat{\gamma}_{1t} \end{pmatrix} \qquad (14.34)$$

are usually taken as the final estimator.

In some studies, betas are estimated from a rolling window of past data. In this case, $X$ will be time-varying. The Student $t$-statistic traditionally used for assessing the significance of factor pricing when an OLS estimator is used is computed as:

$$\hat{t}_1 = \frac{\hat{\gamma}_1}{\hat{s}_1/\sqrt{T}} \qquad (14.35)$$

where $\hat{\gamma}_1$ and $\hat{s}_1$ are the sample mean and standard deviation of the time-series $\hat{\gamma}_{1t}$, $t = 1, \ldots, T$. However, the $t$-statistics suffers from an errors-in-variables problem since the estimation errors of the betas are ignored in its computation. Shanken (1992) corrects this problem, and Shanken and Zhou (2007) provide alternative estimators and tests for the Fama-MacBeth two-pass procedure.

**Table 14.2**
Testing the CAPM With Five Industry Portfolios

| Panel A: Regressions | $\alpha$ | $\beta$ | $R^2$ |
|---|---|---|---|
| Consumer | 0.0011 | 0.9290 | 0.8747 |
| | (0.0006) | (0.0112) | |
| | [1.77] | [82.79] | |
| Manufacturing | 0.0008 | 0.9857 | 0.9237 |
| | (0.0005) | (0.0090) | |
| | [1.54] | [109.01] | |
| High Tech | 0.0003 | 0.9473 | 0.8203 |
| | (0.0008) | (0.0141) | |
| | [0.34] | [66.95] | |
| Health Care | 0.0026 | 0.8545 | 0.6488 |
| | (0.0011) | (0.0201) | |
| | [2.33] | [42.59] | |
| Other | −0.0008 | 1.1161 | 0.8716 |
| | (0.0008) | (0.0137) | |
| | [−1.12] | [81.66] | |
| Panel B: GRS Multivariate Test | | | |
| | GRS | 4.6827 | (0.0003) |
| Panel C: Two-pass Market Risk Premium Estimate | | | |
| | $\gamma_1$ | −0.0061 | [−1.21] |

*Note:* The values shown in the parentheses are the standard errors of the coefficient estimates, and those in brackets are the *t*-statistics.

## 14.9.2   A Simple Application

For better understanding the test methodologies, we provide a simple example.

### 14.9.2.1   *Time-Series Tests: Univariate and GRS Tests*

Consider again the five industry portfolios—Consumer, Manufacturing, High Tech, Health Care, and Other—used in the previous chapter. Hence, there are $N = 5$ assets and as explained in the previous chapter there are $T = 984$ observations for each of the five series. The market index is taken as the value-weight of all NYSE, AMEX, and NASDAQ stocks.

We now compute the excess returns on consumer industry portfolio and those on the market index by subtracting the returns from the one-month Treasury bill rate, and then run a regression of the excess consumer industry portfolio returns on the market index excess returns. Any standard OLS regression software can produce the regression coefficients, $\alpha$ and $\beta$, 0.0011 and 0.9290, as provided in Table 14.2.[8] The standard errors of the estimates are underneath the respective estimated values. A value of 0.0006 is not too small, so that the *t*-statistic is only 1.77. We cannot reject the hypothesis that the alpha is zero at the usual 5% significance level. The standard

---

[8] The data are available for free downloading from http://mba.tuck.dartmouth.edu/pages/faculty/ken.french/data_library.html.

error of the beta is 0.0112, which is clearly small compared to the estimate. The $t$-statistic is a huge number of 82.79, suggesting strongly that the beta is nonzero, and important in explaining the Consumer industry portfolio returns.

Similarly regressions can be run for other four industries. In this way, we obtain all the results in Panel A of Table 14.2. Interestingly, based on the univariate regressions, only the alpha of the Health Care industry portfolio is statistically different from zero. Thus, it is only in the case of this industry that the null hypothesis of the CAPM is rejected. In contrast, the GRS test, which is a multivariate test, reaches a different conclusion. Specifically, a test of all the alphas being zero by using the GRS test yields a GRS statistic of 4.6827, with a $p$-value of 0.0003, far less than 5%. So, the null hypothesis of the CAPM being true is strongly rejected.

The CAPM is about the values of the alphas in the regressions. Although the alphas differ significantly from zero, the regressions fit the data well since the regression $R^2$, reported in the last column of Table 14.2 ranges from 65% to 92%. In other words, the market return does have strong power in explaining the industry return variations, although the alphas are not what the CAPM predicts them to be.

### 14.9.2.2 Cross-Sections Test: Fama-MacBeth Test

The Fama-MacBeth two-pass procedure calls for running the following second-pass regression in each month for the five excess industry portfolio returns on the betas:

$$\begin{pmatrix} r_{1t} - r_{ft} \\ \vdots \\ r_{5t} - r_{ft} \end{pmatrix} = \gamma_0 + \begin{pmatrix} 0.9290 \\ \vdots \\ 1.1161 \end{pmatrix} \gamma_1 + \begin{pmatrix} \varepsilon_{1t} \\ \vdots \\ \varepsilon_{5t} \end{pmatrix}$$

Note that the estimated betas for each industry portfolio are obtained from Table 14.2.

Here $N = 5$ acts as the sample size in the above regression. Then, the standard OLS estimate for $\gamma_1$ in each month is easily computed, whose average as computed based on equation (14.34), over all the months is the market risk premium estimate. The result is an unrealistic number of $-0.0016$ with a $t$-statistic of $-1.21$, as reported in Table 14.2. In contrast, the time-series average of the market excess return data, $(r_{mt} - r_{ft})$'s, provides a market risk premium estimate of about a 7% annual return over the 82-year period. The contradiction between this and the two-pass estimate simply says that the market return does not cross-sectionally price the assets well.

## 14.9.3 Empirical Results Reported in the Literature

The poor performance of the CAPM from the earlier example is typical of empirical studies of the CAPM reported by researchers. It is perhaps easy to see such results graphically. The CAPM predicts that the security market line (SML) holds, that is, a plot of portfolios returns and beta risks should be along a straight line, with an intercept equal to the risk-free rate, $r_f$, and a slope equal to the expected excess return on the market, $E(r_m) - r_f$. As discussed in Section 14.5.2, this is also true for any portfolio. Figure 14.5 is, however, more striking to the contrary of the CAPM. When stocks sorted annually based on book-to-market equity ratios (B/M, the ratio of the book value of a common stock to its market value), the average returns and their betas

## FIGURE 14.5
### BOOK-MARKET PORTFOLIOS AND BETA

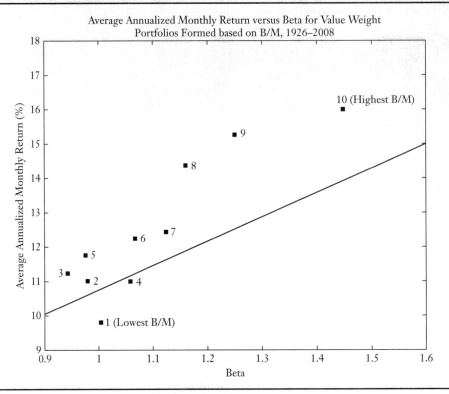

Average Annualized Monthly Return versus Beta for Value Weight Portfolios Formed based on B/M, 1926–2008

are not related closely at all. The highest B/M portfolio with medium beta achieves the highest average returns. Similar patterns can also be found when stocks are sorted based their size (market value). Fama and French (1992, 1993, 2004) discuss the implications of these results for the CAPM. The empirical problems associated with the CAPM are not only present in testing the CAPM for U.S. equities, but are also found in subsequent studies testing the CAPM for international equity markets.

All empirical tests of economic theories face various difficulties, both theoretical problems and statistical ones. In response to the failure of studies to support the CAPM, there have been several explanations as to why empirical tests of the CAPM are flawed. We discuss these critiques next.

### 14.9.3.1 Critiques of CAPM Empirical Tests

Despite the poor performance of the CAPM, Roll (1977) argues that this may not speak to the true CAPM, which has never been tested and probably never will be. One reason is that the market portfolio is neither theoretically precisely defined, nor empirically well approximated. Theoretically, the asset holdings of investors may include residential property and human capital, among others. Empirically, due to data availability, an equity index is often used, which is at most a proxy of the true and unobservable market portfolio. Even if the CAPM is true, errors in the proxy for the market portfolio can lead to problems. On the other hand, even if a proxy holds that prices all the assets with zero alpha, it still does not speak to whether or not the true market portfolio does so. Subsequent to the publication of this important critique by Roll, tests of the CAPM are now interpreted as tests of the efficiency of the given proxy.

### 14.9.3.2  *Multifactor Explanation*

A major explanation for the failure of the CAPM is provided by an alternative pricing theory: the *multifactor asset pricing theory*. For example, Merton (1973) provides an intertemporal capital asset pricing model (ICAPM), which is an extension of the traditonal CAPM, which has only one factor, the market, into multiple factors. Based on the ICAPM, one may interpret the tests described earlier as misspecified with missing factors, and they do not necessarily reject the multifactor ICAPM. In the ICAPM, investors are concerned not only with their end-of-period payoff, but also with the opportunities about how to consume or invest these payoff in the future. Hence, when choosing a portfolio today, they consider not only how their wealth might vary with future state variables tomorrow such as labor income, the prices of consumption goods, and future stock expected return, but also expectations about the labor income, consumption, and investment opportunities available after tomorrow. As a result, there are *extra-market sources of risk*, and the expected return on any asset should be related to all of them. Fama (1996) further elaborates on the "multifactor" nature of the risks.

Therefore, theoretically, we have the following extension of the CAPM:

$$Er_j = r_f + \beta_j[E(r_m) - r_f] + \sum_{s=1}^{S} \beta_{sj}[E(r_s) - r_f] \tag{14.36}$$

where $S$ = the total number of state variables in the economy

  $r_s$ = the return on state $s$ mimicking portfolio (i.e., the portfolio that has the maximum correlation with state);

  $\beta_{sj}$ = asset $j$'s beta related to $r_s$

In contrast to the standard CAPM as given by equation (14.11), the expected return on asset $j$ now has an extra risk premium, which is the sum of its risk premiums on its exposure to all the state risks. The states $S$ serve as $S$ additional factors, beyond the market, in determining the equilibrium asset's expected return.

Another example of a rational asset pricing theory is the Arbitrage Pricing Theory (APT) model as formulated by Ross (1976). Since the APT is the subject of the entire next chapter, so we only mention it briefly here. As with the ICAPM, the APT model assumes that there are multiple factors that determine an asset's expected returns. Assume that we can have a general $K$-factor model that determine stock returns:

$$r_{it} - r_{ft} = \alpha_i + \beta_{i1}f_{1t} + \cdots + \beta_{iK}f_{Kt} + \varepsilon_{it} \tag{14.37}$$

where $f_{jt}$ is the realization of the $j$-th factor in period $t$ and $\varepsilon_{it}$ = the disturbances or random errors. The $K$-factor are systematic since they affect all the stock returns. The $\varepsilon_{it}$ can be regarded as firm-specific factors or idiosyncratic risks. Then, under the assumption of no arbitrage and others discussed in detail in the next chapter, we have that:

$$E[r_i] = r_f + \gamma_1 \beta_{i1} + \cdots + \gamma_K \beta_{iK} \tag{14.38}$$

where $\gamma_1, \ldots, \gamma_K$ are factor risk premiums associated with the factors. For example, $\gamma_1$ is the expected return for a stock return if this stock has only risk exposure to the first factor with unit beta risk. If another stock has twice beta risk in $f_1$, its return should be $2\gamma_1$. The CAPM can then viewed as a special case of the APT with $K = 1$, $f_1 = r_m - r_f$, and $\gamma_1 = E(r_m) - r_f$.

In light of the empirical problems of the CAPM, Fama and French (1993) propose their famous three-factor model:

$$r_{it} - r_{ft} = \alpha_i + \beta_{im}(r_{mt} - r_{ft}) + \beta_{is}SMB_t + \beta_{ih}HML_t + \varepsilon_{it} \tag{14.39}$$

where $SMB_t$ and $HML_t$ are two factors in additional to the market. The terms $SMB_t$, which stand for "small minus big," are defined as the (time-varying) differences between the returns on diversified portfolios of small and big stocks. The size factor here refers to the market capitalization (cap), small means small cap stocks, and big meaning large cap stocks. The terms $HML_t$ refer to "high minus low" and are defined as the difference between the returns on diversified portfolios of high and low B/M stocks. The introduction of these factors is intended to capture much of the systematic variation in average return for portfolios formed on size and book-to-market that cause problems for the CAPM. The factor betas, or slopes of the regressions, then measure the stock's exposure to these systematic factors. Note that the regression given by equation (14.39) is always true because one can always write a regression for one random variable on a set of others, but the alpha is not necessarily zero. In contrast, the asset pricing theory says that the alphas are zero, and so the expected returns are a linear function of the factor risk premiums:

$$E[r_i] = r_f + \beta_{im}[E(r_{mt}) - r_{ft}] + \beta_{is}E[SMB_t] + \beta_{ih}E[HML_t] \qquad i = 1, \ldots, N \tag{14.40}$$

in which the alphas disappear and the earlier factors are replaced by their risk premiums. Since equation (14.40) can be the implication of other multifactor theoretical models, such as Merton's ICAPM or Ross's APT (with two factors), the $SMB_t$ and $HML_t$ factors may then be interpreted as proxies to the two factors in those models.

Besides the size and book-to-market factors, subsequent studies attempt to add more factors into the model. Notably, Carhart (1997) adds a momentum factor (the difference between the returns on diversified portfolios of short-term winners and losers[9]) to the three-factor Fama-French model. Another one is to add liquidity as a factor (see Pastor and Stambaugh, 2003). These are examples of abstracting from

---

[9] There are various studies that have examined momentum in stock prices. The empirical tests of momentum studies involve defining winner and loser stocks, the former being defined as stocks that have performed the best by some measure and the latter being stocks that performed the worst by the same measure.

known patterns in average returns to uncover systematic factors. However, since the momentum effect is short-lived and the liquidity effect is not terribly relevant to passive investors, these extended factors models are not as widely used.

### 14.9.3.3 A Behavioral Explanation

Behavioral finance provides another explanation for the failure of the CAPM. It explains that stocks with high B/M ratios, known as value stocks, are often those firms that have fallen on bad times, while low B/M stocks are usually firms associated with growth opportunities, known as growth stocks. When investors overreact to the bad news, and when these overreactions are later corrected, we observe high returns for value stocks and low returns for growth stocks.

### 14.9.3.4 The Bottom Line

Empirically, the Fama and French three-factor model improves the performance of the CAPM significantly, and is popular in academic studies and practical applications. The availability of the factor data from Kenneth French's website makes the model much easier to apply. In practice, the bottom line is that the CAPM provides the profound insight that only systematic risks are rewarded by the financial markets. It is not a matter of getting the best model. What is important is to obtain a model that is better than others, so that it can be used, studied, and improved further. But despite its wide use, the Fama-French three-factor model is still not adequate for understanding and estimating the expected returns in many applications. The three factors are not sufficient in explaining the expected returns for a large set of assets, and hence more factors are needed, as discussed in the next chapter.

## KEY POINTS

- The CAPM makes a number of assumptions about investor behavior and about the capital market. The key assumptions are that investors have the same information set, and the capital markets are completely competitive and frictionless (i.e., a perfect capital market).
- Under the CAPM assumptions, the optimal portfolios of all investors must be on the security market line. That is, they are combinations of the market portfolio and the risk-free asset.
- Under the CAPM assumptions, the expected security excess return and beta must be on the security market line. The higher the beta risk, the higher the expected return is.
- Under the CAPM, the expected return on any asset is the sum of the risk-free rate return plus the security's risk premium given by the product of the security's beta with the expected market excess return.
- The beta of a portfolio is a weighted average of the betas of the securities held in the portfolio.

- The CAPM is also true for any portfolio of the securities; that is, the expected return on any portfolio is the sum of the risk-free rate return plus the product of portfolio beta with the expected market excess return.
- According to the CAPM, the risk of a portfolio can be decomposed into systematic risk and unsystematic risk. Systematic risk, also referred to as non-diversifiable risk, is the risk relative to the market and is measured by beta. Unsystematic risk is the risk that can be diversified away.
- The CAPM asserts that the only risk for which investors will be compensated is systematic risk, not unsystematic risk.
- Under the CAPM, the alpha empirically estimated by regressing any security excess return on the market excess return must be zero. Otherwise, an investor can be better off by holding the market portfolio and the risk-free asset if the alpha is not zero.
- The CAPM provides a way to estimate not only the expected return on an investment project, but also the expected returns on assets for forming portfolios.
- There are numerous studies investigating the validity of the CAPM. There are mainly two types of tests, time series and cross-sectional. The tests generally find that the expected asset returns are not perfectly in line with their beta risks, leading to rejection of the CAPM.
- Models with factors in additional to the market factor tend to do much better in explaining the cross-section asset expected returns than the CAPM.

## QUESTIONS

1. Explain whether the following statements about the CAPM are correct or not.
   a. The CAPM says that a stock with zero beta risk (no exposures to systematic risk) should have zero return.
   b. The CAPM assumes that the beta risk of any asset is constant.
   c. The beta in the CAPM is a measure of total risk exposure of a stock.
   d. According to the CAPM, an investor who desires a higher level of expected return must be willing to accept a higher risk of inflation.
   e. According to the CAPM, two stocks with the same beta must have the same return.

2. In the CAPM, what is meant by the market risk premium?

3. What is the difference between systematic risk and unsystematic risk?

4. a. What are the various names for unsystematic risk?
   b. How can a portfolio's unsystematic risk be eliminated in theory?
   c. Why in the real world might it be difficult to completely eliminate unsystematic risk?

5. What is the difference between the security market line and the capital market line?

6. Assume that the market has an expected return of 12% and volatility (risk or standard deviation) of 20%. Suppose the CAPM accurately describes the data one is using. IBM has a 0.90% correlation with the market and 50% volatility. The risk-free rate is 3%.

   a. What is the covariance between IBM and the market?

   b. What is IBM's beta?

   c. What is the expected return on IBM?

   d. What percentage of IBM's total variance risk is specific (nonsystematic)?

   e. Suppose you want to take only 15% risk on your investment portfolio. What is the best you can do if you invest in only IBM and the risk-free asset?

   f. How much better can you do if you add in the market portfolio in part e?

7. One problem with the CAPM is that it assumes lending and borrowing rates are the same. If this assumption is violated, is the CAPM useless? If not, why not?

8. In practice, to estimate an asset's alpha and beta, the following linear regression is usually estimated:

$$r_j - r_{ft} = \alpha_j + \beta_j(r_{mt} - r_{ft}) + \varepsilon_j$$

   where $r_j$ is the asset return, $r_{ft}$ the risk-free rate, and $r_{mt}$ the market return.

   a. If the CAPM accurately describes the data one is using, should the estimated alpha be zero?

   b. If the estimated alpha is statistically different from zero, is the CAPM true or not?

   c. If the asset return is that of a mutual fund, and if the alpha is positive, does it mean that the mutual fund beat the market (i.e., outperformed the market)?

   d. If we run the regression over all the stocks (i.e., if the regression is run successively for each of the available stocks), what can we say about the average alpha, beta, and idiosyncratic risk?

9. Suppose that there are only two stocks in the stock market. Stock A sells for $20 and has 100 shares outstanding. Stock B sells for $40 and has 200 shares outstanding. Assume that there is a risk-free asset.

   a. What is the market portfolio in this hypothetical economy?

   b. If the beta of stock A is 1.2, what is the beta of stock B?

   c. If the stocks have volatilities 20% and 30%, and if all investors have quadratic utility so that the CAPM accurately describes the data being used, what is the equilibrium expected return (or equilibrium expected return or the CAPM implied expected return as practitioners call it) on the stocks in excess of the risk-free asset?

10. How do the following explain the failure of empirical studies to support the CAPM?

    a. The failure to use the true market portfolio in empirical tests.

    b. The presence of other factors ignored by the CAPM.

    c. Behavorial finance theory.

11. (Based on the appendix to the chapter.) Suppose that there are $I$ investors in the economy all of whom have a quadratic utility:

$$u_i = a_i W_i - \frac{b_i}{2} W_i^2$$

where $a_i > 0$ and $b_i > 0$ are constant parameters of individual $i$, and $W_i$ is the wealth. Provide a proof of the CAPM without the normality assumption.

---

• • • **APPENDIX 14.1: RUBINSTEIN'S PROOF OF THE CAPM**

Assume there are $I$ investors, and each of them has a differentiable utility $u_i$, $i = 1, 2, \ldots, I$. If we let $W_0^i$ be investor $i$'s initial wealth, then his wealth next period will be his initial wealth times the sum of the return on risk-free asset and on the risky assets. Therefore, the investor's optimization problem is to maximize his expected utility of wealth $u_i(W_i)$ with:

$$W_i = W_0^i (1 - \sum_j w_{ij})(1 + r_f) + \sum_j w_{ij}(1 + r_j) \tag{14.A1}$$

where $w_{ij}$ is the portfolio weight on risky asset $j$. Taking the derivative of $E[u_i(W_i)]$ with respective to the portfolio weights, we get the first-order condition,

$$E[u_i'(W_i)(r_j - r_f)] = 0 \tag{14.A2}$$

which holds for all $j$, $j = 1, 2, \ldots, N$. Since the covariance, $cov(a, b)$, of any two random variable is $E(ab) - E(a)E(b)$, equation (14.A2) can be written as:

$$cov(u_i', r_j) = -E[u_i']E(r_j - r_f) \tag{14.A3}$$

or

$$E(r_j) - r_f = cov[u_i', W_i]/E[u_i'] \tag{14.A4}$$

The next key step is to use Stein's Lemma, which computes the covariance of any function of a normal random variable with another normal random variable by the product of the two random variable with an adjustment by the expectation of the derivative of the function, $cov[g(a), b] = E[g'(a)]cov(a, b)$. Since the returns are assumed normal, so must the wealth. Then the application of Stein's Lemma implies that:

$$E(r_j) - r_f = \theta_i cov(W_i, r_j) \qquad (14.A5)$$

where $\theta_i = -E[u'']/E[u_i']$. Dividing both sides of equation (14.A5) by $\theta_i$, and summing over all $i$, we have

$$\left(\sum_i \frac{1}{\theta_i}\right)(E(r_j) - r_f) = cov(W_m, r_j) \qquad (14.A6)$$

where $W_m = \sum_i W_i$ is the market wealth, and is given by $W_{m0}(1 + r_m)$, with $W_{m0}$ the initial market wealth. Therefore, we obtain

$$E(r_j) - r_f = W_{m0}\left(\sum_i \frac{1}{\theta_i}\right)^{-1} cov(r_m, r_j) \qquad (14.A7)$$

Now, multiplying equation (14.A7) by the market weight on asset $j$, and summing over assets, we have

$$E(r_m) - r_f = W_{m0}\left(\sum_i \frac{1}{\theta_i}\right)^{-1} cov(r_m, r_m) \qquad (14.A8)$$

Finally, taking the ratio of the equations (14.A7) and (14.A8), and then multiplying both sides by $E(r_m) - r_f$, we obtain the CAPM relation given by equation (14.11) that concludes the proof.

## REFERENCES

Black, Fischer. (1972). "Capital Market Equilibrium with Restricted Borrowing," *Journal of Business* **45**: 444–455.

Carhart, Mark. (1997). "On Persistence in Mutual Fund Performance," *Journal of Finance* **52**: 57–82.

Fama, Eugene F. (1996). "Multifactor Portfolio Efficiency and Multifactor Asset Pricing," *Journal of Financial and Quantitative Analysis* **31**: 441–465.

Fama, Eugene F., and Kenneth R. French. (1992). "The Cross-Section of Expected Stock Returns," *Journal of Finance* **47**: 427–465.

Fama, Eugene F., and Kenneth R. French. (1993). "Common Risk Factors in the Returns on Stocks and Bonds," *Journal of Financial Economics* **33**: 3–56.

Fama, Eugene F., and Kenneth R. French. (2004). "The Capital Asset Pricing Model: Theory and Evidence, " *Journal of Economic Perspectives* **18**: 25–46.

Fama, Eugene F., and James D. MacBeth. (1973). "Risk, Return, and Equilibrium: Empirical Tests," *Journal of Political Economy* **81**: 607–636.

Gibbons, Michael R., Stephen A. Ross, and Jay Shanken. (1989). "A Test of the Efficiency of a Given Portfolio," *Econometrica* **57**: 1121–1152.

Lintner, John. (1965). "The Valuation of Risk Assets and the Selection of Risky Investments in Stock Portfolios and Capital Budgets," *Review of Economics and Statistics* **47**: 13–37.

Merton, Robert C. (1973). "An Intertemporal Capital Asset Pricing Model," *Econometrica* **41**: 867–887.

Mossin, Jan (1966). "Equilibrium in a Capital Asset Market," *Econometrica* **35**: 768–783.

Pastor, Lubos, and Robert F. Stambaugh (2003). "Liquidity Risk and Expected Stock Returns," *Journal of Political Economy* **111**: 642–685.

Perold, Andre F. (2004). "The Capital Asset Pricing Model," *Journal of Economic Perspectives* **18**: 3–24.

Roll, Richard R. (1977). "A Critique of the Asset Pricing Theory's Tests Part I: On Past and Potential Testability of the Theory," *Journal of Financial Economics* **4**: 129–176.

Ross, Stephen A. (1976). "The Arbitrage Theory of Capital Asset Pricing," *Journal of Economic Theory* **13**: 341–360.

Rubinstein, Mark. (1973). "The Fundamental Theorem of Parameter-Preference Security Valuation," *Journal of Financial and Quantitative Analysis* **8**: 61–69.

Rubinstein, Mark. (2006). *A History of the Theory of Investments: My Annotated Bibliography.* Hoboken, NJ: John Wiley & Sons.

Shanken, Jay. (1992). "On the Estimation of Beta-Pricing Models," *Review of Financial Studies* **5**: 1–33.

Shanken, Jay, and Guofu Zhou. (2007). "Estimating and Testing Beta Pricing Models: Alternative Methods and Their Performance in Simulations," *Journal of Financial Economics* **84**: 40–86.

Sharpe, William F. (1964). "Capital Asset Prices: A Theory of Market Equilibrium under Conditions of Risk," *Journal of Finance* **19**: 425–442.

Shleifer, Andrei, and Robert W. Vishny. (1997). "The Limits of Arbitrage," *Journal of Finance* **52**: 35–55.

Treynor, Jack L. (1962). "Toward a Theory of Market Value of Risky Assets," Unpublished manuscript. Final version published in *Asset Pricing and Portfolio Performance*, 1999, Robert A. Korajczyk, ed. London: Risk Books, pp. 15–22.

Wagner, Wayne H., and Sheila Lau. (1971). "The Effect of Diversification on Risks," *Financial Analysts Journal* **26**: 414–453.

Zhou, Guofu. (2008a). "On the Fundamental Law of Active Portfolio Management: What Happens if Our Estimates Are Wrong?" *Journal of Portfolio Management* **34**: 26–33.

Zhou, Guofu. (2008b). "On the Fundamental Law of Active Portfolio Management: How to Make Conditional Investments Unconditionally Optimal? *Journal of Portfolio Management* **35**: 12–21.

# 15

# ARBITRAGE PRICING THEORY AND FACTOR MODELS

*I*n this chapter, we continue with our coverage of *asset pricing models* by explaining the arbitrage pricing theory (APT) formulated by Ross (1976). As indicated in the previous chapter, the APT is a general multifactor model for pricing assets. We begin by discussing a special case of a one-factor model for motivation, and then prove the general form of the APT. Regardless of the APT's validity, in practice, factor models are useful for estimating expected asset returns and their covariance matrix, which in turn are valuable for both portfolio management and risk analysis. Consequently, we provide a detailed treatment of factor models and their estimation.

## 15.1 APT AND CAPM

One of the fundamental problems in finance is to explain the cross-section differences in asset expected returns. Specifically, what factors can explain the observed differences? Since those factors that systematically affect the differences in expected returns are the risks investors are compensated for, the term *factors* is used interchangeably with the term *risk factors*.

The Capital Asset Pricing Model (CAPM) developed in the previous chapter asserts that expected returns are linearly related to a single systematic source, the risk of the market portfolio. Beta is a relative measure of market portfolio risk and we referred to this as beta risk. In contrast and also as mentioned at the end of the previous chapter, the APT asserts that the expected returns are linearly related to $K$ systematic factors and the exposure to these factors is measured by factor betas. That is,

$$E[\tilde{r}_i] = r_f + \gamma_1 \beta_{i1} + \cdots + \gamma_K \beta_{iK} \tag{15.1}$$

where $\beta_{ik}$ is the beta or risk exposure on the $k$-th factor, and $\gamma_k$ is the factor risk premium, for $k = 1, 2, \ldots, K$. When $K = 1$ and $f_1$ is the market portfolio factor, the APT implies the CAPM. If the first asset has only a unit beta risk on the second factor, that is, $\beta_{i2} = 1$ and zero betas on all other factors, then its expected return will be $E[r_1] = r_f + \lambda_2$ according to equation (15.1), the risk-free rate increased by an extra return to compensate for taking the factor risk on $f_2$. This is why $\lambda_2$ is called the *factor risk premium* on $f_2$, or the extra return one earns by taking one unit beta risk on the factor. Interpretations for other $\lambda$'s follow the same way.

There are, however, some key differences in the assumptions of the CAPM and the APT. The CAPM is based on mean-variance theory and assumes that only means and variances (whose calculations include covariances) matter in portfolio choice. This requires restrictions on either the statistical distribution of the asset returns, such as normality, or on the form of the utility function, such as the quadratic form. In contrast, the APT does not impose as strong distributional assumption as the CAPM. It assumes that only the asset returns are affected by a few factors. Moreover, it does not impose any restrictions on the form of utility functions except the trivial assumption that investors prefer more to less.

In the CAPM, all investors are informed about the true means, variances, and covariances of the asset returns, and they all use Markowitz portfolio theory to make their optimal investment decisions. As a result, all investors hold the same market portfolio of risky assets and differ only, depending on their risk aversions, in the allocation of their total wealth between the risk-free asset and the market portfolio. In contrast, the APT assumes that it is sufficient for only some investors to be able to take advantage of arbitrage opportunities. If the assets are mispriced so that the expected returns of these assets deviate from what is accounted for by their beta risk, smart investors can construct an arbitrage portfolio to make abnormal returns, as detailed below. In a competitive market, we can assume that there are no "free lunch" arbitrage opportunities because, if there were any, they would be exploited quickly by the smart investors. Hence, the assets in the economy must be rewarded only by their beta risk exposures, and therefore the APT holds. Higher asset expected returns are associated with higher systematic risks.

Technically, the APT assumes a $K$-factor model. That is, the asset returns are influenced by $K$ factors in the economy via linear regression equations,

$$\tilde{r}_{it} - r_{ft} = \alpha_i + \beta_{i1}\tilde{f}_{1t} + \cdots + \beta_{iK}\tilde{f}_{Kt} + \tilde{\varepsilon}_{it} \tag{15.2}$$

where $\tilde{f}_1, \tilde{f}_2, \ldots, \tilde{f}_K$ are the systematic factors that affect all the asset returns on the left-hand side, $i = 1, 2, \ldots, N$; and $\tilde{\varepsilon}_{it}$ is the asset-specific risk. Note that we have placed a tilde sign (~) over the random asset returns, factors, and specific risks. If the tilde is present, it means the factors are random variables, whereas the same notation without the tilde refers to the variables' realizations (data). This makes it easier to follow the estimation below.

Theoretically, under the assumption of no arbitrage, the asset pricing relation of the APT as given by equation (15.1) must be true. Before embarking on the proof of the APT, we note two important points. First, the return-generating process, equation (15.2), is fundamentally different from the asset pricing relation. The return-generating process is a statistical model used to measure the risk exposures of the asset returns. It does not require drawing an economic conclusion, nor does it say anything about what the expected returns on the assets should be. In other words, the alphas ($\alpha_i$'s) in the return-generating process can statistically be any numbers. Only when the no-arbitrage assumption is imposed can one claim the APT, which says that the alphas should be linearly related to their risk exposures (betas).

The APT does not provide any specific information about what the factors are, nor does it make any claim regarding the number of factors. (In contrast, the CAPM claims a single factor and that factor is the market.) The APT simply assumes that the returns are driven by the factors, and if the smart investors know the betas (via learning or estimating), then an arbitrage portfolio, which requires no investment but yields a positive return, can be formed if the APT-pricing relation is violated in the market. Hence, in equilibrium if there are no arbitrage opportunities, we should not observe deviations from the APT-pricing relation.

## 15.2 APT IN A SPECIAL ONE-FACTOR MODEL

To see the intuition of the APT, consider a one-factor model in which there are two assets and suppose the factor model has no errors. In particular,

$$\tilde{r}_1 = \mu_1 + 0.8\tilde{f}$$

and

$$\tilde{r}_2 = \mu_2 + 1.6\tilde{f}$$

where $\tilde{f}$ is the single factor that affects the return on both assets with $E(\tilde{f}) = 0$, and $\mu_1$ and $\mu_2$ are the expected asset returns for assets 1 and 2, respectively. For example, for the asset 1:

$$E(\tilde{r}_1) = \mu_1 + 0.8E(\tilde{f}) = \mu_1 + 0.8 \times 0 = \mu_1$$

The question is how $\mu_1$ and $\mu_2$ are related to their betas, 0.8 and 1.6.

With two assets and one factor, a suitable portfolio consisting of the two assets can eliminate the single factor risk. With the current beta values, 0.8 and 1.6, one such portfolio (which we call portfolio z) is:

$$\tilde{z} = 2\tilde{r}_1 - \tilde{r}_2 = 2\mu_1 - \mu_2$$

This portfolio is risk free with a constant return $2\mu_1 - \mu_2$. Assume as in the two previous chapters that there is a risk-free asset in the market with rate of return $r_f$. An *arbitrage opportunity* then exists if two risk-free investments have different returns. In this illustration, let's suppose that $r_f$ is 5%. Portfolio $z$ is risk-free so its return should also be 5%. Suppose instead that portfolio $z$ has a 6% return. That is, $2\mu_1 - \mu_2 = 6\%$. If this situation existed in the market, then investors can borrow funds at the risk-free rate of 5% and invest the borrowed funds in the risk-free asset portfolio earning 6%. This would result in a 1% sure profit without any initial investment. Suppose, instead, portfolio $z$ has a return of 4% (i.e., $2\mu_1 - \mu_2 = 4\%$). In this case, investors can short the asset portfolio and invest the proceeds in the risk-free asset earning 5%, once again making a 1% sure profit without any initial investment. Either case gives rise to a sure profit that is clearly unlikely to be available in a competitive market. In asset pricing theory, we typically make the assumption that there are no such sure profit arbitrage opportunities since if they ever occur, some smart investors will jump in to eliminate them quickly.

Because the risk-free portfolio $z$ should have the same return as the risk-free asset, we have:

$$2\mu_1 - \mu_2 = r_f$$

which can be rewritten as:

$$\frac{\mu_1 - r_f}{0.8} = \frac{\mu_2 - r_f}{1.6} \tag{15.3}$$

This says that the ratio of the excess expected returns on the two assets divided by their betas should be equal. Let $\lambda_1$ be the proportional coefficient, then equation (15.3) implies:

$$\mu_1 = r_f + 0.8\lambda_1$$
$$\mu_2 = r_f + 1.6\lambda_1$$

Similarly, the same beta pricing relation holds for any asset; that is,

$$\mu_i = r_f + \beta_i\lambda_1 \tag{15.4}$$

where $\mu_i$ is the expected return on a risky asset with beta risk $\beta_i$ (as long as the one-factor model assumption, $\tilde{r}_t = \mu_i + \beta_i\tilde{f}$, is true, and there is no arbitrage). Equation (15.4) says that the expected excess asset returns are proportional to their beta risks, and is exactly the claim of the APT in the one-factor case. Equation (15.4) resembles the CAPM, but is derived here under assumptions different from those of the CAPM.

## 15.3 APT IN THE MULTIFACTOR MODEL

Consider now the $K$-factor model, equation (15.2), or equivalently,

$$\tilde{r}_{it} - r_{ft} = \mu_i + \beta_{i1}\tilde{f}_{1t} + \cdots + \beta_{iK}\tilde{f}_{Kt} + \tilde{\varepsilon}_{it} \tag{15.5}$$

where we assume that the factors have zero means (or the means are subtracted from the factors, as often done in the context of the APT factor model), so that the expected excess asset returns are given by the $\mu_i$'s. Now we want to examine under what conditions the pricing relation:

$$E[\tilde{r}_i] = \mu_i = r_f + \gamma_1\beta_{i1} + \cdots + \gamma_K\beta_{iK} \tag{15.6}$$

is true. In contrast to the special one-factor model, here we have $K$ risk factors and also the presence of the unsystematic risk $\tilde{\varepsilon}_{it}$ (i.e., noise).

Nevertheless, the argument for beta pricing in the one-factor case can be extended to the $K$-factor model. To see this, consider again the previous one-factor example. For any portfolio weights $w_1$ and $w_2$,

$$w_1 + w_2 = 1 \tag{15.7}$$

that satisfy the condition of no risk:

$$w_1\beta_1 + w_2\beta_2 = 0 \tag{15.8}$$

(in our example, $\beta_1 = 0.8$ and $\beta_2 = 1.6$), the portfolio:

$$\tilde{z} = w_1\tilde{r}_1 + w_2\tilde{r}_2$$

will be riskless as before. Hence, it has the risk-free rate of return so that,

$$w_1\mu_1 + w_2\mu_2 = r_f$$

Using this portfolio condition, equation (15.7) can be rewritten as:

$$w_1(\mu_1 - r_f) + w_2(\mu_2 - r_f) = 0 \tag{15.9}$$

Note that any portfolio satisfying equation (15.8) is a portfolio that eliminates factor risk. In terms of linear algebra, equation (15.8) says that the portfolio vector is orthogonal to the beta vector [that is, their inner product as expressed by equation (15.9) is zero].[1] Equation (15.9) says that any vector orthogonal to the beta vector will also be orthogonal to the expected excess return vector. This can only be true if the expected excess return vector can be generated by the betas, that is, the expected excess return vector must be a linear function of the betas. The result is the earlier equation (15.4). What we just provided here is the general reasoning that is applicable to the $K$-factor case.

To see why the beta-pricing relation remains true in the $N$ assets case, consider the portfolio:

$$
\begin{aligned}
\tilde{r}_p &= \sum_{i=1}^{N} w_i\tilde{r}_i \\
&= \left(\sum_{i=1}^{N} w_i\beta_{i1}\right)\tilde{f}_{1t} + \cdots + \left(\sum_{i=1}^{N} w_i\beta_{iK}\right)\tilde{f}_{Kt} + \sum_{i=1}^{N} w_i\tilde{\varepsilon}_{it}
\end{aligned} \tag{15.10}
$$

---

[1] See Web-Appendix O for an explanation of what is meant by orthogonal and inner product.

Suppose now that the portfolio weights are orthogonal to all the betas,

$$\sum_{i=1}^{N} w_i \beta_{ik} = w_1 \beta_{1k} + w_2 \beta_{2k} + \cdots + w_N \beta_{Nk} = 0, \quad k = 1, 2, \ldots, K \quad (15.11)$$

Then the portfolio has only unsystematic risk by equation (15.10),

$$\tilde{r}_p = \sum_{i=1}^{N} w_i \tilde{\varepsilon}_{it} \quad (15.12)$$

Under certain conditions, this risk will be approximately zero. To see why, assume all the unsystematic risks are independent across assets and they have the same variance $\sigma_u^2$. Then the variance of $\tilde{r}_p$ is:

$$\sigma^2(\tilde{r}_p) = (w_1^2 + w_2^2 + \cdots + w_N^2)\sigma_u^2 \quad (15.13)$$

When there are a large number of assets, the weights can be roughly of the same magnitude of $1/N$, and hence $\sigma^2(\tilde{r}_p)$ should be of magnitude of:

$$(1/N)^2 \times N \times \sigma_u^2 = \sigma_u^2/N$$

which approaches zero as $N$ approaches infinity. This implies that $\tilde{r}_p$ is almost risk free. Hence, in the absence of arbitrage, the return on $\tilde{r}_p$ should be approximately $r_f$, or

$$w_1(\mu_1 - r_f) + w_2(\mu_2 - r_f) + \cdots + w_K(\mu_K - r_f) \approx 0 \quad (15.14)$$

As in the one-factor case, this implies an approximate beta-pricing relation. Under some additional assumptions, such as a finite upper bound on the variances of all the risky assets and some property on the utility, the approximate relation can be exact as given by equation (15.6).

## 15.4 FACTOR MODELS

From a practical point of view, the APT is abstract in that it does not tell where the investors should go to find the factors and estimate the associated beta risks. On the other hand, this is precisely the generality of the theory. In investing in a group of assets, say in certain sectors or industries, the theory allows investment managers to identify important factors that affect the assets of interest, and to examine whether there are any mispricing opportunities.

More importantly, factor models are widely used in practice as a tool for estimating expected asset returns and their covariance matrix, regardless of the validity of the APT. This is because if market participants can identify those true factors that drive asset returns, they will have much better estimates of the true expected asset returns and the covariance matrix, and hence can form a much better portfolio than otherwise possible. Hence, there is considerable research devoted to analyzing factor models in practice by the investment community. There is an intellectual "arms race" to find the best portfolio strategies to outperform competitors. In addition, factor models can be used not only for explaining asset returns, but also for predicting future returns.

Factor model estimation depends crucially on whether the factors are identified (known) or unidentified (latent), and depends further on the sample size and the number of assets. In this section, we review the factor models in the case of known and latent factors in order to provide an overview, then discuss the details of estimation in Section 15.5.

## 15.4.1 Known Factors

The simplest case of factor models is where the $K$ factors are assumed known or observable, so that we have time-series data on them. In this case, the $K$-factor model for the return-generating process,

$$\tilde{r}_{it} - r_{ft} = \alpha_i + \beta_{i1}\tilde{f}_{1t} + \cdots + \beta_{iK}\tilde{f}_{Kt} + \tilde{\varepsilon}_{it} \tag{15.15}$$

is a multiple regression for each asset, and is a multivariate regression if all of the individual regressions are pooled together. For example, if one believes that the gross domestic product (GDP) is the driving force for a group of stock returns, one would have a one-factor model,

$$\tilde{r}_{it} - r_{ft} = \alpha_i + \beta_{i1}\tilde{GDP}_t + \tilde{\varepsilon}_{it}$$

The above equation corresponds to equation (15.15) with $K = 1$ and $f_1 = \tilde{GDP}$. In practice, one can obtain time-series data on both the asset returns and GDP, and then one can run regressions to obtain all the parameters, including in particular the expected returns. Another popular one-factor model is the market model regression (introduced in the previous chapter):

$$\tilde{r}_{it} - r_{ft} = \alpha_i + \beta_{i1}(\tilde{r}_{mt} - r_{ft}) + \tilde{\varepsilon}_{it}$$

where $\tilde{r}_{mt}$ is the return on a stock market index.

To understand the covariance matrix estimation, it will be useful to write the $K$-factor model in matrix form:

$$\tilde{R}_t = \alpha + \beta\tilde{f}_t + \tilde{\varepsilon}_t \tag{15.16}$$

or

$$\begin{bmatrix} \tilde{R}_{1t} \\ \vdots \\ \tilde{R}_{Nt} \end{bmatrix} = \begin{bmatrix} \alpha_1 \\ \vdots \\ \alpha_N \end{bmatrix} + \begin{bmatrix} \beta_{11} & \cdots & \beta_{1K} \\ \vdots & \ddots & \vdots \\ \beta_{N1} & \cdots & \beta_{NK} \end{bmatrix} \begin{bmatrix} \tilde{f}_{1t} \\ \vdots \\ \tilde{f}_{Kt} \end{bmatrix} + \begin{bmatrix} \tilde{\varepsilon}_{1t} \\ \vdots \\ \tilde{\varepsilon}_{Nt} \end{bmatrix}$$

where

$\tilde{R}_t$ = an $N$-vector of asset excess returns

$\alpha$ = an $N$-vector of the alphas

$\beta$ = an $N \times K$ of betas or factor loadings

$\tilde{f}_t$ = a $K$-vector of the factors

$\tilde{\varepsilon}$ = an $N$-vector of the model residuals

For example, we can write a model with $N = 3$ assets and $K = 2$ factors as:

$$\begin{bmatrix} \tilde{R}_{1t} \\ \tilde{R}_{2t} \\ \tilde{R}_{3t} \end{bmatrix} = \begin{bmatrix} \alpha_1 \\ \alpha_2 \\ \alpha_3 \end{bmatrix} + \begin{bmatrix} \beta_{11} & \beta_{12} \\ \beta_{21} & \beta_{22} \\ \beta_{31} & \beta_{32} \end{bmatrix} \begin{bmatrix} \tilde{f}_{1t} \\ \tilde{f}_{2t} \end{bmatrix} + \begin{bmatrix} \tilde{\varepsilon}_{1t} \\ \tilde{\varepsilon}_{2t} \\ \tilde{\varepsilon}_{3t} \end{bmatrix}$$

Taking the covariance of both sides of equation (15.16), we obtain the return covariance matrix:

$$\Sigma = \beta' \Sigma_f \beta + \Sigma_\varepsilon \tag{15.17}$$

where $\Sigma_f$ is the covariance matrix of the factors, and $\Sigma_\varepsilon$ is the covariance matrix of the residuals. The matrix $\Sigma_f$ can be estimated by using the sample covariance matrix from the historical returns. This works for $\Sigma_\varepsilon$ too if $N$ is small relative to $T$. However, when $N$ is large relative to $T$, the sample covariance matrix of the residuals will be poorly behaved.

Usually an additional assumption that the residuals are uncorrelated is imposed, so that $\Sigma_\varepsilon$ becomes a diagonal matrix, and can then be estimated by using the sample variances of the residuals. Plugging the estimates of all the parameters into the right-hand side of equation (15.17), we obtain the covariance matrix needed for applying the mean-variance portfolio analysis.

In the estimation of a multifactor model, it is implicitly assumed that the number of time series observations $T$ is far greater than $K$, the number of factors. Otherwise, the regressions will perform poorly. For the case in which $K$ is close to or larger than $T$, some special treatments are needed, and will be addressed later in this chapter.

### 15.4.1.1 Examples of Multifactor Models with Known Factors

Let's briefly describe some multifactor models where known factors are used: (1) Fama-French three-factor model,[2] (2) MSCI Barra fundamental factor model,[3] (3) the Burmeister-Ibbotson-Roll-Ross (BIRR) macroeconomic factor model,[4] and (4) the Barclay Group Inc. factor model.[5] The first three are equity factor models and the last is a bond factor model.

---

[2] See Fama and French (1993). Carhart (1997) extended the Fama-French Model to four factors by including a momentum factor.

[3] See Bender and Nielsen (2010).

[4] See Burmeister, Roll, and Ross (1993).

[5] A description of this factor model is provided in Chapter 23 in Fabozzi (2009).

The Fama-French three-factor model that we described in the previous chapter is a special case of equation (15.15) with $K = 3$,

$$\tilde{r}_{it} - r_{ft} = \alpha_i + \beta_{im}(\tilde{r}_{mt} - r_{ft}) + \beta_{is}\tilde{SMB}_t + \beta_{ib}\tilde{HML}_t + \tilde{\varepsilon}_{it}$$

where $\tilde{SMB}_t$ and $\tilde{HML}_t$ are the book-market and size factors, respectively. These factors are supported by studies that suggest that market capitalization and stocks classified as either growth or value impact excess returns.

*Fundamental factor models* use company and industry attributes and market data as "descriptors." Examples are price-earnings ratios, book-price ratios, estimated earnings growth, and trading activity. The estimation of a fundamental factor model begins with an analysis of historical stock returns and descriptors about a company. In the MSCI Barra model, for example, the process of identifying the factors begins with monthly returns for hundreds of stocks that the descriptors must explain. Descriptors are not necessarily the risk factors themselves, but are rather candidates for risk factors. The descriptors are selected in terms of their ability to explain stock returns. That is, all of the descriptors are potential risk factors but only those that appear to be important in explaining stock returns are used in constructing risk factors. Once the descriptors that are statistically significant in explaining stock returns are identified, they are grouped into "risk indices" to capture related company attributes. For example, descriptors such as market leverage, book leverage, debt-to-equity ratio, and company's debt rating are combined to obtain a risk index referred to as "leverage." Thus, a risk index is a combination of descriptors that captures a particular attribute of a company. For example, in the MSCI Barra fundamental multifactor model, there are 13 risk indices and 55 industry groups. The 55 industry classifications are further classified into sectors.

In a *macroeconomic factor model*, the inputs to the model are historical stock returns and observable macroeconomic variables. In the BIRR macroeconomic multifactor model, the macroeconomic variables that have been successful in explaining excess returns and that are therefore included in the market are:

- *The business cycle*: Changes in real output that are measured by percentage changes in the index of industrial production.
- *Interest rates*: Changes in investors' expectations about future interest rates that are measured by changes in long-term government bond yields.
- *Investor confidence*: Expectations about future business conditions as measured by changes in the yield spread between high- and low-grade corporate bonds.
- *Short-term inflation*: Month-to-month jumps in commodity prices, such as gold or oil, as measured by changes in the consumer price index.
- *Inflationary expectations*: Changes in expectations of inflation as measured by changes in the short-term risk-free nominal interest rate.

Additional variables, such as the real GDP growth and unemployment rates, are also among the macroeconomic factors used by asset managers in other macroeconomic multifactor models. Moreover, some asset managers also have identified technical variables such as trading volume and market liquidity as factors.

The Barclay Group Inc. (BGI) bond factor model (previously the Lehman bond factor model) uses two categories of systematic risk factors: term structure and non-term structure risk factors. The former include changes in the level of interest and changes in the shape of the yield curve. The latter include sector risk, credit risk, optionality risk (i.e., risk associated with bonds with embedded options), and a series of risks associated with investing in mortgage-backed securities.

The search for factors is a never-ending task of asset managers. In practice, many popular investment software packages use dozens of factors. Some academic studies, such as Ludvigson and Ng (2007), even use hundreds of them.

## 15.4.2   Latent Factors

While some applications use observed factors, some use entirely latent factors, that is, they take the view that the factors $f_t$ in the $K$-factor model:

$$\tilde{R}_t = \alpha + \beta \tilde{f}_t + \tilde{\varepsilon}_t$$

are not directly observable. An argument for the use of latent factors is that the observed factors may be measured with errors or have been already anticipated by investors. Without imposing what $f_t$ are from our likely incorrect belief, we can statistically estimate the factors based on the factor model and data.

It is important to understand that the field of statistics incorporates a methodology known as "factor analysis" in which the model employed is referred to as a "factor model." These are not, of course, the same factors as we have been discussing, but rather represent basic underlying causes referred to here as latent factors. The latent factor models serve two main purposes: (1) they reduce the dimensionality of models to make estimation possible and/or (2) they find the likely true causes that drive data. In the following discussion of multifactor models, we shall try to determine the latent factors.

While the estimation procedures for determining the set of factors will be discussed in the next section, it will be useful to know some of the properties of the factor model here. First, the factors are not uniquely defined in the model, but all sets of factors are linear combinations of each other. This is because if $\tilde{f}_t$ is a set of factors, then, for any $K \times K$ invertible matrix $A$, we have:

$$\tilde{R}_t = \alpha + \beta \tilde{f}_t + \tilde{\varepsilon}_t = \alpha + (\beta A^{-1})(A \tilde{f}_t) + \tilde{\varepsilon}_t \tag{15.18}$$

which says that if $\tilde{f}_t$ with regression coefficients $\beta$ (known as a *factor loading* in the context of factor models) explains well the asset returns, so does $\tilde{f}_t^* = A \tilde{f}_t$ with loadings $\beta A^{-1}$. The linear transformation of $\tilde{f}_t$, $\tilde{f}_t^*$, is also known as a *rotation* of $f_t$.

The second property is that we can assume all the factors have zero mean, that is, $E[\tilde{f}_t] = 0$. This is because if $\mu_f = E[f_t]$, then the factor model can be written as:

$$\tilde{R}_t = \alpha + \beta \tilde{f}_t + \tilde{\varepsilon}_t = (\alpha - \beta \mu_f) + \beta(\tilde{f}_t - \mu_f) + \tilde{\varepsilon}_t \tag{15.19}$$

If we rename $\alpha - \beta \mu_f$ as the new alphas, and $f_t - \mu_f$ as the new factors, then the new factors will have zero means, and the new factor model is statistically the same as the old one. Hence, without loss of generality, we will assume that the mean of the factors are zeros in our estimation in the next section.

Note that the return covariance matrix formula, equation (15.17) and repeated here as

$$\Sigma = \beta'\Sigma_f\beta + \Sigma_\varepsilon \qquad (15.20)$$

holds regardless of whether the factors are observable or latent. However, through factor rotation, we can make a new set of factors so as to have the identity covariance matrix. In this case with $\Sigma_f = I_K$, we say that the factor model is *standardized*, and the covariance equation then simply becomes:

$$\Sigma = \beta'\beta + \Sigma_\varepsilon \qquad (15.21)$$

In general, $\Sigma_\varepsilon$ can have nonzero off-diagonal elements, implying that the residuals are correlated. If we assume that the residuals are uncorrelated, then $\Sigma_\varepsilon$ becomes a diagonal matrix, and the factor model is known as a *strict factor model*. If we assume further that $\Sigma_\varepsilon$ has equal diagonal elements, that is, $\Sigma_\varepsilon = \sigma^2 I_N$ for some $\sigma > 0$ with $I_N$ an $N$ dimensional identity matrix, then the factor model is known as a *normal factor model*.

## 15.4.3 Both Types of Factors

Rather than taking the view that there are only observable factors or only latent factors, we can consider a more general factor model with both views,

$$\tilde{R}_t = \alpha + \beta\tilde{f}_t + \beta_g\tilde{g}_t + \tilde{\varepsilon}_t \qquad (15.22)$$

where $\tilde{f}_t$ is a $K$-vector of latent factors, $\tilde{g}_t$ is an $L$-vector of observable factors, and $\beta_g$ are the betas associated with $\tilde{g}_t$. This model makes intuitive sense. If we believe a few fundamental and macroeconomic factors are the driving forces, we will use them to create the $\tilde{g}_t$ vector. Since we may not account for all the possible factors, we need to add additional $K$ unknown factors, which are to be estimated from the data.

The estimation of the above factor model given by equation (15.22) usually involves two steps. In the first step, a regression of the asset returns on the known factors is run in order to obtain $\hat{\beta}_g$, an estimate of $\beta_g$. This allows us to compute the residuals,

$$\hat{u}_t = R_t - \hat{\beta}_g g_t \qquad (15.23)$$

that is, the difference of the asset returns from their fitted values by using the observed factors for all the time periods. Then, in the second step, a factor estimation approach is used to estimate the latent factors for $\hat{u}_t$,

$$\tilde{u}_t = \alpha + \tilde{\beta}f_t + \tilde{v}_t \qquad (15.24)$$

where $\tilde{u}_t$ is the random differences whose realized values are $\hat{u}_t$. The estimation method for this model is the same as estimating a latent factor model, and will be detailed in the next section. With the factor estimates, we can treat the latent factors as known, and then use equation (15.22) to determine the expected asset returns and covariance matrix.

### 15.4.4 Predictive Factor Models

An important feature of factor models is that they use time $t$ factors to explain time $t$ returns. This is to estimate the long-run risk exposures of the assets, which are useful for both risk control and portfolio construction. On the other hand, portfolio managers are also very concerned about time-varying expected returns. In this case, they often use a predictive factor model such as the following to forecast the returns:

$$\tilde{R}_{t+1} = \alpha + \beta \tilde{f}_t + \beta_g \tilde{g}_t + \tilde{\varepsilon}_t \qquad (15.25)$$

where as before $\tilde{f}_t$ and $\tilde{g}_t$ are the latent and observable factors, respectively. The single difference is that the earlier $\tilde{R}_t$ is now replaced by $\tilde{R}_{t+1}$. Equation (15.25) uses time $t$ factors to forecast future return $\tilde{R}_{t+1}$.

Computationally, the estimation of the predictive factor model is the same as for estimating the standard factor models. However, it should be emphasized that the regression $R^2$, a measure of model fitting, is usually very good in the explanatory factor models. For example, as we recall from the regression of the market return on the five industry portfolio returns in the previous chapter, the $R^2$ ranges from 65% to 92%, indicating a good fitting or strong explanatory power. In contrast, if a predictive factor model is used to forecast the expected returns of various assets, the $R^2$ rarely exceeds 2%. This simply reflects the fact that assets returns are extremely difficult to predict in the real world. For example, Rapach et al. (2011) find that the $R^2$ are mostly less than 1% when forecasting industry returns using a variety of past economic variables and past industry returns.

## 15.5 FACTOR MODEL ESTIMATION

In this section, we provide first a step-by-step procedure for estimating the factor model based on the popular and implementable approach, the *principal components analysis* (PCA), to which a detailed and intuitive introduction is provided in Web-Appendix P. PCA is a statistical tool that is used by statisticians to determine factors with statistical learning techniques when factors are not observable. That is, given a variance-covariance matrix, a statistician can determine factors using the technique of PCA. Then, after understanding the computational procedure, we provide an application to identify three factors for bond returns. Finally, we outline some alternative procedures for estimating the factor models.

### 15.5.1 Computational Procedure

Following our discussion in Section 15.4, we need to consider only how to estimate the latent factors $\tilde{f}_t$ from the $K$-factor model,

$$\tilde{Y}_t = \beta \tilde{f}_t + \tilde{\varepsilon}_t \tag{15.26}$$

where both the dependent variables and the factors have zero means,

$$E(\tilde{f}_t) = 0, \quad E[\tilde{Y}_t] = 0$$

This version of the factor model is obtained in two steps. First, we substract the factor $f_t$ from its mean so that the alphas are the expected returns of the assets. Second, we substract the asset returns from their means.[6] In other words, we let $\tilde{Y}_t = \tilde{R}_t - \alpha$.

In practice, suppose that we have return data on $N$ risky assets over $T$ time periods. Then the realizations of the random variable $\tilde{Y}_t$ can be summarized by a matrix:

$$Y = \begin{pmatrix} Y_{11} & Y_{21} & \cdots & Y_{N1} \\ \vdots & \vdots & \vdots & \vdots \\ Y_{1T} & Y_{2T} & \cdots & Y_{NT} \end{pmatrix} \tag{15.27}$$

where each row is the $N$ asset returns after subtracting their sample means at time $t$ for $t = 1, 2, \ldots, T$. Our task is to estimate the realizations (unobserved) on the $K$ factors, $\tilde{f}_t$, over the $T$ periods:

$$F = \begin{pmatrix} F_{11} & F_{21} & \cdots & F_{K1} \\ \vdots & \vdots & \vdots & \vdots \\ F_{1T} & F_{2T} & \cdots & F_{KT} \end{pmatrix} \tag{15.28}$$

We will now apply PCA estimation methodology. There are two important cases, each calling for a different method of application. The first case is the one of traditional factor analysis in which $N$ is treated as fixed, and $T$ is allowed to grow. We will refer to this case as the "fixed $N$" below. The second case is where $N$ is allowed to grow and $T$ is either fixed or allowed to grow. We will refer to this case simply as "large $N$."

*Case 1: Fixed N.* In this case, we have a relatively small number of assets and relatively large sample size. Then the covariance matrix of the asset returns, which is the same as the covariance matrix of $\tilde{Y}_t$, can be estimated by the sample covariance matrix:

$$\Psi = \frac{Y'Y}{T} \tag{15.29}$$

which is an $N$ by $N$ matrix since $Y$ is $T$ by $N$. For example, if we think there are $K$ (say $K = 5$) factors, we can use standard software to compute the first $K$ eigenvectors of $\Psi$

---

[6] The process of subtracting the mean of a variable from the variables value is referred to as "de-meaning."

corresponding to the first $K$ largest eigenvalues of $\Psi$, each of which is an $N$ vector. Let $\hat{\beta}$ be the $N$ by $K$ matrix formed by these $K$ eigenvectors. Then $\hat{\beta}$ will be an estimate of $\beta$. Based on this, the factors are estimated by:

$$\hat{F}_t = \hat{Y}_t \hat{\beta}, \quad t = 1, 2, \ldots, T \tag{15.30}$$

where $Y_t$ is the $t$-th row of $Y$, and $\hat{F}_t$ is the estimate of $F_t$, the $t$-th row of $F$. The $\hat{F}_t$'s are the estimated realizations of the first $K$ factors. The reason why the $\hat{F}_t$'s are good estimates of the true but unobserved factor realizations is provided in Section 15.5.2. However, while theoretically they are close, they will not necessarily converge to the true values as $T$ increases, unless the factor model is normal. Nevertheless, despite this problem, the procedure is widely used in practice.

*Case 2: Large N.* In this case, we have a large number of assets. We now form a new matrix based on the product of $Y$ with $Y'$:

$$\Omega = \frac{YY'}{T} \tag{15.31}$$

which is a $T$ by $T$ matrix since $Y$ is $T$ by $N$. Given $K$, we use standard software to compute the first $K$ eigenvectors of $\Omega$ corresponding to the first $K$ largest eigenvalues of $\Omega$, each of which is a $T$ vector.[7] Letting $\hat{F}$ be the $T$ by $K$ matrix formed by these $K$ eigenvectors, the PCA says that $\hat{F}$ is an estimate of the true and unknown factor realizations $F$ of equation (15.28), up to a linear transformation. Connor and Korajczyk (1986) provided the first study in the finance literature to apply the PCA as described above. The large $N$ method is also termed *asymptotic PCA* since it allows the number of assets to increase without bound. Recall that in contrast, the first and traditional PCA method keeps $N$ fixed, while allowing the number of time periods $T$ to be large.

Theoretically, if the true factor model is the strict factor model or is not much too different from it (i.e., the residual correlations are not too strong), Bai (2003) shows that $\hat{F}$ converges to $F$ up to a linear transformation when both $T$ and $N$ increase without limit. The estimation errors are of order the larger of $1/T$ or $1/\sqrt{N}$, and converge to zero as both $T$ and $N$ grow to infinity. However, when $T$ is fixed, we need the stronger assumption that the true factor model is close to a normal model, in which case the estimation errors are of order of $1/\sqrt{N}$. Intuitively, given that there are only a few factors pricing many assets, at each time $t$ we should have enough information to back out the factors accurately.

Based on the estimated factors, the factor loadings are easily estimated from equation (15.26). For example, we can obtain the loadings for each asset by running a standard ordinary least squares (OLS) regression of the asset returns on the factors. Mathematically, this is equivalent to computing all the loadings from the formula:

$$\hat{\beta}' = (\hat{F}'\hat{F})^{-1}\hat{F}'X \tag{15.32}$$

---

[7] See Web-Appendix O for an explanation of eigenvalues and eigenvectors.

Under the same conditions above, $\hat{\beta}$ also converges to $\beta$ or a linear transformation of $\beta$.

The remaining question is how to determine $K$. In practice, this may be determined by trial and error depending on how different $K$'s perform in model fitting and in meeting the objectives where the model is applied. From an econometrics perspective, there is a simple solution in Case 2. Bai and Ng (2002) provide a statistical criterion:

$$IC(K) = \log(V(K)) + K\left(\frac{N+T}{NT}\right)\log\left(\frac{NT}{N+T}\right) \qquad (15.33)$$

where

$$V(K) = \sum_{i=1}^{N} \sum_{t=1}^{T} (Y_{it} - \hat{\beta}_{i1}\hat{f}_{1t} - \hat{\beta}_{i2}\hat{f}_{2t} - \cdots - \hat{\beta}_{iK}\hat{f}_{Kt})^2 \qquad (15.34)$$

For a given $K$, $V(K)$ is the sum of the fitted squared residual errors of the factor model across both asset and time. This is a measure of model fitting. The smaller the $V(K)$, the better the $K$-factor model in explaining the asset returns. So we want to choose such a $K$ that minimizes $V(K)$. However, the more the factors, the smaller the $V(K)$, but this improvement is obtained at a cost of estimating more factors with greater estimation errors. Hence, we want to penalize too many factors. This is the same as the case in linear regressions where we also want to penalize too many regressors. The second term in equation (15.33) plays this role. It is an increasing function of $K$. Therefore, the trade-off between model fitting and estimation errors requires us to minimize the $IC(K)$ function. Theoretically, assuming that the factor model is indeed true for some fixed $K^*$, Bai and Ng (2002) show that the $K$ that minimizes $IC(K)$ will converge to $K^*$ as either $N$ or $T$ or both increase to infinity.

## 15.5.2 An Application to Bond Returns

To illustrate the procedure, consider an application of the PCA factor analysis to the excess returns on Treasury bonds with maturities 12, 18, 24, 30, 36, 42, 48, 54, 60, 120, and beyond 120 months. Hence, there are $N = 11$ assets. With monthly data from January 1980 to December 2008, available from the Center for Research in Security Prices of the University of Chicago's Booth School of Business, we have a sample size (i.e., number of data points) of $T = 348$. Since $N$ is small relative to $T$, this is a case of fixed $N$.

Now:

$$\Psi = \frac{Y'Y}{348}$$

is an 11 by 11 matrix. We can easily compute its eigenvalues and eigenvectors. The largest three eigenvalues are:

$$(\lambda_1, \lambda_2, \lambda_3) = 10^{-2}(0.2403, 0133, 0012)$$

**TABLE 15.1**

FACTOR LOADINGS AND EXPLANATORY POWER

| | $\beta_1$ | $\beta_2$ | $\beta_3$ | $R^2\ (F_1)$ | $R^2\ (F_1 \text{ and } F_2)$ | $R^2$ (all three) |
|---|---|---|---|---|---|---|
| 12 month | 0.0671 | −0.1418 | 0.4046 | 0.67 | 0.80 | 0.96 |
| 18 month | 0.1118 | −0.2057 | 0.4227 | 0.79 | 0.84 | 0.99 |
| 24 month | 0.1524 | −0.2455 | 0.3371 | 0.85 | 0.87 | 1.00 |
| 32 month | 0.1932 | −0.2876 | 0.3199 | 0.88 | 0.89 | 1.00 |
| 38 month | 0.2269 | −0.2851 | 0.2101 | 0.91 | 0.92 | 1.00 |
| 42 month | 0.2523 | −0.2621 | −0.0813 | 0.94 | 0.94 | 0.99 |
| 48 month | 0.2837 | −0.2415 | −0.2531 | 0.95 | 0.96 | 1.00 |
| 54 month | 0.3072 | −0.1920 | −0.3762 | 0.97 | 0.97 | 1.00 |
| 60 month | 0.3368 | −0.1819 | −0.3246 | 0.97 | 0.98 | 0.99 |
| 120 month | 0.4038 | 0.0426 | −0.1507 | 0.99 | 0.99 | 0.99 |
| Over 120 | 0.5966 | 0.7173 | 0.2394 | 0.92 | 0.93 | 1.00 |

whose sum is more than 99% of the sum of all the eigenvalues. Thus, it is enough to consider $K = 3$ factors and use the first three eigenvectors, PCAs, as proxies for the factors. Denote them as $F_1$, $F_2$, and $F_3$.

Consider now the regression of the 11 excess bond returns on the three factors:

$$R_{it} = \alpha_i + \beta_{i1} F_{1t} + \beta_{i2} F_{2t} + \beta_{i3} F_{3t} + \varepsilon_{it}$$

where $i = 1, 2, \ldots, 11$. The regression $R^2$'s of using all the factors for each of the asset are reported in the last column of Table 15.1. All but one is 99% or above, confirming the eigenvalue analysis that three factors are sufficient to explain almost all the variations of the bond returns. However, when only the first two are used, the $R^2$'s are smaller, although the minimum is still over 80%. When only the first factor is used, the $R^2$'s range from 67% on the first bond return to 99% on the 10th. Overall, the PCA factors are effective in explaining the asset returns.

The factor loadings or regression coefficients on the factors are also reported in Table 15.1. It is interesting that the loadings on the first factor are all positive. This implies that a positive realization of $F_1$ will have a positive effect on the returns of all the bonds. It is clear, however, that $F_1$ affects long-term bonds more than short-term bonds. As an approximation, $F_1$ is usually interpreted as a *level effect* or *parallel effect* that roughly shifts the returns on bonds plotted against their maturity (i.e., the yield curve).

The second factor has a different pattern from the first. A positive realization of $F_1$ will have a negative effect on short-term bonds, and a positive effect on the long-term ones. This is equivalent to an increase in the slope of the yield curve. Therefore, $F_2$ is commonly identified as a *steepness* factor.

Finally, a positive realization of $F_3$ will have a positive effect on both short- and long-term bonds, but a negative effect on the intermediate ones. Hence, $F_3$ is usually interpreted as a *curvature* factor. Litterman and Scheinkman (1991) appear among the first to apply the PCA to study bond returns, and to have identified the above three factors. Although the data we used here are different, the three factors we computed share the same properties as those identified by them.

## 15.5.3 Alternative Approaches and Extensions

The standard statistical approach for estimating the factor model is the maximum likelihood (ML) method that maximizes the ML or density function of the data. Consider the same factor model, equation (15.26) or:

$$\tilde{Y}_t = \beta \tilde{f}_t + \tilde{\varepsilon}_t$$

where

$$E(\tilde{f}_t) = 0, \quad E(\tilde{Y}_t) = 0$$

The de-meaned returns and standardized factors are usually assumed to have normal distributions. In addition, the factors are usually standardized so that $\Sigma_f = I_K$, and the residuals are assumed uncorrelated so that $\Sigma_\varepsilon$ is diagonal. Then the log likelihood function (the log density function) of the returns is:

$$\log L(\beta, \Sigma_\varepsilon) = -\frac{NT}{2}\log(2\pi) - \frac{T}{2}\log|\beta'\beta + \Sigma_\varepsilon| - \frac{1}{2}\sum_{t=1}^{T} Y_{t'}(\beta'\beta + \Sigma_\varepsilon)^{-1} Y_t \quad (15.35)$$

The ML estimator of the parameters $\beta$ and $\Sigma_\varepsilon$ are those values that maximize the log likelihood function. Since $\beta$ enters into the function in a complex nonlinear way, finding an analytical solution to the maximization problem is very difficult. Numerically, it is still difficult if one attempts to maximize $\log L(\beta, \Sigma_\varepsilon)$ directly.

There is, however, a data-augmentation technique, known as the *expectation maximization* (EM) algorithm, that can be applied.[8] Lehmann and Modest show that the EM algorithm can be used effectively to solve the maximization problem numerically. The idea of the EM algorithm is simple, but the key difficulty here is that the factors are unobserved. But conditional on the parameters and the factor model, we can learn them. Consider that given the factors $\tilde{f}_t$, the log likelihood function conditional on $f_t$ is:

$$\log L_c(\beta, \Sigma_\varepsilon) = -\frac{NT}{2}\log(2\pi) - \frac{T}{2}\log|\Sigma_\varepsilon| - \frac{1}{2}\sum_{t=1}^{T}(Y_t - \beta f_t)'\Sigma_\varepsilon^{-1}(Y_t - \beta f_t) \quad (15.36)$$

Because this is conditional on $f_t$, the factor model is the usual linear regression. In other words, integrating out $f_t$ from equation (15.36) yields the unconditional $\log L(\beta, \Sigma_\varepsilon)$. The beta estimates conditional on $f_t$ are straightforward. They are the usual OLS regression coefficients, and the estimates for $\Sigma_\varepsilon$ are the residual variances. On the other hand, conditional on the parameters, we can learn the factors by using their conditional expected values that are obtained easily from their joint distribution with the returns. Hence, we can have an iterative algorithm. Starting from an initial guess

---

[8] Lehmann and Modest (1988) were the first in finance to apply the EM algorithm to study factor models and the APT.

of the factors, we maximize the conditional likelihood function to obtain the OLS $\beta$ and $\Sigma_\varepsilon$ estimates, a procedure called the M-step. Based on these estimates, we update a new estimate of $f_t$ using their expected value, a procedure called the E-step. Using the new $f_t$, we learn new estimates of $\beta$ and $\Sigma_\varepsilon$ in the M-step. With the new estimates, we can update again the $f_t$. Iterating between the E and M steps, the limits converge to the unconditional ML estimate and the factor estimates converge to the true ones.

Alternative to the ML method, Geweke and Zhou (1996) propose a Bayesian approach, which treats all parameters as random variables.[9] It works in a way similar to the EM algorithm. Conditional on parameters, we learn the factors, and conditional on the factors, we learn the parameters. Iterating after a few thousand times, we learn the entire joint distribution of the factors and parameters, which are all we need in a factor model. The advantage of the Bayesian approach is that it can incorporate prior information and can provide exact inference. In contrast, the ML method cannot use any priors, nor can it obtain the exact standard errors of both parameters and functions of interest due to complexity of the factor model. Nardari and Scruggs (2007) extend the Bayesian approach to allow a more general model in which the covariance matrix can vary over time and the APT pricing restrictions can be imposed.

Finally, we provide two important extensions of the factor model, which are useful in practice. Note that the factors we discussed thus far assume identical and independently distributed returns and factors. These are known as *static factor models*. The first extension is to use *dynamic factor models* that allow the factors to evolve over time according to a vector autoregression:

$$\tilde{f}_t = A_1 \tilde{f}_{t-1} + A_2 \tilde{f}_{t-2} + \cdots + A_m \tilde{f}_{t-m} + \tilde{v}_t \tag{15.37}$$

where the $A$'s are the regression coefficient matrices, $m$ is order of the autoregression that determines how far past factor realizations still affect today's, and $v_t$ is the residual. In practice, many economic variables are highly persistent, and hence, it will be important to incorporate this as above.[10]

The second extension is to allow the case with a large number of factors. Consider our earlier factor model:

$$\hat{R}_t = \alpha + \beta \tilde{f}_t + \beta_g \tilde{g}_t + \tilde{\varepsilon}_t \tag{15.38}$$

where $\tilde{f}_t$ is a $K$ vector of latent factors, $\tilde{g}_t$ is an $L$ vector of observable factors. The problem now is that $L$ is large, about 100 or 200, for instance. This requires at least a few hundred time-series observations for the regression of $R_t$ on $g_t$ to be well behaved, and this can cause a problem due to the lack of long-term time-series data or due to concerns of stationarity. The idea is to break $\tilde{g}_t$ into two sets, $\tilde{g}_{1t}$ and $\tilde{g}_{2t}$, with the first having a few key variables and the second having the rest. We then consider the

---

[9] For a discussion of Bayesian methods and their applications to finance, see Rachev, Hsu, Bagasheva, and Fabozzi (2008).

[10] Amengual and Watson (2007) and references therein discuss the estimation for dynamic factor models.

modified model:

$$\tilde{R}_t = \alpha + \beta \tilde{f}_t + \beta_{g1}\tilde{g}_{1t} + \beta_{h1}\tilde{h}_t + \tilde{\varepsilon}_t \tag{15.39}$$

where $\tilde{h}(t)$ has a few variables that represent a few major driving forces that summarize the potentially hundreds of variables of $\tilde{g}_{2t}$ via another factor model:

$$\tilde{g}_{2t} = B\tilde{h}_t + \tilde{u}_t \tag{15.40}$$

where $\tilde{u}_t$ is the residual. This second factor model provides a large dimension reduction that transforms the hundreds of variables into a few, which can be estimated by the PCA. In the end, we have only a few factors in equation (15.39), making the analysis feasible based on the methods we discussed earlier. Ludvigson and Ng (2007) appear the first to apply such a model in finance. They find that the model can effectively incorporate a few hundred variables to make a significant difference in understanding stock market predictability.

# KEY POINTS

- The APT makes weaker assumptions than the CAPM.
- In contrast to the CAPM, which claims a single factor and the factor is the market, the APT does not provide any specific information about what the factors are. Moreover, the APT does not make any claims on the number of factors either.
- Like the CAPM, the APT says that only taking systematic risks are rewarded. Unsystematic risks are not rewarded because they can be diversified away.
- The APT simply assumes that if the returns are driven by the factors, and if investors know the betas for the factors, then an arbitrage portfolio, which requires no investment but yields a positive return, can be formed if the APT pricing relation is violated in the market. In equilibrium, therefore, if there are no arbitrage opportunities, deviations from the APT pricing relation should not be observed.
- In practice, factor models are widely used as a tool for estimating expected asset returns and their covariance matrix, regardless of the validity of the APT. The reason is that if investors can identify the factors that drive asset returns, they will have much better estimates of the true expected asset returns and the covariance matrix, and hence, will form a much better portfolio than otherwise possible.
- Factor model estimation depends crucially on (1) whether the factors are identified (known) or unidentified (latent) and (2) the sample size and the number of assets. Furthermore, factor models can be used not only for explaining asset returns, but also for predicting future returns.
- The simplest case of factor models is where the factors are assumed to be known or observable, so that time-series data are those factors that can be used to estimate the model.
- In practice three commonly used equity multifactor models where known factors are used: (1) Fama-French three-factor model, (2) MSCI Barra fundamental factor

model, and (3) the Burmeister-Ibbotson-Roll-Ross macroeconomic factor model. Fundamental factor models use company and industry attributes and market data as descriptors. In a macroeconomic factor model, the inputs to the model are historical stock returns and observable macroeconomic variables.

- An argument for the use of latent factors is that the observed factors may be measured with errors or have been already anticipated by investors. Without imposing their possibly incorrect prior beliefs on what the factors might be, asset managers can statistically estimate the factors based on the factor model and data.

- Two important extensions of the static factor model used in practice are (1) dynamic factor models, which allow the factors to evolve over time according to a vector autoregression and (2) allowance for a large number of factors. This second factor model provides a large dimension reduction that transforms the hundreds of variables into a few, which can be estimated by the principal components analysis.

- Principal component analysis is a statistical approach that can be applied to estimate a factor model easily and effectively.

## QUESTIONS

1. Explain whether the following statements about the arbitrage pricing theory (APT) are true or false.
   a. APT requires that the market portfolio be efficient.
   b. APT builds upon Markowitz mean-variance portfolio theory.
   c. APT assumes that there are both an uncountable number of assets and an uncountable number of systematic factors in the economy.
   d. APT assumes the absence of any arbitrage opportunities in the market.
   e. APT requires that there is a bound on the variance of idiosyncratic risks.

2. Suppose there are two risky assets in the economy whose returns are related to a single risk factor by:

$$\tilde{r}_1 = \mu_1 + \beta_1 \tilde{f}$$
$$\tilde{r}_2 = \mu_2 + \beta_2 \tilde{f}$$

   Let $r_f$ be the return on the risk-free asset.
   a. How do you eliminate the factor risk?
   b. If there is no arbitrage, and if $\beta_1 \neq \beta_2$, show that there exists a parameter $\lambda$ (factor risk premium) for the linear pricing rule:

$$\mu_j = r_f + \beta_j \lambda, \quad j = 1, 2$$

   c. Suppose that

$$\mu_2 = r_f + \beta_2 \lambda + \eta$$

   where $\eta > 0$, whereas the linear pricing rule holds for $\mu_1$. Show how an arbitrage profit can be made.

3. What is a fundamental factor model?

4. What is factor analysis and what purpose does it play in construction of factor models?

5. **a.** What is the meant by a latent factor?
   **b.** Why would you use a latent factor rather than an observed factor?

6. Consider the Fama-French (1993) three-factor model:

$$\tilde{r}_{it} - r_{ft} = \alpha_i + \beta_{im}(\tilde{R}_{mt} - r_{ft}) + \beta_{is}\tilde{SMB}_t + \beta_{ih}\tilde{HML}_t + \tilde{\varepsilon}_{it}$$

where $\tilde{R}_{mt}$, $\tilde{SMB}_t$, and $\tilde{HML}_t$ are the market, book-market, and size factors, respectively. To analyze one stock, you run the above regression on the three factors and obtain $\alpha_i = 1\%$, $\beta_{im} = 0.9$, $\beta_{is} = 0.3$, and $\beta_{ih} = 0.2$.

Assume that the market beta is the same if you get it from either the CAPM or the three-factor regression. (In practice, the values are close.)

Suppose that the risk-free interest rate is 3%, and that the market, book-market, and size premiums are 12%, 5%, and 6%, respectively.
   **a.** What is the required rate of return on the stock if you believe the CAPM to be an accurate descriptor?
   **b.** What would your answer be if you believed the three-factor model were a more nearly accurate descriptor?
   **c.** What would your answer be if you do not believe factor models are valid?

7. How can you standardize the Fama-French three-factor model given in the previous question?

8. Suppose you believe that the 500 stocks in the S&P 500 index are driven by five factors, and you have 10 years of monthly data on the returns in excess of the risk-free interest rate. Provide a detailed approach on which you can estimate the five unknown factors.

9. How do you determine the required rate of return for taking the five factor risks in the previous question?

10. In question 8, assume that you believe the S&P 500 index itself is a factor. How do you find the other four factors, and how do you determine the required rate of return in this case?

## REFERENCES

Amengual, Dante, and Mark Watson. (2007). "Consistent Estimation of the Number of Dynamic Factors in a Large N and T panel," *Journal of Business and Economic Statistics* **25**: 91–96.

Bai, Jushan. (2003). "Inferential Theory for Factor Models of Large Dimensions," *Econometrica* **71**: 135–172.

Bai, Jushan, and Serena Ng. (2002). "Determining the Number of Factors in Approximate Factor Models," *Econometrica* **70**: 191–221.

Bender, Jennifer, and Frank Nielsen. (2010). "The Fundamentals of Fundamental Factor Models," *MSCI Research Insight*, June.

Burmeister, Edwin, Richard Roll, and Stephen A. Ross. (1994). "A Practitioner's Guide to Arbitrage Pricing Theory," in *A Practitioner's Guide to Factor Models*. Charlottesville, VA: Institute of Chartered Financial Analysts.

Carhart, Mark M. (1997). "On Persistence in Mutual Fund Performance," *Journal of Finance* **52**: 57–82.

Connor, Gregory, and Robert Korajzcyk. (1986). "Performance Measurement With The Arbitrage Pricing Theory: A New Framework For Analysis," *Journal of Financial Economics* **15**: 373–394.

Fabozzi, Frank J. (2009). *Institutional Investment Management*. Hoboken, NJ: John Wiley & Sons.

Fama, Eugene F., and Kenneth R. French. (1993). "Common Risk Factors in the Returns on Stocks and Bonds," *Journal of Financial Economics* **33**: 3–56.

Geweke, John, and Guofu Zhou. (1996). "Measuring the Pricing Error of The Arbitrage Pricing Theory," *Review of Financial Studies* **9**: 557–587.

Lehmann, Bruce N., and David M. Modest. (1998). "The Empirical Foundations of The Arbitrage Pricing Theory," *Journal of Financial Economics* **21**: 213–254.

Litterman, Robert, and Jose Scheinkman. (1991). "Common Factors Affecting Bond Returns," *Journal of Fixed Income* **1**: 54–61.

Ludvigsona, Sydney C., and Serena Ng. (2007). "The Empirical Risk-Return Relation: A Factor Analysis Approach," *Journal of Financial Economics* **83**: 171–222.

Nardari, Federico, and John Scruggs. (2007). "Bayesian Analysis of Linear Factor Models With Latent Factors, Multivariate Stochastic Volatility, and APT Pricing Restrictions," *Journal of Financial and Quantitative Analysis* **42**: 857–892.

Rapach, David E., Jack K. Strauss, Jun Tu, and Guofu Zhou. (2011). "Industry Return Predictability: Is It There Out of Sample" Working paper, Washington University in St. Louis.

Rachev, Svetlozar T., John S. J. Hsu, Biliana Bagasheva, and Frank J. Fabozzi. (2008). *Bayesian Methods in Finance*. Hoboken, NJ: John Wiley & Sons.

Ross, Stephen A. (1976). "The Arbitrage Theory of Capital Asset Pricing," *Journal of Economic Theory* **13**: 341–360.

# 16

# GENERAL PRINCIPLES OF ASSET PRICING

*I*n this chapter, we discuss the general principles of asset pricing. Previously, we have discussed them only in special cases. Our focus here is to analyze asset pricing in a more comprehensive setup. Due to its generality, this chapter is inevitably abstract and challenging, but important for understanding the foundations of modern asset pricing theory. After extending the state-dependent contingent claims discussed in Chapter 10 to allow for an arbitrary number of states, we then introduce the economic notions of complete market, the Law of One Price, and arbitrage. Then, we provide the fundamental theorem of asset pricing that ties these concepts to asset pricing relations. Subsequently, we discuss stochastic discount factor models, providing the unified framework of asset pricing theories, including the Capital Asset Pricing Model (CAPM) and Arbitrage Pricing Theory (APT) as special cases. We also explain the Hansen-Jagannathan bound on the volatility of possible stochastic discount factors and apply it to analyze the equity risk premium.

## 16.1 ONE-PERIOD FINITE STATE ECONOMY

Recall from Chapter 10 that if a security has payoffs,

$$\tilde{x} = \begin{cases} \$1, & up \\ 0, & down \end{cases}$$

it means that the economy will have two states next period, up or down, and the security will have a value of $1 or 0 in the up and down states, respectively. Similarly, as a simple extension, we can think that the economy has three states next period: good, normal, and bad. Then, any security in this economy must have three possible payoffs corresponding to the three states. For example,

$$\tilde{x} = \begin{cases} \$3, & good \\ \$2, & normal \\ \$1, & bad \end{cases}$$

is a security in the three-state economy with values of $3, $2, and $1, in the respective states. For notational brevity, we sometimes use the transposed vector dropping the dollar sign $(3, 2, 1)'$ to denote the payoff of this security, where the prime $(')$ indicates transpose.

In general, we can consider an economy with an arbitrary number of *s states and N securities*. In this economy, the payoff of any security can be expressed as:

$$\tilde{x} = \begin{cases} v_1, & \text{State } 1 \\ v_2, & \text{State } 2 \\ \vdots & \vdots \\ v_s, & \text{State } s \end{cases} \tag{16.1}$$

where the $v$'s are the values of the security in the $m$ states. For example, if $s = 4$, then a security with payoff $(1.10,1.10,1.10,1.10)'$ is well-defined in the four-state economy. If the current price of this security is $1, then the security earns $0.10 or 10% ($0.1/ $1) regardless of the state. Hence, it is risk free with a rate of return equal to 10% regardless of the state of the economy.

Suppose now that there are a total of $N$ securities, $\tilde{x}_1, \ldots, \tilde{x}_N$, in an economy of $s$ states. We can summarize the payoffs next period of all the $N$ securities by using the following matrix,

$$X = \begin{pmatrix} v_{11} & \cdots & v_{1N} \\ \vdots & \ddots & \vdots \\ v_{s1} & \cdots & v_{sN} \end{pmatrix} \tag{16.2}$$

where each of the $N$ columns represents the values of the securities. It is evident that matrix $X$ summarizes all possible payoffs of all the securities, and hence, determines their future values completely.

The asset pricing question is how to determine the price for each of the securities. Mathematically, the pricing mechanism can be viewed as a mapping $\rho$ from the $j$-th security (or the $s$ vector, the possible payoffs obtained from owning the security), to a price $p$ that an investor is willing to pay today,

$$\rho(\tilde{x}_j) = p_j \tag{16.3}$$

As it turns out, simple economic principles imply many useful properties of the mapping, which will be discussed below. The properties comprise the *general principles of asset pricing*.

---

## 16.2  PORTFOLIOS AND MARKET COMPLETENESS

In evaluating securities, a key principle is to evaluate them as a whole, and not in isolation. To do so, consider a portfolio of the $N$ securities,

$$\tilde{x}_p = \varphi_1 \tilde{x}_1 + \varphi_2 \tilde{x}_2 + \cdots + \varphi_N \tilde{x}_N \tag{16.4}$$

where the $\varphi$'s are portfolio weights that represent the units of the securities we purchase in the portfolio, and $\tilde{x}_p$ is the vector of payoffs to the portfolio, a vector that simply adds up the individual values. Note that the weights can be either positive or negative. A negative weight on a security is a *short* position. If no short sales are allowed, the weights are restricted to be positive.

Note that previously the portfolio weights were the percentages of money we invest in the securities, where prices were given and we were interested in the return on a portfolio. In contrast, we focus here on the weights in terms of units because we are interested in determining securities prices. However, once the prices are obtained, the weights in terms of either units or percentages are easily related as shown below. To see this, if we express a portfolio in term of returns, rather than payoffs as above, then the portfolio return is:

$$R_p = w_1 R_1 + w_2 R_2 + \cdots + w_N R_N \tag{16.5}$$

where

$$R_j = \frac{\tilde{x}_j}{p_j}$$

is the gross return on security $j$; that is, one plus the usual percentage return. Equation (16.5) holds for the usual percentage return as well as discussed in Chapter 13. The relation between the $\varphi$'s and the w's is:

$$w_j = \frac{\varphi_j p_j}{\varphi_1 p_1 + \cdots + \varphi_N p_N} \tag{16.6}$$

where the numerator is the amount of money we spent on security $j$, and the denominator is the total amount of money invested in the securities. Hence, the w's are the percentage weights as before.

Consider the following two securities in a two-state economy,

$$\tilde{x}_1 = \begin{cases} 1, & up \\ 0, & down \end{cases}, \qquad \tilde{x}_2 = \begin{cases} 0, & up \\ 1, & down \end{cases}$$

Suppose their prices today are $1. Then, with an investment of $1 that buys 0.5 units of each security, one obtains a portfolio:

$$\tilde{x} = \varphi_1 \tilde{x}_1 + \varphi_2 \tilde{x}_2 = 0.5 \tilde{x}_1 + 0.5 \tilde{x}_2$$

with payoff:

$$\tilde{x} = \begin{cases} 0.5, & up \\ 0.5, & down \end{cases}$$

With an initial amount of $1, one can also buy 2 units of the first security, and short one unit of the second security, in which case the resulting portfolio is:

$$\tilde{x} = 2\tilde{x}_1 + (-1)\tilde{x}_2$$

with payoff:

$$\tilde{x} = \begin{cases} 2, & up \\ -1, & down \end{cases}$$

Note that the payoff of the portfolio is negative, −$1, in the down state. This means that when the economy is down, one has to buy back the second security at a price of $1 (its value in the down state) to cover the short position. In contrast to the portfolio where equal dollar amounts were invested in both securities, this portfolio with short sales permitted has a higher payoff of $2 in the up state, which compensates for the loss in the down state.

### 16.2.1 Redundant Assets

A portfolio is uniquely determined by its portfolio weights as summarized by the $N$-vector:

$$\varphi = (\varphi_1, \varphi_2, \ldots, \varphi_N)'$$

The portfolio's payoffs are uniquely determined by the $s$-vector,

$$\text{Payoff} = X\varphi \tag{16.7}$$

For example, one can easily verify that this is true in our first illustration in which $X$ is simply equal to the identity matrix.

A portfolio $\varphi$ is said to be *replicable* if we can find another portfolio with different weights, $\omega$, such that their payoffs are equal,

$$X\omega = X\varphi, \quad \omega \neq \varphi \tag{16.8}$$

In particular, if one of the $x$'s can be replicated by a portfolio of others, it is called a *redundant asset* or *redundant security*. In an economy, redundant securities can be eliminated without affecting the properties of all the possible portfolios of the remaining assets. Sometimes, in order to distinguish the securities, the $x$'s that define the economy and all its possible portfolios, we will refer to the $x$'s as *primitive securities* because all other portfolios are composed of them.

Consider the following two state economy,

$$\tilde{x}_1 = \begin{cases} 1, & up \\ 0, & down \end{cases}, \quad \tilde{x}_2 = \begin{cases} 2, & up \\ 0, & down \end{cases}$$

with prices for both securities being \$1 today. The portfolio with weight vector $\varphi = (0.5, 0.5)'$ is:

$$\tilde{x} = 0.5\tilde{x}_1 + 0.5\tilde{x}_2$$

This portfolio is replicable because it is also equal to:

$$\tilde{x} = 1.5\tilde{x}_1$$

The primitive asset $x_2$ is redundant here because its payoff is simply double the payoff of the first asset.

## 16.2.2 Complete Market

In an economy with $N$ risky securities and $s$ states, a security market is formed if arbitrary buying and short sales are allowed, creating the possibility of infinitely many portfolios. We say the market is *complete* and is hence referred to as a *complete market*, if for any possible payoff, there is a portfolio of the primitive securities to replicate it. That is, for any desired payoff $\tilde{x}$, we can find portfolio weights such that:

$$\varphi_1\tilde{x}_1 + \varphi_2\tilde{x}_2 + \cdots + \varphi_N\tilde{x}_N = \tilde{x} \tag{16.9}$$

A complete market not only allows investors to obtain any desired payoff in any state (with a price), but also permits unique security pricing, as will be clear later.

For example, the two securities in our first example will form a complete market. This is because for any possible payoff:

$$\tilde{x} = \begin{cases} a, & up \\ b, & down \end{cases}$$

the portfolio:

$$a\tilde{x}_1 + b\tilde{x}_2$$

yields the payoff. To see why, if one investor wants to get a \$2 payoff in the up state and \$3 in the down state, buying 2 units of the first security and 3 units of the second security will provide exactly what is desired. However, the two securities in our second example above form an incomplete market. This is because for any possible portfolio consisting of the two securities, it will be impossible to create a payoff of \$1 in the down state.

In terms of matrix and vector notation, a complete market requires that, for any payoff vector, we can find portfolio weights $\varphi$ to solve the linear equation with $\varphi$ as the unknown variable,

$$X\varphi = y \tag{16.10}$$

Note that $X$ is an $s$ by $N$ matrix and $y$ is an $s$-vector. Recall from linear algebra that the number of independent columns of $X$ is called the *rank* of the matrix $X$, denoted as rank$(X)$ below. If rank$(X) = s$, the linear combinations of these columns will generate all possible $s$-vectors. That is, since a portfolio of those securities whose payoffs are those independent columns is capable of producing any possible payoffs, the market must be complete. Conversely, if the above linear equation has a solution for any $y$, it must do so for $s$ independent $y$'s, say, the $s$ columns of the $s$-dimensional identity matrix, which is an $s$ by $s$ matrix with diagonal elements 1 and 0 elsewhere. For example, if $s = 2$, the $y$'s corresponds to the payoffs of the two securities in our first example. This means that linear combinations of the columns of $X$ are capable of yielding $s$ independent columns. So, the number of independent columns must be greater than or equal to $s$. Since $X$ is an $s$ by $N$ matrix, its number of independent columns, rank$(X)$, cannot be greater than $s$. Then the only possibility is equal to $s$. We can summarize our discussion in the following proposition:

> *Market Completeness Proposition*: The market is complete if and only if the rank of the $s$ by $N$ payoff matrix $X$ is $s$, that is,

$$\text{rank}(X) = s \tag{16.9}$$

Consequently, for $s$ possible states, we should have at least $N \geq s$ primitive assets for the market to be complete. One can verify that the rank condition holds for the two securities in our first example, but not in our second example.

## 16.3 THE LAW OF ONE PRICE AND LINEAR PRICING

In this section, we discuss first the Law of One Price and its relation to the linear pricing rule. We then introduce the concept of state prices and relate it to the Law of One Price.

### 16.3.1 Linear Pricing

The *Law of One Price* (LOP) says that two assets with identical payoffs must have the same price. In international trade, in the absence of tariffs and transportation costs, an apple sold in New York City must have the same price as an apple sold in London after converting the money into the same currency. This provides an economic channel through which to tie the currencies together. In the financial markets, the LOP says that one should not be able profit from buying the same security at a higher price and selling it at a lower price.

Mathematically, under LOP, if two portfolios have the same payoffs,

$$X\varphi = X\omega \tag{16.12}$$

then their prices today must be the same:

$$\rho(X\varphi) = \rho(X\omega) \tag{16.13}$$

where, as we recall from the Section 16.1, $\rho$ is the mapping that maps the payoff of an asset or of a portfolio into its price.

A simple necessary and sufficient condition for the LOP to hold is that every portfolio with zero payoff must have a price of zero. To see that the condition is necessary, suppose that there is an asset with zero payoff that sells at a nonzero price, say, $0.01. We can combine this asset with any other asset to form a new asset without changing the payoff, but the price of this new asset is $0.01 higher than before packaging the two assets. The LOP says that the old one and the new one must have the same price, which is, of course, a contradiction. To see that the condition is sufficient, suppose two portfolios with an identical price were to be sold at different prices, say $2.01 and $2. Then buying the one with the price of $2.01, and shorting the one with a price of $2 creates an asset with zero payoff, but a price of $0.01. This is not possible from the zero price condition.

The LOP essentially prevents an asset from having multiple prices, which gives rise to its name. Only when it is true, is it possible for there to be rational pricing with a unique price. The most important theoretical implication is that the price mapping $\rho$ must be linear,

$$\rho[X(a\varphi + b\omega)] = a\rho(X\varphi) + b\rho(X\omega) \tag{16.14}$$

That is, the price of a portfolio must be equal to a portfolio of the component prices. Intuitively, the price of two burgers must be two times the price of one, and the price of a burger and a coke must be the same as the sum of the two individual prices. The linear pricing rule is fundamental in finance. It implies that if the share price of a company is the price of its future cash flows, then no matter how one slices the cash flows, the price will remain unchanged and is equal to the values of the slices added together.

The linear pricing rule clearly implies the LOP. The price mapping is uniquely determined by the payoffs only, and so it must be the case that the prices are identical if the payoffs are. Conversely, if the LOP is true, paying the price of the left-hand side of equation (16.14) will result in a portfolio with identical the payoff of the right-hand side, and hence, their prices must be the same. A formal statement of this is as follows:

*Linear Pricing Rule*: The Law of One Price is valid if and only if the linear pricing rule holds.

## 16.3.2 State Price

In asset pricing, the concept of a state price is fundamental. In our hypothetical economy there are $s$ states. The *state price* in state $i$ is the price today investors are willing to pay to obtain one unit of payoff in that state, and nothing in other states. The state price is also known as the *Arrow-Debreu price*, named in honor of the concept's originators. A *state price vector* will then be an $s$-vector of all the prices in all the states. If there exists a state price vector $q = (q_1, q_2, \ldots, q_s)'$, then we can write the asset price for each primitive security as:

$$p_j = q_1 v_{1j} + q_2 v_{2j} + \cdots + q_s v_{sj} \tag{16.15}$$

In words, this equation says that the price of the $j$-th security is equal to its payoffs in each of the states times the price per unit value in that state.

The state price is useful both for linking the payoffs of the primitive securities to their prices, and for pricing other assets, including stocks, bonds, other contingent claims, and derivatives in the economy. All we need to do is to identify the payoffs of these assets and then sum the products of the payoffs with their state prices to obtain asset prices.

The question is whether the state price vector always exists. We rewrite the state pricing relation (16.15) in matrix form as:

$$p = X'q \tag{16.16}$$

The existence of the state price vector $q$ is the existence of solution $q$ to the linear equation given by equation (16.16). In our state's economy here, we can show that the LOP is necessary and sufficient for the existence of the state price (in more complex economies, say those with an infinite number of assets and an infinite number of states, some auxiliary condition may be needed):

> *Existence of State Price Condition*: The Law of One Price is valid if and only if the state price vector exists.

The proof of the above follows from linear algebra. If the state price vector exits, then:

$$p'\varphi = qX\varphi = qX\omega = p'\omega$$

which says that the price of the portfolio with weights $\varphi$ is the same as the price of another portfolio as long as their payoffs are identical. Conversely, if the LOP is true, then for any portfolio weights $w$ with zero payoff or satisfying $X'\varphi = 0$, we must have zero price or $p'\varphi = 0$. This means that $p$ is orthogonal to every vector that is orthogonal to $X$.[1] Now projecting $p$ on the entire $N$-dimensional space, $p$ must then be a linear combination of the columns of $X$. The combination of coefficients is exactly equal to $q$, which is what we are looking for. The proof is therefore complete.

As an example, consider the following two securities in a two-state economy,

$$\tilde{x}_1 = \begin{cases} 1, & up \\ 0, & down \end{cases}, \qquad \tilde{x}_2 = \begin{cases} 2, & up \\ 0, & down \end{cases}$$

where the first security has a price of \$1, and the second of \$2. Clearly the prices are consistent with the LOP. In this case, a state price of $(1,0)'$ can price all portfolios of the two securities:

$$1 = 1 \times 1 + 0 \times 0$$

---

[1] See web-Appendix O for a definition of orthogonal.

and

$$2 = 1 \times 2 + 0 \times 0$$

Another state price $(1,2)'$ can also do the same. A more subtle case is in an economy where:

$$\tilde{x}_1 = \begin{cases} 1, & up \\ 1, & down \end{cases}, \qquad \tilde{x}_2 = \begin{cases} 2, & up \\ 2, & down \end{cases}$$

with the same prices of \$1 and \$2. Then $(0.5,0.5)'$ and $(0.2,0.8)'$ both, among others, price the two primitive securities and all their portfolios correctly.

Under what conditions will the state price be unique? To find the conditions, recall the matrix form of the state pricing relation:

$$p = X'q$$

The LOP is equivalent to the existence of the state price vector $q$. If in addition the market is complete, then $q$ in the above equation can be uniquely solved as:

$$q = (XX')^{-1}Xp \tag{16.17}$$

Note that $X$ is $s$ by $N$, so its inverse is undefined unless $s = N$. But the inverse of the $s$ by $s$ matrix, $XX'$, is well defined. Equation (16.17) leads to our next proposition.

*Uniqueness of State Price Proposition*: If the Law of One Price holds, and if the market is complete, the state price must exist and be unique.

For example, consider the following two securities in a two-state economy,

$$\tilde{x}_1 = \begin{cases} 1, & up \\ 2, & down \end{cases}, \qquad \tilde{x}_2 = \begin{cases} 3, & up \\ 4, & down \end{cases}$$

where the first security has a price of \$4, and the second of \$10. We can check that both the rank and LOP conditions are true. The unique state price vector is then given by equation (16.17),

$$\begin{bmatrix} q_1 \\ q_2 \end{bmatrix} = \begin{pmatrix} 5 & -3.5 \\ -3.5 & 2.5 \end{pmatrix} \begin{pmatrix} 1 & 3 \\ 2 & 4 \end{pmatrix} \begin{bmatrix} 4 \\ 10 \end{bmatrix} = \begin{bmatrix} 2 \\ 1 \end{bmatrix}$$

It can be verified that these prices indeed work for pricing the two primitive securities.

## 16.4  ARBITRAGE AND POSITIVE STATE PRICING

Asset pricing theories rely on assuming the absence of arbitrage. When there are free lunches, or what economists refer to as *arbitrage opportunities*, asset prices are not well related to each other, and in these circumstances investors are likely to be able to correct the prices by exploiting the arbitrage opportunities. Eventually these opportunities will disappear, and the prices will reflect the equilibrium values with which asset pricing theory is concerned.

In our states economy, the concept of arbitrage can be formally defined. Indeed, there are two types of arbitrage. The first type exists if there is a portfolio strategy that requires no investment today (i.e., what we referred to earlier as zero-investment strategy) and yet yields nonnegative payoffs in the future, and positive (or not identical to zero) at least in one of the states. Mathematically, this type of arbitrage can be expressed as:

$$X\varphi \geq 0, X\varphi \neq 0$$

with

$$p_1\varphi_1 + p_2\varphi_2 + \cdots + p_N\varphi_N \leq 0$$

The second type of arbitrage is one by which a portfolio strategy earns money today, and yet has no future obligations. We can express this mathematically as follows:

$$X\varphi \geq 0$$

with

$$p_1\varphi_1 + p_2\varphi_2 + \cdots + p_N\varphi_N < 0$$

Consider as an example the following two securities in a two-state economy,

$$\tilde{x}_1 = \begin{cases} 1, & up \\ 2, & down \end{cases}, \quad \tilde{x}_2 = \begin{cases} 2, & up \\ 4.1, & down \end{cases}$$

with prices \$1 and \$2. If we follow a strategy that involves shorting two units of the first security, and buying one unit of the second security, then our net investment will be zero, but the payoffs will be:

$$-2 \times \tilde{x}_1 + 1 \times \tilde{x}_2 = \begin{bmatrix} 0 \\ 0.1 \end{bmatrix}$$

This is an arbitrage of the first type. However, there is no arbitrage of the second type. This is because for any weights $\varphi_1$ and $\varphi_2$, if the cost is negative, that is,

$$\varphi_1 + 2\varphi_2 < 0$$

then the payoff in the up state of the portfolio,

$$\varphi_1 + 2\varphi_2$$

will be negative too.

To illustrate arbitrage of the second type, consider the following two securities in a two-state economy,

$$\tilde{x}_1 = \begin{cases} 1, & up \\ -1, & down \end{cases}, \qquad \tilde{x}_2 = \begin{cases} 2, & up \\ -2, & down \end{cases}$$

with prices $1 and $1.9. If we short two units of the first security, and buy one unit of the second security, then our net investment will be:

$$(-2) \times 1 + 1 \times 1.9 = -0.1$$

but the payoffs will be:

$$-2 \times \tilde{x}_1 + 1 \times \tilde{x}_2 = \begin{bmatrix} 0 \\ 0 \end{bmatrix}$$

This example showing arbitrage of the second type does not display arbitrage of the first type. This is because for any weights $\varphi_1$ and $\varphi_2$, the arbitrage requires the portfolio payoffs be nonnegative,

$$\varphi_1 + 2\varphi_2 \geq 0$$

and

$$-\varphi_1 - 2\varphi_2 \geq 0$$

in the two states, respectively. The only nonnegative payoffs for both the states is the zero payoff in this case. So, there cannot be an arbitrage of the first type.

Note that the pricing operator maps the payoffs of an asset to its price, and it provides the state price if the payoff is $1 in that state and nothing in other states. If the state price in one state is zero, there will clearly be an arbitrage opportunity as an investor can get future payoffs in this state while paying a zero price today. To rule out arbitrage opportunities in the economy, it is hence necessary to require the state prices be positive. When the pricing operator is both linear and implies all positive state prices, we call it a positive linear pricing rule. As shown below, the existence of such a positive linear pricing rule is equivalent to the absence of arbitrage opportunities in the economy.

Arbitrage is also related to the LOP. If there is no arbitrage, the LOP must hold. If two portfolios with two identical payoffs were sold at different prices, a "buy low and sell high" strategy would lead to the construction of a portfolio with zero payoffs in the future, but with positive proceeds today—an arbitrage of the first type. Thus, the no-arbitrage condition implies the LOP. Indeed, the assumption of no arbitrage is crucial, as explained next by the fundamental theorem of asset pricing.

# 16.5 THE FUNDAMENTAL THEOREM OF ASSET PRICING

Consider now an investor's utility maximization problem. Assume the investor prefers more to less, so that the utility function is monotonically increasing in consumption. Given an initial wealth $W_0$, and given trading opportunities, the investor's future consumption, as a vector in the $s$ states, will be:

$$C_1 = W_1 + (W_0 - C_0) \times R_p$$

where

$C_0$ = consumption (measured in dollars) today

$R_p$ = return on a portfolio of assets that can be optimally chosen by the investor maximizing his utility

$W_1$ = the investor's income from other sources next period, such as labor income

The utility function $u(C_0, C_1)$ is assumed to be a monotonic function of both $C_0$ and $C_1$.

Then the following theorem ties altogether the no arbitrage, positive linear pricing rule, and the utility maximization problem.

*The Fundamental Theorem of Asset Pricing:* States that the following are equivalent:

1. absence of arbitrage
2. existence of a positive linear pricing rule
3. existence of an investor with monotonic preference whose utility is maximized

We provide a simplified proof here.[2]

To see that the absence of arbitrage implies existence of a positive linear pricing rule, note first that Section 16.4 provides for the existence such a pricing rule. The state prices must be positive in the absence of arbitrage. This is because, if there is a zero or negative state price in some state, then the payoffs in this state are free lunches, so arbitrage opportunities can arise. Conversely, if the state prices are positive, every single payoff in each state has a positive price, and there cannot be any free lunch.

Mathematically, this can also be easily demonstrated. If $\varphi$ is an arbitrage portfolio so that its price is zero or negative, then:

$$0 \geq p'\varphi = (X'q)'\varphi = q'(X\varphi)$$

---

[2] A more rigorous proof is provided in Dybvig and Ross (1987).

where the first equality is the linear pricing rule, and the second equality holds by matrix multiplication rules. Because of positive state prices, all components of $q$ are positive. If $p'\varphi$ is zero, $X\varphi$ must be all zeros, and if $p'\varphi$ is negative, $X\varphi$ must have strictly negative components. Both contradict the assumption that $\varphi$ is an arbitrage portfolio. Hence, there are no arbitrage opportunities when the state prices are positive.

To see how the existence of a positive linear pricing rule implies existence of a monotonic utility that is maximized, the consumption of the investor in each state must be finite because the investor has finite wealth, and faces a binding budget constraint (due to the positive state prices). Next, the existence of an investor with monotonic preference whose utility is maximized clearly implies the absence of arbitrage. This is because adding an arbitrage portfolio (i.e., a free lunch) to the investor's portfolio will only strictly increase his utility without affecting his budget, contradicting the fact his utility is maximized to begin with. This concludes the proof.

The fundamental theorem provides an important insight into what we need for models of asset pricing. In deriving pricing formulas, many theoretical equilibrium asset pricing models assume all investors behave rationally and have indentical information sets. (Recall from Chapter 14 that these were Assumptions 2 and 4 for the CAPM.) The theorem says that, to rationally price assets or to ensure market pricing efficiency, we do not need to assume that all investors are smart. What we need is a few smart investors or traders who can capitalize on any arbitrage opportunities. Then, the equilibrium prices should reflect no arbitrage opportunities.

## 16.5.1 The Discount Factor

The concept of the *discount factor* is related to the fundamental theorem. Indeed the discount factor is a common feature of almost all asset pricing models, as will become evident in the next section. Let $\theta_i > 0$ be the probability that state $i$ will occur. The linear pricing rule given by equation (16.15), can be rewritten as:

$$\begin{aligned} p_j &= \theta_1(q_1/\theta_1)v_{1j} + \theta_2(q_2/\theta_2)v_{2j} + \cdots + \theta_s(q_s/\theta_s)v_{sj} \\ &= E(mv_j) \end{aligned} \tag{16.18}$$

where $m$ is a random variable whose value in state $s$ is equal to:

$$m_s = \frac{q_s}{\theta_s} \tag{16.19}$$

Equation (16.18) says that the price for asset $j$ is given by the expected value of its payoff multiplied by a random variable $m$, where $m$ is common for all assets.

Suppose now that there is a risk-free asset in the economy that can earn a risk-free interest rate $r$, and that the price of this risk-free asset today is \$1 (we can scale the asset unit if necessary). Then the payoff of this risk-free asset's price in the next period will be $1 + r$ in all states. So, by equation (16.18), we have the following expected payoff for this risk-free asset:

$$1 = E[m(1+r)]$$

and therefore,

$$E[m] = \frac{1}{1+r} \tag{16.20}$$

If there were no risks in the economy, and if there were no arbitrage opportunities, it is clear that all assets should earn the same risk-free rate of return. Hence, assets should be priced by the present values of their cash flows; the prices are equal to the discounted cash flows using the discount factor $1/(1+r)$. When there is risk as is the case now, the payoffs are multiplied by the random variable $m$ whose mean is $1/(1+r)$. This is why $m$ is also known as a *stochastic discount factor* because (1) it is random and (2) it extends the risk-free discounting to the risky asset case.

Consider, for example, three securities in a three-state economy with prices $5, $5, and $6, and with the following payoff matrix,

$$X = \begin{pmatrix} \$10 & \$20 & \$30 \\ \$10 & \$10 & \$10 \\ \$10 & \$ 5 & \$ 5 \end{pmatrix}$$

In this economy, the first asset is the risk-free asset since it has a constant payoff of $10 regardless of the future state. Moreover, the risk-free rate is 100% because the asset is sold at a price of $5. The state price vector can be solved using equation (16.17) and is $q = (0.1, 0.2, 0.2)'$. Assume the probability for each state is ⅓. Then the linear pricing rule can be expressed as:

$$\$5 = p_1 = \frac{1}{3} \times (0.3 \times \$10) + \frac{1}{3} \times (0.6 \times \$10) + \frac{1}{3} \times (0.6 \times \$10)$$

$$\$5 = p_2 = \frac{1}{3} \times (0.3 \times \$20) + \frac{1}{3} \times (0.6 \times \$10) + \frac{1}{3} \times (0.6 \times \$5)$$

$$\$6 = p_3 = \frac{1}{3} \times (0.3 \times \$30) + \frac{1}{3} \times (0.6 \times \$10) + \frac{1}{3} \times (0.6 \times \$5)$$

Let $m$ be a random variable that has values 0.3, 0.6, and 0.6 in the three possible states. Then the above says that, for each asset, the price is the expected value of the discounted payoff. The mean of the discount factor is:

$$E[m] = \frac{1}{3} \times 0.3 + \frac{1}{3} \times 0.6 + \frac{1}{3} \times 0.6 = 0.5 = \frac{1}{1+100\%}$$

This verifies equation (16.20).

The state price vector, or equivalently the discount factor, is not only useful for pricing primitive assets, but also for any other assets, and portfolios consisting of them. For example, consider a call option that grants the owner of the option the right to buy one unit of the second asset at a price of $10.[3] This option will have a value in state 1 equal to $10 (the price of the second asset in state 1 reduced by the price that must be paid to acquire asset 1 as provided for by the option, $10. The payoff to the option is therefore $10, the difference $20 − $10 in state 1). In the other two states, the payoff to the option is no greater than $10. Hence, it would not be economic for the owner of the option to exercise. Then the price of this call option is:

$$\text{Price of Call} = \frac{1}{3} \times (0.3 \times \$10) + \frac{1}{3} \times \$0 + \frac{1}{3} \times \$0 = 1$$

The discount factor prices the assets by taking the expectation under the true probabilities.

## 16.5.2 Pricing Using Risk-Neutral Probabilities

One can also price the assets under a probability measure known as the *risk-neutral probabilities*. The approach is especially useful when we discuss pricing derivatives in Part V. The reason is that the risk-neutral payoffs are easy to determine, while finding the discount factor in a general case is more complex.

To see how the risk-neutral approach works here, applying the linear pricing rule given by equation (16.15) to the risk-free asset, we have:

$$1 = q_1(1+r) + q_2(1+r) + \cdots + q_s(1+r)$$

so that

$$q_1 + q_2 + \cdots + q_s = \frac{1}{1+r} = q$$

which says the sum of state prices must be equal to the present value of $1 today. Denote by $q$ the sum of the individual $q$'s. Since now all the state prices are positive, the ratio of each to $q$ can be considered a probability. Since the ratios sum to one, the probability is well defined. (As explained below, this is known as the risk-neutral probability.) However, this is not the objective probability of the states, but rather an economic magnitude that will be useful for pricing derivatives and other assets.

Suppose now, without loss of generality, that the risk-free asset is the first one. Then the pricing relation for the other assets are:

$$p_j = q_1 v_{1j} + q_2 v_{2j} + \cdots + q_s v_{sj}$$
$$= \frac{1}{1+r}\left(\frac{q_1}{q}v_{1j} + \frac{q_2}{q}v_{2j} + \cdots + \frac{q_2}{q}v_{sj}\right) \qquad (16.21)$$
$$= \frac{1}{1+r}E^Q[v_j]$$

---

[3] We will discuss derivatives such as option in much more detail in Chapters 18 and 19.

that is, the price is the present value discounted at the risk-free rate of the risk-adjusted expected payoff of the asset, where $E^Q$ denotes the expectation taken under the risk-neutral probability. In other words, for any risky asset, we compute its value in two steps. In the first step, the risk-neutral payoff is calculated. In the second step, treating this payoff as riskless, the payoff is discounted at the risk-free rate to obtain the price. Consequently, the probability we are now using is also often referred to as the *risk-neutral probability measure*.

For example, for the assets in our previous example, the sum of the state prices is:

$$0.1 + 0.2 + 0.2 = \frac{1}{1 + 100\%} = 0.5$$

Moreover, the risk-neutral probabilities are ⅕, ⅖, and ⅖. So the expected payoff of the earlier call option is:

$$E^Q(call) = \frac{1}{5} \times \$10 + \frac{2}{5} \times \$0 + \frac{1}{5} \times \$0 = \$2$$

Discounting the $2 at the risk-free rate (100% in our example), we get the price of $1 = [\$2/(1 + 1)]$. This price is, of course, the same as computed above using the discount factor to price the call option computed under the true probability.

## 16.6 DISCOUNT FACTOR MODELS

In this section, we provide the discount factor models in a more general setup by allowing the asset returns be arbitrarily distributed, not necessarily over a finite set of states as in the previous section. Then we derive a lower bound on the variance of all the possible discount factors, known as the Hansen-Jagannathan bound, and analyze its implications for some problems in finance.

### 16.6.1 Stochastic Discount Factors

Consider now a more general problem of an investor who is interested in maximizing his utility over the current and future values of consumption,

$$u(C_t, C_{t+1}) = u(C_t) + \delta E[u(C_{t+1})]$$

where the first term is the utility of consumption today, the second term is the utility of future consumption, and $\delta$ is the subjective time-discount factor of the investor that captures the investor's trade-off between current and future consumptions. Note that the second term has an expectation operation since future consumption is unknown today, and the investor can only maximize the expected utility with the expectation taking over all possible random realizations of the future consumption.

Besides the quadratic utility, another popular form of utility function is the power utility,

$$u(C_t) = \frac{C_t^{1-\gamma}}{1-\gamma}$$

where $\gamma$ is the Arrow-Pratt coefficient of absolute risk-aversion. (Compare this problem and its solution with the one presented in Section 2.1.5 in Chapter 2.) The higher the $\gamma$, the more the risk averse the investor. In practical application, a value of about 3 for $\gamma$ is sometimes said to be reasonable.

For notational brevity, we assume there is only one risky asset. Unlike earlier sections in this chapter where a finite number of states was assumed, we now assume the payoff of the risky asset can have an arbitrary probability distribution so long as the expectation is well defined. (In particular the distribution may be continuous.) The budget constraints for maximizing the utility can be written as:

$$C_t = W_t - p_t w$$
$$C_{t+1} = W_{t+1} + X_{t+1} w$$

where $W_t$ and $W_{t+1}$ are the investor's wealth from other sources, $w$ is the number of units of the risky asset the investor purchases today at time $t$, $p_t$ is the security price, and $X_{t+1}$ is the payoff.

Plugging the budget constraints into the utility function, and taking the derivative with respect to $w$, we obtain the first-order condition (FOC),

$$p_t u'(C_t) = E_t[\delta u'(C_{t+1}) X_{t+1}]$$

or

$$p_t = E_t[m X_{t+1}], \qquad m = \delta \frac{u'(C_{t+1})}{u'(C_t)} \qquad (16.22)$$

This equation says that the price today is the expected value of the discounted payoff, and $m$ is the discount factor. In the case of the power utility,

$$m = \delta \left( \frac{C_{t+1}}{C_t} \right)^{-\gamma} \qquad (16.23)$$

which is a power function of the consumptions.

What we have derived in equation (16.22) is called a *consumption-based asset pricing model*, so-named because the theory is based on the perspective of consumption. This perspective is different from the earlier no arbitrage arguments that yield equation (16.18). Yet, the pricing equations have the same form except that the discount factor now takes a new specification.[4]

---

[4] Indeed, most if not all, asset pricing models are of the discount factor form, and different theories may specify the $m$ differently.

For the particular specification of $m$ given by equation (16.22), $m$ is also known as the *marginal rate of substitution* because it is the ratio of the marginal utilities, as first pointed out in Section 2.1.5 of Chapter 2. Intuitively, when the marginal rate of substitution is high, the value of future consumption will be high, and an investor is willing to pay more for the asset if the asset's payoff is high in this case. This is why the price, as given by equation (16.22), is high.

The discount factor representations of asset prices are often expressed as returns. Let $R_t$ be the gross return on the asset where the gross return is equal to one plus the usual return (i.e., percentage return). That is, $R_t = X_{t+1}/p_t$. Then the pricing relation in equation (16.22) is equivalent to:

$$1 = E_t[mR_{t+1}] \tag{16.24}$$

If an asset price is scaled to be equal to $1, the payoff will be its return, and then the expected discounted return must be equal to $1, its price today. When there are $N$ risky assets, we can write the discount factor model as:

$$1 = E_t[mR_{j,\,t+1}] \tag{16.25}$$

where $R_{j,t+1}$ is the return on the asset $j$.

Note that the expectation in equation (16.25) is conditional on all information available at time $t$ and therefore, the pricing relation is known as the *conditional form of the discount factor model*. Taking expectation on both sides of equation (16.25), we obtain:

$$1 = E[mR_{j,\,t+1}] \tag{16.26}$$

which is known as the *unconditional form of the discount factor model*. A conditional expectation equality implies an unconditional expectation equality, but the converse is not necessarily true, and so equation (16.26) is a weaker form of the model.

## 16.6.2  Application to CAPM and APT

To see the generality of the discount factor model, consider now its relation to the CAPM and APT. As explained shortly, one can write these two asset pricing models as follows:

$$E[R_j] = \tau + \lambda_1\beta_{j1} + \cdots + \lambda_K\beta_{jK} \tag{16.27}$$

where $R_j$ is the gross return on asset $j$, $\beta_{jk}$ is its beta or risk exposure to the $k$-th factor $f_k$, $\lambda_k$ is the factor risk premium, for $k = 1, 2, \ldots, K$, and $\tau$ is a constant.

Although equation (16.27) is now written out in terms of gross returns to conform with discount factor notations, it can be reduced to have exactly the same expression in terms of returns as in the previous two chapters. For example, the CAPM specifies $K = 1$, $\tau$ as the gross risk-free rate $1 + r$, $\lambda_1 = E[R_m] - 1 - r$, and $R_m$ is the gross return on the market portfolio. In this case, $\lambda_1$ is same as the usual market return in excess of the risk-free rate since the ones in their difference will be canceled out.

We next show that if the stochastic discount factor is a linear function of the

We next show that if the stochastic discount factor is a linear function of the factors,

$$m = a + b_1 f_1 + \cdots + b_K f_K \tag{16.28}$$

we will obtain equation (16.27). Conversely, if equation (16.27) is true, the discount factor must be a linear function of the factors. Therefore, the CAPM and APT are special cases of the discount factor models.

To see why, it is sufficient to analyze the case of $K = 1$. For simplicity, we drop the subscripts so that we want to show:

$$m = a + bf \tag{16.29}$$

and

$$E[R_j] = \tau + \lambda \beta_j \tag{16.30}$$

are equivalent. The latter is often referred to as a *beta pricing model*. In the proof below, we can assume $E[f] = 0$, since we can always move the mean of $f$ into $a$. Recall the simple statistical formula that the covariance between any two random variables can be written as a sum of the expectation of their product and the product of their expectations,

$$cov(x, y) = E[xy] + E[x]E[y] \tag{16.31}$$

Using this formula and $E[f] = 0$, we have, if equation (16.29) is true,

$$\begin{aligned} 1 = E[mR_j] &= aE[R_j] + bE[fR_j] \\ &= aE[R_j] + bcov(R_j, f) - bE[R_j]E[f] \\ &= aE[R_j] + bcov(R_j, f) \end{aligned}$$

Solving for $E[R_j]$, we obtain:

$$E[R_j] = \frac{1}{a} - \frac{b}{a} cov(R_j, f) \tag{16.32}$$

Comparing this equation with equation (16.30), it follows that:

$$\tau = \frac{1}{a}, \qquad \lambda = -\frac{b}{a} \sigma^2(f) \tag{16.33}$$

where $\sigma^2(f)$ is the variance of the factor. Hence, if the discount factor model is true, it must imply the beta pricing model. Conversely, if the beta pricing model is true, we can solve $a$ and $b$ from equation (16.33) to get the discount factor model.

### 16.6.3   Hansen-Jagannathan Bound

As we discussed, an asset pricing model is a specification of the discount factor. The question is what properties all the possible discount factors $m$ must have. Hansen and Jagannathan (1991) show that the variance of the discount factors has to be bounded below. In other words, $m$ must be volatile enough with respect to the asset returns to be priced.

The discount factor relation, equation (16.26), ties the return $R_t$ of an asset to its price via the expectation of its product with $m$. It will be useful to separate $R_t$ out to understand further the relation between $m$ and $R_t$. Using again the covariance formula, equation (16.31), we have:

$$1 = cov[m, R_{t+1}] + E[m]E[R_{t+1}] \tag{16.34}$$

Suppose that a risk-free asset with gross return $R_f = 1 + r$ is available, where $r$ is the usual risk-free rate. Applying equation (16.34) to the risk-free asset, the first term will be zero, and hence:

$$E[m] = \frac{1}{1+r} \tag{16.35}$$

Note that this equation is true for all possible discount factors, and is an extension of earlier equation (16.20). In other words, for all possible stochastic discount factors, their mean must be equal to $1/(1+r)$ to price the risk-free asset.

Now we multiply equation (16.34) by $R_f$ on both sides, and obtain:

$$E[R_{t+1}] - R_f = -R_f cov[m, R_{t+1}]$$

This says that an asset's return in excess of the risk-free rate will be higher if it has a larger negative covariance with $m$. Recall the covariance is related to correlation and standard deviations by:

$$cov[x, y] = \sigma(x) \times \sigma(y) \times corr(x, y)$$

where $\sigma(\cdot)$ denotes the standard deviation function. Since the correlation is always between $-1$ and 1, we have from the earlier equation that:

$$|E[R_{t+1}] - R_f| = R_f |cov[m, R_{t+1}]| \leq R_f \times \sigma(m) \times \sigma(R_{t+1})$$

Separating terms on $m$ from those on $R_{t+1}$, we have a lower bound on the standard deviation of $m$ as denoted by $\sigma(m)$,

$$\frac{\sigma(m)}{E[m]} \geq \frac{|E[R_{t+1}] - R_f|}{\sigma(R_{t+1})} \tag{16.36}$$

The right-hand side, the ratio of the expected return on a risky asset to its standard deviation, is the Sharpe ratio that measures the extra return beyond the risk-free rate per unit of asset risk. The relationship given by equation (16.36) says that, for any discount factor that prices the assets, it must have enough variability so that its standard deviation divided by its mean must be greater than the Sharpe ratio of any risky asset in the economy.

The above lower bound on $\sigma(m)$ is known as the *Hansen-Jagannathan bound*. It is an important result since if an asset pricing model fails to pass this bound, then the proposed asset pricing model can be rejected. For example, to test the validity of either the discount factor model given by equation (16.18) for a finite state economy, or the consumption-based asset pricing given by equation (16.22), or the CAPM and the APT discussed in Chapters 14 and 15, respectively, one can test first whether it satisfies the bound given by equation (16.36). No further testing will be necessary of it fails the Hansen-Jagannathan bound. Theoretically, Kan and Zhou (2006) show that the Hansen-Jagannathan bound can be tightened substantially with the use of information regarding the state variables affecting the stochastic discount factor.

## 16.7 EQUITY RISK PREMIUM PUZZLE

Now we are ready to bring the theory to data to explain what economists refer to as the *equity risk premium puzzle*. The *equity risk premium* is defined as the return on the stock market or market portfolio in excess of the risk-free rate. It is the extra compensation investors receive by taking market risk. The sample mean of post–World War II data for the United States suggests that the equity risk premium is about 8% (per annum), while the risk or standard deviation is about 16% (per annum). This gives rise to a Sharpe ratio, the right-hand side of inequality equation (16.36), a value of about 0.5.

Consider the case when the theory is applied to a representative consumer of the economy who has a power utility function. The consumption level is then replaced by using per capita consumption. Assuming that the consumption growth rate is approximately normally distributed, then the power form of $m$ given by equation (16.23) allows a simple approximation of inequality (16.36) as follows:[5]

$$0.5 = \frac{|E[R_{t+1}] - R_f|}{\sigma(R_{t+1})} \leq \frac{\sigma(m)}{E[m]} \approx \gamma \times \sigma(c) \qquad (16.37)$$

where $\sigma(c)$ is the standard deviation of the consumption growth rate. Economists often use a risk-version parameter of about 3 for the power utility function. Since the U.S. consumption volatility is about 1% (per annum), the right-hand side of inequality equation (16.37) will only have a value of 0.05 even if we use a risk-aversion parameter of $\gamma = 5$. The result is of an order of magnitude smaller than what the theory requires on the left-hand side. To make the relationship given by equation (16.37) literally true, we need an incredibly large risk-aversion parameter of about 50!

So, if one is to take the theory seriously, it means that the U.S. equity risk premium is too high to be explained by the standard theory. That is why it is called the

---

[5] See, for example, Cochrane (2001).

equity premium puzzle, first pointed out by Mehra and Prescott (1985). The equity premium puzzle stimulated a number of economist to develop various new asset pricing models. We discuss here two of the recent most promising models that are successful in explaining the equity risk premiums: Campbell-Cochrane model and Bansal-Yaron model.

Campbell and Cochrane (1999, 2000) propose a model with the following stochastic discount factor:

$$m = \delta \left( \frac{S_{t+1}}{S_t} \frac{C_{t+1}}{C_t} \right)^{-\gamma} \tag{16.38}$$

where $S_t = (C_t - X_t)/C_t$ and $X_t$ is the habit level of consumption relative to which an investor assesses his consumption (he does not consider solely the absolute level of consumption as before). In the Campbell-Cochrane model, $X_t$ is determined by aggregate consumption history and evolves slowly. The idea is that investors now want their consumption level to be more stable relative to the market aggregate. This introduces friction to the change of their consumptions and lowers their utility more when asset prices drop. As a result, while they still have the same power utility, they will demand higher expected return than before, leading to the resolution of the risk premium puzzle.

Bansal and Yaron (2004) provide another model that resolves the risk premium puzzle. There are two key features of the Bansal-Yaron model. First, the power utility function is replaced by Epstein-Zin recursive utility function,

$$u_t = \left[ (1-\delta)C_t^{(1-\gamma)/\theta} + \delta(E_t u_{t+1}^{(1-\gamma)})^{1/\theta} \right]^{\theta[(1-\gamma)]} \tag{16.39}$$

where $\gamma$ is the risk-aversion parameter as before, and $\delta = (1-\gamma)/(1-1/\psi)$ with $\psi$ as the elasticity of intertemporal substitution. The utility function is recursive because future expected utility enters the second term.[6] Second, Bansal and Yaron introduce a long-run risk component $X_t$, which affects both consumption and dividend growth, $\log(C_{t+1}/C_t)$ and $\log(D_{t+1}/D_t)$ via regressions,

$$\begin{aligned} \log(C_{t+1}/C_t) &= \mu_c + X_t + \sigma_t \eta_{t+1} \\ \log(D_{t+1}/D_t) &= \mu_d + \varphi X_t + \varphi_d \sigma_t u_{t+1} \end{aligned} \tag{16.40}$$

where $X_{t+1} = \alpha X_t + \varphi_x \sigma_t e_{t+1}$ follows an autoregression time-varying, so does the variance process $\sigma_t$; $\eta_{t+1}, u_{t+1}$, and $e_{t+1}$ are independent shocks drawn from the standard normal distribution.

---

[6] However, in the special case of $\gamma = 1/\psi$, the utility function is mathematically equivalent to the power utility function. The restriction $\gamma = 1/\psi$ of the power utility has the unattractive feature that it cannot separate the concept of risk aversion (desire to smooth consumption across states of nature) from that of elasticity of intertemporal substitution (desire to smooth consumption over time). In the recursive utility, the two effects are captured by $\gamma$ and $\psi$ separately.

The intuition behind the Bansal-Yaron model is that $X_t$ captures the long-run growth prospects of the economy. Shocks in both long-run $X_t$ and short-run $\eta_{t+1}$ drive the consumption growth and asset prices. The fear for adverse long-run growth requires a high-risk premium to compensate. Along with the long- and short-run shocks in dividend growth, asset prices can be very volatile. As a result, the Bansal-Yaron model can successfully explain the equity risk premium and related puzzles. This model has recently received a lot of attention in the finance literature. Zhou and Zhu (2009) extend this model further by allowing long-run and short-run variances/volatilities, in order to explain additional stylized facts about the equity market such as the predictability of stock returns by consumption and dividends, and negative risk premium of market volatility.

---

# KEY POINTS

- A complete market is one in which any desired future payoff can be generated by a suitable portfolio of the existing assets in the economy.
- In a world where the number of states (future scenarios) is finite, a market is complete if and only if this number is equal to the rank of the asset payoff matrix. In particular, it is necessary for the number of assets be greater than the number of states.
- The Law of One Price states that any two assets with identical payoffs in the future must have the same price today.
- A linear pricing rule means that the price of a basket of assets is equal to the sum of the prices of those assets in the basket. The Law of One Price is true if and only if the linear pricing rule is true.
- The state price is the price one has to pay today to obtain a one dollar payoff in a particular future state and nothing in other states. The existence of the state price is equivalent to the validity of the Law of One Price. It will be unique if the market is complete.
- There are two types of arbitrage opportunities. The first is paying nothing today and obtaining something in the future, and the second is obtaining something today and incurring no future obligations.
- The Fundamental Theorem of Asset Pricing asserts the equivalence of three key issues in finance: (1) absence of arbitrage; (2) existence of a positive linear pricing rule; and (3) existence of an investor who prefers more to less and who has maximized his utility (no more free lunches to pick up from the economy).
- Due to risk, a rational investor will not pay a price equal to the expected value of an asset, and will instead discount it by a suitable factor for the risk. A stochastic discount factor is a random variable such that the expected value of its product with the asset payoffs is the rational price of the asset. The stochastic discount extends the risk-free discounting (time value of money) to the risky asset case, and is the same for pricing all the assets in the economy.
- The CAPM and APT are special cases of stochastic discount factor models in which the discount factor is a linear function of the market factor or APT factors.

Moreover, almost all asset models can be formulated as stochastic discount factor models.

- The Hansen-Jagannathan bound provides a simple lower bound on the variance of a stochastic discount factor, so that one can examine whether the stochastic discount factor satisfies some basic restrictions of the data. If not, we can reject it without further analysis.

- The equity risk premium puzzle in the United States refers to the fact that the equity risk premium, about 8% (per annum), is too high to be explained by asset pricing models developed prior to the 1990s. However, recent models can explain this puzzle.

## QUESTIONS

1. What is meant by a redundant asset?

2. Arbitrage opportunities include only situations where an investor can realize something of economic value today at no cost and incur no future obligations. Explain whether you agree or disagree.

3. Consider an economy with two stocks. Stock A has a price of $50 today, and will be either $60 or $40 next year, and stock B, with a price of $40, will be either $52 or $28 next year.

   a. In terms of the finite state economy in Section 16.1, what are the number of assets and states, and what is the payoff matrix?

   b. With $100 to invest, how do you purchase the equal-weighted portfolio?

   c. Suppose that there is an 80% chance for the first state (up state) to obtain. What is the expected return and risk of the equal-weighted portfolio?

   d. Suppose there is in addition a risk-free asset that pays you $105 for sure for a $100 investment. How does that alter your answer to part a?

   e. Suppose that there is a new stock available that will pay you $250 or $150 next year. Is this stock redundant and if so, why?

   f. If the new stock in part d has a price of $201 today, is there an arbitrage opportunity and if so why?

4. Assume a finite state economy with three assets whose payoff matrix is given by

$$X = \begin{bmatrix} \$30 & \$20 & \$10 \\ \$20 & \$15 & \$ 0 \end{bmatrix}$$

   a. What are the payoffs of the third asset?
   b. Is the third asset redundant and why?
   c. Is the second asset redundant and why?
   d. Is the market complete?

e. Suppose the prices of the three assets are $25, $17, and $8. Does the Law of One Price hold in this market?

f. What should be the price of a new asset that provides payoffs of $20 or nothing in the two states?

5. In a finite state economy with three assets, assume that the payoff matrix is given by

$$X = \begin{bmatrix} \$30 & \$20 & \$50 \\ \$20 & \$15 & \$30 \end{bmatrix}$$

a. Suppose that the asset prices are $28, $18, and $46, respectively. Is there an arbitrage opportunity in the market?

b. If the third asset has a payoff of $35 instead of $30, is there an arbitrage opportunity in the market?

6. Assume a finite state economy with three assets whose payoff matrix is given by

$$X = \begin{bmatrix} \$30 & \$20 & \$50 \\ \$20 & \$15 & \$35 \end{bmatrix}$$

a. Suppose that the asset prices are $28, $18, and $47, respectively. Is there an arbitrage opportunity in the market?

b. If the price of the third asset reduces to $46, is there an arbitrage opportunity in the market?

7. Assume a finite state economy with three assets whose payoff matrix is given by

$$X = \begin{bmatrix} \$110 & \$100 & \$48 \\ \$110 & \$ 50 & \$40 \\ \$110 & \$ 40 & \$36 \end{bmatrix}$$

a. Is there a risk-free asset in the market?

b. Suppose that asset prices are $100, $70, and $40. Is there an arbitrage opportunity in the market?

c. Suppose there is an asset that hedges the downside risk with $10 payoff in the third (down) state and nothing in other two states. What should the price of this asset be?

d. What are the risk-neutral probabilities?

e. Using the risk-neutral valuation approach, recalculate the asset that hedges the downside risk with a $10 payoff in the third (down) state and nothing in other two states.

8. What is the implication of the linear pricing rule regarding a firm's share price?

9. What is the significance of the Hansen-Jagannathan bound in testing asset pricing models?

**10.** As discussed in the chapter, asset prices can usually be expressed as

$$1 = E[mR_{j,\,t+1}]$$

where $m$ is the discount factor and $R_{j,t+1}$ is the return on asset $j$. Suppose that there are $N$ risky assets with expected return $\mu$ and covariance matrix $\Sigma$. Denote by $\mu_m = E[m]$ the mean, and $\sigma_m^2$ the variance of the discount factor.

  **a.** Let

$$m_0 = \mu_m + (1_N - \mu_m \mu)' \Sigma^{-1} (R_{t+1} - \mu)$$

where $1_N$, is an $N$-vector of ones. Prove that

$$1_N = E[m_0 R_{t+1}]$$

that is, $m_0$ is also a discount factor, where $R_{t+1}$ is an $N$-vector of the returns on the $N$ risky assets.

  **b.** Using the Cauchy-Schwarz inequality, show that:

$$\sigma_m^2 \geq var[m_0] = (1_N - \mu_m \mu)' \Sigma^{-1} (1_N - \mu_m \mu)$$

a general form of the Hansen-Jagannathan bound that extends equation (16.36) in the chapter. The Cauchy-Schwarz inequality is $[cov(x,y)]^2 \leq \sigma_x^2 \, \sigma_y^2$ for any random variables $x$ and $y$.

  **c.** Suppose now that $m = m(x)$ is a function of an economic variable $x$, and that $R_{t+1}$ is now jointly normally distributed with $x$. Prove that:

$$\sigma_m^2 \geq \frac{1}{\rho_{x,m_0}^2} var[m_0]$$

where $\rho_{x,m_0}$ is the correlation coefficient between $x$ and $m_0$. This is an improvement of the Hansen-Jagannathan bound in the case where $m = m(x)$.

---

### ⬢ ⬢ ⬢    REFERENCES

Bansal, Ravi, and Amir Yaron. (2004). "Risks for the Long Run: A Potential Resolution of Asset Pricing Puzzles," *Journal of Finance* **59**: 1481–1509.

Campbell, John Y., and John H. Cochrane. (1999). "By Forces of Habit: A Consumption-Based Explanation of Aggregate Stock Market Behavior," *Journal of Political Economy* **107**: 205–251.

Campbell, John Y., and John H. Cochrane. (2000). "Explaining the Poor Performance of Consumption-Based Asset Pricing Models," *Journal of Finance* **55**: 2863–2878.

Cochrane, John H. (2001). *Asset Pricing*. Princeton, NJ: Princeton University Press.

Dybvig, Philip H., and Stephen A. Ross. (1987). "Arbitrage," in J. Eatwell, M. Milgate, and P. Neuman (eds.), *The New Palgrave: A Dictionary of Economics*. London: Macmillan, 100–106.

Hansen, Lars P., and Ravi Jagannathan. (1991). "Implications of Security Market Data for Models of Dynamic Economies," *Journal of Political Economy* **99**: 225–262.

Kan, Raymond, and Guofu Zhou. (2006). "A New Variance Bound on the Stochastic Discount Factor," *Journal of Business* **79**: 941–961.

Mehra, Rajnish, and Edward C. Prescott. (1985). "The Equity Premium: A Puzzle," *Journal of Monetary Economics* **15**: 145–161.

Mehra, Rajnish, and Edward C. Prescott. (2003). "The Equity Premium in Retrospect," in George Constantinides, Milton Harris, and René M. Stulz (eds.), *Handbook of the Economics of Finance: Vol. 1B, Financial Markets and Asset Pricing* Amsterdam: Elsevier, 887–936.

Zhou, Guofu, and Yingzi Zhu. (2009). "A Long-Run Risks Model with Long- and Short-Run Volatilities: Explaining Predictability and Volatility Risk Premium," Working Paper, Washington University in St. Louis.

# 17

# Pricing Corporate Securities

*F*inanciers and investors spend much of their time establishing the values of financial instruments. For example, a financier needs to assess the value of a loan contract in order to determine the extent to which funds can profitably be advanced against it, and a trader needs an estimate of what a security might be worth before bidding to acquire it. Since risks can vary greatly across financial instruments, it is important to determine how risk and value are related. It would be even more important to have systematic ways of recognizing how uncertainty affects the valuation (or pricing) of a financial instrument, but this part of financial theory is still relatively underdeveloped, partly because the effects of uncertainty are largely unquantifiable.

In the first four chapters of Part IV of this book, we have focused on methods for valuing financial instruments under risk in markets where all opportunities for arbitrage have been taken up. This provides a point of departure for studying securities price relations in real-world financial markets. Some highly active financial markets exhibit price relations that conform closely to the results of financial theory, while other markets exhibit large and persistent deviations from theoretical predictions. Financial research is actively concerned with assessing the pricing effects of influences like informational differences, but a practical explanation of asset price relations in different markets is still far from being fully realized. Nevertheless, it is possible to present some qualitative guidelines for valuing financial instruments in practice.

Perhaps the most straightforward way of pricing a security is to compare its price to those of other similar securities when profitable trading opportunities have been eliminated. Thus, in this chapter we explain the pricing of corporate securities in the assumed absence of arbitrage opportunities. We described the different types of arbitrage in Chapter 16. The prices derived when the absence of arbitrage is assumed are referred to as *arbitrage-free prices*. Conveniently, arbitrage-free prices are related to each other by an underlying measure known as a risk-neutral probability that we also introduced in Chapter 16. In this chapter, we show how the values of securities with different risks can be calculated using risk-neutral probabilities. In particular, we demonstrate how debt and equity can be used to divide up the risks of the earnings generated by a given asset, and how the values of financial instruments are related to the value of the underlying asset generating those earnings. In addition, we show how the same risk-neutral probabilities can be used to address some of the valuation problems presented by bonds.

In the two chapters in Part V of this book, our focus shifts to the pricing of derivative instruments. We use the neoclassical paradigm to show how to value both corporate securities (in this chapter) and derivative instruments (in the next two chapters). That is, our focus is on valuation under the assumption of no arbitrage opportunities. In Chapters 20 and 21, we drop the no-arbitrage assumption and tackle market relations when there are impediments or limits to arbitrage.

## 17.1  PROFIT-SEEKING ELIMINATES ARBITRAGE OPPORTUNITIES

A financial asset's value is based on the timing and the probability distribution of the payments it promises. As discussed in the previous chapters, financial theory establishes that payments to be received in the future can be converted to their present value using appropriate discount factors. For example, the appropriate interest rate for discounting payments to be received with certainty is the risk-free interest rate.[1] In a market where agents are risk averse, the appropriate discount factors for risky payments use interest rates greater than the risk-free rate. The differences between rates are referred to as *risk premia*. In this section, we show how asset values are related to each other when there are no remaining arbitrage possibilities, and how differing risks of receiving payments are reflected in the risk premia.

To calculate asset prices under the assumption of no remaining arbitrage opportunities, the neoclassical paradigm inquires how they would be related at equilibrium. For example, suppose there are two assets with identical payment streams, streams known either with certainty or to have identical probability distributions. Since there are no differences between the two payments streams, the two assets should both have the same market value,[2] and this result must hold at equilibrium in a competitive market with no transactions costs. If it did not, profit-seekers would buy the cheaper asset and sell the dearer, thereby earning arbitrage profits. Such profit opportunities could not persist indefinitely, but neither would arbitrage-based trading end before the prices of the two assets converged. In other words, profit-oriented trading will eliminate arbitrage opportunities when there are no impediments to trading the assets in question.[3]

---

[1] The risk-free interest rate may change from period to period, as some of the illustrations presented later in this chapter demonstrate.

[2] The assumption of identical probability distributions means equality of such concepts as market risk and default risk, as will later be shown.

[3] In Chapter 16, we explained the two forms of arbitrage. Unfortunately, in practice, market professionals describe some transactions as "risk arbitrage". Although this term is used in practice, it is not used in theoretical discussions because it refers to a transaction as having some risk that is perceived by the transactor to be "small". An example of where one often hears the term *risk arbitrage* used is in transactions involving companies that are involved in a merger. One might think of risk arbitrage as something akin to being a "little pregnant".

## 17.1.1   Financial Market Efficiency and the Absence of Arbitrage Opportunities

Financial market efficiency can lead to an absence of arbitrage opportunities, but efficiency is actually a different concept because it examines value in relation to underlying information about an asset's payoffs. Since as we explained in Chapter 2 the underlying information will not necessarily be distributed evenly among all market participants, possible differences in the distribution of information are described as leading to strong, semi-strong, or weak forms of efficiency.

Asset prices in a *strong-form efficient market* fully reflect all available information, both publicly available and privately. The *efficient market hypothesis* based on strong-form efficiency states that any investment strategy based on all available information cannot outperform the market after adjusting for risk and transaction costs.[4] Because all available public information is accounted for in prevailing security prices. In particular, tools commonly employed by market participants such as fundamental security analysis and technical analysis will not lead to strategies that can outperform the efficient market.

*Fundamental security analysis* involves the analysis of a company's operations to assess its economic prospects. The analysis begins with the financial statements of the company in order to investigate the earnings, cash flow, profitability, and debt burden.[5] The analyst who focuses on fundamentals will look at the major product lines, the economic outlook for the products (including existing and potential competitors), and the industries in which the company operates. The results of this analysis will be the growth prospects of earnings. Based on these prospects, fundamental analysis attempts to determine the fair value of the stock. *Technical analysis*, in contrast, ignores company information regarding the economics of the firm. Instead, technical analysis focuses on price and/or trading volume of individual stocks, groups of stocks, and the overall market resulting from shifting supply and demand. This type of analysis is not only used for the analysis of common stock, but it is also a tool used in the trading of commodities, bonds, and futures contracts.

Stock prices in a semi-strong-form efficient market reflect all available public information, while stock prices in a weak-form efficient market reflect only the influence of past prices. Therefore, neither technical analysis nor fundamental security analysis can be expected to produce abnormal returns (i.e., returns that are in excess of what would be expected after adjusting for risk and transaction costs) in a semi-strong-form efficient market. If the market is weak-form efficient, then investors cannot earn abnormal returns by trading on the information embodied in past prices, since that information is already reflected in current prices. That is, technical analysis is futile. However, weak-form efficiency does not rule out the possibility that fundamental

---

[4] This conclusion leads to the Grossman-Stiglitz (1980) paradox: If information has no value why would anyone collect it? In theory the paradox is resolved by assumptions that mean only some information is reflected in equilibrium prices.

[5] The father of traditional fundamental analysis is Benjamin Graham, who espoused this analysis in his classic book, *Security Analysis*. There have been several editions of this book. The first edition was printed in 1934 and coauthored with Sidney Cottle. A more readily available edition is a coauthored version with David Dodd (Graham, Dodd, and Cottle, 1962). The writings and teachings of Graham had a powerful impact on Warren Buffet.

security analysis can be used to identify undervalued and overvalued stocks that can lead to abnormal returns. Therefore, profits can be earned by keen investors looking for profitable companies by researching the financial statements.

Although practitioners and academicians subscribe to a wide range of viewpoints as to how market efficiency varies across markets for different types of assets, a considerable body of empirical evidence indicates that most markets are at least weak-form efficient. Additionally, the more liquid the market, the more active the trading in it, and the more homogenous the instruments traded, the stronger the form of market efficiency that is likely to prevail.

## 17.2  Pricing Securities Relative to Each Other

The absence of arbitrage opportunities is a necessary condition[6] for market equilibrium. If any arbitrage opportunities were to remain, trading would continue and prices would keep adjusting until the opportunities were eliminated. Consequently, at market equilibrium the prices of different financial instruments offering the same promised payments with the same probability distributions will have the same value, at least as long as any financial instrument can be exchanged for any other without payment of transaction costs. As will be shown shortly, this observation has important implications: The absence of arbitrage opportunities makes it possible to calculate the value of any security from any other, as long as the relations between the security's promised payments can be described exactly. To illustrate the usefulness of these results, we first consider some simple examples, and then demonstrate how financial theory can be used, still in the absence of arbitrage opportunities, to calculate prices for all securities.

Consider first whether there are any practical differences between five dollars in coins and a five-dollar bill. If it is only total buying power that matters, there are no practical differences between the two: the coins should exchange freely for the bill, and vice versa. On the other hand, any impediments to free exchange of the coins for the bill, or vice versa, can frustrate the principle's workings. For example, if you have $50 worth of pennies, a bank may not exchange them for a $50 bill. Rather, they are likely to impose a service charge for making the exchange. You will see the same thing in supermarket machines that accept your coins in exchange for paper currency. Usually the machine is programmed to deduct a fee for making the exchange.

As a second example, suppose one security promises to pay the amounts specified by the risky asset S whose payoffs are shown in Table 17.1. Suppose that a second security Y, also shown in Table 17.1, promises exactly twice the amounts specified by S. That is, each outcome is twice as large, but occurs with the same probabilities as for the original security. In the absence of arbitrage opportunities, the second security must then have a value that is exactly twice that of the original risky security. The payments from holding 2S are exactly the same as the payments from holding Y, regardless of which outcome is actually realized. Since the positions

---

[6] Most of the time, we shall simply assume the absence of arbitrage opportunities but do not specify whether or not an equilibrium exists.

**TABLE 17.1**
PAYOFFS OF TWO RISKY SECURITIES: S AND Y

|  | *Payoff at Time 2* | *Payoff at Time 2* | *Probability* |
|---|---|---|---|
| Good Scenario | $100 | $200 | $p$ |
| Bad Scenario | $ 95 | $190 | $1 - p$ |
| Time 1 Values | $S_1 = Y_1/2$ | $Y_1 = 2S_1$ | |

are the same, the value the security holder places on either of them is also the same. This implies that the time zero price of the security, $S_1$, must equal $Y_1/2$, where $Y_1$ is the price of Y.

It is possible to utilize the same ideas for assets that are related in more complicated ways, but in order to establish the possibility it is convenient to define some tools that will help the discussion to proceed.

## 17.3 CALCULATING RISK-NEUTRAL PROBABILITY MEASURES

The absence of arbitrage opportunities can be used to organize valuation calculations in an especially convenient way. The procedure involves the *risk-neutral probabilities* that we described in Chapter 16, and use in several examples here. As noted in Chapter 16, despite the name risk-neutral probabilities, the method actually takes risk into account because risk premia are embodied in the securities prices used to calculate the probabilities. Formally, a risk-neutral probability distribution is defined so that the expected value of an asset's payments, when discounted at the risk-free rate, equals the asset's current market value.[7] Moreover, if that current market value is determined in a risk-averse market, it incorporates a risk premium.

The calculations involve the following ideas. Begin with a security's value at the current time, here denoted as time 1, and assume a value for the risk-free interest rate between time 1 and time 2, the time at which securities' payoffs will be realized. For any given security, when viewed from the perspective of time 1, the time 2 payoffs are assumed to be describable by a probability distribution. For example, suppose a security whose time 1 value is $S_1 = \$92$, might pay off either $95 or $105 at time 1. Only one of the payoffs will actually be realized, but from the time 1 perspective no one knows which it will be. Suppose also that the risk-free interest rate between time 1 and time 2 is 5%, so that if we discount time 2 payoffs at the risk-free interest rate to find their time 1 value, we arrive at $95/1.05 for the smaller possible payoff and $105/1.05 for the larger.

---

[7] If the asset has only two possible outcomes, its time 1 value and time 2 payoff are sufficient for determining the risk-adjusted probability distribution whenever the risk-free interest rate is known. If assets have three outcomes, the values of two instruments will be needed to find the risk-adjusted probability distribution, and so on. More formal details of the approach are given in Section 17.4.

If we now assume that the price $S_1$ is a price that admits no arbitrage opportunities,[8] the risk-neutral probabilities $q$ and $1 - q$ are defined to satisfy:[9]

$$\$92 = q(\$105/1.05) + (1 - q)(\$95/1.05)$$

Solving, we find that $q = 0.16$ and $1 - q = 0.84$ satisfy the above condition. Shortly, we will show how the same risk-neutral probabilities can be used to value other securities.[10]

Formally, when there are only two possible future states of the world, finding the risk-neutral probabilities means finding a vector:

$$\mathbf{q} \equiv (q, 1 - q)'$$

whose components are both positive and satisfy the value calculation:

$$S_1 = E^Q[S_1/(1 + r)|\Im_1] \tag{17.1}$$

The right-hand side of equation (17.1) means "take the expectation, under the risk-neutral probability, of the discounted value of the time 1 payoffs." The effect of the risk-free interest accumulation from time 1 to time 2 is described by $1 + r$, so that risk-free discount factor is $1/(1 + r)$. The symbol $\Im_t$ means the expectation is to be taken conditionally on the basis of what is known at time $t$, and in the present example $t = 1$. When it is not necessary to show conditional notation regarding the information set, the notation "$|\Im_t$" will be dropped for simplicity.

To see how risk-neutral probabilities are used to value securities, suppose $q$, $1 - q$, and the risk-free interest rate are all given. In the absence of arbitrage opportunities, it would be correct to use these data to calculate the value of $S_1$. The calculations look exactly like discounted expected value calculations.[11] Since $1 + r = 1.05$,

$$S_1 = [\$105q + \$95(1 - q)]/1.05$$

---

[8] The no-arbitrage condition means that all securities traded in the market have prices that do not admit opportunities. After showing how a risk-neutral probability is calculated, we will use it to price other securities, and at that point the usefulness of the no-arbitrage opportunities assumption will become clearer.

[9] If there are two possible payoffs, we say there are two possible future states of the world. In this case there are two risk-neutral probabilities, one for each state. Moreover, since there are only two states, one of them must actually be realized at time 1, and so the probabilities for the two states must add to unity.

[10] The theoretical rationale for making the calculations in this way is developed in such works as Pliska (1997). For a full discussion of the relations between no-arbitrage opportunities, the absence of dominant trading strategies, and the Law of One Price, see Pliska (1997, pp. 4–10).

[11] It is important to reiterate that risk-neutral valuation does not mean that interest rates on risky assets have no risk premium. Risk-neutral probabilities incorporate a risk adjustment whenever the market is risk averse. If the market were risk neutral, the asset's price $S_1$ would be $\$100/1.10$ rather than $\$97.90/1.10$. Moreover, the risk-neutral probabilities would then equal the underlying objective probabilities, here assumed to be $\frac{1}{2}$.

Substituting the value of $q$ into the last line:

$$S_1 = [\$105(0.16) + \$95(0.84)]/1.05 = \$92$$

Of course, the calculations must lead to the time 1 value of the asset, because the risk-neutral probabilities were defined to give that result. But the importance of risk-neutral probabilities is that once they have been obtained, they can also be used to value other related financial instruments—as long as the financial instruments' prices admit no arbitrage opportunities.

One way to see that risk-neutral probabilities can be used to value different financial instruments (other validity checks will be presented later) is to recalculate the value by which $S_1$ exceeds the $95/1.05$ (i.e., the amount a bank would lend against the financial instrument at the risk-free interest rate of 5%). If the financial instrument has a high time 2 payoff, there will be $10 (= \$105 − \$95)$ left over after the debt repayment has been made. However, if the financial instrument has a low time 2 payoff, there will be just enough to pay the bank; nothing will be left over for the asset's owners. Thus, according to the risk-neutral probability calculation, the value of the financial instrument over and above the time 1 value of the debt, $95/1.05 = \$90.48$, is:

$$[q(\$105 − \$95)/1.05] = [0.16(\$10) + (0.84)\$0]/1.05 = \$1.52$$

Finally, adding up the values of the debt and the equity gives.

$$\$90.48 + \$1.52 = \$92$$

which is exactly the total asset value, verifying the manner in which the $1.52 was obtained.

## 17.4 USING RISK-NEUTRAL PROBABILITIES FOR SECURITIES VALUATION

As shown Chapter 16, if at a given time the prices for all securities traded in a market admit no arbitrage opportunities, then the risk-neutral probabilities defined above will exist and can be used to value any risky asset. For example, suppose there are four states of the world and the values of $\mathbf{q}$ for the four states are respectively 0.15, 0.20, 0.35, and 0.30. (The values of $\mathbf{q}$ can be obtained using equation (16.17).) If the risk-free interest rate is 3%, then the time 1 value of a contingent claim on state 1 is 0.15 ($1)/1.03$. If a security offers a time 2 payoff distribution of $3, $7, $0, and $2 in the four states, then the time 1 value of that security will be:

$$[\$3(0.15) + \$7(0.20) + \$0(0.35) + \$2(0.30)]/1.03 = \$2.38$$

Note that if state 2 is realized, the value of the security at time 2 will be $7, but if state 3 is realized, the value of the security at time 2 will be zero—the example is that of a risky investment whose payoffs vary according to an underlying probability distribution.

## 17.5 DEBT VERSUS EQUITY

Financial instruments of different sorts present different kinds of risks, but under the absence of arbitrage opportunities their values can still be related to each other using risk-neutral probability calculations. For example, the payoffs to risky assets can be divided using debt and equity, and the two instruments have payoffs with different risk characteristics.

### 17.5.1 How are Risks Divided with Debt and Equity?

Let us now interpret the asset payoffs $S_2$, introduced in Section 17.3, as cash flows generated by a firm (e.g., the net earnings from its operations). Suppose that a bank lender (or purchaser of a bond issued by the firm[12]) believes the firm's realized earnings will either be $105 or $95 as before. Also, suppose the current market value of the firm's assets is $89. If the loan is to be repaid from the realized cash flow, there is a maximum amount the banker will lend on a risk-free basis. Assuming the risk-free rate of interest to be 10%, that maximal amount is $95/1.10. (If the total of the principal and interest to be repaid one year from now is exactly $95, the proceeds are valued today at $95/1.10 = $86.36.) Given the assumed distribution, by advancing no more than $95/1.10, the lender is assured of getting back $95 at time 1 whether the firm does well or badly. With such a deal the lender is assured of earning 10% without risk. A loan for more than $95/1.10 could not be always repaid in full from the firm's cash flows, because in the less favorable scenario the firm will only have a cash flow of $95. In other words, loans with a promised repayment of more than $95 are subject to default risk.

Assuming the firm does raise $95/1.10 on a risk-free basis, consider what happens one year later when the firm's cash flows are realized and the loan is due to be repaid. The promised $95 principal and interest will be paid to the lenders, and any cash flows in excess of $95 will be available as a return to the firm's shareholders. Symbolically, this division of payoffs into debt and equity can be written *Value* ≡ *Debt* + *Equity*, where *Value* represents the asset's payoffs or firm value, *Debt* the principal and interest payments to debt holders, and *Equity* the payments to shareholders. The data for the present example are shown in Table 17.2. The values are shown both at time 1 and at time 2.

The column headings of Table 17.2 indicate the available funds and the amounts paid to the two classes of security holders for the two possible values for the security. Each of the first two rows represents a scenario, the first showing the payoffs to be received if the firm does well, the second if it does badly. By summing across a row of Table 17.2, it can be seen that the combined payoffs to debt and equity exactly equal

---

[12] For simplicity both bonds and bank loans are assumed to perform the same function in this example. However, in practice bank loans differ from bond investments in that the bank typically has greater governance capability than the bond investor.

TABLE 17.2
VALUING DEBT AND EQUITY

|  | Value (Firm Value) | Debt | Equity |
|---|---|---|---|
| Time 2 High Payoffs | $105 | $95 | $10 |
| Time 2 Low Payoffs | $ 95 | $95 | $ 0 |
| Time 1 Values | $ 97.90/1.10 = $89 | $95/1.10 = $86.36 | $ 2.90/1.10 = $2.64 |

the payoffs to the firm as a whole. However, note also that the payments to the debt holders are the same whether the firm does well or badly. Thus, the debt in the current example has a risk-free payoff, but the equity does not. Instruments with different risk characteristics will command different expected rates of return, as we shall see when we apply the risk-neutral probabilities to their valuation.

## 17.5.2 Valuing Debt and Equity

The principle for determining prices in the absence of arbitrage opportunities can be used to value the debt and equity payoffs defined above. First, the fact that the row payoffs in columns *Debt* and *Equity* sum to the row payoff in column *Value* in Table 17.2 means that in the absence of arbitrage opportunities, the time 1 values in columns *Debt* and *Equity* must also sum to their time 1 values. That is, only two of the columns' time 1 values need to be known in order to determine the third—as long as the assumption of pricing in the absence of arbitrage opportunities is maintained. Continuing to assume the risk-free interest rate is 10%, the market value of a risk-free investment in the firm is $95/1.10. Assuming further that the market value of the whole firm continues to be $89, it follows from the absence of arbitrage opportunities that the value of the equity in the project must equal the difference between the value of the whole firm and the value of its debt. (This is known as the Modigliani-Miller Theorem, which we discussed in Chapter 5.) That is, the equity is worth:

$$E^Q[Value_1/(1+r)|\Im_1] - Debt_1/(1+r) = \$89 - \$95/1.10$$
$$= [\$97.90 - \$95]/1.10 = \$2.64$$

Table 17.2 verifies the following observations. The $89 at the value column is given by assumption, and the value $86.36 at the bottom of the debt column must be the value of the risk-free debt if interest rates are 10%. (The debt is risk-free because it has the same payoff whether the firm does well or badly.) It can be seen that under either the high or the low payoff scenario, the payoffs to the equity are exactly the same as the payoffs to the whole firm minus the payoffs to the debt holders. It follows that, in the absence of arbitrage opportunities, the value of the equity equals the value of the whole firm less the value of the debt.

## 17.5.3 Risky Debt

Now suppose the firm issues debt with a promised repayment of more than $95. It is clear from the total payoff distribution shown in the value column of Table 17.2 that

**TABLE 17.3**

VALUING DEBT AND EQUITY WHEN DEBT PROMISES TO PAY $99

|  | *Value* (Firm value) | *Debt* | *Equity* |
|---|---|---|---|
| Time 2 High Payoffs | $105 | $99 | $6 |
| Time 2 Low Payoffs | $ 95 | $95 | $0 |
| Time 1 Values | $ 89 | $87.42 | $1.58 |

the firm will not always be able to redeem such a promise in full. For example, suppose the firm issued debt that nominally promised to pay $99 in principal and interest at time 2. Assuming the firm has no other resources, and that there are no additional costs of default, the payoffs to the security holders would be as shown in Table 17.3.

In this case, the debt is not riskless. The amount that can be repaid is $99 if the firm does well, but is only $95 if earnings turn out badly. The value displayed for the debt, $87.42, will be calculated shortly.

Since the two possible realized outcomes are assumed to be equally likely in the present example, the expected discounted value of the time 2 payments to the debt holders is:

$$E[Debt/(1+r)|\Im_1] = (1/2)[(\$99) + (1/2)(\$95)]/1.10 = \$88.18$$

where $E$ means "take the expected value," in this case using the objective rather than the risk-neutral probabilities. In the absence of arbitrage opportunities, the time 1 value of the debt must be less than $97/1.10 = $88.18, since discounting an expected value at the risk-free interest rate is not sufficient to adjust for the debt being risky.

To put the matter another way, the firm cannot become worth more just because it has changed the amount it promises to pay debt holders. Investors look at what the firm can earn, and will value its securities in relation to those earnings, no matter what the nominal promises made by the firm are. Thus, to obtain the value of the debt, it is only necessary to value the equity and subtract that amount from the value of the firm. Given the two payoffs of $105 and $95, the risk-free interest rate of 10%, and the current market value of the firm as $89, the risk-neutral probabilities, calculated as in Section 17.3, are respectively $q = 0.29$ and $1 - q = 0.71$. Hence, the value of the equity is:

$$E^Q[Equity/(1+r)|\Im_1] = (0.29)[\$6]/1.10 = \$1.58$$

as shown in the lower right-hand corner of Table 17.3. It then follows immediately that the value of the debt must be $89.00 - $1.58 = $87.42. Continuing to suppose that the two earnings scenarios are equally probable, the expected debt repayment is:

$$E[Debt|\Im_1] = (1/2)[(\$99) + (1/2)(\$95)] = \$97$$

Therefore, the discount rate applied to the debt is:

$$(\$97 - \$87.42)/\$87.42 = 0.1096 = 10.96\%$$

Since the risk-free rate has been assumed to be 10%, the risk premium on this particular debt issue is 0.96% or 96 basis points.

---

## 17.6  APPLICATION: BOND VALUATION AND MARKET RISK

Although in practice corporate bonds are regarded as lower risk securities than equities, they are not riskless. First, and as the immediately preceding example has shown, corporate bonds can be subject to default risk, meaning that the corporate issuer may not repay the principal and interest as set forth in the debt agreement. In practice, default risk is gauged by the credit rating as assigned by commercial rating companies. Second, even if the issuer of a corporate bond has a high credit rating and default risk is very low, the return realized from investing in the bond can still vary randomly if the risk-free discount rate varies, or if the discount rate is affected by changes in price levels. These types of risk are forms of market risk, and will be examined in this chapter.

### 17.6.1  Valuation with Risk-Neutral Probabilities

Changes in interest rates can create market risk in bond values, even if the bonds have no default risk. The following example, based on Pliska (1997), shows how stochastic evolution of the risk-free interest rate can create this form of market risk. The example also indicates how risk-neutral probabilities can be used to determine bond values.[13] While the valuation procedure is not conceptually different from that of the previous section, it is now applied to random changes in interest rates rather than directly to changes in payoff as before.

Suppose there are two zero-coupon bonds[14] each promising to repay a principal amount of $1, the first at time 1 and the second at time 2. The present time is 1, and the risk-free interest rates that are assumed to prevail between time 1 and time 2 (denoted by $r_{12}$) as well as between time 2 and time 3 (denoted by $r_{23}$) are shown in Table 17.4. The time 1-2 interest rate is assumed to be known with certainty at time one, but the time 2-3 interest rate is known only probabilistically at time 1, and will not become known with certainty until time 2. The risk-neutral probabilities for the rates between times 2 and 3, assumed to have been calculated at time 1, are shown in the last column of Table 17.4.

Now consider how a zero-coupon bond issued at time 1 and maturing at time 2 will be valued. At time 2 it will be redeemed for the principal amount, $1, and at time 1 it will be worth the present value of the time 2 payment, discounted at the 6%

---

[13] For a more extended discussion of the methods involved, see Pliska (1997, Chapter 6).

[14] Using zero-coupon bonds simplifies the example. The calculations for a bond with a coupon can be set up as a valuation exercise for a zero-coupon bond representing the principal and another for a bond (or bonds) representing the coupon payment(s).

**TABLE 17.4**
INTEREST RATES AND PROBABILITIES

| $r_{12}$ | $r_{23}$ | Risk-neutral probabilities of the time 2-3 rates |
|---|---|---|
| | 0.09 | 0.3000 |
| 0.06 | 0.06 | 0.3000 |
| | 0.03 | 0.4000 |

**TABLE 17.5**
VALUES OF A ZERO-COUPON BOND MATURING AT TIME 2

| Time 1 | Time 2 |
|---|---|
| $1/1.06 = $0.9434 | $1.00 |

**TABLE 17.6**
VALUES OF A ZERO-COUPON BOND MATURING AT TIME 3

| Time 1 | Time 2 | Time 3 |
|---|---|---|
| | ($1/1.09) × 0.3000 = $0.2752 | $1 |
| | ($1/1.06) × 0.3000 = $0.2830 | $1 |
| | ($1/1.03) × 0.4000 = $0.3883 | $1 |
| Time 1 market value = $0.9465/1.06 = $0.8929 | Time 2 market value just before $r_{23}$ becomes known = $0.9465 | |

interest rate certain to prevail from time 1 to time 2. (Because the relevant interest rate is known with certainty, the 6% interest rate is treated as occurring with a risk-neutral probability of 1.) Thus, as shown in Table 17.5, the time 1 value of the one-period bond is $0.9434.

Now consider valuing a two-period bond. At time 3 it is worth the promised payment of $1, no matter what the prevailing interest rate is. If the interest rate $r_{23}$ could be known with certainty at time 2, the bond value at time 2 would then be the time 3 value discounted by the known rate. However, at time 2 (just before the realized rate $r_{23}$ becomes known), the time 2 market value is the sum of the three possible values associated with the three possible interest rate outcomes, each multiplied by its respective risk-neutral probability. The calculations are shown in the second column of Table 17.6. The time 1 value of the bond is its time 2 value discounted by 1.06, as shown on the bottom line of the first column. Note the example shows that if an investor buys a two-period bond and resells it at time 2, the bond will be subject to price risk, determined by the value of the time 2-3 interest rate that obtains when the investor sells the bond.

## 17.6.2 Bond Prices and Expected Inflation

Bonds exhibit market risk for another reason as well: Their prices can be affected by expected inflation. Whatever the underlying pattern of real interest rates (rates adjusted to allow for changes in purchasing power), nominal interest rates can be affected by changes in the expected rate of inflation. This second sort of change may or may not be predictable. For example, a sudden burst of inflation can disturb usual interest rate patterns because it can take time to be fully reflected in nominal rates. In particular, nominal rates may change sluggishly with the result that following a burst of inflation, posted real rates of interest may become negative for a time. However, once the adjustment of nominal rates is complete, real rates should and usually do revert to more customary levels.[15]

To illustrate the effect of inflation on nominal interest rates, suppose for simplicity that the real interest rate is known with certainty and remains unchanged. Suppose also that an investor buys a three-year bond and intends to hold it to maturity. The bond is assumed to pay no interest over its lifetime, and to be redeemable for the lump sum of $1,000 at the end of three years. If it were known that inflation would be zero and that the risk-free interest rate would remain unchanged at 4% over each of the next three years, the bond would sell at time 1 for $1,000/$(1.04)^3 = \$889$. An investor purchasing the bond for $889 would earn a real interest rate of 4%, compounded annually if the bond is held it to maturity.

Now suppose that even though price levels have not been expected to increase, the inflation rate actually does increase by 1% per annum, compounded annually. This means in turn that, if nominal interest rates are used for discounting purposes, they will be affected by inflation. Consequently the investor who did not anticipate the inflation and paid the purchase price of $889 would earn substantially less than a real interest rate of 4% on the investment in this bond. In terms of purchasing power, the investor will only be repaid $1,000/$(1.01)^3$ when the bond matures. Since the unanticipated inflation was not taken into account, the real interest rate realized on the investment is found by solving the following equation for $r$:

$$\$889 \, (1+r)^3 = \$1,000/(1.01)^3$$

Solving we get $r = 2.9703\%$. The real interest rate on the bond has been decreased by the unexpected change in inflation.

The preceding example shows that a bond's real interest earnings can be affected by unanticipated changes in the rate of inflation. Moreover, an investor cannot escape this risk by selling the bond as and when expectations regarding inflation are revised. For as soon as expectations are revised,[16] bond prices will change accordingly, at least in a liquid market. Suppose that in the previous example the inflation forecast changes from 0% to 1% just after our investor has purchased the bond. When the change is reflected in the market, the bond price will fall from its original:

$$\$1,000.00/(1.04)^3 = \$889$$

to

$$\$1,000/(1.01)^3(1.04)^3 = \$862.85$$

---

[15] The process may be lengthy in some economies. For example, Japan witnessed lengthy periods of negative real interest rates in the late 1990s and the 2000s.
[16] As mentioned above, revisions can sometimes be subject to lags.

that is, by 2.94% of its original capital value! And once bond prices have changed, it is too late for the investor to sell the bond without suffering the capital loss illustrated in the last calculation.

## KEY POINTS

- The value of a financial asset is based on the timing and the probability distribution of the payments it promises.
- According to financial theory, payments to be received in the future from a financial asset can be converted to their present value using appropriate discount factors.
- Asset prices are calculated under the assumption of no-arbitrage opportunities. The neoclassical paradigm inquires how they would be related at equilibrium.
- In a strong-form efficient market, asset prices fully reflect all available information, both publicly available and privately. Tools commonly employed by market participants such as fundamental security analysis (analysis of a company's operations to assess its economic prospects) and technical analysis (analysis of price and/or trading volume of individual stocks, groups of stocks, and the overall market resulting from shifting supply and demand) will not lead to strategies that can outperform the efficient market.
- The absence of arbitrage opportunities is a necessary condition for market equilibrium and therefore at market equilibrium the prices of different financial instruments offering the same promised payments with the same probability distributions will have the same value, at least as long as any financial instrument can be exchanged for any other without payment of transaction costs.
- The absence of arbitrage opportunities can be used to organize valuation calculations using risk-neutral probabilities. The calculations take risk into account because risk premia are embodied in the securities prices used to calculate the probabilities.
- If at a given time the prices for all securities traded in a market admit no arbitrage opportunities, then the risk-neutral probabilities will exist and can be used to value any risky asset.
- Any security can be regarded as a package of unit contingent claims.
- The values of financial instruments that are characterized by different kinds of risk can still be related to each other in the absence of arbitrage opportunities using risk-neutral probability calculations.
- The principle for determining prices in the absence of arbitrage opportunities can be used to value the debt and equity instruments based on their expected payoffs.

## QUESTIONS

1. What are the three types of market described in the efficient market hypothesis?

2. In risk-neutral pricing, why is it unnecessary to consider the investor's risk preference?

3. Which interest rate is closer to being risk-free: the one-month Treasury rate or LIBOR?

4. For the following table reproduced from Table 17.3 in the chapter, when calculating the time 1 value of debt, we subtract the value of equity from the value of the firm. Recalculate the debt value based on risk-neutral pricing.

VALUING DEBT AND EQUITY WHEN DEBT PROMISES TO PAY $99

|  | *Value* (Firm value) | *Debt* | *Equity* |
|---|---|---|---|
| Time 1 High Payoffs | $105 | $ 99 | $ 6 |
| Time 2 Low Payoffs | $ 95 | $ 95 | $ 0 |
| Time 1 Values | $ 89 | $ 87.42 | $ 1.58 |

5. Identify at least three factors that would affect a bond's price.

6. Suppose that the current price of a stock is $92 and the expectation is that three months from now the price will be either $95 or $105. Assume that the three-month risk-free interest rate is 2% and that an investor can borrow and lend at that rate.

   a. Assuming that there are no transaction costs, explain why there is an arbitrage opportunity.

   b. Explain how to construct a portfolio to exploit this opportunity.

7. (This question deals with options, the subject of the next chapter.) Assume that the current stock price is $30, and it is expected in one year to be worth either $28 or $35. There is a European call option with a strike price of $30 and a maturity of one year. Apply no-arbitrage arguments to calculate the price of this European call option given $\Delta$ shares of stock and M amount of cash. Assume that the one-year risk-free interest rate is constant at 10%.

8. Suppose that today a firm's value is $80 million and it is expected to be either $85 million or $90 million one year from now, depending on actual sales of new products that the firm has developed. Now a firm's mangers have decided to issue a one-year debt obligation wherein the payment to the debt holders is as follows:

   • If the firm's value one year from now is $85 million (the lower expected firm value), investors would receive $84 million.

   • If the firm's value reaches the high expectation of $90 million, it would pay creditors $88 million.

   a. Assuming that the one-year risk-free rate is 10%, calculate the risk-neutral probability for this debt obligation.

   b. Create a table to illustrate the debt and equity facing the firm in time 2 (i.e., one year from now).

9. A zero-coupon bond promising to repay the principal of $1 at time 4 is available in the market. Today (time 1), the risk-free interest rate between time 1 and time 2

(denoted by $r_{12}$) is constant at 0.02. However, the interest rates $r_{23}$ and $r_{34}$ are only known probabilistically at time 1. The interest rates and probabilities are as follows:

INTEREST RATES AND PROBABILITIES

| $r_{12}$ | $r_{23}$ | $r_{34}$ | Risk-neutral probability for each state |
|---|---|---|---|
| | 0.07 | 0.09 | 0.6000 |
| 0.02 | 0.03 | 0.06 | 0.2000 |
| | 0 | 0.04 | 0.2000 |

10. Suppose that the current inflation expectation for the next three years is 2%. There is a three-year inflation-adjusted bond that pays bondholders an interest rate equal to a fixed rate of 2% plus the rate of inflation, with coupon payments made semiannually. Suppose you purchase this bond and immediately after the purchase, a major scientific breakthrough was announced that could cut energy costs in half one year from now. In reaction, the inflation expectation for the next two years suddenly drops from 2% to 1%. What would be the bond price before and after the news is announced? Use the bond yield as the discount rate and assume that the bond par value is 100.

11. A fund manager hopes to buy a corporate bond to maximize the portfolio's return; however, the corporate issuer has a default probability of 30%, under which circumstance the investors would get nothing back. To hedge the risk, the portfolio manager buys insurance on the bond, which would pay the manager 80% of the bond's par value at maturity. What is the risk-neutral price of the insurance? Assume the risk-free rate is 10% and the bond is a one-year zero-coupon bond.

12. In his book *The Alchemy of Finance*, George Soros—a renowned hedge fund manager—proposed a theory called *reflexivity*. This theory asserts that prices influence fundamentals and that these newly influenced set of fundamentals then proceeds to change market expectations, thus influencing prices. Because the pattern is self-reinforcing, markets tend towards disequilibrium. Sooner or later the market reaches a point where the sentiment is reversed and negative expectations become self-reinforcing in a downward direction, thereby explaining the familiar pattern of boom and bust cycles. Contrast this view with the efficient market hypothesis.

# REFERENCES

Graham, Benjamin, David L. Dodd, and Sidney Cottle. (1962). *Security Analysis* (4th ed.). New York: McGraw-Hill.

Grossman, Sanford and Joseph Stiglitz. (1980). "On the Impossibility of Informationally Efficient Markets," *American Economic Review Finance* **70**: 393–408.

Pliska, Stanley R. (1997). *Introduction to Mathematical Finance: Discrete Time Model*. Malden, MA: Blackwell.

# PART V
# DERIVATIVE INSTRUMENTS

# PRICING DERIVATIVES BY ARBITRAGE: LINEAR PAYOFF DERIVATIVES

*A* *derivative instrument* is a financial instrument whose value depends on some underlying asset. The term "derivative" is used to describe this product because its value is derived from the value of the underlying asset. The *underlying asset*, simply referred to as the *underlying*, can be either a commodity, a financial instrument, or some reference entity such as an interest rate or stock index, leading to the classification of commodity derivatives and financial derivatives. *Commodity derivatives* have as their underlying traditional agricultural products and are distinguished by hard and soft commodities. *Hard commodities* are products from the energy (e.g., oil and gasoline), precious metals (e.g., gold, platinum, and silver), and industrial metals (aluminium, copper, and zinc) sectors. *Soft commodities* are typically weather-dependent, perishable commodities for consumption from the agricultural sector, such as grains, soybeans, or livestock (e.g., cattle or hogs). *Financial derivatives* are a relatively new entrant into the derivatives market in comparison to commodity derivatives. Included in the realm of financial derivatives are derivatives on individual stocks, stock indexes, interest rates, bonds, and currencies.

Although there are close conceptual relations between derivative instruments and such cash market instruments such as debt and equity, the two classes of instruments are used differently: Debt and equity are used primarily for raising funds from investors, while derivatives are primarily used for dividing up and trading risks.[1] Moreover, debt and equity are direct claims against a firm's assets, while derivative instruments are usually claims on a third party. A derivative's value depends on the value of the underlying, but the derivative instrument itself represents a claim on the "counterparty" to the trade.

Derivatives instruments are classified in terms of their payoff characteristics: linear and nonlinear payoffs. The former include forward, futures, and swap contracts while the latter include options. In this chapter and the next, we continue with the development of pricing financial instruments in the absence of arbitrage. We look at

---

[1] There are, however, exceptions. Some debt issues are accompanied by option-like instruments called warrants designed to improve the marketability of the debt. Other debt issues are convertible, meaning they have a built-in option to exchange the debt for equity.

the pricing of derivative instruments with linear payoffs in this chapter and those with nonlinear payoffs in the next chapter. We begin this chapter with an explanation of what we mean by derivative instruments with linear and nonlinear payoffs.

## 18.1 LINEAR VERSUS NONLINEAR PAYOFF DERIVATIVE INSTRUMENTS

To understand the classification of derivatives in terms of their payoffs, consider a corn farmer and a food manufacturer who are concerned about the price of corn in the future. The former is concerned that after the corn has been harvested in the future, the price of corn will decline below the current market price; the latter is concerned that when corn is needed for production in the future, the price of corn will be higher than the current market price. The risk that the farmer and food manufacturer face is price risk: The price of corn may move adversely at the time corn must be sold (in the case of the corn farmer) or purchased (in the case of the food manufacturer). Derivatives allow both parties to manage this risk. Moreover, derivative instruments provide two types of arrangements and this is what leads us to the classification of linear and nonlinear derivatives.

### 18.1.1 Linear Payoff Derivative Instruments

One way to manage risk is to enter into a contract where two parties agree to a fixed price at which to transact (i.e., buy and sell) at some future date. For example, suppose the farmer and the food manufacturer agree to exchange 10,000 bushels of corn three months from now at a fixed price of $3 per bushel. That is, the farmer agrees to sell 10,000 bushels of corn for $3 per bushel three months from now and the food manufacturer agrees to buy 10,000 bushels of corn for $3 per bushel three months from now. Thus, both parties have eliminated price risk for corn.[2]

Basically, the agreement is a *risk sharing arrangement* since both are sharing the risk that the price of corn will move adversely three months from now. Suppose corn increases to $3.50 per bushel three months from now. Although both parties have achieved their risk management objective of locking in a price of $3.00 per bushel, the food manufacturer gains in the sense that corn can be purchased for $0.50 less because the price of corn is $3.50; the farmer loses in the sense that he could have sold corn for $0.50 more per bushel than the $3.00 price specified in the agreement.

Let's consider the same risk sharing arrangement assuming two parties A and B, where A agrees to sell (deliver) corn under the terms of the contract and B agrees to buy corn under the terms of the contract. Party A is said to sell the contract or to be "short" the contract. Party A would enter this contract if he or she thought the price of corn would fall three months from now. Party B is said to buy the contract or to be "long" the contract. Party B would do so if he or she believes the price of corn will rise three months from now.

---

[2] Of course, they have not eliminated opportunity risk. If the price changes over the three months, one of the parties will be worse off (and the other better off) than if the contract had not been struck. These details are explored next.

Consider what happens for every $1 per bushel change in the price of corn three months from now. For every $1 per bushel decrease in the price of corn, Party A gains because that party can buy corn in the market for $2 per bushel and sell it under the terms of the contract to Party A for $3 per bushel, realizing a gain of $1 per bushel. More generally, the party with the short position realizes a gain when the price of the underlying decreases. Since the exchange is a zero-sum game (aside from transaction costs, here assumed to be zero), the long (Party B) realizes a loss. If instead the price of corn increases by $1 per bushel three months from now, Party B realizes a $1 per bushel gain because corn can be purchased for $3 per bushel under the terms of the contract and then sold in the market for $4 per bushel; Party A realizes a $1 loss. Thus, if the price of the underlying increases, for this type of derivative instrument the long realizes a profit and the short realizes a loss.

For this reason, this type of instrument is referred to as *linear payoff derivative* because the payoff is characterized by a $1 for $1 gain or loss. A linear payoff derivative is also referred to as a *symmetric payoff derivative*. This type of contract is the subject of this chapter and includes forwards, futures, and most swaps. Also notice that in this risk sharing arrangement, both parties are obligated to perform.

## 18.1.2 Nonlinear Derivative Payoff Instruments

Now consider another and more obvious type of contract for protecting against price risk. Suppose that the food manufacturer can find someone who is willing to insure that the firm will not have to pay more than $3 per bushel for 10,000 bushels of corn three months from now. The insurance contract would specify that for a price, called an *insurance premium*, the food manufacturer is guaranteed not to have to pay more than $3 per bushel for 10,000 bushels of corn three months from now. Let's assume that the insurance premium is $0.10 per bushel. Now suppose that the price of corn increases to $3.50 per bushel three months from now. Then the food manufacturer will require the insurer to sell the firm 10,000 bushels of corn for $3 per bushel. Effectively, the food manufacturer is setting a maximum price for corn of $3.10 per bushel, the price of $3 under the insurance contract plus the cost of the contract (the insurance premium) of $0.10 per bushel. Suppose, instead, that the price of corn three months from now falls by $0.50 per bushel to $2.50. Obviously, the food manufacturer would want to buy the corn at the prevailing market price three months from now at $2.50 per bushel. The contract with the insurer gives the food manufacturer the right but not the obligation to transact with the insurer. If the market price is $2.50 per bushel three months from now, the food manufacturer would literally tear up the contract and buy the corn in the market. Hence, the food manufacturer loses the $0.10 insurance premium but gets to buy the corn at the lower price.

Suppose instead of a food manufacturer, Party C believes that the price of corn three months from now will increase by more than $0.10. Instead of the insurance company, the counterparty in our illustration is Party D who does not believe that will happen or does not believe that the price will increase enough to offset the fee that Party D would charge Party C to enter into the contract. The fee is the equivalent of the insurance premium in our earlier illustration.

Let's look at what happens if the price of corn changes three months from now. Suppose that the price of corn rises to $3.50 per bushel. Party C can now by contract purchase from Party D corn for $3 per bushel and then sell the corn in the market for $3.50 per bushel. From the sale, Party C realizes a gain of $0.50 per bushel. However, that gain must be reduced by the fee paid to Party D ($0.10) per bushel. Thus, the gain per bushel for Party C is $0.40 per bushel. Suppose, instead, that the price of corn three months from now falls by $0.50 per bushel to $2.50. Party C is not obligated to perform. That is, Party C does not have to purchase the corn. By doing nothing, Party C realizes a loss of $0.10 per bushel (the fee paid to Party D).

Notice for Party C that the payoff from this insurance type derivative instrument is nonlinear. For example, for each $1 increase in the price per bushel of corn, the maximum loss remains unchanged at the cost of the fee but gains $1. Hence, this is a *nonlinear payoff derivative*. Equivalently, it is an *asymmetric payoff derivative*. Notice that unlike a linear payoff derivative, one party is required to perform: the party providing the insurance. Derivatives with this type of payoff are called options and the pricing of this type of derivative instrument is the subject of the next chapter.

## 18.2  FORWARD CONTRACTS

Forward contracts are one of the simplest forms of instruments used for trading an asset's future price risk. In essence, a forward contract specifies that an asset can be bought or sold at a given future date for a stipulated price. Since the asset's cash price will likely be different from the contract's stipulated price when the contract matures, the instrument serves to separate the risk of price change from the price stipulated in the contract.

### 18.2.1  What is a Forward Contract?

A forward contract is an agreement under which an investor assumes an obligation to trade a specified asset, at a given time, and for a given price. The stipulated price is called the *forward price*. Taking a *long position in a forward contract* means assuming an obligation to purchase a specified asset at the forward price to be paid on the future date specified in the contract. This date is called the *delivery date* or *settlement date*. Similarly, taking a *short position in a forward contract* means assuming an obligation to sell the specified asset, again at the forward price. The principal purpose of taking a position in a forward contract is to trade the risk of price changes between the time the contract is originated and its delivery date. The parties entering the contract may or may not own the asset when the contract is originated, and they may or may not intend to take physical possession of the asset on the delivery date.

The gross profit or loss on a forward contract, and consequently the contract's value, depends on the relation between the forward price specified by the contract and the asset's actual cash price on that date. A long position in a forward contract conveys an opportunity to profit if the asset's cash price turns out to be more than the forward price. For example, if a party to a forward contract has agreed to buy an asset for $100, and if the asset actually turns out to be worth $111 on the delivery date, the holder of the long position can turn an immediate gross profit[3] of $11 by purchasing the asset according to the terms of the forward contract, and then reselling it in the cash

---

[3] That is, a profit calculated without taking account of transactions costs.

market. By the same token, taking a long position incurs a loss if the asset's future cash price turns out to be less than the forward price. For example, if the holder of a forward contract has agreed to buy an asset for $100, and if the asset turns out to be worth only $91 on the delivery date, the holder loses $9. Since a short position is the reverse of a long position, the gross profit or loss to a party with a short position are exactly the opposite of those realized by the party with the offsetting long position.

There are two types of forward contracts: marked-to-market (MTM) and non-marked-to-market (non-MTM) forward contracts.[4] At the outset of a trade, the counterparties may be required to post initial collateral. The purpose of the collateral is reduce counterparty risk; that is, the risk of the counterparty to the contract defaulting on its obligation. Default means that either the party taking the long position fails to buy the underlying asset at the delivery date or the party taking the short position fails to make delivery of the underlying asset at the delivery date. By marked-to-market is meant that at times specified in the forward contract, the values of the counterparties' positions are recorded. The forward contract may specify that this is done daily, weekly, or monthly, for example. There is a clearly specified procedure agreed to by the counterparties for determining the value of the position for marking the positions to market. If the value of the position of one of the counterparties declines below a level specified in the contract, that party must post additional collateral. Moreover, if the value of the position of one of the counterparties increases above a predetermined level, that counterparty can withdraw collateral. As explained later in this chapter, a futures contract is similar to a marked-to-market forward contract because the value of the position of both parties is marked to market at the end of each trading day. However, in the case of a futures contract the exchange where the contract is traded specifies the procedure for determining how the value of the position is calculated for the purpose of marking a position to market.

Where the counterparties are both high-credit-quality entities, they may agree not to mark positions to market. In our illustration of the valuation of a forward contract, we will first look at only the valuation of non-marked-to-market contracts. However, if one or both of the parties are concerned with the counterparty risk of the other, then positions will be marked to market. The interim cash flows resulting from marking positions to market as the value of the position changes stochastically over time makes the valuation of marked-to-market forward contracts more difficult.

## 18.2.2 Valuing a Forward Contract

A forward contract is written to separate trading profits or losses from the current expectation of the asset's price. In order to trade this risk of price change, the parties must strike a contract that is acceptable to them both. To see conceptually how such a contract might be set up, consider again the payoffs to a risky asset discussed in Chapter 17:

| Possible market value (cash price) at time 2 | Objective probability of realizing this price |
|---|---|
| $105 | 0.5 |
| $ 95 | 0.5 |

---

[4] Many books mistakenly state that a forward contract is not marked to market. That is not the case.

TABLE 18.1
PROFITS OR LOSSES ON A FORWARD CONTRACT WITH FORWARD PRICE OF $100 (THE FORWARD PRICE IS TO BE PAID AT TIME 2)

| | S (Asset Payoff) | O (Forward Price) | S − O (Gross gain or loss) |
|---|---|---|---|
| Time 2 High Price | $S_2 = \$105$ | $O_2 = \$100$ | $S_2 - O_2 = \$5$ |
| Time 2 Low Price | $S_2 = \$95.00$ | $O_2 = \$100$ | $S_2 - O_2 = -\$5$ |
| Time 1 Values | $S_2 = \$89.00$ | $O_2/1.10 = \$90.91$ | $S_1 - O_2/1.10 = -\$1.91$ |

Here $S_2$ is assumed to represent the distribution of the asset's possible market values at time 2, and the objective probabilities shown in the above table indicate that either outcome is equally likely.[5] Suppose you have taken a long position in a forward contract at time 1, specifying that you will buy the asset at time 2, and that your contract specifies a forward price of $100. The first question about such a contract is what gain or loss does it represent to you? A second question is what is the potential gain or loss worth to you now?

Although industry practice is to create contracts whose initial value is zero, it is useful for explanatory purposes to begin by showing the present contract starts out with a non-zero market value. The third column of Table 18.1 shows the gross profits or losses that your long position will realize at time 2. The time 2 payoffs represented by $S_2$ are quantities whose value will only be realized at time 2. However, the forward price $O_2$ is set at time 1 and is a known quantity from that moment on. (The time 2 subscript indicates the time the payment is to be made, not the time the contract is written.) In this example the risk-free interest rate is assumed to be 10%, so the risk-free discount factor $1/1.10 = 0.9091$.

If you take a long position in the forward contract at time 1, you agree to pay $100 for the asset at time 2. This means you will realize a gross profit of $5 if the asset price turns out to be high at the delivery date, but a gross loss of $5 if it is low at the delivery date. In essence, Table 18.1 says that a forward contract divides the risky payoffs represented by $S_2$ into a sure payment $O_2$ and a random profit or loss $(S_2 - O_2)$. Symbolically, this division of the original risk can be expressed as:

$$S_2 \equiv O_2 + (S_2 - O_2)$$

where $S_2$ represents the asset payoffs
    $O_2$ = forward price
    $S_2 - O_2$ = gross gain or loss to the (long) forward position

Adding the symbols corresponds to adding across each row of Table 18.1. In effect, the equation summarizes the information in the table: The forward contract represents a division of payoffs no matter which value of the asset is actually realized. The holder of the long position agrees to pay a fixed price, and the counterparty

---

[5] The probabilities used for valuation purposes are the risk-neutral probabilities and differ from the objective probabilities; see below.

assumes the gain or loss (calculated between times 1 and 2) to any price change between the specified forward price and the cash price.

What will be the time 1 value of assuming the price risk? The answer clearly depends on the forward price. In the present example, taking a long position in the contract means you will pay $100 for the asset, come what may. In the absence of any arbitrage opportunities, the time 1 value of the forward contract must equal the difference between the time 1 value of the asset and the time 1 value of the certainty payment,[6] $100. Suppose as before that the asset has a time 1 value of $89. Also suppose that the risk-free interest rate is 10%, implying that a certainty payment of $100 has a time 1 value of $90.91. Therefore, in the absence of arbitrage opportunities it follows that the payoff to the forward contract in Table 18.1 must have a time 1 value of:

$$\$89 - \$90.91 = -\$1.91$$

This negative value means that, given the asset price of $89 and the risk-free interest rate of 10%, the counterparty will have to pay you $1.91 at time 1 to induce you to enter into this forward contract.[7] The value calculations are summarized in the last row of Table 18.1.

## 18.2.3   How a Forward Price is Determined

As already mentioned, forward contracts usually specify a forward price that gives the contract a value of zero at the time it is written. In the present example, the forward price will have to be less than $100 if the contract is to have a market value of zero at time 1. Since the asset is worth $89 today, its certainty equivalent value must be $89 (1.10) = $97.90 one year from now (time 2). If the forward contract stipulates paying this amount one year from now, the present value of the payment is $89, the same as the current market value of the asset. That is, with a forward price of $97.90, the contract has a present value of zero.

As shown in Table 18.2, this contract yields a gain of $7.10 if the asset price turns out to be high, and a loss of $2.90 if the asset price turns out to be low. If the underlying asset has a market price today of $89, and if the risk-free interest rate is 10%, the time 2

**TABLE 18.2**
VALUING A CONTRACT WITH A FORWARD PRICE OF $97.90

|  | $S$ | $O$ | $S - O$ |
|---|---|---|---|
| Time 2 High Payoffs | $105 | $97.90 | $7.10 |
| Time 2 Low Payoffs | $ 95 | $97.90 | −$2.90 |
| Time 1 Values | $ 89 | $89 | $0 |

---

[6] The example ignores any possibility of defaulting on the $100 payment; that is, it ignores counterparty risk.

[7] The price of $1.91 that you require is determined under the assumption that the individual promising to buy the asset will not default. If there were some possibility the contracting individual might default on his obligation to you, you would require more to enter the contract.

payments in the third column must have a time 1 market value of zero. As we have already determined, the forward price that makes the contract worth zero at time 1 is today's price, accumulated at the risk-free interest rate (i.e., \$89(1.10) = \$97.90). The value calculations are summarized in the last row of Table 18.2.

The risk-neutral probabilities found in Chapter 17, $q = 0.29$ and $1 - q = 0.71$, can be used to check that the new forward contract indeed has a present value of zero:

$$E^Q[(S_2 - O_2)/1.10 \,|\, \mathfrak{I}_1] = (0.29)(\$7.10)/1.10 - (0.71)(\$2.90)/1.10 = \$0$$

It is now time to generalize the insights of the previous example. In writing forward contracts, standard practice stipulates a forward price that implies the contract has an initial value of zero. Let the contract origination time be denoted time 1, and the contract delivery date time $T$. Let $O_T$ be the forward price (to be paid at time $T$, but set at time 1). Let $S_T$ be the price of the underlying asset at time $T$, and let $B_T$ be the value of \$1 accumulated at the risk-free interest rate from time 1 to time $T$. In the absence of arbitrage opportunities, the forward price must be such that:

$$E^Q[(S_T - O_T)/B_T \,|\, \mathfrak{I}_1] = 0 \tag{18.1}$$

where $Q$ is the risk-neutral probability measure, and $\mathfrak{I}_1$ means the risk-neutral probability measure is established using information available at time 1. From the time 1 perspective, the forward price $O_T$ is known with certainty, while the asset price $S_T$ is a random variable. The risk-free interest rate effect represented by $B_T$ is assumed to be known with certainty.[8] Rewriting equation (18.1) gives:

$$E^Q[S_T/B_T \,|\, \mathfrak{I}_1] = O_T E^Q[(1/B_T) \,|\, \mathfrak{I}_1] = S_1 \tag{18.2}$$

The forward price can be taken outside the expectation sign because it is assumed to be a deterministic value at time 1.

Rewriting equation (18.2), the calculations for the forward price on a contract with delivery date $T$ can be expressed as:

$$O_T = S_1/E^Q[(1/B_T) \,|\, \mathfrak{I}_1] \tag{18.3}$$

Equation (18.3) says that if interest rates are random, the forward price equals the current asset price accumulated at the expected interest rate, where the expectation is taken under the risk-neutral probability. Notice that the interest effects are calculated by taking the expectation of the discount factors, which is not the same thing as taking the expectation of the interest rates themselves. Nor is it the same thing as the reciprocal of the expected interest rate.

If interest rates are deterministic as currently assumed, $B_T$ can be taken outside the expectation sign and equation (18.3) reduces to:

$$O_T = S_1/B_T \tag{18.4}$$

---

[8] Although we generally assume the risk-free interest rate is deterministic, we show shortly how this assumption can be relaxed without inordinately complicating the valuation exercise. For a further discussion, see Pliska (1997).

With a deterministic interest rate, the expression for the forward price is straight-forward: It is the current asset price, accumulated at the deterministic interest rate until the delivery date. Since the interest rate in the example is deterministic, equation (18.4) can be used to calculate:

$$O_T = S_1/(1/B_2) = \$89/(1 \div 11/10)$$
$$= \$89 \div 10/11 = \$89 \times 11/10 = \$97.90$$

the value found before.

## 18.2.4 Arbitrage Without Risk-Neutral Pricing

The discussion above to show the pricing of a forward contract can be determined from risk-neutral probabilities is useful to understanding how arbitrage principles can be used to price this instrument. However, we can also derive the theoretical price of a forward contract, still using arbitrage principles, but without relying on risk-neutral probabilities.[9] We will do so by first using an illustration to demonstrate the price of a hypothetical forward contract and then go on to show the general case.

We make the following assumptions for a forward contract:

*Assumption 1*: For the underlying asset, there are no payments made over the life of the forward contract.

*Assumption 2*: The forward contract is not marked to market during the life of the contract.

*Assumption 3*: There is a risk-free interest rate at which market participants can borrow and lend.

*Assumption 4*: There is no counterparty risk.

The first two assumptions mean that there are no interim cash flows (cash in or cash out) that we need be concerned with in valuing the forward contract. We will modify some of the assumptions later and look at the impact on the theoretical value of the forward contract.

In this illustration we will once again assume that (1) the cash market price of the underlying is $89, (2) the delivery date is one year from now, and (3) the risk-free interest rate is 10%.

Suppose that the price of the forward contract in the market is $105. Let's see if that price can be sustained in the market. Consider the following trading strategy:

- Sell the forward contract in the market at $105.
- Buy the underlying asset in the cash market for $89.
- Borrow the proceeds to purchase the underlying asset at 10%.

---

[9] The result is not surprising. Both the derivation of the risk-neutral probabilities and the value calculations presented here are consequences of there being no arbitrage opportunities. So clearly, the values obtained by either method of calculation should be the same.

This strategy requires at the delivery date the sale of the underlying asset for a price of $105 and the repayment of the $89 borrowed plus interest of $8.90 (10% of $89). Hence, the proceeds of $105 exceed the cost to purchase the $97.90. There will be a profit from this strategy of $7.10.

The profit of $7.10 from this strategy is guaranteed regardless of what the cash price of the underlying asset is one year from now (the delivery date). This is because in the preceding analysis of the outcome of the strategy, the cash price of the underlying asset one year from now never enters the analysis. Moreover, this profit is generated with no investment outlay; the funds needed to acquire the underlying asset are borrowed when the strategy is executed. The profit in the strategy we have just illustrated arises from a riskless arbitrage between the price of the underlying asset in the cash market and the price of the underlying asset in the futures market.

In a well-functioning market, arbitrageurs who could realize this arbitrage profit for a zero investment would implement the strategy described above. By selling the forward contract and buying the underlying asset in order to implement the strategy, this would force the forward price down so that at some price for the forward contract, the arbitrage profit is eliminated.

This strategy that resulted in the capturing of the arbitrage profit is referred to as a *cash-and-carry trade*. The reason for this name is that implementation of the strategy involves borrowing cash to purchase the underlying asset and "carrying" that underlying to the delivery date of the forward contract.

From the cash-and-carry trade we see that the price of the forward contract cannot be $105. Suppose instead that the price of the forward contract in the market is $95 rather than $105. Let's try the following strategy to see if that price can be sustained in the market:

- Buy the forward contract at $95.
- Sell (short) the underlying asset for $89.
- Invest (lend) $89 received from the short sale for one year earning the risk-free interest rate of 10%.

We assume that there is no cost to selling the asset short and lending the proceeds received from the short sale.[10] Given these assumptions, there is no initial cash outlay for the strategy just as with the cash-and-carry trade. At the delivery date, the underlying asset is purchased to settle the long position in the forward contract. The underlying asset is accepted for delivery and then used to cover the short position in the cash market.

Thus, at the delivery date, the underlying asset is purchased for $95. The cash received from the investment is $89 plus interest of $8.90. Hence, $97.90 is received and $95 paid. The profit from this trading strategy is $2.90.

---

[10] It is assumed in this strategy that the proceeds from the short sale are received and reinvested. In practice, for individual investors, the proceeds are not received, and, in fact, the individual investor is required to deposit margin (securities margin and not futures margin) to short sell. For institutional investors, the underlying may be borrowed, but there is a cost to borrowing. This cost of borrowing can be incorporated into the model by reducing the cash yield on the underlying asset that we describe below.

As with the cash and carry trade, the $2.90 profit from this strategy is an arbitrage profit. This strategy requires no initial cash outlay, but will generate a profit whatever the price of the underlying asset in the cash market at the delivery date. In real-world markets, this opportunity would lead arbitrageurs to buy the forward contract and short the underlying asset. The implementation of this strategy would be to raise the forward price until the arbitrage profit disappeared.

This strategy that is implemented to capture the arbitrage profit is known as a *reverse cash-and-carry trade*. That is, with this strategy, the underlying is sold short and the proceeds received from the short sale are invested.

We can see that the forward price cannot be $95 or $105. What is the theoretical forward price given the assumptions in our illustration? It can be shown that if the forward price is $97.90, there is no opportunity for an arbitrage profit. That is, neither the cash-and-carry trade nor the reverse cash-and-carry trade will generate an arbitrage profit.

Equivalent to equation (18.3), the formula for determining the theoretical forward price given the assumptions of the model is:

Theoretical forward price = Cash market price $(1 + \text{risk-free interest rate})$   (18.5)

In our illustration, since the cash market price for the underlying is $89 and the risk-free interest rate is 10%, then we have:

$$\text{Theoretical forward price} = \$89(1.10) = \$97.90$$

While the result is the same as derived earlier using the risk-neutral probabilities, the reasoning of the present example provides additional intuition regarding ways to obtain the theoretical forward price.

Note that at the delivery date of the forward contract, the forward price must equal the cash market price. The reason is that a forward contract with no time left until delivery is equivalent to a cash market transaction. Thus, as the delivery date approaches, the forward price will converge to the cash market price. This fact is evident from the formula for the theoretical forward price given by equation (18.5). The interest earned approaches zero as the delivery date approaches.

### 18.2.4.1 *Taking into Account Cash Flows from the Underlying Asset*

An assumption that was made in deriving the theoretical forward price is that the underlying asset did not provide any cash flow over the life of the forward contract. For example, if the underlying asset is a share of common stock, dividends could be paid over the life of the forward contract. When the underlying is a bond, interest is likely to be paid over the life of the forward contract. Let's see how the theoretical forward price as given by equations (18.3) and (18.5) must be modified if there is a cash flow generated by the underlying asset.

To simplify, we will assume that the cash flow is realized only at the delivery date. More specifically, in our illustration we will assume that a payment of 2% of the cash price of the underlying asset will be made at the end of one year. (We refer to this as the *cash yield*.) That is, there will be a cash payment of $1.78 at the end of one year. Let's now look at both the cash-and-carry trade and the reverse cash-and-carry trade.

Recall that the cash-and-carry trade is:

- Sell the forward contract in the market at $105.
- Buy the underlying asset in the cash market for $89.
- Borrow the proceeds to purchase the underlying asset at 10%.

The following occurs at the delivery date:

| | |
|---|---:|
| Proceeds from sale of underlying asset to settle forward contract | =$ 105.00 |
| Cash flow from the underlying asset | =$ 1.78 |
| Proceeds received | =$ 106.78 |
| Repayment of principal of loan | =$ 89.00 |
| Interest on loan | =$ 8.90 |
| Total outlay | =$ 97.90 |

Therefore, the arbitrage profit form the cash-and-carry strategy is $8.80. Hence, the forward price of $105 cannot prevail in the forward market.

Consider the reverse cash-and-carry trade analyzed earlier:

- Buy the forward contract at $95.
- Sell (short) the underlying asset for $89.
- Invest (lend) $89 received from the short sale for one year earning the risk-free interest rate of 10%.

The following occurs at the delivery date:

| | |
|---|---:|
| Proceeds paid to purchase the underlying asset to settle the contract | =$ 95.00 |
| Payment of the cash flow of the underlying asset | =$ 1.78 |
| Proceeds paid | =$ 96.78 |
| Proceeds from short sale of the underlying asset | =$ 89.00 |
| Interest received from the proceeds invested | = 8.90 |
| Proceeds received | =$ 97.90 |

Hence, the arbitrage profit for this strategy is $1.20. Consequently, a forward price of $95 cannot be sustained. As can be verified by employing both trades and finding that there is no profit or loss, it can be demonstrated that the price is $96.12.

In general, the formula for the theoretical forward price is:

$$\text{Theoretical forward price} = \text{Cash market price} \, (1 + \text{risk-free interest rate} - \text{cash yield}) \tag{18.6}$$

In our illustration, the cash yield on the underlying asset is 2%. Therefore,

$$\text{Theoretical forward price} = \$89 \, (1 + 0.10 - 0.02) = \$96.12$$

The spread between the risk-free interest rate and the cash yield is called the *net financing cost*. Notice from equation (18.6) the following relationship between the cash price and the forward price based on the net financing cost:

| If the net financing cost is | then |
|---|---|
| positive | forward price > cash price |
| negative | forward price < cash price |
| zero | forward price = cash price |

A more commonly used term by market participants for the net financing cost is the *cost of carry* or simply *carry*. Carry is said to be positive if what is earned on the underlying asset (i.e., the cash yield) exceeds the cost of borrowing to purchase the underlying asset to the delivery date. Carry is said to be negative if the cost of borrowing to purchase the underlying asset to the delivery date is greater than the cash yield. Based on carry, the following relationship exists between the cash price and the forward price:

| If carry is | then |
|---|---|
| positive | forward price < cash price |
| negative | forward price > cash price |
| zero | forward price = cash price |

### 18.2.4.2  Borrowing and Lending Rates are Different

One feature of a perfect capital market is that the borrowing rate and the lending rate are equal. Obviously, that assumption is unwarranted since in such a capital market, lenders could not survive. In real-world capital markets, the lending rate is higher than the rate. The impact on pricing is that there is not a theoretical forward price but a band for the futures price where no arbitrage opportunity exists.

Specifically, in the cash-and-carry trade, the theoretical forward price as given by equation (18.6) becomes:

$$\text{Theoretical forward price} = \text{Cash market price } (1 + \text{borrowing rate} - \text{cash yield}) \tag{18.7}$$

For the reverse cash-and-carry trade, it becomes:

$$\text{Theoretical forward price} = \text{Cash market price } (1 + \text{lending rate} - \text{cash yield}) \tag{18.8}$$

Equations (18.7) and (18.8) together provide a band between which the actual forward price can exist without allowing for any arbitrage profit. Equation (18.7) establishes the upper value for the band, while equation (18.8) provides the lower value for the band. For example, assume that the borrowing rate is 10% per year, while the lending rate is 8% per year. Using equation (18.7), the upper value for the theoretical forward price is $96.12. Using equation (18.8), the lower value for the theoretical forward price is $94.34.

## 18.3   FUTURES PRICING

In this section we examine futures contracts. We discuss how and why futures and forward contracts are different, and then explain how futures contracts can be valued. Valuing a futures contract is a more complex exercise than valuing a non-MTM forward contract because the futures price changes stochastically during its life, and because the contract provides for periodic payment of capital gains or losses realized during the life of the contract. Moreover, we will look at specific types of futures contracts to see how the pricing model must be modified to account for the features of a specific contract.

### 18.3.1   What is a Futures Contract?

A futures contract is like a MTM contract. Futures contracts are standardized agreements as to the delivery date (or month) and quality of the deliverable, and are traded on organized exchanges. A forward contract differs in that it is usually non-standardized (that is, the terms of each contract are negotiated individually between buyer and seller), there is no clearinghouse, and secondary markets are often non-existent or extremely thin. A futures contract is an exchange-traded product, while a forward contract is an over-the-counter instrument.

We noted earlier in this chapter that the parties to a forward contract are exposed to counterparty risk, the risk that the other party to the transaction will fail to perform. The counterparty risk arises in part because there is no clearinghouse that guarantees the performance of a counterparty in a forward contract. Associated with every futures exchange is a clearinghouse which performs several functions. One of these functions is to guarantee that the two parties to the transaction will perform. Because of the clearinghouse, the two parties need not worry about the financial strength and integrity of the other party taking the opposite side of the contract. After initial execution of an order, the relationship between the two parties ends. The clearinghouse interposes itself as the buyer for every sale and as the seller for every purchase. Thus, the two parties are then free to liquidate their positions without involving the other party in the original contract, and without worry that the other party may default.

### 18.3.2   Margin Requirements

When an investor first takes a position in a futures contract, she must deposit a minimum dollar amount specified by the exchange. This amount, called *initial margin*, is required as a deposit for the contract. The initial margin may be in the form of an interest-bearing security such as a Treasury bill. The initial margin is placed in an account, and the amount in this account is referred to as the *investor's equity*. As the price of the futures contract fluctuates each trading day, the value of the investor's equity in the position changes.

At the end of each trading day, the exchange determines the "settlement price" for the futures contract. The settlement price is different from the closing price, which is the price of the final trade of the day (whenever that trade occurred during the day). By contrast, the settlement price is that value the exchange considers to be representative of trading at the end of the day. The exchange uses the settlement price to mark to market the investor's position, so that any gain or loss from the position is quickly reflected in the investor's equity account.

A *maintenance margin* is the minimum level (specified by the exchange) by which an investor's equity position may fall as a result of unfavorable price movements before the investor is required to deposit additional margin. The maintenance margin requirement is a dollar amount that is less than the initial margin requirement. It sets the floor that the investor's equity account can fall to before the investor is required to furnish additional margin. The additional margin deposited, called *variation margin*, is an amount necessary to bring the equity in the account back to its initial margin level. Unlike initial margin, variation margin must be in cash, not interest-bearing instruments. Any excess margin in the account may be withdrawn by the investor. If a party to a futures contract who is required to deposit variation margin fails to do so within 24 hours, the futures position is liquidated by the clearinghouse.[11]

To illustrate the marked-to-market procedure, let's assume the following margin requirements for asset XYZ:

- Initial margin $7 per contract.
- Maintenance margin $4 per contract.

Suppose that Bob buys 500 contracts at a futures price of $100, and Sally sells the same number of contracts at the same futures price. The initial margin for both Bob and Sally is $3,500, which is determined by multiplying the initial margin of $7 by the number of contracts, 500. Bob and Sally must both put up $3,500 in cash or Treasury bills or other acceptable collateral. At this time, $3,500 is the equity in each of the two parties' accounts.

The maintenance margin for each of the two positions is $2,000 (the maintenance margin per contract of $4 multiplied by 500 contracts). That means the equity in the account may not fall below $2,000. If it does, the party whose equity falls below the maintenance margin must put up additional margin, which is the variation margin. Regarding the variation margin, note two things. First, the variation margin must be cash. Second, the amount of variation margin required is the amount to bring the equity up to the initial margin, not just to the maintenance margin.

## 18.3.3 Relations Between Futures and Non-Marked-to-Market Forward Prices

To value a futures contract, one must take into account the possibility that the futures price embodied in the instrument will be changed as realized capital gains or losses

---

[11] Although there are initial and maintenance margin requirements for buying securities on margin, the concept of margin differs for securities and futures. When securities are acquired on margin, the difference between the price of the security and the initial margin is borrowed from the broker. The security purchased serves as collateral for the loan, and the investor pays interest. For futures contracts, the initial margin, in effect, serves as "good-faith" money, an indication that the investor will satisfy the obligation of the contract. Normally, no money is borrowed by the investor.

are credited to the parties' trading accounts due to marking to market of the positions of both counterparties. Although a complete investigation of the issues in valuation is a complex subject beyond the scope of this chapter, the following example shows how to compare future prices and non-MTM forward prices. This technical difference reduces the possible costs of default (i.e., counterparty risk) and also has particular valuation effects if interest rates are uncertain. So in our discussion below, when we refer to a forward contract, we mean a forward contract that is not marked to market.

First, compare the cash flows from going long in either a forward or a futures contract when the two contracts will remain outstanding for two periods.[12] The futures contract will be revalued at time 2, while the terms of the analogous forward contract remain unchanged at that point. The cash flows from the two contracts are shown symbolically in Table 18.3.

**TABLE 18.3**
FORWARD AND FUTURES CONTRACTS

|  | Time 1 | Time 2 | Time 3 |
|---|---|---|---|
| Cash Flow from Forward Contract | 0 | 0 | $S_3 - O_{13}$ |
| Cash Flows from Futures Contract | 0 | $U_{23} - U_{13}$ | $S_3 - U_{23}$ |

In the table, $O_{13}$ is the forward (fOrward) price, set at time 1 and referring to delivery at time 3. Similarly, $U_{13}$ is the futures (fUtures) price,[13] set at time 1 and referring to delivery at time 3. In addition, $U_{23}$ is the futures price after the contract, still specifying delivery at time 3, has been marked to market at time 2. Finally, $S_3$ refers to the price of the asset at time 3.

As is evident from Table 18.3, the difference between the long positions in the two contracts is the cash flow (positive or negative) on the futures contract, which results from its being marked to market at time 2. If the cash flow is positive, we assume it can be invested at the then-prevailing risk-free interest rate, while if it is negative, we assume funds can be borrowed at the risk-free rate.

Let

$$B_2 = (1 + r_{12})$$

where $r_{12}$ is the interest rate between time 1 and time 2 and

$$B_3 = (1 + r_{12})(1 + r_{23})$$

so that the interest rate between time 1 and time 2 is:

$$(B_3/B_2) - 1 = r_{23}$$

---

[12] We could consider more periods, but to do so would mean having to repeat similar calculations without adding further insights.

[13] The futures price has two subscripts because, even for a contract with fixed maturity, the price itself changes from one period to the next.

The discount factor between times 1 and 2 is then $1/B_2$, and $B_2/B_3$ is the discount factor between times 2 and 3. At time 1, we assume the interest rate between times 1 and 2 is known with certainty, but the interest rate between times 2 and 3 is known only as a random variable[14] until time 2. The assumed randomness of $B_3/B_2$ means that the time 2 cash flow is random when viewed from a time 1 perspective.

Table 18.3 shows why the two contracts have different risks when they are regarded from the perspective of time 1. If the spot price (i.e., the price in the cash market) at time 3 were known, the cash flows from the forward contract could be stated with certainty at time 1. However, the time 1 value of the time 3 cash flows from the futures contract could not be stated with certainty even if the spot price were known, because the present value of the cash flows would still depend on a random interest rate.

## 18.3.4 Finding Futures Prices Using Risk-Neutral Probabilities

The relations determining futures prices, and the differences between forward and futures prices, can be developed further using the ideas of arbitrage-free securities prices and risk-neutral probabilities. Suppose that the contracts call for delivery of one unit of some underlying asset. In any such contract, the amount to be paid on delivery date $T$ is the value of the asset at the time. Suppose also that the asset does not make a cash payment between the present time 1 and the delivery date $T$. Repeating equation (18.3) for convenience, recall that the forward price set at time 1 on a contract with delivery date $T$ is:[15]

$$O_{1T} = S_1/E^Q[1/B_T|\mathfrak{I}_1]$$

and may be rewritten as:

$$O_{1T} = E^Q[(S_T/B_T)|\mathfrak{I}_1]/E^Q[1/B_T|\mathfrak{I}_1] \qquad (18.9)$$

We next show that the futures price is:

$$U_{1T} = E^Q[S_T|\mathfrak{I}_1] \qquad (18.10)$$

First, at time 1, standard market practice is to set the futures prices so that the cash flows from a two-period contract are valued at zero:

$$E^Q[(U_{23} - U_{13})/B_2 + (U_{33} - U_{23})/B_3|\mathfrak{I}_1] = 0$$

However, marking to market also means that at time 2:

$$E^Q[(U_{33} - U_{23})B_2/B_3|\mathfrak{I}_2] = 0 \qquad (18.11)$$

---

[14] The interest rate is called risk-free because it is the market rate of interest on a bond with no default risk. Nevertheless, such a rate can also change randomly from time to time. Our assumptions regarding when the risk-free rate becomes known with certainty mean we are treating it as a predictable process. See Pliska (1997).

[15] For comparison purposes, we now give the forward price two subscripts, reflecting both the date of origination and the delivery date, when the forward price is to be paid.

If the contract allows for no substitutions in the asset to be delivered,[16] $U_{33} = S_3$. But equation (18.11) means that:

$$U_{23} = E^Q[U_{33}|\mathfrak{I}_2] = E_Q[S_3|\mathfrak{I}_2] \tag{18.12}$$

since $U_{23}$, $B_2$, and $B_3$ are all known at time 2. Then substituting equation (18.12) into equation (18.11) gives:

$$E^Q[(U_{23} - U_{13})B_2 + 0 \mid \mathfrak{I}_1] = 0 \tag{18.13}$$

and since $B_1$ is also known at time 1, equation (18.13) can be rewritten as:

$$E^Q[(U_{23} - U_{13})|\mathfrak{I}_1] = 0$$

It then follows immediately that:

$$U_{13} = E^Q[U_{23}|\mathfrak{I}_1] = E^Q\{E^Q[U_{33}|\mathfrak{I}_2]|\mathfrak{I}_1\} = E^Q[U_{33}|\mathfrak{I}_1] = E^Q[S_3|\mathfrak{I}_1] \tag{18.14}$$

establishing equation (18.10) when $T = 3$.

If interest rates are random, the values of $B_T$, $T > 1$, are random when viewed from the perspective of time 1. However, if interest rates are deterministic, the value of $B_T$ is deterministic also. In the latter case, the value of $B_T$ can be taken outside the expectation operator and we obtain:

$$O_{13} = E^Q[(S_T/B_T)|\mathfrak{I}_1]/E^Q[1/B_T|\mathfrak{I}_1] = E^Q[S_T|\mathfrak{I}_1] = U_{13} \tag{18.15}$$

the last equality following from equation (18.13). That is, time 1 forward and futures prices are equal in a world of deterministic interest rates.

Note from equation (18.15) that when interest rates are random the expression for forward prices contains interest terms, but the corresponding equation (18.14) for futures prices does not. You can see why by comparing equation (18.15) with equations (18.13) and (18.14). Under a futures contract, capital gains or losses are received or paid each period, and thus do not need to be equated between time points. Finally, if there is only one time period remaining before the delivery date, the forward price and the futures price[17] are equal, because the two contracts represent the same outcomes at this point in time.

## 18.3.4.1 Examples

Here we present two examples of relations between non-MTM forward and futures prices, both due to Pliska (1997).[18] The first is a one-period example with deterministic interest rates. It verifies that a non-MTM forward and a futures contract

---

[16] Some futures contracts do allow such substitutions. We will discuss one such contract later.

[17] After the futures contract has been marked to market at that point in time.

[18] Note that Pliska does not use the term "non-MTM forward" contract. We use the terms because of our earlier discussion about the actual way in which forward contracts operate.

are the same in this context, and also displays the differences between the forward and futures price equations. Moreover, it shows that despite the differences in the equations, the same value is obtained in the present restricted context. Suppose an asset has a time 1 market value of $5 and pays off either $8 or $4 at time 2 as shown in Table 18.4.

**TABLE 18.4**
ASSET PRICES AND DETERMINISTIC INTEREST RATES

| Time 1 | Time 2 | Risk-Neutral Probability |
|---|---|---|
| $5 | $8 | $q = 7/18$ |
| $5 | $4 | $1 - q = 11/18$ |

Suppose also that $B_2 = 10/9$, a statement equivalent to saying that the risk-free interest rate is 1/9. Assuming the absence of arbitrage opportunities, the risk-neutral probabilities can be found using:

$$S_1 = E^Q[S_2/B_2|\Im_1]$$

Applying the last line to the present example means solving:

$$\$5 = q \times \$8 \times (9/10) + (1 - q) \times \$4 \times (9/10)$$

for $q$. The value of the solution is shown in the first line, third column of Table 18.4. The time 1 determined forward price, to be paid at time 2, is given by:

$$O_{12} = S_0 \times B_1 = \$5 \times (10/9) = \$50/9$$

The futures price is given by:

$$U_{12} = E^Q[S_2|\Im_1] = \$8 \times (7/18) + \$4 \times (11/18) = \$100/18 = \$50/9$$

As already mentioned, these calculations show the essential similarity of one-period non-MTM forward and futures contracts, and also show that with deterministic interest rates the forward and futures prices are the same.

The second of Pliska's examples has two time intervals and random interest rates between times 2 and 3. Each row of Table 18.5 shows a possible evolution of asset prices from time 1, through time 2, to time 3.

**TABLE 18.5**
ASSET PRICES AND RANDOM INTEREST RATES

| Time 1 | Time 2 | Time 3 | Risk-Neutral Probability |
|---|---|---|---|
| $5 | $8 | $9 | 5/24 |
| $5 | $8 | $6 | 1/24 |
| $5 | $4 | $6 | 9/24 |
| $5 | $4 | $3 | 9/24 |

Bond prices are 1 at time 1, 1 at time 2, and either 17/16 or 9/8 at time 3. The price of 17/16 is associated with the events in the first two rows of Table 18.5, and the price of 9/8 is associated with the events in the second two rows. Thus, the interest rate from time 1 to time 2 is zero, while the interest rate from time 2 to time 3 is either 1/16 or 1/9, according to whether the asset price has risen or fallen by time 2. The values of the risk-neutral probability measure, consistent with the assumption of arbitrage-free prices, are here taken as given.

The futures price at time 1 takes on two values, corresponding to the two possible asset prices. If the asset price is $8 at time 2, one knows the asset price must either be $9 or $6 in the next period. The conditional risk-neutral probabilities that reflect these events are respectively $(5/24)/(6/24) = 5/6$ and $(1/24)/(6/24) = 1/6$. In that event the time 2 futures price can be found using (18.14):

$$(U_{23}|S_2 = \$8) = E^Q[S_3|\mathfrak{I}_2] = \$9(5/6) + \$6(1/6) = \$51/6 = \$17/2$$

If the asset price is $4, the conditional risk-neutral probabilities are both equal to ½ and the futures price is:

$$(U_{23}|S_2 = \$4) = E^Q[S_3|\mathfrak{I}_2] = \$6(1/2) + \$3(1/2) = \$9/2$$

Finally, the futures price at time 1 is given by:

$$(U_{13}) = E^Q[S_3|\mathfrak{I}_1] = \$9(5/24) + \$6(1/24) + \$6(9/24) + \$3(9/24) = \$132/24 = \$11/2$$

The futures price at time 1 can also be computed as a conditional expectation, under the risk-neutral probability measure, of the previously calculated time 2 futures prices. Using equation (18.14):

$$U_{13} = E^Q[U_{23}|\mathfrak{I}_1] = (\$17/2)(1/4) + (\$9/2)(3/4) = \$11/2$$

On the other hand, the forward price at time $1^{19}$ is found from equation (18.1):

$$O_3 = 5/[(16/17)(6/24) + (8/9)(18/24)] = 5/[46/51] = 255/46$$

In keeping with the discussion following equation (18.1), the expected discount rates in the previous calculation are:

$$E^Q[(1/B_2)|\mathfrak{I}_1] = (\$16/17)(1/4) + (\$8/9)(3/4) = \$46/51$$

That is, the forward price is the current asset price accumulated at the expected interest rate.

---

[19] It is possible to calculate forward values at time 2, but the contract does not permit delivery at that time.

## 18.3.5 Pricing of Stock Index Futures and Treasury Note and Bond Futures

The theoretical futures price for a futures contract given earlier, equation (18.14), must be modified to take into account the nuances of institutional constraints and the specifications of specific futures contracts. The refinement is necessary because of the assumptions underlying the general pricing model given above. Below we will look at two popular types of futures contracts: stock index futures contracts and Treasury note and bond futures contracts.

### 18.3.5.1 Stock Index Futures

While there are futures contracts on both stock indexes and individual stocks, the most commonly used futures are on the former. Therefore, we will focus only on stock index futures.

The underlying for a stock index futures contract can be a broad-based stock market index or a narrow-based index. Examples of broad-based stock market indexes used as futures contract underlyings are the S&P 500, S&P Midcap 400, Dow Jones Industrial Average, Nasdaq 100 Index, NYSE Composite Index, and the Russell 2000 Index. A narrow-based stock index futures contract is one based on a subsector or components of a broad-based stock index containing groups of stocks or a specialized sector developed by a bank. For example, Dow Jones MicroSector Indexes are traded on OneChicago, an all-electronic exchange of listed security futures. There are 15 sectors in the index.

The dollar value of a stock index futures contract is the product of the futures price and a specified "multiple." That is,

Dollar value of a stock index futures contract = Futures price × Multiple

For example, suppose that the futures price for the S&P 500 is 1410. The multiple for the S&P 500 futures contract is $250. Therefore, the dollar value of the S&P 500 futures contract would be $352,500 (=1410 × $250). If an investor buys an S&P 500 futures contract at 1410 and sells it at 1430, the investor realizes a profit of 20 times $250, or $5,000. If the futures contract is sold instead for 1360, the investor will realize a loss of 50 times $250, or $12,500.

Stock index futures contracts are contracts for which cash will be exchanged in settlement. For example, if an investor buys an S&P 500 futures contract at 1410 and the futures settlement price is 1430, settlement would be as follows. The investor has agreed to buy the S&P 500 for 1410 times $250, or $352,500. The S&P 500 value at the settlement date is 1430 times $250, or $357,500. The seller of this futures contract must pay the investor $5,000 ($357,500 − $352,500). Had the futures price at the settlement date been 1360 instead of 1430, the dollar value of the S&P 500 futures contract would be $340,000. In this case, the investor must pay the seller of the contract $12,500 ($352,500 − $340,000). (Of course, in practice, the parties would be realizing any gains or losses at the end of each trading day as their positions are marked to the market.)

Clearly, an investor who wants to short the entire market or a sector will use stock index futures contracts. The costs of a transaction are small relative to shorting the individual stocks comprising the stocks index or attempting to construct a portfolio that replicates the stock index with minimal tracking error.

The nuances of stock index futures contracts that require a modification of the theoretical futures model are (1) the interim cash flows for the underlying and (2) the deliverable being a basket of stocks rather than a single asset. In the derivation of a basic pricing model, it is assumed that no interim cash flows arise because of changes in futures prices (that is, there is no variation margin). For a stock index, there are interim cash flows. In fact, many cash flows are dependent upon the dividend dates of the component companies. To correctly price a stock index futures contract, it is necessary to incorporate the interim dividend payments, but these patterns are not known with certainty. Consequently, they must first be projected from the historical dividend payments of the companies in the index and then incorporated into the pricing model. The only problem is that the value of the dividend payments at the settlement date will depend on the interest rate at which the dividend payments can be reinvested from the time they are projected to be received until the settlement date. The lower the dividend, and the closer the dividend payments to the settlement date of the futures contract, the less important the reinvestment income is in determining the futures price.

Now let's look at the issue of having a basket of stocks to deliver. The problem in arbitraging stock index futures contracts is that it may be too expensive to buy or sell every stock included in the index. Instead, a portfolio containing a smaller number of stocks may be constructed to track the basket or index (which means having price movements that are very similar to changes in the stock index). Nonetheless, the two arbitrage strategies involve a tracking portfolio rather than a single asset for the underlying, and the strategies are no longer risk-free because the tracking portfolio will not precisely replicate the performance of the stock index. For this reason, the market price of futures contracts based on a stock index is likely to diverge from the theoretical price and have wider bands (i.e., lower and upper theoretical futures price) that cannot be exploited.

### 18.3.5.2 *Treasury Bond and Note Futures Contracts*

Treasury bond and Treasury note futures contracts are traded on an exchange, the Chicago Mercantile Exchange (CME). The underlying instrument for the Treasury bond futures contract is $100,000 par value of a hypothetical 20-year coupon bond. This hypothetical bond's coupon rate is called the *notional coupon*. The notional coupon is 6%. There are three Treasury note futures contracts: 10-year, 5-year, and 2-year. All three contracts are modeled after the Treasury bond futures contract and are traded on the same exchange. The underlying instrument for the 10-year Treasury note contract is $100,000 par value of a hypothetical 10-year 6% Treasury note. The futures price is quoted in terms of par being 100. Since the bond and notes futures contract are similar, for the remainder of our discussion we will focus on the bond futures contract.

We have been referring to the underlying instrument as a hypothetical Treasury bond. While some interest rate futures contracts can only be settled in cash, the seller (the short) of a Treasury bond futures contract who chooses to make delivery rather than liquidate his/her position by buying back the contract prior to the settlement date must deliver some Treasury bond. This begs the question: Which Treasury bond? The CME allows the seller to deliver one of several bonds specified as acceptable for delivery. A trader who is short a particular bond is always concerned with the risk of being unable to obtain sufficient securities to cover their position.

The set of all bonds that meet the delivery requirements for a particular contract is called the *deliverable basket*. The CME makes its determination of the Treasury issues that are acceptable for delivery from all outstanding Treasury issues that have at least 15 years to maturity from the first day of the delivery month. It is important to keep in mind that while the underlying Treasury bond for this contract is a hypothetical issue and therefore cannot itself be delivered into the futures contract, the bond futures contract is not a cash settlement contract. The only way to close out a Treasury bond futures contract is to either initiate an offsetting futures position or to deliver a Treasury issue from the deliverable basket.

The delivery process for the Treasury bond futures contract is innovative and has served as a model for government bond futures contracts traded on various exchanges throughout the world. On the settlement date, the seller of the futures contract (the short) is required to deliver the buyer (the long) $100,000 par value of a 6% 20-year Treasury bond. As noted, no such bond exists, so the seller must choose a bond from the deliverable basket to deliver to the long. Suppose the seller selects a 5% coupon, 20-year Treasury bond to settle the futures contract. Since the coupon of this bond is less than the notional coupon of 6%, this would be unacceptable to the buyer who contracted to receive a 6% coupon, 20-year bond with a par value of $100,000. Alternatively, suppose the seller is compelled to deliver a 7% coupon, 20-year bond. Since the coupon of this bond is greater than the notional coupon of 6%, the seller would find this unacceptable. In summary, how do we adjust for the fact that bonds in the deliverable basket have coupons and maturities that differ from the notional coupon of 6%?

To make delivery equitable to both parties, the CME uses conversion factors for adjusting the price of each Treasury issue that can be delivered to satisfy the Treasury bond futures contract. Given the conversion factor for an issue and the futures price, the adjusted price is found by multiplying the conversion factor by the futures price. The adjusted price is called the *converted price*. That is,

Converted price = Contract size × Futures settlement price × Conversion factor

For example, suppose the settlement price of a Treasury bond futures contract is 110 and the issue selected by short has a conversion factor of 1.25. Given the contract size is $100,000, the converted price is $100,000 × 1.10 × 1.25 = $137,500. The price that the buyer must pay the seller when a Treasury bond is delivered is called the *invoice price*. Intuitively, the invoice price should be the futures settlement price plus accrued interest. However, as just noted, the seller can choose any Treasury issue from the deliverable basket. To make delivery fair to both parties, the invoice price must be adjusted using the conversion factor of the actual Treasury issue delivered. The invoice price is:

Invoice price = Contract size × Futures settlement price × Conversion factor
        + Accrued interest

In selecting the issue to be delivered, the short will select from all the deliverable issues the one that will give the largest rate of return from a cash-and-carry trade as explained earlier. In the case of bond futures contract, a cash-and-carry-trade is strategy in which a cash bond that is acceptable for delivery is purchased with borrowed funds and simultaneously the Treasury bond futures contract is sold. The bond purchased can be delivered to satisfy the short futures position. Thus, by buying the Treasury issue that is acceptable for delivery and selling the futures, an investor has effectively sold the bond at the delivery price (that is, the converted price).

A rate of return can be calculated for this trade. This rate of return is referred to as the *implied repo rate*.[20] Once the implied repo rate is calculated for each bond in the deliverable basket, the issue selected will be the one that has the highest implied repo rate (that is, the issue that gives the maximum return in a cash-and-carry trade). The issue with the highest return is referred to as the *cheapest-to-deliver issue*. This issue plays a key role in the pricing of a Treasury futures contract.[21]

In addition to the choice of which acceptable Treasury issue to deliver— sometimes referred to as the *quality option* or *swap option*—the short has at least two more options granted under CME delivery guidelines. The short is permitted to decide when in the delivery month, delivery actually will take place. This is called the *timing option*. The other option is the right of the short to give notice of intent to deliver up to 8:00 P.M. Chicago time after the closing of the exchange (3:15 P.M. Chicago time) on the date when the futures settlement price has been fixed. This option is referred to as the *wildcard option*. The quality option, the timing option, and the wildcard option (in sum referred to as the *delivery options*), mean that the long position can never be sure which Treasury bond issue will be delivered or when it will be delivered.

Once again, let's look at how the nuances of a futures contract necessitate the refinement of the theoretical futures pricing model. The two assumptions that require a refinement of the model are the assumptions regarding (1) no interim cash flows and (2) the deliverable asset and the settlement date are known.

With respect to interim cash flows, for a Treasury futures contract the underlying is a Treasury note or a Treasury bond. Unlike a stock index futures contract, the timing of the interest payments that will be made by the U.S. Department of the Treasury for an acceptable issue is known with certainty and can be incorporated into the pricing model. However, the reinvestment interest that can be earned from the payment dates to the settlement of the contract is unknown and depends on prevailing interest rates at each payment date.

Now let's look at the implications regarding a known deliverable and known settlement date. Neither assumption is consistent with the delivery rules for some futures contracts. For U.S. Treasury note and bond futures contracts, for example, the contract specifies that any one of several Treasury issues can be delivered to satisfy the contract. Such issues are referred to as *deliverable issues*. The selection of which deliverable issue to deliver is an option granted to the party who is short the contract (that is, the seller). Hence, the party that is long the contract (that is, the buyer of the contract) does not know the specific Treasury issue that will be delivered. However, market participants can determine the cheapest-to-deliver issue from the issues that

---

[20] Repo is short for "repurchase agreement." This agreement is the most commonly used form of collaterized borrowing by traders and portfolio managers. The interest rate on a repurchase agreement is called the repo rate.

[21] While a particular Treasury bond may be the cheapest to deliver today, changes in interest rates, for example, may cause some other issue to be the cheapest to deliver at a future date.

are acceptable for delivery, and this issue is used in obtaining the theoretical futures price. The net effect of the short's option to select the issue to deliver to satisfy the contract is that it reduces the theoretical future price by an amount equal to the value of the delivery option granted to the short.

Moreover, unlike other futures contract, the Treasury bond and note contracts do not have a delivery date. Instead, there is a delivery month. The short has the right to select when in the delivery month to make delivery. The effect of this option granted to the short is once again to reduce the theoretical futures price. More specifically,

Theoretical futures price adjusted for delivery options

$= $ Cash market price $+$ (Cash market price) $\times$ (Financing cost $-$ Cash yield)

$-$ Value of the delivery options granted to the short

## 18.4 Swaps

A *swap* is an agreement whereby two parties (called *counterparties*) agree to exchange periodic payments. The dollar amount of the payments exchanged is based on some predetermined dollar principal, which is called the *notional principal amount* or simply *notional amount*. The dollar amount each counterparty pays to the other is the agreed-upon periodic rate times the notional amount. The only dollars that are exchanged between the parties are the agreed-upon payments, not the notional amount.

A swap is an over-the-counter contract. Hence, the counterparties to a swap are exposed to counterparty risk. The most popular type of swap is an interest rate swap. We explain this type of swap in this section and explain its pricing.

### 18.4.1 Mechanics of an Interest Rate Swap

An *interest rate swap* is a linear payoff derivative. In such a swap, the counterparties swap payments in the same currency based on an interest rate. In the most common type of interest rate swap, one of the counterparties pays a fixed interest rate and the other party a floating interest rate. This type of swap is called a generic interest rate swap. The floating interest rate is commonly referred to as the *reference rate*.

For example, suppose the counterparties to a swap agreement are Farm Equip Corporation (a manufacturing firm) and JPMorgan. The notional amount of this swap is $100 million and the term of the swap is five years. Every year for the next five years, Farm Equip Corporation agrees to pay JPMorgan 5% per year, while JPMorgan agrees to pay Farm Equip Corporation one-year LIBOR as the reference rate.[22] This means that every year, Farm Equip Corporation will pay $5 million (5% times $100 million) to JPMorgan. The amount JPMorgan will pay Farm Equip Corporation depends on LIBOR. For example, if one-year LIBOR is 3%, JPMorgan will pay Farm Equip Corporation $3 million (3% times $100 million).

---

[22] In practice, interest rate swaps typically involve a quarterly exchange of payments and the reference rate is then three-month LIBOR, the London Interbank Offered Rate.

## 18.4.2 Interpretation of an Interest Rate Swap

If we look carefully at an interest rate swap, we can see that it is not a new derivative instrument. Rather, it can be decomposed into a package of the derivative instruments that we have already discussed. To understand this, consider our hypothetical interest rate swap. Every year for the next five years Farm Equip Corporation agrees to pay JPMorgan 5% and JPMorgan agrees to pay Farm Equip Corporation the reference rate, one-year LIBOR. Since the notional amount is $100 million, Farm Equip Corporation agrees to pay $9 million. Alternatively, we can rephrase this agreement as follows: Every year for the next five years, JPMorgan agrees to deliver something (one-year LIBOR) and to accept payment of $5 million. Looked at in this way, the counterparties are entering into multiple forward contracts: One party is agreeing to deliver something at some time in the future, and the other party is agreeing to accept delivery. The reason we say that there are multiple forward contracts is that the agreement calls for making the exchange each year for the next five years.

While a swap may be nothing more than a package of forward contracts, it is not a redundant contract for several reasons. First, in many markets where there are forward or futures contracts, the longest maturity does not extend out as far as that of a typical swap. Second, a swap is a more transactionally efficient instrument. By this we mean that in one transaction an entity can effectively establish a payoff equivalent to a package of forward contracts. The forward contracts would each have to be negotiated separately. Third, the liquidity of certain types of swaps has grown since the inception of swaps in 1981; swaps now are more liquid than many forward contracts, particularly long-dated (i.e., long-term) contracts.

## 18.4.3 Pricing of Interest Rate Swaps

The pricing of a swap follows from its interpretation: A swap's value is equal to the value of a package of forward contracts with each forward contract maturing on the swap payment date. That is, if there are forward contracts available in the market so that a swap can be synthetically recreated, the value of the swap would be equal to the value of the forward contracts. Unfortunately, even for the most commonly traded swaps, interest rate swaps, forward contracts with a maturity beyond two years are unavailable or not reliable for pricing because they are highly illiquid.

In the case of interest rate swaps, however, there are interest rate futures contracts that are available with maturities going out long enough to be able to synthetically create an interest rate swap.[23]

---

⬧ ⬧ ⬧   ## KEY POINTS

- A derivative instrument is a financial instrument whose value depends on some underlying asset.
- The underlying asset for a derivative instrument can be either a commodity, a financial instrument, or some reference entity such as an interest rate or stock index.

---

[23] For an explanation of how this is done, see Fabozzi (2009).

- Derivatives instruments are classified in terms of their payoff characteristics: linear payoff derivatives (which include forward, futures, and swap contracts) and nonlinear payoff derivatives (which include options).

- Linear payoff derivatives have a payoff that is characterized by a $1 for $1 gain or loss when the price of the underlying changes; a linear payoff derivative is also referred to as a symmetric payoff derivative.

- Linear payoff derivatives are risk sharing arrangements.

- A forward contract is an agreement for the future delivery of something at a specified price at the end of a designated period of time but differs from a futures contract in that it is nonstandardized and traded in the over-the-counter market.

- A futures contract is an agreement between a buyer (seller) and an established exchange or its clearinghouse in which the buyer (seller) agrees to take (make) delivery of something at a specified price at the end of a designated period of time.

- A futures contract is required to be marked to market; a forward contract may or may not be marked to market.

- An investor who takes a long futures/forward position realizes a gain when the futures price increases; an investor who takes a short futures position realizes a loss when the futures price decreases.

- The theoretical price of a futures/forward contract is determined by arbitrage arguments with any departures for the theoretical price being brought into line by using either a cash-and-carry trade or a reverse cash-and-carry trade.

- The theoretical price of a futures/forward contract is equal to the cash or spot price plus the cost of carry.

- The cost of carry is equal to the cost of financing the position less the cash yield on the underlying asset.

- The underlying for a stock index futures contract is a broad-based stock market index or a narrow-based index.

- Stock index futures contracts are cash settlement contracts.

- The nuances of stock index futures contracts that require a modification of the theoretical futures model are (1) the interim cash flows for the underlying and (2) the deliverable being a basket of stocks rather than a single asset.

- For the Treasury bond futures contract the underlying instrument is $100,000 par value of a hypothetical 20-year 8% Treasury coupon bond.

- Conversion factors are used to adjust the invoice price of a Treasury bond futures contract to make delivery equitable to both parties.

- The short in a Treasury bond futures contract has several delivery options: quality option (or swap option), timing option, and wild card option.

- The cheapest-to-deliver issue is the acceptable Treasury bond issue that has the largest implied repo rate.

- For Treasury bond futures contracts, the delivery options granted to the seller reduce the theoretical futures price below the theoretical futures price suggested by the standard arbitrage model.

- An interest rate swap is an agreement specifying that the parties exchange interest payments at designated times based on a notional principal amount.

- In a generic interest rate swap, one party agrees to make fixed-rate payments and receive floating-rate payments and the counterparty agrees to make floating-rate payments and receive fixed-rate payments.
- Interest rate swaps are over-the-counter instruments.

---

## ••• QUESTIONS

1.  **a.** From the perspective of counterparty risk, what is the difference between a futures and a forward contract?
    **b.** Comment on the following statement: Unlike a forward contract, a futures contract requires marking to market.
    **c.** Under what conditions are futures and forward prices the same?

2.  In a futures contract, initial margin is required when first taking a position in the contract. If the equity in the account drops below the maintenance margin, how much must be posted to maintain the position?

3.  Interpret equation (18.14) that is reproduced below:

$$U_{13} = E^Q[U_{23}|\mathfrak{I}_1] = E^Q\{E^Q[U_{33}|\mathfrak{I}_2]|\mathfrak{I}_1\}$$

from a financial perspective rather than mathematical deduction.

4.  **a.** Why is it not straightforward to price a stock index futures contract?
    **b.** Can the divergence between the theoretical future prices and market price for the futures be exploited? Be sure to explain your answer.

5.  **a.** For Treasury bond futures contracts, what are the three main delivery options?
    **b.** How do they impact the theoretical futures price?

6.  Why do market participants prefer to use interest rate swaps instead of a package of future/forward contracts to accomplish some risk management objective?

7.  Suppose that there is a forward contract on a non-dividend paying stock. The spot price of the stock is $80, and it would be either $85 or $78 in the next time period. The forward price is $83. The risk-free interest rate is constant at 5%.
    **a.** What is the value of the forward contract?
    **b.** Given the answer to (a), is there an arbitrage opportunity available?
    **c.** If there is an arbitrage opportunity, provide a strategy to exploit the arbitrage.

8.  Suppose that the current index value for a stock index is 10000. The expected annual dividend yield for the stock index is 3% annually. What is the theoretical index value of a six-month futures contract on this stock index if the annual risk-free interest rate for borrowing and lending is 6%?

9.  A one-year futures contract on a non-dividend-paying stock is entered into when the cash price for the stock is $30 and the risk-free interest rate is 10%.

**a.** What is the futures price today and what is the value of this futures contract?

**b.** Six month later, the stock price rises to $35 and the risk-free interest rate rises to 8%. What is the futures price and what is the value of this futures contract at that time?

10. In an arbitrage-free market, there are two time intervals and random interest rates between time 2 and time 3. Assume that an asset would pay no dividends during these two intervals. Each row of the following table shows a possible evolution of asset prices from time 1 to time 3.

EVOLUTION OF ASSET PRICES

| Time 1 | Time 2 | Time 3 |
|--------|--------|--------|
| $5 | $6 | $8 |
| $5 | $6 | $5 |
| $5 | $3 | $5 |
| $5 | $3 | $3 |

The interest rate between time 1 and time 2 is 10%; the interest rate for the first two situations between time 2 and time 3 is 12%, and 8% for the last two situations.

**a.** Calculate all the risk-neutral probabilities between time interval 1 and 2 as well as time interval 2 and 3.

**b.** Calculate the future and future prices.

11. The cheapest to deliver bond for a Treasury bond futures contract is the one for which:

Quoted cash bond price − Quoted futures price × Conversion factor

is the least. Suppose the quoted Treasury bond futures price is $100. Which of the following three bonds is the cheapest to deliver?

| Bond | Quoted Bond Prices | Conversion Factor |
|------|--------------------|--------------------|
| 1 | $125 | 1.20 |
| 2 | $131 | 1.25 |
| 3 | $120 | 1.10 |

# REFERENCES

Fabozzi, Frank J. (2009). *Bond Markets, Analysis and Strategies*. Hoboken, NJ: John Wiley & Sons.

Pliska, Stanley R. (1997). *Introduction to Mathematical Finance*. Malden, MA: Blackwell.

# 19

# PRICING DERIVATIVES BY ARBITRAGE: NONLINEAR PAYOFF DERIVATIVES

*I*n this chapter, we examine the pricing of derivatives with nonlinear payoffs, a special case of which are the payoffs of standard call and put options on stocks. Since the valuation methods are the same for all types of options, we will focus on stock options to understand better the pricing properties of general derivatives with nonlinear payoffs.

## 19.1 BASIC CONCEPTS

An *option* is a contract that gives the buyer the right, but not the obligation, to buy or to sell a particular asset (the underlying asset) on or before the option's expiration date, at an agreed price. The agreed price is called the *strike price* or *exercise price*. A *call option* is the right to buy the underlying asset and a *put option* is the right to sell it. The act of buying or selling the underlying asset by using the option is referred to as *exercising the option*. An *American option* can be exercised any time prior to or on the expiration date. A *European option* can be exercised only on the expiration date. Hence, there are four main types of options: an American call, an American put, a European call, and a European put.[1]

The option buyer must pay the seller of the option (also called the option writer) a fee to enter into the agreement. This fee is called the *option price* or *option premium*. Notice two important differences between a futures or forward contract compared to an option. First, in an option one of the parties must always compensate the other for entering into the contract at the trade date: The option buyer must pay the seller the option price. Second, only one party to an option is required to perform, not both parties as is the case with a futures or forward contract. In the case of an option, only the option seller is required to perform and that occurs when and if the option buyer

---

[1] There are also options that allow for exercise on some but not all trading dates prior to maturity.

exercises the option. However, after paying the option price the buyer need only exercise if he wishes. Otherwise, he can walk away from the option with no further obligation.

The option valuation on the expiration day is easy to calculate. For example, consider a call and put on IBM with strike price of $100. On the expiration day, if IBM's stock price is $110, the call is worth $10 (= $110 − $100), but the put is worth nothing. On the other hand, if IBM's stock price is $80, then the call is worthless, but the put is worth $20 ($100 − $80).

The value of a call on the expiration date, time $T$, is the larger of the stock price minus the exercise price or zero,

$$C_T = \max(S_T - X, 0) = (S_T - X)^+ \tag{19.1}$$

where

$(S_T - X)^+$ is a common shorthand notation for $\max(S_T - X, 0)$
$S_T$ is the stock price at maturity
$X$ is the strike price

Similarly, the value of a put option on the expiration date is:

$$P_T = \max(X - S_T, 0) = (X - S_T)^+ \tag{19.2}$$

Note that if we double the terminal stock price, the payoffs will not necessarily be doubled. For example, consider the call option on IBM stock with a strike price of $100 and compare the payoff if the stock price at the expiration date is $100 and $200. When the terminal stock price is $100, the payoff for the call option is zero. However, when the terminal stock price is $200, the payoff is $100. Hence, option payoffs are nonlinear. Here we see another difference between an option and a futures and forward contract. For futures and forward contracts, doubling the terminal price of the underlying doubles the contract's payoff. As discussed in Chapter 18, futures and forward contracts have linear payoffs.

In practice, option investors are interested in their potential profits at all possible stock prices. For the above IBM option, Figure 19.1 plots the potential profits of the call at the option expiration date. Let's assume that the option price for the IBM call option is $5. The option buyer's profit is $5 (assume zero interest for simplicity) when the stock price ends up at $S_T = \$110$ on the expiration day. The option buyer realizes $10 by exercising the call option. However, this amount must be reduced by the option price of $5, so the net profit from exercising the option is $5 = ($10 − $5). The profit is $15 when $S_T = 120$. However, if $S_T \leq 100$, the buyer will not exercise the call and consequently incurs a maximum loss of $5, the purchase price. Figure 19.2 is a similar plot for the potential profits of the put option.

At any time $t$ from today to expiration, an option holder can take one of three actions: (1) hold the option; (2) exercise (if the terms of the option permit early exercise); or (3) sell it. We say a call is:

*out-of-the-money* if the stock price is below the strike price, $S_t < X$
*at-the-money* if the stock price is equal to the strike price, $S_t = X$
*in-the-money* if the stock price is above the strike price, $S_t > X$

## FIGURE 19.1
### CALL VALUE AT EXPIRATION

Profit at $T$: on a long position of a call on IBM with strike price = $100. The cost of the call is = $5, and the time since purchase is $T$ years.

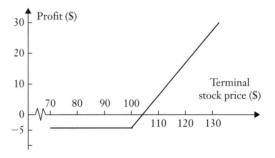

## FIGURE 19.2
### PUT VALUE AT EXPIRATION

Profit at $T$: on a long position of a put on IBM with strike price = $100. The cost of the put is = $4, and the time since purchase is $T$ years.

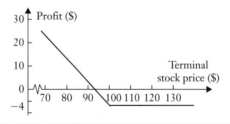

For a put option, the same definitions follow, but with the inequalities reversed.

Clearly, the option buyer will only exercise an option when it is in-the-money. For example, for the IBM call option with a strike price of $100 (i.e., $X = \$100$), the option buyer only exercises it when the stock price is above $100. This exercise value is known as the option's *intrinsic value*. In general, $\max(S_t - X, 0)$ is the intrinsic value for a call, and $\max(X - S_t, 0)$ for a put. It should be noted that the intrinsic values are zero for out-of-the-money and at-the-money options.

Prior to expiration, the option buyer does not have to exercise the option when it is in-the-money. If the option buyer wants to realize the intrinsic value, all that need be done is to sell the option in market. Simple arbitrage assures that the option's price is at least as high as the value if it were to be exercised (i.e., the intrinsic value) and will usually be higher. The purpose of the option pricing theory discussed later in this chapter is to determine the fair price of an option.

## 19.2 SIMPLE USES OF OPTIONS

Why do we care about options? They are tools for both hedging and speculation. If an investor owns IBM stock, for example, and worries about the downside price risk for that stock, he can simply buy put options on IBM. For example, if the investor has one share of IBM stock with a price of $100 today and wants to avoid the risk of the price dropping to $80, he can buy a put with a strike price of $80. Then no matter how the stock price moves between the purchase date and the expiration date, the investor can always sell the stock for at least $80. In other words, with the put option, the floor value of the stock position is $80 over the life of the option. If he has a higher risk appetite, he can buy a put with strike price of $50. Buying a put is analogous to buying insurance, where the strike price is effectively the minimum price that will be received for an asset and the difference between the current price of the asset and the strike price is the deductible that the insurance buyer is willing to accept. Of course, the option price is the insurance premium (hence, the use of the term option premium as a synonym for the term option price). For example, suppose the stock price is $100 and the investor purchases a put option with a $70 strike price. The investor is willing to accept a loss of up to $30 if the price falls. Thus, the $30 is effectively the deductible. If, instead, the investor buys a put with a strike price of $80, he is only willing to accept a loss of $20 should the price fall and the deductible is $20. As with insurance, the greater the deductible the insurance buyer is willing to accept (i.e., the lower the strike price), the lower the cost of the insurance. In the case of a put, a put with a strike price of $70 (a deductible of $30) will cost less than a put with a strike price of $80 (a deductible of $20).

Consider now a speculative use for options. Suppose that IBM stock price is currently at $100, and a call with a strike price of $110 sells at $5 (i.e., option price). If an investor has $5,000, he can buy 1,000 options.[2] Then, if the stock price rises to $150 on the expiration day, each option will be worth $40 or a total of $40,000 for the 1,000 options. Hence, the return on the $5,000 invested in the call option position is 700% [= ($40,000 − $5,000)/$5,000]. In contrast, if he had invested directly in the stock, the investor can buy 50 shares (= $5,000/$100), realizing a profit of $50 on each share or $2,500 on all 50 shares. The return in this case would be 50% [= ($5,000 − $2,500)/$5,000].

---

[2] In the real world, stock options typically involve 100 shares of the underlying stock. However, for simplicity we will assume each option is for one share.

While the investment in the call option generated a far superior return than investing directly in the stock, there is also a disadvantage of greatly increased risk. To see this, suppose that the stock price goes up to $105 rather than $150. The stock investment will generate a 5% return, but the option investment will suffer a 100% loss since all the call options will expire worthless. This simple example highlights the high risk and high return nature of option trading.

There are countless ways in which options can be used. For example, a popular bet is on news or earning announcements. Suppose that, prior to an announcement, it is unknown whether the news is good or bad. If one believes that a large stock price movement will follow the announcement, he can buy both a call and put on the stock, each with at-the-money (ATM) strike prices. In this way, whether the stock moves up or down, he can make money as long as the movement is sizable enough to cover the option price. This strategy is known as a *straddle strategy*, which is clearly difficult to do without the use of options. Moreover, since ATM options are more expensive than out-of-the money ones, the investor can buy the latter instead. Then the strategy is known as a *strangle strategy*.

## 19.3  PUT-CALL PARITY

The prices of a *European* call and a *European* put cannot be arbitrary. Rather, arbitrage possibilities mean they are related by the *put-call parity* relationship:

$$S + P = C + D + PV(X) \tag{19.3}$$

where $D$ is the present value of dividends paid by the underlying stock over the life of the option, and $PV(X)$ is the present value of the strike price. The intuition is that buying a stock and a put has upside potential and limited downside, as shown by the left-hand side of (19.3), and so is buying a call with risk-free investment of certain cash, as shown by the right-hand side of (19.3). Since both have the same payoffs in the future, in the absence of costless arbitraging[3] their prices today must be the same. Note that although the formulation of put-call parity is in terms of options on individual stocks, the relationship holds for options on stock indexes and bonds. In the case of bonds, the dividends are replaced by coupon interest payments over the life of the option.

A rigorous proof of the put-call parity relation works as follows. Assume for simplicity that there are no dividends. Consider the payoffs of two portfolios. Portfolio $A$ contains one share of the stock and a put. Portfolio $B$ contains a call and an investment of the present value of $X$. Let $S_T$ be the stock price at expiration. Then, as shown below, the two portfolios will always have the same payoffs on the expiration day regardless of the stock price:

---

[3] Trading commissions and illiquidity can inhibit arbitrage possibilities and hence, prevent an exact put-call parity relationship from being established.

|  | Value on the Expiration Date |  |
|---|---|---|
| If | $S_T \leq X$ | $S_T > X$ |
| **Portfolio A:** | | |
| Buy the stock | $S_T$ | $S_T$ |
| Buy one put | $X - S_T$ | $0$ |
| Total | $X$ | $S_T$ |
| | | |
| **Portfolio B:** | | |
| Buy one call | $0$ | $S_T - X$ |
| Invest PV of X | $X$ | $X$ |
| Total | $X$ | $S_T$ |

Therefore, the two portfolios must have the same price today if there is no arbitrage. This implies that the put-call parity must hold.

In option pricing, we usually use a continuously compounded interest rate. (See Web-Appendix J.) If today is time 0, and the time to expiration is $T$, then:

$$PV(X) = Xe^{-rT}$$

where $r$ is the continuously compounded risk-free rate (annualized).

The application of put-call parity is straightforward. For example, suppose that a firm's stock sells at $50. Suppose that a put option, with strike price $45 and a maturity of 6 months is selling in the market at $3. Assume further that $r = 5\%$. What price should a call option sell for?

Now we have:

$$S = \$50, \ X = \$45, \ P = \$3, \ r = 5\%, \ T = 0.5, \ D = 0$$

so the PV of the strike price is:

$$PV(X) = \$45 \times e^{-0.05 \times 0.5} = \$43.89$$

By put-call parity, we have:

$$C = S + P - PV(X) = \$50 + \$3 - \$43.89 = \$7.12$$

Note that the above put-call parity holds exactly for European options, but only approximately for American options. One reason is that either an American put or an American call may be exercised prior to maturity, while the other is still out-of-the-money.

## 19.4 KEY IDEA FOR VALUATION

The fundamental insights that lead to almost all option valuation formulae (i.e., formulae for determining the theoretical value of an option) are

- A suitable portfolio (called a *replicating portfolio*) of the stock and bond replicates the payoff of the option.
- A suitable portfolio (called a *hedging portfolio*) of the option and stock is risk free.

Then, if there is no arbitrage, the cost of the first portfolio (i.e., the replicating portfolio) must be the option price, and the return on the second portfolio (i.e., the hedging portfolio) must be the risk-free rate.

To obtain an option price, we have to make an assumption on how the stock price will move from today until the time when the option expires. Given such an assumption, we can obtain the theoretical option price based on either of the insights, used together with the assumption that there are no arbitrage opportunities.

## 19.5 SINGLE-PERIOD BINOMIAL MODEL

In this section, we provide a simple option valuation based on the key insights. To make the ideas and methods as easy to understand as possible, we assume a one-period and two-state model for the stock price. These assumptions will be relaxed later.

### 19.5.1 Replicating Portfolio

Suppose that a stock's price is $50 today, and that it can have one of two possible values next month: either $60 in the "up" state or $40 in the "down" state. Consider a European call option to buy the stock next month at the strike price of $55. If the monthly interest rate is $r = 1\%$, what should the call price be?

Note that the call will be worth $5 if the stock is up, and $0 if the stock is down. Figure 19.3 illustrates the stock price tree and the payoffs to the option. Now we want to replicate the payoffs to the call. Consider a portfolio of 0.25 shares of the stock and the sale of a bond of $9.90. Selling the a bond is a means of obtaining funds (i.e., borrowing) to invest and is denoted by −$9.90. The construction of the portfolio consisting of the 0.25 shares of stock and the amount of bonds to be sold will be derived later.

**FIGURE 19.3**
REPLICATING PORTFOLIO

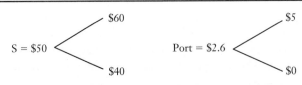

If the stock goes up to $60, the 0.25 shares of the stock will be worth $60 × 0.25 = $15. The sale of the bond means that not only must the $9.90 be repaid, but there is interest of $0.90 (1% interest for the month). So $10 must be paid to satisfy the bond obligation. Thus, the portfolio is worth the difference between the value of the shares ($15) and the bond repayment ($10) or $5. If, instead, the stock price goes down, the 0.25 shares of the stock is worth $10, which is just enough to pay the borrowing, so the portfolio is worth $0.

We have shown that the above portfolio replicates the payoff of the call. If there is no arbitrage, the cost of the portfolio must be equal to the cost of the call, implying that:

$$0.25 \times \$50 - \$9.90 = \$2.60$$

must be the call price.

The remaining question is: How do we construct the replicating portfolio? Suppose we need $\Delta$ shares of the stock and $B$ amount of bonds, then we want:

$$\$60 \times \Delta + (1.01) \times B = \$5 \quad \text{in the up state}$$
$$\$40 \times \Delta + (1.01) \times B = \$0 \quad \text{in the down state}$$

to replicate the payoff of the call. By solving the above two equations, we get $\Delta = 0.25$ and. $B = -\$9.90$.

The replicating portfolio says that, holding a call option is equivalent to the portfolio of holding $\Delta$ shares of the stock and a loan of amount $B$, that is,

$$C = S\Delta + B \tag{19.4}$$

In words, this says that:

> Value of being long the call option
> $=$ Value of being long the underlying asset $+$ Borrowing     (19.5)

That is, the call can be synthetically created by a portfolio of stocks and leverage such that the payoff of the portfolio replicates the payoff of the call, and this is why the portfolio is called the replicating portfolio (also referred to as the *equivalent portfolio*).

In general, if a stock with price $S$ today will either go up to $(1 + u)S$ or go down to $(1 + d)S$, where $u > r$ and $d < r$, we solve

$$(1 + u)S \times \Delta + (1 + r) \times B = C_u, \quad \textit{up state}$$
$$(1 + d)S \times \Delta + (1 + r) \times B = C_d, \quad \textit{down state}$$

for the replicating portfolio, where $C_u$ and $C_d$ are the call values in the up and down states, respectively. The solution is easily obtained,

$$\Delta = \frac{C_u - C_d}{S(u - d)}, \quad B = \frac{(1 + u)C_d - (1 + d)C_u}{(u - d)(1 + r)} \tag{19.6}$$

Equation (19.6) is the general formula for finding the composition of a replicating portfolio. Using equation (19.6) along with equation (19.4), we can write the call price as:

$$C = \frac{pC_u + (1-p)C_d}{1+r}, \quad p = \frac{r-d}{u-d} \tag{19.7}$$

As will become clear later, the risk-neutral probability $p$ can be interpreted as the probability from the perspective of a risk-neutral investor. Hence, the call price is simply the present value of its expected payoff, calculated under the risk-neutral probability. Equation (19.7) is a special case of the theory discussed in Chapter 16. Note also that the same formula is also applicable to a put option once the call payoffs are replaced by the put values. Alternatively, one can compute the put price by using the put-call parity.

Now, to value the previous call option, we can apply equation (19.7) directly without computing the replicating portfolio. We have $u = 20\%$, $d = -20\%$, and so:

$$p = (0.01 + 0.20)/(0.20 + 0.20) = 0.525$$

Thus,

$$C = \frac{0.525 \times \$5 + (1 - 0.525) \times \$0}{1 + 0.01} = \$2.60$$

the same answer as before, as it should be.

## 19.5.2  Hedging Portfolio

Consider now the position of a market maker who sells a call to an investor and would like to buy $\Delta$ shares of the stock to hedge. That is, he has a portfolio consisting of (1) a short position in one call and (2) a long position in $\Delta$ shares of the stock. The value of this portfolio next month will be ($60 \Delta - \$5$) if the stock goes up and $\$40\Delta$ if the stock goes down.

How can the market maker arrange a risk free portfolio? If he buys $\Delta = 0.25$ shares, then the value of the portfolio will be:

$$(\$60\Delta - \$5) = \$40\Delta = \$10$$

regardless of which state is realized, that is, regardless of whether the stock goes up or down! Assuming as usual that there are no arbitrage opportunities in the economy, this portfolio must earn the same return as the risk-free rate. Since the cost of the portfolio is ($\$50 \times 0.25 - C) = (\$12.5 - C)$, where $C$ is the call price and $-C$ represents "negative" cost because the option market maker receives money from selling the call, we must have:

$$\frac{\$10 - (\$12.5 - C)}{\$12.5 - C} = 1\%$$

or $C = \$12.5 - \$10/(1 + 1\%) = \$2.60$.

Note that the replicating portfolio and the hedging portfolio are closely related. If $S\Delta + B$ replicates the payoff of a call $C = S\Delta + B$, then $S\Delta - C$ must be the hedging portfolio because $S\Delta - C = B$ is risk free. The converse is also true. Hence, the number of shares $\Delta$ of the hedge portfolio (known as the *hedge ratio*), can be computed from equation (19.6) for hedging an arbitrary call.

## 19.5.3 Risk-Neutral Valuation

The replicating and hedging portfolio valuations provide profound insights into how option prices are determined. In particular, option prices have been shown to be independent of investors' risk tolerance. Intuitively, no matter what level of risk tolerance an investor has, he will take any possible arbitrage opportunities because by definition such opportunities are riskless. Then, since the absence of arbitrage does not depend on investors' risk tolerance, neither do option prices, which also rely on the absence of any possible arbitrage opportunities.

The fact that option prices do not depend on investors' risk tolerance is of fundamental importance, leading to the so-called *risk-neutral valuation*. We can compute the option price in the real world (where investors have different levels of risk tolerance) by computing it in an imagined *risk-neutral* world where (1) all investors care only about the expected returns (not the risk as measured by standard deviations) and (2) the expected returns on all risky investments are the same as the risk-free rate.

Risk-neutral valuation is a simple method for computing option prices easily and quickly. Consider now how we apply it to compute the earlier call price of $2.6. In a risk-neutral world, the expected return on the stock must be the risk-free rate of 1% per month, so:

$$p\$60 + (1 - p)\$40 = \$50(1 + 1\%)$$

where $p$ is the *risk-neutral probability* that the stock to go up, and $(1 - p)$ is the risk-neutral probability for the stock to go down. Solving the above equation, we have:

$$p = 0.525$$

Now, using this probability, we can compute the expected payoff on the call option,

$$0.525 \times \$5 + (1 - 0.525) \times \$0 = \$2.625$$

Since the option should produce the risk-free return in a risk-neutral world, its present value discounted by $r$ should be its price today, that is,

$$C = \frac{0.525 \times \$5 + (1 - 0.525) \times \$0}{1 + r} = \frac{\$2.625}{1 + 1\%} = \$2.60$$

In general, if a stock price either goes up to $(1 + u)S$ or goes down to $(1 + d)S$, the risk-neutral probability must satisfy:

$$p \times (1 + u)S + (1 - p) \times (1 + d)S = S \times (1 + r)$$

Then:

$$p = \frac{r - d}{u - d} \qquad (19.8)$$

The expected payoff on a call option is then:

$$pC_u + (1 - p)C_d$$

and so the call price is the discounted expected payoff,

$$C = \frac{pC_u + (1 - p)C_d}{1 + r} \qquad (19.9)$$

This is the same formula as equation (19.7). Note that the risk-neutral probability is a function of the stock growth rates (i.e., the amount by which the stock can go up or down) and $r$, but does not depend on any call or put features.

For a further clarification, consider another example. A firm's stock sells at $100. It is known that the price will be either $125 or $75 a year from now. Thus, $u$ is 0.25 and $d$ is $-0.25$. Assume that the annual risk-free interest rate is 4%. What price should a European call option with a strike price of $110 and a maturity of one year sell for? One can solve the problem in three steps. First, find the risk-neutral probability,

$$p = (r - d)/(u - d) = (0.04 + 0.25)/(0.25 + 0.25) = 0.58$$

Second, find the expected payoff of the option at the time of its expiry,

$$p \times \$15 + (1 - p) \times \$0 = \$8.70$$

Third, get the time 0 option price by discounting the expected payoff,

$$C = \$8.7/(1 + 0.04) = \$8.37$$

## 19.6 BLACK-SCHOLES FORMULA

In this section, we provide the famous Black-Scholes option valuation formula. We first lay out the key assumption that the stock price follows a lognormal distribution, then compute the option price based on the no-arbitrage principle. Finally, we discuss various features of the formula.

## 19.6.1 Lognormal Stock Price

We have so far computed option prices by assuming stock prices can change according to two states of the world, clearly a simplistic assumption. Another model for describing the movement in stock prices is a *random walk*, in which a stock price is assumed to evolve according to:

$$S_{t+1} = S_t + \varepsilon_{t+1} \qquad (19.10)$$

where $\varepsilon_{t+1}$ is a noise term. This model says that tomorrow's stock price is today's price plus a random noise. The noise $\varepsilon_{t+1}$ is a normal random variable with zero mean and standard deviation $\sigma$. The standard deviation $\sigma$ reflects the magnitude of fluctuations in the price. For example, assume today's price is $S_0 = \$50$ and the standard deviation of $\varepsilon_{t+1}$ is 2. Some good and bad news may successively shock the stock price by, say, $\varepsilon_1 = 0.85$, $\varepsilon_2 = -1.34$, $\varepsilon_3 = 0.28$, and so on. Then the price will be $S_1 = 50 + 0.85 = \$50.85$, $S_2 = 50.85 - 1.34 = \$49.51$, $S_3 = 49.51 + 0.28 = \$49.79$, and so on.

To understand better the random walk model, it will be useful to review two definitions of the rate of return before proceeding further. The first definition is the *discrete return* or *simple return* given by:

$$R_t = (S_{t+1} - S_t)/S_t = S_{t+1}/S_t - 1 \qquad (19.11)$$

the percentage change in price. The second is the *continuously compounded return*, given by:

$$R_t^* = \ln(S_{t+1}/S_t) \qquad (19.12)$$

the rate of change in price expressed as a natural logarithm. If today's price of $50, and if the future price is either $25 and 0, then the simple returns are $-50\%$ or $-100\%$. A simple return of $-200\%$ does not make any sense, since the simple return is both bounded from below and asymmetric. On the other hand, the continuously compounded return is well defined for any value. For example, the continuously compounded returns of $-50\%$, $-100\%$, and $-200\%$ mean the future stock price is $33.33 ($= 50e^{-0.5 \times 1}$), $18.40, and $6.77, respectively. In pricing derivatives, continuously compounded returns are used instead of simple returns to be consistent with the assumption that prices move continuously over continuous time. The continuously compounded return is often assumed to be normally distributed, further implying that it is symmetric around 0. In addition, the volatility used in derivatives is the standard deviation of the continuously compounded return, not that of the simple return.

Going back to the the random walk model given by equation (19.10), despite its popularity, there are two problems. The first is that the normal random variable has a positive probability of realizing a large negative number. For instance, in the earlier example with $S_0 = \$50$, $\varepsilon_1$ can be less than $-\$50$ with positive probability, and then $S_1 < 0$. This is clearly not possible in the real world. A simple way to resolve the negative stock price problem is to assume that the logarithm (log) of the price is a random walk. That is,

$$\ln(S_{t+1}) = \ln(S_t) + \varepsilon_{t+1} \qquad (19.13)$$

In this case, the future price $S_{t+1} = S_t e^{\varepsilon_{t+1}}$ will always be positive if today's price is positive.

The second problem with the random walk model is that the expected return of the stock is zero, which is also unrealistic. Suppose $\mu$ is the annual expected return. We can add it into the above equation (19.13) to obtain:

$$\ln(S_{t+1}/S_t) = \mu + \varepsilon_{t+1}, \quad \varepsilon_{t+1} \sim N(0, \sigma^2) \tag{19.14}$$

where $N(0, \sigma^2)$ denotes the normal distribution with mean zero and variance $\sigma^2$.

The last two changes lead us to the next fundamental assumption underlying the famous Black-Scholes formula:

*Assumption 1:* The continuously compounded stock returns, $\ln(S_{t+1}/S_t)$, are independent over time, and identically normally distributed with mean $\mu$ and variance $\sigma^2$.

This assumption is also known as the *geometric random walk model, geometric Brownian motion,* and *lognormal stock price model.* Figure 19.4 is helpful in understanding the assumption. Assume that the stock price is $50 today, and its average growth rate or expected return is $\mu = 16\%$, with 20% annual size of fluctuations (i.e., annual volatility). In the absence of risks, the stock should grow at 16%, that is,

**FIGURE 19.4**
PRICE UNDER LOGNORMAL ASSUMPTION

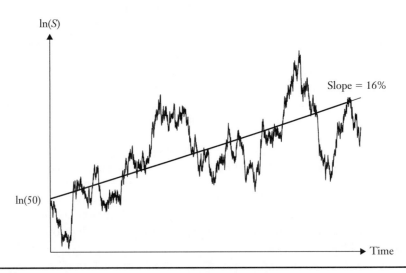

Assume    $S_0 = 50$,  $\mu = 16\%$,  $\sigma = 20\%$

$\mu$ is the expected return of the stock (mean of the return)
$\sigma$ is the volatility of the stock (standard deviation of the return)

its prices over time should be the straight line with slope 16%. However, as good and bad news is released along the way, the actual price path is the up and down curve, with the size of annual fluctuation being normally distributed with an annual volatility of 20%.

The lognormal assumption is additive in that the sum of two lognormal returns remains lognormal. Suppose today is time 0. Over $T$ periods, the total return is:

$$R_T^* = \sum_{t=1}^{T} \ln(S_{t+1}/S_t) = \mu T + \sum_{t=1}^{T} \varepsilon_t \tag{19.15}$$

The expected return and variance are:

$$E[R_T^*] = \mu T, \quad var[R_T^*] = \sigma^2 T \tag{19.16}$$

This says that the expected return grows linearly with time $T$, but the standard deviation (known also as volatility) grows at $\sigma\sqrt{T}$. Since $R_T^* = \ln(S_{t+1}/S_t)$, we can also write the lognormal assumption as:

$$\ln(S_T) \sim N[\ln(S_0) + \mu T, \sigma^2 T]$$

Taking exponential on the both sides, we have the assumption in terms of price,

$$S_T = S_0 e^{\mu T + \sigma\sqrt{T}\tilde{z}} \tag{19.17}$$

where $\tilde{z}$ is a standard normal random variable with mean zero and variance 1. This equation will be useful later.

## 19.6.2 The Formula

Recall that in our one-period–two-states model, a call option price is given by:

$$C = \frac{pC_u + (1-p)C_d}{1+r} \tag{19.18}$$

i.e., the price takes the form of an expected payoff discounted at the riskless rate. This is also the risk-neutral valuation principle discussed in Chapter 16. Hence, even under the lognormal assumption, we still have:

$$C = e^{-rT}E(\tilde{C}_T) \tag{19.19}$$

where $r$ is the continuously compounded risk-free rate (usually annualized) and $T$ is the time (from today) to maturity of the option (usually measured in years). The key now is to compute the expected payoff, $E(\tilde{C}_T)$, under the lognormal assumption.

Since $\tilde{C}_T = (S_T - X, 0)^+$, we can decompose $E(\tilde{C}_T)$ into two terms,

$$E(\tilde{C}_T) = E(S_T - X|S_T \geq X) + E(0|S_T < X)$$
$$= [E(S_T|S_T \geq X) - X] \; prob(S_T \geq X). \qquad (19.20)$$

By transforming $\ln S_T$ into the standard normal random variable, we can then compute the two terms explicitly (see the appendix to this chapter), and hence, obtain the most useful and famous *Black-Scholes formula* for option pricing for the price of a European call,

$$C = SN(d_1) - Xe^{-rT} \; N(d_2) \qquad (19.21)$$

where

$$d_1 = \frac{\ln(S/X) + (r + \sigma^2/2) T}{\sqrt{\sigma^2 T}}, \quad d_2 = d_1 - \sqrt{\sigma^2 T}$$

and

$$N(d) = prob(\tilde{z} < d) = \int_{-\infty}^{d} \frac{1}{\sqrt{2\pi}} e^{-z^2/2} dz$$

is the cumulative normal distribution function, that is, the probability that a standard normal random variable $\tilde{z}$ is less than a given number $d$. In practice, $N(d)$ can be easily computed by using the Excel function *normsdist*. For example, $N(0) = $ normsdist $(0) = 0.5$, $N(1) = $ normsdist$(1) = 0.8413$, etc.

The Black-Scholes formula given by equation (19.21) provides a price of a European call option on a non-dividend-paying stock (the dividend case will be discussed later). To compute the call price, there are five parameters to supply:

1. $S = $ current stock price
2. $X = $ exercise or strike price
3. $r = $ risk-free rate (continuously compounded) over the life of the option
4. $\sigma = $ standard deviation (volatility) of (continuously compounded) stock returns
5. $T = $ time to expiration date or maturity

Note that $S$, $X$, and $T$ are directly observable, but $r$ and $\sigma$ are not. They have to be estimated, which will be discussed later.

Consider now how to implement the Black-Scholes formula. Assume a stock that pays no dividends for the next three months is selling at $30. The annual risk-free rate is estimated to be 6% and volatility is estimated to be 50%. We ask two questions. First, what is the price of a call with strike $35 and time to expiration three months? Second, what is the price of a put option with the same strike and time to expiration? Here we have

$$S = \$30, \quad X = \$35, \quad T = 3 \text{ months}, \quad \sigma = 0.5, \quad r = 0.06$$

Since $r$ is here assumed to be the continuously compounded annual interest rate, $T$ should also be in annual form; that is, $T = 3/12 = 0.25$ years.

To obtain the price of the call, we compute first $d_1$ and $d_1$:

$$d_1 = \frac{\ln(\$30/\$35) + (0.06 + 0.5^2/2) \times 0.25}{\sqrt{0.5^2 \times 0.25}} = -0.4316$$

$$d_2 = -0.4316 - \sqrt{0.5^2 \times 0.25} = -0.6816$$

Then, by using Excel or a relevant software package, we get the values of the cumulative normal distribution function,

$$N(d_1) = N(-0.4316) = 0.3330$$
$$N(d_2) = N(-0.6816) = 0.2477$$

Then, plugging these into the Black-Scholes formula given by equation (19.21), we have:

$$C = \$30 \times N(d_1) - \$35 \times e^{-0.06 \times 0.25} \times N(d_2)$$
$$= \$30 \times 0.3330 - \$35 \times e^{-0.06 \times 0.25} \times 0.2477$$
$$= \$1.45$$

Given the price of the call, we now use put-call parity to get the price of the put as follows:

$$P = C + PV(X) - S$$
$$= \$1.45 + \$35 e^{-0.06 \times 0.25} - \$30$$
$$= \$5.93,$$

where we have computed the present value of the strike price using continuous discounting, because $r$ is the continuously compounded interest rate.

How do we interpret the terms in the Black-Scholes formula? The same replicating portfolio interpretation,

$$C = S\Delta + B \tag{19.22}$$

holds in both the previous binomial model and in the lognormal model here. It is just that the two models imply different forms of $\Delta$ and $B$. Now we have $\Delta = N(d_1)$, which is the delta or hedge or the number of shares one needs to buy today to replicate the payoff of the call. This is also roughly the amount of money the buyer of the call makes when $S$ goes up by \$1. In the example here, the call seller should purchase $N(d_1) = 0.333$ shares of the stock to hedge the call.

The term $X e^{-rT} N(d_2)$ is the analogue to $B$ in equation (19.22), the amount of money one borrows to finance the purchase of the stock in the replicating portfolio. Note that both $d_1$ and $d_2$ are transformations to link the log stock price to the standard normal random variable, and they have no obvious economic interpretations.

In addition, based on the proof in the appendix to this chapter, $N(d_2)$ is the risk-neutral probability for the option to make money. It is 24.77% in the previous example. However, it should be pointed out that this is different from the true probability, $N(d_2^*)$, where:

$$d_2^* = (\ln(S/X) + \mu T)/(\sqrt{\sigma^2 T}) \tag{19.23}$$

is a function of $\mu$, the expected continuously compounded return on the stock. The expected return is $\mu = r - \sigma^2/2$ if the risk-neutral probability is the same as the true probability. The derivation of $N(d_2^*)$ is the same as $N(d_2)$, except now the objective probability is used. In the earlier example, if $\mu = 15\%$, then $d_2^* = -0.4666$ and $N(d_2^*) = 33.3\%$. Intuitively, the objective probability is what risk-averse investors believe the stock will exceed the strike price, and in a risk-averse world it must be higher than the risk-neutral probability.

The Black-Scholes formula is the first model recognizing that options are replicable assets and can be priced given the underlying asset price and other parameters. It provides profound insights for subsequent derivatives theory and practice.[4]

## 19.6.3 Accounting for Dividends

The Black-Scholes formula assumes no dividends. But stocks do pay dividends in practice. It is clear, however, that only those dividends over the life of the option will matter in the option price. We consider two types of dividends here. The first is *discrete* where the dividends are paid over a finite number of dates prior to maturity. This is the case for individual stocks in practice. The second is *continuous* dividends where the dividends can be viewed as being paid continuously, such as holding a stock index or a foreign currency (the foreign interest rate plays the role of dividends).

For European options, dividends can be accommodated straightforwardly. We can simply apply the Black-Scholes formula to the dividend-adjusted price, that is, the stock price excluding the present value of the dividends. The reason is that when the dividends are fully anticipated, the stock price will drop each time by the amount of dividends that are paid out. One can imagine that there are two identical firms. One pays out all the dividends today by its present value and another pays out sequentially. Since both firms pay out the same present value of dividends, their values must be identical on the option expiration day, which is what matters for the European option holder. Hence, the option on the second firm must be identical to that on the first, but the second has no dividends over the life of the option.

If dividends are discrete and paid according to a known series, $\{D_1, D_2, \cdots, D_m\}$, to be paid at $0 < t_1, t_2, \ldots, t_m \leq T$, then the dividend-adjusted stock price is

$$S_D = S - D_1 e^{-rt_1} - D_2 e^{-rt_2} - \cdots - D_m e^{-rt_m} \tag{19.24}$$

---

[4] After several rejections by academic journals, the Black-Scholes paper was finally published in 1973. Merton (1973) provided further insights of their model along with important extensions. Scholes and Merton received the 1997 Nobel Prize in economics for their contributions, while Black was ineligible for the prize because of his death in 1995.

The option price is then:

$$C = S_D N(d_1) - X e^{-rT} N(d_2) \qquad (19.25)$$

where

$$d_1 = \frac{\ln(S_D/X) + (r + \sigma^2/2) T}{\sqrt{\sigma^2 T}}, \quad d_2 = d_1 - \sqrt{\sigma^2 T}$$

For example, suppose that $S = \$50$, $X = \$50$, $T = 0.25$, $\sigma = 50\%$, $r = 6\%$ and the stock pays \$2 dividend in one month, that is, $D_1 = 2$ with $t_1 = 1/12$. Then $S_D = S - D_1 e^{-0.06 \times 1/12} = \$48.01$. Applying the Black-Scholes formula given by equation (19.21) for $S_D$, the call price is \$4.24. A put price is computed similarly. For example, the put price with the same strike is

$$P = C - S_D + PV(X) = \$4.24 - \$48.01 + \$50 e^{-0.06 \times 3/12} = \$5.49$$

Note that the put-call parity relation applied here is the one without dividends, because $S_D$ has already adjusted for the dividends. One can also apply the version with dividends, but then $S$ has to to used. The answer will obviously be the same.

For European options with continuous dividends, the present value of the dividends is:

$$D = S(1 - e^{-\delta T}) \qquad (19.26)$$

where $\delta$ is the annual dividend yield rate. Then, the dividend-adjusted price is:

$$S_D = S - D = S e^{-\delta T} \qquad (19.27)$$

Plugging this into the Black-Scholes formula and rearranging terms, we obtain:

$$C = S e^{-\delta T} N(d_1) - X e^{-rT} N(d_2) \qquad (19.28)$$

where

$$d_1 = \frac{\ln(S/X) + (r - \delta + \sigma^2/2) T}{\sqrt{\sigma^2 T}}, \quad d_2 = d_1 - \sqrt{\sigma^2 T}$$

For the price of a European put a similar formula,

$$P = X e^{-rT} N(-d_2) - S e^{-\delta T} N(-d_1)$$

holds.

### 19.6.4 Estimating $r$

The Black-Scholes formula is a function of five parameters, $S$, $X$, $r$, $\sigma$, and $T$ (and a sixth, $\delta$ if there are dividends), of which the risk-free rate $r$ and volatility $\sigma$ have to be estimated in practice. It is easy to estimate $r$ from financial market data. For short-term (less than 1 year) options, a proxy for $r$ may be chosen as the continuously compounded annual rate of return for holding a U.S. Treasury bill. For example, suppose that the face value of a 90-day Treasury bill is $100 and the cash price is $99.30. Then $r$ is obtained by solving $\$100 = \$99.30e^{r \times 90/365}$, that is, $r = 2.85\%$. For long-term options, $r$ is extracted from Treasury note prices.

Theoretically, $r$ is the rate of U.S. Treasury security whose maturity matches the remaining life of the option. So, for short-term options, the maturity of the Treasury bill should be close to the maturity of the option. This, however, seldom matters because the option price is fairly insensitive to the risk-free rate. To see this, consider our earlier example with $S = \$30$, $X = \$35$, $T = 0.25$, $\sigma = 0.5$, $r = 0.06$, $d = 0.0$, the call price is $1.45. Allowing the risk-free rate to go up from 1% to 10%, we have:

| $r$ | 1% | 2% | 3% | 4% | 5% | 6% | 7% | 8% | 9% | 10% |
|---|---|---|---|---|---|---|---|---|---|---|
| Call price ($) | 1.34 | 1.36 | 1.39 | 1.41 | 1.43 | 1.45 | 1.47 | 1.49 | 1.51 | 1.54 |

The above results show how the call price varies with the risk-free rate. Small differences or estimation errors in $r$ do not make a substantial difference in the option price.

### 19.6.5 Estimating $\sigma$

In contrast, the call price is very sensitive to the value of volatility. In the above example, if we allow $\sigma$ to vary, we have:

| $\sigma$ | 10% | 20% | 30% | 40% | 50% | 60% | 70% | 80% | 90% | 100% |
|---|---|---|---|---|---|---|---|---|---|---|
| Call price | 0.001 | 0.12 | 0.46 | 0.92 | 1.45 | 2.01 | 2.58 | 3.17 | 3.77 | 4.36 |

We see from the above the call price varies from virtually worthless to $1.45 at the true volatility of 50%. For the same percentage of estimation error in $\sigma$, it has a much greater impact on the option price than the error in $r$. It is, hence, very important to estimate the volatility accurately in practice.

In the Black-Scholes formula, the volatility is the standard deviation of the continuously compounded stock returns over the life of the option. It is both one of the most important factors in determining an option price, and one of the most difficult to estimate. This is because no one knows what future volatility will be for the remaining life of the option. Nevertheless, there are two widely used methods for its estimation. The first is to use historical stock prices and obtain the so-called *historical volatility*. The second is to use an observed option price to back out a volatility at which the

Black-Scholes formula price is equal to the observed option price. This volatility is implied by the option price, and so it is called the *implied volatility*.

### 19.6.5.1 Estimating Historical Volatility

The computation of the historical volatility can be carried out in four steps:

*Step 1*: Decide whether to use daily, weekly, or monthly prices, and how many of them.

*Step 2*: Compute the continuously compounded returns as follows

$$R_i^* = \ln[(S_i + Div_i)/S_{i-1}], \quad i = 1, 2, \ldots, n$$

where $S_0, S_1, S_2, \ldots, S_n$ are the stock prices, and $Div_i$ is zero or the amount of the dividends at $i$ if there are any.

*Step 3*: Use Excel or other computer software to obtain the standard deviation of $R_i^*$, say $s$.

*Step 4*: Transform the historical volatility $s$ into annual form,

$$\hat{\sigma} = \sqrt{\tau} s$$

where $\tau$ is the number of the intervals of the data in a year. For example, $\hat{\sigma} = \sqrt{365} s$, $\hat{\sigma} = \sqrt{52} s$, and $\hat{\sigma} = \sqrt{12} s$ for daily, weekly, and monthly data, respectively. However, investors usually adjust the daily volatility by the number of trading days rather than by the number of the calendar days. Following this convention, $\hat{\sigma} = \sqrt{252} s$ should be used for daily data. For example, if the estimated daily standard deviation is 1%, then $\hat{\sigma} = \sqrt{252} \times 1\% = 15.9\%$. Since all parameters of the Black-Scholes formulas are usually measured in annual form, it is important to remember to annualize the standard deviation.

### 19.6.5.2 Estimating Implied Volatility

Consider now how to compute the implied volatility. This is best understood by using an example. On one day, Microsoft's stock price was $\$80\frac{3}{8}$, and the call option with strike $85 sold at $\$2\frac{7}{8}$. With the following additional information,

$$S = \$80.375, \quad X = \$85, \quad T = 0.1945, \quad r = 2.79\%, \quad d = 0.0$$

we are ready to compute the call price by using the Black-Scholes formula for any given value of $\sigma$. Although now we know $C = \$2.875$, $\sigma$ is unknown and needs to be backed out.

To find $\sigma$, we can start from a low value of $\sigma$ and a high value of $\sigma$. A value of $\sigma = 10\%$ roughly says that the stock return is likely to be 10% up or down from the coming year, and is probably a low estimate for the volatility of most stocks. On the other hand, $\sigma = 100\%$ is a high estimate. Computing the call price at $\sigma = 10\%$, denoted as $C(\sigma = 0.10)$, and doing the same for $\sigma = 100\%$, we have:

$$C(\sigma = 0.10) = \$0.2278, \quad C(\sigma = 1.00) = \$12.4018$$

Note that the observed price $C = \$2.875$ is between $C(\sigma = 0.10)$ and $C(\sigma = 1.00)$, the volatility has to be between 0.10 and 1.00 because the call price is an increasing function of the volatility.

Now computing the call price at the middle point between 0.10 and 1.00, we have:

$$C(\sigma = 0.55) = \$6.0472$$

Because the observed price $C = \$2.875$ is between $C(\sigma = 0.10)$ and $C(\sigma = 0.55)$, the volatility has to be between 0.10 and 0.55. Computing the call price at the middle point between 0.10 and 0.55, we have:

$$C(\sigma = 0.325) = \$2.9168$$

Because the observed price $C = \$2.875$ is between $C(\sigma = 0.10)$ and $C(\sigma = 0.325)$, the volatility has to be between 0.10 and 0.325. Computing the call price at the middle point between 0.10 and 0.325, we have:

$$C(\sigma = 0.2125) = \$1.4361$$

Because the observed price $C = \$2.875$ is between $C(\sigma = 0.2125)$ and $C(\sigma = 0.325)$, the volatility has to be between 0.2125 and 0.325.

Proceeding in the process as above, we will find that:

$$
\begin{aligned}
0.2688 &= (0.2125 + 0.325)/2, & C(\sigma = 0.2688) &= \$2.1620 < \$2.875 \\
0.2969 &= (0.2688 + 0.325)/2, & C(\sigma = 0.2969) &= \$2.5368 < \$2.875 \\
0.3109 &= (0.2969 + 0.325)/2, & C(\sigma = 0.3109) &= \$2.7262 < \$2.875 \\
0.3180 &= (0.3109 + 0.325)/2, & C(\sigma = 0.3180) &= \$2.8214 < \$2.875 \\
0.3215 &= (0.3180 + 0.325)/2, & C(\sigma = 0.3215) &= \$2.8929 > \$2.875 \\
0.3232 &= (0.3180 + 0.3215)/2, & C(\sigma = 0.3232) &= \$2.8929 > \$2.875 \\
0.3224 &= (0.3180 + 0.3232)/2, & C(\sigma = 0.3224) &= \$2.8810 > \$2.875 \\
0.3219 &= (0.3180 + 0.3224)/2, & C(\sigma = 0.3219) &= \$2.87502 \approx \$2.875
\end{aligned}
$$

So, the implied volatility is $\sigma = 0.3219 = 32.19\%$. It is easy to program the above procedure, referred to as the *bisection method*, into a computer to find the implied volatility quickly.

A more efficient (but less intuitive) procedure is the Newton-Raphson algorithm. The algorithm finds the root of a function; that is, a solution to $f(x) = 0$, successively by iterating from any initial value $x_0$ via:

$$x_{i+1} = x_i - f(x_i)/f'(x_i)$$

where $i = 0, 1, 2, 3, \ldots$, till convergence. Since now the implied volatility is the solution to $C(\sigma) - \$2.875 = 0$, we compute:

$$\sigma_{i+1} = \sigma_i - [C(\sigma = \sigma_i) - C]e^{d_1^2/2}\sqrt{2\pi}/(S\sqrt{T})$$

based on an arbitrary starting value, say, $\sigma_0 = 1.0$. Then, $\sigma_1 = 0.3225$, $\sigma_2 = 0.32192$, and $\sigma_3 = 0.32192$. The algorithm finds the answer in two steps.

While traders may come up with different estimates of the historical volatility, their estimates of the implied volatility should be the same if they agree with the Black-Scholes formula. The implied volatility represents the current market's assessment of the volatility of the underlying security, whether it is a stock, a commodity, or a stock index. This is useful not only for option traders, but also to stock investors for estimating the current riskiness of the market.

With the use of implied volatility, the price given by the Black-Scholes model is matched to the option's market price. A question is why we compute the volatility by using the option price, and not the other way around as we usually do. The answer is that the option market contains the information about the stock volatility of all traders, and this is reflected in the traded option price. Based on one such option price that provides the current assessment of volatility, the Black-Scholes formula can then help to price all other options, with different strikes and maturities, on the same stock and options on assets closely related to the stock.

## 19.6.6 Measuring Price Sensitivity to Inputs: The Greeks

As we have seen, the following factors determine the option's price: (1) current stock price, (2) strike price, (3) interest rate, (4) volatility in the stock price, (5) time to expiration, and (6) cost of carry (dividends for stocks). Given these factors, we can use the Black-Scholes formula to compute the price of any European option. This section investigates how changes in these factors will affect the option price.

Consider how the stock price affects a call based on the Black-Scholes formula with continuous dividends. The intuition is that a call option allows one to obtain a stock in the future for a fixed price (strike price). Other things being equal, the higher the stock price, the more valuable the call option and, therefore, the higher should the call price be. Mathematically, the partial derivative of the call with respect to the stock price, known as the *option's delta*, is:

$$\Delta = \frac{\partial C}{\partial S} = e^{-\delta T} N(d_1) > 0 \tag{19.29}$$

where the right-hand side is the partial derivative of the Black-Scholes call price, equation (19.28), taken with respect to the stock price. The $\Delta$ is also the *hedge ratio* that measures the changes in a call price due to the changes in a stock price.

The *option's gamma*, denoted by $\Gamma$, measures the rate of change in the option's delta with respect to change in the stock price,

$$\Gamma = \frac{\partial^2 \Delta}{\partial S^2} = \frac{n(d_1)e^{-\delta T}}{S\sigma\sqrt{T}} > 0 \tag{19.30}$$

where $n(d_1) = N'(d_1) = e^{d_1^2/2}/\sqrt{2\pi}$. This says that the delta increases as the stock price goes up. If $\Gamma$ is small, delta changes slowly with respect to $S$. If $\Gamma$ is large, the delta is more sensitive to changes in $S$.

The call price is clearly a decreasing function of the strike price,

$$\frac{\partial C}{\partial X} = -e^{-rT}N(d_2) < 0 \tag{19.31}$$

Intuitively, the higher the payment for exercising a call option (i.e., the higher the strike price), the less valuable the option.

The effect of the changes in the interest rate, referred to the *option's rho* and denoted by $\rho$, is:

$$\rho = \frac{\partial C}{\partial r} = TXe^{-rT}N(d_2) > 0 \tag{19.32}$$

This says that the value of a call is positively related to the level of interest rates. Intuitively, the higher the interest rate, the lower the present value of the payment for exercising the option to buy a stock whose value remains the same, and so the more valuable the option.

Volatility is the key factor determining the option price. The change in the option price with respect to the change in volatility is referred to as an *option's vega* and is usually denoted by:

$$Vega = \frac{\partial C}{\partial \sigma} = S\sqrt{T}e^{-\delta T}n(d_1) > 0 \tag{19.33}$$

This states the well-known fact that the call price rises as the volatility goes up. The Vega of a put is also positive. Intuitively, a stock may go up or down. A call or put allows one to obtain either the upside or downside potential while risking only the premium (the money paid for the call or put before the change in the volatility takes place). The greater the volatility, the greater the upside or downside movement. Thus, a larger volatility allows a greater potential payoff. Hence, the call or put must be more valuable if the volatility rises.

The impact of the changes in time to expiration is called the *option's theta*, denoted by $\Theta$, and is measured by:

$$\Theta = \frac{\partial C}{\partial T} = Se^{-\delta T}\frac{\sigma n(d_1)}{2\sqrt{T}} - \delta Se^{-\delta T}N(d_1) + rXe^{-rT}N(d_2) \tag{19.34}$$

and can be either positive or negative. Intuitively, the longer an option's life, the higher the stock price may grow, and so the more valuable the option. On the other hand, the stock price may not grow at all if it pays too much in dividends. However, the dividends for stocks are usually small, and when this is the case, theta is unambiguously positive. Indeed, in practice, it is almost always the case that the longer the life of the option, the more valuable the option.

TABLE 19.1
IMPACT OF PARAMETERS ON OPTION VALUE

|  | Call price | Put price |
|---|:---:|:---:|
| 1. current stock price $(S)$ | + | − |
| 2. exercise price $(X)$ | − | + |
| 3. interest rate $(r)$ | + | − |
| 4. volatility in stock price $(\sigma)$ | + | + |
| 5. time to expiration $(T)$ | + | + |
| 6. dividend $(\delta)$ | − | + |

Finally, the impact of dividend changes is measured by

$$\frac{\partial C}{\partial \delta} = -TSe^{-\delta T}N(d_1) < 0 \qquad (19.35)$$

This says that the relationship between the call price and the cost of carry is positive. Intuitively, the higher the dividend, the more money goes to the shareholders, and hence, the less valuable the call option.

All the above partial derivatives, which measure how the option price will change as one of the six parameters varies, are known as Greeks.[5] The qualitative relationships are summarized in Table 19.1.

## 19.7  BINOMIAL MODEL

In this section, we extend the earlier one-period binomial model to multiple periods. The model complements the Black-Scholes formula. It not only converges to the Black-Scholes price for European options, but is also applicable to American options.

### 19.7.1  Multiple Periods

The one-period binomial model allows only two possible values of the stock price at the expiration date, assumed here to be one month. As already noted, this is an unrealistic assumption, and we would like to increase the number of possible values. To get three possible values, we can extend the one-period model to a two-period model by assuming that the stock with price $S$ will either go up to $(1 + u)S$ or go down to $(1 + d)S$ in the first half of the month; (1) if it goes up to $(1 + u)S$, it may go up again to $(1 + u)[(1 + u)S] = (1 + u)^2 S$ or go down to $(1 + d)[(1 + u)S] = (1 + d)(1 + u)S$ in the second half of the month; (2) if it goes down to $(1 + d)S$, it may go up to $(1 + u)[(1 + d)S] = 1 + d)(1 + u)S$ or go down

---

[5] Unlike the other five measures, Vega is not a letter of the Greek alphabet.

again to $(1+d)[(1+d)S] = (1+d)^2 S$ in the second half. Thus, at the end of the month we have three possible values of the stock price:

$$(1+u)^2 S, \quad (1+d)(1+u)S, \quad (1+d)^2 S$$

This is illustrated in Figure 19.5.

**FIGURE 19.5**
**A TWO-PERIOD BINOMIAL MODEL**

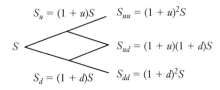

The question is how do we price a call option now. The idea of recursive discounting is widely used in practice for the valuation of complex derivatives. We can apply the one-period model recursively to discount the payoffs back period by period till today. The call prices in the half month when the stock is up or down are:

$$C_u = \frac{pC_{uu} + (1-p)C_{ud}}{1+r}, \quad C_d = \frac{pC_{du} + (1-p)C_{dd}}{1+r} \tag{19.36}$$

where $p = (r-d)/(u-d)$ and $C_{ud} = C_{du}$. Thus, the call price today is the discounted expected payoff:

$$C = \frac{pC_u + (1-p)C_d}{1+r} \tag{19.37}$$

Mathematically, one can verify that the replicating portfolio costs exactly $C$ today. Although the portfolio will adjust next period, no future inflow or outflow of capital is needed since on the expiration date, its payoffs will equal the option payoffs in all three states of the world.

For example, consider a stock selling at $50 that will either go up at the rate of $u = 25\%$ or go down at the rate of $d = -25\%$ in each month for the next two months. Assume the constant risk-free rate is 1% per period. Then from equation (19.37) the risk-neutral probability is $p = (0.01 + 0.25)/(0.25 + 0.25) = 0.52$. For a call with a strike of $55, its payoff (1) when the stock price is up next period is $C_u = (p \times 23.125 + (1-p) \times 0)/1.01 = \$11.91$, and (2) when the stock price is down is $C_d = \$0$. Hence, the price today must be $C = (p \times 11.91 + (1-p) \times 0)/1.01 = \$6.13$. For a put option with the same strike price, we can either compute its value the same way by replacing the payoffs of calls in each node of the tree by those of the put or by using the put-call parity. In the latter case,

$$P = C - S + D + PV(X) = \$6.13 - \$50 + \$0 + \$55/(1+r)^2 = \$10.05$$

where $(1+r)^2$ is used to compute the present value of the strike price because there are now two periods to expiration.

The two-period binomial model allows three terminal values of the stock price. To allow four possible values, we need a three-period binomial model. In this case, the terminal values in the third period are:

$$(1+u)^3(1+d)^0 S, \ (1+u)^2(1+d)^1 S, \ (1+u)^1(1+d)^2 S, \ (1+u)^0(1+d)^3 S$$

In general, we can model the movement of a stock price to have $(n+1)$ values in the $n$-th period by using the $n$-period binomial model. The terminal values are:

$$(1+u)^n(1+d)^0 S, \ (1+u)^{n-1}(1+d)^1 S, \ (1+u)^{n-2}(1+d)^2 S,$$
$$\cdots, \ (1+u)^1(1+d)^{n-1} S, \ (1+u)^0(1+d)^n S$$

To obtain the call price in this case, similar to the 2-period binomial model, we can work backward from the tree and obtain the call price.

For example, consider a stock selling at $40 that will either go up at the rate of $u = 15\%$ or go down at the rate of $d = -5\%$ each month for the next three months. Assume the constant risk-free rate is 1% per month. In a 3-period model, for the price of a call option with a strike $42 and three months to maturity, we compute first the stock price tree forward, and then the option price tree backward. The results are shown in Figure 19.6. For instance,

$$C_{uu} = (0.3 \times \$18.835 + (1 - 0.3) \times \$8.255)/(1 + r) = \$11.316$$

and

$$C = (0.3 \times \$5.061 + (1 - 0.3) \times \$0.728)/(1 + r) = \$2.01$$

**FIGURE 19.6**
A THREE-PERIOD CALL VALUATION

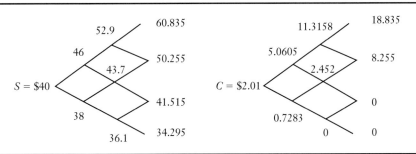

## 19.7.2 Relation to Black-Scholes Formula

Given $S, X, r, \sigma$, and $T$, we can compute the price of a European call option on a non-dividend-paying stock by using the Black-Scholes formula. Alternatively, we can compute the price by using the binomial model. The question is how the two prices are related to each other.

To match the lognormal assumption of the Black-Scholes formula, we choose:

$$\Delta T = T/n, \quad u = e^{\sigma\sqrt{\Delta T}} - 1, \quad d = e^{-\sigma\sqrt{\Delta T}} - 1, \quad p = \frac{e^{r\Delta T} - 1 - d}{u - d} \qquad (19.38)$$

in an $n$-period binomial model with $\Delta T$ as the per period time.[6] Then, the larger the $n$ (the greater the number of periods we use in the binomial model), the closer the binomial tree to the lognormal price, and so the closer the binomial price to the Black-Scholes price. In the limit, they are equal.

For example, consider the earlier call with:

$$S = \$30, X = \$35, T = 0.25, \sigma = 0.5, r = 0.06, d = 0.0$$

The Black-Scholes price is \$1.45. Now, with using the $n$-period binomial model, we obtain the call price:

| $n$ | 10 | 20 | 30 | 40 | 50 | 60 | 70 | 80 | 90 | 100 | 110 |
|---|---|---|---|---|---|---|---|---|---|---|---|
| Call price (\$) | 1.38 | 1.47 | 1.46 | 1.44 | 1.45 | 1.46 | 1.46 | 1.45 | 1.44 | 1.44 | 1.45 |

Theoretically, the price converges to \$1.45 with an error of order $1/n$, but the error oscillates, that is, it does not decrease monotonically with $n$.

Analytically, note that if the terminal stock price does not go up enough, the value of the call, $\max[(1 + u)^{n-j}(1 + d)^j S - X, 0]$, is zero. Let $a$ be the smallest nonnegative integer such that $a \geq \ln[(1 + u)^n S/X]/\ln[(1 + u)/(1 + d)]$, then $\max[(1 + u)^{n-j}(1 + d)^j S - X, 0] = 0$ when $j \geq a$ and $S - X$ when $j < a$. So, we can compute the call price as:

$$C = \frac{1}{(1 + r^*)^n} \sum_{j=0}^{a} \binom{n}{j} p^{n-j}(1 - p)^j \left[(1 + u)^{n-j}(1 + d)^j S - X\right]$$

$$= S\Phi(n) - X(1 + r^*)^{-n}\Psi(n)$$

where $r^* = e^{r\Delta T} - 1$,

$$\Phi(n) = \sum_{j=0}^{a} \binom{n}{j} p^{n-j}(1 - p)^j(1 + u)^{n-j}(1 + d)^j(1 + r^*)^{-n}, \quad \Psi(n) = \sum_{j=0}^{a} \binom{n}{j} p^{n-j}(1 - p)^j$$

---

[6] They are obtained by matching the mean and variance of the binomial model to the lognormal model. Among alternatives, and following Cox, Ross, and Rubinstein (1979), we use $1 + u = 1/(1 + d)$.

By the central limit theorem of probability theory, one can show that $\Phi(n) \to N(d_1)$ and $\Psi(n) \to N(d_2)$ as $n \to \infty$. That is, the binomial price converges to the Black-Scholes price with the parameter choice as given by equation (19.38).

### 19.7.3 Accommodating Dividends

The binomial model is far more flexible than the Black-Scholes formula. It can both deliver the Black-Scholes formula result, and also be easily generalized to compute options on assets that pay either discrete or continuous dividends. For discrete dividends, one can build the binomial tree with enough periods so that the dividends are paid at the end of periods in the tree. Then, one can compute the option prices the usual way by using the ex-dividend stock prices.

For example, assume that a stock with price $100 will either go up at $u = 10\%$ or go down at $d = -10\%$ for the next two months. The stock will pay a $3 dividend next month and $r = 1\%$. Let's demonstrate how to price a call with strike $X = 100$ and maturity of two months. We first compute the stock price tree forward. The price next month will be either $100 or $90. The only difference from before is that now the price will grow from its ex-dividend price, $107 or $87 to the second month. The final stock price is on the left-hand side of Figure 19.7. Computing the call payoffs at expiration as usual by taking the differences between the stock prices and the strike, we obtain those values on the right-hand side of Figure 19.7. Discounting them back period by period as before, we get the call price today as $5.25.

For continuous dividends, one can build the binomial tree the same way as before. However, the risk-neutral probability needs be adjusted as follows:

$$p = \frac{e^{(r-\delta)\Delta T} - 1 - d}{u - d} \qquad (19.39)$$

This adjustment is needed because, under the risk-neutral probability, the stock price appreciation combined with the dividends should earn the risk-free rate, and so the price should grow at a rate of $(r - \delta)\Delta T$ per period, that is,

$$pu + (1 - p)d = Se^{(r-\delta)\Delta T}$$

**FIGURE 19.7**
A CALL ON A DIVIDEND-PAYING STOCK

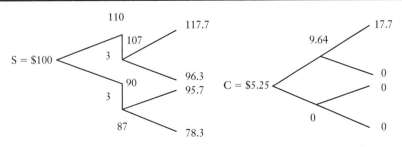

The solution to this equation leads to equation (19.39), which reduces to equation (19.38) when $\delta = 0$. Then the valuation will be the same as the case when there are no dividends.

## 19.8 AMERICAN OPTIONS

For ease of study, our discussion so far focused on European options. Many real-world options, such as options on the S&P 500, are indeed European options where the option holder can only exercise the option on the expiration day. However, individual stock options, options on the S&P 100 (the most actively traded index option), and many others are American type where the option holder can exercise the option any time up to and including the expiration day. By incorporating the early exercise feature into our previous analysis, we can come up with the value of American options.

First, we note that the value of an American option should be at least as large as that of the corresponding European option on the same terms. This is because the American option has all the privileges of the European option and the additional privilege of early exercise. Using lowercase letters for European option prices and uppercase letters for American option prices with the same terms, we have:

$$C = c + \varepsilon_C$$
$$P = p + \varepsilon_P$$

where $\varepsilon_C$ and $\varepsilon_P$ are both nonnegative quantities called *early exercise premiums*.

For American calls on non-dividend-paying stocks, a somewhat surprising result is that it will never be optimal to exercise early and so the early exercise premium is zero. That is, the American call and European call have the same value in the zero dividend case. To see this, assume an American on a stock with strike $45 is available. The stock price is $S = \$50$. Consider (a) a portfolio consisting of the call and $45 cash, and (b) a portfolio consisting of the stock. On the expiration day, portfolio (a) will have the value of at least the stock plus interest income from investing the $45 of cash and so the cost of portfolio (a) must be higher than that of portfolio (b); that is, $C + \$45 > \$50$ or $C > \$5$. By exercising the call, only $5 is realized. So the option holder should not exercise the call. If the option holder needs the money or thinks the stock is going to drop, he should sell the call for $C > 5$ in the option market.

However, there always exists the possibility of early exercise for American puts even on non-dividend-paying stocks, implying that American puts are never worth less than European puts. For example, suppose a put with strike $100 was purchased awhile ago when the stock price was $120. It is always possible for the price to drop dramatically to $S = \$1$ today. Assume the option still has a year to maturity. If the option holder waits to the expiration day, the maximize value is $100. But if the option holders exercises the option today, $99 can be realized which, in turn, can be invested at the risk-free rate, say 3%. Consequently, by exercising the option holder will get more than $100 next year. Hence, the option holder will exercise the option early and this is always possible.

As mentioned earlier, the binomial model is flexible and can be easily adapted to compute the price of American options. In contrast with European options, the key here is that on any node of the tree, the value of an American option is the maximum of its discounted expected payoff or its exercise value. The same holds for the put. That is,

$$C_i = \max \left[ S_i - X, \frac{pC_{iu} + (1-p)C_{id}}{1+r} \right],$$

$$P_i = \max \left[ X - S_i, \frac{pP_{iu} + (1-p)P_{id}}{1+r} \right]$$

$$(19.40)$$

To see why, notice that the option holder can either wait or exercise the option at the node. If the option holder waits, he gets the discounted expected payoff. If he exercises, he gets the exercise value. The option holder will select the course of action that provides the higher value.

For example, in Figure 19.7, if the call is now an American style one, and if we exercise in the first month when the stock price is up, we exercise prior to the dividend payout to get $10 (= $110 − $100). If we wait, the *wait value* is the European value of $9.64 = $(p \times $17.7 + (1 − 0.55) \times $0)/(1 + 0.01)$, which is lower. Hence, the American value at the node should be $10 rather than $9.64. Discounting back, we obtain the American call price as $5.45, which is $0.20 greater than the European call.

---

## 19.9 Arbitrary Payoffs and General Models

While our analysis has been focused on standard option payoffs, the risk-neutral valuation method is straightforwardly applied to compute any European type option with an arbitrary payoff function $V_T = V(S_T)$, where $V(\cdot)$ is a function of the terminal stock price. In a binomial tree model, we simply discounted the payoffs of $V_T$ successively back to today. In the lognormal model, we compute now the discounted expected payoff under the risk-neutralized lognormal distribution,

$$V_0 = e^{-rT} E(\tilde{V}_T) \qquad (19.41)$$

where $V_0$ is the value today at time 0 of the derivative, and the tilde sign, as usual, emphasizes that the payoff is random. This equation is the same as before, that is, we replace $\tilde{C}_T$ in equation (19.19) by $\tilde{V}_T$. However, we cannot derive a simple expression like the Black-Scholes formula for a general function $V(\cdot)$.

Numerically, one can easily compute $V_0$ via Monte Carlo simulation.[7] The key is to compute the expected payoff of the derivative. Since equation (19.41) uses the risk-neutralized expected payoff, we must also use the risk-neutral distribution of the stock

---

[7] Slavinsky and Neave (2011) provide combinatorial methods they argue give more nearly accurate results, and more quickly, than the typical simulation.

price rather than the true or objective distribution. To do so, we can simply use equation (19.17) with the risk-neutralized mean $\mu = r - \sigma^2/2$. By using simulation software, we can simulate a normal random variable $\tilde{z}$, and then can use equation (19.17) to compute a random terminal stock price. We can do this thousands of times to get thousands of prices. The average of the discounted payoffs over all of these prices will be a good approximation to $V_0$. The approximation error is random, but its standard error converges to zero at a rate inversely related to the square-root of the number of simulated prices.

The payoff function $V(\cdot)$ can also depend on the path of the asset price. In addition, the asset price can be allowed to move over time with jumps, and the volatility can also be allowed to change stochastically. The above methods can be adapted to accommodate all these extensions.[8]

## Appendix 19.1 Derivation of the Black-Scholes Formula

In this appendix, we derive the Black-Scholes formula. Note first that the risk-neutral valuation is generally valid, as shown for the single-period binomial model in Section 19.8 and for the finite states model in Chapter 16. For the lognormal or Brownian motion prices, a rigorous proof requires stochastic calculus.[9]

Given the risk-neutral valuation method, we need to find the distribution of the stock price under the risk-neutral probability. Since:

$$E(e^{a\tilde{z}}) = \int_{-\infty}^{+\infty} e^{az} \frac{1}{\sqrt{2\pi}} e^{-z^2/2} \, dz = e^{a^2/2} \int_{-\infty}^{+\infty} e^{-(a-z)^2/2} \frac{1}{\sqrt{2\pi}} \, dz = e^{a^2/2} \quad \text{(A19.1)}$$

We have, from equation (19.17), that:

$$E(S_T) = S_0 e^{(\mu + \sigma^2/2)T}$$

Under the risk-neutral probability, the expected return should be the risk-free rate, and hence, $\mu = r - \sigma^2/2$ or $S_T = Se^{(r - \frac{1}{2}\sigma^2)T + \sigma\sqrt{T}\tilde{z}}$.

To derive the Black-Scholes formula, we need only to compute the two expected values in equation (19.20). Denote by $f(S_T)$ the lognormal density function of $S_T$. Then:

$$Prob(S_T \geq X) = \int_X^{+\infty} f(S_T) \, dS_T = \int_{\frac{\ln(X/S) - \mu T}{\sigma\sqrt{T}}}^{+\infty} n(z) \, dz$$

$$= \int_{-\infty}^{\frac{\ln(S/X) + \mu T}{\sigma\sqrt{T}}} n(z) \, dz = N(d_2) \quad \text{(A19.2)}$$

---

[8] There are many textbooks, such as Hull (2007) and McDonald (2005), that specialize in derivatives. For an advanced mathematical treatment, Shreve (2004) and its references are a good starting point.

[9] See, for example, Shreve (2004), for details.

where $\mu = r - \sigma^2/2$. The first step follows from the definition for computing the probability, the second makes a transformation of variable,

$$z = \frac{\ln(S_T/S) - \mu T}{\sigma\sqrt{T}}$$

the third reverses the direction of the integral, and the final step follows from the definition of $N(d_2)$. In addition,

$$E(S_T \mid S_T \geq X) = \int_X^{+\infty} S_T f(S_T)\, d\, S_T = \int_{\frac{\ln(X/(S) - \mu T}{\sigma\sqrt{T}}}^{+\infty} S e^{\left(\mu - \frac{1}{2}\sigma^2\right)T + \sigma\sqrt{T}z}\, n(z)\, dz$$

$$= S e^{rT} \int_{\frac{\ln(S/X) + \mu T}{\sigma\sqrt{T}}}^{+\infty} e^{-(\sigma\sqrt{T} - z)^2/2}\, \frac{1}{\sqrt{2\pi}}\, dz$$

$$= S e^{rT} \int_{-\infty}^{\frac{\ln(S/X) + \mu T}{\sigma\sqrt{T}} + \sigma\sqrt{T}} e^{-y^2/2}\, \frac{1}{\sqrt{2\pi}}\, dy = S e^{rT} N(d_1)$$

$$(\text{A19.3})$$

where the steps are similar to the previous one.

---

# KEY POINTS

- In contrast to futures and forward contracts, which have a linear payoff function, option payoffs are nonlinear functions of the underlying asset price. The fundamental valuation principle of option valuation is the absence of arbitrage opportunities.
- The fundamental insight is that option payoffs can be replicated by suitable positions in the underlying asset and the risk-free asset. Hence, the option price must be equal to the cost of the replicating portfolio.
- The hedging portfolio is a risk-free portfolio consisting of a short position in an option and a suitable holding of the underlying asset. It is closely related to the replicating portfolio.
- The price of a European call option is tied to the price of a European put with same underlying, strike price, and expiration date by a relationship called put-call partity. This relationship is only approximately true for American options.
- Risk-neutral valuation is used to compute the option price as its discounted expected payoff with the risk-free rate as the discount rate, while the payoff is adjusted for risk by using the risk-neutral probability.
- In a binomial model of the stock price, the option price can be computed backwards successively by discounting the expected future payoffs period by period.

- In a lognormal model of the stock price, the option price for a European call can be computed by using the Black-Scholes formula, and the European put price can then be computed using put-call parity.
- For European options on a dividend-paying stock, the Black-Scholes formula can still be employed by applying it to the dividend-adjusted price, which is the current stock price less the present value of the expected dividends.
- The volatility used in the Black-Scholes formula is the standard deviation of the continuously compounded stock return over the life of the option. It is the most important parameter that determines an option price, and can be estimated by either using historical volatility or implied volatility.
- With compatible choice of parameters in the binomial model, the binomial price converges to the Black-Scholes price as the number of periods approaches infinity.
- An American option on a non-dividend-paying stock will not be optimally exercised prior to expiration, and hence, its price will be identical to the corresponding European call. However, for a dividend-paying stock, the American call price will in general be greater than the corresponding European call price.
- An American put option has a positive probability of being exercised regardless if dividends are expected, and hence, its price is always greater than that of the corresponding European put.
- While the Black-Scholes formula is not applicable to American options except for non-dividend-paying stocks, American options can be evaluated by using the binomial tree model by taking the larger of the exercise value or wait value along the nodes of the tree. Monte Carlo simulation may also be used.
- Both the binomial tree and Monte Carlo approaches are applicable to derivatives with arbitrary nonlinear payoffs.

## QUESTIONS

1. If an investor wants to protect against the decline in the value of an asset and both puts and calls are available for that asset, which should the investor buy?

2. Consider a put option on a stock with a strike price of $50. What is the value of the put at expiration if the stock price is
   a. $55?
   b. $46?
   c. $50?

3. Consider a call option on a stock with a strike price of $50. What is the value of the call at expiration if the stock price is
   a. $55?
   b. $46?
   c. $50?

4. Why is a put option analolgous to buying insurance?

5. What is meant by put-call parity?

6. A firm's stock sells at $50. A European call option with a strike price of $55 and a maturity of three months is selling at $2. Assume the continuously compounded risk-free annual interest rate is 5%.

   a. What price should a European put option with the same strike price and maturity sell for?

   b. If the call price is under-valued by the market, will the put be under-valued or over-valued?

   c. What can we say about the price of a put option with a strike price of $50?

7. In determining the theoretical value of an option, what is

   a. the replicating portfolio?

   b. the hedging portfolio?

8. A firm's stock sells at $50. The stock price will be either $65 or $45 three months from now. Assume the 3-month risk-free rate is 1%.

   a. What is the price of a European call with a strike price of $50 and a maturity of three months?

   b. What is the price of a European call with a strike price of $55 and a maturity of three months?

   c. What is the price of a European put with a strike price of $50 and a maturity of three months?

   d. Find a portfolio of the stock and bond (a position in risk-free borrowing) such that buying the European call with a strike $50 is equivalent to holding this portfolio. Compare the cost of this portfolio with the call price.

9. Consider the valuation of a European call on stock XYZ with a strike price of $110 and a term to maturity of three months. Assume the stock price is $100 today and it has a lognormal distribution with volatility of 40% over the life of the option. In addition, the continuously compounded risk-free rate is 2% per year. Using the Black-Scholes formula, answer the questions below.

   a. What is the theoretical value of the call?

   b. If the stock will pay a $4 dividend next month, what should the theoretical call price be?

   c. What is the risk-neutral probability that you will exercise the option at maturity?

   d. If the expected stock return is 20%, what is the true probability that the call option will be exercised prior to maturity?

10. From an online quote system, you know a 5-week European call option with a strike price of $40 sells at $7⁄8, whereas the stock sells at $37. Assume that the continuously compounded risk-free rate is 3% per year, and there are no

dividends for the next five weeks. What is the market's assessment of the volatility (the implied volatility) of the stock?

**11.** A stock selling at $100 will either go up at the rate of $u = 10\%$ or go down at the rate of $d = -10\%$ each month for the next two months. The constant risk-free rate is 1% per month. Consider the evaluation of a European call and put on the stock with strike $X = \$95$ and maturing in two months.

    **a.** If there are no dividends, what are the prices of the call and put?

    **b.** If the stock will pay a dividend of $10 next month, what are the prices of the call and put with a strike price of $90?

**12.** A stock selling at $100 will either go up at the rate of $u = 20\%$ or go down at the rate of $d = -20\%$ each month for the next two months. The constant risk-free rate is 1% per month. The stock will pay a dividend of $20 next month.

    **a.** What is the price of an American call with a strike price of $75 and a maturity of two months?

    **b.** What is the price of an American put with a strike price of $110 and a maturity of two months?

**13.** Assume that a non-dividend-paying stock satisfies all the conditions of the Black-Scholes formula, especially that the stock price is lognormally distributed. Recall that the payoff function of the standard call option is $\max(S_T - X, 0)$. Consider now a derivative that will pay you at maturity $V_T$.

    **a.** If $V_T = S_T^2$ (i.e., the squared stock price) can we apply the Black-Scholes formula to compute the price? If not, derive a formula for it.

    **b.** What is the price of if the payoff function is $V_T = f(S_T)$, where $f(\cdot)$ is an arbitrary continuous function?

---

### ⬥ ⬥ ⬥    REFERENCES

Black, Fischer, and Myron Scholes. (1973). "The Pricing of Options and Corporate Liabilities," *Journal of Political Economy* **81**: 630–654.

Cox, John C., Stephen A. Ross, and Mark Rubinstein. (1979). "Option Pricing: A simplified Approach," *Journal of Financial Economics* **7**: 229–263.

Hull, John C. (2007). *Options, Futures and Other Derivative Securities* (7th ed.). New York: Prentice-Hall.

McDonald, Robert L. (2005). *Derivatives Markets* (2nd ed.). New York: Addison Wesley.

Merton, Robert C. (1973). "Theory of Rational Option Pricing," *Bell Journal of Economics and Management Science* **4**: 141–183.

Shreve, Steven E. (2004). *Stochastic Calculus for Finance II: Continuous-Time Models*. New York: Springer-Verlag.

Slavinsky, Serge and Edwin H. Neave. (2011). "Efficient Valuation of Prepayment and Default Risky Securities," *Journal of Applied Finance* **2**: 1–17.

# PART VI

# CAPITAL MARKET IMPERFECTIONS AND THE LIMITS TO ARBITRAGE

# 20

# CAPITAL MARKET IMPERFECTIONS AND FINANCIAL DECISION CRITERIA

*I*n this chapter we recognize a variety of capital market imperfections and then outline their consequences for the financial theories we have so far developed. *Capital market imperfections* have a potential for creating important consequences for financial decision making. However, these consequences depend both on the nature and on the ubiquitousness of the imperfections. These are matters related more closely to applications than to theory and we will explore applications further in the book's remaining parts. But first it is useful to outline how the theory itself is changed by the phenomena we now recognize.

We shall argue that the major imperfection affecting financial market prices involves the collection and dissemination of information that seems often to be distributed quite unevenly. At the same time, auction markets like the stock exchanges are clearly efficient despite the presence of such imperfections as transactions costs. Thus, in the sequel we shall pay considerable attention to heterogeneously distributed information and less to issues involving explicit charges such as flotation and brokerage costs. We also argue, on occasion, that markets may be incomplete in the sense of Chapter 16, and the effects of incompleteness will, from time to time, augment the effects of heterogeneously distributed information.

## 20.1 TYPES OF CAPITAL MARKET IMPERFECTIONS

There are several kinds of capital market imperfections whose existence appears to be potentially important for explaining real-world financial decisions. We first categorize these imperfections, then investigate their importance.

### 20.1.1 Heterogeneous Expectations

In a risky world, differences of opinion regarding the probability distributions characterizing future events may arise. That is, investors may have *heterogeneous expectations.* Even if we assume all investors are privy to the same data regarding past events, they might form different probability distributions regarding possible future events. Accordingly we must consider the implications of possibly differing probability distributions, both for financial theory and for the decisions they prescribe.

We use the concept of a contingent claim discussed in Chapter 10 to develop the essence of the argument. We assume there are two possible future states of the world, and that our task is to assess the effects of a contingent claim's differing values under the following three sets of conditions:

Condition 1. *Homogeneous expectations and risk neutrality.* Assume that everyone agrees on the following data for the contingent claim and the associated objective probabilities:

| State | Probability | Contingent claim |
|-------|-------------|------------------|
| 1     | $p$         | 1                |
| 2     | $1 - p$     | 0                |

Also, assume that the one-period risk-free rate is $r$. Then the time 1 value of the contingent claim, denoted by $C(1)$ is:

$$C(1) = [p(1) + (1 - p)(0)]/(1 + r)$$

because risk-neutral investors capitalize the risky prospects' expected values at the risk-free rate of interest. The assumption of investor agreement implies that the time 1 value will also be the market price of the claim.

Condition 2. *Homogeneous expectations, risk-averse investors.* In a perfect capital market, we can estimate risk-neutral probabilities from market price data. In this case, the value of claim one can be calculated as:

$$C^*(1) = [q(1) + (1 - q)(0)]/(1 + r) < C(1)$$

assuming that the (estimated) risk-neutral probability $q < p$ and[1] that the risk-free rate is the same as before. Again, because of investor agreement, the value $C^*(1)$ will be the market price of the claim. But $C^*(1) < C(1)$, reflecting the risk premium demanded by the market.

Condition 3. *Heterogeneous expectations, risk-averse investors.* We now assume each investor $i$ attaches her own risk-neutral probability $q_i$ to state 1 and $1 - q_i$ to state 2. We continue to suppose that all investors agree on the risk-free rate. Under these assumptions, the value of the contingent claim to investor $i$ is:

$$C_i^*(1) = [q_i(1) + (1 - q_i)(0)]/(1 + r)$$

---

[1] This will normally be the case in a two-state world if state 1 is associated with favorable economic conditions.

and $C_i^*(1)$ may be either less than or greater than $C^*(1)$. That is, each investor's valuation of a contingent claim varies according to the subjective value of the risk-neutral probability she attaches to state 1. The time 1 market value of contingent claims then depends on the number of different investors, their demands for claims as implicitly defined by the foregoing equation, and the supply of claims. It is convenient to elaborate these effects on market value by using a more extended example.

Let us now suppose that there are $N$ contingent claims outstanding in the capital market and that each investor may buy at most one such claim. (The claim prices are now chosen for convenience and are not calculated from the data of the earlier example.) Each investor $i$ will buy a claim if his or her valuation of claim $C_i(1)$ is at least as great as the claim's market price, denoted $C_m(1)$. Assuming $N$ to be 4, we assume the data shown in Table 20.1, from which Figure 20.1 is drawn.[2] Under the assumption that investors differ in their subjective estimates of risk-neutral probabilities, the stepped line of the figure indicates the demand function of all potential investors at various market prices for the contingent claims. Note that as the price of the contingent claims falls, more investors are willing to purchase a claim. The horizontal straight line shows the market demand function for the claims if all investors agree regarding their probability assessments. We show the two demand curves intersecting at the same price for the average investor. This means that when

TABLE 20.1
DATA FOR FIGURE 20.1

| Investor number | Homogeneous expectations, claim valued at | Heterogeneous expectations, claim valued at[a] |
|---|---|---|
| 1 | 0.50 | 0.60 |
| 2 | 0.50 | 0.58 |
| 3 | 0.50 | 0.56 |
| 4 | 0.50 | 0.54 |
| 5 | 0.50 | 0.52 |
| 6 | 0.50 | 0.50 |
| 7 | 0.50 | 0.48 |
| 8 | 0.50 | 0.46 |
| 9 | 0.50 | 0.44 |
| 10 | 0.50 | 0.42 |
| 11 | 0.50 | 0.40 |
| | Equilibrium price if 4 claims outstanding is 0.50. | Equilibrium price if 4 claims outstanding is 0.54. |

[a]The calculation of value uses the same method as in condition 3 above.

[2] The thinking underlying this example is due to Edward Miller (1977). Compare Miller's Figure 1.

FIGURE 20.1

MARKET-CLEARING VALUE OF CONTINGENT CLAIM UNDER HETEROGENEOUS
EXPECTATIONS

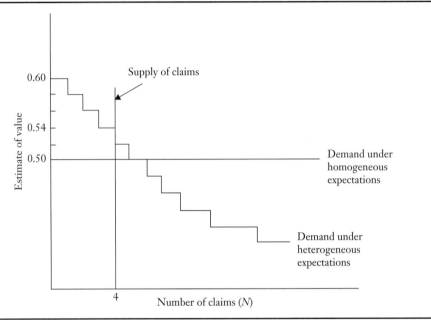

expectations differ, about as many investors attach a high value to the stock as the number attaching a low value. The vertical line at $N = 4$ represents the available supply when no short selling is permitted, and the market-clearing price is established by the intersection of the market supply and demand curves. When $N$ is small relative to the number of potential investors, the market price will be higher than it is under homogeneous expectations, at least if enough of the investors are more optimistic than the average, as in our example.

The reasoning applied to contingent claims can be applied to any security. When it is applied to stocks, several conclusions follow from this model of heterogeneous expectations:[3]

1. As long as the entire supply of shares can be absorbed by a minority of the potential purchasers, the market-clearing price will be above the mean evaluation of the potential investors.

2. Under condition 1, an increase in *divergence of opinion*[4] will increase the market-clearing price, and a decrease will reduce the market-clearing price. (When the divergence of opinion decreases to the point where there is no disagreement, we are back to the case of homogeneous expectations.)

---

[3] Miller (1977, p. 1153). We cite only some of the conclusions reached in the original article. For extension of this work, see Miller (2004a, 2004b, 2004c).

[4] This means an increase in dispersion of opinions while the mean of the distribution remains constant.

3. If potential investors make unbiased estimates of the distribution of mean returns from possible investments and make investments on the risk-return basis of standard portfolio theory, the market-clearing price of shares will exceed the willingness to pay of an investor with perfect information about the probability distribution of returns.

4. Under condition 3, if firms make their investment decisions to maximize the market value of their shares, there will be excess investment in those firms and industries about which there is the greatest divergence of opinion, and these may well be the riskier alternatives.

In the foregoing discussion we assumed the supply of securities to be small relative to the number of potential investors. This may not be so if markets are somehow segmented: For example, if large private placements are sold to a small number of institutional investors. In these contrary cases, heterogeneous expectations would lower rather than raise prices. This may be a partial explanation for why certain classes of firms, such as new ventures, frequently seem to have considerable difficulty raising finance capital.

In any event, with heterogeneous expectations our reliance on models like the contingent claims model (just mentioned) or like the CAPM is weakened, because a market equilibrium price is much less easily predicted. Unless we have more details about how opinion diverges, we cannot say whether price will be higher or lower than that predicted by a model like the CAPM. Nevertheless, we do not regard these statements as saying that our earlier theories should be abandoned. Rather, it seems that they may still provide approximately correct pictures of real-world conditions, at least for portfolios of stocks. Thus, if we wish to assume heterogeneous expectations, the task becomes one of assessing the degree of approximation involved in a given financial decision problem.

## 20.1.2 Unequally Distributed Information

The situation regarding risky future outcomes is actually more complex than a discussion of heterogeneous expectations suggests. For not only may investors have different expectations regarding the future, they may not even share the same information about the past. For example, a seller of fire insurance, knowing that a client has lodged a claim for fire damage, will not always be able to tell (at least for any reasonable cost) whether the client deliberately set the fire or not. Of course, the client has this information, but a dishonest client cannot be expected to admit culpability.

To give another example more closely related to financial management, an investor may not have the same information about either a firm's history or its prospects as does the firm itself. Moreover, the latter may not wish or perhaps even be able completely to convey available information.[5] The last problem is especially important in cases where a public offering of securities is made. In these cases most legal jurisdictions have securities regulations stipulating that the company's plans be

---

[5] These situations are examples of a condition termed information impactedness, and the insurance scenario also illustrates a situation known as moral hazard that we mentioned in Chapter 1 and discuss further in the next chapter. For further discussion of these important concepts, see Williamson (1975).

outlined in a prospectus. But there are well-known difficulties to incorporating all relevant information, especially that of a qualitative nature, in such a document. For these reasons, it may be difficult for potential investors to assess accurately the nature of the risks involved in purchasing the securities of some firms. Accordingly, potential investors may not all have the same data with which to make assessments of the firm's future, and even if they do, all investors may not assume the same probability distributions in describing a firm's prospects. A similar situation may obtain in negotiated markets where borrowers' credit risks may be difficult to establish.[6]

## 20.1.3   Transactions Costs and Tax Differentials

If when making financial transactions an investor must pay charges other than interest rates (e.g., loan application charges, brokerage charges on stock sales), the ability to move along a wealth constraint of equal present values is impaired. In particular, any profile of cash flows different from that determined by income receipts may have a lower present value than that of the income receipts themselves, because the investor might have to pay transactions charges to make the conversion from one cash flow profile to another.

To see the effects of transactions charges, suppose that all investors are risk neutral, that an investor has an income stream with expected values of $800 and $770 at times 1 and 2, respectively, and that interest rates are 10%. Then the present value of this income stream is $1,500. Now suppose the investor wishes to spend $1,000 at time 1. In a perfect capital market this means the expenditure stream is ($1,000, $550), which also has a present value of $1,500. But if markets are imperfect in the sense that to borrow the $200 to finance time 1 consumption the investor must pay, in addition to interest charges, a commission having a time 1 value of $10, then the expenditure stream is $1,000 and $539) in times 1 and 2, respectively, with a present value of $1,490. Hence, the investor cannot move freely along the wealth constraint, shown as a solid line in Figure 20.2, but must instead accept a reduction in net present value to reallocate income in the fashion indicated. Hence, this investor is not indifferent between the income stream $800 and $770, and the income stream $1,000 and $550 (both for times 1 and 2, respectively) even though the streams both have the same net present value when transaction charges are not paid.

A similar conclusion applies to selling shares. An investor may prefer dividend income to realizing capital gains through share price appreciation, if in the latter case brokerage charges to sell shares must be paid. On the other hand, the problem is the same but the conclusions may be reversed with respect to the effects of taxation. If, for example, income taxes are levied but capital gains are taxed at a lower rate than ordinary income, investors will not be indifferent between dividend and share price increases; they may have a distinct preference for the latter.

For all the foregoing reasons, the separation of managers' wealth-maximizing decisions from the consumption decisions of their firm's stockholders is no longer always possible. The implications of this are considered further in Section 20.3.

---

[6] See Jaffee and Russell (1976).

FIGURE 20.2
EFFECT OF TRANSACTIONS CHARGE ON THE WEALTH CONSTRAINT

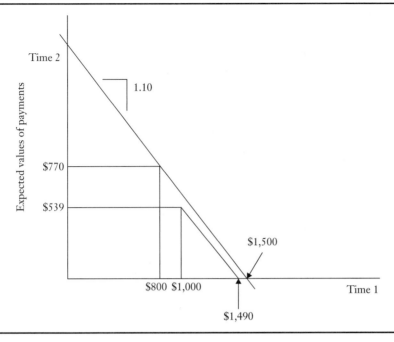

## 20.1.4 Costs of Unsystematic Risk

The CAPM predicts that firms will be valued solely on the basis of their risk contribution to the market portfolio because unsystematic risk can be diversified away in a perfect capital market (see Chapter 14). Important to this result is the absence of costs that might impede sufficient diversification from taking place and hence might also impede the reduction of unsystematic risk to levels where it does not affect decision making. Therefore, such market imperfections as transactions costs might well imply that stockholders could be concerned with unsystematic risk.

Moreover, even in the absence of transactions costs impeding diversification, managers of particular firms might not take the CAPM view of the firm's risk if their own career prospects are related to an individual firm's unsystematic risk.[7] This is a way of saying that even in a perfect capital market, the markets for managers' services might not also be perfect. In these circumstances, a downward deviation in the earnings of a given firm might not be important to the holders of a diversified portfolio, but the career of the managers of that particular firm might be jeopardized. Hence, managers might be tempted to take decisions that do not maximize the firm's market value if by so doing career risks could be avoided. In other words, when the markets for managerial

---

[7] This point takes on special importance when it is recognized that employers (boards of directors) may not always know exactly the capacities of their employees (the firm's management). For discussions of difficulties with such agency relations, see Akerlof (1976) and Salop (1976).

services are imperfect, say because of monitoring costs, it is quite possible that managers will not follow the dictates of the market value criterion exactly. We shall look at this question further in the next chapter.

## 20.2  SOME EFFECTS OF CAPITAL MARKET IMPERFECTIONS

In this section we consider how some of our previously established theoretical conclusions are altered by the presence of the market imperfections whose nature we have just indicated.

### 20.2.1  Absence of a Criterion Function

In a perfect capital market, the market value of the firm serves as a criterion function for its managers because, as we have seen, there is nothing more that the manager can do for a firm's stockholders than to maximize their wealth. That in turn means maximizing the market value of securities investors own, which itself implies maximizing the market value of the firm.

The situation changes when capital markets are not perfect, for in this case the market value of the firm is not always well defined. For one thing, if interest rates differ in ways other than predicted by a model (say the CAPM), the market value of the firm is not uniquely determined, as Figure 20.3 shows. In the figure we assume risk-neutral investors, so that all payments are valued by discounting their expectations. We further assume in the figure that borrowing is costlier than lending, with the result that the market value of the firm depends on which discount rate is applied

FIGURE 20.3
EFFECT OF DIFFERENT BORROWING AND LENDING RATES

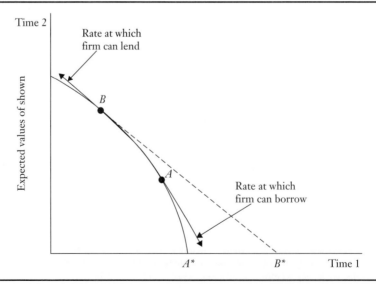

to earnings. That is, the market value of the firm at time 1 is $0A^*$ if the firm's earnings are capitalized at the borrowing rate but $0B^*$ if the firm's earnings are capitalized at the lending rate. Hence, we can no longer rely on a unique market value as providing the sole standard for managers to utilize.

Figure 20.3 also shows that financial and operating decisions are no longer separable, because the value of the firm depends on both the operating decision and the manner in which any necessary funds are raised. Since the very fact of borrowing or lending has itself an impact on the firm's market value, operating and financial decisions are no longer separable. The lack of separability means that investment decisions cannot be taken with reference to a single cost of capital, because the cost of capital is dependent on the investment decisions implemented. Hence, the effects of investment and financing decisions must be assessed in combination.

## 20.2.2 Absence of a Theory of Share Price Determination

Additional complications also arise. Heterogeneous expectations alone need not destroy the CAPM notion of a risk-return trade-off,[8] but in their presence the risk-return trade-offs faced by a given investor may not correspond to those of the capital market line.[9] Different investors might thus attach different values to the securities of the same firm, making it difficult to ascertain the firm's market value, as described in Section 20.1. Moreover, inasmuch as there may be only a small number of buyers for a given firm's securities, there may be client effects to the pricing of the firm's securities, effects due either to unequally distributed information or to heterogeneous expectations, even if information is equally distributed. These possibilities, taken alone or in conjunction with the differing interest rates previously mentioned, mean that the market value of a firm is not uniquely determined by a fixed relationship between risk and return. Managers thus have no ready way of using market rates of return to judge how their actions might affect the well-being of the firm's stockholders. Managers might still be well advised to use a model like the CAPM as a guide, but cannot be certain that its predictions provide more than an approximate indication of a given decision's effects.

## 20.2.3 Financing Decisions and the Firm's Market Value

Another implication of capital market imperfections is that the firm does not necessarily have an unique cost of capital which it can use as a hurdle rate in deciding on the acceptability of investment projects. Indeed, as already mentioned, capital budgeting and financing decisions cannot any longer be determined separately as in a perfect market. Moreover, even if the cost of capital could still be defined as independent of the firm's operating plans, it might also depend on the particular lender advancing the funds. If investors have differing expectations regarding the firm's prospects, they might charge different effective rates for the same investment arrangement. In these circumstances, if information about different sources of credit

---

[8] See Lintner (1969). The market price of risk becomes, in effect, a weighted average of individual investors' risk-return trade-offs. The security market line is explained in Chapter 14.

[9] Miller (1977, p. 1157) summarizes evidence suggesting that the riskiest stocks in the market will tend to plot below the capital market line. For further discussion, see Friend and Bicksler (1977).

is costly to obtain, a manager might never be able to ascertain whether the firm's funds were being raised at the lowest cost consistent with the risk involved. For this reason also the manager cannot know if market value is actually being maximized.

Finally, as we have already mentioned, the cost of a given kind of capital may depend, in any time period, on the amount raised. As and when this is so, it means that the market value of the firm depends on the timing and amount of financial decisions as well as on all the other variables discussed. Because costs may depend on the amount borrowed in any time period, a firm's manager may find that a policy of distributing borrowings over several time periods will lower financing costs from what they would be if all required funds are borrowed at once.

## 20.2.4  Restricted Applicability of a Firm's Utility Function

The usefulness of the market value rule in a perfect capital market is its ability to provide a standard reflecting the best interests of all the firm's stockholders. When this standard is impaired because of capital market imperfections, it is natural to ask whether the stockholders' utility functions can be used instead. Certainly, this will be the case for the entrepreneurial firm: A decision maker can estimate the single owner's utility function, consider the terms of the various operating and financial transactions the firm can enter, and select decisions to maximize the owner's expected utility. Essentially, the same procedures can be employed if either the firm has many owners whose tastes are identical or the owners have identical expectations. But a difficulty arises in knowing what to do if a firm's owners have conflicting preferences. For in these cases management needs a rule that will reconcile conflicting preferences, but no such rule, satisfying reasonable conditions, may exist. For example, stockholder voting schemes may, at least in principle, be unable to resolve certain kinds of conflicts. The foregoing is not to say that there will never be unexceptionable actions for management to take. But it does say that in some circumstances management may not be able to select any single decision that will be in the best interests of all stockholders.[10]

## 20.2.5  A Role for Mutual Funds and Other Financial Intermediaries

In a perfect capital market investors do not need the diversification provided by financial intermediaries because they can achieve it on their own. In imperfect capital markets investors may well patronize financial intermediaries for the reason that the intermediaries may be able, because of transactions costs, scale economies, and unequally shared information, to create and manage investment portfolios more cheaply than can individuals. Hence, as Part II of this book has argued, the rationale for the existence of financial intermediaries actually rests on the capital market imperfections we are now examining. Most commonly, we might think of mutual funds as the kinds of financial intermediaries that provide such financial services. Certainly the notion of the market portfolio suggests a role for mutual funds in creating such investment opportunities, and explains the reason for the creation of *index funds*—

---

[10] These results will be established in Section 20.4.

mutual funds whose investment objective is to replicate some broad-based stock market index. However, other financial intermediaries also transform the nature of their lending risks when carrying out their functions (e.g., a bank's loans to individual businesses involve different credit risks than do depositors' loans to the bank, even if the latter are not covered by deposit insurance). In doing so, financial intermediaries may both save on transactions costs and mitigate problems of gathering transaction information. Therefore we might interpret the roles of a whole spectrum of financial intermediaries as those of overcoming at least some of the market imperfections whose existence we have recognized. In addition, by transforming risks, intermediaries might create securities whose return distributions differ from those of other companies and thus contribute to mitigating market incompleteness.

## 20.2.6   A Role for Conglomerates

In imperfect capital markets with unequally shared information a role for *conglomerate* enterprise is also suggested. If we define conglomerate activity as that involved in setting up a financial holding company to control unrelated businesses, there would be no economic advantage to such an activity in a perfect market because it would only create a diversified portfolio, which individual investors could create as cheaply on their own. But if conglomerate activity allows closer supervision of investments than can be exercised through the securities markets, and if the informational differences between borrowers and lenders described in Section 20.1.2 exist, then conglomerates can create financial portfolios that could not otherwise be created, at least for the same costs. Conglomerates might also be able to create more highly diversified portfolios by saving on several types of transactions costs.[11] Finally, in imperfect markets unsystematic risk may also be important, and conglomerate activity might be able to reduce unsystematic risk both by intensive governance and by combining negatively correlated earnings streams.[12]

## 20.3   NEED FOR AN INTEGRATED APPROACH TO FINANCIAL DECISION MAKING

The discussion of this chapter means in effect that the management of a firm operating in imperfect markets must maximize a criterion function by choosing operating and financial decisions in combination. The criterion is not necessarily the maximization of market value, and operating decisions cannot necessarily be separated from financing decisions. Moreover, the results of these decisions cannot always be assessed using a simple measure of market value, because stockholders may distinguish between

---

[11] This argument is due to Williamson (1975). On the other hand, Miller (1977, p. 1162) suggests that with heterogeneous expectations, the total market value of two otherwise independent firms can be lowered by a conglomerate merger.

[12] If the amounts of funds involved are large, alternative organizations such as investment clubs with many members might not be able to perform the same task. Moreover, an investment club will not usually have the same supervisory capabilities as a conglomerate headquarters staff. Williamson (1975) attaches considerable weight to conglomerates' supervisory capabilities.

different cash flow profiles having the same present value. Finally, the management of the firm may have to deal with unevenly distributed information in two ways—providing it to investors through signals on the one hand, and obtaining it about investments through contingency planning on the other. In essence, then, the firm's management faces the difficult problems of determining what criterion to employ, of having to solve a complex multiperiod programming problem after selecting a criterion function, and of dealing with differing informational conditions while so doing. We do not mean to overemphasize these difficulties. Perfect capital market theory has improved our understanding and may serve as a practical guide even in imperfect markets. The important operational questions are the extent to which perfect capital market theory may prove only a rough guide and why this might be so in a particular circumstance. Some observers conjecture, and we agree, that informational differences are likely to prove of greater practical importance than other types of transactions costs such as flotation costs and brokerage or loan application charges.

## 20.4  CHOOSING CRITERIA FOR FINANCIAL DECISIONS

We conclude this chapter by discussing some tools that management can use in making financial decisions when the firm's market value is not uniquely defined. As a practical matter, it might be well for decisions to be taken with a view to improving market value in such cases, even if it is not known whether market value is the best criterion to use. However, it is also desirable to be aware of alternative criteria that can be used, as in this way management can judge whether a given criterion such as market value might indicate actions different from those that would be selected by another criterion, such as expected utility maximization.

Alternative available criteria take a number of forms. One is the firm's utility function, although in using a utility, the question of whether it even exists must be faced. If such a utility does exist, the question of how to estimate the function must also be faced, although in some instances the utility's form need only be known in a general way. These circumstances arise when it is possible to rank the payoffs from decisions using the techniques of stochastic dominance discussed in Chapter 12. Finally, given a criterion, the question of whether a manager will be motivated to maximize it must be considered. This involves the question of providing incentives for managers to make decisions in the stockholders' interests. Therefore, in our discussion in this section we describe several possible approaches to choosing decision criteria in imperfect markets, each useful in particular circumstances.

### 20.4.1  A Firm's Utility Function Does Not Always Exist: Arrow Possibility Theorem

In imperfect capital markets where the value of the firm is not uniquely defined, management will not always know how to select investment projects that are in the best interests of all stockholders. In particular, management will be aware that different cash flow profiles, even if they have the same present value, can yield different levels of satisfaction to individual stockholders, for the reasons outlined earlier in this chapter.

In these circumstances, and knowing that the utility functions discussed in Chapter 11 can be estimated, a firm's management might be tempted to choose a utility intended to be somehow representative of stockholders' preferences. Unfortunately, however, an aggregate utility that represents the best interests of all stockholders need not always exist, because the conflicting preferences of individual stockholders are not always capable of being resolved, at least in any democratic fashion.

To suggest the nature of the difficulties involved, suppose a firm has three stockholders (or stockholder classes) who are asked to choose among three projects. The stockholders' rankings of the projects are shown in the body of Table 20.2. For example, stockholder B ranks the second project lowest in terms of preferences. In order for a firm's utility function to exist, it must rank actions in a manner consistent with the rankings of individual stockholders. The problem thus becomes one of devising such an aggregated ranking. But democratic schemes for resolving differences, using rules such as voting on paired comparisons, will not necessarily be able to effect a resolution. Indeed, Arrow (1951) has shown that it is not generally possible to resolve conflicting preferences without acting in an essentially dictatorial fashion.

While the technical nature of Arrow's argument lies far beyond the scope of this book, an example can be used to illustrate something of the difficulties that arise in attempting to construct a firm's utility function. Table 20.3 tabulates the votes each project would receive if votes reflecting the preferences in Table 20.2 were made on a paired comparison basis. Such a basis is, at least to some persons, one reasonable way of attempting to resolve stockholder conflict. However, in the example given the approach fails. For in considering project 2 versus project 3, stockholders A and C would vote for project 2 and B for project 3. Other pairs are similarly ranked, as the table shows. But the table then indicates the presence of an intransitivity, because as a group the stockholders (when the votes are counted) prefer project 1 over project 2, 2 over 3, and 3 over 1. This means that as a group stockholders' preferences are not consistent; the transitivity axiom (see Chapter 11) necessary for existence of a utility function is not satisfied. For this reason, a group utility function cannot exist in the present case, and

**TABLE 20.2**
STOCKHOLDER RANKINGS OF MUTUALLY EXCLUSIVE PROJECTS[a]

| Project Stockholder | 1 | 2 | 3 |
|---|---|---|---|
| A | 1 | 2 | 3 |
| B | 2 | 3 | 1 |
| C | 3 | 1 | 2 |

[a]A ranking of 1 indicates the stockholder's most preferred project.

**TABLE 20.3**
STOCKHOLDER VOTING ON A PAIRED COMPARISON BASIS

| Comparison Stockholder | 1 vs. 2 | 2 vs. 3 | 3 vs. 1 |
|---|---|---|---|
| A | 1 | 2 | 1 |
| B | 1 | 3 | 3 |
| C | 2 | 2 | 3 |

management cannot resolve the conflicting preferences to the satisfaction of all stockholders. Arrow's work shows that all democratic schemes for resolving conflicts, such as the voting scheme just examined, can encounter this same difficulty.

## 20.4.2  When a Firm's Utility Function Does Exist

While a firm's utility function does not always exist, we can say that it will, if, loosely speaking, the stockholders are not too dissimilar in their preferences. On the one hand, this statement means that if stockholders use roughly similar rankings, conflicts can be resolved. The same is true if stockholders are exactly similar in either their attitudes toward risk or in their expectations regarding the future. We next examine each of these cases in turn. This provides some information about the conditions under which managers can be reasonably confident of acting in the shareholders' best interests even if the market value criterion is not used.

### 20.4.2.1  Single-Peakedness Condition

To explain the notion of similarity between rankings, consider Figure 20.4, which plots each stockholder's ranking of the preferences indicated in Table 20.2 against the projects, which are arranged in numerical order. In the graph, we plot each stock-holder's rankings against the project numbers.[13] We can see that project 2 is the least

**Figure 20.4**
STOCKHOLDER B'S PREFERENCES DO NOT EXHIBIT THE SINGLE-PEAKEDNESS PROPERTY

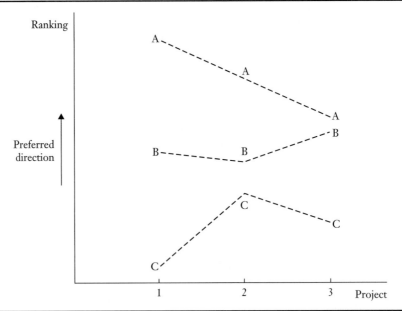

---

[13] The height of a particular stockholder's preferences is not relevant. The essential feature of the graph is how a given stockholder ranks the projects relative to each other, that is, the slope of the individual stockholder's graph showing preferences.

preferred of the three by stockholder B and the most preferred of the three by stockholder C. It can be shown by advanced methods, beyond the scope of this text, that in the present case our difficulty with paired comparison schemes resides in the attitudes of stockholder B. Moreover, it can be shown that if B's preferences are such that B's graph has a single high point (rather than a single low point as in Figure 20.4), then voting according to the paired comparison schemes will yield a transitive ranking that management can use in deriving a firm utility function. To see this by an example, suppose in Table 20.2 the rankings of stockholder B are replaced either by those of A or of C or by ranking the three projects in reverse order, that is, 3, 2, 1. If B uses any one of these three rankings, then paired voting will select a single project as most preferred by all three stockholders. If the ranking is 3, 2, 1, then in Table 20.3 stockholder B's votes would be recorded under 2 in the first comparison, under 3 in the second, and again under 3 in the third. This means the group now prefers 2 to 1, 2 to 3, and 1 to 3, so that project 2 can be selected by management.

Accordingly, the example has suggested that if in a graph like Figure 20.4 no stockholder's ranking displays a low point in the middle of the set of projects ranked (technically if every stockholder's preferences are single-peaked), then a voting scheme to resolve conflicts of interest can be used. That is, the difficulties discovered by Arrow do not obtain when preferences are single-peaked. Hence, in such cases management can act in the best interests of all stockholders by following procedures along the lines indicated above. While such an approach might not be at all easy to put into practice, at least it does show that management will not always be paralyzed by inconsistent stockholder preferences. The importance of this possibility to practical decision making has been pointed out by Scott (1978).

Under more restrictive conditions than single peakedness, more can be said about a firm's utility function. A well-defined utility function for the firm exists either if (1) all stockholders' preferences are identical, or if (2) their preferences are not identical but their expectations about the future are exactly the same.

### 20.4.2.2  *Implications of Using a Firm's Utility Function*

We have now identified three conditions that may justify substituting a firm utility function for the market value of its shares. These conditions are (1) that every stockholders' preferences are single-peaked, or (2) that all stockholders' preferences are identical, or (3) that if condition 2 does not hold, then stockholder expectations about the future must all be the same. Of course, if (2) does hold, a utility will also exist if stockholder expectations are identical. The point is that one of conditions (1), (2), or (3) must be satisfied for a utility to exist. Then, if both (2) and (3) are satisfied, the utility will certainly exist. Moreover, in the second and third instances we have indicated how the firm's utility is related to that of the individual stockholders.[14]

The foregoing conditions may obtain if either the past actions of the firm's management have attracted like-minded investors, or past policies have induced a particular set of expectations. To the extent that such conditions are satisfied, they tend to argue for gradual changes in financial policy so that dissatisfied investors can adjust their investment positions over time. It is probably most helpful if a firm's policy changes can be

---

[14] For a full discussion, see Wilson (1968).

announced in advance, since given advance knowledge dissatisfied investors might be able to adjust their positions at lower transactions costs than would otherwise be the case.

### 20.4.3 Using Utilities When it is Possible

When a utility function for the firm does exist, management can use expected utility maximization as a decision criterion. That is, management can select actions that maximize the firm's expected utility rather than its market value. As we showed in the previous section, the manager considers the effects of actions on the distribution of cash flows, performs expected utility calculations for the distributions implied by available alternative actions (including different levels of investment), and selects an act that maximizes expected utility.

The use of expected utility maximization is more practical than it may first appear because such calculations can be approximated using risk-adjusted rates of return. To see this, consider the following example. Suppose the utility function is given by:

$$u(w) = w^{1/2}$$

and consider a lottery, X, that pays $1 and $4 at time 2 with equal probability. Then:

$$E[u(x)] = \frac{1}{2}[u(\$1) + u(\$4)]$$

A certainty equivalent $c$ is defined by the condition:

$$u(c) = \frac{1}{2}[u(\$1) + u(\$4)]$$

Replacing the utility function by its explicit form, we obtain:

$$c^{1/2} = \frac{1}{2}\left[(1)^{1/2} + (4)^{1/2}\right]$$

Squaring both sides of the above equation then gives:

$$c = \frac{1}{4}\left\{1 + 4 + 2[(1)(4)]^{1/2}\right\} = \frac{1}{4}(1 + 4 + 4) = \frac{9}{4}$$

But $E(X) = \frac{5}{2} = \frac{10}{4}$, so that the implied risk premium is $\frac{10}{4} - \frac{9}{4} = \frac{1}{4}$. The risk premium is measured at time 2, so that $\frac{9}{4}$ is a certainty equivalent value at time 2. Also suppose that the investment's certainty equivalent has a time 1 value[15] of $\frac{8}{9}\left(\frac{9}{4}\right)$, that is, the risk-free rate is 0.125 = $\frac{1}{8}$. Based on these assumptions, the risk-adjusted rate of return for the project is:

$$\frac{\frac{10}{4} - \frac{8}{9}\left(\frac{9}{4}\right)}{\frac{8}{9}\left(\frac{9}{4}\right)} = \frac{10 - 8}{8} = 25\%$$

---

[15] That is, if the risk-free rate is 0.125 = 1/8.

Accordingly, using expected utilities in one-period problems gives results similar to those obtained using risk-adjusted discount rates.[16] The main problem with this approach is that unless the utility function's form is known, the firm's management does not know which risk-adjusted rate of return to choose. But if projects are acceptable over a range of risk-adjusted discount rates, management can be reasonably confident of their acceptability to the firm's stockholders. Note, moreover, that the lowest rate of discount the manager should use for risk-averse stockholders is certainly not less than the risk-free rate, that is, the rate that would be used by risk-neutral stockholders.

At this point one might ask whether there is really any difference between the present interpretation of expected utility maximization as implying risk-adjusted discount rates or the use of the CAPM to find the risk-adjusted rates according to which share prices are determined by discounting expected future earnings. From a policy point of view, there may not appear to be substantial differences between the two approaches—in both cases the size of the risk adjustment increases with the risk of the lottery being valued. Thus, the differences between the approaches are mainly conceptual, although the utility function approach does not require using any specific description of risk such as a covariance. Rather, the project distribution of return is used.

The real importance of our discussion of risk-adjusted rates thus becomes the implicit question of whose risk adjustment is to be used. If the CAPM is valid, market risk adjustments are to be used; if the expected utility model for a group of stockholders is valid, it is their risk adjustments that are of greatest importance to a firm's management. In either case, the tools we have developed indicate how to approach the problem of calculating the adjustments.

## 20.4.4  Using Dominance Criteria When Utilities are not Fully Specified

While in Section 20.4.3 it was suggested that the prescriptions of expected utility maximization could be approximated by risk-adjusted discount rates, there are also circumstances in which management can make decisions without knowing a great deal about stockholders' utilities. Some, but not all, probability distributions can be compared for any utility function that, say, merely exhibits risk aversion.[17] Thus, when management can only make weak assumptions about individual stockholders' preferences (rather than postulate the exact nature of their utilities), decisions can sometimes still be made on behalf of them all in the knowledge that the stockholders would all approve. To see how this thinking applies to risk-averse stockholders, we consider first a simple situation applying whenever stockholders can be assumed to be materialistic in the sense of preferring more money to less. No assumptions about risk aversion will be required in this first example. However, after having considered this simple case, we shall then discuss a rule for use by management acting on behalf of risk-averse stockholders.

---

[16] Caution: The use of risk-adjusted rates in multiperiod models can lead to incorrect decisions unless carefully interpreted. We discuss these issues in Chapter 25.

[17] See also the discussion of stochastic dominance in Chapter 12.

If management is willing only to assume that every stockholder's utility increases with wealth, there are still some lotteries that are clearly better than others irrespective of the utilities' particular forms. For example, consider the following two lotteries, A and B, with payoffs and associated probabilities shown:

|  | *Lottery A* | | *Lottery B* | |
| --- | --- | --- | --- | --- |
| Payoffs | $1 | $3 | $0 | $2 |
| Probability | 0.5 | 0.5 | 0.6 | 0.4 |

From Figure 20.5 it appears that lottery A would be preferred to lottery B, because lottery A always offers outcomes below a given fixed amount with lower probability than does lottery B (the downside risk of lottery A is lower).

To verify that this result is true for any decision maker whose utility increases with wealth, consider:

$$E[u(A)] = \frac{1}{2}u(\$1) + \frac{1}{2}u(\$3)$$

$$E[u(B)] = \frac{6}{10}u(\$0) + \frac{4}{10}u(\$2)$$

Then, under the assumption that utility increases in wealth,

$$E[u(B)] = \frac{6}{10}u(\$0) + \frac{4}{10}u(\$2) < \frac{6}{10}u(\$1) + \frac{4}{10}u(\$3) < \frac{1}{2}u(\$1) + \frac{1}{2}u(\$3) = E[u(A)]$$

**FIGURE 20.5**
**FIRST-DEGREE STOCHASTIC DOMINANCE**

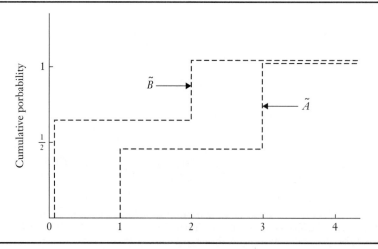

so that

$$E[u(A)] = E[u(B)]$$

As the example suggests, a choice between two lotteries can be made on the basis of these ideas whenever their respective distributions do not cross.[18] Hence, if this were the only available ranking rule, in many cases it would mean that no comparisons could be made. However, sometimes this inability to compare distributions whose graphs cross can be resolved by imposing additional assumptions about stockholder preferences.

Hence, we now suppose all stockholders are risk averse in addition to preferring more wealth to less. Then we assume that management must compare lotteries C and D with the payoffs and probabilities shown below:

|  | Lottery C | | | Lottery D | |
|---|---|---|---|---|---|
| Payoffs | $0 | $2 | $4 | $1 | $4 |
| Probability | 1/3 | 1/3 | 1/3 | 1/2 | 1/2 |

These are lotteries whose cumulative distributions cross as shown in Figure 20.6. As we showed in Chapter 9 (pages 187–188), in this case Lottery D is preferred by second degree stochastic dominance. For convenience the reasoning is repeated here. Notice first that $E(D) = \$\frac{5}{2}$ and $E(C) = \$2$, so the risk-neutral stockholder at least would prefer lottery D. Note also that the worst outcome of lottery D is at least as good as (in fact better than) the worst outcome[19] from lottery C. This means that in terms of the greatest possible downside risk, lottery D is never quite as bad as lottery C.

To see how it might be shown formally that lottery D is actually preferred by any risk-averter, let us ask if $E[u(D)] = E[u(C)]$. If it were, we would have:

$$\frac{1}{2}u(\$1) + \frac{1}{2}u(\$4) > \frac{1}{3}u(\$0) + \frac{1}{3}u(\$2) + \frac{1}{3}u(\$4)$$

which may also be written as:

$$\left(\frac{1}{3} + \frac{1}{6}\right)u(\$1) + \left(\frac{1}{3} + \frac{1}{6}\right)u(\$4) > \frac{1}{3}u(\$0) + \left(\frac{1}{6} + \frac{1}{6}\right)u(\$2) + \frac{1}{3}u(\$4)$$

Then after cancelling common terms and regrouping, we would have:

$$\frac{1}{3}[u(\$1) - u(\$0)] + \frac{1}{6}[u(\$4) - u(\$2)] > \frac{1}{6}[u(\$2) - u(\$1)]$$

---

[18] The relationship between lottery A and lottery B is in this case expressed by saying lottery A dominates lottery B in the first degree. See Hadar and Russell (1969) for a proof of the general result.

[19] These are necessary conditions for the ranking we are now establishing, second-degree dominance. They are necessary to prevent lottery D from being rejected by risk-averters who are especially heavily influenced by worst-case thinking. Note that these necessary conditions do not imply $\sigma^2(D)$ must always be smaller than $\sigma^2(C)$.

But $u(\$1) - u(\$0) > u(\$2) - u(\$1)$ by the diminishing marginal utility characteristic of risk-averters, so the original inequality will certainly be satisfied if we can show that

$$\frac{1}{6}[u(\$1) - u(\$0)] + \frac{1}{6}[u(\$2) - u(\$1)] + \frac{1}{6}[u(\$4) - u(\$2)] > \frac{1}{6}[u(\$2) - u(\$1)]$$

But this expression reduces to

$$\frac{1}{6}[u(\$1) - u(\$0)] + \frac{1}{6}[u(\$4) - u(\$2)] > 0$$

which is obviously true. Accordingly, it is now easy, by working backward from the last line, to verify that $E[u(D)] > E[u(C)]$; that is, lottery D is preferred to lottery C by all risk-averse decision makers.

The test for this relationship, known as second-degree stochastic dominance, which was described in Chapter 12, can be made systematically as follows. If, proceeding from the left in a graph like Figure 20.6, the area accumulated from the left of the graph and between the two distributions never changes sign,[20] the distribution beginning on the right is said to be preferred according to the

**FIGURE 20.6**
SECOND-DEGREE STOCHASTIC DOMINANCE (START EVALUATION AT LEFT-HAND SIDE OF THE DIAGRAM BECAUSE RISK-AVERSE INVESTORS ATTACH A GREATER NEGATIVE WEIGHT TO DOWNSIDE RISK THAN THEY DO TO UPSIDE POTENTIAL)

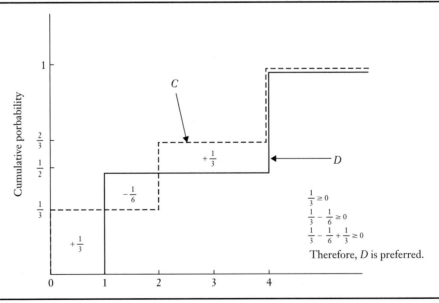

---

[20] Individual components of the accumulated area may differ in sign, as Figure 20.7 shows. It is only the accumulated area that must always have the same sign.

FIGURE 20.7
CHECKING FOR SECOND-DEGREE DOMINANCE

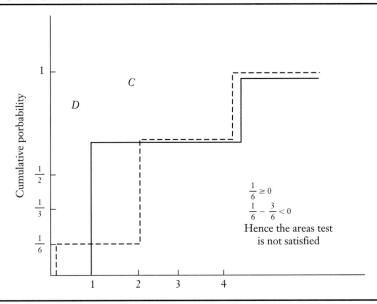

relationship of second-degree stochastic dominance.[21] The method of making the calculations is displayed in the figure.

Not everything can be ranked by second-degree dominance, for there are pairs of distributions such that the area of the difference between the distributions does change sign as these areas are cumulated from the left. For example, consider Figure 20.7, drawn to indicate the distributions for the two lotteries that have the same payoffs as lotteries C and D but different probability distributions:

|  | *Lottery C* | | | *Lottery D* | |
|---|---|---|---|---|---|
| Payoffs | $0 | $2 | $4 | $1 | $4 |
| Probability | 1/6 | 1/2 | 1/3 | 2/3 | 1/3 |

Note that $E(C) = \$\frac{14}{6} > E(D) = \$2$, so that on the basis of the mean (but not on the basis of lowest outcomes) lottery C might prove to be a dominant lottery. But Figure 20.7 shows that the areas test is not satisfied, so that we cannot choose between lottery C and lottery D without knowing more about the decision maker's preferences. A risk-neutral decision maker would prefer lottery C, but lottery D has a better lowest outcome than lottery C, so that a highly risk-averse[22] decision maker would prefer lottery D. Hence, neither lottery C nor lottery D satisfies the two conditions necessary for one to dominate the other.

---

[21] Formal proofs of this result are given in Hadar and Russell (1969).
[22] Technically this holds if the decision maker's index of absolute risk aversion is sufficiently large.

**FIGURE 20.8**
PREFERENCE RELATIONS AND RANKING POSSIBILITIES

Preferences

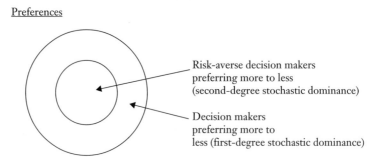

Risk-averse decision makers
preferring more to less
(second-degree stochastic dominance)

Decision makers
preferring more to
less (first-degree stochastic dominance)

Random variables

All distributions
ranked by
(first-degree
stochastic dominance)

All distributions
ranked by
(second-degree
stochastic dominance)

All distributions

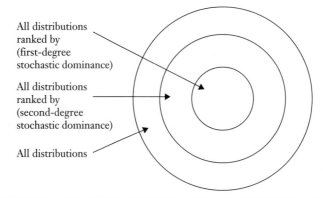

The findings may be summarized as follows. Management can rank some probability distributions by making only minimal assumptions about the preferences of stockholders on whose behalf the distributions are ranked. While not all distributions can be ranked by either of the criteria discussed here, more can be compared as the assumptions about stockholder preferences are made more specific. The relations between assumptions regarding preferences on the one hand and the classes of variables that can be ranked are displayed schematically in Figure 20.8. That is, the more things we are willing to specify about stockholders' preferences, the larger the set of distributions we can compare. For example, if we assume stockholders are risk averse, we can use second-degree stochastic dominance[23] to make at least some comparisons among prospects on behalf of the risk-averse stockholders.

---

[23] For further discussion of the dominance concepts, see Chapter 12.

## 20.5 Motivating Managers to Meet Owners' Objectives: Agency Theory

If it is not easy to monitor the activities of managers, say because information about their performance is difficult to obtain, it becomes important to motivate managers to act in the best interests of the stockholders. Essentially, the problem is to ensure that management is motivated to maximize the criterion stockholders prefer. Incentive schemes can create this motivation by rewarding the manager for following stockholders' preferences. For example, a stock option plan for management gives managers greater incentive to maximize share price than does a fixed salary arrangement that is independent of the firm's profit performance.

However, such schemes resolve the motivation problem only partially. One reason for a potential conflict between stockholders' and managers' objectives, even with stock options[24] or other forms of profit sharing, is that a manager's compensation may be tied entirely to the fortunes of the firm. Recall that we earlier divided the firm's standard deviation of return into diversifiable and nondiversifiable components. Since stockholders normally purchase a firm's shares as part of a portfolio, only a stock's systematic risk is of concern to them, at least in markets that are perfect or nearly so. But if managers are less able to diversify their personal investments,[25] they may be concerned with unsystematic risk as well. This could lead them to make operating (investment) decisions that are less risky than would be optimal from the stockholders' viewpoints.[26]

This problem has been studied using the economic theory of agency.[27] The stockholders' (principal's) problem is to design a compensation scheme that will lead an expected utility-maximizing manager (agent) to maximize the principal's expected utility. The current state of the approach is rather abstract and thus beyond the scope of this text. Nevertheless, it does suggest that the owners' problem of contracting for the services of a manager may fruitfully be examined as a problem in buying information. In this case the information purchased is the manager's opinion regarding possible excess returns from the operation, and its price is the manager's fee. The fee to be paid will depend on whether the owner can evaluate the excess returns correctly. If so, the fee will be less than otherwise (the owner and manager engage in the form of bargaining known as bilateral monopoly, so the outcome is indeterminate a priori). The analysis by Heckerman (1975) shows that if the manager is allowed to invest in the firm (stock option), he will value the option less as the standard deviation of the firm's return increases, requiring a larger fixed fee in compensation. The owner's protection lies in keeping the fixed fee small enough so that the manager will accept

---

[24] Companies are rethinking the use of stock options, in part because of backdated options scandals. A backdated option is an executive option grant in which the date of the grant has been manipulated to provide greater benefits to the executive and to minimize taxes. Such manipulation, however, violates financial disclosure and tax laws.

[25] This is because through a stock option plan their major investment may be in the firm they manage.

[26] In terms of the transformation curve of Chapter 2, it is not shifted up and to the right as far as it could be. Recall we stated that it was the manager's technical knowledge of the firm's operations that established the position of this curve.

[27] See Heckerman (1975).

the contract only if the manager believes the excess return is large enough to protect the owner. Such a participatory contract between an owner and a manager will require a higher rate of return for investment decisions than otherwise to compensate the owner for the costs of obtaining the information needed to design the contract.

Another approach emphasizing the costs of monitoring agency relationships has been developed by Jensen and Meckling (1976). These authors argue that managers of firms can always take some of their income in kind, since the cost to the stockholders of monitoring an agent's every action would be prohibitively great. The problem, then, becomes one of balancing off incentives paid to agents against the costs of monitoring those actions for which incentives to act in the stockholders' best interests are not provided.

## KEY POINTS

- Capital market imperfections have far-reaching implications for financial decision making.
- There are several kinds of capital market imperfections: heterogeneous expectations, unequally distributed information, transactions costs, tax differentials, and the costs of unsystematic risk.
- With heterogeneous expectations, investors have differences of opinion regarding the probability distributions of future events.
- Assuming heterogeneous expectations weakens but does not destroy the CAPM notion of a risk-return trade-off. However, the risk-return trade-offs faced by a given investor may not correspond to those of the capital market line.
- In addition to heterogeneous expectations regarding the future, investors may not even share the same information about the past. Therefore, it may be difficult for potential investors to accurately evaluate the nature of the risks involved in purchasing the securities of some firms. Similarly, in debt markets it may be difficult for lenders to assess accurately the credit risk of borrowers.
- The major imperfection affecting market prices appears to involve the collection and dissemination of information that seems often to be distributed quite unevenly.
- When capital markets are not perfect, the market value of the firm is not always well defined and therefore management action to maximize stockholder value is not always as clear as in the case of a perfect capital market.
- In an imperfect capital market, financial and operating decisions are no longer separable, because the value of the firm depends on both the operating decision, which determines the amount of financing needed, and the manner in which the funds are raised. Therefore, the effects of investment and financing decisions must be assessed in combination.
- In a world of capital market imperfections, a firm's market value is not uniquely determined by a fixed relationship between risk and return, because management has no ready way of using market rates of return to judge the effect of its actions on the well-being of the firm's stockholders.

- In an imperfect capital market, firm investing decisions are more difficult for management because the firm does not necessarily have a unique cost of capital that it can use as a hurdle rate in deciding on the acceptability of investment projects.
- While the usefulness of the market value rule in a perfect capital market is its ability to provide a standard reflecting the best interests of all the firm's stockholders, this standard is impaired because of capital market imperfections.
- In an imperfect capital market, the difficulty faced by management is in knowing what to do if a firm's owners have conflicting preferences, because under reasonable conditions regarding preferences no rule for resolving conflicts may exist.
- When operating in an imperfect capital market, a firm's management must maximize a criterion function by choosing operating and financial decisions in combination.
- Two ways for management to deal with unevenly distributed information are via signals and through contingency planning.
- A firm's utility function representing the best interests of all stockholders need not always exist. The conflicting preferences of individual stockholders are not always capable of being resolved, at least in any democratic fashion. In fact, it has been shown that it is not generally possible to resolve conflicting preferences without acting in an essentially dictatorial fashion.
- There are conditions that may justify substituting a firm's utility function for the market value of its shares. If a firm's utility function can be employed, management can use expected utility maximization as a decision criterion.
- The expected utility maximization approach that management can follow in an imperfect capital market could be approximated by using a risk-adjusted discount rate. Moreover, there are circumstances in which management can make decisions without knowing a great deal about stockholders' utilities.
- Incentive schemes (such as stock option plans) must be designed to motivate managers for following the preferences of stockholders. The stockholders' (principal's) problem is to design a compensation scheme that will lead an expected utility-maximizing manager (agent) to maximize the principal's expected utility.

## QUESTIONS

1. What are some circumstances in which differences in expectations might result in stock prices being lower than in the case of investor agreement?

2. What are the implications of unequally distributed information for investors and the management of a firm?

3. Because of a concern with unsystematic risk, a firm's management might be tempted to operate the firm in a manner not wholly consistent with stockholder interests. Can you think of a financial arrangement that might partly alleviate this problem?

4. If mutual funds can effect diversification more cheaply than individual investors, they might be able to earn greater returns on a portfolio of given risk than

would individual investors. Assuming this to be true, who would be likely to receive the excess returns, and why? (Hint: Specify carefully the market conditions in which the mutual funds are assumed to trade.)

5. Why is there a need for an integrated approach to financial decision making?

6. What are the conditions that may justify substituting the market value of a company's shares for its utility function?

7. In an imperfect capital market, can the managers of a firm still use the market value of the company as a rule for making decisions? If not, what other criterion can they use to make financial decisions?

8. The management of Minuscule Investments Ltd. is considering two investment proposals, X and Y, either of which may be had for $10 million. Because of a limited capital budget, only one of the two can be selected. Their one-period payoffs are, respectively,

|  | Investment X | | Investment Y | | |
|---|---|---|---|---|---|
| Payoffs | $15 | $25 | $18 | $20 | $22 |
| Probability | 1/2 | 1/2 | 1/3 | 1/3 | 1/3 |

Which set of payoffs is preferable and why? (Hint: Consider second-degree stochastic dominance in answering this question.)

9. You are asked to compare the following probability distributions of cash flows:
   a. A versus B:

|  | Cash flow A | | Cash flow B | | |
|---|---|---|---|---|---|
| Payoffs | $7 | $9 | $2 | $5 | $8 |
| Probability | 1/2 | 1/2 | 1/6 | 1/3 | 1/2 |

   b. C versus D:

|  | Cash flow C | | | Cash flow D | | |
|---|---|---|---|---|---|---|
| Payoffs | $10 | $30 | 50 | $20 | $40 | $60 |
| Probability | 1/3 | 1/3 | 1/3 | 1/2 | 1/3 | 1/6 |

   c. E versus F:

|  | Cash flow E | | | Cash flow F | | |
|---|---|---|---|---|---|---|
| Payoffs | $10 | $30 | $50 | $11 | $21 | $60 |
| Probability | 1/3 | 1/3 | 1/3 | 1/2 | 1/3 | 1/6 |

What comparisons can you make in each case, and why?

10. The stockholders' utility function for a firm is $u(x) = x^{\frac{1}{2}}$. Assuming that the risk-free rate is 10%, determine the risk-adjusted return of a lottery that pays $2 with probability $\frac{1}{3}$ and $6 with probability $\frac{2}{3}$.

11. Let's suppose that the risk adjustment of investors is 0.05% and the risk-free rate is 4%. Determine the time 1 value of the following contingent claim in the different cases:

| State | Probability | Contingent Claim |
|-------|-------------|------------------|
| 1 | 1/6 | 10 |
| 2 | 1/2 | 4 |
| 3 | 1/3 | 1 |

a. Homogenous expectations and risk-neutral investor
b. Homogenous expectations and risk-averse investor
c. Now suppose a market with two identical claims and three investors and let's assume that an investor can hold at most one claim. Let's also suppose that the investors have the following view of the contingent claim:

| State | Probability investor 1 | Probability investor 2 | Probability investor 3 |
|-------|------------------------|------------------------|------------------------|
| 1 | 1/6 | 1/3 | 1/4 |
| 2 | 1/2 | 1/6 | 1/2 |
| 3 | 1/3 | 1/2 | 1/4 |

What will be the price of the contingent claim in this market?

# REFERENCES

Akerlof, George A. (1976). "The Economics of Caste and of the Rat Race and Other Woeful Tales," *Quarterly Journal of Economics* **90**: 599–617.

Arrow, Kenneth J. (1951). *Social Choice and Individual Value*. New York: John Wiley & Sons.

Friend, Irwin, and James R. Bicksler. (1977). *Risk and Return in Finance*. Cambridge, MA: Ballinger.

Hadar, Josef, and William R. Russell. (1969). "Rules for Ordering Uncertain Prospects," *American Economic Review* **59**: 24–35.

Heckerman, Donald G. (1975). "Motivating Managers to Make Investment Decisions," *Journal of Financial Economics* **2**: 273–292.

Jaffee, Dwight M., and Thomas Russell. (1976). "Imperfect Information, Uncertainty, and Credit Rationing," *Quarterly Journal of Economics* **90**: 651–666.

Jensen, Michael C., and William M. Meckling. (1976). "Theory of the Firm: Managerial Behavior, Agency Costs, and Ownership Structure," *Journal of Financial Economics* **3**: 305–360.

Lintner, John. (1969). "The Aggregation of Investors' Diverse Judgments and Preferences in Purely Competitive Security Markets," *Journal of Financial and Quantitative Analysis* **4**: 347–400.

Miller, Edward M. (1977). "Risk, Uncertainty, and Divergence of Opinion," *Journal of Finance* **32**: 1151–1167.

Miller, Edward M. (2004a). "Restrictions on Short Selling and Exploitable Opportunities for Investors," in Frank J. Fabozzi (ed.), *Short Selling: Strategies, Risks, and Rewards*. Hoboken, NJ: John Wiley & Sons.

Miller, Edward M. (2004b). "Implications of Short Selling and Divergence of Opinion for Investment Strategy," in Frank J. Fabozzi (ed.), *Short Selling: Strategies, Risks, and Rewards*. Hoboken, NJ: John Wiley & Sons.

Miller, Edward M. (2004c). "Short Selling and Financial Puzzle," in Frank J. Fabozzi (ed.), *Short Selling: Strategies, Risks, and Rewards*. Hoboken, NJ: John Wiley & Sons.

Salop, Joanne and Steven Salop. (1976). "Self-Selection and Turnover in the Labor Market," *Quarterly Journal of Economics* **90**: 619–627.

Scott, William R. (1978). "Group Preference Orderings for Audit and Valuation Alternatives: The Single-Peakedness Condition," *Accounting Review* **53**: 120–137.

Williamson, Oliver E. (1975). *Markets and Hierarchies: Economic Analysis and Antitrust Implications*. New York: Free Press.

Wilson, Robert. (1968). "The Theory of Syndicates," *Econometrica* **36**: 119–132.

# 21

# IMPEDIMENTS TO ARBITRAGE

$\mathcal{T}$his chapter explores market relations when there are impediments to arbitrage. It begins by explaining how markets differ in providing liquidity. If all markets were perfectly liquid and there were no transactions costs, asset prices would be related as in the no-arbitrage world. However, with differing degrees of information, of liquidity, and in the presence of transactions costs, asset price relations become very much less well defined, as Chapter 20 indicated. Furthermore, these same market imperfections can lead to a number of phenomena, including credit rationing equilibria, market segmentation, market failure, and financial system externalities.

In an arbitrage-free world, securities are always liquid, all market transactions are linked by arbitrage, externalities (i.e., third-party effects) and market failures are assumed away. The assumptions are important both in their own right and for analyzing some of the complications arising when the assumptions do not hold. Market imperfections can imply that market prices are no longer completely linked to each other, that the liquidity of securities can vary, and that externalities (third-party effects) may influence prices. Sometimes equilibrium prices may not be attainable; in other cases, market failure can occur and no transactions will take place at all.

Despite the foregoing complications, the prices determined in arbitrage-free markets can still serve as a guide to value, although depending on circumstances the guide can range from being helpful to being unreliable. In this chapter, we trace some of the ways in which the benchmarks' reliability can be affected by different forms of imperfections. We begin by examining market liquidity and its determinants, and then examine the following issues: market linkages and market segmentation, financial system externalities, credit-rationing equilibria, and market failure.

## 21.1 SECURITIES MARKETS AND LIQUIDITY

Traders act as dealers by taking instruments into inventory, but act as brokers when they arrange transactions between counterparties without taking a position themselves. The existence of dealers, and consequently the degree to which the market provides liquidity, depends in part on the inventory risk-reward ratio for a typical transaction, as will be explained below. The specialists on exchanges like the New York Stock Exchange (NYSE) function as dealers, as do the market makers on exchanges such as the NASDAQ market.

The role of the stock exchange specialist was first examined by Baumol (1965) and by Demsetz (1968). Their work indicates that making a market involves assembling information regarding both the company whose shares are being traded and its business environment. Agents using a market maker's services do not need to acquire information themselves, but can pay the market maker to do so for them. To Demsetz, one of the main roles of the market maker is to supply *immediacy of trading*. Since the market maker holds an inventory of the security, in effect he provides a form of insurance against temporary order imbalances (i.e., when during some time period buy orders for a specific security substantially exceed sell orders for the same security or sell orders substantially exceed buy orders). The market maker also insures a potential trader against entering the market without success—at least as long as the agent is ready to trade at or near the current market price. The specialist buys at a price below the market and sells at a price higher than the market. The price spread covers the specialist's costs of providing trade immediacy services, as well as its risk and any other operating costs.

One of the most important risks faced by a market maker is the risk of inventory price change. Since market makers have limited capital, they can be quite sensitive to these risks. Baumol (1965) argues that when market makers infer from order imbalances and other information that conditions may be changing, they change prices more frequently and reduce their price quotations to the minimum amounts of trading allowed in order to limit their inventory risks. Market makers also face the risk of trading with better-informed parties, in which case they can suffer the effects of adverse selection. On average, market makers will lose when trading with better-informed parties, and will have to cover those losses through the bid-ask spreads they set when trading with uninformed parties.

Liquidity differences among markets depend on such factors as differences in market structure, the nature of the instruments traded, and the kinds of obligations the instruments represent. This section, based on Grossman and Miller (1988), considers how the economics of dealing in a marketplace can influence the number of active market makers whose presence contributes to liquidity. Grossman and Miller explain why liquidity differs among markets and show that the number of active market makers can be used to measure market liquidity. To do so, the model links the observed presence of market specialists to the profits they can expect to earn in different markets. For example, making a market for securities issued by the U.S. Department of the Treasury, called Treasury securities, can prove profitable. On the other hand, making a market for residential homes will likely not be, as discussed further in the next section.

The model considers a group of market makers and a group of outside customers trading in a single stock. If customers wish to sell their stock, they can either sell immediately to market makers, or wait until later to determine if additional potential buyers might respond with a more favorable offer. Selling immediately brings a certainty price, typically lower than the price customers might expect to realize from waiting. On the other hand, waiting for a possibly higher price also means bearing a risk of adverse price change. Grossman and Miller refer to customers' willingness to sell at once as their demand for immediacy, and postulate that the demand for immediacy depends on both the volatility of the stock price and any possibilities they might have to diversify against adverse price moves.

Market makers who stand ready to buy are said to supply immediacy services, and their supply function is determined by the economics of market making. Gross returns from market making must cover both the costs and risks of holding an inventory and the opportunity costs of standing ready to buy whenever sellers demand their services.[1] First, making a market means assuming a price risk, described analytically by price variance. From a market maker's point of view, an increase in price variance increases both the risk of holding inventory and the possibility of earning trading profits. Second, market makers must cover their operating costs. In recognition of their costs and the risks they face, market makers will buy at prices lower than the prices they expect to realize when reselling the inventory.

Differences in the supply of and demand for immediacy jointly determine market liquidity. The greater the demand for immediacy, and the lower the market makers' costs, the larger will be the proportion of transactions channeled through market makers. The larger the proportion of transactions so channeled, the greater will be the degree of market liquidity.

## 21.1.1 Liquidity Differences in Practice

We described futures contracts in Chapter 18. Successful futures markets offer an example of markets where both the demand for immediacy and the supply of market-making services are relatively great, and consequently these markets exhibit a relatively high degree of liquidity. The futures markets' demands for immediacy stem from the fact that delaying futures trades can be highly risky, especially when a trade is part of a portfolio adjustment strategy. Since futures markets also stimulate hedging, Grossman and Miller argue that the demand for immediacy is both urgent and sustained. At the same time, the supply of market-making services is relatively great because market makers' costs and inventory risks are relatively low.

On the other hand, markets for retail transactions in residential homes are highly illiquid. Sellers of individual homes are less concerned with immediacy than with making sure that all potential buyers (i.e., the largest possible set it is economic to inform) are notified of the intended sale. Moreover, the supply of market-making services is limited both by the opportunity costs of maintaining a presence in a thin market and by a very high degree of inventory risk. The inventory risk can also be affected by moral hazard if the seller has adverse private information about the property's condition. As a consequence, almost all residential homes are traded by brokers (who do not take inventory positions) rather than by market makers.

Stock markets lie between the two extremes just outlined. For a few widely held and very actively traded stocks, the NYSE[2] comes close to the futures markets in

---

[1] Inventory risk may be a more important factor in the short run; opportunity cost is a more important factor in the longer run.

[2] Now NYSE Euronext. However, the two markets still maintain separate trading facilities, known as the NYSE and Euronext, respectively.

providing a high degree of liquidity, and for much the same reasons. However, the same is not true for NYSE-listed stocks that are less actively traded. For these stocks, a specialist trader is granted a trading monopoly in exchange for an obligation to stand ready to buy or sell during exchange business hours, at least if the proposed orders are relatively small.[3] For larger transactions the specialist can, with the permission of the exchange, suspend trading while searching for counterparties. This search will likely involve participants in the upstairs market, discussed next.

The upstairs market is an institutional market for block trades. The upstairs market originally emerged in the 1960s as a facility aimed at finding institutional traders whose spreads were lower than the commissions then charged by exchange specialists. Since the late 1960s upstairs market participants have taken increasingly larger inventory positions, thereby increasing the liquidity of the market. Since the early 1980s, upstairs market participants have been able to sell off some of their inventory risks by using futures and index options, offsetting some of the previously assumed inventory risks. As a result, market making has become more economic, and upstairs market liquidity has increased still further.

When they were originally set up, OTC markets handled stocks whose trading was too thin to merit listing, even on a regional exchange. At the outset, OTC markets functioned mainly as bulletin boards on which market makers could list price quotes valid for minimum order amounts. For at least some stocks, lower computing and communications costs have changed the supply of market-making services, stimulating the emergence of more market makers. At the same time, and particularly in the late 1990s with the emergence of electronic computer networks, both the number of OTC participants and the demand for liquidity services have increased. As a result, the OTC markets are now more liquid than previously,[4] and some large stocks that formerly traded on organized exchanges now trade OTC.

## 21.2  LIMITS TO ARBITRAGE

As Chapter 7 explained, financiers are usually described as seeking out profitable arbitrage opportunities, both within a given market and between markets. Through trading, financiers link securities prices to each other. The linkages are strengthened by market operators who strive to attract business through executing trades quickly and at the lowest possible charges. Market trading is at its most active when deal terms are standardized, when agents have ready access to the same information, and when transactions costs comprise a relatively small percentage of trades' values.

Trading among complementary securities is usually less active than among close substitutes. For example, there is relatively little or no trading between government

---

[3] While the specialist's position creates a potential for the exercise of monopoly power, stock exchange regulations are designed to limit the potential for exploiting the monopoly.

[4] The same comment can be made regarding the electronic markets known as Alternative Trading Systems (ATS). Although the literature does not usually so describe them, the OTC markets can be regarded as constituting the first ATSs. Moreover, the largest and best known of the original OTC markets, the NASDAQ, is now and has been for many years large enough and liquid enough to qualify as another exchange.

and corporate securities of similar maturities. Corporate securities are less liquid than governments, and there is usually less information regarding the creditworthiness of the corporations involved. Accordingly, interest rates on government and corporate securities markets are less closely related than interest rates on different maturities of government securities. In addition, some trading practices can impede arbitraging and frustrate efforts to attract order flow. For example, in attempts to minimize the adverse selection effects of trading large positions, some traders prefer to remain anonymous and to conceal the amounts they are ready to trade. As still another example, while it can be easy and cheap to switch between exchanges when trading stocks, it is not equally easy and cheap to switch between stock and futures exchanges. This difference means there are stronger linkages between markets for actively traded stocks than there are for actively traded futures contracts (Bookstaber 2007).

Shleifer and Vishny (1997) point out that while textbook arbitrage requires no capital and entails no risk, in practice arbitraging transactions almost always require capital and can entail varying degrees of risk, depending on the nature of the particular transaction. In addition, professional arbitrage is carried out by a relatively small number of agents, who must raise capital from investors to finance their activities. Moreover, professional arbitrageurs raise capital by demonstrating that their strategies have produced trading profits in the past. Hence, professional arbitrageurs have an incentive to avoid positions that expose them to the possibility of liquidating the portfolio under pressure from investors in the fund. When professional arbitrageurs find it difficult to finance emerging arbitrage opportunities, they may avoid the opportunities as being too risky, and market-pricing anomalies can persist.

Since both incentives and impediments to trade differ in kind and degree among markets, at any point in time the financial system exhibits a complex mixture of market linkages. Where there are no impediments to trading or intermediation, effective interest rates on deals will be closely related. On the other hand, where trading or intermediation is impeded, the affected parts of the financial system are likely to be segmented to a degree that depends on the severity of the impediments.

## 21.3 MARKET SEGMENTATION

When trading is severely inhibited by market imperfections, the result is called *market segmentation*, and presents the possibility of carrying out the same transaction at different effective interest rates in different markets, after duly adjusting for such differences as risk, tax rates, and maturity. Market segmentation is likely indicated when instruments representing the same risk persistently trade at different rates of interest.

Market segmentation occurs if neither arbitrageurs nor intermediaries discern profit opportunities to linking different transactions through trading, but the segmentation may not always be total. For example, transaction costs usually impede the search for arbitrage profits and thereby weaken linkages, but they do not necessarily destroy the relationships entirely. Indeed, much effort has been devoted to testing derivative securities pricing theories, and when transactions costs are taken into account the theories provide relatively good predictions of prices for the most actively traded derivatives. The overwhelming empirical evidence on the pricing efficiency of the stock options market, for example, suggests that, after considering transactions costs, the market appears to be efficient.

Nevertheless, price relationships among markets will not be maintained if existing opportunities are not perceived or if financiers do not have the technical knowledge to eliminate them. Trading can also be impeded if agents do not have access to the same information, if the counterparties are unknown to each other, or if the financial instruments traded are not guaranteed by a third party and therefore require individual assessment of their credit risk. Finally, financial instruments representing incomplete contracts are much more difficult to trade than financial instruments representing complete contracts.[5]

In some cases, transactions costs may frustrate profitable trading because financiers lack the technical knowledge needed to reduce these costs. If market segmentation is due to a lack of technological knowledge, its effects may eventually be mitigated by learning, although the process can be lengthy. In some cases, information differences and transactions costs can remain high enough to affect price relationships more or less permanently. For example, trading can be impeded if the financial instruments in a given market are not all written according to an agreed standard, because then transactions costs are higher than they would be with standardized financial instruments.

Market segmentation may also be observed in relatively small markets if the traders who would potentially enter the market cannot spread their fixed entry costs over a sufficiently large volume of deals. For example, if screening is subject to scale economies, intermediaries may not find it profitable to develop the screening capability needed to serve a small market.

In sum, markets are segmented when the types of services that traders offer differ from the types of services that clients demand. A particular market organization will serve some clients better than it serves others, and when the benefits from differentiation to some clients exceed the benefits from consolidation, markets tend to be linked less strongly. For example, some traders are impatient to trade, and are therefore willing to pay for liquidity as discussed in Section 21.1. Other traders are patient and willing to wait until they can obtain what they regard as a fair market price for the asset in question.

In sophisticated and highly developed economies, strong and persistent examples of market segmentation are difficult to find, especially in the markets for actively traded stocks. On the other hand, segmentation appears to arise more frequently, and to be relatively more important, in less-developed countries. As one example, some Asian financial markets exhibited a very strong form of market segmentation prior to the 1970s when it was not possible to raise funds for agricultural projects yielding annual returns in excess of 40%, while export businesses yielding returns of less than 6% were readily able to obtain financing. McKinnon (1973) argues that a combination of inadequate geographical diffusion of financial services and political conditions enabled well-connected exporters to obtain funds more easily than could agricultural

---

[5] See Chapter 7 for a discussion of complete and incomplete contracting.

borrowers. Governance considerations strengthened the effects of the market segmentation. It was more difficult for banks to obtain credit information about rural borrowers than about well-known exporters, and the assets of the latter were usually more liquid than those of the former. As a result, potential agricultural investment projects faced more severe credit limitations than did such other businesses as the export trade.

Regulation can contribute to market segmentation, at least temporarily, by restricting the kinds of businesses permitted.[6] On the other hand, financiers have strong incentives to find ways of circumventing regulations that limit profit opportunities. In the 1960s and 1970s the U.S. Federal Reserve Board's Regulation Q attempted to limit the maximum interest rates paid on deposits with U.S. banks, but the larger clients of these banks circumvented the regulation by placing funds in Eurodollar deposits, sometimes with overseas branches of U.S. banks. At the time these banks could offer higher rates in cities (e.g., London) outside the Fed's jurisdiction, but not within the United States.

## 21.3.1 Consequences of Segmentation

Market segmentation creates problems of allocative inefficiency. For example, in the case of common stock, the prices of less actively traded, smaller or neglected companies do not always conform to the predictions of asset pricing theory. The term "neglected firms" is used to refer to stocks whose price-earnings ratios—a measure of relative valuation commonly used by market participants—are judged to be atypically low, given the degree of risk they represent. Such shares are likely to be issued by relatively small companies, and their low price-earnings ratios can be attributed in part to informational asymmetries stemming from a lack of institutional research.[7] Since it is uneconomic for larger institutions to trade smaller issues, it is also uneconomic for them to conduct research on small companies, and as a result, the neglected share phenomenon is likely to persist.

At the same time, segmentation can contain the seeds of its own destruction. The very impediments that create segmentation present potential profit opportunities to financiers who can find profitable ways of overcoming the impediments. Such potential opportunities might be exploited by designing new securities issues or by developing new kinds of transactions. If profitable forms of deals can be found, funds will be moved from low-yield opportunities to higher-yield ones.[8] As and when these opportunities are discovered, existing forms of market segmentation will weaken or disappear. For example, the market for speculative grade corporate bonds (also known as non-investment grade or junk bonds) evolved as a way of mobilizing institutional funds for investment in high credit risk bonds. In cases where the impediments cannot be overcome, markets remain segmented and effective interest differentials persist.

---

[6] For example, Domowitz, Glen, and Madhavan (1998, p. 190) find that "ownership restrictions effectively segment the equity market in Mexico."

[7] See Arbel and Strebel (1983).

[8] Assume the comparison takes possible differences in risk into account.

Some potential opportunities may exist for relatively long periods of time without being viewed as potentially profitable, while others are exploited soon after they are discovered. New means of exploiting opportunities can arise either from new sources of information or from technological change that increases net transaction revenue. As and when innovative agents can find such opportunities, they may well be able to earn above normal rates of return on them, at least temporarily. At the same time, the innovators' profit-making actions are quite likely to attract competition, and as a result, the above normal rates of return will only persist until the original market segmentation is weakened or eliminated.

Should it not prove possible to realize profits on private transactions by moving funds between segmented markets, the segmentation will likely persist unless and until legislative action is taken to deal with it. However, public sector intervention to deal with segmentation is only rarely justified, and even when it is, the form of intervention must be carefully designed to ensure its effectiveness.

## 21.4 INFORMATIONAL ASYMMETRIES AND CREDIT MARKET EQUILIBRIA

Informational asymmetries can have effects additional to those created by persistent arbitrage opportunities. They can also affect credit markets, and even lead to a credit rationing equilibrium; that is, an equilibrium in which only some potential clients can raise funds at market rates of interest. Other clients presenting the same risks, and seeking the same terms, cannot obtain credit.

While it is commonly believed that changes in interest rates will always equate supply with demand, there are circumstances under which the customarily expected adjustment will not take place. The situation occurs if potential clients take on increased risks when their financing costs are increased, and if intermediaries' profit maximization depends on both the prevailing interest rate and average risk. There is no reason to suppose that the demand for credit at the profit-maximizing interest rate will just equal the amount of credit supplied. If demand exceeds supply, intermediaries will lend to some but not to all borrowers; that is, intermediaries will ration credit.

There are three issues associated with equilibrium credit rationing: (1) client reactions to borrowing terms, (2) adverse selection and backward bending supply, and (3) moral hazard and backward bending supply. We discuss each below.

### 21.4.1 Client Reactions to Borrowing Terms

It is useful to begin a discussion of credit rationing with a model of client reactions to the terms of the lending arrangement offered by lenders. The model shows that lenders can, in certain circumstances, create perverse results by proposing more stringent repayment schemes.

Consider the scenario shown in Table 21.1. It assumes that a group of lenders advance the time 0 market values of the scheduled repayment denoted by $R$ to a party whom we refer to as simply the "borrower." The borrower will use the funds to invest in some project. The scenario in the table further assumes that the project has two possible payoffs, $H$ or $L$, where $H > R > L$. Thus, in state 1 the borrower can repay in full, but in state 2 the borrower partially defaults and can pay only $L$. Given these data along with the objective and risk-neutral probabilities shown, the proposed repayment scheme has an expected value of $(R + L)/2$. The market value of the payments is $(0.45H + 0.55L)/(1+r)$, where $r$ is the risk-free interest rate. The borrower's payoff is $H - R$ in state 1, zero in state 2, and has a market value at time 0 of $0.45(H - R)/(1+r)$. Assume these rewards are just equal to the level at which the borrower is just willing to borrow in order to take on the project. We refer to this level as the "borrower's reservation level."[9]

**TABLE 21.1**
SCENARIO 1 AND PAYOFFS FOR ILLUSTRATION

| States | Objective Probability | Risk-Neutral Probability | Asset Payoffs | Actual Debt Repayment | Borrower's Payoff |
|---|---|---|---|---|---|
| 1 | 0.50 | 0.45 | $H$ | $R$ | $H-R$ |
| 2 | 0.50 | 0.55 | $L$ | $L$ | $0$ |
| Time 1 Expected Values | | | $(H+L)/2$ | $(R+L)/2$ | $(H-R)/2$ |
| Time 0 Market Values | | | $(0.45H+0.55L)/$ $(1+r)$ | $(0.45R+0.55L)/$ $(1+r)$ | $0.45(H-R)/$ $(1+r)$ |

The scenario in Table 21.1 assumes that the lenders propose a larger repayment $R + 1$ (i.e., increase in the interest rate charged) that would, unless compensated for, reduce the borrower's payoff below the reservation level. Assume the borrower can offset this possibility by increasing the variance of the asset payoffs (i.e., increase the risk), while holding the mean payoff constant.[10] The result of the combined actions is to decrease the market value of the assets, and the market value of the promised repayments to the lenders, but to maintain the value of the borrower's payoff as shown in Table 21.2.

**TABLE 21.2**
SCENARIO 2 AND PAYOFFS FOR ILLUSTRATION

| States | Objective Probability | Risk-Neutral Probability | Asset Payoffs | Actual Debt Repayment | Borrower's Payoff |
|---|---|---|---|---|---|
| 1 | 0.50 | 0.45 | $H+1$ | $R+1$ | $H-R$ |
| 2 | 0.50 | 0.55 | $L-1$ | $L-1$ | $0$ |
| Time 1 Expected Values | | | $(H+L)/2$ | $(R+L)/2$ | $(H-R)/2$ |
| Time 0 Market Values | | | $(0.45H+0.55-0.10)$ $/(1+r)$ | $(0.45R+0.55L-0.10)/$ $(1+r)$ | $0.45(H-R)/$ $(1+r)$ |

---

[9] In states where firm payoffs do not permit full debt repayment, it is assumed that lenders receive the value of the firm and there is costless default of the remaining unpaid amount.

[10] For simplicity we also assume the risk-neutral probabilities are unaffected by the change.

The net effect on the lenders' position depends on whether they are aware of the change in risk and, if so, whether they adjust the amount they will lend. If they are not aware of the moral hazard problem presented by the borrower's reaction, they might advance the same amount as in the first scenario. If so, expected earnings of the lender would be unchanged, but the market value of the repayments is decreased and consequently the value of the position of the lenders is impaired.

In summary, the attempt by the lenders to extract a larger repayment can be frustrated by the borrower's reactions. As will be shown in the rest of this chapter, in these kinds of circumstances, the lender's profit-maximizing solution may involve credit rationing.

## 21.4.2 Adverse Selection and Backward Bending Supply

We can now employ the insights from the model just presented to investigate further the effects of borrowers' responding to more stringent repayment terms. For example, credit rationing can occur at equilibrium if the expected return on a bank loan for a given class of borrowers is not a monotonically increasing function of the nominal interest rate charged on the loan. The supply curve for credit can be backward bending if an increase in the required repayment (and hence in the effective interest rate charged) can lead borrowers to respond by taking greater risks. Thus, the result of proposing an increase in repayments could mean that lenders end up advancing the same amount of funds to riskier borrowers, as demonstrated by Stiglitz and Weiss (1981). In such circumstances there is no incentive for financiers to raise the interest rate, and a form of credit rationing may instead be used to equate demand with supply.

To illustrate the circumstances explicitly, suppose now that borrowers differ by a risk parameter $\theta$. Borrowers know the value of their own $\theta$, but financiers do not. Therefore, financiers offer all firms (i.e., borrowers) a standard debt contract based on an average value of $\theta$ and calling for all firms to repay $R$ per unit amount of financing raised. If a firm cannot make a scheduled repayment, its current cash flow $y$ will be seized by the lenders. On the basis of this contract, financiers advance a fixed amount to each firm they accommodate. The realized value of the cash flow to the firm is thus:

$$\pi(y) = \max(0, y - R) \qquad (21.1)$$

Assuming that the firm uses an expected value criterion, this model will exhibit adverse selection if its expected profit:

$$E[\pi(y|\theta)] \qquad (21.2)$$

increases in $\theta$. The assumption means that when firms take on riskier projects, the expected profits to them are increased. (In the example of Section 21.5.1 the expected profits to the firm's owners remained constant, but the market value decreased.) As a result, there is at most one value of $\theta$, say $\theta^*$, that satisfies:

$$E[\pi(y|\theta^*)] = \pi_{\min} \qquad (21.3)$$

where $\pi_{min}$ is the reservation level of profit that will induce the firm to adopt the project. If firms cannot take on a certain degree of risk, they cannot generate their reservation earnings, and do not operate.

The lending banks' expected profits depend on the contracted repayment $R$ and on the quality distribution of firms applying for credit. Given that the amount advanced is fixed, an interest rate increase means $R$ is increased because the amount of interest increases. Then the firm's profit expectations for any given value of $\theta$ decrease because for any given value of $\theta$:

$$E[\pi(y|\theta)] = E[(\max(0, y - R))|\theta] \qquad (21.4)$$

is a decreasing function of $R$.

To compensate for the decrease in expected profit, each firm will consider adopting riskier projects; that is, a firm's management will consider adopting projects with a larger value of $\theta$. As a result, the critical value $\theta^*$ defined in equation (21.3) increases, meaning that the population of firms now finding it worthwhile to seek credit bearing the new and more stringent repayment terms is riskier than before. Thus, an increase in interest rates can decrease the demand for loans, but as the demand decreases the less risky firms drop out of the market. In these circumstances, the increase in interest rates need not necessarily increase expected profits of banks, and to maximize profits banks may ration the amount of credit made available to the remaining clients.

To illustrate, let the measure of credit risk be $\theta$ as indicated in column 1 of Table 21.3. The second column in the table shows the value of the cash flow $y(\theta)$

## TABLE 21.3
### EXAMPLE OF BANK PROFIT FUNCTION AND ASSOCIATED SUPPLY CURVE

| Credit risk $\theta$ | $y(\theta)$ | $p(\theta)$ | $R$ | Demand for credit[1] | Expected Repayment[2] | Expected return to lending[3] | Supply of deposits, equal to supply of credit[4] |
|---|---|---|---|---|---|---|---|
| 1 | $ 1 | 0.9 | $ 1 | $10 | $4.5 | −0.55 | $0 |
| 2 | 2 | 0.8 | 2 | 9 | 7.2 | −0.20 | 0 |
| 3 | 3 | 0.7 | 3 | 8 | 8.4 | 0.05 | 1 |
| 4 | 4 | 0.6 | 4 | 7 | 8.4 | 0.20 | 4 |
| 5 | 5 | 0.5 | 5 | 6 | 7.5 | 0.25 | 5 |
| 6 | 6 | 0.4 | 6 | 5 | 6.0 | 0.20 | 4 |
| 7 | 7 | 0.3 | 7 | 4 | 4.2 | 0.05 | 1 |
| 8 | 8 | 0.2 | 8 | 3 | 2.4 | −0.20 | 0 |
| 9 | 9 | 0.1 | 9 | 2 | 0.9 | −0.55 | 0 |
| 10 | 10 | 0.0 | 10 | 1 | 0.0 | −1.00 | 0 |

[1]Suppose $R = \$7$. Then only firms with $y(\theta)$ equal to $7, $8, $9, or $10 will go into operation.
[2]For example, if $R = \$7$, the lender will receive an expected payment of $7(0.3 + 0.2 + 0.1) = \$4.2$.
[3]For example, if $R = \$7$, four loans of $1 are made, and ($4.2 − $4)/$4 = 0.05$.
[4]The supply of deposits increases with the expected return to lending. Thus, if $R = \$7$, for example, only one of the four borrowers applying can be accommodated.

if the project is successful. An unsuccessful project brings in zero as discussed above. The probability $p(\theta)$ with which a positive cash flow $y(\theta)$ is realized is shown in the table's third column. In accordance with the previous discussion, $p(\theta)$ decreases as $y(\theta)$ increases in $\theta$.

To keep the calculations simple, we suppose the firm's reservation profit is zero so that any firm required to make a payment $R \leq y(\theta)$ will operate, but if $R > y(\theta)$, the firm has no incentive to operate. Any firm that commences operations seeks a loan equal to one unit of capital. Suppose for simplicity there is exactly one firm in each credit risk class. Then, setting repayments to the integral values as shown in the fourth column of Table 21.3, the demand for credit as a function of $R$ takes on the values shown in the fifth column. For example, if the required repayment is set to $7, only firms with credit risk of $7 or greater will apply for loans, so the demand for credit will be $4. The expected repayments are shown in the sixth column. For example, if the required repayment is $7, the applying firms have credit risks $7, $8, $9, and $10.

The firm in credit risk class 7 repays its loan of $1 with probability 0.3, the firm in credit risk class 8 with probability 0.2, and so on. The expected value of all positive repayments when the scheduled repayment amount is $7 thus becomes:

$$\$7(0.30 + 0.20 + 0.10 + 0) = \$4.20$$

as shown in the sixth column of the table. For later use, note that the last calculation is exactly equal to a calculation using the total amount to be repaid and the average repayment probability:

$$(\$7 \times 4) \times \{(0.30 + 0.20 + 0.10 + 0)/4\} = (\$28) \times \{0.15\} = \$4.20$$

The expected return to lending is calculated in the next-to-the-last column. For example, if $R = \$1$, the calculation is:

$$(\$4.50 - \$10)/\$10 = -0.55 = -55\%$$

Suppose the bank does not hold any cash reserves, operates at a zero profit, and can attract deposits according to a supply function that is linear in the expected interest rate on loans. An expected return of 0.5 brings in deposits totalling 1 unit of capital, a return of 0.20 brings in 4 units, and so on. Negative interest rates are assumed to bring in zero deposits.

The supply and demand functions for credit are shown in Figure 21.1. Since demand is greater than supply at all values of $R$, the supply and demand functions do not intersect. The bank will have to practice credit rationing, accommodating some borrowers but turning down others with exactly the same characteristics.

In contrast, if the function relating banks' expected cash flow to the scheduled repayment were always increasing, the effect would not occur. And nor would the effect occur if it were somehow possible for banks to sort out the quality of the different borrowers applying for credit.

**FIGURE 21.1**
DEMAND AND SUPPLY OF CREDIT

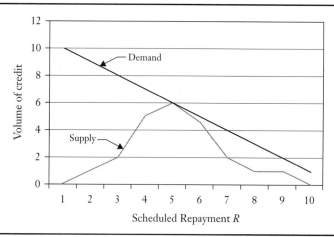

### 21.4.2.1  *Stiglitz-Weiss Adverse Selection Model*

Let's now look at a model proposed by Stiglitz and Weiss (1981) depicting adverse selection. This model will be also be used to depict moral hazard. Suppose all firms are identical and have a choice of two projects, either of which requires financing in the amount of $1. If successful, the projects yield B and G, respectively. Any project that is unsuccessful yields zero, regardless of its type. Suppose $B > G$ but the success probabilities are $p_B$ and $p_G$, respectively, with $p_B < p_G$. Thus, project B is a riskier project than is project G. The model depicts adverse selection if the announcement of lending terms is interpreted as meaning that only firms with project B will seek funding unless the repayment terms are set appropriately. This interpretation applies to an entire population of B and G firms, and it is supposed the selection occurs ex ante.

If a firm is indifferent between projects G and B at repayment $R^*$, then:

$$(B - R^*)p_B = (G - R^*)p_G \qquad (21.5)$$

that is,

$$R^* \equiv (p_G G - p_B B)/(p_G - p_B) \qquad (21.6)$$

Whenever equation (21.5) is satisfied, the return to the bank is not monotonic in $R$. The return to the bank is $p_G R$ for $R \le R^*$, then $p_B R$ for $R^* \le R < B$. Thus, the interest return increases for $R < R^*$, falls sharply when $R = R^*$, then increases again for $R^* < R \le B$. For $R < R^*$ firms choose the safe project, while for $R \varepsilon (R^*, B]$ firms choose the risky project.

The maximum repayment the bank could require and still induce investment in project G is $R^*$. The maximum expected return to the bank also occurs at $R^*$ if and only if

$$p_B B < p_G R^* \qquad (21.7)$$

where $R^*$ is given in equation (21.6). Whether or not equation (21.7) holds, the non-monotonicity of return means the bank chooses a repayment amount that will maximize its effective return. There is no reason to suppose the chosen repayment amount will equate demand with supply, and hence there may be credit rationing.

### 21.4.3 Moral Hazard and Backward Bending Supply

As already indicated, the moral hazard interpretation can use the same model as did the adverse selection discussion. However, now the individual firm is viewed as being able to switch clandestinely from project G to project B after obtaining a commitment for funds from the bank. Again, financiers cannot observe which technology firms actually choose, and must therefore specify that all firms promise the same repayment $R$ in order to borrow the single unit of capital needed to acquire the technology. Also assume:

$$p_G G > p_B B \qquad (21.8)$$

while $B > G$. In combination, these assumptions mean that:

$$p_B < p_G \qquad (21.9)$$

the bad technology is riskier than the good one. The firm will choose the good technology if and only if:

$$p_G(G - R) \geq p_B(B - R) \qquad (21.10)$$

that is, if and only if:

$$R \leq (p_G G - p_B B)/(p_G - p_B)$$

As before, there is a largest feasible repayment:

$$R^0 \equiv (p_G G - p_B B)/(p_G - p_B) \qquad (21.11)$$

and potential borrowers will only select the good project if $R \leq R^0$. If $R \leq R^0$ the expected return to the lender is $\pi_G R$, but if $R > R^0$, then the expected return to the lender is $\pi_B R$.

Suppose there is an infinitely elastic supply of funds at expected rate $r$; that is, any amount can be borrowed by paying the market interest rate. Then if:

$$p_G R^0 > 1 + r > p_B R^0$$

there can be two different loan quantities at which the credit market clears. That is, there may be some $R^{00} > R^0$ such that $\pi_B R^{00} = 1 + r$. At the same time there may be some other repayment $R^{000} \leq R^0$ for which it is also true that $\pi_G R^{000} = 1 + r$.

On the other hand, if the supply of credit function attains only a local maximum at $R^0$, the credit market may not clear, just as in the adverse selection case explained earlier. Rationing will occur whenever the quantity of credit demanded at $R^0$ exceeds the quantity of credit supplied.

## 21.5 MARKET FAILURE

Informational differences can sometimes be extreme enough to lead beyond credit rationing to *market failure*. For example, if a newly appointed loan officer of a bank cannot distinguish good from bad clients, he may decide that it is profitable only to lend against collateral, in which case the market for unsecured loans in the business area covered can be said to have failed. As another example, it may be difficult to resell the shares of a small business at a price reflecting its value as a going concern because the purchaser cannot verify the information on which a going concern value would be based.

## 21.6 FINANCIAL SYSTEM EXTERNALITIES

Financial system performance can be assessed from either a private or a societal point of view. The criteria of private cost and benefit are used to assess the private value of economic activity. A private optimum occurs when the activity is pursued to the point at which privately determined marginal costs, reflected in the prices of resources employed, rise to a point at which they are just equal to privately determined marginal benefits[11] (as reflected in output prices).

The criterion of social costs and benefits is used to reflect society's (possibly differing) assessment of the same activity. A social optimum occurs when an activity is pursued until marginal social costs rise to the point that they just equal marginal social benefits. It will not always be the case that marginal social benefits equal marginal social costs at the level of activity for which marginal private benefits equal marginal private costs.

The term *externality* refers to the impact of an economic activity whose market price, based on calculations of private cost and private benefit, does not fully reflect the activity's balance of social benefits and social costs.[12] For example, a market-determined price may not fully reflect the costs of resources used by the firms producing the good or service in question. Similarly, when a good or service is sold at a market-determined price, the private revenue firms realize may not equal the social value of the goods produced.

While externalities are not ubiquitous, and while they are not always significant even when they do occur, there are circumstances in which they can be important enough to merit remedial attention. In financial markets the most important instances of externalities occur when social benefits go unrealized because the quantities of funds advanced are smaller than is socially optimal. The problem usually arises because

---

[11] This assumes that only a unique optimum obtains.
[12] The theoretical model of a competitive equilibrium has the desirable property that prices exactly cover both the social and the private costs of production.

it is unprofitable for private sector lenders to extend a socially optimal quantity of funds.[13]

In developed economies it is not usually easy to find instances where externalities are present. Moreover, even if externalities are present, it may not be possible to find cost-effective ways of securing the social benefits currently being foregone. However, export credit insurance offers one example of a situation where society may have benefited from intervention. Social benefits may well stem from the jobs created by expanding export-oriented businesses, but it is sometimes difficult or costly for an exporting firm privately to insure against possible default losses on international shipments made on credit. Exporters may need the credit to secure the business, and private sector insurance companies may regard it uneconomic to provide credit insurance. In these circumstances, it may be worthwhile for the public sector to increase the amount of insurance provided and thus capture social benefits that would otherwise be foregone.

In the turbulent markets of 2007–2008, numerous financial institutions were rescued by national governments on the grounds that the failure of these financial institutions would create severe externalities for the world's financial systems. In these circumstances it has been shown to be theoretically desirable to use public sector intervention to offset the negative externalities that would otherwise be suffered. Moreover, public sector intervention can also be practically desirable. For example, the 2008 failure of Lehman Brothers shattered the confidence of financial market agents and drastically affected the prices of many financial assets; that is, it created substantial negative externalities. Subsequently, when other financial institutions faced the same possibilities of failing, the authorities intervened to offset further declines in confidence and asset prices.

---

## ● ● ●    KEY POINTS

- In the idealized world of financial markets where there is perfect liquidity and no transactions costs, asset prices are related as in the no-arbitrage world.
- If financial market participants face differing degrees of information, of liquidity, and of positive transactions costs, then asset price relations become very much less well defined. Moreover, market imperfections can lead to such phenomena as credit rationing equilibria, market segmentation, market failure, and financial system externalities.
- The reasons why liquidity differences exist include differences in market structure, the nature of the instruments traded, and the kinds of obligations the instruments represent.
- Market makers stand ready to buy assets and therefore are said to supply immediacy services; the supply of and demand for immediacy jointly determine market liquidity.

---

[13] The point is not that the interest rate is somehow incorrect, but that it does not reflect the net social gain or cost to the transaction. The example of the export industry in the next paragraph argues that a bank's interest earnings on a loan to finance exports will not typically reflect such social benefits as the employment creation following on the growth of export business made possible by bank lending.

- Usually financiers seeking out profitable arbitrage opportunities do so through trading and this, in turn, links asset prices to each other. The linkages are strengthened by market operators who strive to attract business through executing trades quickly and at the lowest possible charges.

- Market trading is at its most active when deal terms are standardized, when agents have ready access to the same information, and when transactions costs comprise a relatively small percentage of trades' values.

- Textbook arbitrage requires no capital and entails no risk, but in practice arbitraging transactions almost always require capital and can entail varying degrees of risk, depending on the nature of the particular transaction.

- Professional arbitrage is carried out by a relatively small number of agents, who must raise capital from investors to finance their activities and do so by demonstrating to suppliers of capital that they have produced trading profits in the past.

- Professional arbitrageurs have an incentive to avoid positions that expose them to the possibility of liquidating the portfolio under pressure from investors in the fund. Market pricing anomalies can persist because when professional arbitrageurs find it difficult to finance emerging arbitrage opportunities, they may avoid the opportunities as being too risky.

- Market segmentation arises when trading is severely inhibited by market imperfections.

- Market segmentation offers the opportunity for carrying out the same transaction at different effective interest rates in different markets, after duly adjusting for such differences as risk, tax rates, and maturity.

- Market segmentation occurs if neither arbitrageurs nor intermediaries discern profit opportunities to linking different transactions through trading. The segmentation may not always be total and can also change through time.

- Trading can also be impeded if agents do not have access to the same information, if the counterparties are unknown to each other or if the financial instruments traded are not guaranteed by a third party and therefore require individual assessment of their credit risk.

- Financial instruments representing incomplete contracts are much more difficult to trade than financial instruments representing complete contracts.

- In some cases, transactions costs can frustrate profitable trading because financiers lack the technical knowledge needed to reduce these costs.

- Informational asymmetries can have effects additional to those created by persistent arbitrage opportunities. They can affect credit markets as well, and even lead to a credit rationing equilibrium; that is, an equilibrium in which only some potential clients can raise funds at market rates of interest. In such a situation other clients presenting the same risks, and seeking the same terms, cannot obtain credit.

- There are three issues associated with equilibrium credit rationing: (1) client reactions to borrowing terms, (2) adverse selection and backward bending supply, and (3) moral hazard and backward bending supply.

- Informational differences can sometimes be extreme enough to lead beyond credit rationing to market failure.

- The impacts of an economic activity whose market price, based on calculations of private cost and private benefit, do not fully reflect the activity's balance of social benefits and social costs are referred to as externalities.
- Although externalities are not always significant even when they do occur, there are circumstances in which they can be important enough to merit remedial attention.

---

## ◈ ◈ ◈ QUESTIONS

1. What are the assumptions of an arbitrage-free world?

2. What is the role of market makers and what are the risks that they face?

3. Order the following markets from the most liquid to the most illiquid and explain why: Futures market, market for retail transactions in residential homes, and stock market.

4. **a.** When is market trading the most active?
   **b.** Why may new arbitrage opportunities persist in the market despite their presence being known to professional arbitrageurs?

5. **a.** What is meant by market segmentation?
   **b.** When does market segmentation occur?

6. What are "neglected firms"?

7. Explain the concepts of market failure and externality.

8. Calculate the expected repayment in each of the following cases:
   **a.** In this case, each firm borrows $1 and is required to repay $5

   | Firm | Probability of repayment |
   | --- | --- |
   | A | 0.2 |
   | B | 0.5 |
   | C | 0.4 |

   **b.** Each firm borrows $1 but the amount repaid depends on the probability of repayment

   | Firm | Amount repaid (in $) | Probability of repayment |
   | --- | --- | --- |
   | A | 4 | 0.2 |
   | B | 3 | 0.5 |
   | C | 2 | 0.7 |

9. Assume that a bank does not hold any cash reserves (i.e., invests all the funds it receives in deposits) and operates at a zero profit (i.e., the return earned on the

amount it lends is equal to the interest rate which it pays depositors). Suppose further that the bank can attract deposits according to the following supply function that is linear in the interest rate that it pays. That is,

| Interest rate offered on deposits | Amount of funds from deposits |
|---|---|
| 6% | $1 |
| 12% | $2 |
| 18% | $3 |
| and so on | |

Because there are no cash reserves, the amount of the deposits will be the amount of capital available for lending.

In each case below, calculate the expected returns from lending to firms and determine whether there will be a rationing of credit.

**a.** Each firm has borrowed $1 and must repay $4:

| Firm | Probability of repayment |
|---|---|
| A | 0.5 |
| B | 0.4 |
| C | 0.3 |

**b.** Each firm borrows $1 and repays the amounts shown below:

| Firm | Amount repaid (in $) | Probability of repayment |
|---|---|---|
| A | 10 | 0.1 |
| B | 7 | 0.2 |
| C | 5 | 0.3 |
| D | 2 | 0.6 |
| E | 1 | 0.8 |

**10.** In the model of credit rationing, how can a lender's position decrease by increasing the interest rate charged?

**11.** What are the three issues associated with equilibrium credit rationing?

# REFERENCES

Arbel, Avner, and Paul Strebel. (1983). "Pay Attention to Neglected Firms!" *Journal of Portfolio Management* **9**: 37–42.

Baumol, William J. (1965). *The Stock Market and Economic Efficiency.* New York: Fordham University Press.

Bookstaber, Richard. (2007). *A Demon of Our Own Design*. New York and London, John Wiley & Sons.

Demsetz, Harold. (1968). "The Cost of Transacting," *Quarterly Journal of Economics* **82**: 33–53.

Domowitz, Ian, Jack D. Glen, and Ananth Madhavan. (1998). "Country and Currency Risk Premia in an Emerging Market," *Journal of Financial and Quantitative Analysis* **33**: 189–216.

Grossman, Sanford J., and Merton H. Miller. (1988). "Liquidity and Market Structure," *Journal of Finance* **43**: 617–637.

McKinnon, Ronald I. (1973). *Money and Capital in Economic Development*. Washington, D.C. Brookings Institution.

Neave, Edwin H. (2009). *Modern Financial Systems: Theory and Applications*. Hoboken, NJ: John Wiley & Sons.

Shleifer, Andrei, and Robert W. Vishny. (1997). "The Limits of Arbitrage," *Journal of Finance* **52**: 35–55.

Stiglitz, Joseph, and Andrew Weiss. (1981). "Credit Rationing in Markets with Imperfect Information," *American Economic Review* **71**: 393–410.

# PART VII

# CAPITAL STRUCTURE DECISIONS IN IMPERFECT CAPITAL MARKETS

# 22

# WHEN CAPITAL STRUCTURE MATTERS

*I*n Chapter 4, we investigated the conditions under which changes in capital structure cannot affect firm value. We showed that in a perfect capital market, although debt is usually less risky than equity, and therefore has a lower cost than equity, it does not follow that using more and apparently lower-cost debt will necessarily lower the firm's weighted average cost of capital. The conclusion in Chapter 4 was that in a perfect capital market without corporate taxation, splitting up the cash flow among the different claim holders of the firm does not affect the firm's value. Put quite simply: The capital structure decision is irrelevant. As a result, in a perfect capital market there is no optimal capital structure.

In this chapter, we will look at conditions under which a firm's value will indeed be affected by its capital structure by relaxing the perfect capital market assumption. We begin by showing how debt offers a tax advantage that can affect the firm's cost of capital. This result would suggest that the capital structure is relevant and suggests that management use the maximum amount of debt. But we then take a look at other factors that management should consider before it pursues a policy of maximum financial leverage. Specifically, we discuss how bankruptcy costs can limit the tax advantage of debt. We make similar arguments regarding agency costs and heterogeneous expectations. The importance of these factors for the theory of dividend payments is then examined.

For expositional clarity, in this chapter we focus primarily on financing decisions under the assumption that operating decisions (i.e., production and investment decisions) have been chosen and fixed in advance. Most of the traditional literature studies capital structure problems in the context of long-term and unchanging operating decisions, and seeks a permanent solution to the capital structure problem. However, recent theoretical work emphasizes the dynamics of changing capital structure over time, and in this chapter we summarize this recent line of investigation. At the end of the chapter, we return to the notion of an optimal capital structure. When our investigation is finished, we shall have a complete statement of why, under what conditions, and to what extent, management should be concerned with leverage. The next chapter examines how the theory of capital structure can be applied to financing decisions in practice.

## 22.1 Effect of Corporate Taxation on Leverage

As explained in Chapter 4, the effects of leverage on a firm's value change dramatically if corporate income is taxed and interest on outstanding debt may be deducted from the firm's taxable income.[1] In these circumstances, the perfect capital market model predicts that the effects of leverage are so important that, unless something else offsets them, the firm will be financed only with debt.[2] For the more debt the firm issues, the greater the tax saving it can realize—a conclusion that applies whether the debt is risky or not. After developing this argument, we shall of course consider features of capital structure that limit the value creation role of debt. But, it is helpful to consider the different effects one at a time.

Consider two firms, one levered and one unlevered, with the same underlying earnings distribution.[3] Then, continuing with the notation used in Chapter 4 and considering our usual two points in time and assuming a corporate tax rate $\tau$, the after-tax earnings of the unlevered firm will be:

$$V(2)(1 - \tau)$$

assuming tax to be paid at rate $\tau$ on any level of realized earnings. The after-tax earnings of the levered firm before payment of bond interest $R(1)$ will be:

$$V(2) - \tau[V(2) - R(2)]$$

The expression assumes that bond interest can always be paid from earnings and that it will be paid before the bond issue's outstanding principal amount is reduced. Now, the investor buying proportion $\alpha$ of the equity of the levered firm pays a price of:

$$\alpha[V(1) - B(1)] \tag{22.1}$$

where $B(1)$ is the bond issue's market value at time 1, to obtain title to:

$$\alpha\{V(2) - \tau[V(2) - R(2)] - [R(2) + B(2)]\}$$

The largest possible value of $B(2)$ is the promised amount, that is, the principal amount outstanding.[4] In contrast, the investor buying proportion $\alpha$ of the unlevered firm pays $\alpha S(1) = \alpha V(1)$ to be entitled to earnings of $\alpha V(2)(1 - \tau)$. If this investor

---

[1] We suppose also that the firm's income is large enough that interest can in fact be charged against it. That is, we assume that the firm can use the interest deduction for tax purposes.

[2] Modigliani and Miller (1963) corrected their original analysis to take into account the tax treatment of the interest paid by a firm.

[3] This first part of this section depends heavily on Fama and Miller (1972).

[4] In the case of technical insolvency, the firm will not necessarily pay the bondholders the full principal amount.

borrows funds promising to pay $\alpha[R(2) + B(2) - \tau R(2)]$, the investment position at time 1 will be the same as that of the investor in the levered firm. But the time 1 value of the position taken by the investor in the unlevered firm is:

$$\alpha\{V^*(1) - [B(1) - \tau V_R(1)]\} \tag{22.2}$$

where $V^*(1)$ is the time 1 value of the unlevered firm and $V_R(1)$ is the time 1 value of interest $R(2)$ payable at time 2.

Since any investor can arrange either position, the two investments are perfect substitutes and hence have the same market value at time 1. This means equations (22.1) and (22.2) are equal, from which it follows that:

$$V(1) = V^*(1) + \tau V_R(1) \tag{22.3}$$

Equation (22.3) then says that the value of the levered firm is the value of the unlevered firm plus the present value of the tax subsidy realized by issuing bonds. Since for a profitable firm the value of the tax subsidy increases with the amount of debt outstanding, it follows that if it is possible to effect such a scheme, the firm will minimize the cost of funds raised by having a capital structure that is 100% debt.

To see the effects in greater detail, we present an example showing that as the proportion of debt in the capital structure increases, the firm's effective cost of funds falls. The example assumes that the firm will be operated for one period and then sold. We further assume that corporate tax rates are 40%, that they apply to the entire distribution of earnings except for the portion used as bond interest. Given the earnings distribution before taxes as shown below, the distribution of market values in a 100% equity-financed (i.e., unlevered) firm after taxes is as shown below:

| State | Probability | V(2) (pretax) | V(2) (post-tax) |
|-------|-------------|---------------|-----------------|
| 1     | 0.5         | $1,769        | $1,056          |
| 2     | 0.5         | $1,320        | $ 792           |

The expected value of the firm is then $E[V(2)] = \$924$, which is assumed to be discounted at 10% to give $V(1) = \$840$.

Now suppose $200 worth of risk-free debt having a time 2 market value of $200 and bearing interest at the prevailing risk-free rate of 5% is issued. Without the tax saving accruing to the debt, we know the value of the equity at time 2 would be $640, because in a perfect capital market the value of debt plus that of the equity equals the market value of the firm. Allowing for the tax savings gives the following post-tax earnings:

| State | Probability | V(2) (post-tax) |
|-------|-------------|-----------------|
| 1     | 0.5         | $1,060          |
| 2     | 0.5         | $ 796           |

because in these circumstances the $10 interest charge reduces the firm's tax liability by $4, so that at a discount rate of 10%, $V(1)$ is just a little less than $844.[5]

If the debt is increased still further to $400, the after-tax distribution of values becomes

| State | Probability | $V(2)$ (post-tax) |
|---|---|---|
| 1 | 0.5 | $1,064 |
| 2 | 0.5 | $ 800 |

so that $V(0)$ is just a bit less than $848.[6] Since the example indicates that the value of the firm rises with riskless debt (because of the tax saving), the cost of capital must be falling as leverage increases.[7]

The situation changes again if, in addition to corporate taxes, we assume that investors in the firm must also pay income taxes. This situation is investigated in Miller (1977), who observes first that gains from leverage are reduced by the presence of a higher personal income tax rate that investors pay on bond interest than against income on stocks (dividends and capital gains). Miller observes this is the most likely situation under the tax laws of many countries. In such a situation, bond investors will require higher interest payments than would otherwise be the case, and it is reasonable to argue that this higher cost of bond financing may well offset the gains from leverage, once again leaving the firm's market value unchanged by leverage. That is, the introduction of realistic personal tax rate assumptions can offset the corporate tax advantage to using debt.

Whether or not Miller's argument turns out to be empirically valid, the capital structure arguments offered to this point leave open the question of whether an optimal level of debt exists. What we have shown is that with taxes on corporate income, the firm may be better off if it is more highly levered. Yet the next section shows that other effects mean that a firm can also issue too much debt; that is, there can also be costs to increasing leverage.

## 22.2 CAPITAL STRUCTURE AND FINANCIAL DISTRESS

A company that has difficulty making payments to its creditors is in financial distress. Not all companies in financial distress ultimately incur legal bankruptcy, but extreme financial distress may very well lead to it. While bankruptcy is often a result of financial difficulties arising from problems in paying creditors, some bankruptcy

---

[5] We know that 10% is not the exact rate to use any longer, but it is a close enough approximation to examine the rough nature of the effect. The reader should be able to explain why the exact value for $V(2)$ would be ($924/1.10) + ($4/1.05) = $843.81.

[6] In exact terms it is ($924/1.10) + ($8/1.05).

[7] The cost will fall linearly with an increasing debt-equity ratio while the debt is riskless. After interest payments on the debt become risky, the cost will fall at a decreasing rate.

filings are made prior to distress when a large claim is made on assets (for example, class action liability suit).

## 22.2.1 Costs of Financial Distress

The costs associated with financial distress in the absence of legal bankruptcy can take different forms. For example, to meet creditors' demands, management may take on investment projects expected to provide a quick payback. In doing so, management may select an investment project that decreases owners' wealth. Similarly, management may forgo a profitable investment project that has a long-term payback.

Another cost of financial distress is the cost associated with lost sales. If a company is having financial difficulty, potential customers may shy away from its products because they may perceive the company unable to provide maintenance, replacement parts, and warranties, a recent example being car buyer concerns with General Motors and Chrysler in 2009. Lost sales due to customer concerns represent an opportunity cost of financial distress—something of value (sales) that the company would have had if it were not in financial difficulty.

Still another example of a cost of financial distress is the cost associated with suppliers. If there is concern over a company's ability to meet its obligations to creditors, suppliers may be either unwilling to extend trade credit at all, or they may extend it only at unfavorable terms. Also, suppliers may be unwilling to enter into long-term contracts to supply goods or materials. This increases the uncertainty that the company will be able to obtain these items in the future and raises the costs of renegotiating contracts.

## 22.2.2 The Role of Limited Liability

*Limited liability* limits owners' liability for obligations to the amount of their original investment in the shares of stock. Limited liability for owners of some forms of business creates a valuable right and an interesting incentive for stockholders. The valuable right is the right to default on obligations to creditors—that is, the right not to pay creditors. Because the most shareholders can lose is their investment, there is an incentive for the company to take on very risky projects: If the projects turn out well, the company pays creditors only what it owes and keeps the remainder and if the projects turn out poorly, it pays creditors what it owes—if there is anything left.[8]

The fact that owners with limited liability can lose only their initial investment—the amount they paid for their shares—creates an incentive for owners to take on riskier projects than if they had unlimited liability: They have little to lose and much to gain. Owners of a company with limited liability have an incentive to take on risky investment projects since they can only lose their investment in the company. But they can benefit substantially if the payoff on the investment is high.

For companies whose owners have limited liability, the more the assets are financed with debt, the greater the incentive to take on risky projects, leaving creditors "holding the bag" if the projects turn out to be unprofitable. This is a problem: a

---

[8] This phenomenon is a form of moral hazard, a topic discussed in Chapter 7.

conflict of interest between shareholders' interests and creditors' interests. The investment decisions are made by management (who represent the shareholders) and, because of limited liability, there is an incentive for management to select riskier investment projects that may harm creditors who have entrusted their funds (by lending them) to the company.

The right to default is a call option: The owners have the option to buy back the entire company by paying off the creditors at the face value of their debt. As with other types of options, the option is more valuable the riskier the cash flows. However, creditors are aware of this and demand a higher return on debt (and hence, a higher cost to the company). Jensen and Meckling (1976) analyze the agency problems associated with limited liability. They argue that creditors are aware of the incentives the company has to take on riskier project. Creditors will demand a higher return and may also require protective provisions in the loan contract. The result is that shareholders ultimately bear a higher cost of debt.

## 22.2.3   Bankruptcy and Bankruptcy Costs

When a company is having difficulty paying its debts, there is a possibility that creditors will foreclose (that is, demand payment) on loans, causing the company to sell assets that could impair or cease the company's operations. But if some creditors force payment, this may disadvantage other creditors. So what has developed is an orderly way of dealing with the process of the company paying its creditors—the process is called *bankruptcy*.

Bankruptcy in the United States is governed by the Bankruptcy Code, which is found under U.S. Code Title 11. A company may be reorganized under Chapter 11 of this Code, resulting in a restructuring of its claims, or liquidated under Chapter 7. Chapter 11 bankruptcy provides the troubled company with protection from its creditors while it tries to overcome its financial difficulties. A company that files bankruptcy under Chapter 11 continues as a going concern during the process of sorting out which of its creditors get paid and how much. On the other hand, a company that files under Chapter 7 bankruptcy, under the management of a trustee, terminates its operations, sells its assets, and distributes the proceeds to creditors and owners.

We can classify *bankruptcy costs* into direct and indirect costs. *Direct costs of bankruptcy* include the legal, administrative, and accounting costs associated with the filing for bankruptcy and the administration of bankruptcy. *Indirect costs of bankruptcy* are more difficult to evaluate. Operating a company while in bankruptcy is difficult, since there are often delays in making decisions, creditors may not agree on the operations of the company, and the objectives of creditors may be at variance with the objective of efficient operation of the company.

Another indirect cost of bankruptcy is the loss in value of certain assets. If the company has assets that are intangible or for which there are valuable growth opportunities or options, it is less likely to borrow because the loss of value in the case of financial distress is greater than, say, a company with marketable assets. Because many intangible assets derive their value from the continuing operations of the company, the disruption of operations during bankruptcy may change the value of the company. The extent to which the value of a business enterprise depends on intangibles varies among industries and among companies; so the potential loss in value from financial distress varies as well. For example, a drug company may experience a greater disruption in its business activities than, say, a steel manufacturer, since much of the value of the drug company may be derived from the research and development that leads to new products.

## 22.3 FINANCIAL DISTRESS AND CAPITAL STRUCTURE

The relationship between financial distress and capital structure is simple: As more debt financing is used, fixed legal obligations increase (interest and principal payments), and the ability of the company to satisfy these increasing fixed payments decreases. Therefore, as more debt financing is used, the probability of financial distress and then bankruptcy increases. For a given decrease in operating earnings, a company that uses debt to a greater extent in its capital structure (that is, a company that uses more financial leverage) has a greater risk of not being able to satisfy the debt obligations and increases the risk of earnings to owners.

Another factor to consider in assessing the probability of financial distress is the business risk of the company. The *business risk* of a firm is the risk associated with the earnings from operations. The business risk interacts with the financial risk to affect the risk of the company.

Management's concern in assessing the effect of financial distress on the value of the company is the present value of the expected costs of financial distress. And the present value depends on the probability of financial distress: The greater the probability of financial distress, the greater the expected costs of financial distress.

The present value of the costs of financial distress increases with the increasing relative use of debt financing because the probability of financial distress increases with increases in financial leverage. In other words, as the debt ratio increases, the present value of the costs of financial distress increases, lessening the value gained from the use of tax deductibility of interest expense.

In summary, the factors that influence the present value of the cost of financial distress are:

- The probability of financial distress increases with increases in business risk.
- The probability of financial distress increases with increases in financial risk.
- Limited liability increases the incentives for owners to take on greater business risk.
- The costs of bankruptcy increase the more the value of the company depends on intangible assets.

Management does not know the precise manner in which the probability of distress increases as the debt-to-equity ratio increases. Yet, it is reasonable to think that:

- The probability of distress increases as a greater proportion of the company's assets are financed with debt.
- The benefit from the tax deductibility of interest increases as the debt-to-equity ratio increases.
- The present value of the cost of financial distress increases as the debt-to-equity ratio increases.

## 22.3.1 Probability of Technical Insolvency

The possibility of technical insolvency (i.e., inability to meet contractual payments) can, if dealing with insolvency is costly, cause the weighted average cost of capital to increase as more debt is issued. We next provide an example of this effect. Consider a firm with a time 2 distribution of values given by:

| State | Probability | $V(2)$ (pretax) |
|---|---|---|
| 1 | 0.5 | $3,870 |
| 2 | 0.5 | $1,470 |

Suppose the entire distribution $V(2)$ is taxable at 50% and that the costs of becoming insolvent[9] are $150, deducted at time 2 from value realized, if state 2 occurs. Finally, suppose the time 1 prices of (unit) contingent claims for the two states of the world are each 0.45. Then, assuming in the first instance that the firm has 100% equity financing, the after-tax distribution of values is:

| State | Probability | $V(2)$ (post-tax) |
|---|---|---|
| 1 | 0.5 | $1,935 |
| 2 | 0.5 | $ 735 |

In this case the time 1 value of the firm is:

$$V(1) = \$1,935(0.45) + \$735(0.45) = \$1,201.50$$

If we suppose the two states occur with equal probability, then in this case $EV(2)] = \$1,335$ and the firm's weighted average cost of capital can be calculated as

$$\frac{\$1,335 - \$1,201.50}{\$1,201.50} = 11.11\%$$

Now let there be $600 worth of debt issued bearing interest at 10%, the interest being deductible from taxable income. From this, the following can be calculated (1) the distribution of taxable incomes after deducting the interest of $60, (2) the distribution of income available to the investors after taxes and interest have been deducted, and (3) the after-tax distribution, including interest, that is available to the investors:

---

[9] We recognize that following technical insolvency a firm can either reorganize or declare bankruptcy. We assume in the remainder of this discussion that the cheaper of these two alternatives is chosen. See Barnea, Haugen, and Senbet (1985).

| State | Probability | V(2) (pretax) | V(2) (post-tax) | V(2) (post-tax plus interest) |
|---|---|---|---|---|
| 1 | 0.5 | $3,810 | $1,905 | $1,965 |
| 2 | 0.5 | $1,410 | $ 765 | $ 765 |

Under these assumptions, the market value of the firm at time 1 is given by valuing the payments to all investors:

$$\$1,965(0.45) + \$765(0.45) = \$1,228.50$$

The market value of debt is:

$$\$660(0.45) + \$660(0.45) = \$594.00$$

and of equity is:

$$\$(1,965 - \$660)(0.45) + (\$765 - \$660)(0.45) = \$634.50$$

Again, assuming that either state can be realized with equal probability, we compute the weighted average cost of capital as before.

| State | Probability | V(2)(post-tax plus interest) | Debt Holders | Shareholders |
|---|---|---|---|---|
| 1 | 0.5 | $1,965 | $660 | $1,305 |
| 2 | 0.5 | $ 765 | $660 | $ 105 |

As shown in the above table, the expected payments to equity investors are $\frac{1}{2}(\$1,305 + \$105) = \$705$.

However, from the firm's point of view the expected debt payments must be assessed in terms of both interest costs and tax savings. Accordingly, from the firm's point of view, the debt payments are $\$660 - (0.5 \times \$60) = \$630$ because interest on the bonds is deductible from taxable income. Therefore, the weighted average cost of capital is:

$$\frac{\$634.50}{\$1,228.50}\left(\frac{\$705 - \$634.50}{\$634.50}\right) + \frac{\$594}{\$1,228.50}\left(\frac{\$630 - \$594}{\$594}\right)$$

$$= \frac{\$634.50}{\$1,228.50}(11.11) + \frac{\$594}{\$1,228.50}(6.06) = 8.67\%$$

Because of the tax advantage, the cost of capital is now lower than when the firm was financed with 100% equity. Naturally, management will wish to take advantage of this possibility whenever it is available.

If levering were to be continued beyond the point where the debt repayment could be made with probability 1, an insolvency cost to be paid to third parties before the debt holders receive their funds might well be incurred whenever the promised debt payments could not be made. To see the implications of this possibility, consider a third situation in which debt in the amount of $800 is issued at the nominal interest rate of 10%. Then we have the following distributions for (1) taxable income after deducting the interest of $60 and (2) the distribution of income available to the investors after taxes and interest have been deducted:

| State | Probability | V(2) (pretax) | V(2) (post-tax) |
|-------|-------------|---------------|-----------------|
| 1 | 0.5 | $3,790 | $1,895 |
| 2 | 0.5 | $1,390 | $ 695 |

But now in state 2 the principal amount of the debt cannot be wholly repaid, and so after taxes and interest, insolvency costs of $150 are incurred. (We assume for simplicity that incurring the insolvency cost does not affect the firm's tax liability.) This means the distribution available to investors, including interest but deducting tax payments and insolvency costs, is:

| State | Probability | V(2) (post-tax plus interest less insolvency costs) |
|-------|-------------|------------------------------------------------------|
| 1 | 0.5 | $1,975 |
| 2 | 0.5 | $625 |

The value in the second state of $625 is computed from $695 + $80 − $150. The time 1 market value of the firm is now:

$$(\$1,975 + \$625)(\$0.45) = \$1,170$$

This is less than before. The market value of the debt is ($880 + $625)(0.45) = $677.25 and of equity $1,095(0.45) = $492.75. In determining the market value of the debt, only payments received by holders of the debt are included.

Again assuming that either state occurs with probability ½, the expected value of payments to equity investors is (1/2)($1,095 + $0) = $547.50. However, the expected cost of debt when regarded from the firm's viewpoint is computed using (1/2) [$840 + ($695 + $40)] = $787.50, because the firm considers insolvency costs to be a part of the cost-of-debt issue. Accordingly, the weighted average cost of capital is:

$$\frac{\$492.75}{\$1,170}\left(\frac{\$547.50 - \$492.75}{\$492.75}\right) + \frac{\$677.25}{\$1,170}\left(\frac{\$787.50 - \$677.25}{\$677.25}\right)$$

$$= \frac{\$492.75}{\$1,170}(11.11) + \frac{\$677.25}{\$1,170}(16.28) = 14.10\%$$

Hence, the possibility of incurring insolvency costs can cause the weighted average cost of capital to increase once some level of debt in the capital structure has been exceeded.

The situations we have considered indicate that when both corporate taxes and insolvency costs are taken into account, there can be an optimal degree of leverage and hence a definite minimum value for the cost of capital.[10] This is illustrated in Figure 22.1. In this instance, the optimal degree of leverage is such that tax advantages are realized by issuing debt up to the point where the risk-free portion of earnings is entirely used in making the promised debt repayment. Issuing more debt would result in incurring the $150 insolvency costs with some positive probability, and this would more than offset any further incremental tax advantages offered by the deductibility of interest. The foregoing examples thus suggest that in choosing the debt-equity ratio corporate management is involved in weighing the costs and benefits of the choice of balancing tax advantages against possible insolvency costs.

The analysis assumes that the risk premia associated with bankruptcy costs do not change. In contrast, Almeida and Philippon (2007) consider implications of risk premia changing over time in response to changing market and economic conditions.

**FIGURE 22.1**
EXISTENCE OF OPTIMUM CAPITAL STRUCTURE IN PRESENCE OF INSOLVENCY COSTS

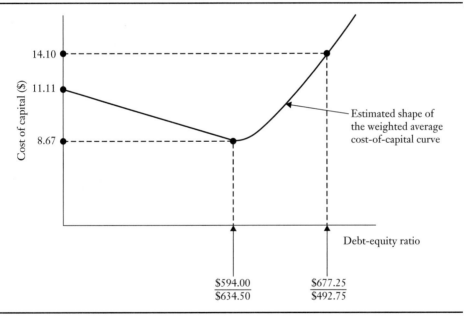

## 22.4 HETEROGENEOUS EXPECTATIONS

Even in an otherwise perfect capital market, differing opinions among lenders and borrowers may have an impact on a given firm's cost of capital. Lenders or equity

---

[10] The attainable minimum is actually to the right of the lowest point plotted in Figure 22.1, because that point was computed for an amount of risk-free debt slightly less than the attainable maximum.

investors are less likely to be optimistic than borrowers and are also less likely to have the detailed information regarding the company's prospects that management possesses, as we discussed in Chapter 21. In these circumstances, the interest rates demanded by lenders or returns expected by equity investors may appear unwarrantedly high to a firm's management, with the result that from a managerial point of view the firm's cost of capital would rise if lender terms were to be accepted.

To see the effects of heterogeneous expectations, consider another example. In this example, a perfect capital market scenario without taxes is assumed so that we can study the impact of heterogeneous expectations in isolation. Suppose that stockholder expectations regarding the firm's operating earnings are (X) while bondholders expectations are (Z), as shown next:

| State | Probability | X | Z |
|---|---|---|---|
| 1 | 0.5 | $1,000 | $900 |
| 2 | 0.5 | $ 300 | $200 |

We suppose further that any bonds sold can only be sold at a price determined by the distribution Z.

We assume all investors are risk neutral and first consider 100% equity financing. Moreover, we suppose the risk-free rate $r_f = 5\%$. The assumption of risk-neutral investors means that all earnings are capitalized at 5%. Then, from the stockholders' point of view, the value of the firm is:

$$V(1) = \frac{\$1,000(0.5) + \$300(0.5)}{1.05} = \frac{\$650}{1.05}$$

Now suppose the same firm undertakes $200 debt financing at 5%. The value of the bonds is:

$$\left[\$210\left(\frac{1}{2}\right) + \$200\left(\frac{1}{2}\right)\right]/1.05 = \$205/1.05$$

because the possibilities the bonds represent are priced by bondholders using the distribution Z. But from the stockholders' point of view, the cost of bonds so valued is:

$$[\$210 - (\$205/1.05)]/(\$205/1.05) = (\$220.5 - \$205)/\$205 = 7.5\%$$

The stockholders then also calculate that the value of the equity (based on X) is:

$$\left[(\$1,000 - \$210)\left(\frac{1}{2}\right) + (\$200 - \$210)\left(\frac{1}{2}\right)\right]/1.05 = \$440/1.05$$

Hence, the actual market value of the firm becomes ($440 + $205)/1.05 = $645/1.05, although the stockholders still believe it to be worth $650. The pessimism of the bondholders has reduced the market value of the firm and hence raised the firm's cost of capital when the latter is assessed from the stockholders' point of view.

To see how the cost-of-capital calculations are made, we proceed as follows. In the first case of 100% equity financing, the cost of capital is clearly 5%. In the second example, the stockholders' valuations are used, so that the calculation is:

$$\frac{\$440}{\$650}(0.05) + \frac{\$210}{\$650}(0.075) = 5.8\%$$

The second case also demonstrates the possibility that differing expectations are enough to place an upper limit of $200/1.05 on the debt's time 1 market value. After this amount has been issued, the value of the firm (as judged from the stockholders' point of view) is diminished by further debt issues, because bondholders will no longer pay the amounts for bonds that shareholders believe the bonds to be worth. But up to that point, the value of the firm is unaltered by changing the capital structure. Under these circumstances our calculations have assumed (i.e., without considering any tax advantage), the stockholders will believe there is a desirable upper limit to the amount of debt issued. If there were also some tax advantage to debt, this would encourage leverage up to the point where the tax advantage was offset by the disadvantage due to differing expectations.

To at least some extent, this view related to heterogeneous expectations may be borne out by practical management's use of a technique known as *break-even analysis*.[11] When in practice financial managers employ this technique, they usually ask about the amount of (cheaper) debt that can be issued without impairing the certainty of meeting interest payments out of income, that is, without incurring the possibility of technical insolvency. In such circumstances, management may implicitly be recognizing that investors could have a conservative view of the distribution of firm earnings. If so, by not issuing debt beyond a certain point, management is trying to lower the average cost of funds without incurring the cost implicit in investors' conservative expectations.

Another view of the effects attributable to heterogeneous expectations is developed by Ross (1977). His analysis begins with the observation that the marketplace values its perceptions of a firm's earnings stream, as did our earlier examples in this section. But Ross then argues that managerial actions may be able to affect the perceptions of the marketplace, a possibility not considered in our previous example. In particular, Ross suggests that managers might be able to create more optimistic expectations about the value of a particular firm if the managers lever the firm more highly than would be warranted for a firm with less favorable prospects. If managers are successful in thus altering expectations, the value of the firm would increase. Hence, Ross at least partly resolves the earlier question of why firms might wish to lever even if there were no tax advantage to issuing debt. Since none of the previous examples explored was capable of offering this explanation and since, as Jensen and Meckling (1976) observe, firms have been known to lever even in the absence of a tax

---

[11] Of course, this is just one explanation for the use of break-even analysis. If a financial market were perfect, management's use of the technique on the grounds mentioned would be mistaken; in an imperfect market it might also be justified on any of the other increasing costs to debt arguments that we have raised.

advantage, the possibility of managers' affecting marketplace perceptions through signals taking the form of a changed debt-equity ratio seems deserving of serious consideration.

## 22.5 AGENCY EFFECTS

Taking on additional debt may enhance the value of the firm by reducing agency costs.[12] By this we mean that management might not always be motivated to maximize shareholder value, preferring to use company revenue to enhance management's personal well-being. Debt can reduce this motivation because the contractual arrangements regarding debt create difficulties for the firm if the repayments are not made. In other words, a firm that takes on debt may make more effective use of its free cash flows (as discussed further in Chapter 23), thus reducing agency costs. Taking on additional debt also provides a second management performance incentive: Creditors and rating agencies will be monitoring the firm's performance and hence its ability to pay its debt obligations.

Another agency issue that arises with regard to the use of debt is its use as a takeover defense. A *takeover defense* is any mechanism that discourages or prevents a hostile takeover. By taking on additional debt, a company can make itself unattractive to potential suitors. Some companies borrow to repurchase their common shares specifically as an anti-takeover device, increasing financial leverage dramatically. Whether this is beneficial to the company depends on a number of factors. Most research into the effects of takeover defenses concludes that the use of takeover defenses may reduce the value of the company, especially if motivated by self-interest on the part of the target company's management. Jandik and Makhija (2005) conclude in their study of unsuccessful takeovers that if the increase in debt results in better monitoring, the company benefits from the increase in debt. However, if the increase in debt results in management entrenchment, the effect on the company's value is adversely impacted.

## 22.6 THEORY OF DIVIDEND PAYMENTS

In a perfect capital market, even under risk, the dividend declared by the board of directors of a corporation is irrelevant to determining the firm's market value. While many individuals are quite unwilling to believe that this particular piece of the capital structure argument describes how dividend policy affects share price in the real world, the proposition is nonetheless a useful one. For, it says to managers that if dividends are to matter, they must look for reasons other than those provided by perfect market theory.

To express this in another way, in a perfect capital market it makes no difference whether the firm raises capital from internally generated sources (by using profits to finance new investment rather than to pay dividends) or from the sale of additional

---

[12] See Jensen (1986).

shares. Either source is discounted at the market rate of return appropriate to the firm's business risk. That is, the market-required rate of return is used both to price new shares and to value earnings retained by the firm. This means, in turn, that the value of the existing stockholders' interest in a firm will not be diminished by a new share issue because the existing stockholders would price the new share issue so it yields exactly the appropriate market-required return. Moreover, at this price buyers would be willing to purchase the shares because such shares offer the same return as any other investment of equal risk in the assumed perfect capital market.

However, the foregoing perfect markets story of dividend irrelevance[13] is not the whole of dividend theory. The *bird in the hand theory* put forth by Gordon (1959) argues that investors might prefer a certain dividend stream to no dividends and uncertain appreciation of the stock price. Moreover, signaling explanations hold that dividends provide a way for management to inform investors regarding its view of the firm's future prospects.[14] Still further, the previously discussed agency explanation holds that the payment of dividends forces the firm to seek more external financing, which in turn subjects the firm to the scrutiny of investors and thus provides an incentive for management to perform as effectively as possible.

Differential tax rates and transactions charges are also relevant to determining dividend policy. First, suppose income taxes are levied on stockholders and that tax rates differ according to whether the income is received in the form of dividends (ordinary income) or share price appreciation (capital gains). Suppose further that taxation of ordinary income occurs at higher rates than does taxation of capital gains. Under these circumstances, unless there are buyers of the firm's shares who can entirely escape taxation, the declaration of a dividend reduces the wealth position of stockholders more than does allowing stockholders to realize capital gains through share sales. In these circumstances, declaring a dividend is not irrelevant either to stockholders or to potential stockholders, and hence the market value of the firm can be altered by a dividend's being paid unless stockholders have some means of escaping the heavier tax rates. In the absence of such possibilities, paying a dividend results in a transfer of wealth from stockholders to the jurisdiction levying the tax. Some observers argue that due to the way dividends are taxed, investors should prefer the retention of funds to the payment of dividends.

While transactions costs are (by definition) assumed to be zero in a perfect capital market, it is also easy to see that, if there were charges for issuing new shares, the declaration of a dividend would not be a matter of indifference to stockholders even if markets were otherwise perfect. For if a dividend is declared and the firm raises funds to finance capital acquisitions through a new share issue, it incurs flotation charges (i.e., legal and registration fees) on the issue. As and when this happens, the resources over which the firm has command are reduced by flotation costs, with the result that the firm's market value is lower than it would have been in the absence of the dividend.

A similar argument can be made regarding the effect on stockholders if a dividend is not paid, and the stockholders must then sell shares to finance their current

---

[13] The dividend irrelevance results are a consequence of the Modigliani-Miller theorem discussed above. See, for example, Fama and Miller (1972).

[14] See Ambarish et al. (1987).

consumption expenditures. For if brokerage charges must be paid to complete the sale, and if there are not other effects such as differential tax rates to be recognized, stockholders are not as well off as they would have been if they had received a dividend.

At certain times management may have the option of repurchasing the firm's shares. In a perfect capital market we can conclude that securities repurchased, like dividend payments, are irrelevant to determining the firm's market value.

## 22.7 Is there an Optimal Capital Structure?

Our focus in this chapter has been to explain the factors corporate management should recognize as affecting a firm's capital structure. The question that arises is whether there is an optimal capital structure (i.e., a structure that maximizes the value of the firm). For the reasons suggested in this chapter, it seems that the capital structure is relevant but quantitatively it is difficult to identify a single point where the capital structure might maximize firm value.

Even if the optimal capital structure cannot be determined precisely, corporate management should understand that there is an economic benefit from the tax deductibility of interest expense, but eventually this benefit may be reduced by the costs of financial distress. While corporate management may not be capable of specifying the company's optimal capital structure, we do know the factors that affect the optimum. The discussion in this chapter demonstrates that there is a benefit from taxes and the discipline of debt but, eventually, these benefits reduce financial flexibility and may increase the likelihood of financial distress. The factors are summarized below:

| Advantages of debt financing | Disadvantages of debt financing |
|---|---|
| Interest tax shield | Financial flexibility |
| Governance value | Financial distress and/or bankruptcy |

## 22.8 Dynamic Models

Dynamic models focus on the ways capital structure can change through time as firms adjust both to new developments in their own positions and to new information about market conditions. Models of this type frequently specify a *target capital structure* defined by the factors discussed above, and then consider how the firm may benefit by taking decisions to deviate, at least for a time, from that chosen target structure. For example, Morellec and Schuerhoff (2007) develop a real options model in which the timing of investment, the composition of the firm's capital structure, and any decision to default on previously issued securities are endogenously and jointly determined. (We discuss real options in Chapter 26.) In their model, differential tax treatment of capital gains and income can adversely affect a firm's policy choices. For example, by providing a hedge for poor corporate performance, capital loss offsets erode the option value of waiting and induce firms to speed up investment. The model also predicts that firms optimally employ more equity financing as the firm's stock price increases. Still further, the worse the firm's performance history, the more equity financing it will optimally employ.

In a second model, Morellec and Schuerhoff (2009) analyze the effects of asymmetric information on firms' investment and financing decisions as the firms raise external funds. In this model, corporate insiders can signal private information to outside investors by altering either the timing of investment, the firm's debt-equity mix, or both. Informational asymmetries can erode the option value of waiting to invest, inducing firms with good prospects to speed up investment. Moreover, informational asymmetries may not translate into a traditional financing hierarchy. For example, informational asymmetries can render equity issues more attractive than debt issues even if firms have ample debt capacity.

Tserlukevich (2008) notes that while traditional models commonly invoke financial transactions costs in order to explain leverage fluctuations, lumpy investment opportunities can create similar fluctuations even in the absence of those costs. In simulations, Tserlukevich shows that firms' leverage ratios can be negatively related to profitability, exhibit mean reversion, and also depend on past stock returns. Incorporating the frictions of lumpy investments can increase models' explanatory power because Tserlukevich shows that both gradual and lumpy adjustments to leverage positions can occur in the absence of financial transactions costs.

Lambrecht and Myers (2008) show that bankruptcy costs can distort both capital investment and disinvestment. Managers' personal wealth constraints can lead both to delaying the firm's investment and to increased reliance on firm debt financing. Changes in cash flow can then cause further changes in investment by tightening or loosening the wealth constraints. Finally, the authors identify a moral hazard effect: Firms with weaker investor protection adopt higher debt levels.

## KEY POINTS

- Moving from a perfect capital market to real-world factors that management must recognize leads to theories of how capital structure can affect firm value.

- The factors include the effect of corporate taxation, probability of technical insolvency, heterogeneous expectations, and agency effects.

- Taxes and financial distress costs result in a trade-off: For low debt ratios, the benefit of tax reduction more than overcomes the present value of the costs of financial distress, resulting in increases in the value of the company for increasing debt ratios. But beyond some debt ratio, the benefit of tax reduction is overcome by the costs of financial distress; the value of the company decreases as debt is increased beyond this point.

- The possibility of incurring direct and indirect costs of financial distress discourages management from taking on high levels of debt.

- Limited liability creates a valuable right and an interesting incentive for shareholders. More specifically, the ability of shareholders to default on the company's debt and face only limited liability can be viewed as a call option: The owners have the option to buy back the entire company by paying off the creditors at the face value of the company's debt.

- In an agency relationship, the agent has the responsibility of acting for the principal. There is concern that management (the agent) will not act in the best interests of the shareholders (the principals).

- Agency costs are the costs associated with any effort to minimize the potential for conflict between the owners and management and include monitoring costs, bonding costs, and residual loss.

- Heterogeneous expectations may contribute to a decrease in the weighted average cost of capital when leverage is first increased, and may also contribute to an increase in the weighted average cost of capital if leverage continues to increase beyond a conventional level.

- Dynamic theories have begun to clarify relations between target capital structures and opportunistic deviations from them over time as new information about the firm itself and macro conditions become available.

- Some of the dynamic theories of capital structure also explain the simultaneous determination of investment and financing opportunities, choices that have traditionally been regarded separately.

## QUESTIONS

1. Suppose that XYZ Corporation
   - operates in a perfect capital market,
   - faces a 40% corporate tax, and
   - has a current asset value of $1,000.

   Management expects operating earnings (i.e., earnings before interest and taxes) of $200 in the coming year.
   a. Calculate the total expected income available to the suppliers of capital for the following three capital structures:
      *Capital structure* 1: 100% equity
      *Capital structure* 2: 70% equity and 30% debt with an annual interest of 10%
      *Capital structure* 3: 30% equity and 70% debt with an annual interest of 10%
   b. What's the optimal capital structure for this company? Assume that the annual interest of 10% applied to any amount of debt.
   c. If an individual income tax is introduced into this market and income tax on bond interest is much higher than that on dividends, how will the optimal capital structure of this company be affected and why?

2. a. What is meant by financial distress?
   b. Identify three common forms of costs associated with financial stress.

3. Consider a company with an asset value of $1 million and a capital structure consisting of 50% equity and 50% debt, and management's objective is to

maximize shareholders' wealth. Assume that the interest to the bondholders is negligible.

**a.** Which one of the following two projects (project A and project B) will be more likely to be chosen by management? Why?

| | | Profit/Loss ($ millions) | |
| | Probability | Project A | Project B |
| --- | --- | --- | --- |
| State 1 | 50% | 0.5 | 1.0 |
| State 2 | 50% | −0.3 | −0.8 |

**b.** If instead the company's capital structure consists of 90% equity and 10% debt, will the company be more likely or less likely to choose project B compared to the scenario when capital structure is 50% equity and 50% debt?

**c.** What do parts (a) and (b) suggest about the relationship between shareholders' limited liability and a company's capital structure?

**4. a.** What is meant by direct cost of bankruptcy?

**b.** What is meant by the indirect cost of bankruptcy?

**5. a.** What is meant by technical insolvency?

**b.** How does the possibility of technical insolvency affect capital structure?

**c.** Explain briefly the relationship between financial distress and capital structure.

**6.** Explain the mechanism of using financial leverage as a takeover defense tool.

**7.** In a perfect capital market, a company's dividend policy is irrelevant in determining the firm's market value. That is, it does not make any difference whether the company raises capital from retained earnings (i.e., not paying dividends) or from the sale of additional shares (due to paying dividends). The following are some factors/theories that may make the dividend choice relevant:

- Bird in the hand theory
- Signaling
- Agency theory
- Taxation on ordinary income and taxation on capital gain
- Flotation costs of issuing new shares
- Brokerage charges on the purchase of common stock shares

Which of these factors/theories could be used to support the argument that a company's management should pay dividends and obtain financing by issuing new shares? Be sure to explain why.

**8.** Which of the following are advantages of debt financing and which of them are disadvantages?

- Governance value
- Financial flexibility
- Interest tax shield
- Financial distress/bankruptcy

9. Consider a firm in a two period (time 1 and time 2) setting with the following distribution of values at time 2:

| State | Probability | Values ($t = 2$) |
|-------|-------------|------------------|
| 1 | 0.5 | $3,600 |
| 2 | 0.5 | $1,600 |

Suppose the corporate tax rate is 50%. If the firm becomes insolvent at time 2, the costs incurred would be $200, which is deducted from the firm's value. Suppose further that time 0 prices of (unit) contingent claims for the two states of the world are each 0.45.

a. What is the firm's weighted average cost of capital if the firm's capital is 100% equity financed?

b. If there is $600 worth of debt-bearing interest rate of 10% in the firm's capital, what is the firm's weighted average cost of capital?

c. If there is $1,000 worth of debt-bearing interest rate of 10% in the firm's capital, what is the firm's weighted average cost of capital?

---

◈ ◈ ◈  # REFERENCES

Almeida, Heitor, and Thomas Philippon. (2007). "The Risk-Adjusted Cost of Financial Distress," *Journal of Finance* **62**: 2557–2586.

Ambarish, Ramasastry, Kose John, and Joseph Williams. (1987). "Efficient Signaling with Dividends and Investments," *Journal of Finance* **42**: 321–343.

Barnea, Amir, Robert A. Haugen, and Lemma W. Senbet. (1985). *Agency Problems and Financial Contracting.* Englewood Cliffs, NJ: Prentice-Hall.

Fama, Eugene F., and Merton H. Miller. (1972). *The Theory of Finance.* New York: Holt, Rinehart and Winston.

Gordon, Myron J. (1959). "Dividends, Earnings and Stock Prices," *Review of Economics and Statistics* **41**: 99–105.

Jandik, Tomas, and Anil Makhija. (2005). "Debt, Debt Structure and Corporate Performance After Unsuccessful Takeovers: Evidence From Targets That Remain Independent," *Journal of Corporate Finance* **11**: 882–914.

Jensen, Michael C. (1986). "Agency Costs of Free Cash Flow, Corporate Finance, and Takeovers," *American Economic Review* **76**: 323–329.

Jensen, Michael, and William Meckling (1976). "Theory of the Firm: Managerial Behavior, Agency Costs, and Ownership Structure," *Journal of Financial Economics* **3**: 305–360.

Lambrecht, Bart M., and Stewart C. Myers (2008). "Debt and Managerial Rents in A Real-Options Model of the Firm," *Journal of Financial Economics* **89**: 209–231.

Miller, Merton H. (1977). "Debt and Taxes," *Journal of Finance* **32**: 261–275.

Modigliani, Franco, and Merton H. Miller. (1963). "Taxes and the Cost of Capital: A Correction," *American Economic Review* **53**: 433–443.

Morellec, Erwan, and Norman Schuerhoff. (2007). "Personal Taxes, Leverage, and Real Investment," available at http://ssrn.com/abstract=559003.

Morellec, Erwan, and Norman Schuerhoff. (2009). "Dynamic Investment and Financing under Asymmetric Information," Swiss Finance Institute Working Paper.

Ross, Stephen A. (1977). "The Determination of Financial Structure: The Incentive-Signalling Approach," *Bell Journal of Economics* **8**: 23–40.

Tserlukevich, Yuri. (2008). "Can Real Options Explain Financing Behavior?" *Journal of Financial Economics* **89**: 232–252.

# 23

# FINANCING DECISIONS IN PRACTICE

*I*n Chapters 4 and 22, we considered such major factors affecting capital structure as taxes, bankruptcy costs, and agency effects. This chapter considers further practical aspects of choosing financial arrangements, including (1) estimating the costs of different financing sources; (2) timing securities issues when management will not be able to maintain an optimal capital structure at all times; (3) how the views of creditors and investors might affect the timing and amount of securities issued; (4) the significance of insolvency costs for capital structure choices; (5) considerations in developing a dividend policy; and (6) considerations in repurchasing equity and issuing equity via a preemptive rights offering.

## 23.1  ESTIMATING THE COSTS OF DIFFERENT FUNDING SOURCES

The theory of capital structure provides a framework for analyzing how management can estimate the costs of raising funds from different sources (i.e., new equity or debt). The theory predicts that if additional equity is issued by a firm with both debt and equity in its capital structure, the debt-equity ratio will necessarily fall, and the discount rate applied to all the outstanding equity will usually also fall. On the other hand, an increase in the debt-equity ratio due to the issue of additional riskless debt (assuming it is actually possible to issue more riskless debt) will increase the discount rate applied to the equity but will not affect the rate applied to the debt.

For the reasons just mentioned, an attempt to forecast the cost of raising additional funds from different funding sources must be made with some care if it is not to be misleading. We will illustrate the analysis using additional equity. Suppose for the sake of exposition that a firm expands its activities while keeping its business risk the same. Then the rate of discount the market applies to the firm's earnings will not change. However, the rates of discount applied to debt and stock issues only remain the same if the proportion of debt to equity is unaltered. If the debt-equity ratio is altered, the discount rates prevailing after the financing will also change.

As an example, suppose a firm's earnings distribution at time 2, prior to expanding operations, is:

| State | Probability | Earnings |
|-------|-------------|----------|
| 1 | 0.5 | $2,000 |
| 2 | 0.5 | $1,080 |

Hence, expected earnings for time 2 are $1,540. Suppose this earnings distribution is discounted at 10%, implying the current value of the firm is $1,400. Suppose further that the firm has issued $400 in riskless debt and equity of $1,000. Assuming the riskless debt bears a market interest rate of 5%, the interest cost is $20 (5% times $400). Then in the absence of corporate income taxes the stockholders are entitled to all earnings exceeding $420—the $400 repayment of debt plus $20 interest. Thus,

| State | Probability | Available to stockholders |
|-------|-------------|---------------------------|
| 1 | 0.5 | $1,580 |
| 2 | 0.5 | $ 660 |

The expected dollar return to the stockholders is $1,120. Thus, since the value of equity is $1,000, the market is applying a discount rate of ($1,120 − $1,000)/$1,000 = 12% when the $400 in riskless debt has been issued.

Suppose now that if management can raise $300 of additional capital, the firm can expand its earnings distribution next year to:

| State | Probability | Earnings |
|-------|-------------|----------|
| 1 | 0.5 | $2,500 |
| 2 | 0.5 | $1,350 |

which has an expected earnings of $1,925 and which will also be discounted at 10% (since the earnings distribution has been expanded proportionately) so that the time 0 market value of the firm is $1,750.

Suppose further that there were originally 1,000 shares outstanding, each with a market value of $1, and that the new financing of $300 is to be effected via the sale of only equity. The new distribution of value that accrues to the stockholders is, assuming existing debt remains outstanding,

| State | Probability | Available to stockholders |
|-------|-------------|---------------------------|
| 1 | 0.5 | $2,080 |
| 2 | 0.5 | $ 930 |

which is found by subtracting $420 (principal repayment and interest) from the earnings in each state. Since the current market value of the firm is $1,750 and the value of the debt is $400, the current value of equity is $1,350. Given the expected return to stockholders is $1,505, the discount rate applied by the market to the equity will fall to ($1,505 − $1,350)/$1,350 = 11.5%. Thus, as a result of raising $300 via an equity offering, the discount rate on the equity declines because of the reduction in the debt-equity ratio.

The remaining problem is for management to set the terms of the new equity issue so that the existing stockholders reap the capital gains from the expansion, while new stockholders obtain just the appropriate market rate of return on their investment. The expansion will increase the value of the firm by $1,750 − $1,400 − $300 = $50, and existing stockholders are entitled to this additional amount. Since the current total value of the equity will be $1,350, because the value of the new shares issued must be $300 and the 1,000 old shares are now outstanding, we can express the required conditions as:

$$P(1,000 + n) = \$1,350$$

and

$$Pn = \$300$$

where $P$ is the share price and $n$ the number of new shares to be issued. These two conditions give us $1,000P = \$1,050$, so $P = \$1.05$ can be chosen as the market price of shares subsequent to the expansion. Since there are initially 1,000 shares outstanding (i.e., old shares) and the new shares are sold for $0.05 more than the current price, the old stockholders do indeed capture the $50 ($0.05 × 1,000) increase in value. Then, since $300 must be raised through the new stock issue, the required number of new shares to be sold to new investors[1] is $300/$1.05 or approximately 286.

Note that an attempt to price the equity on the basis of the old cost of equity capital, 12% in our example, would be erroneous. It would work to the detriment of existing stockholders because the firm's asking price for the new shares would be too low. Note also that the firm can choose either the number of shares to be issued, or the share price, but not both.

● ● ●   ## 23.2  TIMING THE ISSUANCE OF DEBT

In imperfect capital markets, the issuance of a new security incurs underwriting costs (referred to as *flotation costs*) that usually have a large fixed component. Hence, a cost-conscious management is likely to issue new securities relatively infrequently. However, the additional costs associated either with short-term borrowing or with investing surplus cash that has already been raised by long-term borrowing imply that

---

[1] Or to existing investors at the higher price.

the issuance of new securities cannot take place too frequently either. Hence, the timing of new issues becomes a question requiring management consideration.

In the case of the issuance of new debt securities, the effects of issue size on interest costs imply that regularly chosen times for their issuance might be advisable. On the other hand, fixed issurance costs provide an incentive to reduce the number of times a firm offers new debt securities to the market. Hence, management faces the problem of balancing these opposing considerations. To see how this might be achieved, we consider an example of balancing flotation costs against the interest costs of long-term debt. The total cost of issues is assumed to be given by:

$$\frac{FD}{N} + VD + \frac{N(r_L - r_B)}{2} \tag{23.1}$$

where
$F$ = fixed cost of issuing a debt obligation
$D$ = amount of funds raised during a given time interval
$N$ = size of individual issue
$D/N$ = number of issues during time interval
$V$ = variable cost of flotation
$r_L$ = rate on long-term debt obligations
$r_B$ = rate on short-term debt obligations

Here the objective assumed is just that of minimizing interest and flotation costs,[2] and we assume for simplicity that interest costs do not depend on the size of an issue. Moreover, interest rates are assumed to be unchanging over the entire planning period.

We can find the minimum of equation (23.1) by differentiating with respect to $N$ and setting the derivative equal to zero:

$$\frac{-FD}{N^2} + \frac{r_L - r_B}{2} = 0$$

$$\frac{FD}{N^2} = \frac{r_L - r_B}{2}$$

$$N^* = \left(\frac{2FD}{r_L - r_B}\right)^{1/2}$$

The last expression then gives us the size of an issue that best balances flotation and interest costs.

---

[2] Much more detailed, and complex, models of the bond flotation and refunding problems have been developed. As our purpose is merely to cite the basic aspects of these developments, we do not present these details.

As an example,[3] suppose the following data characterize the problem:

$$D = \$50,000,000 \text{ over 3 years}$$

$$F = \$100,000$$

$$r_L = 7\% \text{ per annum}$$

$$r_B = 5\% \text{ per annum}$$

$$r_L - r_B = 0.02/3 \text{ (for a 3-year planning horizon)}$$

$$N^* = \left[ \frac{2(\$100,000)(\$50,000,000)}{0.06} \right]^{1/2}$$

$$= \$12,909,000$$

Accordingly, about four issues ($50,000,000/$12,909,000), one every nine months represents a strategy minimizing the sum of interest and flotation costs.

A second feature of timing has to do with the possibility that market interest rates may at times be unrepresentatively high due to expectations of high inflation or large credit spreads in the credit market. If management can discern such effects, either unaided or with the investment banker's advice, it may prove economic to time the issue with a view to minimizing the costs incurred thereby.

## 23.2.1 Effects of Upward-Sloping Supply Curves

Debt obligations or stock prices usually fall a little when a new issue is floated, contrary to the assumptions of a perfect market. Moreover, the extent to which these prices fall may depend on the amount of funds raised. Hence, effective interest rates can increase with the amount of funds raised, as Figure 23.1 indicates. Over any given time interval, only a certain amount can be raised at or near market rates. On these grounds some firms may find issuing securities more or less continuously to be an economic strategy for raising capital. This appears to be characteristic, for example, of public utilities with lengthy expansion or refitting programs to carry out.

## 23.2.2 Target versus Actual Capital Structures

Given the existence of both upper and lower limits on the amounts of securities that can economically be floated in any period, it is clear that the firm may not be able to adhere exactly to an optimal capital structure at all points in time. Instead, the firm is likely to stipulate an optimal structure as a target, making episodic adjustments to keep it reasonably near this value. Thus, while the firm's leverage may on average equal some chosen value, at any point in time it may deviate from that average.

---

[3] This illustration is taken from Van Horne (1977).

**FIGURE 23.1**
IMPERFECT MARKETS VIEW OF SUPPLY CURVE FOR A GIVEN TYPE OF CAPITAL

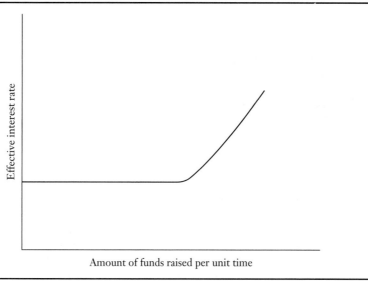

Amount of funds raised per unit time

DeAngelo, DeAngelo, and Whited (2009) estimate a model in which firms have target capital structures but respond to investment opportunity shocks by issuing transitory debt obligations that represent deviations from their target. In the DeAngelo and Whited model, the average amount of outstanding debt differs predictably from a target capital structure chosen to reflect the value of options to issue transitory debt. The optimal leverage path reflects time-varying and state-contingent transitory debt whose usage is determined by current and prospective shocks to the firm's investment opportunities. The model also displays sluggish mean reversion in leverage, reflecting the opportunity cost of utilizing debt capacity rather than the transactions costs of debt issuance.

## 23.3 CREDITORS, INVESTORS, AND CAPITAL STRUCTURE CHOICES

If during a given time interval a firm can borrow only a limited amount at or near market rates of interest, the firm's management may wish to maintain emergency borrowing powers and consequently limit the debt-equity ratio. Moreover, if there is a question about the firm's ability to meet fixed charges, the firm may have difficulty obtaining trade credit, and this may in turn impair its ability to generate sales and eventually earnings, providing another reason for management to limit the debt-equity ratio.

The perfect capital market predictions depend on the assumption that both individuals and firms can borrow on the same terms and without payment of transactions costs. In reality, transactions costs are likely to limit individual investors' ability to offset firms' decisions (at least in the short run because these costs impede marginal adjustments), and this possibility may be exacerbated by individuals' inability to borrow on the same terms as firms. Similarly, investors in high tax brackets might prefer capital gains to dividends, because the tax rate applicable to the former is less. In order to minimize the impacts of transactions costs and differential tax rates, investors might prefer that the firm adopt a specific debt-equity ratio. Hence, if these factors are regarded as important by a firm's management, it seems plausible that firms might adopt financial risk postures suitable to the average investor.

In offering explanations of why particular debt-equity ratios might be desirable, we emphasize that the arguments developed are tentative. They are still the center of substantial controversy in financial theory, and the eventual resolution of the controversy may well alter details of the present explanations. Nonetheless, we believe the explanations reflect the thrust of current thinking and that our conjectures at least indicate directions in which current thinking is likely to evolve. In any event, for reasons of the sort just mentioned, the question of how the firm's cost of capital actually behaves with respect to leverage remains an open one.

Leary (2009) examines capital structure choices under changing financial environments. He studies financing data relevant to the 1961 expansion of bank credit due to the emergence of the market for negotiable certificates of deposit, and also the contraction associated with a credit crunch in 1966. Leary shows that these changes in market liquidity contribute to several capital structure reactions. Leary finds that the leverage ratios of bank-dependent firms decrease (increase) following bank credit contraction (expansion). Bank-dependent firms also shift toward equity when bank debt becomes scarce. On the other hand, non-bank-dependent firms shift between bank debt and public debt markets. Leary's results indicate that observed leverage ratios and debt placement structures are determined by a combination of (1) firms' demand for capital structures and (2) supply frictions in the credit markets, frictions that particularly affect bank-dependent firms. That is, the capital market imperfections that create a link between the banking sector and economic growth also create a link between credit conditions and firms' financial structures.

Rauh and Sufi (2008) investigate a data set that records individual debt issues on the balance sheets of a large random sample of rated public firms. The authors find that debt heterogeneity provides still further insights into the determinants of corporate capital structure. The data show that relative to high-credit-quality firms, low-credit-quality firms are more likely to have a multi-tiered capital structure consisting of both secured bank debt with tight covenants and subordinated non-bank debt with looser covenants. Thus, while high-credit-quality firms can employ a variety of discretionary and flexible sources of finance, low-credit-quality firms rely on tightly monitored secured bank debt.

An empirical study by Lewis and Verwijmeren (2009) finds that relatively complex securities issues are chosen with several goals in mind. Firms select security designs with a view to: reducing corporate taxes, minimizing refinancing costs, and mitigating the cost of managerial discretion. Apparently some firms also choose securities issues that enhance the firm's ability to report particularly favorable earnings patterns.

# 23.4  Significance of Technical Insolvency

Having examined the manner in which insolvency costs might affect the firm's cost of capital in Chapter 22, we now attempt to assess their nature and significance.[4] If a firm is unable to meet its contracted payments, it is technically insolvent. In these circumstances the first decision to be made by management is whether the firm should be reorganized or whether it should be liquidated and the assets sold for whatever they will bring. Presumably management will choose between these alternatives on the basis of which appears better from the investors' point of view. Bankruptcy proceedings in the United States are governed by the bankruptcy code. A *reorganization* under Chapter 11 of the bankruptcy code involves changing the firm's capital structure, while a *liquidation* under Chapter 7 of the code involves the sale of the firm's assets and payment of the proceeds to various classes of investors.

Bankruptcy proceedings can be both lengthy and expensive. In the case of a liquidation, the assets of the firm may have to be sold at distress prices, incurring losses that might have been unnecessary had the firm not borrowed so much as to be forced into technical insolvency. Even if the firm is reorganized and no assets are sold, production may be temporarily halted, employees may resign, and contracts with either suppliers, customers, or both may have to be renegotiated—all with resulting economic costs. In addition, there may be indirect costs borne by the distressed firm even if bankruptcy does not actually occur. The mere possibility of a bankruptcy may increase personnel costs if it is costly for employees to relocate and find new jobs. For example, upper-level management stand a greater chance of losing their jobs in the event of technical insolvency, and if this appears to be an important possibility, they may require either greater compensation or more costly monitoring if they are to be deterred from acting in their own best interests. Likewise, costs of obtaining supplies may increase because suppliers will be reluctant to establish business relations with a firm that is likely to become insolvent.[5]

Even if the firm's market opportunities do not change as a result of an increased probability of insolvency, the operating decisions of management may change so as to alter the pattern of net operating income. Just how their decisions change will depend on (1) how management attempts to trade off between their own positions and the value of equity, and (2) the countervailing actions taken by stockholders to restrain management.

If the senior managers of the firm consider their own economic interest when making operating decisions, and if managers' incomes are not well diversified, increasing the firm's financial leverage will increase the risk of a salary reduction or loss of employment, raising the consequent problem of finding new jobs with the stigma of a questionable management record. To minimize this possibility, management may be induced to make low-risk–low-profitability decisions. On the other hand, equity-oriented management may be tempted to accept more risky projects that have a large chance of loss but a small chance of a very large gain.

---

[4] Evidence of the importance of these costs is inconclusive; see Warner (1977a, 1977b).

[5] At least unless payment is guaranteed in advance (a practice more costly than the usual arrangement of establishing a trade account).

The foregoing analysis has assumed that the risk premia associated with bankruptcy costs do not change. However, Almeida and Philippon (2007) point out that risk premia are known to vary in response to changing market and economic conditions. They argue that financial distress is more likely to happen in bad times, and that consequently calculating the present value of financial distress can depend on changing risk premia. They estimate the present value of financial distress using risk-adjusted default probabilities derived from corporate bond spreads. For a BBB-rated firm, their benchmark calculations show that the net present value (NPV) of distress is 4.5% of pre-distress value. In contrast, a valuation that ignores changes in risk premia generates an NPV of only 1.4%. Thus, Almeida and Philippon conclude that marginal distress costs can be as large as the marginal tax benefits of debt, meaning that recognizing the effects of changing risk premia can help explain why firms appear to use debt more conservatively than has been suggested by other studies.

## 23.5 Restrictive Covenants and Agency Costs

Restrictive covenants are constraints accepted by the firm's management as a part of the terms of raising debt. For example, a covenant may limit additional debt issues, changes in the firm's working capital ratio, changes in dividends, changes in management salaries, and the like. All these types of limitations are imposed on firms by investors attempting to improve the security of their investment positions. Jensen and Meckling (1976) regard these arrangements as agency costs incurred to protect bondholders from having their wealth positions diminished by actions of stockholders.

To see how such a possibility might arise, we reproduce an example developed by Copeland and Weston (1979). Suppose, unknown to potential lenders or investors, that a firm has two different investment projects, yielding time 1 payoffs in the two possible states of the world as indicated below:

| | Payoff | |
|---|---|---|
| Project | State 1 | State 2 |
| X | $9,000 | $11,000 |
| Y | $2,000 | $18,000 |

To make the calculations as simple as possible, assume risk neutrality on the part of all investors. If the firm shows only project X to prospective bondholders and can borrow $7,000 to finance it, the firm's managers (or stockholders) would have an incentive to switch to project Y unless the bondholders had stipulated that such actions could not be taken. For if restrictions of this sort are not imposed and if no other costs are involved, the $7,000 borrowed on the basis of a project X that guarantees repayment with interest in both states of the world could instead be used to finance a project Y that would be highly rewarding to stockholders if state 2 obtained, but highly detrimental to bondholders if state 1 obtained.

Billett, King, and Mauer (2007) investigate the effect of growth in investment opportunities on firms' choices of leverage, debt maturity, and covenants. Large sample evidence from a database of detailed debt covenant information shows that covenant protection increases in growth opportunities, debt maturity, and leverage. The normally negative relation between leverage and growth opportunities is significantly attenuated by covenant protections, suggesting that covenants can mitigate the agency costs of debt for high-growth firms. In other words, restrictive covenants appear to reflect the sorts of expectational differences discussed above. To the extent that contractual limitations are inadequate to deal with uncertainties that concern lenders, it might also be expected that higher interest rates will be demanded on any securities that lenders agree to acquire.

## 23.6 DIVIDEND POLICY

Most dividends take the form of cash payments to shareholders, and are paid on all outstanding shares of stock. A few companies pay special or extra dividends occasionally—identifying these dividends as distinct from regular dividends.

### 23.6.1 Dividend Policy

Management may express such differing dividend policies as:

- No dividends
- Low regular dividends with periodic extra dividends
- Constant growth in dividends per share
- Constant ratio of earnings to be paid out as dividends

Corporations that do not pay dividends are usually younger, faster-growing companies. For example, Microsoft Corporation was founded in 1975 and went public in 1986, but did not pay a cash dividend until January 2001. U.S. corporations that pay dividends tend to pay either constant or increasing dividends per share. Dividends tend to be lower in industries that have many profitable opportunities to invest their earnings. But as a company matures and finds fewer and fewer profitable investment opportunities, a greater portion of its earnings are paid out in dividends.

Many corporations are reluctant to cut dividends because the corporation's share price usually falls following any dividend reduction. For example, the U.S. auto manufacturers cut dividends during the recession in the early 1990s. However, as earnings per share declined the automakers did not cut dividends until earnings per share were negative—and in the case of General Motors, not until it had experienced two consecutive loss years. But as earnings recovered in the mid-1990s, dividends were increased. (General Motors increased dividends until cutting them once again in 2006 when it incurred substantial losses.) Corporations tend to raise their regular quarterly dividend only when they are sure they can keep it up in the future. By giving a special or extra dividend, the corporation is able to provide more cash to the shareholders without committing itself to paying an increased dividend each period into the future.

### 23.6.2  Dividend Reinvestment Plans

Many U.S. corporations allow shareholders to reinvest automatically their dividends in the shares of the corporation paying them. A *dividend reinvestment plan* (DRP) is a program that allows shareholders to buy additional shares of company stock instead of receiving a cash dividend payment. A DRP offers benefits to both shareholders and the corporation. Shareholders buy shares without transactions costs—brokers' commissions—and at a discount from the current market price. The corporation is able to retain cash without incurring the cost of a new stock issue. Alas, even though the shareholders never see the dividend, the dividend payments are taxed as income before they are reinvested. The result is similar to a dividend cut, but with a tax consequence for the shareholders: The cash flow that would have been paid to shareholders is plowed back into the corporation. Many corporations are finding high rates of participation in DRPs, raising the question that if so many shareholders want to reinvest their dividends—even after considering the tax consequences—why is the corporation paying dividends? The observation suggests some other rationale such as signaling compels corporations to pay dividends.

### 23.6.3  Stock Splits and Stock Dividends

A *stock split* increases the number of existing shares, and is thus something like a stock dividend. For example, in a 2:1 split each shareholder gets two shares for every one owned. If an investor owns 1,000 shares and the stock is split 2:1, the investor then owns twice as many shares—and so does every other shareholder. If the investor owned 1% of the corporation's stock before the split, the investor still owns 1% after the split. So why split? Like a stock dividend, the split reduces the trading price of shares. If an investor owns 1,000 shares of the stock trading for $50 per share prior to a 2:1 split, the shares should trade for $25 per share after the split.

Aside from a minor difference in accounting, stock splits and stock dividends are essentially the same. The stock dividend requires a shift within the stockholders' equity accounts, from retained earnings to paid-in capital, for the amount of the distribution; the stock split requires only a memorandum entry. A 2:1 split has the same effect on a stock's price as a 100% stock dividend, a 1.5 to 1 split has the same effect on a stock's price as a 50% stock dividend, and so on. The basis of the accounting rules is related to the reasons behind the distribution of additional shares. If firms want to bring down their share price, they tend to declare a stock split; if firms want to communicate news, they often declare a stock dividend.

How can investors tell what the motivation is behind stock dividends and stock splits? They cannot, but they can determine how other investors interpret these actions by looking at how the corporation's share price responds to an announcement of a stock dividend or other action. If the share price tends to rise when the announcement is made, the decision is probably good news; if the price tends to fall, the stock dividend is probably bad news. This is supported by evidence that indicates corporation's earnings tend to increase following stock splits and dividends.

The share price of companies announcing stock distributions and stock splits typically increases by 1% to 2% when the split or stock dividend is announced. When the stock dividend is distributed or the split is effected (on the "ex" date), the share's price typically declines according to the amount of the distribution. Suppose a firm announces a 2:1 split. Its share price may increase by 1% to 2% when this is announced, but when the shares are split, the share price will go down to approximately half of its presplit value. The most likely explanation is that this distribution is interpreted as good news—that management believes that the future prospects of the company are favorable or that the share price is more attractive to investors.

## 23.7 REPURCHASING THE FIRM'S COMMON STOCK

Corporations sometimes repurchase common stock from their shareholders. A corporation repurchasing its own shares is effectively paying a cash dividend, with one important difference: its tax impact. Cash dividends are treated as ordinary taxable income to the shareholder, but a share repurchase is treated as a capital gain or loss for the shareholder, and thus its tax impact depends on the shares' original purchase price. In addition, the resulting capital gains are usually subject to lower taxation rates than is ordinary income.

The company may repurchase its own stock by any of three methods: (1) a tender offer, (2) open market purchases, and (3) a targeted block repurchase. A *tender offer* is an offer made to all shareholders, with a specified deadline and a specified number of shares the corporation is willing to buy back. The tender offer may be a fixed-price offer, where the corporation specifies the price it is willing to pay and solicits purchases of shares of stock at that price.

A tender offer may also be conducted as a *Dutch auction* in which the corporation specifies a minimum and a maximum price, soliciting bids from shareholders for any price within this range at which they are willing to sell their shares. After the corporation receives these bids, they pay all tendering shareholders the maximum price sufficient to buy back the number of shares they want. A Dutch auction reduces the chance that the firm pays a price higher than needed to acquire the shares. Dutch auctions are gaining in popularity relative to fixed-price offers. For example, Wendy's International announced in October 2006 that it would buy back shares in a Dutch auction tender offer. In this offer, the company specified the range of prices it is willing to pay—in this case $31.00 to $36.00 per share—and the number of shares. The company then allowed the auction mechanism to work to determine the price. As a result of this auction, Wendy's bought back 22.4 million shares at $35.75 per share in November of 2006, representing 19% of the company's outstanding common stock. There were 27.9 million shares tendered, but only 22.4 million shares at or below the purchase price.

A corporation may also buy back shares directly in the open market, a transaction that involves using a broker as an intermediary to carry out the purchases. A corporation that wants to buy shares may have to spread its purchases over time so as not to drive the share's price up temporarily by buying large numbers of shares.

A third method of repurchasing stock is to buy it from a specific shareholder. This method is referred to as a *targeted block repurchase*, since there is a specific shareholder (the "target") and there are a large number of shares (a "block") to be purchased at one time. Targeted block repurchases, also referred to as "greenmail," were used in the 1980s to fight corporate takeovers.

Corporations repurchase their stock for a number of reasons. First, a repurchase is a way to distribute cash to shareholders at a lower effective cost to both the firm and the shareholders than that of using dividends. If capital gains are taxed at rates lower than ordinary income, which until recently has been the case with U.S. tax law, repurchasing is a lower cost way of distributing cash. However, since shareholders have different tax rates—especially when comparing corporate shareholders with individual shareholders—the benefit is mixed. The reason is that some shareholders' income is tax-free (e.g., pension funds), some shareholders are only taxed on a portion of dividends (e.g., corporations receiving dividends from other corporations), and some shareholders are taxed on the full amount of dividends (e.g., individual taxpayers).

Another reason to repurchase stock is to increase earnings per share. A company that repurchases its shares increases its earnings per share simply because there are fewer shares outstanding after the repurchase. But there are two problems with this motive. First, cash is paid to the shareholders, so less cash is available for the corporation to reinvest in profitable projects. Second, while the earnings pie is sliced into fewer pieces after the repurchase, the pie itself remains the same size unless and until operations are also changed.

Still another reason for stock repurchase is that it could tilt the debt-equity ratio so as to increase the value of the company. By buying back stock—thereby reducing equity—the company's assets are financed to a greater degree by debt. To see this, suppose a corporation has a balance sheet consisting of assets of $100 million, liabilities of $50 million, and $50 million of equity. That is, the corporation has financed 50% of its assets with debt, and 50% with equity. If this corporation uses $20 million of its assets to buy back stock worth $20 million, its balance sheet will have assets of $80 million financed by $50 million of liabilities and $30 million of equity. It now finances 62.5% of its assets with debt and 37.5% with equity.

If the benefits from deducting interest on debt outweigh the cost of increasing the risk of bankruptcy, repurchasing stock may increase the value of the firm. But financing the firm with more debt can decrease value if the risk of financial distress—difficulty paying legal obligations—outweighs the benefits from tax deductibility of interest. Hence, any benefits to repurchasing shares must really be judged on a case-by-case basis to determine if the action is beneficial or detrimental.

One more reason for a stock repurchase is that it reduces total dividend payments because the corporation can still pay the same amount of dividends per share, but the total dividend payments are reduced. At the same time, if the shares are correctly valued in the market (there is usually no reason to believe otherwise), the payment for the repurchased shares equals the reduction in the value of the firm—and the remaining shares are worth the same as they were before. Some argue that a repurchase is a signal about future prospects. That is, by buying back the shares, management is communicating to investors that the company is generating sufficient cash to be able to buy back shares. But if the company has profitable investment opportunities, the cash could be used to finance these investments, instead of paying it out to the shareholders.

A stock repurchase may also reduce agency costs by reducing the amount of cash the management has on hand. Similar to the argument suggested for dividend payments, repurchasing shares reduces the amount of free cash flow and, therefore, reduces the possibility that management will invest it unprofitably. Many companies use stock buybacks to mitigate the dilution resulting from executive stock options, as well as to shore up their stock price. According to a press releases by Standard & Poor's (2005, 2006), companies in the S&P 500, for example, repurchased a record dollar amount of shares in 2005 and 2006, as much as they spent on capital expenditures. The effect of these buybacks has been to increase earnings per share for the S&P 500 by 20% in 2006.

Repurchasing shares tends to shrink the firm: Cash is paid out and the value of the firm is smaller. Can repurchasing shares be consistent with wealth maximization? Yes. If the best use of funds is to pay them out to shareholders, repurchasing shares maximizes shareholders' wealth. If the firm has no profitable investment opportunities, it is better for a firm to shrink by paying funds to the shareholders than to shrink by investing in lousy projects.

So how does the market react to a company's intention to repurchase shares? A number of studies have looked at how the market reacts to such announcements. In general, the share price goes up when a firm announces it is going to repurchase its own shares. It is difficult to identify the reason the market reacts favorably to such announcements since so many other things are happening at the same time. By piecing bits of evidence together, however, we see that it is likely that investors view the announcement of a repurchase as good news—a signal of good things to come.

## 23.8 PREEMPTIVE RIGHTS OFFERING

The current shareholders of a corporation may be concerned that their economic interest in terms of profits and dividends will be diluted by management's issuing new shares of stock. In some cases, current shareholders may also be concerned that management might diminish their voting rights by selling new shares. Consequently, shareholders may seek a provision in new securities issues to protect against these possibilities. The provision, called a *preemptive right*, grants current shareholders the right to purchase some proportion of new shares issued at a price below market value. The price at which the new shares can be purchased is called the *subscription price*. When such preemptive right exists, management must first offer new stock to current shareholders and the offering is said to be a *preemptive rights offering*.

In the United States, some states provide that current shareholders have this right automatically. For example, the general corporation law of the state of Delaware requires that preemptive rights be granted to shareholders. However, even in such states a corporation is entitled to alter or abolish preemptive rights by amending its certificate of incorporation. In other states, preemptive rights are not granted as a matter of law but must be specifically granted in a corporation's state filings with the terms and conditions set forth in the shareholders' agreement. For example, New Jersey's corporate statutes specify that corporations organized after January 1, 1969, shall not have preemptive rights unless the certificate of incorporation provides otherwise. Corporations organized prior to January 1, 1969, had to have preemptive rights unless a bylaw duly adopted by the shareholders provides otherwise.

In the United States, the practice of issuing common stock via a preemptive rights offering is uncommon since typically preemptive rights are either not given or abolished by amending the certification of incorporation. In other countries it is much more common and in some, it is the only means by which a new offering of common stock may be sold.

For shares sold via a preemptive rights offering, the underwriting services of an investment banker are not needed, hence, there is savings in transaction costs. However, the issuing corporation may use the services of an investment banker for the distribution of unsubscribed common stock. In such instances, a *standby underwriting arrangement* will be used. This arrangement calls for the investment banking firm or firms to purchase the unsubscribed shares. The issuing corporation pays a *standby fee* to the investment banking firm.

To demonstrate how a rights offering works, the effect on the economic wealth of shareholders, and how the terms set forth in a rights offering affects whether or not the issuer will need an underwriter, we will use an illustration. Suppose that the market price of the stock of Company W is $20 per share and that there are 30,000 shares outstanding. Thus, Company W's market capitalization is $600,000. Suppose that the company's management is considering a rights offering in connection with the issuance of 10,000 new shares. Each current shareholder would receive one right for every three shares owned. The terms of the rights offering are as follows: For three rights and $17 (the subscription price) a new share can be acquired. The subscription price must always be less than the market price or the rights will not be exercised. However, as we will see, the amount of the discount (i.e., the difference between the market price and subscription price) is relevant. In our illustration, the subscription price is 15% ($3/$20) below the market price.[6]

In addition to the number of rights and the subscription price, there are two other important elements of a rights offering. First is the choice to transfer the rights by selling the rights in the open market. As we will see, this is critical because the rights have a value and that value can be captured by selling them. The second element is the time when the rights expire (that is, when the rights can no longer be used to acquire the stock). Typically, the time period before rights expire is short.

The value of a right can be found by calculating the difference between the price of a share before the rights offering and the price of a share after the rights offering.[7] That is,

$$\text{Value of a right} = \text{Pre-rights offering price} - \text{Post-rights offering price}$$

---

[6] Note that the same results can be achieved by issuing one right per share but requiring three rights plus the subscription price for a new share (except for rounding off problems and implications for the value of one right discussed below).

[7] Alternatively, the value of a right can be found as follows:

$$\frac{\text{price after rights offering-subscription price}}{\text{number of rights required to buy a share}}.$$

**TABLE 23.1**
ANALYSIS OF RIGHTS OFFERING ON THE MARKET PRICE OF COMPANY W'S STOCK

| Before rights issue | |
|---|---|
| 1. Capitalization | $600,000 |
| 2. Number of shares | 30,000 |
| 3. Share price (rights on) | $20.00 |
| **After issuance of shares via rights offering** | |
| 4. Number of shares | 40,000 (=30,000 + 10,000) |
| 5. Capitalization | $770,000 (=$600,000 + 10,000 × $17) |
| 6. Share price (ex rights) | $19.25 (=$770,000/40,000) |
| 7. Value of one right | $0.75 (=$20.00 − $19.25) |
| **Net gain or loss to initial stockholder** | |
| 8. Loss per share due to dilution | $0.75 (=3.75% × $20) |
| 9. Gain per share from selling or exercising a right | $0.75 |
| 10. Net gain or loss | $0 |

Or, equivalently,

$$\text{Value of a right} = \text{Share price rights on} - \text{Share price rights}$$

Table 23.1 shows the impact of the rights offering on the price of a share. The price after the rights offering will be $19.25. Therefore, the value of a right is $0.75 ($20.00 − $19.25).

The difference between the price before the rights offering and after the rights offering expressed as a percentage of the original price is called the *dilution effect of the rights issue*. In the present case, the dilution effect is $0.75/$20, or 3.75%. The dilution is larger, the larger the ratio of old and new shares, and the larger the discount.[8]

The last section of Table 23.1 shows the net gain or loss to the initial shareholder as a result of the rights offering. The loss per share due to dilution is $0.75, but that is exactly equal to the value of a right, which, if the shareholder desires, can be sold in the market. This result is important because it shows that the rights offering as such will not affect the sum of the value of the share without rights (referred to as ex rights) plus the value of the rights the current shareholder receives, no matter how much the

---

[8] Specifically:

$$\text{dilution effect} = \frac{\text{discount \%}}{1 + (\text{ratio of old to new shares})}.$$

In our illustration the discount is 15% and the ratio of old to new shares is 30,000/10,000 or 3, so the dilution effect is 0.15/4, or 3.75%.

dilution or the initial discount offered. This is because a larger dilution is exactly compensated for by the increase in the value of the rights.

However, this does not mean that the size of the discount and dilution is irrelevant for the welfare of the stockholders. On the contrary, the value of one right will, in general, not be constant during the period over which the rights may be exercised. In our example, it is $0.75 on the day the rights begin trading and are exercisable. However, for any successive day between this day and the last day that the rights may be exercised, the value of the rights will tend to be equal to the difference between the market price of the stock at that date and the subscription price. This is because in a perfect capital market, with no transaction costs, any difference can be arbitraged, forcing the stock and the right to be priced consistently. Thus, suppose that just after the rights issuance the price of Company W's stock is at $19.25 as expected, but at the same time the price of a right is underpriced and selling at only $0.60. Then one can arbitrage by buying the underpriced rights, exercising them by paying the subscription price of $17, and receiving shares at the cost of $18.80, which can be simultaneously sold at $19.25, for a gain of $0.45 per share. This arbitrage activity will drive the price of the shares and the rights to be priced consistently so as to eliminate any arbitrage profit.

However, in reality arbitrage incurs transaction costs, including at least the round-trip commission (i.e., buying and selling securities). Therefore, the price of the right may remain somewhat lower than the difference between the market price of the shares and the subscription price. This has two implications. First, if the market price of the stock were to fall by more than the initial value of the rights, then the rights would become worthless and remain worthless as long as the market price remained below that critical level. From the point of view of the issuing company, this would mean that some rights would fail to be exercised and therefore the firm would be unable to raise the amount of financing it intended to. For this reason it has been suggested that the firm should rely on the services of an investment banker who would commit to buy any unsold shares at the subscription price.

The risk of a rights offering failing will depend on the value of the right relative to the volatility of the stock price. But the value of the right (given the shares to be issued) depends on the discount chosen in designing the issue. Now suppose that the subscription is to occur within one month and the monthly price volatility (as measured by the standard deviation) can be estimated. Then, by the choice of an appropriately high discount and resulting value of the right, the issuer can make the probability of failure as small as desired (at least if there are no other constraints on the discount, which we discuss below). Therefore, we conclude that if the rights offering can be so designed that the services of an investment banker are not needed, the cost of the issue to shareholders[9] can be substantially reduced.

There is another consideration that suggests the desirability of designing the rights offering with a relatively high discount. We have already seen that the value of the right will be unfavorably affected by transaction costs. In addition, these costs will

---

[9] The value of the rights is also affected by the choice described in the previous footnote. Clearly, the value of one right is larger if a shareholder is given one right per three shares than if the shareholders are each given one right per three shares and are required to buy one unit of the stock. In other words, the value of rights is enhanced by giving one right to each holder of $1/y$ shares rather than one right to each holder of one share and then requiring $1/y$ rights to buy one new share.

reduce the net amount received by a stockholder who decides to sell his rights rather than exercise them. For both reasons it is desirable to keep transaction costs low. Since transaction cost per dollar transacted increases as the share price decreases, it is desirable to design the offering so that the right has a large unit value, which means a relatively high discount.

There is potential disadvantage, however, to designing a rights offering with a high discount. Some stockholders fail either to exercise or to sell their rights. This may occur because they did not receive notice of the rights offering and its terms or because, for some reason, they simply elected not to act. Stockholders who fail to act will suffer a net loss per share equal to the value of the right per share times the number of shares held (or equivalently equal to the dilution times the value of the holdings, which dilution is no longer compensated for from the proceeds from the sale of the rights) and thus increases with the value of the rights. On the other hand, it can be argued that when the rights have greater value, stockholders are less likely to fail to make use of their opportunity, although there seems to be no empirical evidence on this point. In any event, it seems safe to conclude that there is a strong case for a design that makes the value of the rights substantial. Then, the greater the value, the more it behooves the board of directors to make efforts to ensure that stockholders are apprised of the economic value of their rights. Without going into further detail, we merely note here that the proportion of stockholders that are "hard to locate" will differ from one circumstance to the other. There are a variety of ways for reaching hard-to-locate stockholders, and they have differential costs, making the problem of choice among alternatives a nontrivial one.

Note, finally, that when there is no investment banker acting as the residual buyer, and a positive probability that at least some of the stockholders will fail either to exercise or sell their rights, there is a risk that some of the stock will remain unsold. This danger can be eliminated by giving the stock to those who will exercise the right—the privilege of over-subscribing (i.e., of buying additional shares at the subscription price) in proportion to their purchases. If there are then some non-exercised rights, they are allocated to the over-subscribers. There are various possible criteria for this allocation. One reasonable gauge may be to allocate what is available first to the stockholders of record before the issue, ensuring that at least a portion of the losses to the non-exercisers will remain within the stockholder family. Because one over-subscription is worth as much as one right, there is a substantial possibility that the abundance of over-subscription will absorb the entire number of shares not exercised during the primary offering.

## 23.9 CONTINGENCY PLANNING AND CAPITAL STRUCTURE CHOICES

We introduced contingency planning in Chapter 10. Contingency planning relates to capital structure decisions in two ways:

* Maintaining a reserve of liquid assets over the short run
* Maintaining reserve financing capacity over somewhat longer time periods

In the short run, a certain level of liquid assets provides the firm with an ability to cover such contingencies as unanticipated shortfalls in cash inflows used to meet regular expenses. The maintenance of a liquidity reserve carries an opportunity cost in terms of lost revenues, to be sure, but it also reduces costs associated with being unable to make payments on time. Consider, for example, the problems management would face with its labor force if it could not meet a payroll on the normally scheduled date. As another example, a firm that cannot meet scheduled interest payments is technically insolvent and could face the problem of declaring bankruptcy. The kind of contingency planning needed to determine an appropriate level of liquid assets balances the revenues foregone by investing in assets of this type against the costs, exact or implied, of being unable to meet scheduled payments.

With respect to maintaining reserve debt capacity, the costs incurred result from maintenance of a higher proportion of equity in the capital structure than would otherwise be necessary. The anticipated benefits are those of being able quickly to adjust to technological developments or other unpredictable environmental changes by having quick access to debt funds permitting the financing of such investments. Without reserve debt capacity, it might not be possible to adopt new projects when opportunities first arise. Moreover, raising the necessary financing might take a longer time or involve the need to pay higher interest rates.[10]

## KEY POINTS

- Management can use the theory of capital structure as a guide for estimating the costs of raising funds from different sources (i.e., new equity or debt).
- According to the theory of capital structure, raising additional equity funds results in a decline in the debt-equity ratio, further resulting in a lower discount rate applied to all the outstanding equity. An increase in the debt-equity ratio resulting from the sale of additional risk-free debt results in a higher discount rate applied to the equity but will not affect the rate applied to the debt. Issuing additional risky debt will typically increase the cost of debt financing.
- In issuing new equity, management should set the terms of the offering in such a way that the existing stockholders reap the capital gains from the expansion, while new stockholders obtain just the appropriate market rate of return on their investment.
- Management attempting to price a new equity issue on the basis of the pre-existing cost of equity capital could lead to setting the asking price for the new shares too low. This kind of error would work to the detriment of the existing stockholders.
- The timing of new issues becomes a question requiring management consideration because it involves balancing the trade-off between issuing securities on a regular basis due to the effect of size on interest costs on the one hand, and

[10] As with the bond refunding and flotation problems, stochastic dynamic programming can be used to compute the best ways of deviating from target capital structures over time.

reducing the number of new issues due to the fixed costs associated with each issuance.

- In order to minimize the impacts of transactions costs and differential tax rates, investors might prefer that the firm adopt a specific debt-equity ratio.

- Because of the need to time new issues, management may not be able to adhere exactly to the optimal proportions of debt and equity at all points in time. It will instead stipulate its optimal structure as a target and aim to approach the target as closely as possible given the limitations to and costs of raising funds.

- If management believes that it can only issue a limited amount in a given time period (at or near market rates of interest), management may wish to maintain emergency borrowing powers and hence limit the debt-equity ratio for this reason also.

- Bankruptcy proceedings in the United States are governed by the bankruptcy code. A reorganization under Chapter 11 of the code involves changing the firm's capital structure, while a liquidation under Chapter 7 of the code involves the sale of the firm's assets and payment of the proceeds to various classes of investors.

- Bankruptcy proceedings can be both lengthy and expensive and lead to indirect costs that make it difficult for management to operate the firm and thereby have an adverse impact on new operating income.

- How management adjusts to technical insolvency will depend both on whether management tries to enhance either their own positions or those of the debt-holders, as well as on the countervailing actions taken by stockholders.

- Restrictive covenants are constraints accepted by the firm's management as a part of the terms of raising debt, the purpose of which is to protect bondholders from having their wealth positions diminished by the actions of stockholders.

- A dividend policy specifies the basis on which a corporation intends to pay cash dividends to shareholders.

- Management will periodically repurchase the firm's common stock from their shareholders via a tender offer, open market purchases, or a targeted block repurchase.

- The major reasons for stock repurchase are: (1) it is a means to distribute cash to shareholders at a lower cost to both the firm and the shareholders than dividends, resulting in favorable capital gains tax treatment compared to payment of cash dividends; (2) it will increase earnings per share; (3) it could tilt the debt-equity ratio so as to increase the value of the company; (4) it reduces total dividend payments because the corporation can still pay the same amount of dividends per share, but the total dividend payments are reduced; and (5) it may reduce agency costs by reducing the amount of cash management has on hand.

- A number of studies have found that the market reacts by increasing the share price when a firm announces it is going to repurchase its own shares.

- A preemptive right grants current shareholders the right to purchase some proportion of new shares issued at a price below market value.

- In the event of a preemptive rights offering, management must first offer new stock to current shareholders.

- If a preemptive rights offering can be structured to dispense with the services of an investment banker, there is savings in transaction costs. However, the issuing corporation may still use the services of an investment banker for distributing, via a standby underwriting arrangement, any common stock that is not subscribed.
- The rights granted to existing shareholders have a value that can be captured by selling the rights in the market.
- The terms of a preemptive rights offering must be designed carefully with the risk of a rights offering failing depending on the value of the right relative to the volatility of the stock price. In turn, the value of the right (given the shares to be issued) depends on the discount chosen by management in designing the issue.
- By selecting an appropriately high discount and resulting value of the right, the issuer can make the probability of failure as small as desired so that in general the rights offering can be so designed that the services of an investment banker are not needed.

## QUESTIONS

1. Consider a firm in a two-period (time 1 and time 2) setting with the following distribution of earnings at time 2:

| State | Probability | Earnings ($t = 2$) |
|---|---|---|
| 1 | 0.5 | $2,300 |
| 2 | 0.5 | $ 920 |

Suppose the firm value at time 1 is the earnings discounted at 15% and the firm has issued $400 debt with an interest rate of 10%. Assume there is no corporate tax.

a. What is the discount rate applied by the market on equity?

b. If the market value of a share of equity is $1, how many shares are there in the market?

c. Suppose that management can raise $400 of additional capital and that by raising those funds the firm can expand its earnings distribution to:

| State | Probability | Earnings ($t = 2$) |
|---|---|---|
| 1 | 0.5 | $2,990 |
| 2 | 0.5 | $1,196 |

What is the discount rate applied by the market on equity?

d. If the management decides to finance the needed $400 capital by issuing new shares and it wants the existing shareholders to have the entire capital gains from the expansion, how should management set the price and the number of shares of the new shares?

  **e.** What will be the price of new issuance if management still uses the old cost of equity capital—the result of part a? Why is using the old cost of equity capital not good for the existing shareholders?

**2.** List a few factors that make the timing and frequency of the issuance of new debt securities important for management.

**3.** What is the major difference between Chapter 7 and Chapter 11 of the U.S. bankruptcy code?

**4.** Explain how operating decisions of management may be affected by the probability of the firm's technical insolvency and why the magnitude of the influence may depend on whether management is more self-interest oriented or more shareholder-oriented.

**5.** What is meant by restrictive covenants?

**6.**  **a.** What is a dividend reinvestment plan?
  **b.** What is the benefit of this plan to the firm and to the shareholders?

**7.**  **a.** What are stock splits and stock dividends?
  **b.** If a firm's stock price is $120 and the number of existing shares is 1 million, what will be the number of shares and share price after a 3:1 stock split?
  **c.** What will be the number of shares and share price after a 100% stock dividend? Alternatively, how much stock dividend should the company issue to have the same effect as a 3:1 stock split?

**8.** There are three common methods for a company to repurchase its stock. What are these three methods? Explain each method briefly.

**9.** List a few reasons why corporations repurchase their stock.

**10.** Suppose the market price of Corporation ABC's stock is $30 per share and that there are 40,000 shares outstanding. Suppose the company's management is considering a preemptive rights offering in connection with the issuance of 10,000 shares. Each current shareholder would receive one right for every four shares owned. The terms of the rights offering are as follows: For four rights and $25 (the subscription price) a new share can be acquired.

 **a.** What is a preemptive right?
 **b.** What is the value per right?
 **c.** Often a rights offering is designed to have a relatively high value per right. What is the firm's consideration behind it?

**11.** Contingency planning relates to capital structure decisions in two ways: (i) maintaining a reserve of liquid assets over the short run and (ii) maintaining reserve financing capacity over somewhat longer time periods. What are the benefits and costs of each?

## REFERENCES

Almeida, Heitor, and Thomas Philippon. (2007). "The Risk-Adjusted Cost of Financial Distress," *Journal of Finance* **62**: 2557–2586.

Billett, Matthew T., Tao-Hsien Dolly King, and David C. Mauer. (2007). "Growth Opportunities and the Choice of Leverage, Debt Maturity, and Covenants," *Journal of Finance* **62**: 697–730.

Copeland, Thomas E., and J. Fred Weston. (1979). *Financial Theory and Corporate Policy.* Reading, MA: Addison-Wesley.

DeAngelo, Harry, Linda DeAngelo, and Toni M. Whited. (2009). "Capital Structure Dynamics and Transitory Debt," available at http://ssrn.com/abstract=1262464.

Jensen, Michael, and William Meckling. (1976). "Theory of the Firm: Managerial Behavior, Agency Costs, and Ownership Structure," *Journal of Financial Economics* **3**: 305–360.

Leary, Mark T. (2009). "Bank Loan Supply, Lender Choice, and Corporate Capital Structure," *Journal of Finance* **64**: 1143–1185.

Lewis, Craig M., and Patrick Verwijmeren. (2009). "Convertible Design and Contract Innovation," Available at SSRN: http://ssrn.com/abstract=1352503.

Rauh, Joshua D., and Amir Sufi. (2008). "Capital Structure and Debt Structure," NBER Working Paper 14488.

Van Horne, James C. (1977). *Financial Management and Policy* (4th ed.). Englewood Cliffs, NJ: Prentice-Hall.

# 24

# Financial Contracting and Deal Terms

*I*n Chapter 7, we described deal terms. Corporate management in need of external funds must design and negotiate terms with financiers. The formalization of the terms of the agreement between the supplier and demander of funds is memorialized in a contract. The process is referred to as *financial contracting*.[1] The literature on financial contracting seeks to explain what kinds of deals are made between financiers and corporate management and helps us understand why different forms of contractual relations are observed in practice between firms and financiers (i.e., investor groups). Basically, financial contracting seeks the optimal security design for overcoming conflicts between financiers and those entities seeking funding. Much of the focus in the application of financial contracting has not been on large public firms but, instead, primarily on small entrepreneurial firms.

We first explain how the informational conditions under which a deal (i.e., a financing) is originated—and the likely evolution of that information—have important implications for selecting deal terms. When deals are arranged under risk, they can be formulated as complete contracts. In addition, when they are arranged under conditions of symmetric information, it is relatively easy to select appropriate terms. However, if the deals are arranged under conditions of information asymmetry, they usually present potential complications of moral hazard and adverse selection. Each can be governed effectively, but at the expense of incurring additional costs. Finally, when deals are arranged under uncertainty, the contracts are necessarily incomplete, and as a result their governance requires different methods and terms.

We also examine how deal terms are used to fine-tune agreements between a financier and the management of a firm seeking funding. The discussion emphasizes the financier's perspective, since typically a financier proposes a standard set of terms to be negotiated. If the management of a firm seeking funds finds the terms generally acceptable, management may propose additional negotiation to resolve any remaining differences. As negotiations proceed, the financier may also propose additional

---

[1] For a survey of financial contracting, see Roberts and Sufi (2009).

conditions intended to enhance the deal's safety, profitability, or both. Finally, if both parties are agreed on the conditions, the deal will be struck and the financing extended.

## 24.1 Costs of Deals

Deals with differing attributes will usually be arranged at differing interest rates in order to compensate for the risk or uncertainty involved. The difference between the effective interest rate[2] charged to a firm and the interest cost of funds to the financier will vary according to the deal's particular attributes, the governance capabilities of the financier, and the competitiveness of the environment in which the financing is arranged. For example, a market exchange of bonds is usually a risky deal based on information publicly available to both parties. In such a transaction the difference between financiers' total interest cost and the effective rate paid by the firm will not usually be large, especially if the market is competitive. On the other hand, financing a new business venture represents a deal under uncertainty, and the parties are likely to have quite different information about possible payoffs. The interest premium for facing uncertainty, and for incurring transactions and information processing costs, is therefore likely to be greater —in some cases very much greater—than in the bond deal. Moreover, the markets for financing business ventures are not as likely to be competitive, meaning that financier profit margins will likely be higher than in the first example.

### 24.1.1 Transactions Costs

The client seeking financing considers both direct and indirect costs in assessing a deal's total transactions costs. Direct costs are those the client pays to the financier. Indirect costs are those paid to others, but the outlays still comprise part of management's expenses. For example, the owner of a small business might look long and hard to find someone interested in investing long-term capital in his business, and would have to bear the costs of continuing to search for an accommodating financier until one is found.

From the financier's point of view, a deal's costs include the financier's costs of raising the funds, the marginal costs of assessing the deal, a contribution to the financier's fixed costs, and an allowance for a profit margin. The magnitude of the charges depends on the financier's efficiency, the competitiveness of the market served, and the kind of deal information that must be obtained, both at the outset when the deal is being negotiated (*ex ante* information obtained by screening) and subsequently as the deal is being worked through (*ex post* information obtained from monitoring). If a financier is to stay in business over the longer term, all costs must be recovered, whether through interest charges, explicit fees, or a combination of the two.

### 24.1.2 Screening and Monitoring Costs

*Screening costs* are the *ex ante* costs a financier incurs to assess a funding proposal, while *monitoring costs* are the *ex post* costs involved in the deal's continuing governance. Since

---

[2] Although some of the charges may actually be specified as lump sums, for comparative purposes it is usually convenient to convert them to effective interest rates.

screening costs are usually the sum of a fixed set-up cost and an *ex ante* variable cost, the average cost of screening individual deals can be expected to decline as the number of deals screened increases. The same is likely to be true of monitoring costs.

The average cost of administering a deal is the sum of its screening and monitoring cost, along with the cost of making any adjustments that monitoring indicates would be desirable. While scale economies explain why this average cost function will likely decline with transaction volume, other factors can affect the function's position and how it is likely to shift. First, the position of the screening cost function will be higher for deals with greater informational differences between clients and financier. Second, the screening cost function may shift downward as financiers gain experience with a particular type of deal and, thereby, learn how to screen it more efficiently. Monitoring costs differ according to the kinds of informational differences involved, and a financier's monitoring cost function can also shift as a result of learning. Finally, as shown in both this chapter and in Chapter 21 where we discussed markets with impediments to arbitrage, both screening and monitoring costs can be greater in deals where it is necessary to manage the effects of asymmetric information.

The potential volume of a given deal type is determined by the intersection of the demand and supply curves for the financing type. If demand from businesses is relatively great, many deals are likely to be completed, and per deal screening costs will be low because financiers can take advantage of both scale economies and learning effects. However, the economics of screening can work to deter the entry of a new supplier to a market, especially if the cost function shifts downward as the number of completed deals increases. In such circumstances, the financier who first enters a market can gain a first mover advantage over subsequent entrants, particularly if the skills the financier acquires are experiential and therefore difficult to communicate.[3] Potential new entrants may not be willing to set up innovative financing arrangements because they see existing financiers as having entrenched advantages that are difficult to overcome.

The economics of screening can also work to inhibit the viability of new deals. First, financiers have to incur costs to determine whether the deal is viable. Moreover, financiers' perceptions of economic viability depend in part on the skills they have already acquired. To illustrate, there are high fixed costs to setting up venture capital firms, both because the personnel in a new firm need to learn how to screen prospects, and because any one person can only supervise a limited number of venture investments. Even if a venture firm has some personnel with screening experience, their skills are acquired principally through experience rather than in a classroom setting. As a result any new employees have to gain similar experience, and at any given time existing firms may not be able to accommodate the entire market's demands for financing. Nevertheless, unless there is enough unsatisfied demand to cover the fixed costs of setting up a new firm, the supply deficiency may persist.

---

[3] Practical knowledge—"know-how"—can be more difficult to transmit than theoretical knowledge—"know-why."

## 24.2 Informational Conditions

The information available to a financier affects his estimate of a deal's profitability and determines the kinds of reports he will require from the client. When financiers take on familiar deals, they are likely to treat the transactions routinely, especially in the absence of informational asymmetries. For example, the purchaser of a U.S. Treasury bill has access to almost all potentially relevant information when the purchase is made. On the other hand, the venture capitalist investing in a growing firm has much less precise *ex ante* information, particularly when the firm's principal asset is the talent of its owner-manager. Moreover, the venture capitalist is much more likely to refine *ex post* estimates of firm's potential profitability over the investment's life than is the purchaser of a Treasury bill.

If a financier has less information than her client, she will try to determine whether it is cost-effective to obtain more details. If he thinks it would be, he may incorporate his informational requirements in the terms of the deal, as illustrated later in this chapter when we discuss the renegotiation of a bank loan. Some information may be available *ex ante* while other information may only be obtainable *ex post*. For example, a retail client borrowing against accounts receivable might be asked to submit quarterly statements of accounts receivable outstanding, thus keeping fresh the lender's information about the quality of the security.

### 24.2.1 Information and Contract Types

As Table 24.1 indicates, financiers select governance mechanisms according to each deal's informational conditions. Deals arranged under risk are easier to govern than deals under uncertainty, because they present situations in which complete contracting is possible. The terms of deals arranged under uncertainty cannot usually be specified quantitatively. For example, if the relevant states of nature are observable but not verifiable, it will not be possible to write a complete contract. In still more complex situations it may not even be possible to define the relevant states of nature.

Financings arranged under uncertainty usually provide for the exercise of discretion to compensate for contract incompleteness. For example, the arrangements may provide for relatively intensive monitoring over the deal's life, as well as for flexibility of response to evolving information. If an unforeseen contingency does occur, it may not have been possible to specify in advance what the appropriate

TABLE 24.1
DEAL ATTRIBUTES AND GOVERNANCE STRUCTURES

| Informational Attribute | Governance Structure |
| --- | --- |
| Risk | Complete contract. Rule based; little or no provision for monitoring and subsequent control. |
| Uncertainty | Incomplete contract. Structure allows for discretionary governance. Details of monitoring and control are typically negotiated. |

adjustments would be.[4] Basically, there is a relationship between management and financiers that is not static but changes over time. Over the course of time, future states of the world may be redefined, or contingencies may arise that could not have easily been foreseen at the time a financial contract was entered into. A contract between the parties that has these attributes (i.e., fail to specify all future contingencies and thereby the consequences to the parties) is called an *incomplete contract*. Many such incomplete contracts are expressed in terms of the principles to be followed in making adjustments if and when the need for them becomes apparent. Hart (2001) observes that one way of coping with such eventualities is through different forms of financial structure. For example, equity gives shareholders decision rights if the firm is solvent, but debt gives creditors those decision rights if the firm is in bankruptcy.[5]

Another possibility is that whatever financial instrument is used, a preamble to the contract may state principles for renegotiation under certain general conditions that by necessity cannot be well specified in advance since the future is "simply too unclear" (Hart 2001, p. 1,083). The possibility of renegotiation implies that financiers' governance costs will increase, and the increased costs will only be warranted if financiers believe they can reduce possible losses at least commensurately. Financiers will also seek larger interest rate premiums for bearing what they perceive to be greater degrees of uncertainty, and will attempt to recover these costs and premiums from firms seeking funding. As a result, the firm presenting a highly risky deal can expect to pay a higher effective interest rate than a firm presenting a less risky deal, and a firm presenting a deal under uncertainty can expect to pay a higher effective interest rate than a firm presenting a deal under risk.

## 24.2.2 Informational Asymmetries

While informational asymmetries are not unknown in public market transactions, they have greater importance in private market and in intermediated transactions, mainly because they are more difficult to resolve in the absence of active market trading. Indeed, in intermediated transactions informational differences may persist even after intensive screening. First, financiers and a firm seeking funds may differ in their estimates of a deal's profitability, in part because they have different information processing capabilities. Second, the parties may have the same *ex ante* information about a deal, but their ability to keep informed about its progress may differ. Finally, financiers are well aware that firms seeking funds sometimes provide biased information in attempts to improve the financing terms they can obtain.

---

[4] As a practical problem, it may be difficult to detect whether or not a contract is incomplete, since it can be difficult to determine whether unanticipated contingencies have arisen

[5] Note how the financial contracting perspective differs from the MM theory of capital structure. In the MM theory, it is assumed that the firm's cash flows are given and debt and equity are then characterized by the type of claim on those cash flows. This is also true in the case of the agency explanation proffered by Jensen and Meckling (1976) described in Chapter 23, but the distribution of the firm's cash flows impact the value of a firm via the types of incentives established for management. Despite the fact that control and rights are important to management, both the MM theory and the incentive theory fail to take into account these factors.

It is much more difficult to reach a satisfactory agreement when financiers and a firm seeking funds differ greatly over a project's viability than it is when they share the same view. If the asymmetries are great enough, it may only be possible to do the deal at nonmarket interest rates. In other cases, it may not be possible to reach agreement at any interest rate. For example, in the early 1980s opinion regarding the value of the troubled Continental Illinois Bank's loan portfolio varied so greatly that counterparties found it difficult to agree on a mutually satisfactory price for the bank's shares. As a second example, the parties attempting to exchange mortgage-backed securities collateralized by subprime loan portfolios in 2007 and 2008 found that, as the instruments became increasingly illiquid, getting any estimate of the value of these securities was difficult.

Sufi and Mian (2009) explore some of the ways that information asymmetry influences loan syndicate structure and membership.[6] First, lead bank and borrower reputation mitigates, but does not eliminate information asymmetry problems. Moreover and consistent with moral hazard in monitoring, the syndicate's lead bank both retains a larger share of the loan and invites fewer other syndicate members when the borrower requires more intense monitoring. When information asymmetry is potentially severe, accommodating lenders are likely closer to the borrower, both geographically and in terms of previous lending relationships. The models presented in the rest of this chapter further illustrate some of the ways financiers attempt to cope with the effects of informational asymmetries.

## 24.2.3 Third-Party Information

Financiers can sometimes reduce information costs through purchasing information rather than producing it in-house. Deal information will be provided by third parties if they can turn a profit doing so. For example, rating agencies like Moody's, Standard & Poor's, and Fitch monitor the creditworthiness of public companies' debt issues and publish their ratings. Companies seeking funds will pay to be rated if by so doing they can reduce their financing costs more than commensurately. Benson (1979) argues that by producing bond rating information and then finding investors interested in purchasing the bonds, underwriters can reduce financing costs to less than they would be if buyers produced the information individually. In the United States, municipal bond insuring agencies serve as another type of information producer.

Even though information is collected and used privately by the insurers, other members of the investing public may interpret the issuance of an insurance policy as a signal regarding the municipality's creditworthiness. Similarly, Fama (1985) argues that short-term bank lending may signal a borrowing firm's quality, and that a bank's willingness to extend short-term financing may reduce the firm's total financing costs. As still another example, when a portfolio of loans is securitized, it is quite common for a third party to insure the securities issued against such events as default on their principal amount. In effect, the insurance amounts to a third-party

---

[6] See Web-Appendix B for a description of syndicated loans.

rating of the default risk in the loan portfolio backing the issuance of the new instruments.

## 24.2.4 Asymmetries and Financing Choice: Debt versus Equity

Many writers have addressed the question of why firms use both debt and equity financing. The famous Modigliani-Miller (MM) theorem establishes conditions under which there is no advantage to using one rather than the other. Recall that MM argue that if there are no taxes or bankruptcy costs to defaulting on debt, then financing with a combination of debt and equity rather than with equity alone adds nothing to the value of the firm. In the circumstances envisioned by MM, debt and equity are merely ways of dividing up cash flows and different ratios of debt to equity financing neither create nor destroy firm value. However, subsequent research recognizes that taxes, bankruptcy costs, and other forms of market imperfection can explain why corporate treasurers are not indifferent to the manner in which they raise long-term finance. That is, the costs of long-term finance can be affected by differing ratios of debt to equity when taxes, bankruptcy costs, and other market imperfections are recognized as elements of the financing picture.

Ross (1977) notes that firms used both debt and equity financing even before corporate taxes were levied. Ross suggests that different levels of the debt-equity ratio can reflect management attempts to signal the quality of their firms, and that management can be motivated to signal truthfully as long as they face appropriate incentives. He shows that debt with a fixed face value and a bankruptcy penalty[7] is the optimal contract for maximizing a risk-neutral entrepreneur's expected return, given a minimum expected return to lenders. The Ross explanation is persuasive if management has personal resources to pay the bankruptcy penalties, but such a situation is not typical of an entrepreneur who has invested all available assets in his firm. In addition to Ross's explanation, debt-equity ratios can have value implications because they convey different control possibilities. Hart (2001) points out that while shareholders have decision rights as long as a firm is solvent, those decision rights pass to creditors when the firm is insolvent.

The next example shows still another effect, this time due to informational asymmetries: If financiers and entrepreneurs disagree regarding a firm's prospects, debt can come closer than equity to resolving their differences. The result is first demonstrated numerically and then considered a little more formally. Suppose both owners and financiers are risk neutral, and that interest rates are zero. Suppose also that the owners of a firm are optimistic, while financiers are pessimistic, in the sense reflected in Table 24.2. Owners expect firm earnings to be higher than do financiers; indeed, owners do not expect earnings of $4 can occur at all, and attach equal positive probability to the remaining four scenarios. Financiers do not expect that earnings of 8 are possible, but attach equal positive probability to the other remaining scenarios.

Next, consider the value of the equity in the firm, as viewed by the owner and the financier, respectively. The owner values the equity at ($8 + $7 + $6 + $5)/4 = $6.5,

---

[7] The penalty, borne by management, must be at least as great as any shortfall in the debt payment.

**TABLE 24.2**
OUTCOMES AND PROBABILITIES

| | Firm earnings ($) | Probability estimates of optimistic owner | Probability estimates of pessimistic financier |
|---|---|---|---|
| Scenario 1 | 8 | 0.25 | 0.00 |
| Scenario 2 | 7 | 0.25 | 0.25 |
| Scenario 3 | 6 | 0.25 | 0.25 |
| Scenario 4 | 5 | 0.25 | 0.25 |
| Scenario 5 | 4 | 0.00 | 0.25 |

while the financier's value is ($7 + $6 + $5 + $4)/4 = $5.5. Nevertheless, both parties would agree that the firm's promise to pay 4 can be met all of the time and, therefore, both parties would place the same time 0 value on debt[8] promising to pay $4 at time 1. That is, even though they do not agree on the firm's prospects, the two parties can agree on the value of at least this limited amount of debt.

Now suppose the firm needs to raise $5, and that financiers have the power to set the terms on which they will purchase securities. If financiers were to purchase equity that they regard as being worth $5, they would demand $5.0/$5.5 or 10/11 of the shares. However, the owners regard 10/11 of the shares as having a value of ($6.5) (10/11), or $5.91. Thus, to the owners, equity financing carries a high implicit rate of return, even in the present case where interest rates have been assumed to be zero.

Alternatively, suppose financiers propose a debt issue that promises to pay off $5.5 if the firm has the funds, or whatever funds are available if the firm does not generate cash flows at least equal to $5.5. Financiers would value this debt at ($4.0 + $5.0 + $5.5 + $5.5)/4 = $5.00. The owners, who regard the debt as worth ($5.0 + $5.5 + $5.5 + $5.5)/4 = $5.38, would still think they were paying too much for funds. However, they would also agree that the cost of debt financing was less than the cost of equity financing, since to them the value of the equity that would have to be surrendered is $5.91. Thus, while financiers and owners do not always agree on what the securities are worth, they may still be able to agree that debt reduces the differences in their valuations more than equity. As the example suggests, entrepreneurs will prefer debt to equity if the choice of instrument affects their perceptions of financing costs.

To establish the difference between debt and equity a little more formally, suppose both financiers and entrepreneurs believe the firm can generate one of two possible cash flows. Let the financiers' estimates of these flows be $y_H$ and $y_L$, while entrepreneurs' are $y_H + a$ and $y_L + a$, $a > 0$. To keep the symbolism to a minimum, suppose that financiers and entrepreneurs both believe either outcome can occur with equal probability. Financiers set the price of the instruments, but allow the entrepreneur to choose either the debt or the equity. In addition, suppose that if debt is used, financiers stipulate a repayment amount:

---

[8] This possibility is also discussed in Hart (2001, p. 1,087).

$$y_H > R > y_L$$

It will simplify the analysis to assume in addition that:

$$R > y_L > (y_H - y_L)/2 \tag{24.1}$$

The second inequality in equation (24.1) implies that $y_H < 3y_L$, that is, for purposes of the present analysis the difference between high and low payoffs is limited.

Continuing to assume that financiers accept an interest rate of zero, financiers value the debt instrument at $(y_L + R)/2$. Financiers are also willing to provide equity financing, as long as the proportion of the equity they can obtain has a current market value equal to that of the debt with promised repayment $R$. In order to have the same value as the debt, the proportion of equity issued, $\alpha$, must satisfy:

$$(y_L + R)/2 = \alpha(y_L + y_H)/2$$

Solving the last equation for $\alpha$ gives:

$$\alpha \equiv (y_L + R)/(y_L + y_H) \tag{24.2}$$

Using equation (24.1), equation (24.2) implies:

$$\alpha(y_L + y_H)/2 = (y_L + R)/2 > y_L/2 + (y_H - y_L)/4 = (y_L + y_H)/4 \tag{24.3}$$

so that $\alpha > 1/2$. Then for any repayment $R < y_H$ the borrower's valuation of the debt is less than the borrower's valuation of the equity, as shown by:

$$(y_L + R + a)/2 = \alpha(y_L + y_H)/2 + a/2 < \alpha(y_L + y_H)/2 + 2\alpha a/2$$
$$= \alpha(y_L + y_H + 2a)/2 \tag{24.4}$$

Since financiers will advance the same amount of funds whether debt or equity is offered, the borrower will prefer to use debt, since from the borrower's point of view it lowers financing costs. The argument can be generalized to more outcomes, different probabilities, and more complex differences in the payoff distribution, but for present purposes the simple assumptions used above are sufficient to illustrate the point.

While in the last example the client is assumed to have more information than the financier, the opposite can sometimes be true. Axelson (2007) studies security design when investors rather than managers have private information about the firm, and argues that in such cases it can be optimal to issue equity. A "folklore proposition of debt" from traditional signaling models says that the firm should issue the least information-sensitive security possible, that is, standard debt. However, Axelson finds this proposition to be valid only if the firm can vary the face value of the debt as investor demand varies. If a firm has several assets, debt backed by a pool of the assets is more beneficial for the firm when the degree of competition among investors is low, but equity backed by individual assets is more beneficial when competition is high.

# 24.3 MORAL HAZARD[9]

Moral hazard, a classic consequence of informational asymmetries, frequently affects relations between a financier and an individual client.[10] For example, if a financier does not take appropriate precautions, a firm seeking funds may use the proceeds of a debt issue to substitute a riskier project for the one originally proposed to the financier. The incentive to substitute a riskier project arises from the fact that, unless detected, shareholders of the firm would receive greater benefits from the substitution, while debt holders would bear greater risk. The following model of moral hazard analyzes a complete contract drawn up under conditions of risk.

## 24.3.1 Avoiding Moral Hazard

Consider a situation in which a borrower might substitute a bad project for a good one unless the lender takes steps to prevent it. Suppose that without any preventive measures the lender who advances the single unit of capital needed to implement a project has no further control over the type of project actually chosen. Suppose there is a good project that pays off either $G$ with probability $p_G$; or zero with probability $(1 - p_G)$. There is also a bad project that pays off $B$ with probability $p_B$ or zero with probability $(1 - p_B)$. Suppose in addition that $p_G > 1 > p_B$, so that the good project has the higher expected value. Assume also that the interest rate is zero, the expected present value of the good project positive, and that of the bad project negative. Suppose finally that $B > G$, so that the owners of the firm could benefit from adopting the riskier project. The foregoing assumptions imply $p_G > p_B$, but depending on the size of the repayment, the owners of the firm may find themselves better off by choosing the bad project. They may be able to reap large rewards if the bad project succeeds, and it will be the financiers who suffer if it does not succeed.

The owners of the firm only face an incentive to choose the good project if they will be better off doing so after taking the size of the loan repayment into account. That is, the firm will choose the good project if:

$$p_G(G - R) > p_B(B - R)$$

This last, incentive, condition defines a critical value $R_C$ for the amount of repayment:

$$R < R_C \equiv [p_G G - p_B B]/(p_G - p_B)$$

---

[9] The section "Moral Hazard," and those that follow—"Complete Contracts" and "Incomplete Contracts"—are based on models developed in Freixas and Rochet (1997). Arrow (1974) observes that moral hazard is present in nearly all types of insurance contracts, and suggests that direct control over the actions of the insured and co-insurance are possible ways of mitigating its effects.

[10] In contrast, the adverse selection problem discussed in Chapter 20 affects dealings between a financier and an entire class of fund-seeking firms.

FIGURE 24.1
## FIGURE 24.1
INCENTIVES FOR PROJECT CHOICE VERSUS SIZE OF REPAYMENT

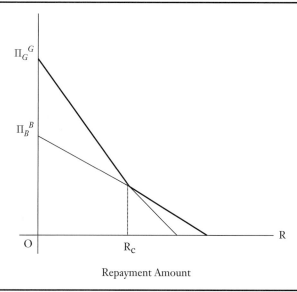

Repayment Amount

*Note:* O- $R_C$: region in which borrower has an incentive to choose the good project.

Note that since $G < B$, the last line also implies that $R_C < G$: The financier cannot demand too high a repayment (i.e., too high an effective interest rate) without creating the possibility that the firm will substitute the bad project for the good one. Figure 24.1 indicates the situation from the firm's point of view. Of course, the repayment that the lender can charge must also be high enough for the lender to profit in an expected value sense. If not, the lender will decline the financing application.[11]

## 24.3.2  Incentives to Repay

Some financiers recognize that gradual revelation of information can be used to their advantage. For example, moral hazard problems can be mitigated if firms with good repayment records can obtain additional funds at lower cost. John and Nachman (1985) show that when a firm has to return repeatedly to the market for financing, it will benefit from considering the effects of its repayment choices on both current and future securities prices.

If the contingencies can be defined in advance, they can be incorporated in the original, complete contract. To illustrate, suppose that firms and financiers are both risk neutral, that the interest rate is zero, and that firms have no initial resources. In each period a firm adopting an investment project will generate a random income $y$, and the possible realizations of $y$ are respectively $y_G$ and $y_B$. If a lender cannot observe

---

[11] Other models can be developed in which the bank can use costly monitoring to ensure that firms do not adopt the bad technology.

**TABLE 24.3**

FIRM CASH FLOWS

A. Time 2 Cash Flows and Payments to Financier

| Time 1 | Time 2 Realized Cash Flow | Time 2 Payments to Financier |
|---|---|---|
| $L$ advanced | $y_B$ | $y_B$ —Arrangement terminated at the end of time 2 since first scheduled repayment not made in full. |
| | $y_G$ | $R$ —A second amount $L$ is advanced since first scheduled repayment made in full. |

B. Times 2 and 3 Cash Flows and Payments to Financier

| Time 2 and Time 3 Realized Cash Flows | Time 2 and Time 3 Payments to Financier |
|---|---|
| $(y_B, y_B)$ | $(y_B, 0)$ |
| $(y_B, y_G)$ | $(y_B, 0)$ |
| $(y_G, y_B)$ | $(R, y_B)$ |
| $(y_G, y_G)$ | $(R, y_B)$ |

the cash flow, the most it will lend in an unsecured single period arrangement is $y_B$. If it were to lend more, the borrower could claim he had only earned $y_B$, and consequently repay only that amount.

Now consider a contract the lender agrees to renew for a second period whenever the borrower makes a payment of more than $y_B$ at the end of the first. However, if only $y_B$ is paid at the end of the first period, the arrangement will be terminated immediately. Assuming there are only two periods, the firm has no incentive to maintain a good reputation after time 2 has passed. Thus, if it has the cash flow to do so, the firm will make a payment larger than $y_B$ at time 2, but not at time 3. The arrangement is detailed in the two parts of Table 24.3.

The lender's expected profit from this arrangement is:

$$\pi = -L + (1 - p_G)y_B + p_G(R + y_B - L) \tag{24.5}$$

as may be determined from Table 24.3. Equation (24.5) can be rewritten as:

$$\pi = -L + y_B + p_G(R - L) \tag{24.6}$$

The lender will profit if $R$ is large enough to ensure that $\pi \geq 0$. The entrepreneur will enter the arrangement if $R$ is small enough that she makes a profit when things turn out well for the firm at time 2; that is, if

$$-R + p_G(y_G - y_B) \geq -y_B \tag{24.7}$$

which is equivalent to:

$$R \leq y_B + p_G(y_G - y_B) = E(Y) \tag{24.8}$$

Any repayment that satisfies both the lender's profit condition and the borrower's incentive conditions will constitute a viable arrangement.

## 24.3.3 Collateral as a Screening Device

Contracts providing for collateral can be used as screening devices to mitigate the effects of informational asymmetries. Suppose loan contracts take the form $(C_k, R_k)$ where $C_k$ is the amount of collateral required, $R_k$ is the corresponding repayment, and $k$ is the type of firm entering the contract, $k \in \{G, B\}$. The symbols $G$ and $B$ refer to firms with good and bad quality projects, respectively. The good project pays off $y$ with a relatively high success probability $p_G$, or 0 with probability $1 - p_G$. The riskier, bad project $B$ pays off $y$ with a relatively low success probability $p_B$ or 0 with probability $1 - p_B$. The risk of the project is defined by its success probability, and borrowers know which type of project they have.

In all except the first instance examined below, lenders do not know which type of project the borrower has selected. All the bargaining power, that is, the power to set terms, is assumed to reside with the lender. The amount the borrower will be required to repay depends on the amount of collateral taken: $R_k = R_k(C_k)$. If the project succeeds, then the realized cash flow is $y$, the lender is repaid $R_k$, and the borrower keeps $y - R_k$. If the project fails, then the realized cash flow is zero, the borrower loses the posted collateral $C_k$, and the financier realizes $\delta C_k$, $0 < \delta < 1$.

If the lender could observe the success probability $p_k$, she would set the repayment amount and collateral so that the borrower's remaining income would just be:

$$p_k(y - R_k) - (1 - p_k)C_k = \pi_{k,\min} \tag{24.9}$$

where $\pi_{k,\min}$ is the minimum amount the borrower must earn in order to undertake the project. Assume that the repayment amount is enough to make the deal attractive to the lender as well. If the lender could not observe $p_k$, the best she could do is to earn an average profit dependent on the proportion of good and bad borrowers who might apply. The proportion will depend on the repayment required. If the repayment amount were sufficiently high, only the bad borrowers would find it worthwhile to apply for financing.

Lender profits can be improved by setting up a contract that will both induce good borrowers to post collateral and induce bad borrowers not to misrepresent themselves as good borrowers. In order for a contract to provide the correct incentives, it must specify repayments $R_G$, $R_B$, and collateral $C_G$, such that it pays type B (high-risk) borrowers to declare themselves honestly as high risk:

$$p_B(y - R_B) \geq p_B(y - R_G) - (1 - p_B)C_G \tag{24.10}$$

At the same time the terms must be such that type $G$ borrowers find it worth their while to declare themselves low risk and post the collateral to back up their declaration:

$$p_G(y - R_G) - (1 - p_G)C_G \geq \pi_{G,\min} \tag{24.11}$$

Inequality (24.11) indicates that the amounts realized by a borrower must exceed her opportunity cost $\pi_{G,\min}$. The repayment $R_G$ required of borrowers declaring themselves to be of good quality will be less than the repayment $R_B$, which means the low-risk borrowers pay a lower effective interest rate. In essence, low-risk borrowers bet they will not fail, post collateral to indicate their confidence, and thereby qualify for a lower interest rate than that paid by high-risk borrowers. High-risk borrowers do not take the same arrangement because to do so they would have to post collateral that, according to their private information, they have a high probability of losing.

---

### 24.4  Complete Contracts

Qian and Strahan (2007) find that in countries with strong creditor protection, bank loans have more concentrated ownership, longer maturities, and lower interest rates. The authors argue that more credit can be extended and on more generous terms when lenders have more credible threats in the event of default. Similar research shows a wide variety in choices of loan terms, but a complete discussion of variations is beyond the scope of this survey. Instead, this section illustrates two elementary choices based on complete contracts. The succeeding companion section provides similar illustrations for incomplete contracts.

#### 24.4.1  Costly Verification

There is a body of literature based on *costly verification* where the design of an optimal contract between firms seeking external funds and financiers is assessed assuming that the profitability of a firm is private information. Although private, the information can be made public at a cost.

Suppose financiers cannot directly observe the firm's cash flow. As a result, financiers must either accept the realized cash flow value as reported by the firm, or conduct a costly audit. It will be worthwhile for financiers to conduct the audit if that costs less than the benefits expected to be gained from the verification. For example, suppose the borrower could report a cash flow $y_R$, even though she actually realized $y > y_R$. The financier could detect a propensity to report falsely by stipulating a repayment function and by designing an audit rule. If the firm's cash flow report is audited, the financier incurs a fixed cost $\gamma$; otherwise auditing costs are zero.

Clearly, an audit rule cannot be efficient unless it minimizes expected audit costs. A first requirement for managing audit costs is to conduct an audit only if repayment is not made in full. A second requirement is to minimize expected auditing costs by writing the contract for a fixed repayment, and setting the repayment size so as to minimize the probability of having to conduct an audit. If both parties are risk neutral, such a debt contract will be both incentive compatible and efficient so long as the firm is required to pay all reportedly available cash flows whenever the announcement is less than the full amount of scheduled debt repayment.[12]

## 24.4.2 Incentives to Report Honestly

Financiers can also try to design incentives for the borrower to report cash flows honestly. Suppose the borrower can be penalized for false reporting, using the penalty function:

$$\gamma(y, y_R) = \gamma|y - y_R| \tag{24.12}$$

where $y$ is the actual cash flow, $y_R$ the reported cash flow, and $\gamma$ the proportional cost the borrower incurs if she does not report truthfully.[13] If $0 < \gamma < 1$, the borrower receives the realized cash flow, less the repayment (based on the reported cash flow) and less any penalty for not reporting truthfully:

$$\pi_B = y - R(y_R) - \gamma|y - y_R| \tag{24.13}$$

The function $R(y_R)$ represents the repayment to the lender. This mechanism is falsification proof if it is maximized at $y_R = y$, a situation that will occur if and only if:

$$-\gamma \le R(y) \le \gamma \tag{24.14}$$

That is, the borrower faces an incentive to report truthfully if the amount by which repayment increases in $y$ is less than the amount by which the penalty increases in $y$.

By limited liability, $R(0) = 0$, which along with equation (24.14) means:

$$R(y) \le \gamma y \tag{24.15}$$

In turn, equation (24.15) means the lender cannot expect to be repaid more than $\gamma E(y)$. Then if $L$ is the original amount lent and $r$ the interest rate, the lender must also ensure that:

$$(1 + r)L \le \gamma E(y)$$

If the borrower is risk averse and the lender risk neutral, the optimal form of repayment is a call option[14] on the cash flow:

$$R(y) = \max(0, \gamma y - \alpha)$$

where $\alpha$ is some positive constant. This contract provides incentives for truthful reporting and can be shown to minimize the probability that it will be necessary to audit the firm if the financier is to receive the expected value of the contract. For

---

[12] See Freixas and Rochet (2008).

[13] The model assumes the penalty will be paid if the borrower reports falsely. However, it does not stipulate how false reporting is detected, or how the penalty is actually collected.

[14] If $\alpha = 0$, the call option has the same payoff as a proportion of the firm's equity.

example, an audit will only be conducted if $\gamma R \leq \alpha/\gamma$; that is, if the borrower does not make the loan payment in full and the financier assumes control of the firm. If $y > \alpha/\gamma$, it is in the borrower's interest to make the scheduled repayment, since that maximize the amount of the proceeds he can retain.

### • • •   24.5   INCOMPLETE CONTRACTS: INTRODUCTION

Diamond (2004) stresses that lenders can face difficulties in legal systems with ineffective enforcement, but if lenders do not attempt to collect from defaulting borrowers, the borrowers have greater incentives to default. Diamond argues that bank lenders would be more prone to enforce penalties if news about defaulting borrowers were to cause bank runs. In other words, tough collection schemes can help banks to retain depositor confidence.

In this section we provide models of such schemes. It first shows how renegotiation can improve bondholder payoffs when cash flows are unverifiable, and how an incomplete contract can overcome what would otherwise be market failure. Another form of incomplete contract allows a bank to renegotiate a deal and extract a greater expected profit from it than could bondholders without the same freedom to renegotiate.

### 24.5.1   Bondholder Threat to Liquidate

A credible threat can improve bondholders' expected payoffs if they were to receive less than a scheduled repayment. The threat may even be effective enough to make viable an otherwise unviable transaction. Assume both the firm and bondholders are risk neutral, and that the interest rate is zero. The firm seeks one unit of money at time 1 in order to finance a project that generates cash flows at both times 2 and 3. At both time 2 and time 3 there are two possible cash flow realizations: $y_H$ with probability $p$ or $y_L$ with probability $(1 - p)$; $y_H > y_L$. Thus, the four possible cash flow patterns over two periods are $(H, H)$, $(H, L)$, $(L, H)$, and $(L, L)$, and they occur with probabilities $p^2$, $p(1 - p)$, $(1 - p)p$ and $(1 - p)^2$, respectively.

The firm operates for two periods unless bondholders shut it down early. The two-period profile of cash flows is assumed to be completely determined at time 1, but the realized values of the flows are assumed not to be verifiable by either party, or even by both parties acting together. Therefore, no lender can write a complete contract contingent on the realized cash flow.[15]

Since interest rates are zero, the present (and the future) value of the firm equals the sum of the realized cash flows in the two periods, less the scheduled loan repayments. The realized cash flow at time 3 is zero if the firm is put out of business, and either $y_H$ or $y_L$ if the firm is allowed to continue operating in the second period. Bondholders can shut down operations after time 2 if they do not receive the full

---

[15] However, it would also be possible to stipulate that the firm would be liquidated if a contracted payment were not made at time 1. In the situation illustrated a complete contract could be written contingent on the size of the repayment received.

amount of the time 2 scheduled repayment. However, if they do receive the time 2 repayment in full, bondholders permit the firm to continue operating until time 3.

In the event of liquidation the bondholders receive the larger of the cash flow $y_L$ or the time 2 liquidation value $A_2$. The time 3 liquidation value is assumed to be $A_3 = 0$, so that the maximal amount a lender can realize at time 3 is just $y_L$. Since the bondholders cannot verify the firm's cash flow, the firm would never repay $y_H$ at time 2. If $A_1 < y_L$, a liquidation threat is not credible, since the firm cannot be forced to repay more than $y_L$. In this case, the bondholders can never expect repayment of more than $2y_L$. Since bondholders must advance 1 to finance the project, and since interest rates are assumed to be zero, the market will fail if $2y_L < 1$. The details are given in Table 24.4.

If $A_2 > y_L$, the liquidation threat is credible. Assuming that bondholders have no powers to renegotiate existing arrangements, they will shut down the firm if a scheduled time 1 payment is not made in full. In what follows we shall assume that the

**TABLE 24.4**
CASH FLOWS AND THEIR DISTRIBUTION

| | Cash Flows | Time 2 Repayments: To Bondholders, Firm | Time 3 Repayments: To Bondholders, Firm | Total Paid to Bondholders | Total Retained by Firm |
|---|---|---|---|---|---|
| **No Credible Threat** | | | | | |
| Firm always operates | $y_H, y_H$ | $y_L, y_H{-}y_L$ | $y_L, y_H{-}y_L$ | $2y_L$ | $2(y_H{-}y_L)$ |
| | $y_H, y_L$ | $y_L, y_H{-}y_L$ | $y_L, 0$ | $2y_L$ | $y_H{-}y_L$ |
| | $y_L, y_H$ | $y_L, 0$ | $y_L, y_H{-}y_L$ | $2y_L$ | $y_H{-}y_L$ |
| | $y_L, y_L$ | $y_L, 0$ | $y_L, 0$ | $2y_L$ | $0$ |
| **Credible Threat** | | | | | |
| Let firm operate | $y_H, y_H$ | $R, y_H{-}R$ | $y_L, y_H{-}y_L$ | $R+y_L$ | $2y_H{-}R{-}y_L$ |
| Shut firm down | | $A_2, 0$ | $0, 0$ | $A_2$ | $0$ |
| Let firm operate | $y_H, y_L$ | $R, y_H{-}R$ | $y_L, 0$ | $R+y_L$ | $y_H{-}R$ |
| Shut firm down | | $A_2, 0$ | $0,0$ | $A_2$ | $0$ |
| Shut firm down | $y_L, y_H$ | $A_2, 0$ | $0, 0$ | $A_2$ | $0$ |
| Shut firm down | $y_L, y_L$ | $A_2, 0$ | $0, 0$ | $A_2$ | $0$ |
| | Assume: $2y_L \le A_2 \le R+y_L$ | | | | |

liquidation value is $A_2$, such that $2y_L < A_2 < y_L + R$. A firm that is shut down at time 1 cannot earn any income at time 2. Therefore, a firm that knows its cash flows will be $(H, H)$ (remember they learn this at time 2) will want to continue operating, and will therefore make the time 2 scheduled repayment. A firm knowing its cash flows to be $(H, L)$ will not default. If the firm were to default, it would get nothing whereas if it pays $R$ the firm gets to keep $y_H - R$ from the first period, but nothing from the second period. When the firm cannot offer more than $yL$ at time 1, the bondholders will shut it down and keep $A_2$.

The ability to threaten closure means that from the lender's point of view the financing will be viable whenever

$$p(R + y_L) + (1 - p)A_2 > 1 \qquad (24.16)$$

The condition in equation (24.16) can be satisfied for sufficiently large values of both $R$ and $A_2$ even if $2y_L < 1$, creating the possibility of market failure in the absence of a credible threat. For example, if $y_L = 1/6$ and $A_2 > 2/6$, then any value of $R > A_2 - 1/6$ will satisfy condition (24.16). Thus, the threat to liquidate can sometimes make market financing viable even if inability to invoke a credible threat would imply market failure.

## 24.5.2  Renegotiating a Bank Loan

Gorton and Kahn (2000) model how a bank might renegotiate with a borrower.[16] Essentially, depending on how the borrower's business evolves, the bank stipulates a right to renegotiate the loan contract, thus permitting it to contemplate a variety of outcomes ranging from full repayment, through extension, to completely forgiving the loan. In the following model, the bank will renegotiate rather than liquidate, if the net present value of its loan repayments can be increased through restructured financing.[17]

The model has three times: 1, 2, and 3. The firm is assumed to borrow 1 at time 1, and agrees to repay $R_1$ at time 3. At time 2, both the borrower and the bank observe a (nonverifiable) signal $z$.[18] At that time a bank with a credible threat to liquidate can force renegotiation, thereby providing the firm with the incentive to choose a good investment project at time 3, and thus improve the prospects of both firm and bank. The timing is shown in Table 24.5.

---

[16] This presentation is adapted from the simplified Gorton-Kahn model developed in Freixas and Rochet (1997, pp. 114–118). The original Gorton and Kahn paper was published in 1993.

[17] This model illustrates one form of continued monitoring, a capability that is a characteristic of bank governance.

[18] If they knew a signal would be available, most lenders would insist on receiving it before agreeing to the loan. The model may therefore be more suitably applied to situations in which lenders and their clients are surprised by the arrival of new information.

**TABLE 24.5**
TIMING OF CONTRACT, RENEGOTIATION DECISION, AND PAYOFFS

| Time 1 | Time 2 | Time 3 |
|---|---|---|
| Contract is signed; $R_1$ determined | $z$ is observed and parties decide whether to renegotiate | Action $G$ or $B$ is chosen, return obtained, and shared between lender and firm. |

The firm can choose between two investment projects. Project $G$ has the returns distribution:

$$zy_G + A_3 \text{ with probability } p_G$$
$$A_3 \text{ with probability } (1 - p_G)$$

Project B has the returns distribution:

$$zy_B + A_3 \text{ with probability } p_B$$
$$A_3 \text{ with probability } (1 - p_B)$$

The assumptions $p_G y_G > p_B y_B$ and $y_G < y_B$ present the moral hazard problems discussed in Chapter 7. If lenders are to avoid the consequences of moral hazard, they must stipulate a repayment $R_1$, such that:

$$p_G(zy_G + A_3 - R_1) \geq p_B(zy_B + A_3 - R_1) \tag{24.17}$$

Note that $R_1$ cannot be made too large without violating the condition in equation (24.17). As described earlier in this chapter, when we covered costly verification (Section 24.4.1), management must be motivated to choose the good project rather than the bad one. If the project fails, management gets nothing since the model assumes $R_1 > A_3$, meaning that financiers claim the entire amount $A_3$.

The condition in equation (24.17) can be satisfied if $z$ is known at the time of setting $R_1$. However, in the assumed circumstances, $z$ is not known when $R_1$ is set, and if the realized value of $z$ is small enough, then at time 1, the condition in equation (24.17) will turn out to be violated for the given value of $R_1$. That is, for any given value of $R_1$ there is a critical value of $z^* = z^*(R_1)$, such that if $z < z^*$ management has an incentive to adopt the bad project. Given $R_1$, $z^*$ is defined as the value of $z$ that makes the condition in equation (24.17) an equality.

If the realized value of $z$ is such that $z < z^*$, there is a potential for the bank to mitigate moral hazard by renegotiating the contract. Let the project have liquidation values $A_2$ and $A_3$ at times 2 and 3, respectively; $A_2 > A_3$.

Suppose the possible realizations of $z$ have a minimum value $z_0$ and suppose $p_B z_0 y_B \geq R_1 > A_3$ so that if the firm is allowed to continue until time 2 the lender will be repaid in full if the project succeeds, but not if it fails. The payments to both parties are illustrated for the case $z < z^*$ in Table 24.6.

Suppose it is time 2 and the bank has no credible threat. In this case the lender cannot renegotiate, and her expected return is:

TABLE 24.6
$z < z^*$, BUT FIRM CONTINUES UNTIL TIME 3

| $z < z^*$ | Project success | Project failure |
|---|---|---|
| Payoff to lender | $R_1$ | $A_3$ |
| Payoff to borrower | $zy_B + A_3 - R_1$ | 0 |
| Total payoff | $zy_B + A_3$ | $A_3$ |

$$Prob\{z > z^*\}[p_G R_1 + (1 - p_G)A_3] + Prob\{z < z^*\}[p_B R_1 + (1 - p_B)A_3] \qquad (24.18)$$

The value of renegotiation lies in its potential to increase the lender's payoff, but in order for the bank to be able to force renegotiation, it must have a credible threat.[19] There is no credible threat if $z > z^*$, but if $z < z^*$, the threat is credible if also

$$A_2 > p_B R_1 + (1 - p_B)A_3 \qquad (24.19)$$

Consider what would happen if equation (24.19) were satisfied. The bank's problem is to decide whether to liquidate early or to reset $R_1$ to a smaller value $R_2$ and allow the firm to continue in business. However, $R_2$ cannot be too large without again incurring moral hazard. The optimal decision is defined to be one that maximizes the bank's expected return,[20] taking account of the moral hazard possibility.

Continue to assume equation (24.19) and suppose the bank has all the negotiating power. Under these assumptions the bank can alter the repayment terms as it sees fit. The bank will liquidate the firm if that offers a higher expected value than other alternatives. However, if continuation has the higher expected value, the bank can maximize its return by providing the borrower with an incentive to pick the better project. Suppose there is some value $R_2 < R_1$, such that:

$$p_G R_2 + (1 - p_G)A_3 \geq A_2 > p_B R_1 + (1 - p_B)A_3 \qquad (24.20)$$

Suppose, for a given value of $z$, that $R_2 = R_2(z)$ satisfies both equations (24.17) and (24.20). Then the bank will choose renegotiation rather than liquidation, because that increases the expected return of both the bank and the firm. For instance, if the bank sets:

$$R_2 < (p_G z y_G - p_B z y_B)/(p_G - p_B) + A_3 \qquad (24.21)$$

then equation (24.17) holds and the firm is motivated to choose the better project. The payoffs to both parties are shown in the two parts of Table 24.7.

---

[19] As a practical alternative to finding a credible threat strategy, a contract might simply provide for renegotiation if the borrower has violated some of the original terms. The effectiveness of the threat is then the effectiveness of imposing legal sanctions.

[20] Although for simplicity the procedure is not developed here, the value of $R_2$ can be determined optimally using backward induction.

**TABLE 24.7**
$z < z^*$ BEFORE AND AFTER RENEGOTIATION

a. Before renegotiation

|  | Project success | Project failure |
|---|---|---|
| Payoff to lender | $R_1$ | $A_3$ |
| Payoff to borrower | $zy_B + A_3 - R_1$ | 0 |
| Total payoff | $zy_B + A_3$ | $A_3$ |

b. After renegotiation

|  | Project success | Project failure |
|---|---|---|
| Payoff to lender | $R_1$ | $A_3$ |
| Payoff to borrower | $zy_B + A_3 - R_1$ | 0 |
| Total payoff | $zy_B + A_3$ | $A_3$ |

The bank will profit from the renegotiation if:

$$p_G R_2 + (1 - p_G)A_3 > p_B R_1 + (1 - p_B)A_3 \qquad (24.22)$$

## 24.6 INCOMPLETE CONTRACTS: FURTHER COMMENTS

In this section we further examine deals under uncertainty. In contrast to the previous section where cash flows were known but not verifiable, we now consider deals in which it is not possible to establish cash flow magnitudes using a probability distribution that is sufficiently precise to be useful. In some cases, parties to the deal are aware that even though they cannot specify future contingencies exactly, the contingencies can still affect the deal's payoffs (see Hart, 2001, p. 1,083). To complete such deals, financiers write contracts providing for adjustments to be made according to guidelines based on certain principles.

### 24.6.1 Uncertainty and Governance

A deal's payoff uncertainty can arise from a variety of sources, including fund seeker's actions, third-party actions, or changes in the economic environment. The different possible sources of uncertainty can affect financier responses. As one example, financiers may try to negotiate with different parties to absorb possible adverse impacts. In natural gas pipeline construction, financiers may request their clients to obtain an advance ruling from the regulatory authorities, permitting the pipeline company to pass on any construction cost increases to consumers by increasing the cost of gas. The advance ruling has the effect of reducing the uncertainty that the project will be able to turn a profit large enough to repay the financiers.

Financiers may interpret management actions as signals indicating the possible gravity of different uncertainties. For example, management's willingness to join an endeavor likely evinces belief in the project's success, particularly if management personnel invest in the project. Equally, of course, resignation of key personnel could be taken as indicating management's lack of faith in project prospects.

Rating agencies are unlikely to play prominent information production roles under uncertainty, since their main function is to refine estimates of risks at relatively low cost. For example, in the subprime meltdown of 2007–2008, it became clear that rating agencies had failed to assign appropriate ratings to complex mortgage-backed securities (MBS) and structured credit products (e.g., collateralized debt obligations, CDOs) until relatively late in the subprime lending boom. Although the rating agencies might not have faced uncertainty initially, they clearly did so after investors lost confidence in the complex investment products. After the loss of confidence, market prices for the instruments sometimes exhibited large discounts attributable at least as much to investor fears as to objective changes in the underlying security.

However, consultants or other experts—observers with specialized knowledge—may be able to determine key implications of a deal's uncertainties. For example, market research experts might offer clients estimates of a product's likely sales volumes under different economic circumstances. This information could in turn affect the phasing of a business's product offerings and ultimately its profitability.

## 24.6.2 *Ex Post* Adjustment

All contracts involve fund seeker-financier interdependence, but the degree of interdependence is greater with an incomplete contract. For an uncertain deal to reach a successful conclusion, financier and fund seeker depend on each other to reveal information and to cooperate more fully than with a complete contract. This interdependence is usually reflected in arrangements that provide for greater flexibility in governance as and when originally unforeseen events occur. For example, the arrangements may include using equity in place of debt in order to obtain voting rights on the board of directions of a corporation seeking funds rather than imposing contractual obligations such as maintaining a given working capital ratio.

*Ex post* adjustments can sometimes benefit both financier and fund-raising entity, as the preceding models of risky deals have indicated. Under uncertainty, *ex post* adjustments can be based on learning about the key profitability features of a deal and how to manage those features effectively. They may also allow the entity seeking funds to learn how to operate the firm more profitably, or to enhance the probability of its long-run survival.[21] On the other hand, debt renegotiation subsequent to a default can be cumbersome and lengthy because it can mean obtaining agreement from a relatively large number of lenders who may not agree on the terms of the renegotiation.

A given set of terms does not necessarily offer net benefits in every possible outcome state; compare Hart (2001). A contract that does not provide for unforeseeable contingencies can be finely tuned to work perfectly under one set of circumstances,

---

[21] For example, some developing countries have found their financiers willing to accept equity in exchange for debt previously issued. The country obtains the advantage of more flexible repayment terms, while the financier may find the value of the existing investment increased. From the country's perspective, equity financing eliminates the technical possibility of default and its attendant renegotiation costs, an important consideration when debt carries fixed interest payments that might become too great for the debtor to bear.

but can work badly if other circumstances are encountered. A more flexible contract that contains provisions for unforeseeable contingencies may not work perfectly under any set of circumstances, but there may be a considerable variety of different circumstances under which it works relatively well. The parties to a deal do not always recognize that their agreement constitutes an incomplete contract. Moreover, a failure of this type can weaken the financiers' ability to profit from the deal. If and when the incompleteness is recognized, financiers will then try to devise adjustments, but they will be in a weaker position than if they had originally foreseen the need for adjustments.

The credit crunch of 2007–2008 offers numerous examples. For instance, banks found themselves forced, for reputational reasons, to take back the default risk on instruments they previously regarded as having been sold. As a second example, credit derivatives (more specifically, one form of credit derivative called a credit default swap) that were originally thought to be safe hedges came to be questioned as the issuing insurance companies' capital dwindled and could not be replaced.

### 24.6.3  Bypassing Uncertainty

One obvious way of dealing with uncertainty is to pass its effects on to another party, say the client. For example, a few Japanese banks, concerned in the later 1980s about the possibility of eventual peaking in the then rapidly rising Japanese real estate prices, were able to securitize some of their property loans using equity instruments. This strategy passed the risk of capital loss on to the purchasers of the equities. Of course, since it also passed on any future capital gains, it may well have been that the sellers placed a lower expected value on possible capital gains than did the purchasers.

Collateral can also be used to bypass the effects of uncertainties, since financing can be secured by the market value of the collateral rather than by the firm's uncertain cash flows, as discussed earlier in this chapter. Still further, various forms of guarantees might also be used for the same purposes. For example, governments frequently provide export credit insurance to businesses engaged in foreign trade. Export credit insurance cannot always be obtained from the private sector, because it may involve insuring shipments against risks that neither the financier nor the client can control, such as losses from acts of war. As a second example, certain actions by management or the board of a corporation can be bonded to cover financiers against losses arising from fraud or malfeasance. As a third example, financings may be insured against such eventualities as death of key management personnel.

### 24.6.4  Research Findings

Davydenko and Strebulaev (2007) examine an aspect of uncertainty in asking whether the strategic actions of borrowers and lenders can affect corporate debt values. They find higher bond spreads for firms that have the capability to renegotiate debt contracts relatively easily: The firm's threat of strategic default depresses bond values *ex ante*. Moreover, the effect of strategic action is greater when lenders are vulnerable to threats, as might occur in the cases of relatively large proportions of managerial shareholding, simple debt structures, and high liquidation costs.

## • • • 24.7 ISSUANCE OF MULTIPLE DEBT CLAIMS

In earlier chapters when we discussed financing, we described the capital structure in terms of debt and equity, where there was only one form of the latter. Yet, firms typically have a more complicated debt structure. Upon recognizing the effects of taxes and the costs of financial distress, the capital structure question becomes: Why should management have a debt structure rather than just one type of debt? That is, what is the economic rationale for partitioning the cash flows generated from among the firm's different debt instruments that have different risk attributes, and how to partition optimally the claims on the firm's asset. Boot and Thakor (1993) tackle this issue. They demonstrate when there is asymmetric information, proceeds raised in external financing are increased by partitioning the firm's cash flow because it makes informed trade of the securities more profitable.

Boot and Thakor formulate a model in which it is assumed that the value of a firm's cash flows is a priori unknown by investors but that value can be revealed by some investors at a cost. In their model there are three types of traders who bid on securities: (1) pure liquidity traders, (2) traders who become informed at a cost about the firm's intrinsic value (i.e., informed traders), and (3) uninformed discretionary traders who could become informed but choose to remain uninformed. The following is also assumed: (1) trading on information should be profitable, (2) the demand from informed traders should be endogenous, and (3) equilibrium prices embody at least some of the information of informed traders.

The Boot-Thakor analysis shows that management can maximize proceeds from an external financing by partitioning the firm's cash flows from assets in place by issuing different financial claims. Basically, this is done by creating two types of securities. The first is an informationally insensitive security designed to include just one debt claim on the cash flows. The second type is an informationally sensitive security designed to include more than one debt claim on the cash flows. Creating these two types of securities allows informed trading to be more profitable because informed traders have the potential to generate a higher return from the production of information by allocating their portfolio to the information-sensitive security. Trading by informed traders will push the more valuable security's equilibrium price closer to its fundamental value. This will then increase the proceeds received by the firm.

## • • • 24.8 SECURITIZATION

Securitization is a form of external financing used by operating corporations who accumulate assets in the course of their business (e.g., receivables and lease receivables), as well as intermediaries such as banks that have assembled a portfolio of loans. The pool of assets is used as collateral for the offering of multiple securities with different priority claims on the cash flows of the asset pool. Securitization is an alternative funding source to using the same pool of assets for the issuance of a bond secured by those assets. In this section, we describe the securitization process and the incentive for those who have assembled a portfolio of assets to issue multiple securities against the portfolio's cash flow.

## 24.8.1 Basics of Securitization

To understand this, let's begin with a brief description of a securitization. With traditional forms of secured bonds, it is necessary for the issuer to generate sufficient earnings to repay the debt obligation. So, for example, if a manufacturer of farm equipment issues a bond in which the bondholders have a first mortgage lien on one of its plants, the ability of the manufacturer to generate cash flow from all of its operations is earmarked to pay off the bondholders. In contrast, in an asset securitization transaction, the burden of the source of repayment shifts from the issuer's cash flow to the cash flow generated by a pool of financial assets, potentially supplemented by a third-party guarantee of the payments should the asset pool not generate sufficient cash flow. For example, if the manufacturer of farm equipment has receivables from installment sales contracts to customers (i.e., a financial asset for the farm equipment company) and uses these receivables in a structured financing as described below, payment to the buyers of the bonds backed by the receivables depends on the ability to collect the receivables. It does not depend on the ability of the manufacturer of the farm equipment to generate cash flow from operations.

The process of creating securities backed by a pool of financial assets is referred to as *asset securitization*. The financial assets included in the collateral for an asset securitization are referred to as *securitized assets*.

## 24.8.2 Illustration of a Securitization

Let's use an illustration to describe an asset securitization transaction. In our illustration, we will use a hypothetical firm, Farm Equip Corporation. This company is assumed to manufacture farm equipment. Some of its sales are for cash, but the bulk of the sales takes the form of installment sales contracts. Effectively, an installment sale contract is a loan to the buyer of the farm equipment who agrees to repay Farm Equip Corporation over a specified period of time. For simplicity, we will assume that the loans are typically for four years. The collateral for the loan is the farm equipment purchased by the borrower. The loan specifies an interest rate that the buyer pays.

The credit department of Farm Equip Corporation makes the decision to extend credit to a customer. That is, the credit department will receive a credit application from a customer and, based on criteria established by the firm, will decide on whether to extend a loan and the amount. The criteria for extending credit or a loan are referred to as underwriting standards. Because Farm Equip Corporation is extending the loan, it is referred to as the originator of the loan. Moreover, Farm Equip Corporation may have a department that is responsible for servicing the loan. *Servicing* involves collecting payments from borrowers, notifying borrowers who may be delinquent and, when necessary, recovering and disposing of the collateral (i.e., farm equipment in our illustration) if the borrower does not make loan repayments by a specified time. While the servicer of the loans need not be the originator of the loans, in our illustration we are assuming that Farm Equip Corporation is the servicer.

Now let's get to how these loans can be used in a securitization transaction. We will assume that Farm Equip Corporation has more than $200 million of installment sales contracts. This amount is shown on the corporation's balance sheet as an asset. We will further assume that Farm Equip Corporation wants to raise $200 million.

Rather than issuing corporate bonds management decides to raise the funds via a securitization.

To do so, the Farm Equip Corporation will set up a legal entity referred to as a *special-purpose entity* (SPE), also referred to as a *special-purpose vehicle* (SPV). The purpose of this legal entity is critical in a securitization transaction because it allows the separation of the assets from the originator and the SPV. In our illustration, the SPE that is set up is called FE Asset Trust (FEAT). Farm Equip Corporation will then sell to FEAT $200 million of the loans. Farm Equip Corporation will receive from FEAT $200 million in cash, the amount it wanted to raise. But where does FEAT get $200 million? It obtains those funds by selling securities that are backed by the $200 million of loans. The securities are called *asset-backed securities*. The asset-backed securities issued in a transaction securitization are also referred to as bond classes or *tranches*.

A simple transaction can involve the sale of just one bond class with a par value of $200 million. We will call this Bond Class A. Suppose that 200,000 certificates are issued for Bond Class A with a par value of $1,000 per certificate. Then, each certificate holder would be entitled to 1/200,000 of the payment from the collateral. Each payment made by the borrowers (i.e., the buyers of the farm equipment) consists of principal repayment and interest. A securitization transaction is typically more complicated.

An example of a more complicated transaction is one in which two bond classes are created, Bond Class A1 and Bond Class A2. The par value for Bond Class A1 is $90 million and for Bond Class A2 is $110 million. The priority rule can simply specify that Bond Class A1 receives all the principal that is paid by the borrowers (i.e., the buyers of the farm equipment) until all of Bond Class A1 has paid off its $90 million and then Bond Class A2 begins to receive principal. Bond Class A1 is thus a shorter-term bond than Bond Class A2. By creating securities with maturities that differ from the maturity of the underlying financial assets, particular investors' needs can be satisfied. For example, if the collateral has a maturity of say five years, bond classes can be created with say, a one-year maturity, two-year maturity, and five-year maturity. This creation of bond classes with different maturities is called *time tranching*.

There are typically structures with more than one bond class, and the classes differ as to how they will share any losses resulting from defaults of the borrowers in the underlying collateral pool. In such a structure, the bonds are classified as *senior bond classes* and *subordinate bond classes*. The structure itself is referred to as a *senior-subordinate structure*. Losses are absorbed by the subordinate bond classes before any are realized by the senior bond classes. The senior bond classes have less credit risk than the subordinated classes. For example, suppose that FEAT issued $180 million par value of Bond Class A, the senior bond class, and $20 million par value of Bond Class B, the subordinate bond class. As long as there are no defaults by the borrower greater than $20 million, then Bond Class A will be repaid fully its $180 million.

The design of a senior-subordinate structure offers an example of redistributing the credit risk of the collateral to different bond classes. Investors seeking a security with high credit quality but who would be unwilling to purchase the individual financial assets in the collateral would be candidates to purchase the senior bond classes. Investors willing to accept greater credit risk would be candidates to purchase the subordinate bond classes. This is process of creating bond classes with different credit risk is referred to as *credit tranching*.

## 24.8.3 Securitization and Funding Costs

Although there are reasons other than cost why a corporation or a financial intermediary might issue securities via a securitization rather than issuing a bond backed by the portfolio of assets, we will confine our discussion to the issue of maximizing proceeds from the issuance of securities backed by the portfolio (i.e., optimal security design).[22]

The implication of the Boot-Thakor model for why a firm would be economically advantaged by creating the multiple debt securities that we described in the previous section is also capable of providing insights as to why the management of an operating corporation would be motivated to issue multiple classes of claims against portfolios of a pool of assets via the securitization process. In the securitization process, management of the firm seeking external funding can structure the transaction so as to create securities with different degrees of information sensitivity. According to the Boot-Thakor model, this can generate greater proceeds than issuing a secured corporate bond.

There are other explanations to explain the benefits from partitioning the cash flow of an asset pool. Gorton and Pennacchi (1990) find that an issuer can make informed investors interested in relatively information-insensitive securities better off by splitting the total asset cash flow from a pool of assets so as to create a liquid asset whose payoff does not embody private information.

DeMarzo (2005) offers another explanation as to how arbitrage profits can be garnered by tranching collateral. He determines the optimal strategy for an entity that owns a pool of assets when that entity has superior information about the value of the underlying assets. When faced with a choice of selling either individual assets or the entire asset pool, he shows that the entity is better off following the former strategy due to the information destruction effect of asset pooling. However, when the capital market allows the entity to issue multiple debt classes (or tranches) collateralized by the pool of assets, then it may be optimal to sell such a structure. Tranching gives the entity the opportunity to exploit the risk diversification effect if the residual risk of each asset in the pool is not highly correlated. This will result in some tranches within the financing structure that have a low risk and are highly liquid.

Brennan, Hein, and Poon (2009) present yet another explanation for creating a structured product with tranches that can potentially generate arbitrage profits. Although the arguments are in terms of CDOs, which employ the securitization technology, the argument applies in full force to asset-backed securities. They set forth a theory of the impact on initial market pricing (i.e., issuance spread) attributable to collateral diversification and tranching. The key assumption underlying

---

[22] There are two other factors about funding cost that are considered. For a financial intermediary securitizing a pool of loans, another motivation could be the desire to remove assets from their balance sheet for risk-based capital purposes. The second motivation could be purely for risk management purposes.

their theory is that some investor groups do not have the capability to evaluate tranches from a structured product, and, as a result, investors that fall into this category are highly dependent on bond ratings. If this is the case and if the rating agencies assign a higher valuation for a tranche than the tranche's fundamental value, then tranches can be marketed and sold based solely on ratings. Brennan, Hein, and Poon then go on to describe the drawbacks of the rating systems employed by the major rating agencies because they rely on either default probabilities (Standard & Poor's and Fitch) or expected losses due to default (Moody's). They argue that both systems can be gamed by bankers in working with clients to generate arbitrage profits.

# KEY POINTS

- Financial contracting attempts to explain the different kinds of deals made between financiers and their clients. In particular, financial contracting seeks to explain the economics of choosing a security design that can mitigate conflicts among the parties.

- The informational conditions under which a deal is arranged affect both the nature of the contract used and the governance mechanism employed to administer the contract. If deals are arranged under risks commonly understood by both parties, a complete contract is relatively easy to arrange. If risks are assessed asymmetrically, the complications of moral hazard and of adverse selection can arise.

- Deals arranged under uncertainty cannot be arranged using complete contracts. Rather, agreement over the principles under which the deal can be conducted is the most that can be determined in advance.

- Deals with differing attributes are usually arranged at different interest rates to compensate for the risk or uncertainty involved.

- The transactions costs of a deal include both the direct costs a client pays a financier and such indirect costs as the search costs involved in finding an accommodating financier.

- Screening costs are the *ex ante* costs a financier incurs to assess a funding proposal, while monitoring costs are the *ex post* costs involved in the deal's continuing governance.

- Financiers select governance mechanisms according to each deal's informational conditions. Risky deals may involve conditions of either informational symmetry or informational asymmetry.

- In the presence of informational asymmetry between financiers and their clients, debt may come closer than equity to resolving their differences.

- Moral hazard is a consequence of informational asymmetries. A financier may be able to manage the effects of moral hazard judiciously, albeit at increased governance costs.

- Even complete contracts arranged under risk can involve costly verification of outcomes.

- The difficulties presented by incomplete contracts can sometimes be mitigated by the use of renegotiation or liquidation schemes.
- Deals arranged under uncertainty create greater interdependence between financier and client, and the effects of interdependence can partially be mitigated by using relatively flexible governance arrangements.
- Firms may employ relatively complex financing structures in order to mitigate effects such as those due to differently distributed information.
- Securitization is a form of external financing used both by operating corporations that accumulate assets in the course of their business and by intermediaries that assemble and refinance portfolios of loans.
- In some cases, the costs of overcoming market imperfections can be reduced by using securitization.

## QUESTIONS

1.  a. What is meant by financial contracting?
    b. What is the objective of financial contracting?

2.  From the client's point of view, a deal's total transaction costs include both direct and indirect costs.
    a. What is meant by direct costs?
    b. What is meant by indirect costs?
    c. From the financer's point of view, what do a deal's costs include?

3.  The average cost of administering a deal is the sum of its screening and monitoring costs, along with the cost of making any adjustments that monitoring indicates would be desirable.
    a. What is meant by screening costs?
    b. What is meant by monitoring costs?
    c. Which of the following factors can lead to A lower average cost of administering a deal? Which ones would lead to A higher average cost?
       - Larger transaction volume
       - Greater informational difference between clients and financier
       - Financiers having more experience with the deal
       - Markets with impediments to arbitrage

4.  a. What is meant by an incomplete contract?
    b. Under which informational conditions will deals be arranged using a complete contract?
    c. Under which informational conditions will deals be arranged with an incomplete contract?

5.  Provide some reasons why informational asymmetries between financier and a firm are difficult to resolve in a private market and in intermediated transactions.

**6.** Suppose the owners of a firm and financiers are risk neutral, and that interest rates are zero. Suppose also that the owners are optimistic, while financiers are pessimistic, and their views about the earnings distributions are shown in the following table. Suppose the firm needs to raise $5.5.

|  | Firm earnings ($) | Probability estimates of optimistic owner | Probability estimates of pessimistic financier |
|---|---|---|---|
| Scenario 1 | 8 | 1/3 | 0 |
| Scenario 2 | 7 | 1/3 | 1/3 |
| Scenario 3 | 6 | 1/3 | 1/3 |
| Scenario 4 | 5 | 0 | 1/3 |

**a.** What is the value of equity from the point view of owners?

**b.** What is the value of equity from the point view of financiers?

**c.** If the firm raises the needed $5.5 through equity, what proportion of the shares would the financiers demand? How much are those shares worth from the point view of owners?

**d.** Alternatively, suppose financiers propose a debt issue that promises to pay off $5.75 if the firm has the funds, or whatever funds are available if the firm does not generate cash flows at least equal to $5.75. How much would the financiers value the debt?

**e.** How much would the owners value the debt?

**f.** Combining all the above results, which form of financing would the owners prefer to raise the needed $5.5, equity or debt? Why?

**7.** Consider a firm that gets the single unit of capital needed to implement a project. Suppose that the owner might substitute a bad project for a good one unless the financier takes steps to prevent it. The payoff distributions of the good project and the bad project are shown in the following table.

|  | Payoff ($) | Probability |
|---|---|---|
| Good Project | 2 | 3/4 |
|  | 0 | 1/4 |
| Bad Project | 3 | 1/6 |
|  | 0 | 5/6 |

**a.** If the financier sets the loan payment as $2, what is the expected payoff to the owner after taking the size of the loan payment into account when selecting the good and bad project, respectively? Which project would the owner choose?

**b.** Consider the situation when the financier sets the loan payment as $1.5. Answer the same questions raised in (a).

**c.** What range should the financier set the loan payment so that the owner does not have an incentive to substitute the bad project for the good one?

8. Suppose that firms and financiers are both risk neutral, that the interest rate is zero, and that firms have no initial resources. In each period a firm adopting an investment project will generate a random income $y$, and the distribution of $y$ is shown in the following table.

| | Payoff | Probability |
|---|---|---|
| $y$ | $y_D = 4.2$ | $p_G = 3/4$ |
| | $y_B = 1.0$ | $p_B = 1/4$ |

Now consider a contract in which the lender advances \$2 and agrees to renew for a second period whenever the borrower makes a payment of more than $y_B$ at the end of the first period. If only $y_B$ is paid at the end of the first period, the arrangement will be terminated immediately. Assuming there are only two periods, the firm has no incentive to maintain a good reputation after time 1 has passed.

What conditions should the loan repayment at time 1 satisfy so that the lender's expected profit is positive and the entrepreneur is willing to enter the arrangement?

9. Explain briefly how collateral can be used as a screening device to mitigate the effects of informational asymmetries.

10. Explain the benefit of *ex post* adjustments used in contracts for deals under uncertainty.

11. Firms typically have a debt structure with more than just one type of debt. Boot and Thakor (1993) show that management can maximize the proceeds from an external financing by partitioning the firm's cash flows from assets in place by issuing different financial claims. Explain briefly how it works.

12. a. What is meant by asset securitization?
    b. What is meant by securitized assets?

# REFERENCES

Arrow, Kenneth J. (1974). *Essays on the Theory of Risk-Bearing*. Amsterdam: North-Holland.

Axelson, Ulf. (2007). "Security Design with Investor Private Information," *Journal of Finance* **62**: 2587–2632.

Brennan, Michael J., Julia Hein, and Ser-Huang Poon. (2009). "Tranching and Rating," *European Financial Management* **15**: 891–922.

Benson, Earl D. (1979). "The Search for Information by Underwriters and Its Impact on Municipal Interest Cost," *Journal of Finance* **34**: 871–885.

Boot, Arnoud, and Anjan V. Thakor. (1993). "Security Design," *Journal of Finance* **48**: 1349–1378.

Davydenko, Sergei A., and Ilya A. Strebulaev. (2007). "Strategic Actions and Credit Spreads," *Journal of Finance* **62**: 2633–2671.

DeMarzo, Peter. (2005). "The Pooling and Tranching of Securities: A Model of Informed Intermediation," *Review of Financial Studies* **18**: 1–35.

Diamond, Douglas W. (2004). "Committing to Commit: Short-Term Debt when Enforcement is Costly," *Journal of Finance* **59**: 1447–1479.

Fama, Eugene F. (1985). "What's Different about Banks?" *Journal of Monetary Economics* **15**: 29–39.

Freixas, Xavier, and Jean-Charles Rochet. (1997). *Microeconomics of Banking.* Cambridge, MA: MIT Press.

Gorton, Gary, and James Kahn. (2000). "The Design of Bank Loan Contracts, Collateral, and Renegotiation," *Review of Financial Studies* **13**: 331–364.

Gorton, Gary, and George Pennacchi. (1990). "Financial Intermediaries and Liquidity Creation." *Journal of Finance* **45**: 49–71.

Hart, Oliver. (2001). "Financial Contracting," *Journal of Economic Literature* **39**: 1079–1100.

Hart, Oliver D., and John Moore (1998). "Default and Renegotiation: A Dynamic Model of Debt," *Quarterly Journal of Economics* **113**: 1–41.

Jensen, Michael, and William Meckling. (1976). "Theory of the Firm: Managerial Behavior, Agency Costs, and Ownership Structure," *Journal of Financial Economics* **3**:305–360.

John, Kose, and David C. Nachman. (1985). "Risky Debt, Investment Incentives, and Reputation in a Sequential Equilibrium," *Journal of Finance* **40**: 863–878.

Kaplan, Steven N., and Per Stromberg. (2004). "Characteristics, Contracts, and Actions: Evidence from Venture Capitalist Analyses," *Journal of Finance* **59**: 2177–2210.

Neave, Edwin H. (2009). *Modern Financial Systems: Theory and Applications.* Hoboken, NJ: John Wiley & Sons.

Qian, Jun, and Philip E. Strahan. (2007). "How Laws and Institutions Shape Financial Contracts: The Case of Bank Loans," *Journal of Finance* **62**: 2803–2834.

Roberts, Michael R., and Amir Sufi (2009). "Financial Contracting: A Survey of Empirical Research and Future Directions," *Annual Review of Financial Economics*: 207–226.

Ross, Stephen A. (1977). "The Determination of Financial Structure: The Incentive Signaling Approach," *Bell Journal of Economics* **7**: 23–40.

Sufi, Amir, and Atif R. Mian. (2009). "The Consequences of Mortgage Credit Expansion: Evidence from the 2007 Mortgage Default Crisis," *Quarterly Journal of Economics* **124**: 1449–1496.

# PART VIII

# INCORPORATING RISK IN CAPITAL BUDGETING DECISIONS

# 25

# CAPITAL EXPENDITURE PLANS IN A RISKY WORLD

*D*ecisions regarding long-term investment projects are referred to as capital budgeting decisions. In Chapter 6 we discussed how management of a firm should make capital budgeting decisions in a perfect capital market when future cash flows can be forecast with certainty. In this and the next chapter we consider projects with risky future cash flows. Such projects require that managers analyze the following factors:

- Each project's incremental future cash flows
- The probability distributions of these cash flows
- The present value of the cash flows, discounted according to the risks they present

In Chapter 6 we saw that a project's incremental cash flows comprise (1) operating cash flows (the change in the revenues, expenses, and taxes) and (2) investment cash flows (the acquisition and disposition of the project's assets). Given estimates of incremental cash flows for a project and an appropriate discount rate, we looked at alternative techniques to select the best of the available projects.

In deciding whether a project increases shareholder wealth, managers must weigh both its costs and its benefits. The costs are the cash flows necessary to create the project (the investment outlay) and the opportunity costs of not otherwise being able to use the cash tied up in the project. The benefits are the future cash flows expected to be generated by the project. But the future is unknown and therefore future cash flows are exposed to risk. As a result, management must evaluate the risk that cash flows will differ from their expected values. Risk and risk measurement were extensively discussed in Chapters 9 through 12, and the methods of those chapters will be applied here.

Risk arises from different sources, depending on environmental conditions, the industry in which the firm is operating, and the type of project being considered. Each of the following factors presents different sources of risk:

- *Economic conditions.* Will consumers be spending or saving? Will the economy be in a recession? Will the government stimulate spending? Will there be inflation?
- *International conditions.* Will the exchange rate between different countries' currencies change? Are the governments of the countries in which the firm does business stable?
- *Market conditions.* Is the market competitive? How long does it take competitors to enter into the market? Are there any barriers, such as patents or trademarks, that will keep competitors away? Is there sufficient supply of raw materials and labor? How much will raw materials and labor cost in the future?
- *Taxes.* What will tax rates be in the future? Will Congress alter the tax system?
- *Interest rates.* What will be the cost of raising capital in future years?

Several further questions also arise. First, management must determine whether a new project's cash flow risks are the same as those of existing projects and if not, determine a suitable adjustment to the discount rate the company currently uses. The question of determining the project's optimal scale must also be resolved. These matters are discussed in Section 25.1. In Section 25.2 we show how, given a fixed operating plan, rates of return to projects are related to those of the entire firm. This matter is further discussed in Section 25.3, where it is related to the required rate of return on a tax saving generated by depreciation. In Section 25.4 we explore issues regarding multi-period planning of capital expenditure programs, and in Section 25.5 we deal with estimating cash flows and their risks in both single-period and multi-period contexts. Finally, in the next chapter we take a closer look at how the riskiness of a project is assessed.

---

## 25.1 A MARKET VALUE CRITERION

In a risky world with a perfect capital market, management can act in the best interests of stockholders without specific knowledge of their preferences because, as shown in Chapter 6, the only constraint on each consumer's decision is the present value of wealth. When there are no transactions costs, a risky cash flow stream's present value determines the consumer's opportunity set: The consumer is concerned with the project's present value rather than the details of the cash flows. For any expenditure profile having the same present value as the project's, cash flows can be rearranged without payment of charges other than interest, which of course entered into determining the value in the first place. Accordingly, the best that management can do for the firm's owners is to maximize the present value of their investments, and that present value is also the investment's market value.

In the context of capital budgeting under risk, a firm's managers can still implement the market value criterion by relating it to the firm's expected earnings and risk characteristics. The Capital Asset Pricing Model (CAPM) explained in Chapter 14 provides one theoretical framework[1] for how risky future cash flows

---

[1] Contingent claims analysis provides an alternative framework.

can be evaluated, and we will use that framework here. Recall that, according to the CAPM, at equilibrium the expected return on securities of firm $i$ is related to risk by:

$$E(r_i) = r_f + \left[E(r_m) - r_f\right] \frac{cov(r_i, r_m)}{\sigma^2(r_m)} \tag{25.1}$$

where

$r_f$ = one-period risk-free interest rate

$E(r_m)$ = expected return on the market porfolio

$cov(r_i, r_m)$ = covariance between the return on security $i$ at time 1 and the market portfolio return at time 1

$\sigma^2(r_m)$ = variance of the market portfolio return

Denote the distribution of project values at time 2 as $V_i$.[2] This distribution may itself be derived from the distributions of many future periods' cash flows. If so, it is derived assuming the firm has an operating plan[3] that will not change. Such a plan defines both the cash flow stream of the firm and its risk characteristics.

Let $P_i$ represent the project's market value at time 1. We have:

$$r_i = \frac{V_i - P_i}{P_i} \quad \text{and} \quad E(r_i) = \frac{E(V_i) - P_i}{P_i} \tag{25.2}$$

Substituting the expression for $E(r_i)$ from equation (25.2) into equation (25.1) and rearranging gives:

$$P_i = \frac{E(V_i) - \left\{[E(r_m) - r_f]\ cov(V_i, r_m)/\sigma^2(r_m)\right\}}{1 + r_f} \tag{25.3}$$

where $cov(V_i, r_m)$ is the covariance between the value of the proposed firm at time 1 and the market portfolio return.

The numerator of the right-hand side of equation (25.3) is referred to as the time 2 *certainty equivalent value of the cash flow* $V_i$.[4] Providing management knows the data on the right-hand side of equation (25.3), the market impact of a capital budgeting decision can be determined through assessment of its effects on cash flows. In other words, equation (25.3) gives management a means of determining whether or not a particular investment decision should be undertaken and if so, at what level.

The foregoing pricing equation can also be used to develop a risk-adjusted discount rate version of the CAPM. Recall that:

---

[2] If we needed to be explicit about the time, we could write $V_i(2)$.

[3] The operating plan consists of planned capital investment and the utilization of those assets with other resources to produce goods or services for sale. The details are similar to those discussed in Chapters 2 and 3, except that earnings now are risky.

[4] The concept of certainty equivalent value is explained in Chapter 11.

$$\frac{cov(V_i, r_m)}{\sigma^2(r_m)} = \frac{P_i cov(r_i, r_m)}{\sigma^2(r_m)} = P_i \beta_i$$

where $\beta_i$ is the beta risk of firm $i$. We can then rewrite equation (25.3) in terms of beta risk as:

$$P_i = \frac{E(V_i) - \left[E(r_m) - r_f\right]P_i\beta_i}{1 + r_f}$$

Then

$$P_i(1 + r_f) = E(V_i) - P_i\beta_i\left[E(r_m) - r_f\right]$$

$$P_i\left[1 + r_f + \beta_i\left[E(r_m) - r_f\right]\right] = E(V_i)$$

$$P_i = \frac{E(V_i)}{1 + r_f + \beta_i\left[E(r_m) - r_f\right]} \tag{25.4}$$

The numerator of equation (25.4) is equal to one plus the risk-adjusted rate of return required by the market. Subtracting one from the numerator gives the *risk-adjusted rate of return*:

$$r_f + \beta_i\left[E(r_m) - r_f\right]$$

equal to the risk-free rate plus a risk adjustment $\beta_i[E(r_m) - r_f]$. Note that the expected value of the cash flow stream is discounted in equation (25.4), whereas its certainty equivalent was discounted in equation (25.3).

Thus far, our framework has been formulated within a single-period setting. In a multi-period context, the risk-adjusted and certainty equivalent ways of determining value require careful treatment if they are to give equivalent results. These issues are discussed later in this chapter.

## 25.1.1 Basic Application to Capital Budgeting in a Risky World

We now provide an example of how certainty equivalent values and risk-adjusted discount rates are used in capital budgeting under risk. Suppose a firm expects to generate $E(V_i) = \$100$ million at time 2 from current operations, and that the firm has a time 1 market value of $90 million. The return on the market portfolio, $E(r_m)$, is assumed to be 15% and the risk-free rate 5%, $r_f$. Hence,

$$\left[E(r_m) - r_f\right] = 0.15 - 0.05 = 0.10$$

Suppose also that a new project available only in unit size and costing $6 million is contemplated. Further, suppose that the new project's expected cash flow one period later, denoted by $E(F_i)$, is $13 million and that $cov(F_i, r_m)/\sigma^2(r_m)$ is $25 million. The foregoing numerical values are obtained under the assumption that the new project will be put to best use according to a fixed plan of operations that defines cash flows with the stated expected value and risk characteristics.

Should management undertake the new project? First, we can determine $cov(V_i, r_m)/\sigma^2(r_m)$ for the firm prior to adopting the new project. We do this by substituting the assumed numerical data into equation (25.3), which gives:

$$\$90,000,000 = \frac{\$100,000,000 - 0.10 \; cov(V_i, r_m)/\sigma^2(r_m)}{1.05}$$

so that:

$$\frac{cov(V_i, r_m)}{\sigma^2(r_m)} = \$55,000,000$$

Now we may use the property of sums of random variables described in Web-Appendix L to write:

$$cov(V_i + F_i, r_m) = cov(V_i, r_m) + cov(F_i, r_m)$$

so that dividing the above equation by $\sigma^2(r_m)$ we get:

$$\frac{cov(V_i + F_i, r_m)}{\sigma^2(r_m)} = \frac{cov(V_i, r_m)}{\sigma^2(r_m)} + \frac{cov(F_i, r_m)}{\sigma^2(r_m)}$$

We just calculated the first ratio on the right-hand side of the above equation to be $55 million. We assumed that the second ratio is $25 million. Therefore,

$$\frac{cov(V_i + F_i, r_m)}{\sigma^2(r_m)} = \$55,000,000 + \$25,000,000 = \$80,000,000$$

The expected value of the firm with the new project is equal to:

$$E(V_i + F_i) = E(V_i) + (F_i)$$

Since it is assumed that $E(V_i)$ is $100 million and $E(F_i)$ is $13 million,

$$E(V_i + F_i) = \$100,000,000 + \$13,000,000 = \$113,000,000$$

If the new project is undertaken, then the time 1 value of the total cash flow generated by the firm (exclusive of investment cost) will be, again using equation (25.3),

$$\frac{\$113,00,000 - 0.10(\$80,000,000)}{1.05} = \$100,000,000$$

If the project is adopted, the market value of the firm is then expected to be $100 million. Recall that the market value prior to the adoption of the project was assumed to be $90 million. By adopting the project, the market value is expected to increase by $10 million. Thus, the $6 million investment cost would be more than compensated for, and the project should be undertaken.

The calculation can be put in another way to show that because the required rate of return on the project is less than its expected internal rate of return,[5] the project has a positive present value to the firm. However, note first that the required rate of return on the new project is not equal to the firm's cost of funds before the project was undertaken. The rate of return required by the market, prior to the firm's adopting the project, is:

$$\frac{\$100,000,000 - \$90,000,000}{\$90,000,000} = 11.1\%$$

Subsequent to adopting the project, the required rate of return becomes:

$$\frac{\$113,000,000 - \$100,000,000}{\$100,000,000} = 13\%$$

Accordingly, the new project is not discounted by the market at 11.1%, but rather has a larger required rate of return, one that is in fact equal to 30%. To see this, note that the market value of the new project, using equation (25.3) to value it separately, is:

$$\frac{\$13,000,000 - 0.10(\$25,000,000)}{1.05} = \$10,000,000$$

Then, since the new project creates expected cash flows of $13 million, the required rate of return[6] on it is:

$$\frac{\$13,000,000 - \$10,000,000}{\$10,000,000} = 30\%$$

The same calculation can also be put another way. After the new project is adopted, the firm can be regarded as a portfolio of its old and new activities. In terms of market values, the new project accounts for 10% of the firm's activities, so we can stipulate that:

$$\frac{\$90,000,000}{\$100,000,000}(11.11\%) + \frac{\$10,000,000}{\$100,000,000}x$$

where $x$ is an unknown rate of return on the new project. When solved, the foregoing expression gives $x = 30\%$.

---

[5] We explain how the internal rate of return is computed in Chapter 6.
[6] Note that to determine the market-required rate of return we use the project's market value rather than its investment cost.

All the calculated rates of return are based on market values. Now since the new project can be implemented by the firm's existing owners for only $6 million, the internal rate of return on this $6 million investment must be in excess of the rate required by the marketplace, since the project's time 1 market value is $10 million. Nonetheless, if new investors were to purchase shares after the market value of the firm has changed to reflect the new project's adoption, they could earn only 13% on their investment, because the shares of the firm would be priced to yield just that expected return. The value created by the project would be retained by the original stockholders.

As a final point, we show that the firm's cost of capital can be calculated as a weighted average of market-required rates of return, with market values being used as weights. Let us calculate the $\beta$ for the (combined) firm, and from that the overall required rate of return. We use the reasoning employed in obtaining (25.4). Thus:

$$\beta_{\text{original}} = \frac{1}{P_i}\left[\frac{cov(V_i, r_m)}{\sigma^2(r_m)}\right] = \frac{\$55,000,000}{\$90,000,000} = 0.61$$

$$\beta_{\text{project}} = \frac{\$25,000,000}{\$10,000,000} = 2.5$$

Then using market values as weights, we obtain:

$$\beta_{\text{combined}} = \frac{\$90,000,000}{\$100,000,000}(0.61) + \frac{\$10,000,000}{\$100,000,000}(2.5) = 0.8$$

Finally, by equation (25.1) the required rate of return for the combined original firm and new project is:

$$0.05 + (0.15 - 0.05)(0.8) = 0.13 \text{ or } 13\%$$

We have assumed that the values of the firm and the project can be added to obtain the firm's new market value, an assumption that appears to ignore the possibility of synergy. However, this is not in fact the case. First, we can define any change in cash flows to be due to the project, because apart from adopting the project, output levels are assumed to be fixed. Moreover, since the level of the project itself is assumed to be fixed before the described calculations are made, the cash flows associated with the new project can indeed be added to the firm's preexisting cash flows (even if some of those newly created cash flows do result from synergistic effects).

The foregoing calculations establish several conclusions. First, the nature of the firm's business risk is determined by the investment projects it accepts. In the example, adopting the new project changes the firm's business risk, as reflected by the change in $\beta$ and hence in the discount rate applied to the firm's total earnings stream. Second, management should adopt new projects when their internal rate of return exceeds the market-required rate of return for projects with a given measure of risk. Third, because of the possibility of different business risks, the required rate of return on a project is not necessarily the firm's prevailing cost of capital. (In the example it is a larger figure.) Fourth, adoption of a profitable project can alter the firm's overall cost of capital, because the risk of the firm's earnings stream can be altered by a new investment project.

## 25.2 COMPARING NEW AND EXISTING EARNINGS RISKS TO OBTAIN OPTIMAL CAPITAL EXPENDITURE PLANS

We can now use the CAPM to develop optimal capital budgeting rules similar to those discussed in Chapter 6. We consider first the case of projects yielding constant returns to scale, then the case of projects with diminishing returns.

### 25.2.1 Capital Expenditures with Constant Returns to Investment

Using the CAPM, let us consider the question of whether a new firm should be brought into being. As before, let $V_i$ be the distribution of values of the proposed firm at time 2. The market value of the firm at time 1, $P_i$, can be determined using equation (25.3). Alternatively, the market-required rate of return for a firm's cash flows, $E(r_j)$, can be found using equation (25.1).

Suppose that an initial investment of $75 million will be required to set up the new firm, no variation in the size of this investment being permissible. In other words, the optimal size of the investment is either zero or $75 million. Assume further that the distribution for (1) the cash flows to be generated, (2) the corresponding internal rate of returns for the firm ($r_j$), and (3) the market portfolio return ($r_m$) is as follows:

| Probability | Cash flow | $r_j$ | $r_m$ |
|---|---|---|---|
| 0.50 | $97.5 million | 30% | 20% |
| 0.50 | $75.0 million | 0% | 8% |

The estimation of these data is discussed in Section 25.5. From the estimated data, the following can be computed:

$$E(r_m) = 0.14 \qquad \sigma(r_m) = 0.06$$

$$\rho(r_j, r_m) = 1 \qquad \beta_j = \frac{cov(r_j, r_m)}{\sigma^2(r_m)} = 2.5$$

where $\rho(r_j, r_m)$ is the correlation between the return on the proposed firm and the market portfolio.

Assume that the one-period risk-free rate ($r_f$) is 6%. Then applying equation (25.1) to the data, we find that the required rate of return for the proposed firm (i.e., the project) with the cash flow risk assumed is:

$$E(r_j) = r_f + \beta_j[E(r_m) - r_f] = 0.06 + 2.5(0.08) = 0.25 = 25\%$$

However, the proposed firm's expected internal rate of return (as computed from the distribution above) is only 15%, less than the market-required rate of return for an undertaking with the project's risk characteristics. In other words, the proposed firm should not be started because if it were brought into existence, the original investors could not sell the firm for a price as high as the cost of their investment.

The decision of whether an existing firm should adopt a project is a little more complex, as we now show. Suppose that a new project (not necessarily related to the one of the previous example) will expand the firm's time 2 distribution of values by a scale factor $\lambda$. Then, if $V_i$ represents the original time 2 distribution of values, the new distribution is:

$$W_i = (1 + \lambda)V_i$$

It then follows immediately from equation (25.1) that the new time 1 value of the firm is $Q_i = (1 + \lambda)P_i$. It follows further that the market applies the same rate of discount to the augmented cash flows as it did to the original ones. The rate of discount after adopting the project is then:

$$\frac{E(W_i) - Q_i}{Q_i} = \frac{(1 + \lambda)E(V_i) - (1 + \lambda)P_i}{(1 + \lambda)P_i} = \frac{E(V_i) - P_i}{P_i}$$

the discount rate applied to the firm before the project was adopted. Accordingly, adopting new projects such that the firm's distribution of values changes only by a scale factor does not change the market-required rate of return. This situation is technically described as one of an investment yielding *stochastically constant returns to scale*.

Consequently, the rule for projects having the same business risk as the existing firm seems to be that such projects should be adopted, provided they can be implemented at a cost low enough to permit the project to earn at least the required rate of return. However, in this circumstance it is difficult to specify an optimal scale for the project unless one assumes either that the projects are available only in some limited amount or that the projects can only be implemented at increasing unit costs. Otherwise, if the adoption of any such project yields returns in excess of the return required by the marketplace, at what point does the firm's management stop investing in it?[7]

The difficulty lies in our assumption that cash flows expand by a scale factor, an assumption that really means constant internal rates of return are expected to be realized on all additional investments. Since this assumption is useful to illustrate the points developed above, but is at the same time unlikely to describe many practical situations, it will be worthwhile next to explore a scenario in which new project returns decline marginally.

---

[7] There may, of course, be physical limitations to the scale at which the new project can be adopted.

## 25.2.2  Capital Expenditures with Diminishing Marginal Returns to Investment

To consider the case of diminishing marginal returns, suppose that funds invested at time 1 produce cash flows at time 2 according to:

$$Z = I^{1/2}X \tag{25.5}$$

where
$X$ = cash flow at time 2
$I$ = amount invested in the activity at time 1
$Z$ = amount realized at time 2 from that investment

Letting

$$\alpha = \left[E(r_m) - r_f\right]/\sigma^2(r_m)$$

the time 1 value of the cash flow Z ($P_i$) using equation (25.3) is:

$$P_i = \frac{E(Z) - \alpha\, cov(Z, r_m)}{1 + r_f} \tag{25.6}$$

Then equation (25.6) may be rewritten using equation (25.5) as:

$$P_i = \frac{I^{1/2}\left[E(X) - \alpha\, cov(X, r_m)\right]}{1 + r_f} \tag{25.7}$$

as may be seen by applying the results from Web-Appendix L.

In this case the market value maximization objective can be expressed as maximizing the difference between value and investment cost, that is, $P_i - I$. The maximum occurs at an investment cost such that the time 2 internal rate of return falls to just $1 + r_f$. To show this compactly, rewrite equation (25.7) as:

$$P_i = \frac{\gamma I^{1/2}}{1 + r_f}$$

where $\gamma = E(X) - cov(X, r_m)$, and consider:

$$\max_I \left(\frac{\gamma I^{1/2}}{1 + r_f} - I\right)$$

which has a solution given by:

$$(\gamma/2)I^{1/2} = 1 + r_f \tag{25.8}$$

FIGURE 25.1
OPTIMAL INVESTMENT DECISION IN A RISKY WORLD

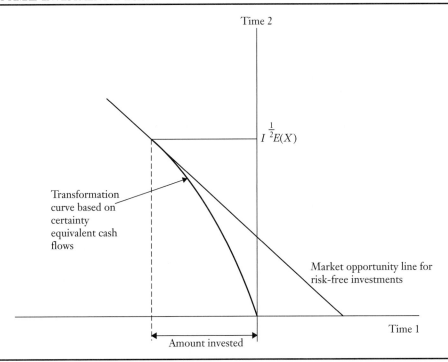

Equation (25.8) is found by differentiating the equation on the previous line with respect to $I$ and setting the result equal to zero. The left-hand term of equation (25.8) equals $1 + r_f$, while the right-hand side is the slope of the market opportunity line for risk-free investments. Thus, when marginal returns to investment diminish, we have obtained a result similar to that in a risk-free situation: Management should invest up to the point where the certainty equivalent marginal internal rate of return equals the risk-free rate of interest. In this form, the situation may be depicted as in Figure 25.1.

The result may also be viewed as showing that at the optimum the expected rate of return on marginal investments is just equal to the rate the market requires for investments having that kind of business risk. To see the result in this manner, rewrite equation (25.8) as:

$$\frac{I^{-1/2}}{2}[E(X) - cov(X, r_m)] = 1 + r_f$$

which can then be manipulated to yield:

$$\left[\frac{I^{-1/2}}{2}E(X)\right] - 1 = r_f + \alpha\left[\frac{I^{-1/2}}{2}cov(X, r_m)\right] \qquad (25.9)$$

That is, the marginal internal rate of return on an invested dollar—the left-hand side of equation (25.9)—equals the marginal rate of return required by the marketplace—the right-hand side of the equation—for cash flows having the risk characteristic indicated by the bracketed part of the second term on the right-hand side of the equation. Accordingly, we see that the rules for capital budgeting in a risky world are (loosely speaking) risk-adjusted analogs of the rules found in Chapter 6. That is, management should raise funds for projects until the marginal internal rate of return on the projects falls to where it equals the rate of interest required by the market.

As we have shown by drawing the transformation curve of Figure 25.1 in certainty equivalent terms that may be related to the market opportunity line for risk-free investments, the introduction of risk does not essentially change the conclusions obtained in Chapter 6. Alternatively, we have shown that the marginal internal rate of return for optimal amounts of investment will be equated to the market-required rate of return. Later in this chapter we shall show that while similar results are obtained for multi-period analyses, they require careful interpretation if erroneous conclusions are to be avoided.

## 25.3 REQUIRED RATES OF RETURN: FIRM, DIVISION, AND PROJECT

In the previous section we showed how the required rate of return on a firm's cash flows could be established, at varying output levels, with the aid of the CAPM. Providing we are now willing to specialize our assumptions by holding output levels fixed, the same approach can be used to relate rates of return on different projects, both to each other and to the market-required rate of return. (The reason for assuming fixed output levels will be discussed shortly.)

We next show that with fixed output levels the firm can be regarded as a portfolio of investment projects. Recalling equation (25.1), if we let the individual projects be defined by the index $k$, then we can write:

$$E(r_j) = \sum_k x_{jk} E(r_{jk}) = \sum_k x_{jk} \left\{ r_f + \left[ \frac{E(r_m) - r_f}{\sigma^2(r_m)} \right] cov(r_{jk}, r_m) \right\}$$

where

$r_j$ = return on project $j$

$x_{jk}$ = the market values of the individual projects relative to the market value of the entire firm

$\sum_k x_{jk} = 1$

This approach shows that the return on the firm is the weighted average of the returns required by the market on each of the individual projects. The details are usefully explored with the aid of an example.

Consider the case of buying, at market value, a single steer. Suppose there are two revenue-producing activities: producing beef (project $b$) and producing hide (project $h$), which we assume generate statistically independent returns. We assume the cost of the steer is $450 and the variable cost of hide production is an additional $50. Moreover, we suppose that the amounts and returns to the two activities are as follows:

| Probability | Producing beef (b) Amount | $r_b$ | Producing hide (h) Amount | $r_b$ |
|---|---|---|---|---|
| ½ | $540 | 0.20 | $54 | 0.08 |
| ½ | $450 | 0 | $50 | 0 |

The returns are calculated on an investment cost basis, but as it will later turn out, investment cost equals market value for the assumed data. Therefore, the returns in this example can also be interpreted as those required by the market. The returns are uncorrelated according to:

$$\rho(r_b, r_m) = 0 \text{ and } \rho(r_b, r_b) = 0$$

where the indices $b$, $h$, and $m$ refer to producing beef or hide and to the market portfolio.

Combining the two activities' returns while recalling their statistical independence, the distribution of returns from investing in the animal, which we denote by $r_c$, is as follows: 0.188, 0.180, 0.008, and 0, where each outcome has a probability of ¼. From this distribution, the expected return from investing in the animal, $E(r_c)$, is equal to 0.094. In order to apply the CAPM, we need more data. We will assume that $r_m$ has two possible outcomes, 0.20 and 0 with equal probability. Then we know that:

$$E(r_m) = 0.10 \text{ and } \sigma(r_m) = 0.010$$

And we will assume that $r_f = 0.04$.

Also suppose that returns on beef production and on the market portfolio are perfectly positively correlated [i.e., $\rho(r_b, r_m) = 1$]. We first apply the CAPM to investing with a view to carrying out both hide and beef production. For this purpose we prepare a table of joint probabilities using the previously stated data as shown below:

| $r_m/r_c$ | 0.20 | 0.00 |
|---|---|---|
| 0.188 | 0.25 | 0.00 |
| 0.180 | 0.25 | 0.00 |
| 0.008 | 0.00 | 0.25 |
| 0.000 | 0.00 | 0.25 |

Then from the table we can calculate, using the definitions from Web-Appendix L,

$$E(r_c, r_m) = 0.0184 \text{ and } E(r_c)E(r_m) = 0.0094$$

so that:

$$E(r_c, r_m) - E(r_c)E(r_m) = cov(r_c, r_m) = 0.0090$$

Therefore, using the calculated covariance in equation (25.1),

$$E(r_c) = 0.04 + \frac{0.10 - 0.04}{(0.10)^2}(0.0090) = 0.094$$

so the required rate of return just equals the expected rate of return we calculated earlier.

Calculation of the required rate of return on the hide production activity means determining $E(r_h)$ according to equation (25.1). Remember $\rho(r_h, r_m) = 0$ so that $cov(r_h, r_m) = 0$. Consequently,

$$E(r_h) = r_f = 0.04$$

Finally, the required rate of return for the beef-producing activity is:

$$E(r_b) = 0.04 + \frac{0.06}{0.10(0.10)}(0.10)(0.10) = 0.10$$

since $\rho(r_b, r_m) = 1$, so that:

$$cov(r_b, r_m) = \sigma(r_b)\sigma(r_m) = 0.10(0.10)$$

Now observe that the return on the combined activity is the weighted average of returns on the individual activities; that is,

$$\tfrac{1}{10}(0.04) + \tfrac{9}{10}(0.10) = 0.094$$

where the weights are computed using the market values of the individual activities. In other words, the required rates of return on the individual activities are related to the required rate of return on the firm in just the same way as the returns on securities are related to portfolio return. Thus, the firm can be regarded as a portfolio of activities when the activities' levels are specified in advance.

While each project will have the same required rate of return regardless of which firm examines it, not all firms will necessarily adopt the project, because firms might have different opportunities. In particular, the costs of adopting the project might vary among firms. That is, in the present example internal rates of return and required rates of return have been set equal for convenience, but this need not always be the case. If the two rates diverge, the portfolio interpretation applies to market values and the rates of return required by the market.

The reason activity levels must be specified in advance is that the calculations just made assumed additivity of the activities' returns. The values of activities held at fixed output levels are additive, but if output levels were allowed to change, the relations between particular activities, values, and the total value produced by the firm might also change, as in the examples of Section 25.2. By fixing output levels prior to performing the analysis, the portfolio approach can be discussed without introducing additional complications.

## 25.4 Depreciation Tax Shield in a Risky World

At one point, Chapter 6 allowed for the effect of the corporate tax depreciation tax shield in calculating cash flows to be evaluated. In that discussion, cash flow from operations was known exactly and when combined with the tax shield, the sum was discounted at the risk-free rate of interest to obtain the net present value (NPV). When operating incomes are risky, a project's depreciation tax shield may have to be considered risky. Nevertheless, and as we now show, the depreciation tax shield will not necessarily present the same risk as the after-tax income from the project. Hence, a project's acceptability is assessed, as in Section 25.3, by applying different discount rates to the cash flows and the tax savings.

Recall from Chapter 6 that the operating cash flows from a project are made up of changes in revenues, changes in expenses, changes in taxes, and changes in working capital. Let's separate the operating cash flow into two components: (1) operating cash flow before the benefits attributable to the depreciation tax shield, which we denote by $X$, and (2) the depreciation tax shield that we will denote by $T$. Hence, the operating cash flow from a project, $Z$, can be expressed as:

$$Z = X + T \qquad (25.10)$$

The present value of $Z$ is:

$$P_Z = \frac{E(Z) - \{[E(r_m) - r_f]cov(Z, r_m)/\sigma^2(r_m)\}}{1 + r_f} \qquad (25.11)$$

Substituting equation (25.10) into equation (25.11) we have:

$$P_Z = \frac{E(X + T) - \{[E(r_m) - r_f]cov(X + T, r_m)/\sigma^2(r_m)\}}{1 + r_f}$$

which by application of the results of Web-Appendix L may be rewritten as:

$$P_Z = \frac{E(X) - \{[E(r_m) - r_f]cov(X, r_m)/\sigma^2(r_m)\}}{1 + r_f}$$
$$+ \frac{E(T) - \{[E(r_m) - r_f]cov(T, r_m)/\sigma^2(r_m)\}}{1 + r_f} \qquad (25.12)$$

We now inquire about the risk characteristics of $T$. If the firm is large and profitable, and the project small in comparison, the ability of the firm to claim the depreciation tax shield is likely unrelated to the outcomes of the particular project and may be regarded as risk free. In that case equation (25.12) reduces to:

$$P_Z = \frac{E(X) - [E(r_m) - r_f]cov(X, r_m)/\sigma^2(r_m)}{1 + r_f} + \frac{T}{1 + r_f} \qquad (25.13)$$

In other words, the depreciation tax shield can be discounted at the risk-free rate, but the cash flows from operations[8] must first be converted to their certainty equivalent value before discounting at the same risk-free rate. This means it is incorrect to add the expected value of the cash flow from operations before the benefits attributable to the depreciation tax shield to the depreciation tax shield and then apply a risk-adjusted discount rate, based on $cov(X, r_m)$, to the sum. However, if the risk of the combination of the two components of the cash flow, $cov(Z, r_m)$, is used to obtain a risk-adjusted discount rate for the combination, it is then correct to discount $E(Z)$ at that rate.

The main purpose in separating the cash flows into components is to display their particular influences on the risk of the combination. Whenever the tax shield is less risky than the project itself, the appropriate discount rate for the tax shield will be different from that for the project.[9]

* * *

## 25.5 SINGLE-PERIOD VERSUS MULTI-PERIOD INVESTMENT MODELS

So far we have considered investment decisions involving only two points in time. We wish now to consider how our previous approach must be altered if the markets for real investment goods are not perfect and if the cash flows the projects generate occur at several points in time.

### 25.5.1 The Market for Capital Goods

To employ the single-period model in a many period context, we need only assume that real capital goods can be bought or sold in a perfect (secondary) market. Under these circumstances, the selection of the optimal level of investment in each period (and particularly the first period) is merely a sequence of independent, single-period decisions that can be taken exactly as we have already specified.[10] The market for capital goods is perfect if there are zero transactions costs, operationally defined to mean that the firm would receive from selling the asset "exactly the same proceeds as

---

[8] Before the benefits attributable to the depreciation tax shield $X$.

[9] This compares exactly with the different required rates of return on stocks and bonds as discussed in Chapter 17.

[10] Fama and Miller (1972, pp. 122–125) discuss this question at some length under conditions of certainty. Recall also our discussion in Chapter 4.

it would have to expend for the (asset's) purchase."[11] Then to determine whether an asset should be purchased at time 1, we need only compare the time 1 investment outlay with the time 2 value of the forecast cash flow, including the secondary market price of the asset. Thus, for those real capital goods having a perfect secondary market, every investment decision can be made using a one-period model, just as in Chapter 4 and the prior discussion in this chapter.

It is also possible that many investment decisions can be made with a one-period model even when there are minor imperfections in the secondary markets. If the firm acquires the asset, the worst possible outcome it may expect is to receive its one-period cash flow and the net salvage value of the asset after the first period. If an asset is acceptable on this basis, it should be acquired, since the firm can only gain by the opportunity to retain it for additional periods. (Note, however, that this does not resolve the problem of the scale at which the asset should be adopted.) On the other hand, many worthwhile projects may have a salvage value at the end of one period that poorly reflects future earning power. In such cases, further periods must be considered in arriving at an investment decision.

## 25.5.2 Multi-Period Valuation in a Risky World[12]

We now rewrite equation (25.3) explicitly introducing time. We suppose time 1 is the current point in time, time 2 the end of the first period, time 3 the end of the second period, and so on up to time $n$, the planning horizon. The equilibrium value of a firm in a single-period world of risk-averse, expected utility-maximizers using the CAPM is:

$$V(1) = \frac{E[V(2)] - \lambda(1)cov[V(2), r_m(2)]}{1 + r_f(1)} \tag{25.14}$$

where

$V(2)$ = the risky time 2 value of the firm

$\lambda(1) = \{E[r_m(2)] - r_f(1)\}/\{\sigma^2[r_m(2)]\}$ = current market price per unit of risk

$r_f(1)$ = current one-period risk-free rate

$r_m(2)$ = return on the market portfolio realized over the period

Consider now a proposed single-period project that will bring an incremental operating cash flow of $X(2)$ and will require a current cash outlay $X(1) = I(1)$. Including the project, the end-of-period value of the firm will be $V(2) + X(2)$, or at the current time, using the valuation model,

$$V(1) + \Delta V(1) = \frac{E[V(2) + X(2)] - \lambda(1)cov[V(2) + X(2), r_m(2)]}{1 + r_f(1)} \tag{25.15}$$

---

[11] Bogue and Roll (1974). Specifically, *zero transactions costs* implies no brokerage costs, free transportation, and no installation or removal costs. This might be approximated by a private sale of an operating plant.

[12] This section depends entirely on the work of Bogue and Roll (1974). The discussion by Fama (1977) of the need for further restrictions on the model is considered below.

where $\Delta V(1)$ represents the time 1 increment to market value (not including investment cost) resulting from the project's adoption. Using the properties of expected value and covariance established in Web-Appendix L, we may write:

$$\Delta V(1) = \frac{E[X(2)] - \lambda(1)cov[X(2), r_m(2)]}{1 + r_f(1)} \tag{25.16}$$

As explained in Chapter 6, if the NPV of this project is positive, that is, if $\Delta V(1) - X(1) > 0$, the project is acceptable because it increases the firm's market value.

The procedure we have used so far is to construct, for a risky cash flow $X(2)$, the certainty equivalent:

$$E[X(2)] - \lambda(1)cov[X(2), r_m(2)]$$

and then discount this time 2 value by the risk-free rate to determine the time 1 market value.

Now consider a project lasting $n$ periods. Let $\Delta V(t)$ be the increments to the firm's value over the project's life, while $X(t)$ are the operating cash flows ($t = 1, \ldots, n$). If we can find an expression for $\Delta V(1)$, our problem is solved, as $\Delta V(1)$ may be compared with $I(1)$ to determine whether the project should be accepted. We proceed by working backward from the last time period to the first time period. For the last period we have:

$$\Delta V(n) = X(n)$$

That is, the value of the project at time $n$ is just the (final) operating cash flow at that time. In the next-to-last period we have a one-period valuation problem as before but with the change that the value we find will be conditional on the state of the world[13] that exists at time $n - 1$, denoted by $S(n - 1)$. The incremental value at time $n - 1$ will be:

$$\Delta V(n-1) = X(n-1) \frac{E[X(n)|S(n-1)] - \lambda(n-1)cov\{[X(n), r_m(n)]|S(n-1)\}}{1 + r_f(n-1)} \tag{25.17}$$

where $E$ now refers to an expectation conditional on state $S(n - 1)$, as denoted by the vertical bars in equation (25.17). The covariance term is also calculated in this conditional manner. Note that not all the terms on the right-hand side of equation (25.17) are observable before time $n$.

Once we have $\Delta V(n - 1)$ calculated, we can use it in an expression just like equation (25.17) to calculate $\Delta V(n - 2)$. We can then continue to apply our single-period valuation model to each period successively so that, in general, we have at time $k$

---

[13] See Chapter 10 where we discuss both contingent claims analysis and states of the world. At time $n - 1$, $S(n - 1)$ is not random. But at times prior to $n - 1$, $S(n - 1)$ is random. As we explain and illustrate in the next chapter, the contingent claims approach provides an alternative to the CAPM approach to capital budgeting.

$$\Delta V(k) = X(k) + \frac{E[\Delta V(k+1)|S(k)] - \lambda(k)cov\{[\Delta V(k+1), r_m(k+1)]|S(k)\}}{1 + r_f(k)},$$

for $k = 1, 2, ..., n-1$

$$(25.18)$$

For a project with an $n$-period life, the technical calculation required by equation (25.18) is that of solving an $n$-stage stochastic dynamic programming problem. In principle,[14] this approach shows how to value assets that can be traded only in imperfect secondary markets.

We shall shortly provide an example of how the approach just outlined can be put to work in solving a multi-period asset acquisition problem, but before doing so, it is instructive to compare the foregoing solution to that obtained when there is a perfect secondary market for real capital assets. A perfect secondary market fully reflects the discounted future earning power of a project at each point in time. That is, just as in the certainty case discussed in Chapter 6, a project's value at any point in time, $\Delta V(k)$, will equal its market price whenever asset markets are perfect. Note also that even if there are not perfect markets for the capital goods themselves, the same result will obtain if claims to the goods (financial instruments conveying ownership rights, such as stocks and bonds) can be sold separately in a perfect capital market. Usually, however, since the capital goods will be only a portion of the firm's assets, financial claims for the separate assets will not be available.

## 25.5.3 Example

Consider a project with only one operating cash flow, to be realized at time 3. First we find the project's incremental value at time 2:

$$\Delta V(2) \frac{E[X(3)|S(2)] - \lambda(2)cov\{[X(3), r_m(3)]|S(2)\}}{1 + r_f(2)}$$

$$(25.19)$$

The time 1 incremental value is then:

$$\Delta V(1) = \frac{E[\Delta V(2)] - \lambda(1)cov[\Delta V(2), r_m(2)]}{1 + r_f(1)}$$

$$(25.20)$$

Transposing the denominator of the right-hand side of equation (25.19) to the left-hand side, taking expectations, and rearranging, we have:

$$E[\Delta V(2)|E[1 + r_f(2)] + cov[\Delta V(2), r_f(2)]$$
$$= E[X(3)|S(2)] - E[\lambda(2)cov\{X(3), r_m(3)|S(2)\}]$$

$$(25.21)$$

---

[14] Even if we only imagine a finite number of possible states of the world, such a problem is often difficult and costly to solve.

Our notation now includes random variables because, while equation (25.20) provides an expression formed from the vantage point of time 2, equation (25.21) views the outcomes from the vantage point of time 1. Such variables as $r_f(2)$, known with certainty at time 2, are known only as random variables at time 1.

Rearranging equation (25.20) into an expression for $E[\Delta V(2)]$, substituting into equation (25.21), and rearranging further, we obtain:

$$
\begin{aligned}
\Delta V(1)&[1 + r_f(1)]E[1 + r_f(2)] \\
&= E[X(3)|S(2)] - E[\lambda(2)cov\{[X(3), r_m(3)]|S(2)\}] \\
&\quad - \lambda(1)cov[\Delta V(2), r_m(2)]E[1 + r_f(2)] - cov[\Delta V(2), r_f(2)]
\end{aligned}
\tag{25.22}
$$

This somewhat complex-looking result has an interesting interpretation. The time 1 value of the single risky operating cash flow two periods in the future is given by the current (conditional) expectation of that flow adjusted by three risk premiums and discounted by the compound amount of the current risk-free rate and expected risk-free rate one period hence.

- By taking the expected cash flow and subtracting the first adjustment on the right-hand side of equation (25.22), effectively we obtain the certainty equivalent value viewed one period hence.
- The second adjustment accounts for the covariation risk of the intermediate value of the project one period hence, compounded to the end of the second period. This term plays the role of a reinvestment opportunity cost, accounting for the possibility that the project could be sold before the final cash flow is realized.
- The third adjustment accounts for the risk of interest rate fluctuation, since possible changes in market interest rates could affect the project's value at intermediate periods even if the other data and forecasts remain unchanged.

In a practical attempt to use this model, we might assume that the risk-free rate and market price of risk would be constant over the relevant planning horizon. This implies that the last term of equation (25.22) (i.e., the interest rate risk adjustment) is zero. We also assume the cash flow forecast is given unconditionally. Then the simplified valuation model is:

$$
\Delta V(1) = \frac{E[X(3)] - \lambda \, cov[X(3), r_m(3)]}{(1 + r_f)^2} - \frac{\lambda \, cov[\Delta V(2), r_m(2)]}{1 + r_f}
\tag{25.23}
$$

This expression can then be compared with the initial investment cost to determine whether the project is acceptable.

One interesting feature of equation (25.23) is that the reinvestment opportunity cost represented by the second right-hand term remains,[15] because the opportunity

---

[15] But compare Fama (1977), who points out that if investors are not to hedge against future changes in portfolio opportunities, the portfolio opportunity set is nonstochastic, so that the only admissible uncertainty is in expected cash earnings as assessed when decisions are made. This further simplifies equation (25.23) by eliminating the second term.

cost of retaining an existing asset has to be considered in deciding whether to retain or sell it. In the general solution, the NPV of this second-period decision must be positive to continue holding the asset. Otherwise the resale value should be used instead. On the other hand, if the real capital good is fixed in the sense that it is installed at time 1 and cannot be resold at any positive price after installation, the second term of equation (25.23) is meaningless and equal to zero.[16]

If there were an intermediate operating cash flow $X(2)$, it should be clear that we would add another one-period valuation expression for it to the right-hand side of equation (25.23) to obtain the appropriate expression for $\Delta V(1)$ in this case.

## 25.5.4 The Source of Risk

Let us rework equation (25.16) to express the value of a single uncertain cash flow $X(t)$ at time $t = 1$:

$$\Delta V(t-1) = \frac{E[X(t)] - \lambda(t)cov[X(t), r_m(t)]}{1 + r_f(t)} \tag{25.24}$$

How we take the next step in working backward in time and write the increment in value at time $t - 2$ depends on where we incorporate risk into the various arguments of equation (25.24). As Fama (1970) and Fama and MacBeth (1974) have shown, in a market where securities are priced each period according to the CAPM, there can be no relationship between risky returns realized at $t - 1$ and risk about the characteristics of the portfolio opportunity set to be observed at $t - 1$ [i.e., the point distribution of returns for period $t$, which in turn implies $\lambda(t - 1)$]. Should such a relationship exist, investors would have an incentive to use their portfolio decisions at time $t - 2$ to hedge against risk regarding portfolio opportunities available at time $t - 1$. These actions imply a pricing process different from the CAPM that we have been using.[17]

Considering the pricing model given by equation (25.24), stochastic variation in $r_f(t)$ and $\lambda(t)$ would, in general, affect the increment in the value of the firm at time $t - 1$, creating the type of relationship between returns realized at $t - 1$ and the parameters of the portfolio opportunity set at $t - 1$, which generally must be ruled out in multi-period applications of the CAPM. Hence, if we wish to continue to apply the CAPM, we must assume that the market parameters do not vary stochastically through time.[18]

Since we have ruled out risk in determining the market parameters, the only remaining source of risk about the incremental value of the firm at earlier points in time must be found with respect to the value of $E[X(t)]$ and to $cov[X(t), r_m(t)]$ prior to time $t$. If we believe that the expected value and covariance are known in all earlier periods, then we may write:

---

[16] Compare Fama and Miller (1972, p. 123).
[17] See Merton (1973) and Long (1974).
[18] This condition was not recognized in the analysis of Bogue and Roll (1974).

$$\Delta V(t-1) = \frac{\Delta V(t-1)}{1 + r_f(t-1)} \tag{25.25}$$

and by repeated application,

$$
\begin{aligned}
\Delta V(1) &= \prod_{k=1}^{t-1} \left[ \frac{1}{1 + r_f(k)} \right] \Delta V(t-1) \\
&= \prod_{k=1}^{t-1} \left[ \frac{1}{1 + r_f(k)} \right] E[X(t)] \left[ \frac{1 - \{\lambda(t)cov[X(t), r_m(t)]/E[X(t)]\}}{1 + r_f(t)} \right] \\
&= \prod_{k=1}^{t-1} \left[ \frac{1}{1 + r_f(k)} \right] \left\{ \frac{1}{1 + E[r(t)]} \right\} E[X(t)]
\end{aligned}
\tag{25.25}
$$

where $E[r(t)]$ is the risk-adjusted discount rate applied to $X(t)$ at time $t$. Note particularly that under the assumption that $E$ and $cov$ are known, the risk-adjusted discount rate is relevant only at $t$ when the cash flow $X(t)$ is to be realized. For the intermediate times, the risk-free rates must be applied. This appears contrary to the intuitive and widely used method of applying a risk-adjusted discount rate during all time periods.

Fama (1977) goes on to propose a *rational expectations adjustment model*, which allows for risk with respect to learning over time[19] about the distribution of $X(t)$. By an argument we shall not repeat here, it is shown that the only admissible risk must be isolated in the expected value of $X(t)$ at earlier times. Under this assumption, it can further be shown that we may write:

$$\Delta V(1) = E(1)[X(t)] \left\{ \frac{1}{1 + E[r(2)]} \right\} \cdots \left\{ \frac{1}{1 + E[r(t)]} \right\} \tag{25.27}$$

duly noting that the expectation operator is itself time subscripted. Further, as argued above, the risk-adjusted discount rates (which are themselves derived from the covariance of the expectation adjustment variable with the market) must be known (i.e., must be non-stochastic).

Equation (25.27) looks more like what we earlier found under certainty in Chapter 6. Note, however, that in order to assume the risk-adjusted rates are non-stochastic, we have had to place heavy restrictions on the market price of risk, the risk-free rate of interest, and the reassessment risk. These restrictions are implicit in the presumption that prices in the capital market are determined each period according to the CAPM. If

---

[19] This should not be taken to imply that the underlying production possibility frontier is stochastic.

we further assume that these parameters are constant over time,[20] then the risk-adjusted discount rates will be the same in each period. This agrees more closely to the cost-of-capital approach presented in introductory textbooks in finance.

To this point, however, we have only considered a single cash flow occurring at some future time $t$. We now extend this to the case of finding the market value of cash flows in each of many future periods. We now rewrite equation (25.27) for a single operating cash flow, adding another subscript to the risk-adjusted discount rates to indicate that they all apply to the particular cash flow to be realized at $t$:

$$\Delta V(t, 1) = E(1)[X(t)] \prod_{\tau=1}^{t} \left\{ \frac{1}{1 + E[r(t,\tau)]} \right\} \qquad (25.28)$$

where $\tau$ runs from $1, \ldots, t$.

The total incremental value of the project then will be the sum of the incremental values of all future cash flows:

$$\Delta V(1) = \sum_{t=1}^{T} \Delta V(t,1) = \sum_{t=1}^{T} E(1)[X(t)] \prod_{\tau=1}^{t} \left\{ \frac{1}{1 + E[r(t,\tau)]} \right\} \qquad (25.29)$$

From equation (25.29) we conclude that in a capital market where prices in each period are set according to the CAPM, the discount rates $E[r(t, \tau)]$ are known but that the rates for the different periods with respect to a particular operating cash flow need not be the same and, further, that the rates for a particular period can vary across cash flows. If the firm is composed of projects of different types, we may first value individual projects as in equation (25.29) and then sum across projects to find the value of the firm. Thus, under the current assumptions, risk-adjusted discount rates can differ (1) across time for the operating cash flow of a given project to be received at a given time, (2) across the operating cash flows of a given project at any particular time, and (3) both ways as well as across the cash flows of different projects. While strictly correct under the current assumptions, equation (25.29) implies a heavy data collection burden on management.

If we write:

$$\beta(t, \tau) = \frac{cov[r(t, \tau), r_m(\tau)]}{\sigma^2[r_m(\tau)]} \qquad (25.30)$$

then we may also write the multi-period security market line as:

$$E[r(t, \tau)] = r_f(t) + \{E[r_m(t) - r_f(t)]\}\beta(t, \tau) \qquad (25.31)$$

Again, pricing according to the CAPM implies that the values of $E[r(t, \tau)]$ and $\beta(t, \tau)$ are already known at time 1 but that they may vary both across the operating cash

---

[20] Note that this still allows a restricted form of learning about the parameters of the distribution of $X(t)$.

flows of different time periods $t$ and across time $\tau$. It may appear convenient to assume that, at least for the cash flows of projects of a given type, the values of $\beta(t, \tau)$ are the same for all $t$ and $\tau$ so that the value of $\beta$ is constant through time. Of course, this is just another way of saying that the required return (cost of capital) for projects with a particular cash flow risk is constant through time.

## KEY POINTS

- Capital budgeting projects typically involve risk, with risk arising from different sources that depend on environmental conditions, the industry in which the firm is operating, and the type of project being considered.
- The sources of risk in capital budgeting include the risks associated with future economic, international, and market conditions, future tax rates, and future interest rates.
- In capital budgeting under risk, a firm's managers can still implement the market value criterion applied in a perfect capital market by relating that criterion to the firm's expected earnings and risk characteristics.
- The Capital Asset Pricing Model provides a theoretical framework for how risky future cash flows can be evaluated in order to assess risky projects.
- In evaluating the cash flows of risky projects, management can use a certainty equivalent approach or a risk-adjusted discount rate approach.
- In evaluating a risk project, the nature of the firm's business risk is determined by the investment projects it accepts; adopting a new project changes the firm's business risk, as reflected by the change in beta and hence in the discount rate applied to the firm's total earnings stream.
- Management should adopt new projects when their internal rate of return exceeds the market-required rate of return for projects with a given measure of risk.
- Because of the possibility of different business risks, the required rate of return on a project is not necessarily the firm's prevailing cost of capital.
- The adoption of a profitable project by management can alter a firm's overall cost of capital because the risk of the firm's earnings stream can be altered by a new investment project.
- The CAPM can be employed to develop optimal capital budgeting rules similar to those rules that management should follow in a perfect capital market.
- The rule that management should follow in assessing projects having the same business risk as the existing firm and has constant returns to scale is that such projects should be adopted provided they can be implemented at a cost low enough to permit the project to earn at least the required rate of return.
- When implementing a project that has diminishing returns to scale, management should invest up to the point where the certainty equivalent marginal internal rate of return equals the risk-free rate of interest.
- Holding output levels fixed, the CAPM can be used to relate rates of return on different projects both to each other and to the market-required rate of return.

- With fixed output levels the firm can be regarded as a portfolio of investment projects and the firm's required return is the weighted average of the returns required by the market on each of the individual projects.
- When operating incomes are risky, a project's depreciation tax shield may have to be considered risky but the depreciation tax shield will not necessarily present the same risk as the after-tax income from the project. As a result, a project's acceptability is assessed by applying different discount rates to the cash flows and the tax savings.
- A project's depreciation tax shield can be discounted at the risk-free rate, but the cash flows from operations must first be converted to their certainty equivalent value before discounting at the same risk-free rate.
- Multi-period formulations of the investment problem are useful in imperfect capital markets when the investment's cash flows occur at several moments in time.
- One way of calculating the present value of a multi-period project is to use dynamic programming to determine values sequentially. The method proceeds backward in time, one period at a time, from the horizon to the first time period. In each period's calculation, future values are added to the current value, thus providing the present value of all the project's cash flows at the first time period.
- A multi-period formulation accounts for the covariation risk of the intermediate value of the project in each of the future periods. The multi-period method in effect provides information regarding reinvestment opportunity cost, accounting for the possibility that the project could be sold before the final cash flow is realized.
- The multi-period method also takes into account the risk of interest rate fluctuation, since possible changes in market interest rates could affect the project's value at intermediate periods even if the other data and forecasts remain unchanged.
- The multi-period method provides for contingency planning, since at each period decisions to change the investment (e.g., increase, abandon) can be taken into account in the calculations, and the changes can be dependent on receiving new information or the realization of other environmental changes.

## QUESTIONS

1. What are the reasons why a firm's management should not always evaluate projects with the net present value (NPV) method by direct cash flow discounting methods using a risk-free interest rate?

2. What are the three terms of the time 1 value of the single risky operating cash flow two periods in the future?

3. In the multi-period valuation model, why does the risk-adjusted discount rate need to apply to cash flow at time $t$, but risk-free rates are applied for the intermediate times under the assumption that the expected value and covariance of the cash flow are known?

4. The market value of a firm at time 1 is $5 million and its estimated beta is 0.4. Suppose that following the adoption of a new capital budgeting project, the required rate of return increases to 9% and the new market value increases to $5.5 million. Using the Capital Asset Pricing Model, what is the required rate of the return for the new project? Assume that the risk-free interest rate is 5% and the expected return on the market is 10%.

5. The market value of CourantRox Corporation is $20 million. There are three mutually exclusive potential projects—A, B, and C—being considered by management. Only one of the projects can be selected. All three projects require the same initial cash investment of $7 million. All three projects have only one cash flow after the project is completed one year from now. The management of CourantRox Corporation has the following information about these three projects:

   - *Project A*: A known single cash flow (i.e., a deterministic cash flow) of $10.5 million immediately after the completion of the project.
   - *Project B*: A risky cash flow (i.e., a stochastic cash flow) of $11 million and the estimated beta for this project is 0.6.
   - *Project C*: A risky cash flow (i.e., a stochastic cash flow) of $12 million and the estimated beta for this project is 2.1.

   The one-year risk-free interest rate (i.e., the relevant interest rate over the life of the three projects) is 5%. Based on the projections of Wall Street analysts, the expected return on the stock market over the next year is 12%.

   Given this information and assuming that the Capital Asset Pricing Model is appropriate for evaluating these three projects, which project should management prefer?

6. A group of investors is considering starting a firm. The joint distribution of the internal rate of return (IRR) for starting the firm $R_j$ and the market portfolio return $R_m$ is assumed to be as follows:

   | $R_j$ | 20% | 10% | $R_m 5\%$ |
   |-------|------|------|------|
   | 30% | 1/8 | 1/16 | 1/16 |
   | 15% | 1/16 | 1/4 | 0 |
   | 0% | 1/8 | 1/16 | 1/4 |

   a. What is the expected return for the market and for the firm?
   b. What is the beta for the firm?
   c. Should the investor group start assuming that the distribution above is correct and the risk-free interest rate is 5%?

7. Assume that funds invested at time 1 produce cash flow at time 2 according to

   $$Z = I^{1/2}X + (1/8)\log(I)X$$

where

$X$ = the cash flow at final time

$I$ = amount invested in the activity at initial time

$Z$ = amount realized at final time from that investment

[This is a modification of equation of (25.5) in the chapter.] Find an appropriate expression for the optimal amount of the investment in the activity at time 1.

8. The operating cash flows from a project consist of two components: (1) operating cash flow before the benefits attributable to the depreciation tax shield denoted by $X$ and (2) the depreciation tax shield denoted by $T$. If the depreciation tax shield is unrelated to the outcomes of that project, using the Capital Asset Pricing Model, what is the present value of the project assuming the expected of the market return is 15% and the expected of the project $E(X)$ is $10 million, assuming that beta is 0.3, $T$ is $2 million, and the risk-free interest rate is 5%?

9. **a.** A project has cash flow at time 3 with an expected value, denoted by $E[X(3)]$, of $5 million. What is the simplified valuation of the time 1 increment to market value, denoted by $V(1)$ (not including investment cost), resulting from the project's adoption, assuming a constant risk-free interest rate of 5% and constant market price of risk of 0.3, the covariance of the cash flow at time 3 and market return is 4, and the covariance of the time 2 incremental value and market return is 2.

   **b.** What is the value of the time 1 increment to market value $V(1)$ if there is another cash flow $X(2)$ with an expected value of $3 million and the covariance of the cash flow at time 2 and market return is 2?

10. Assume the following about an investment project with a cost of $1,500 that is being considered by management:

   - The project will generate cash flow $X(2)$ at time 2 that is normally distributed with mean $1,000, and standard deviation $100.
   - The project will generate cash flow $X(3)$ at time 3 that is normally distributed with mean $1,200 and standard deviation $200.
   - The market return is normally distribution with a mean of 10% and standard deviation 0.005.
   - The correlation between $X(2)$ and the market return is 0.8.
   - The correlation between $X(3)$ and the market return is 0.4.

   How would management value the project if the borrowing and lending rates in the market are 8% and the project cannot be resold?

# REFERENCES

Bogue, Marcus C., and Richard R. Roll. (1974). "Capital Budgeting of Risky Projects with 'Imperfect' Markets for Physical Capital," *Journal of Finance* **29**: 601–613.

Fama, Eugene F. (1970). "Multi-Period Consumption-Investment Decisions," *American Economic Review* **60**: 163–174.

Fama, Eugene F. (1977). "Risk-Adjusted Discount Rates and Capital Budgeting under Uncertainty," *Journal of Financial Economics* **4**: 3–24.

Fama, Eugene F., and James D. MacBeth. (1974). "Tests of the Multi-Period Two-Parameter Model," *Journal of Financial Economics*, **1**: 43–66.

Fama, Eugene F., and Merton H. Miller (1972). *The Theory of Finance*. New York: Holt, Rinehart, and Winston.

Long, John B., Jr. "Stock Prices, Inflation and the Term Structure of Interest Rates," *Journal of Financial Economics* **1**: 131–170.

Merton, Robert C. (1973). "An Intertemporal Capital Asset Pricing Model," *Econometrica* **41**: 867–887.

# 26

# EVALUATING PROJECT RISK IN CAPITAL BUDGETING

*A*s explained in the previous chapter, capital budgeting decisions require management to evaluate each project's future cash flows, their riskiness, and their present value. Managers incorporate risk into their calculations in one of two equivalent approaches: (1) a risk-adjusted discount rate approach, or (2) a certainty-equivalent approach. The latter can be calculated either on an ad hoc basis or under a risk-neutral probability measure that provides a theoretical rationale for determining market value, which is after all a particular form of certainty-equivalent value.

Regardless of the method of estimation, the hurdle that management must overcome in arriving at a certainty-equivalent value involves evaluating project riskiness. To assess the risk of a project, management must first recognize that the firm's existing assets are the result of prior investment decisions, and that the firm is really a portfolio of projects. So when management adds another project to its portfolio, it should consider both the risk of that additional project and the risk of the entire portfolio when the new project is included in it. However, despite its correctness, the portfolio theoretic approach is not always easy to implement in practice, and in applications the focus is frequently on the risk of the individual project.

In this chapter, we look at different techniques for assessing a project's risk. Although the techniques are helpful to management in measuring and evaluating project risk, much of the estimation may be subjective. Judgment, with a large dose of experience, is used to support scientific means of incorporating risk. Is this bad? Well, the scientific approaches to measurement and evaluation of risk depend, in part, on subjective assessments of risk, the objective probability distributions of future cash flows, and judgments about market risk. So it is at least possible, and in many cases quite likely, that supplementing the more technical analyses with subjective assessments may better reflect the project's risk.

This chapter begins by reviewing the risk-adjusted discount rate and the certainty-equivalent approaches to valuing projects. We then look at how to quantify a project's stand-alone risk and market risk. We conclude the chapter with an application of contingency strategies and the real options approach to evaluating projects.

## 26.1 Risk-Adjusted Discount Rate

As explained in Chapter 22, the cost of capital is the cost of funds raised from creditors and owners. The greater the risk of a project, the greater the return that creditors and owners require; that is, the greater the cost of capital for that project. One view of a project's cost of capital regards it as the sum of (1) the risk-free return (which provides compensation for the time value of money) and (2) a risk premium that compensates for project risk.

A commonly used method of estimating a project's cost of capital (i.e., its market-required rate of return) is to use the Capital Asset Pricing Model (CAPM), as explained in the previous chapter. The CAPM specifies that the greater a project's market risk, the greater its market-required return. Finding a project's market-required return requires first determining the market price of risk and then fine-tuning this price to reflect the risk of the project. The market price of risk is the difference between the expected market return on the market portfolio and the risk-free rate of interest. Hence, if management is considering investing in a project whose risk is the same as that of the market portfolio, the project's risk premium should equal the market price of risk. More generally, the risk premium for a given project is the product of the market risk premium and the project's estimated beta. The project's beta adjusts the market risk premium to reflect the risk of the particular project, and adding the adjusted premium to the risk-free interest rate gives the risk-adjusted rate of interest for the project.

Although the foregoing method of applying the CAPM seems quite simple in theory, in practice it may be difficult to estimate the project's beta, and consequently equally difficult to estimate the risk-adjusted interest rate. Another way to estimate the risk-adjusted discount rate for a project is for management to use the company's weighted-average cost of capital (WACC) as a starting point,[1] and then adjust the WACC to suit the perceived risk of the project. For example:

- If a new project being considered is riskier than the average project of the company, the cost of capital of the new project is greater than the average cost of capital.
- If the new project is less risky, its cost of capital is less than the average cost of capital.
- If the new project is as risky as the average project of the company, the new project's cost of capital is equal to the average cost of capital.

However, altering the company's cost of capital to reflect a project's cost of capital requires judgment. How much do we adjust it? If the project is riskier than the typical project, do we add 2%? 4%? 10%? Unless we use the CAPM or another similar method, there is no prescription here. It depends on the judgment and experience of

---

[1] The WACC is the company's marginal cost of raising one more dollar of capital—the cost of raising one more dollar in the context of all the company's projects considered altogether, not just the project being evaluated.

management. But this is where the measures of a project's stand-alone risk, described later in this chapter, can be used to help form that judgment.

Firms whose managements do use risk-adjusted discount rates usually adopt the expedient of classifying projects into risk classes with established costs of capital. For example, management with a cost of capital of 10% may develop from experience the following project classes and discount rates:

| Type of project | Cost of capital |
| --- | --- |
| New product | 14% |
| New market | 12% |
| Expansion | 10% |
| Replacement | 8% |

Given this set of costs of capital, the financial manager need only figure out what class a project belongs to and then apply the discount rate assigned to that class.

## 26.2  CERTAINTY-EQUIVALENT APPROACH AND ITS APPLICATION IN PRACTICE

An alternative to adjusting the discount rate is to adjust the cash flow to reflect risk. As explained in the previous chapter, this is done by converting each risky cash flow into its *certainty equivalent*, the certain cash flow that is considered to be equivalent to the risky cash flow. For example, if in some state of the world the cash flow two periods hence is $1.5 million, the certainty-equivalent value two periods hence is $1.5 million multiplied by the risk-neutral probability for that event. This certainty equivalent could be $1.4 million, $1 million, $0.8 million, or some other amount. The certainty-equivalent value depends on both the state of the world that generates the $1.5 million and the risk-neutral probability associated with that event.[2] The time 1 certainty-equivalent value is then the time 3 certainty-equivalent value discounted by the risk-free rate for the two periods between time 1 and time 3.

The certainty-equivalent approach of incorporating risk into the net present value (NPV) analysis is useful for several reasons.

- It separates the time value of money and risk. Risk is accounted for in the adjusted cash flows while the time value of money is accounted for in the risk-free discount rate.
- It allows each period's cash flows to be adjusted separately for risk. This is accomplished by converting each event's cash flows into a certainty equivalent

---

[2] Unless one can establish that valuations are reached in such a way that no arbitrage opportunities remain, the risk-neutral probability may have to be estimated by management. In such cases, sensitivity analysis can be used to help arrive at useful estimates.

for the relevant time period, then discounting these periods' certainty equivalent back to the present time.[3]

- Management can incorporate different attitudes toward bearing risk. This is done in determining the certainty-equivalent cash flows.

However, there is at least one disadvantage to using the certainty-equivalent approach—the certainty equivalent depends on estimates of the risk-neutral probabilities, and those probabilities are not always easy to estimate. Nevertheless, Chapter 16 showed how to use the risk-neutral probability approach to value assets, and applying risk-neutral probabilities to cash flows discounted at the risk-free rate gives us a certainty-equivalent value that is valid as long as we accept the assumption that the valuations are calculated in a world free of arbitrage opportunities. Even where that assumption is not valid, the risk-neutral probability approach at least gives a benchmark for a project's current market value.

## 26.3 MEASURING A PROJECT'S STAND-ALONE RISK

If management has some idea of a project's future cash flows and their associated objective probabilities, it can develop measures of project risk.[4] Usually this approach measures the project's risk in isolation from the firm's other projects and in that event is referred to as the project's *stand-alone risk*. Since most firms have many assets, a project's stand-alone risk may not be the relevant risk for analyzing the project. A firm is a portfolio of assets, and the assets' returns are not perfectly positively correlated with one another. We are therefore concerned with how the addition of the project changes the firm's asset portfolio risk.

Now let's take it a step further. Shareholders are investors who themselves may hold diversified portfolios. These investors are concerned about how the firm's investments in projects affect the risk of their own personal portfolios. Consequently, as explained in the previous chapter, when owners demand compensation for risk, they seek compensation for the undiversifiable market risk. Recognizing this, management should be concerned with how a new project changes the firm's market risk: The *project's market risk* is relevant for making managerial decisions.

For example, if Microsoft Corporation introduces a new operating system, the relevant risk of the new product is its market risk rather than its stand-alone risk. Microsoft has many computer software products and services in its portfolio of projects. (This illustration is adapted from Fabozzi and Peterson, 2002.) And while its project investments are all related to computers, the products' fortunes are not perfectly correlated. The relevant risk for Microsoft to consider is therefore the product's market risk. Some of the project's stand-alone risk is diversified away at the company level and some at the investors' level, since investors who hold Microsoft common

---

[3] The certainty equivalent values will usually differ for each period and for each event occurring at that time.

[4] In fact, if management has both objective and risk-neutral probabilities, it actually has two distributions that can be used in calculating risk.

stock in their portfolios also own stock of other corporations (and perhaps also own bonds, real estate, or cash).

On the other hand, the project's stand-alone risk should not be ignored. If managers are making decisions for a small, closely held firm whose owners do not hold well-diversified portfolios, the stand-alone risk gives us a good idea of the project's risk. And many small businesses fit into this category. In addition, even if management is making capital budgeting decisions for large corporations that have many products and whose owners are well diversified, the analysis of stand-alone risk is useful. A project's stand-alone risk is both easier to measure than market risk, and may also be so closely related to market risk that it provides a good estimate of the latter.

In any event, we can get an idea of a project's stand-alone risk by evaluating the project's future cash flows. Throughout this book we have described various risk measures. These measures are frequently based on such probability distribution parameters as variance/standard deviation or skewness. However, the calculation of these measures presupposes that a probability distribution for the random variable of interest is available. In the case of capital budgeting, this means that one requires an estimate of a probability distribution for a project's future cash flows. How does management obtain an objective probability distribution for a project's future cash flow? It can be obtained from research, judgment, and/or experience. In addition, analytical tools such as sensitivity analysis and simulation can be employed to aid in deriving a probability distribution of project cash flows.

## 26.3.1  Sensitivity Analysis

Estimates of cash flows are based on assumptions about economic performance, competitors' reactions, consumer tastes and preferences, construction costs, and taxes, among a host of other possible assumptions. One of the first things management must consider about these estimates is how sensitive they are. For example, if the firm can only sell 2 million units instead of 3 million units in the first year, is the project still profitable? Or, if Congress increases corporate tax rates, will the project still be attractive?

Management can analyze the sensitivity of cash flows to changes in underlying assumptions by reestimating the cash flows for different scenarios. *Sensitivity analysis*, also called *scenario analysis* or "what if" analysis, is a method of looking at the possible outcomes, given a change in one of the factors.

To see how sensitivity analysis works, we will use an illustration from Fabozzi and Peterson (2002). The Williams 5 & 10 Company is a discount retail chain, selling a variety of goods at low prices. Business has been very good lately and the Williams 5 & 10 Company is considering opening one more retail outlet in a neighboring town at the end of 20Y0. Management estimates that it would be about five years before a large national chain of discount stores moves into that town to compete with its store. So it is looking at this expansion as a five-year prospect. After five years, it would most likely retreat from this town.

Williams's management has researched the expansion and determined that the building needed could be built for $400,000 and it would cost $100,000 to buy the cash registers, shelves, and other equipment necessary to start up this outlet. Management expects to be able to sell the building for $350,000 and the equipment for $50,000 after five years.

The new store requires $50,000 of additional inventory. Since all sales are in cash, there is no expected increase in accounts receivable. However, the firm anticipates no other changes in working capital. The tax rate is a flat 30% and there are no investment tax credits associated with this expansion. Also, capital gains are taxed at the ordinary tax rate.

The firm's tax staff has determined the depreciation expense for each year to be:

| Year | Building | Equipment | Total |
|------|----------|-----------|-------|
| 20Y1 | $12,698 | $20,000 | $32,698 |
| 20Y2 | 12,698 | 32,000 | 44,698 |
| 20Y3 | 12,698 | 19,200 | 31,898 |
| 20Y4 | 12,698 | 11,520 | 24,218 |
| 20Y5 | 12,698 | 11,520 | 24,218 |
| Total | $63,490 | $94,240 | |

The Williams 5 & 10 extends no credit on its sales and pays for all its purchases immediately. The projections for sales and expenses for the new store for the next five years are:

| | Sales | Expenses |
|------|-------|----------|
| 20Y0 | $200,000 | $100,000 |
| 20Y1 | 300,000 | 100,000 |
| 20Y2 | 300,000 | 100,000 |
| 20Y3 | 300,000 | 100,000 |
| 20Y4 | 50,000 | 20,000 |

The increase in inventory is an investment of cash when the store is opened, a $50,000 cash outflow. That is, management has to invest to maintain inventory while the store is in operation. When the store is closed in five years, there is no need to keep this increased level of inventory. If we assume that the inventory at the end of the fifth year can be sold for $50,000, that amount will be a cash inflow at that time. Since this is a change in working capital for the duration of the project, we include this cash flow as part of the asset acquisition (initially) and its disposition (at the end of the fifth year).

The tax basis of the building and equipment at the end of the fifth year are:

$$\text{Tax basis of building} = \$400,000 - \$63,490 = \$336,510$$

and

$$\text{Tax basis of equipment} = \$100,000 - \$94,240 = \$5,760$$

**TABLE 26.1**
WORKSHEET FOR THE WILLIAM 5 & 10 EXPANSION PROJECT

| | End of year | | | | | |
|---|---|---|---|---|---|---|
| | 20Y0 | 20Y1 | 20Y2 | 20Y3 | 20Y4 | 20Y5 |
| Investment cash flows | | | | | | |
| Purchase and sale of building | ($400,000) | | | | | $350,000 |
| Tax on sale of building | | | | | | −4,047 |
| Purchase and sale of equipment | −100,000 | | | | | 50,000 |
| Tax on sale of equipment | | | | | | −13,272 |
| Change in working capital | −50,000 | | | | | 50,000 |
| Investment cash flows | ($550,000) | | | | | $432,681 |
| | | | | | | |
| Change in operating cash flows | | | | | | |
| Change in revenues | | $200,000 | $300,000 | $300,000 | $300,000 | $50,000 |
| Less: Change in expenses | | −100,000 | −100,000 | −100,000 | −100,000 | −20,000 |
| Less: Change in depreciation | | −32,698 | −44,698 | −31,898 | −24,218 | −24,218 |
| Change in taxable income | | $67,302 | $155,302 | $168,102 | $175,782 | $5,782 |
| Less: taxes | | −20,191 | −46,591 | −50,531 | −52,735 | −1,735 |
| Change in income after tax | | $47,111 | $108,711 | $117,671 | $123,047 | $4,047 |
| Add: Change in depreciation, | | 32,698 | 44,698 | 31,898 | 24,218 | 24,218 |
| Change in operating cash flows | | $79,809 | $153,409 | $149,569 | $147,265 | $28,265 |
| **Net cash flows** | **−$550,000** | **$79,809** | **$153,409** | **$149,569** | **$147,265** | **$460,946** |

Since management expects to sell the building for $350,000 and the equipment for $50,000 after five years, the sale of the building brings a cash inflow of $350,000 at the end of the fifth year. The building is expected to be sold for more than its tax basis, creating a taxable gain of $350,000 − $336,510 = $13,490. The tax on this gain is $4,047. The sale of the equipment generates a cash inflow of $50,000. The gain on the sale of the equipment is $50,000 − $5,760 = $44,240. The tax on this gain is 30% of $44,240, or $3,272.

The pieces of this cash flow puzzle are assembled in Table 26.1, which identifies the cash inflows and outflows for each year, with acquisition and disposition cash flows at the top and operating cash flows below.

Now let's vary the assumptions. Suppose that the tax rate is not known with certainty, but may be any one of 20%, 30%, or 40%. The tax rate that we assume affects all the following factors:

- The expected tax on the sale of the building and equipment in the last year;
- The cash outflow for taxes from the change in revenues and expenses; and
- The cash inflow from the depreciation tax-shield.

Each different tax assumption changes the project's cash flows as follows:

| | Cash flow | | |
|---|---|---|---|
| Year | Tax rate = 20% | Tax rate = 30% | Tax rate = 40% |
| Initial | −$550,000 | −$550,000 | −$550,000 |
| 2001 | +86,540 | +79,909 | +73,079 |
| 2002 | +168,940 | +153,409 | +137,879 |
| 2003 | +166,380 | +149,569 | +132,759 |
| 2004 | +164,844 | +147,265 | +129,687 |
| 2005 | +467,298 | +460,946 | +489,987 |

We can see that the value of this project, and hence any decision based on this value, is sensitive to what we assume will be the tax rate.

We could take each of the "what if" tax rate assumptions and recalculate the value of the project in terms of NPV. The impact on the NPV is shown below assuming a cost of capital of 5%:

| Tax rate | NPV |
|---|---|
| 20% | $331,134 |
| 30% | $276,679 |
| 40% | $249,954 |

But when we do this, we have to be careful because the NPV requires discounting the cash flows at a rate that reflects risk, and that is what we are trying to figure out! So we shouldn't be using the NPV method in evaluating a project's risk in our sensitivity analysis. An alternative is to recalculate the internal rate of return (IRR) under each "what if" scenario as shown below:

| Tax rate | IRR |
|---|---|
| 20% | 20.20% |
| 30% | 17.77% |
| 40% | 16.32% |

And this illustrates one of the attractions of using the IRR to evaluate projects. Despite its drawbacks in the case of mutually exclusive projects and in capital rationing, as pointed out in Chapter 6, the IRR is more suitable for use in assessing a project's attractiveness under different scenarios and, hence, that project's risk. This is because the NPV method requires management to use a cost of capital to arrive at a project's value, but the required return or cost of capital is what we set out to determine! Management would be caught in a vicious circle if it used the NPV method in sensitivity analysis. But the IRR method does not require a cost of capital or required return; instead, management can look at the possible IRRs of a project and use that information to measure a project's risk.

If we can specify the objective probability distribution for tax rates, we can put sensitivity analysis together with well-known statistical measures of risk. Suppose that in the analysis of the project management determines that it is most likely that tax rates will be 30%, although there is a slight probability that tax rates will be lowered and a chance that tax rates will be increased. Suppose further that the market is risk-neutral, in which case objective probabilities and risk-neutral probabilities coincide. More specifically, the table shows the probability distribution of future tax rates and the resulting IRR for the project:

| Probability | Tax rate | IRR |
| --- | --- | --- |
| 10% | 20% | 20.20% |
| 50% | 30% | 17.77% |
| 40% | 40% | 16.32% |

From the above distribution, it can be determined that the expected value for the IRR for this project is 17.433% and the standard deviation is 1.148%. Management could then judge whether the project's expected return is sufficient considering its risk (as measured by the standard deviation).

Management could also use these statistical measures to compare this project with other projects. However, although there is a measure of how widely dispersed the possible outcomes are from the expected value, it does not allow a comparison of standard deviations of different projects' cash flows if they have different expected values. This is because comparing their standard deviations is meaningless without somehow adjusting for the scale of cash flows. Management can make comparisons by using a statistical measure known as the *coefficient of variation*. This measure translates the standard deviation of different probability distributions (because their scales differ) so that they can be compared. The coefficient of variation for a probability distribution is the ratio of its standard deviation to its expected value.

As can be seen from this illustration, sensitivity analysis allows management to assess the effects of changes in assumptions. But, because sensitivity analysis focuses only on one change at a time, it is not very realistic. We know that not one, but many factors can change throughout a project's life. In the case of the project considered by the management of Williams 5 & 10, there are a number of assumptions built into the analysis that are random variables, including the sales prices of the building and equipment in five years and the entrance of competitors no sooner than five years, to name only two.

## 26.3.2  Simulation Analysis

Sensitivity analysis becomes unmanageable if we change several factors at the same time. A manageable approach to changing two or more factors at the same time is simulation. *Simulation analysis* allows management to develop a probability distribution of possible outcomes, given a probability distribution for each variable that may change.

Suppose, for example, management is analyzing a project having the following three random variables: sales (number of units and price), costs, and tax rate. Suppose further that the initial outlay for the project is known with certainty and so is the rate of depreciation. From the firm's marketing research, management estimates a probability distribution for dollar sales. And from the firm's engineers and production staff and purchasing agents, management estimates the probability distribution for costs, which depends, in part, on the number of units sold. The firm's economists estimate the probability distribution of possible tax rates.

Management then has three probability distributions to work with. Now management needs a simulation model that can:

- Randomly select a possible value of unit sales for each year, given the probability distribution
- Randomly select a possible value of costs for each year, given the unit sales and the probability distribution of costs
- Randomly select a tax rate for each year, given the probability distribution of tax rates

Computers can be programmed to randomly select values based on whatever probability distribution is provided by management. Once the computer selects the number of units sold, the cost per unit, and the tax rate, the cash flows are calculated, as well as its IRR. Management now has one IRR or what is referred to as a "trial." Then the computer starts all over by repeating this process, calculating an IRR each time. After a large number of trials, management will have a frequency distribution for the IRRs. A *frequency distribution* is a description of the number of trials the computer arrived at each different IRR value. Using the frequency distribution, management can calculate the expected value, the standard deviation, and coefficient of variation of the IRRs.[5]

To illustrate, let's use a simulation taken from Fabozzi and Peterson (2002). Suppose that management is considering the acquisition of $80 million in equipment for a new product. Through research with the marketing and production management, management has determined the expected price and cost per unit, as well as the number of units to produce and sell. Along with these estimates, management has developed standard deviations from past experience that provide information on the risk associated with these estimates. For simplicity, assume that these three random variables—price, cost, and number of units—are distributed normally with the means and standard deviations as estimated by management. The company's accounting department has provided an estimate of the range of possible tax rates during the product's life; in this example, a uniform distribution for these rates is assumed. This analysis has produced the following:

| Variable | Number of units | Price per unit | Expense per unit | Tax rate | |
|---|---|---|---|---|---|
| Mean | 10,000,000 | $14 | $0.75 | Minimum | 35% |
| Standard deviation | 1,000,000 | $ 2 | $0.05 | Maximum | 45% |

---

[5] In this analysis we can either use estimated risk-neutral probabilities or assume risk neutrality and use objective probabilities.

**FIGURE 26.1**
HISTOGRAM FOR SIMULATION ILLUSTRATION

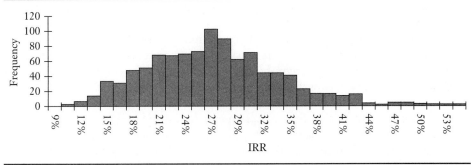

Assuming that the product will be produced and sold for the foreseeable future and using Microsoft Excel, 1,000 draws were simulated (i.e., 1,000 random selections from each of the four variables' distributions) using the above information. The new product's IRR is calculated for each of these draws, resulting in 1,000 IRRs or trials. The result is a distribution of possible IRRs, which are shown in the histogram in Figure 26.1. The height of this distribution is the number of draws (out of the possible 1,000 trials) for which the IRR fell into the range of IRRs depicted on the horizontal axis. In terms of risk, the wider the dispersion of possible IRRs relative to the expected IRR, the greater the new product's risk.

Simulation analysis is more realistic than sensitivity analysis because it introduces risk for many variables in the analysis. But this analysis may become complex since there are many interdependencies, both among variables in a given year and among the variables in different time periods. However, simulation analysis looks at a project in isolation, focusing instead on a single project's total risk. And simulation also ignores the effects of diversification for the owners' personal portfolio. If owners hold diversified portfolios, then their concern is how a project affects their portfolio's risk, not the project's total risk.

## 26.4  MEASURING A PROJECT'S MARKET RISK

If management is looking at an investment in another firm, it could compare the potential acquisition's stock returns and the returns of the market over the same period of time as a way of measuring that stock's market risk. While this is not a perfect measurement, it at least provides management with an estimate of the sensitivity of that particular stock's returns as compared to the returns of the market. But what if management is evaluating the market risk of a new product it is considering introducing? Management cannot look at how that new product has affected the stock return of its own firm! So what does management do in such situtations?

### 26.4.1  Market Risk and Financial Leverage

Though management cannot look at a new project's returns and see how they relate to the returns on the market, management may be able to do the next best thing:

estimate the market risk of the stock of *another firm* whose only line of business is the same as the project's. If management could identify such a company, it could look at the stock market risk of that company and use that as a first step in estimating the project's market risk.

Based on the CAPM, we will let $\beta$ represent market risk. As the reader will recall from Chapter 14, $\beta$ is a measure of the sensitivity of an asset's returns to change in the returns of the market. To distinguish the beta of an asset from the beta used for a firm's stock, we refer to an asset's beta as $\beta_{\text{asset}}$ and the beta of a firm's stock as $\beta_{\text{equity}}$. If a firm has no debt, the market risk of its common stock is the same as the market risk of its assets, and for that firm $\beta_{\text{equity}}$ equals $\beta_{\text{asset}}$.

Financial leverage is created by the use of fixed payment obligations, such as notes or bonds, to finance a firm's assets. As we demonstrated in Chapter 5, the greater the use of debt obligations, the more financial leverage and the greater the risk associated with cash flows to owners. So the effect of using debt is to increase the risk of the firm's equity. If the firm has debt obligations, the market risk of its common stock is greater than its assets' risk (i.e., $\beta_{\text{equity}} > \beta_{\text{asset}}$), due to financial leverage. Let's see why.

For any given firm, $\beta_{\text{asset}}$ depends on the asset's risk, but not on how the firm chooses to finance it. As we have already mentioned, if management finances the firm with equity only, $\beta_{\text{asset}} = \beta_{\text{equity}}$. But what if management chooses to finance the firm partly with debt and partly with equity? Then the creditors and the owners share the risk of the assets, but because of the nature of the claims, not equally. Creditors have seniority and receive a fixed amount (interest and principal), so there is less risk associated with a dollar of debt financing than a dollar of equity financing of the same asset: The market risk borne by the creditors differs from the market risk borne by owners.

Representing the market risk of creditors as $\beta_{\text{debt}}$ and the market risk of owners as $\beta_{\text{equity}}$, the asset's market risk is the weighted average of $\beta_{\text{debt}}$ and $\beta_{\text{equity}}$. If the proportion of the firm's capital from creditors is $w_{\text{debt}}$ and the proportion of the firm's capital from owners is $w_{\text{equity}}$, then:[6]

$$\beta_{\text{asset}} = \beta_{\text{debt}} \left( \begin{array}{c} \text{proportion of assets} \\ \text{financed with debt} \end{array} \right) + \beta_{\text{equity}} \left( \begin{array}{c} \text{proportion of assets} \\ \text{financed with equity} \end{array} \right)$$

or

$$\beta_{\text{asset}} = \beta_{\text{debt}} \, w_{\text{debt}} + \beta_{\text{equity}} \, w_{\text{equity}}$$

But interest on debt is deducted to arrive at taxable income, so the claim that creditors have on the firm's assets does not cost the firm the full amount, but rather the after-tax claim, so the burden of debt financing is actually less due to interest

---

[6] The process of breaking down the firm's beta into equity and debt components is attributed to Hamada (1972).

deductibility. Further, the beta of debt is generally assumed to be zero (i.e., there is no market risk associated with debt). With D representing the market value of debt, E representing the market value of equity, and $\tau$ the marginal tax rate, the relation between the asset beta and the equity beta is:

$$\beta_{asset} = \beta_{debt} \frac{(1 - \tau)D}{[(1 - \tau)D] + E} + \beta_{equity} \frac{E}{[(1 - \tau)D] + E}$$

Assuming $\beta_{debt} = 0$,

$$\beta_{asset} = \beta_{equity} \frac{E}{[(1 - \tau)D] + E}$$

Rearranging,

$$\beta_{asset} = \beta_{equity} \left[ \frac{1}{\left( 1 + \left( (1 - \tau)\frac{D}{E} \right) \right)} \right]$$

This means that an asset's beta is related to the firm's equity beta, with adjustments for financial leverage. If a firm does not use debt, $\beta_{equity} = \beta_{asset}$ and if the company does use debt, $\beta_{equity} > \beta_{asset}$.

Therefore, $\beta_{equity}$ may be translated into $\beta_{asset}$ by removing the influence of the firm's financial risk. To accomplish this, the following must be known:

- The firm's marginal tax rate
- The amount of the firm's debt financing in market value terms
- The amount of the firm's equity financing in market value terms

The process of translation is referred to as "unlevering" because the effects of financial leverage are removed from the equity beta, $\beta_{equity}$, to arrive at a beta for the firm's assets, $\beta_{asset}$. This therefore is an estimate of the market risk of a firm's assets.

To illustrate the unlevering of the equity beta, consider the following three companies:

| Company | Marginal tax rate | Debt | Equity | $\beta_{equity}$ |
|---------|-------------------|------|--------|------------------|
| Company A | 40% | $100 | $200 | 1.5 |
| Company B | 30% | $100 | $400 | 1.5 |
| Company C | 40% | $100 | $200 | 1.0 |

Then,

$$\beta_{asset} \text{ for Company A} = 1.5 \left[ \frac{1}{(1 + (1 - 0.40)\frac{\$100}{\$200}} \right] = 1.15$$

$$\beta_{asset} \text{ for Company B} = 1.5 \left[ \frac{1}{(1 + (1 - 0.30)\frac{\$100}{\$400}} \right] = 1.28$$

$$\beta_{asset} \text{ for Company C} = 1.0 \left[ \frac{1}{(1 + (1 - 0.40)\frac{\$100}{\$200}} \right] = 0.77$$

## 26.4.2 Using a Pure-Play Firm

There are many instances in which management invests in assets with differing risks and is therefore faced with estimating the cost of capital of a project. Using the firm's asset beta would not be appropriate because the asset beta reflects the market risk of all of the company's assets and this may not reflect the risk of the project being evaluated. One approach to dealing with this dilemma is to estimate the cost of capital for a company with a single line of business similar to the project under consideration. Such a company is referred to as a *pure-play firm*.

One method of estimating the pure-play firm's equity beta is to regress the pure-play firm's stock returns against the returns on the market portfolio. Once the pure-play firm's equity beta is calculated, management then "unlevers" it by adjusting it for the financial leverage of the pure-play firm.

Examples of pure-play equity betas in 1994 are shown in Table 26.2. The firms listed in this table have one primary line of business. Using the information for Alcan Aluminum and assuming a marginal tax rate of 35%, we see that the asset beta for aluminum products is 0.748:

$$\beta_{asset} = 1.088 \left( \frac{1}{1 + (1 - 0.35)0.700} \right) = 0.748$$

A firm such as Gap, Inc. with little debt relative to equity will have an asset beta that is close to its equity beta.

**TABLE 26.2**
EQUITY AND ASSET BETAS FOR SELECTED FIRMS WITH A SINGLE LINE OF BUSINESS
("PURE PLAYS"), 1994

| Company | Line of Business | Equity Beta | Debt-to-Equity Ratio | Asset Beta |
|---|---|---|---|---|
| Alcan Aluminum | Aluminum | 1.088 | 0.700 | 0.748 |
| Dillard Department Stores | Retail | 0.709 | 0.643 | 0.500 |
| Gap, Inc. | Apparel | 1.295 | 0.125 | 1.197 |
| Mattel | Toy manufacturing | 0.872 | 0.220 | 0.763 |
| McDonald's | Food service | 1.092 | 0.248 | 0.941 |
| Office Depot | Specialty retailer | 1.711 | 0.188 | 1.525 |

Note: The book value of debt is used in place of the market value of debt since the latter is not readily available. The market value of equity is the product of the number of shares outstanding and the closing share prices as of the end of the year. A 35% tax rate is assumed.

If an appropriate pure-play firm can be identified, this method can be used in estimating a project's cost of capital.[7] However, since many U.S. corporations have more than one line of business, finding an appropriate pure-play firm may be difficult. Care must be taken by management to identify firms whose lines of business are similar to the project's.

## 26.4.3 Adjusted Present Value

The use of the project's cost of capital to discount the cash flows of a project to the present is one method of incorporating the effect of financial leverage into the evaluation of a project. Another method is the *adjusted present value* (APV) *method*, which involves separating the value of the project's leverage from the value of the project itself.[8] In other words,

Adjusted present value

$$= \left( \begin{array}{c} \text{PV of the project} \\ \text{if all-equity financed} \end{array} \right) + \left( \begin{array}{c} \text{PV of the tax} \\ \text{benefits from debt} \end{array} - \begin{array}{c} \text{PV of expected costs} \\ \text{of financial distress} \end{array} \right)$$

The value of the project if all-equity financed is the present value of the project's cash flows, discounted at the asset beta, $\beta_{asset}$.

The value of the tax benefits from debt is the present value of the tax-shield from interest deductibility. Using the company's capital structure as a measure of the anticipated debt financing relevant to consider for this project and indicating

---

[7] Estimating a pure-play asset beta is useful in many other applications, including both valuing divisions or segments of a business and valuing small businesses.

[8] The adjusted present value method is based on the work of Myers (1974).

the marginal tax rate as $\tau$, the after-tax cost of debt as $r_d^*$ and the amount of debt as D, the present value of the tax shields is:[9]

$$\text{Value of the tax benefits from debt} = \frac{\tau \, r_d^* \, D}{r_d^*} = \tau \, D$$

If we assume that the company finances its projects similar to its target debt-equity ratio, D/E, then:[10]

$$\text{Project debt} = (\text{PV of project's outlays})\left(\frac{D/E}{1 + D/E}\right)$$

The present value of the expected costs of financial distress is the present value of the probability-weighted costs of bankruptcy:

$$\begin{array}{l} \text{PV of expected costs} \\ \text{of financial distress} \end{array} = \left(\begin{array}{l} \text{Probability of} \\ \text{financial distress} \end{array}\right)\left(\begin{array}{l} \text{PV of costs of} \\ \text{financial distress} \end{array}\right)$$

Suppose management is evaluating a project that has a required initial outlay of $6 million and expected cash flows of $1 million per year for each of the next 10 years. And suppose that the marginal tax rate is 35%, the company's capital structure has a D/E ratio of 60%, an after-tax cost of debt of 3.25%, and a cost of equity of 8%. The cost of equity is estimated by using the company's beta of 1.5, an expected risk-free rate of interest of 3%, and an expected return on the market of 6.4%. In the traditional NPV method, the project's cost of capital is:

$$\text{Project cost of capital} = (0.375)(0.0325) + (0.625)(0.08) = 6.2188\%$$

and the value of the project is $1.2844 million.

Using the APV method, it is first necessary to unlever the equity beta to remove the effects of leverage:

$$\beta_{\text{asset}} = 1.5\left[\frac{1}{(1 + ((1 - 0.35)0.6))}\right] = 1.21$$

---

[9] This is not presuming that each project has its own financing. Rather, this debt represents the additional debt that the company would need to take on as it finances new projects. Unless there is a reason to do otherwise, it is assumed that the amount of debt for the project is calculated as the product of the amount of total financing for the project and the proportion of debt in the capital structure.

[10] This amount of debt is the cost of the project multiplied by the proportion of debt in the company's capital structure. The proportion of debt can be calculated as the ratio of the debt-equity ratio (D/E) to one plus the debt-equity ratio.

Therefore, the cost of equity is:

$$r_e = 0.03 + 1.21(0.064 - 0.03) = 0.03 + 0.04114 = 0.07114 \text{ or } 7.114\%$$

The value of the all-equity financed project is therefore $0.9867 million.

The debt for the project is the project cost, $6 million, multiplied by the debt-asset ratio:

$$\text{Project debt} = \$6\left(\frac{D}{D+E}\right) = \$6\left(\frac{D/E}{1+D/E}\right) = \$6\left(\frac{0.6}{1.6}\right) = \$2.25$$

The present value of the tax shields from debt are:

$$\text{Value of the tax benefits from debt} = (0.35)\$2.25 = \$0.7875$$

Without considering the effect of financial distress, the APV is:

$$\text{APV} = \$0.9867 + 0.7875 = \$1.7742$$

The challenge is therefore to incorporate the cost of financial distress. If it is assumed that there is a 10% chance the company could experience financial distress and that financial distress would result in a loss of 100% of the project's value, the present value of the costs of financial distress are:

$$\text{PV of the costs of financial distress} = (0.10)(\$0.9867) = \$0.09867$$

The APV considering the effect of financial distress is therefore:

$$\text{APV} = \$0.9867 + 0.7875 - 0.09867 = \$1.6558$$

The NPV and APV methods produce different values for the project: $1.2844 versus $1.6558.[11] This is typically the case in comparing the two methods because the NPV method incorporates the benefit of taxes and the costs of financial distress in the project's cost of capital, whereas the APV adjusts for these separately.

What are the advantages of using the APV approach? In the traditional method the effects of the tax deductibility of interest and of financial distress are reflected in the costs of capital. The APV segregates those effects, thus requiring mangement to focus specifically on incorporating both the probability and the costs of financial distress.[12] The APV method also allows for more flexibility in specifying the debt level anticipated in the future.

---

[11] However, if the probability of financial distress in this example is higher than 75%, the entire benefit from taxes is offset.

[12] However, the costs and probabilities of financial distress are difficult to measure. If the value effects of financial distress are ignored, the APV is overstated, and hence, the value added of the project is overstated.

## 26.5 Contingency Planning of Capital Expenditures

In our Chapter 10 discussion of contingent claims and contingent strategies we explained how management decisions can differ in different states of the world, and how payoffs may be improved by making decisions that are contingent on the currently prevailing state of the world. We also explained how contingent strategies provide ways to manage risks and information about them.[13]

Chapter 10 provided an example of a contingency strategy for a firm planning to select a location and build a factory that might later be expanded. In this section, we provide a second example in which contingency planning can commit the firm to successive stages of an investment program as more information is gleaned regarding the proposed project.[14] We assume for simplicity that the particular decision can be assessed separately from others the firm will take and that management uses expected present value maximization as a criterion function. We shall later illustrate how to take risk into account as well.

### 26.5.1 Example

Here is the setup for the example. The Perils of Pauline Cereals, Inc. has recently developed a new product. Pauline Cereals is now attempting to determine whether marketing the product would be a financially sound decision and, if so, what type of marketing strategy should be employed.

Introduction of the new product would require an initial cash outlay of $725,000 to prepare a production setup with a useful producing life of about one year. The production setup would have a capacity great enough to meet the production requirements of any of the possible plans for product introduction that marketing has developed. Apart from initial cash requirements, discrepancies between revenue and cash flows during the year can be financed at short-term rates, the costs of which are included in the estimates we shall give. The $725,000 is not recoverable if plans are later cancelled; as an alternative these funds could be invested in another project almost certain to yield 7%.

The Marketing Department has prepared a variety of plans for different marketing conditions. These involve either the initial introduction of the product on a national scale or a plan for test marketing, following the results of which a decision to terminate the sales effort or to distribute the product nationally can be made. If the test market plan is followed, there is a possibility that a competitor's product will appear and cut into sales. Furthermore, the probability of competition appearing is increased if the test marketing plan is successful. However, because of the timing involved, immediate national distribution would rule out the possibility of competition.

Marketing has prepared certain estimates of market conditions and the probability of a competitor's product appearing. The Marketing Department believes that

---

[13] Contingent strategies are similar to option instruments in that they recognize management can make decisions that differ according to circumstances.

[14] In this setting the firm can regard the commitment to the full investment program as an option to be exercised in the event of receiving favorable information regarding market conditions.

## TABLE 26.3
### STRATEGIES' PAYOFFS AND PROBABILITIES

| 1. National distribution without testing | Payoff | Probability of this payoff |
|---|---|---|
| National distribution if market is "good" | $2,262,000 | 0.5 |
| National distribution if market is "bad" | −600,000 | 0.5 |

| 2. With successful test and competing product | Payoff | Conditional probability of this payoff |
|---|---|---|
| National distribution if market is "good" | $1,200,000 | 0.625 |
| National distribution if market is "bad" | 800,000 | 0.375 |
| No further distribution after test marketing | 50,000 | 1.000 |

| 3. With successful test and no competing product | Payoff | Conditional probability of this payoff |
|---|---|---|
| National distribution if market is "good" | $2,000,000 | 0.8 |
| National distribution if market is "bad" | 800,000 | 0.2 |
| No further distribution after test marketing | 75,000 | 1.0 |

| 4. With unsuccessful test and competing product | Payoff | Conditional probability of this payoff |
|---|---|---|
| National distribution if market is "good" | $800,000 | 0.1 |
| National distribution if market is "bad" | −400,000 | 0.9 |
| No distribution after test marketing | −100,000 | 1.0 |

| 5. With unsuccessful test and no competing product | Payoff | Conditional probability of this payoff |
|---|---|---|
| National distribution if market is "good" | $1,200,000 | 0.3 |
| National distribution if market is "bad" | 700,000 | 0.7 |
| No further distribution after test marketing | −100,000 | 1.0 |

the probability a test marketing campaign will be successful[15] is about 0.5. If the test market campaign is successful, Marketing judges that the probability of a competing product appearing is 0.8, but if the test marketing campaign is unsuccessful, the probability of a competing product appearing is only 0.4.

The Controller's Division, working with the Marketing Department, has prepared the estimates of payoffs from the different plans as shown in the first panel of Table 26.3. The payoffs are realized after the expenditure of $725,000 and take into account the fact that the national market can (without testing) be characterized as being either a "good" market or a "bad" one. Each payoff is expressed in terms of a lump sum available one year from now and includes all costs and revenue (including any necessary short-term financing) except for the initial $725,000.

---

[15] As before, we can either interpret the probabilities as risk-neutral probabilities or assume that the market is risk-neutral, in which case objective and risk-neutral probabilities coincide.

## FIGURE 26.2
### DECISION TREE FOR PERILS OF PAULINE PROBLEM

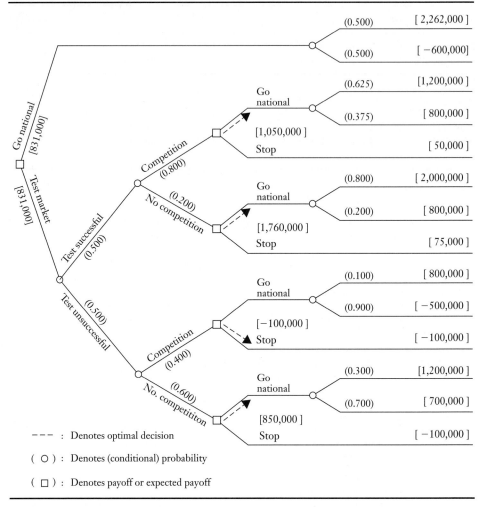

--- : Denotes optimal decision

( ○ ) : Denotes (conditional) probability

( □ ) : Denotes payoff or expected payoff

Similarly, the Controller's Division has prepared the various forecasts of the realizable payoffs after test marketing strategies have been followed and their outcomes ascertained. These payoffs are shown in the the panels in Table 26.3. Once again, the Controller's Division has found it convenient to classify post-test market strategies as either "good" or "bad." However, these conditions (and hence their payoffs) are not directly related to those forecast without test marketing, because the test marketing approach itself, being a learning experience, has an effect on payoffs that can subsequently be earned.

What plan of action should the management follow? Why?

The Perils of Pauline problem can be structured in the form of a decision tree as shown in Figure 26.2. The important characteristics of such a tree are that all possible choices of the decision maker, as well as all possible outcomes of the random variables, are displayed in their logical order as branches of the tree. Note that events are depicted in their natural sequence and that distinctions are made between branches which can be selected by the decision maker, and branches which are selected through the realization of a random variable. The branches at which choices can be made by the decision maker are indicated by nodes with rectangular boxes drawn around them. The dollar payoffs from decision-outcome sequences are recorded at the ends of the branches. Note how the tree displays the notion of contingent strategies as a part of its logic. For example, the second upward-pointing branch of the tree shows that even if the test marketing strategy is successful, management need not commit the firm to a national distribution decision until after it has been determined whether or not a competitor will enter the market.

The solution technique for finding the best contingent strategy involves working backward through the tree, writing down at each decision node the payoff to be earned by following the *best* branch of the tree from that point on, and using that information in calculations for earlier points in time.[16]

To see the logic of the solution technique, consider the second branch from the upper side of the tree in Figure 26.2, depicting the decisions either to introduce the product nationally or to stop. If the company were on the lower twig of this branch, the expected value of going national would be:

$$0.8(\$2,000,000) + 0.2(\$200,000) = \$1,640,000$$

while the expected value of stopping would be \$75,000. Clearly, if the management finds itself in this situation, the best way to continue is by introducing the product nationally, as is shown by the arrow and the value of \$1,640,000 in brackets.

The same calculations are made for each possible decision point at which the firm could arrive when the second decision must be made, and they are then carried backwards in time to the decisions, which, if initially taken, could have placed the company in that position. Thus, for example, the four decision points that could be reached by following a test market strategy are shown in the lower half of the tree and have (at the time one of these four decisions must be taken) the values \$1,050,000, \$1,640,000, \$100,000, and \$850,000. Multiplying these values by the conditional probabilities of their occurring, the expected payoff from the test market strategy is seen to be:

$$0.4(\$1,050,000) + 0.1(\$1,760,000) + 0.2(-\$100,000) + 0.3(\$850,000)$$
$$= \$420,000 + \$176,000 - \$20,000 + \$255,000 = \$831,000$$

In Figure 26.2 the best decisions are indicated by the arrows. The two best strategies in terms of expected value, as calculated from the tree, are given in Table 26.4 along with their payoff distributions. The fact that the two uncertain payoffs have identical expected values reflects the contrived nature of the example and will be used for

---

[16] This is a complete enumeration method of solving the stochastic dynamic programming problem posed by our scenario.

TABLE 26.4
DISTRIBUTION OF PAYOFFS FOR STRATEGIES A AND B

*Distribution of payoff following strategy A (noncontingent strategy)*

| Strategy A | Payoff | Probability |
|---|---|---|
| Engage in immediate | $2,262,000 | 0.50 |
| national distribution | − 600,000 | 0.50 |
| Expected payoff = $831,000 | | |

*Distribution of payoff following strategy B (contingent strategy)*

| Strategy B | Payoff | Probability |
|---|---|---|
| First, test the market | $1,200,000 | 0.25 |
| | 800,000 | 0.15 |
| Then if test successful | 2,000,000 | 0.08 |
| go national | 800,000 | 0.02 |
| If test unsuccessful and if competing | −100,000 | 0.20 |
| product appears, stop | | |
| If test unsuccessful and | 1,200,000 | 0.09 |
| if no competing product | 700,000 | 0.21 |
| appears, go national | | |
| Expected payoff = $831,000 | | 1.00 |

further discussion shortly. Note, however, that the immediate national distribution strategy is actually a noncontingent strategy in that it merely prescribes acting on the basis of the most likely outcome when no test marketing is conducted.

In this example the advantage of the test marketing (contingent) strategy is not a higher expected payoff but rather the lower risk with which that payoff is earned. Indeed, the equality of expected payoffs in the example was designed to emphasize the point that expected values may not capture all relevant aspects of probabilistic payoffs if the decision maker is risk averse. Formally, of course, the difficulty is dealt with by assuming utility functions that are additive or multiplicative in different periods' payoffs and using dynamic programming or other routines to compute expected utility. However, it is sometimes possible to rank probabilistic payoffs using only the knowledge that the decision maker is risk averse. As explained next, the method of stochastic dominance, which performs such rankings, is useful in problems that have only terminal payoffs.[17]

## 26.5.2 Application of Stochastic Dominance

To see how the concept of stochastic dominance is relevant to the example, recall that we showed in Chapter 12 how two probability distributions may be ordered by

---

[17] While stochastic dominance calculations could be performed for vector random variables, the fact that vectors themselves can only be partially ordered restricts the applicability of this approach even further than does the fact that stochastic dominance is itself a partial ordering.

**FIGURE 26.3**
CUMULATIVE DISTRIBUTIONS OF PAYOFFS FROM STRATEGIES A AND B

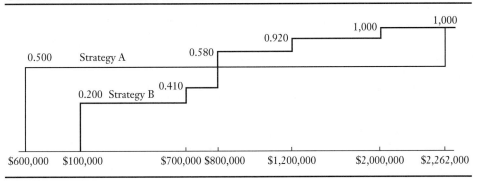

**TABLE 26.5**
STOCHASTIC DOMINANCE CALCULATIONS FOR STRATEGIES A AND B (VALUES EXPRESSED IN HUNDREDS OF THOUSANDS)

|  |  | Incremental area | Total area |
|---|---|---|---|
| $500(0.50) | = | +250 | +250 |
| 800(0.30) | = | +240 | +490 |
| 100(0.09) | = | +9 | +499 |
| 400(0.08) | = | −32 | +467 |
| 800(0.42) | = | −336 | +131 |
| 262(0.50) | = | −131 | 0 |

second degree dominance for any risk-averse decision maker.[18] Using the results of Chapter 12, we find that the payoffs earned from following strategy B would be preferred to those earned from following strategy A by every risk-averse decision maker.

The stochastic dominance calculations comparing A and B are given in Figure 26.3 and Table 26.5. Strategy B and the certain alternative, C, cannot be compared using stochastic dominance because in the latter case the criterion exhibits a sign change. Thus, even though alternative A can be eliminated because it is in effect riskier than alternative B, two alternatives still remain. Either B or C should be selected by a given decision maker on the basis of a more closely specified attitude toward risk.

---

[18] Stochastic dominance calculations are used here mainly for illustrative purposes. If one assumes risk neutrality, dominance calculations are technically irrelevant because decision makers then care only about expected value. If one assumes the existence of risk-neutral probabilities, again the dominance calculations are technically irrelevant because decision makers then care only about market value. Nevertheless, in either case stochastic dominance calculations do show additional dimensions to the risks being taken.

## 26.6 Real Options Valuation

Using a decision tree to analyze a risky project provides one example of *real options valuation* (ROV). The option in the previous example is to expand in stages if the test marketing strategy is successful.[19] Consider other typical options inherent in an investment opportunity:

- Most every project has an option to abandon, though there may be constraints (e.g., legally binding contracts) that affect when this option can be exercised.
- Many projects have the option to expand.
- Many projects have an option to defer investment, putting off the major investment outlays to some future date.

So how should we analyze these options? As our example has already shown, one approach is to use decision tree analysis, associating probabilities to each of the possible outcomes for an event and mapping out the possible outcomes and the value of the investment opportunity associated with these different outcomes. While this approach is workable when there are few options associated with a project, option pricing theory offers a method of analysis that provides additional useful information.

The basic idea of ROV is to recognize that the value of a project extends beyond its value as measured by a noncontingent calculation of NPV; in other words, the value of project is supplemented by the value of the contingent strategies represented as options. Since options are considered to be strategic decisions, the NPV based on contingency strategies is often referred to as *strategic NPV*. Consider an investment opportunity that has one option associated with it. The strategic NPV is the sum of the traditional NPV—referred to as the *noncontingent NPV* or *static NPV*—and the value of the option:

$$\text{Strategic NPV} = \text{Noncontingent NPV} + \text{Value of the option}$$

### 26.6.1 Options on Real Assets

The valuation of options is simple in concept, as both Chapter 19 and the Perils of Pauline example have already illustrated. However, although the underlying concepts are the same as those already illustrated, it may appear substantially more complex to apply traditional forms of option pricing theory, such as the Black-Scholes model (1973). The Black-Scholes model is based on five factors that have been shown to be important in valuing an option:

1. The value of the underlying asset, $P$
2. The exercise price or strike price of the option, $E$
3. The risk-free rate of interest, $r$
4. The volatility of the value of the underlying asset, $\sigma$
5. The time remaining to the expiration of the option, $T$

---

[19] In another early example, Myers (1977) recognized the importance of considering investment opportunities as growth options.

**TABLE 26.6**

RELATION BETWEEN THE FACTORS THAT AFFECT THE VALUE OF A STOCK OPTION AND THOSE THAT AFFECT A REAL OPTION

| Parameter | Option on a stock | Option on a real asset |
|---|---|---|
| $P$ | The stock's price | The present value of cash flows from the investment opportunity (e.g., cash-out price) |
| $E$ | The strike price of the option | The present value of the delayed capital expenditure or future cost savings |
| $R$ | The risk-free rate of interest | The risk-free rate of interest |
| $\sigma$ | Volatility of stock's price | Uncertainty of the project's cash flows |
| $T$ | The time to expiration | Project's useful life |

*Source:* Fabozzi and Peterson (2002).

In Chapter 19, we examined the relation between each of these factors and the value of a stock option. Our focus here is to map these factors into a real option setting. Like other options, real options can be calls (options to buy assets), puts (options to sell assets), or compound options (options on other options). And, like other forms of option instruments, real options may be European (capable of exercise only on the expiration date) or American (capable of exercise at any time on or before the expiration date).

In general terms, the relation between the factors that affect the value of a stock option and those that affect a real option correspond as shown in Table 26.6. Of course, the factors that correspond to a specific option can be better described when we examine the particular option. Consider the option to abandon. In this case, the underlying asset is the value of continuing operations. The strike or exercise price for this option is the exit value or salvage value of the asset. A number of common real options are described in Table 26.7.

**TABLE 26.7**

EXAMPLES OF REAL OPTIONS

| Option | Type | Value of Underlying Asset | Exercise Price |
|---|---|---|---|
| To abandon | American put | The present value of the cash flows from the abandoned assets | The exit or salvage value |
| To defer an investment | American call | The present value of completed project's net operating cash flows | The deferred investment outlay |
| To abandon during construction | Compound option | The present value of the completed project's cash flows | The investment outlay necessary for the next stage |
| To contract the scale of a project | European put | The present value of potential cost savings | The costs of re-scaling the project |
| To expand | European call | The present value of incremental net operating cash flows | The additional investment outlay |
| To switch inputs or outputs | American put | The present value of the incremental cash flows from the best alternative use | The cost of retooling production or distribution |

*Source:* Fabozzi and Peterson (2002).

Identifying the options associated with an investment opportunity is the first step. The second step is to value these options. Consider an investment opportunity to defer an investment. This investment opportunity is similar to what a firm experiences in their investment in research and development (R&D): an expenditure or series of expenditures are made in R&D, and then sometime in the future depending on the results of the research and development, the actions of competitors, and the approval of any regulators, the firm can then decide whether to go ahead with the investment opportunity.

## 26.6.2   Real Options: An Example

Let's put some numbers to the analysis of this project using an illustration from Fabozzi and Peterson (2002). Suppose that research and development is expected to cost $2.5 million for each of the first four years. And suppose that at the end of the fifth year the firm has an option to either go ahead with the product or simply abandon it. If the firm goes ahead with development of the product, this will require an investment of $80 million at the end of the fifth year. To make the analysis simpler, let's assume that we can sell the investment in the product—that is, cash out—at the end of the fifth year for $100 million.[20]

Using a discount rate of 20% (continuously compounded), the NPV of this investment opportunity is −$1.36 million as shown below:[21]

| | | | Year | | | |
|---|---|---|---|---|---|---|
| | *0* | *1* | *2* | *3* | *4* | *5* |
| Investment | ($2.50) | ($2.50) | ($2.50) | ($2.50) | ($2.50) | ($80.00) |
| Terminal value | $0.00 | $0.00 | $0.00 | $0.00 | $0.00 | $100.00 |
| Net cash flow | ($2.50) | ($2.50) | ($2.50) | ($2.50) | ($2.50) | $20.00 |
| | | | | | | |
| PV investment | ($2.50) | ($2.05) | ($1.68) | ($1.37) | ($1.12) | ($29.43) |
| PV terminal value | $0.00 | $0.00 | $0.00 | $0.00 | $0.00 | $36.79 |
| PV of net cash flow | ($2.50) | ($2.05) | ($1.68) | ($1.37) | ($1.12) | $7.36 |
| | | | | | | |
| Net present value | ($1.36) | | | | | |

Using traditional capital budgeting, the foregoing analysis suggests that we should reject the project because its NPV is less than zero. But we have not yet considered the valuable option of the deferred investment. Management can wait

---

[20] If this were not a cash out scenario, the value here would be the present value of future cash flows.
[21] To be consistent with the valuation of the Black-Scholes option pricing model, continuous compounding is used throughout this example.

until the end of the fifth year to decide whether it wants to commit the additional $80 million. Meanwhile, management invests in the R&D in each of the first four years.

So how much is this option worth? We need to make a couple of assumptions regarding the risk-free rate of interest and volatility. Suppose that the risk-free rate of interest is 5%, the market risk premium is 6%, and the volatility (i.e., the standard deviation of the project's cash flows) is 2.5 times that of the market volatility. Since the market volatility is 20%, the option volatility is 50%. The cost of capital is calculated as follows using the risk-free rate and the market risk premium is 20%:

$$\text{Cost of capital} = 5\% + 6\%(50\%/20\%) = 5\% + 15\% = 20\%$$

The value of the factors that are considered in the option valuation are then as follows:

| Parameter | Value |
| --- | --- |
| Value of underlying asset | $36.79 million |
| Exercise price | $80 million |
| Risk-free rate of interest | 5% |
| Volatility | 50% |
| Number of periods to exercise | 5 years |

The value of the underlying asset is the present value of the additional outlays needed to go ahead with the project, discounted at a continuously compounded rate of 20%:

$$\text{Value of underlying asset} = \$100 \text{ million } e^{-.20(5)} = \$36.79 \text{ million}$$

Using the Black-Scholes option pricing formula,[22] the value of this option is $10.24 million. Does this change the decision of whether to invest? The strategic NPV is:

$$\text{Strategic NPV} = \text{Static NPV} + \text{value of the option}$$
$$\text{Strategic NPV} = -\$1.36 \text{ million} + \$10.24 \text{ million}$$
$$\text{Strategic NPV} = \$8.88 \text{ million}$$

Hence, the project has a positive NPV considering the valuable option that is associated with it.

---

[22] The reader may wonder whether it is objective probability or risk-neutral probability that underlies the Black-Scholes model. But in fact, Black-Scholes valuation is based on a differential equation that is independent of risk preferences, and hence, the solution is also independent of risk preferences (Hull, 2003, p. 245). In particular, using this solution is consistent with assuming all investors are risk neutral, in which case objective and risk-neutral probabilities coincide, as assumed earlier.

### 26.6.3   Challenges in Implementing ROV

We used a straightforward example to illustrate the importance of considering options. Now let's examine a couple of the challenges in incorporating ROV into an actual investment opportunity analysis.[23]

The first challenge has to do with the parameters of the model. Focusing just on the estimate of volatility, we can see that the value added of the option is sensitive to the estimate of volatility. Though we simply assumed that the volatility is 50%, it is not a simple matter to determine the volatility of a project's future cash flow. We experience the same problems that we did in trying to determine the beta of a project—it just isn't measurable directly. The volatility of an investment opportunity's cash flows affects two key elements of the strategic value: (1) the volatility has a positive relation to the value of the option (i.e., the greater the volatility, the greater the value of the option), and (2) the volatility has a negative relation to the static NPV (i.e., the greater the volatility, the greater the cost of capital, and hence the lower the static NPV). If we take this last example and calculate the strategic NPV with volatility of 60% and 40%, as well, we see that the value of the option is affected by the choice of volatility:

| | *Volatility* | | |
| --- | --- | --- | --- |
| | *50%* | *60%* | *40%* |
| Static NPV | ($1.36) | ($1.98) | ($0.61) |
| Value of the option | 10.24 | 13.47 | 6.97 |
| Strategic NPV | $8.88 | $11.49 | $6.36 |

Second, most investment projects have several options, and some of them interact. For example, if a firm is investing in R&D over a period of years in the development of a new product, there exists at least two options: the option to abandon during development and the option to defer investment. The valuation problem in the case of multiple options is not simply carried out by adding the separate values because the value of one option may affect the value of other options. Solving for the value of options in the case of multiple, interacting options can be quite difficult, requiring the application of numerical methods.[24]

* * *

## KEY POINTS

- To evaluate the riskiness of a project, management must begin by recognizing that the assets of a firm are the result of its prior investment decisions and hence, that the firm is a portfolio of projects.

---

[23] For a further discussion of the issues related to applying real option analysis see Moore (2001), Amram and Kulatilaka (1999), and Trigeorgis (1993).

[24] For a discussion of these issues and an example of option interaction, see Trigeorgis (1991).

- Although management should consider how a given project increases asset portfolio risk, in practice, management typically focuses on measuring the stand-alone risk of the individual project.
- One approach to evaluating a risky project is to use a risk-adjusted discount rate.
- Within the risk-adjusted discount rate approach, a commonly used method for estimating a project's cost of capital or market-required rate of return is to use the CAPM. That requires specifying the premium for bearing the average amount of risk for the market as a whole and then, using a measure of market risk, fine-tuning this to reflect the project's risk.
- Because in practice it is not simple to estimate a project's beta, an alternative is for management to begin with the weighted-average cost of capital and adjust it based on the project's perceived risk.
- The certainty-equivalent approach is an alternative to the risk-adjusted discount rate. Using risk-neutral probabilities is one way to calculate a project's market value—a particular form of certainty-equivalent value.
- A project's total risk or stand-alone risk can be estimated based on the objective probability distribution for the risky cash flows. It is a project's market risk that is relevant to the management in making a capital budgeting decision.
- A project's beta risk can be estimated by looking at the market risk of firms in a single line of business similar to that of the project, a pure-play.
- An alternative to finding a pure-play is to classify projects according to the type of project (e.g., expansion) and assign costs of capital to each project type according to subjective judgment of risk.
- Sensitivity analysis and simulation analysis are tools that can be used in conjunction with statistical measures to evaluate a project's risk. Both techniques give us an idea of the relation between a project's return and its risk.
- Contingent strategies provide an alternative framework to evaluate risky projects.
- The real options valuation approach involves estimating the options associated with an investment opportunity and helps management identify value in a project that is not reflected using traditional capital budgeting techniques. Real options can be valued using either decision trees or option pricing formulae.
- There are options associated with every investment opportunity, including the option to defer the investment and the option to abandon the investment.
- The valuation of a single option is straightforward but the valuation of multiple options, especially if they interact, can be quite difficult.

# QUESTIONS

1. What is the difference between sensitivity analysis and simulation analysis?

2. Why is the internal return method a better method to employ in capital budgeting analysis than the net present value method when evaluating/assessing a project's attractiveness under different scenarios?

3. **a.** What are the difference between net present value and the adjusted present approaches?
   **b.** What are the advantages of using the APV approach?

4. The XYZ Company has a financial structure that includes debt and equity. There is no preferred stock in the capital structure. The portion of the capital structure financed by debt is 55%. Management estimates that the beta of the debt is 0.3 and the beta of the total assets is 0.5. What is the beta of XYZ Company's equity?

5. What is the relationship between the volatility of an investment opportunity's cash flows with its static net present value and value of the option?

6. Suppose the beta of a firm's assets is $k$ and the tax rate is 40%. What is the debt-to-equity ratio if the beta of the equity is 4 times the beta of the assets?

7. Suppose management of Company ABC is evaluating a project which has an initial outlay of $10 million and an expected cash flow of $3 million per year for each of the next five years. Assume that the company's (i) marginal tax rate is 40%, (ii) debt-to-equity ratio equal to 1, and (iii) after-tax cost of debt of 4% and a cost of equity of 6%. The cost of equity is estimated using the Capital Asset Pricing Model assuming a beta of 1.2, a risk-free interest rate of 3%, and an expected return on the market of 7%.

   **a.** What is the net present value for this project?
   **b.** What is the adjusted present value for this project if the effect of financial distress is ignored?

8. Consider once again the information in question 7 and now consider the cost of financial distress. Assume that management believes there is 20% and 30% chance that financial distress would result in a loss of 80% and 40%, respectively, of the project's value. Recalculate the adjusted present value of the project.

9. Suppose that a project costs $1 million for each of the first five years. At the end of the fifth year, the firm can either abandon the project or continue to operate it. If the project is continued, the expected payoff is $6 million as of the end of the end of the fifth year applying the Black-Scholes option pricing model. For the value of this option to abandon or continue is $3 million. What is the strategic net present value of this project if the cost of capital is 5%?

10. Management is considering entering into a contract to produce a product. The product will be sold at the end of second year for a price of $8. Below is the cash flow of a product under consideration by management. At the end of the second year, management has the option to abandon the project or continue with the development of the project for another investment of $6 million at the end of the second year.

| Year | 0 | 1 | 2 |
|---|---|---|---|
| Investment ($) | −1 | −1 | 2 |

If the cost of the capital is 15% by continuous compounding, the risk-free rate is 5% and the volatility is 0.3. What is the Static NPV and what is the Strategic NPV?

## REFERENCES

Amram, Martha, and Nalin Kulatilaka. (1999). *Real Options*. Boston: Harvard Business School Press.

Black, Fischer, and Myron Scholes. (1973). "The Pricing of Options and Corporate Liabilities," *Journal of Political Economy* **81**: 637–659.

Fabozzi, Frank J. and Pamela P. Peterson. (2002). *Financial Management and Analysis*. Hoboken, NJ: John Wiley & Sons.

Hull, John. (2003). *Options, Futures, and Other Derivatives* (5th ed.). Upper Saddle River, NJ: Pearson.

Moore, William. (2001). *Real Options and Option-Embedded Securities*. Hoboken, NJ: Wiley.

Myers, Stewart C. (1974). "Interactions in Corporate Financing and Investment Decisions— Implications for Capital Budgeting," *Journal of Finance* **29**: 1–25.

Myers, Stewart C. (1977). "Determinants of Corporate Borrowings," *Journal of Financial Economics* **5**: 147–176.

Trigeorgis, Lenos. (1991). "A Log-Transformed Binomial Numerical Analysis Method for Valuing Complex Multi-Option Investments," *Journal of Financial and Quantitative Analysis* **26**: 309–326.

Trigeorgis, Lenos. (1993). "Real Options and Interactions with Financial Flexibility," *Financial Management* **22**: 202–214.

# SUBJECT INDEX

# AUTHOR INDEX